TEACHING ELEMENTARY SCHOOL MATHEMATICS

TEACHING ELEMENTARY SCHOOL MATHEMATICS

Charles D'Augustine
C. Winston Smith, Jr.

Ohio University, Athens

HarperCollins*Publishers*

Photo Credits: p. 14, Jean-Claude Lejeune/Stock Boston; p. 23, Laima Druskis/Stock Boston; pp. 30, 55, 96, 118, 192, 218, 285, 378, Elizabeth Crews/The Image Works; p. 172, Richard Hutchings/InfoEdit; p. 259, Stephen McBrady/PhotoEdit; p. 330, Paul Conklin/PhotoEdit; p. 355, Jeffry W. Myers/Stock Boston.

Executive Editor: Christopher Jennison
Project Editor: Diane Rowell
Design Supervisor: Jaye Zimet
Text Design: Glen Edelstein
Cover Design: Jaye Zimet
Photo Researcher: Carol Parden
Production: Kathleen Donnelly/Beth Maglione
Compositor: Waldman Graphics, Inc.
Printer and Binder: Courier Companies, Inc.
Cover Printer: The Lehigh Press, Inc.

Teaching Elementary School Mathematics

Library of Congress Cataloging-in-Publication Data

D'Augustine, Charles H.
    Teaching elementary school mathematics / Charles D'Augustine,
C. Winston Smith, Jr.
        p. cm.
    Includes bibliographical references and index.
    ISBN 0-06-041473-1
    1. Mathematica—Study and teaching (Elementary) I. Smith, C.
Winston (Charles Winston) II. Title.
QA135.5.D29   1992
372.7—dc20   91-19058
                                                          CIP

91 92 93 94 9 8 7 6 5 4 3 2 1

This book is dedicated to the
individuals who contributed to
NCTM's *Curriculum and Evaluation
Standards for School Mathematics*.

CONTENTS

PREFACE

While the writing of this text has been strongly influenced by the recommendations for curriculum and instruction found in the *Curriculum and Evaluation Standards for School Mathematics* published by the National Council of Teachers of Mathematics (1989), the authors have made a conscious effort to write a text that not only can be used by students who will begin their teaching careers in systems that are well along in adopting the Standards, but also by students who will begin their teaching in systems slow to adopt the Standards' recommendations. For example, many of the suggestions in this text for teacher-guided interactive learning activities and independent and small-group learning activities can be incorporated by teachers within the context of almost any mathematics instructional program.

Suggestions for developing the problem-solving process have been written with a full recognition that many new teachers will be utilizing basal series as a starting point for their development of problem-solving skills. This text makes suggestions on how the "story problems" found in basal texts can be restructured into better models for developing the problem-solving process through activities such as acting the "problems" out, solving the "problems" using models (graphs, pictures, experiments, etc.), and by letting the "problems" provide a focus for generating student-created problems.

Recognizing that some teachers may not teach in systems in which calculators and computers are abundantly available to students, suggestions are made in the text to help overcome this deficiency through shared use of technological devices in learning stations and cooperative group settings.

Aware that some curricula may not make specific provisions for some of the mathematics skills and concepts that educators feel are essential for children to have in a technological society (such as estimation and mathematical reasoning skills), the authors have included suggestions for methods of fitting these concepts and skills into the school day.

While the primary emphasis of assessing the child is finding out what a child knows, and assisting the child to broaden this knowledge, attention is also devoted to identifying errors a child may make habitually, and offering techniques for correcting these errors.

Attention is given throughout the text to a wide variety of techniques that assist children who have physical, mental, social, and emotional deficits. In addition, samples of special provisions for children who may be talented or gifted in mathematics are presented. Areas that may present special problems in teaching are pointed out throughout the text.

Recognizing that the lecture-based method of instruction is totally inadequate as a method for teaching mathematics to young children, the text presents a wide variety of techniques for individual and small-group learning activities. When teacher-guided lesson fragments are presented, the lessons are interactive in nature, utilizing student involvement with manipulatives and communications with other students and the teacher. Special effort has been made to incorporate into the teacher-guided interactive learning activities responses that will provide assessment data relating to students, instruction, and the curriculum.

ACKNOWLEDGMENTS

The authors would like to gratefully acknowledge the assistance of Dr. Bonnie Beach and her undergraduate students at Ohio University Lancaster Campus who field tested early drafts of this text. We would also like to acknowledge the professional advice and guidance of Dr. Len Pikaart, the Robert Morton Mathematics Education Professor at Ohio University, Steve Meiring of the Ohio Department of Education, and the following professors who reviewed the text: Charles Allen, University of Pittsburgh; Catherine Brown, Virginia Polytechnic University; Anna O. Graeber, University of Maryland; Virginia R. Harvin, Indiana University; Herbert K. Heger, University of Texas at El Paso; Gordon Johnston, Mississippi State University; Ray Kurtz, Kansas State University; James Overholt, California State University at Chico; and David Wiley at the University of Pittsburgh.

The authors also would like to recognize AnnaBelle D'Augustine and Darlyne Smith, without whose support and patience this book never could have been written.

Charles D'Augustine
C. Winston Smith, Jr.

TEACHING ELEMENTARY SCHOOL MATHEMATICS

CHAPTER 1

ELEMENTARY SCHOOL MATHEMATICS CURRICULUM

INTRODUCTION

An elementary teacher needs to be knowledgeable in each of the following:

- **What** he or she will be teaching (the **mathematics curriculum**)
- **How to facilitate children's learning** of the concepts, skills, and knowledges prescribed in the mathematics curriculum
- **How to evaluate the three elements of the instructional process** (the children, the curriculum, the instruction)

This chapter will examine the nature of the elementary school mathematics curriculum, the skills teachers need to facilitate the learning process including organizational and planning skills, and strategies for promoting one's growth as a teacher. Future chapters will examine the evaluation and assessment process, and how to facilitate the learning process with specific mathematical content, knowledges, and skills.

1.1 THE NATURE OF THE ELEMENTARY MATHEMATICS CURRICULUM

The elementary school mathematics curriculum and its instruction is not a *static* body of information and processes—it evolves constantly to include new findings in the subject area, new information about how individuals learn, and new directions in society. Sometimes the needs of the subject, the learner, or society are not strongly perceived, so change occurs slowly. When there is a strong perception that the mathematics curriculum and/or instruction are not meeting the current and future needs of students, then society demands a more rapid pace of change. The 1990s is one of those periods of rapid change.

In 1989 the National Research Council disseminated a report entitled *Everybody Counts—A Report to the Nation on the Future of Mathematics Education*. In the summary document, the Council proclaimed that:

> Over the next two decades, all of the major components of mathematics education—curricula, teaching, teacher education, testing, textbooks and software—must change significantly. . . .

For those just entering the field of teaching, such a proclamation must be placed in historical perspective, because the mathematics curriculum has been continually changing and evolving since the colonial period. **Table 1.1** illustrates some of the major changes that have taken place in mathematics education since the colonial period when boys were taught to "cipher" numbers so that they could be keepers of the stores for trading companies. (A bibliography is included at the end of this chapter for those students who wish to examine in greater depth the development of mathematics instruction in the United States since the colonial period.)

In the 1980s a number of groups expressed concern about the poor status of mathematics instruction in the United States. (National Research Council, 1989; National Commission on Excellence in Education, 1983; the National Science Board Commission on Precollege Education in Mathematics and Science, 1983; and the National Council of Teachers of Mathematics, 1980). There was a strong consensus of opinion that mathematics instruction could be improved if there were changes made not only in the curriculum but also in the way students were taught mathematics.

1.2 AN OVERVIEW OF THE CURRICULUM AND EVALUATION STANDARDS FOR SCHOOL MATHEMATICS

In 1989, after several years' effort by working groups of the Commission on Standards for School Mathematics, the National Council of Teachers of Mathematics published *Curriculum and Evaluation Standards for School Mathematics* (NCTM, 1989, hereafter referred to as the *Standards*). A preliminary draft was widely circulated prior to publication and feedback from business leaders, mathematicians, mathematics educators, teachers, parents, and other interested parties was solicited before the final draft was printed.

The *Standards* not only recommend concepts, knowledges, and skills that should be developed by the mathematics curriculum, it also suggests instructional processes for facilitating the learning and evaluation procedures.

Because the *Standards* will strongly influence the mathematics curricula adopted by local school boards as well as publication of mathematics materials for teachers and children, it is imperative that prospective teachers be aware of its recommendations. The following paragraphs highlight and summarize *some* of the suggestions to be found in the *Standards*. (To obtain a better understanding of the full implications of this document, the au-

thors recommend that each teacher who plans to teach elementary school mathematics examine the *Standards*.)

General Assumptions of the *Standards*

There are general assumptions for teaching the child in the lower elementary grades that are well established principles of teaching. Some of these principles have gained wide acceptance through the works of people such as Brownell (1945), Bruner (1960), Piaget (1953), Polya (1957), and VanEngen (1965). The *Standards* **assume** that the curriculum will (1) *stress mathematical thinking and reasoning*, (2) *be developmentally appropriate for children*, (3) *involve children in the actual doing of mathematics*, (4) *utilize real problems from the child's environment*, (5) *develop an understanding of mathematical concepts*, (6) *make full use of calculators*, and (7) *emphasize the application of mathematics and the development of the interrelationships of mathematical knowledge*.

Problem Solving as a Process

The elementary school mathematics curriculum will play a major role in developing problem solvers. Problem solving is a process which can be **learned** by students. Pupils should explore strategies within the context of problems arising in everyday situations. As students mature, their problem-solving strategies will develop from mathematical content as well as everyday situations.

The suggestions for developing problem-solving skills represent a marked departure from the way problem solving has been developed in elementary school classrooms. The *Standards* suggest that problem solving be undertaken in extended projects and problems be derived from verbal as well as written communications. Even computational skills and algorithms can be introduced in problem situations. Children will investigate open-ended problems and formulate questions from these situations. Problems may be found in disciplines and real-life applications—not just in mathematics lessons. (For examples of applications of these aspects, see Chapter 3 on Problem Solving.)

Communicating Mathematical Ideas

Pupils must learn to read, write, and speak mathematical ideas. Students should learn in an environment that not only encourages communication,

TABLE 1.1

Period	Characteristics
1700s–1800s	**PRACTICAL MATHEMATICS ERA**

- Youth taught to be "keepers of the store." (Cited in Kilpatrick, 1917; Monroe, 1917; Smith, 1934)

1800s–1900s	**MIND AS A MUSCLE ERA**

- Educators viewed the mind as a "muscle" that would grow stronger with exercise.
- Arithmetic taught to younger children than during colonial period. Textbooks arranged in more efficient sequences of topics. (Cited in Monroe, 1917)
- Practical problems used to motivate students (as cited in Edwards, 1947).
- A few educators advocated arithmetic be taught inductively using manipulative objects (as cited in Cremin, 1961).

1900–1930s	**DRILL THEORY ERA**

- Many educators viewed learning as the "building of bonds" between a stimulus and response (S-R bonding). Teachers used timed drills to build bonds. (Thorndike, 1922)
- Pupils learned mathematics as the "sum of the whole"—learning skills first and then examining how those skills fit together.
- Some educators advocated a curriculum that pupils would encounter in adult life (as cited in Callahan, 1975).

1930s–1950s	**MEANINGFUL MATHEMATICS ERA**

- Educators viewed learning in terms of "gestalt" or field theory of learning. Pupils looked at the "whole picture"—then viewed the parts and how they were related.
- Research showed pupils learned more effectively using an activity-oriented approach than a drill/practice approach.

1950s–1960s	**MODERN MATHEMATICS ERA**

- Mathematics curriculum redesigned to emphasize the structure of mathematics and its principles.
- Teachers used a discovery approach and a precise mathematical vocabulary (as cited in Riedesel, 1987).
- Topics were introduced earlier in the curriculum.
- Mathematical "analysis" was used to explore algorithms.
- Laboratory approach explored.

1970s–1980s	**BACK TO THE BASICS ERA**

- Backlash from parents and concerned citizens caused curriculums to re-focus upon computational skills.
- Concern with individualized instruction (IPI, IGE).
- National Assessment of Educational Progress (1972–73; 77–78; 81–82; 85–86) showed pupils deficient in higher-level skills, especially problem solving.
- In studies comparing U.S. students to other industrialized countries, American pupils lagged behind their foreign counterparts (cited by National Research Council, 1989).

1990s	**THE "STANDARDS" ERA**

- Curriculums examined in terms of "Standards" published by the National Council of Teachers of Mathematics.

but gives them an opportunity to reflect and clarify their thinking. Communication skills will develop as the child works with others in small groups; exchanges ideas with other students; and interacts with the teacher.

First discussions of mathematical ideas utilize the child's own language, but as children mature they will learn to use more formal language and symbolism.

Mathematics as a Process for Reasoning

Primary-level pupils are involved in informal thinking, conjecturing, and validating. Mathematics should be viewed as reasoning, and as such, children will learn to draw logical conclusions and explain their thinking with the aid of models, properties, relationships, and known facts. Part of the reasoning process can be developed through the study of patterns and relationships.

In the upper elementary grades students will be taught to recognize and apply both deductive and inductive reasonings and that reasoning will be extended to include work with proportions and graphs.

Making Mathematical Connections

When making connections the *Standards* suggest not only assisting students to make the obvious connections between areas of mathematics, but also connecting mathematics to the real world and to other disciplines such as art, music, science, and business, and to other curriculum areas.

Extensive Estimation Activities

Estimation has always been a part of the process of teaching computation and measurement topics, but it has not been as widely applied with quantities and problem-solving activities as is currently being proposed. The *Standards* propose an even greater emphasis on estimation, suggesting that children should be **taught** general estimation strategies.

Number Sense and Numeration

Number sense and numeration are best developed through real-world experiences and physical materials. The *Standards* recommend building understanding through counting, grouping, and place-value concepts. While this does not represent a new approach, such procedures are still absent in some elementary school classrooms.

Whole Number Operation Concepts

At the primary grade levels mathematical operations occur first in problem situations. Pupils should use models and discuss their activities. The *Standards* suggest that more precise mathematical language and symbolism should grow from the child's use of informal language. Children must also learn that a wide variety of problem structures can be represented by a single operation.

Reasonable Proficiency with Basic Facts and Algorithms

Pupils need to develop reasonable proficiency with basic facts and written algorithms, but they must also learn to use a calculator as a computational tool. Pupils should be able to select a way to compute a problem and then determine the reasonableness of the results.

Developing Fraction and Decimal Concepts in the Lower Grades

Concepts related to familiar fractions and mixed numerals are to be developed in the primary grades. Models should be used to explore equivalent fractions and operations on fractions. While the *Standards* recommend that young children study decimals only through tenths, some understanding of hundredths will develop as a natural outgrowth of the study of money and metric measurement. In upper grade levels, fraction and decimal concepts are explored in a problem-solving environment, where the students' number sense will be extended to include fraction and decimal notation.

Developing Computation and Estimation Skills in the Upper Grades

In the upper elementary grades, computation and estimation concepts will be developed in many ways. This variety will strengthen the student's ability to compute with different number systems (whole numbers, integers, fractions, decimals, and rational numbers) and to choose a mode appropriate for the task (mental arithmetic, paper and pencil, calculator, and computer). The student should be able to analyze, develop, and explain computational algorithms and use techniques for estimation.

Developing Geometry Concepts and Spatial Sense

In elementary school students will learn to describe, model, draw, and classify two- and three-dimensional figures, recognizing and appreciating the application of these shapes to the real world. Pupil investigations should include predicting the results of various alterations of the shapes (subdividing, combining, and changing). Geometric concepts will be tied to measurement concepts.

At the upper grades, concepts developed in the primary grades will be extended. As children progress through the upper grades they will learn to solve problems using geometric models and understand geometric properties and relationships. In addition, the upper-grade student will be introduced to the transformations of geometric figures.

Measurement

In the lower grades students first explore the attributes of measurement. The concept of units of measurement and the process of measuring with these units will also be developed. In addition to using measurement units in everyday situations, students will learn to estimate measurements.

In addition to the extension of previously explored concepts, the *Standards* recommend that upper grade level pupils use measurement to describe and compare. Learning experiences must promote student understanding of the structure and use of systems of measurement. The concepts of rates, derived and indirect measures, formulas, and procedures for solving problems should also be developed in the upper grades.

Statistics and Probability

Primary children collect, organize, and display data, and use data to make predictions and solve problems. Probability should be studied within the context of how it is applied in everyday life, and activities will include experiments of chance. Upper elementary grade level students will use statistical methods to describe, analyze, evaluate, and make decisions.

Development of Patterns, Relations, and Functions

In the primary grades children should learn to describe, represent, and create a wide variety of functional relationships and patterns. The strategies children use to find solutions to open sentences should include both intuitive and inverse operation strategies. Upper elementary grade students will learn to identify and use functional relationships, and utilize graphs, tables, and rules to describe functional situations and patterns.

Algebraic Explorations

The *Standards* recommend that a foundation be laid in the upper elementary grades for the study of algebra through informal investigations of inequalities and the use of a variety of methods of solving linear equations. As part of that foundation, the student would develop an understanding of variable expressions and equations.

1.3 CONTINUING TRENDS

Even before the publication of the *Standards*, many changes were taking place that were totally compatible with its recommendations. In this section a few of these trends will be examined.

Use of Calculators

Small handheld calculators have significantly influenced society. Before the calculator an individual needed to become very proficient using paper and pencil computation. Today calculators are used for those functions.

Though the use of noncalculator computation has diminished, the need to understand the **meanings** of the computational processes and to be able to **estimate** has increased. Individuals must recognize when answers obtained on a calculator seem unreasonable. Occasionally the data is entered incorrectly or the calculator may not have been cleared from a previous calculation. Some of the curriculum previously allotted to mastery of computational skills may now be used to build **estimation**, **approximation**, and **problem-solving skills**.

Of course, the inclusion of calculators into the curriculum has not been without resistance. Many adults do not recognize the diminishing need for paper and pencil calculations. They also do not understand how helpful the device can be in developing an understanding of **place value** and **algorithms**, skill in **recognizing patterns**, and how it strengthens **estimation** and **problem-solving skills**.

Using the Computer

Once an expensive research tool, computers are now found in governmental offices, banks, large and small businesses, educational institutions, and even homes. Recognizing the important role played by computers in today's world, parents have generally been advocates for the use of computers in the school curriculum. In some school districts parent organizations have purchased computers for every classroom. Local businesses have also taken a leadership role in encouraging school programs to help pupils become literate in computer usage.

Computers have become common in the classroom and now publishers are including software in their catalogs. Where once teachers had to design their own instructional programs using the computer's BASIC language, the selection of commercial and public-domain software reduces this time-consuming chore. Software is inexpensively available for everything from "drill and practice" to sophisticated problem-solving simulations.

There are many ways to use computers in the instructional program. Software programs oriented toward teaching concepts are available. Sometimes the computer is used as a tool to maintain or improve a pupil's skill development. A convenient feature of many programs is the capability of monitoring student progress. By analyzing computer printouts of pupil work, teachers not only can evaluate student progress, but also can detect which pupils are having difficulty.

Meeting the Needs of Individuals

In the 1970s and 1980s mathematics educators explored techniques to meet the needs of individual pupils. Feeling that instruction would be more effective if personalized, systems were developed to provide for individual differences, such as Individual Prescribed Instruction (IPI) and Individually Guided Education (IGE). In the hands of expert teachers these programs were effective instructional vehicles. In some cases, however, individualized instruction became worksheet-oriented. Mathematics became a "lonely" activity with each child working at his or her own rate in a learning carrel.

The individual remains a major concern of the teacher. However, educators now recognize that an exclusive diet of individualized instruction will not meet every goal of mathematics instruction. Being able to communicate mathematical concepts is one important mathematical goal that cannot be developed when children are taught in isolation from their peers. Pupils who are able to share insights and problem-solving strategies gain as much from sharing with others as they do from their own individual problem-solving efforts.

Contemporary programs consider the contribution of small groups of students interacting with other students; the value of teacher-guided instruction that allows students to interact with the teacher as well as other students; and the importance of personal growth in mathematical skills.

Greater Use of Cooperative Learning Settings

Cooperative learning has long been a part of the educational program, especially in kindergarten. However, as students progress through elementary school, working with others usually was found only in the social studies program—not during mathematics instruction. In the past, teachers have constructed mathematics activities so that all pupils worked on the same problem—but independently. Getting assistance from a classmate not only was discouraged, but in many cases called "cheating." When discovery learning activities and laboratory assignments were emphasized during the 1970s, mathematics educators found that pupils could work together in cooperative endeavors without diminishing the learning of individuals. In fact, pupils gained greatly from the interchange of ideas and the "brainstorming" that occurred during these problem-solving activities.

Cooperative learning (working in small groups to solve problems and gain skills) provides an ideal setting for communicating mathematical ideas. In a cooperative learning setting children:

1. Practice and refine their communication skills with mathematics.
2. Explore and share a wide variety of problem-solving strategies within the context of a team.
3. Utilize manipulative materials. (Of course, the use of manipulative materials is not restricted to cooperative learning settings. However, when manipulative materials are limited, cooperative learning settings provide an opportunity for a greater number of pupils to use these resources.)
4. Help each other gain skills through peer instruction. (The success of a cooperative group is generally measured by the ability of

ALL pupils in the group to perform effectively. In such a setting, a more gifted pupil is motivated to help individuals within his/her group gain a skill, since the gifted pupil's performance is evaluated by how well EACH pupil performs. In explaining a process, the stronger student deepens his/her understanding of a concept.)

5. Gain experience in working within a group.

Multistructured Classrooms

Elementary school classrooms were once filled with orderly rows of desks bolted to the floor. Creative teachers found ways to overcome the limitations of such a structure, but it was difficult to group pupils in this environment. Today, most classrooms have moveable desks and chairs so the classroom teacher can vary the seating arrangements. While science, social studies, and language arts make wide use of different seating arrangements, much of the mathematics instruction continues to be directed to orderly rows of desks (even though the children may be seated in groups of four or six).

The "New Math" of the 1960s brought with it discovery learning, encouraging teachers to place children into groups to solve problems. As teachers worked with the "individualized instruction" of the 1970s–1980s, learning stations were arranged around the room and individuals engaged in educational activities away from their desks. "Centers" or "activity tables" were also established in the classroom, encouraging students to use manipulative materials when exploring mathematical ideas.

A contemporary multidirectional approach requires flexible grouping of students and a multistructured classroom, where the "walls" of the classroom extend far beyond the old view of four walls in a school building.

Application of Mathematics

As children progress from kindergarten through grade 12, some develop a distaste for mathematics. They fail to see the direct application of the mathematical skills they are learning. In the past many mathematical concepts have been justified as prerequisites for more advanced topics. Teachers gave few examples of how mathematics was useful in pupils' everyday lives or for their future vocational choices. For the past two decades textbooks have shown how mathematics is used in various occupations. Texts include illustrations of scientists, aviators, sports figures, store clerks, production engineers, dentists, and even shoppers using mathematics to solve problems in their fields.

While this trend was helpful, children still saw mathematics as a skill to be used when they "grew up." Future occupational choices proved to be insufficient motivation for many. Today (as reinforced in NCTM's *Standards*) activities that require the pupil to **use mathematics in the classroom** are incorporated into the mathematics program. Teachers search out opportunities to introduce mathematical skills and concepts in problem-solving situations applicable to the classroom and the child's daily life.

1.4 FACILITATING CHILDREN'S LEARNING

Several recent studies have examined the attributes of expert teachers, comparing them with novice teachers to determine how they differ. These studies—summarized both by the Department of Education in *Research in Brief* (November 1986) and the National Council of Teachers of Mathematics (NCTM) in the *Arithmetic Teacher* (December 1986)—identify several characteristics of the expert teacher. While the two reports differed somewhat, they agreed that expert teachers: (a) know their subject (mathematics); (b) organize their lessons effectively; and (c) use their time wisely.

Expert teachers know their subject. Not only do good mathematics teachers know their subject, they also are sensitive to concepts that may give pupils difficulty. They are familiar with materials that can be used to help students understand the concepts being explored and know when it is appropriate to use these materials. They can use several different ways to explore a topic and are able to select the techniques or materials most appropriate to the topic being taught. The expert teacher avoids ambiguity, seeking precise but easily understood terms.

Expert teachers organize their lessons effectively. Experts know what they are going to teach and how they are going to do it. They develop plans (or agendas) of what will be occurring in the lesson; they mentally think the lesson through. While these plans may appear to be brief, they are intricate and highly structured. The teacher plans a logical flow for the lesson, considers pupil activity, and recognizes decision points where reteaching might be necessary. Though the plans may appear more structured than those of the novice teacher, when teaching the expert will readily modify a lesson to reach an objective.

Expert teachers use their time wisely. Many teachers, particularly the novice, do not use class time efficiently. Time is wasted getting the lesson started, passing out materials, taking up papers, etc. The expert makes efficient use of *routines* so teaching begins promptly. Such a teacher is less distracted by irrelevant pupil comments or actions and is able to maintain a focus upon the task at hand. Logical movement through the lesson keeps pupils involved in the learning process. Experts also make use of "wasted moments"—minutes spent lining up, passing in papers, waiting for special events. When homework is assigned, students practice those things taught that day, thus extending the learning. Expert teachers maintain practice on those skills already mastered, reinforcing the lessons and building pupil confidence.

This section will examine some of the prerequisite skills for becoming an expert teacher of mathematics in the elementary schools. Since teachers require constant renewal to maintain and enhance their skills, this section examines the types of activities that promote renewal.

Becoming a Skilled Teacher of Elementary School Mathematics

There are many areas that must be mastered on the way to becoming a skillful teacher of elementary school mathematics. Before one can plan a lesson, he/she must be knowledgeable of the content (mathematics); recognize the background and abilities of the students and be able to make provisions for these differences; be familiar with and able to appropriately utilize a wide variety of teaching techniques and learning environments; and be able to develop and execute a process for achieving the goals of the mathematics curriculum.

Using This Text to Develop Teaching Skills

This text has several organizational features which can help the novice teacher develop skill in teaching mathematical skills in the elementary school. These features include: sample scope-and-sequence charts; teacher-guided interactive learning activities, in which the students interact with the teacher and other students; small-group activities, individual activities, separation of topics into primary and intermediate-level developments; illustrations showing the use of manipulative materials; a major emphasis on developing problem-solving skills within the context of real-life situations and from a broad range of disciplines (art, anthropology, science, business, etc.); end-of-chapter exercises that guide the reader's study of

the material; sample pupil activities; and a bibliography of supplementary readings and related computer software. While some of these features are self-explanatory, two organizational formats—scope-and-sequence charts and teacher-guided interactive learning activities—need additional discussion to enhance their value to the reader.

In the introduction of each methods chapter a typical scope and sequence is listed. By examining this outline, the teacher can identify the order in which skills are *generally* developed and associate those skills with a grade level. Since pupil abilities differ, students may develop a given skill earlier or later than the grade level indicated. The sequence, however, should serve as a guide to the general order in which the skills are introduced.

Earlier in this section, elements of a skillful teacher were identified. When reading descriptive lesson fragments in this text, one should examine the role each component plays in the lesson. To highlight this aspect of teaching, the acronym **M A T H** is used. (In addition to the lesson fragments, numerous descriptions of individual and small-group learning activities are given throughout the text.)

Mathematical concepts: A skilled teacher understands in depth the mathematical concepts being developed. This includes not only the *why*, but also *how* these concepts are used in problem solving and where they fit into the scope and sequence.

Attributes of the students: A skilled teacher recognizes the attributes and abilities of the group being taught. Not only does the teacher identify the abilities of the group—the differences within the group are also recognized.

Techniques of teaching: A skilled teacher is familiar with many teaching strategies and selects from among these methods, matching techniques (T) to both to the mathematical content (M) and the abilities (A) of the pupils.

Heuristics of teaching: The skilled teacher must consider needs of the mathematical topic, the abilities of the students, and technique to be used—then organize those into a logical, efficient presentation. The teacher is flexible, modifying instruction to provide alternate ways of reaching the objective, providing additional help for those students who cannot grasp the skill within the allotted time period, and periodically reviewing and reteaching as necessary. (More on this aspect of teaching mathematics is presented in the next section.)

Providing for Children Differing in Attributes

Children differ. Sometimes, as in the case of identical twins, these differences may be slight, but generally these differences are major enough to influence both *how* as well as *what* children are taught. Throughout this text illustrations will be given to show how many of these differences can be met. The instructional techniques illustrated will primarily relate to making accommodations for children differing in physical, social, emotional, and mental abilities.

General Methods of Teaching Elementary School Mathematics— An Overview

Some techniques used to teach elementary school mathematics are also used extensively when teaching subjects other than mathematics. Learning stations used in teaching mathematics are also used extensively in language arts, social studies, science, etc. This section will briefly survey some of those techniques, but the focus will be upon the manner in which these methods are used when teaching mathematics. Because these techniques are discussed in a mathematics teaching context only, there may be minor differences in the way the method is described or specific characteristics of the technique.

These general methods, classified by the learning environments, will be examined in the following categories: (1) individual learning activities minimally teacher-controlled; (2) small-group learning activities minimally teacher-controlled; and (3) teacher-guided interactive learning activities (individual and group instruction).

Individual Learning Activities

When a pupil interacts with the environment, reflects on mathematical ideas, engages in the act of problem solving, attempts to bring order out of disorder, studies patterns, or engages in some aspect of mathematics in a recreational activity, he or she develops not only mathematical understandings, but also an appreciation for his or her own ability. In individual learning activities, the pupil works alone—even though he/she may be in a classroom setting. The pupil's thoughts are directed inward. While communication takes place within the individual, the teacher plays a critical role in structuring the environment to maximize and focus the learning activity. In some instances the focus may be general in nature, such as setting up a classroom

or center where pupils can explore materials. A kindergarten teacher may put out blocks or geometric shapes for pupils to explore and use in building roads, houses, and toys. Unstructured activities promote many different mathematical understandings, but an individual child may learn a little or a great deal from the setting. For instance, pouring water or sand from one container to another may lead a pupil to see that different containers can hold the same amount—that two cups will fill one pint—or merely that water sometimes spills on the floor. A teacher, at the right moment, may pose carefully crafted questions to help pupils reflect upon their experiences.

As students progress through the primary grades, independent hands-on explorations with manipulative materials become more focused on specific learning objectives. While many activities are prompted by teacher-structured questions, some are prompted by a discussion with other students during a group activity, leading an individual student to seek out a solution independently. Other individual learning activities may be generated by situations encountered at a learning station; from a problem posed on the bulletin board or problem of the day; or from a problem that another student poses. Exploration of patterns (visual patterns, number patterns, auditory patterns, and physical patterns) is a rich source for independent learning activities. Well-constructed, independent learning activities develop good attitudes towards mathematics and build the student's confidence in his or her ability.

Small-Group Learning Activities (Minimal Teacher Control)

Students should be able to formulate and communicate mathematical ideas. Communication skills are developed interacting with others. When pupils work together to solve problems, there are many opportunities for communication. Pupils can learn much from one another. When pupils are free to discuss how to solve problems they hear strategies suggested by others, evaluate those strategies, and clarify their ideas, refining and improving their logical thought processes.

Small-group learning activities may be organized in a variety of structures. A teacher may assign pupils to small groups and direct all groups to work toward a solution of the same problem. Using laboratory assignment cards, a teacher may assign a different problem to each group. Lab cards may take the form of an experiment where the group sets up conjectures, gathers evidence, and arrives at a solution or resolution to questions. When the teacher uses *cooperative learning groups*, then the "learning groups" or "cells" become collectively accountable for mastered skills.

Games and simulations played by a group of students also promote interaction which fosters mathematical literacy. While somewhat limited by the flexibility of the game and its rules, such activities can be highly motivating. It is important to carefully select simulations and games which build understanding (rather than drill) to ensure that such activities build mathematical concepts.

Small-group learning not only occurs during the mathematics lesson; it also may take place in the context of another discipline. For example, when studying the environment in social studies or science, mathematical understanding may play an essential role in the discussion. Plotting data, reading graphs, and interpreting statistical statements are mathematical skills that become even more significant when used in other areas.

Teacher-Guided Interactive Learning Activities

Even when a teacher guides instruction, **students should be active participants** in the experience. Active engagement may be accomplished in a variety of ways. Encouraging each pupil to use manipulative materials when modeling mathematical operations is widely practiced in elementary classrooms. Materials help a pupil visualize an operation or process and provide a memory referent when recalling the operation or process. Manipulative materials also permit the teacher to accommodate a wide range of learning abilities and styles by directing pupil attention to specific aspects of the materials. For instance, when the kindergarten teacher uses a walk-on number line to build number-number matching skills, a more advanced student may be directed to estimate where a numeral should be placed. The teacher may then provide practice in rational counting to less mature pupils by directing them to *verify* the estimate by walking along the line. (When this technique is illustrated in an interactive lesson fragment, the word *involvement* is used.)

Active engagement does not always require physical movement. Pupils also participate when they give choral or written responses to questions or directions by the teacher. Such an activity is particularly effective when a skill is being reinforced, since students and teacher get immediate feedback. When exploring place value, pupils may be asked to observe the number of tens or ones being displayed and orally respond in unison. On another occasion, students may be asked to write their re-

sponses on individual slates and display them for teacher approval (see Figure 1.1). As pupils respond, the teacher quickly looks at the slates to identify pupils who are having difficulty. (*Choral and written involvement* is the term used when illustrated in lesson fragments.)

If a teacher wishes to reduce the level of abstraction of a particular concept, an explanation may be given in the form of a story or analogy. (The word *Analogy* is used when this technique appears in a lesson fragment.)

Concepts may be introduced by using either definitions or examples. While such a technique may start with a written or oral description, pupils use these examples as they classify figures or objects. For example, a teacher may create figures that are "gobblies" and those that are not "gobblies." (See Figure 1.2) Pupils sort out "gobblies" from a set of cards using the examples and counterexamples. (*Definitions* or *Examples* will be used to identify this technique when used in descriptive lessons.)

Activities may be designed that promote the discovery of a pattern, property, or formula. Discovery generally takes more time than simply explaining the concept to a student, since the activity builds both the mathematical concept and skill in problem solving. To make the procedure more efficient, a teacher may guide the lesson by utilizing carefully constructed problems or by asking leading ques-

Teacher-Guided Interactive Learning Activity

FIGURE 1.1

Individualized Learning Activity

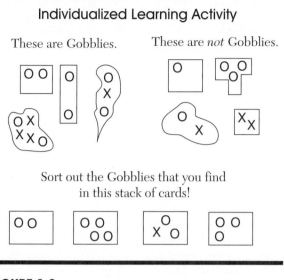

These are Gobblies.   These are *not* Gobblies.

Sort out the Gobblies that you find
in this stack of cards!

FIGURE 1.2

tions. Guiding discovery lessens the frustration level for pupils, but often limits the discovery process. (When this method is used in the interactive lesson fragments, the word *Discovery* will be used.)

Formulating rules based on discovered procedures does not lend itself to as much student participation as the use of manipulative materials. A teacher may increase involvement by using questions which direct pupils back to an originally modeled activity. The process of formulating procedures or rules is then placed in the hands of students by carefully planning or structuring the activities and questions posed by the teacher. For example, after a classification activity where the children sort models into triangles and non-triangles, the teacher may guide the pupils to formulate rules by asking, "What did you look at to decide the figure was a triangle?" ("It is made up of three line segments.") "That's true, but can just any three line segments be a triangle?" etc. (When this technique is illustrated the word *Rules* will be used.)

Since analysis has many problem-solving applications in mathematics and forms an integral structure for the more advanced mathematics, it should be included as an instructional technique when students have sufficient readiness to profit by its use. The analytic process provides a step-by-step answer to why something is logically correct. The more mature student is challenged by this step-by-step explanation of a process, but other pupils may need analytical procedures to be developed using manipulative activities. The teacher should be alert to pupil interest during the lesson and be ready to use a more concrete approach if pupils are unable to comprehend the step-by-step analysis. (When this method is illustrated in interactive lesson fragments the word *Analysis* will be used.)

1.5 PLANNING MATHEMATICS INSTRUCTION

To facilitate student learning a teacher must plan instruction, whether it takes place when the teacher is in direct control of the instructional process or when a student or group of students are working independently.

Teaching mathematics in the elementary school requires more than a knowledge of mathematics, an understanding of the attributes of children, and of techniques of presentation. Good teachers present lessons that are clear and accurate. Their lessons use many examples, demonstrations, and activities that clearly illustrate content. They strive to foster in their students a positive attitude towards mathematics, using an interactive style of teaching which provides for two-way communication between the teacher and students, and among students. Good teachers plan a series of lessons that build concepts in depth. Such lessons require organization and preplanning, especially when students will be working independently or in small non–teacher-directed groups.

While a teacher's manual may suggest materials or procedures, it is the teacher who must decide what is appropriate for the group or individual and what the most effective technique is for presenting that material. The teacher is faced with a PROBLEM: what is the best way to present this material? To solve this problem the teacher must consider many factors. In this text, the word "heuristic" (*H* in the acronym MATH) will be used when talking about the problem-solving strategies used by the teacher in planning and teaching a mathematics lesson. The word "heuristic" comes from the German *heuristisch* which means invent or discover. In its broadest sense, teaching challenges one to discover or invent a way to help children understand a mathematical concept.

This section will examine the planning skills beginning teachers will need when teaching mathematics to elementary school pupils. Some skills and techniques (learning stations, cooperative learning, lesson planning) discussed in this chapter ALSO may be developed in classes and textbooks that deal with general methods of teaching. The material in this section will emphasize the application of these techniques to the teaching of elementary school mathematics.

Selecting Appropriate Mathematics Skills and Sequence

Theoretically, a teacher is responsible for determining the mathematics skills that are needed by students assigned to his/her classroom. In practice, the teacher works within certain guidelines. Each school system chooses specific skills that it feels are vital for the students. These skills are written into objectives and assigned to be reviewed, introduced, or mastered at a specific grade level. These objectives are then printed in a curriculum guide. Using this guide, a committee often reviews elementary mathematics textbooks and/or materials and determines which series (or materials) most nearly corresponds to these objectives. After a school system makes its choice, the teacher uses information about the abilities and achievements of the assigned pupils, along with the curriculum guide and adopted textbook series/materials, to determine what instruction is appropriate.

Using the Curriculum Guide

Curriculum guides generally are compiled by a school system's curriculum committee, which consists of classroom teachers, administrators, curriculum supervisors, parents, and community leaders. Frequently the recommendations of professional organizations and mathematics educators, and publications such as NCTM's *Standards* and state requirements strongly influence the construction of these guides. The committee examines textbooks and materials to see what authors and publishers feel are significant skills. It solicits suggestions from others interested in the school curriculum—especially other classroom teachers. Finally, the committee compiles a list of skills and understandings—generally written in behavioral (or performance) objectives. In some cases, the committee will construct evaluation standards and/or instruments to measure whether the objectives have been met. This material may be sent to classroom teachers for reactions before the guide is submitted to the superintendent and school board for final approval.

Once the curriculum guide is approved by the school board, teachers in that school system are expected to design their instructional program to conform to its recommendations. Objectives in the curriculum guide may be classified as the *introduction* of new skills, concepts, or knowledges; *review and maintenance* of previously introduced skills; or the *mastery* of skills, concepts, or knowledges.

The curriculum guide is a valuable resource for the teacher. The guide lists those skills, concepts, and knowledges which the school system expects the teacher to include in his/her instructional program for the year. Examination of its scope and sequence will help a teacher ascertain which topics have been introduced in previous grades. It also helps the teacher recognize the relationship between the topics taught at that grade level and those which are introduced later in the sequence.

Children enter a class with a wide range of skill levels. Teachers must recognize that some students come to their classroom with a command of skills taught at previous grades, and possibly mastery of topics taught at that current or later grade level. There will be other pupils who have not yet mastered the skills assigned for mastery in previous grades. In spite of these variations in achievement, the teacher must plan a program of instruction to meet the needs of ALL individuals in the classroom and work towards accomplishing the objectives designated in the curriculum guide.

Using the Adopted Textbook/Materials

Some school systems adopt a textbook series or commercial materials to serve as a common foundation for their mathematics program, choosing that which most nearly correspond to the objectives stated in their curriculum guides. *These materials are not the curriculum!* They may not even include material on <u>all</u> of the curriculum objectives. In addition, textbooks may present topics in a sequence that differs radically from the sequence suggested in the curriculum guide, or may include topics that are not a part of the school's curriculum. The structure of the textbook may not lend itself to the kinds of activities needed for individual and small-group learning environments. Because of these differences, teachers need to view textbooks as only one resource which may be utilized to meet the objectives specified in a curriculum guide.

The Teacher's Edition that accompanies the texts used by students is a valuable resource for the teacher. The teacher's manual generally includes facsimiles of pupil text pages, answers to pupil exercises, objectives for teaching the page, suggested teaching procedures, practice assignments, and often enrichment activities. At the beginning of each "chapter" teacher manuals generally present an overview of the unit, objectives, new vocabulary, bulletin board suggestions, activities or games, and suggested teaching schedules for average, above-average, and below-average students. Some publishers include teaching aids, practice worksheets, calculator activities, pre- and post-tests, a year-end test, student and class record charts, individualized assignment and record charts, and even "letters to parents."

In addition to the Teacher's Edition, a text series may also publish supplementary materials that correspond to the objectives taught in the series. While some publishers continue to offer individual "practice workbooks" and "enrichment worksheets," many now publish blackline masters which may be used to reproduce classroom sets of materials. Various types of exercises are available in blackline master format, including problem-solving activities, materials for calculator/computer activities, sheets of challenge problems, activity sheets that focus on skill development, remedial material, supplementary tests, masters for creating transparencies, and materials for independent explorations.

Publishers may also provide supplementary materials in the form of instructional aids. Teachers or school systems may purchase kits that correspond to the materials being illustrated in the text. Such kits may include materials for teacher demonstrations that require an overhead projector, magnetic boards, or flannel-board. Most text series have large wall charts that depict the scope and sequence from kindergarten through grade eight, which are helpful when school systems are trying to match their objectives with those of the textbook series.

Grouping Mathematical Skills for Instruction

Many of the concepts taught in the elementary-school mathematics program require specific prerequisite understandings or skills. To provide an efficient learning environment, the curriculum is arranged in a teaching sequence so that necessary prerequisite skills are mastered prior to instruction in a specific topic. For instance, if addition of 2-digit numbers with regrouping is to be introduced in the second grade, pupils will need to understand the concept of addition, be familiar with the basic addition facts, have experience with positional value of the tens and ones, and be somewhat proficient with addition with 2-digit numbers without regrouping. In order to accomplish this, most of these prerequisite skills are introduced in first grade.

Individual teachers are not required to define an entire curriculum from kindergarten through

high school. This outline is provided by school systems (or textbooks) and printed in their scope and sequence. By examining the scope and sequence, a teacher may quickly determine those skills or concepts which were assigned to be developed before (and after) the present grade.

While the teacher is *guided* by the school's (or text's) scope and sequence, decisions related to the instructional sequence within the year are determined by the teacher. Some skills are more efficiently taught when grouped with similar skills. For instance, a teacher may wish to teach rounding while students are learning place value. Since these topics are closely related, the teacher may combine the two topics into a single "unit" of instruction for several days. The teacher can follow that unit with a unit on subtraction with regrouping. Another teacher may choose to delay instruction in rounding until after regrouping. Both teachers, however, may place regrouping in subtraction after place value since an understanding of positional value is a prerequisite skill for regrouping.

Since units of instruction require differing skills, teachers may change the order in which some topics are explored. For instance, a unit on symmetry does not require the same prerequisite skills as a unit on division. A symmetry unit could be introduced prior to division or it could follow a unit on division. However, a division unit which works with 2-digit quotients generally would not be taught before 1-digit quotients are mastered, since an understanding of 1-digit quotients is a prerequisite skill for the 2-digit quotients.

In children's textbooks, authors group skills by placing them into "chapters" or "units." The placement of skills within textbook chapters indicates the authors' recommended sequence for instruction. Publishers are careful to present a sequence that insures that necessary skills for efficient learning of a new skill have been developed and/or reviewed earlier in that text or series. Since the textbook is just one of many instructional resources used by a teacher, it is not essential that the sequence of chapters be rigorously followed. However, when teachers choose not to follow the textbook's recommended sequence, they must make sure that pupils have the prerequisite skills for each concept being developed.

Effective teachers examine the assigned topics and map out a long-range (or yearly) plan, outlining the approximate length of time that will be devoted to development of each skill. A long-range plan is not a schedule that must be rigidly maintained; it can (and should) be modified as the year progresses. Sometimes pupils master a skill much more easily and in much less time than anticipated. On other occasions, they need additional time—more than anticipated earlier in the year—to become skillful. In spite of the need to constantly revise yearly or semester plans, long-range planning provides direction for the teacher and insures orderly development of the skills identified in the school's scope and sequence.

Developing a Unit and Specific Lessons Within the Unit

The scope and sequence lists the skills appropriate for a given grade level, but it is the teacher's responsibility to determine whether students in his/her classroom have the prerequisite skills. Generally, teachers introduce a new topic by reviewing prerequisite skills with the class. While the review is focused toward the new topic, it also provides the teacher an opportunity to assess student mastery of prerequisite skills. Once students demonstrate readiness for a unit, the teacher will prepare an instructional plan. Some of the key questions a teacher must address in planning the lesson plans that make up a unit are:

How Much Time Should be Allotted for Teaching a Unit?

Factors that should be considered when introducing a new unit include past experience teaching a similar unit; emphasis given the unit in the curriculum guide; amount of development in a basal text when one is used by the school system; abilities of members of the class; student readiness for material presented in the unit; and past success with other mathematics units.

How are Lessons Within the Unit Developed?

If Introducing New Concepts, Skills and Knowledges

- Identify the nature of the mathematics concepts to be taught.
- Identify the desired behavioral outcomes.
- Identify the kinds of activities and procedures (teacher-guided interactive, individual, or group-learning activities) that will promote the desired behaviors.
- Outline how the activities will be conducted, including what and how materials will be used.

If Promoting Students' Mastery of Concepts, Skills, and Knowledges

- Specify the objectives in terms that will indicate what will be accepted as an indication of mastery (pupil performance objectives).
- Identify the kinds of activities and procedures that will promote mastery.
- Outline how the activities will be conducted, including what and how materials will be used.
- Provide a means of evaluating how well concepts are being acquired.
- Provide for remediation activities when habituated errors are detected and for enrichment activities for students who have mastered the objectives.

If Maintaining Previously Developed Concepts, Skills, and Knowledges

- Specify the objectives in terms that will indicate that an acceptable level of mastery has been restored.
- Identify the activities that will be needed to maintain the skills or concepts (individual learning activities, small-group activities such as games, teacher-directed activities).
- Outline how the activities will be conducted, including what and how materials will be used.
- Provide for remediation activities when habituated errors are detected and for enrichment activities when students indicate they have restored their skill to acceptable levels.

Children differ in their ability to handle abstract ideas.

Executing a Planned Lesson

Teaching is a dynamic interactive activity. Both teachers and students shape the actual execution of a lesson. Lesson plans guide the lesson and promote efficient use of the time allocated to teach mathematics. Skilled teachers adjust their teaching plans as the teaching process unfolds. Without lesson plans to maintain direction, it may prove difficult to return from some side exploration that often becomes a normal part as learning is being facilitated, either under teacher-guided interactive learning activities or as the child engages in individual or small-group learning activities. As a matter of fact, without careful planning, the teacher may be unaware of just how far afield the instructional process is straying.

Some **general suggestions** for executing a mathematics lesson are:

- When possible, begin lessons from problems derived from the pupils' environment, or at least by relating the lesson to their experiences. Such a process gives pupils a purpose for learning a skill and an application for the skill. (Most lesson fragments in this text originate from a problem situation.)
- Indicate to pupils, either verbally or, as in the case of learning stations, in writing, exactly what they are expected to get out of the lesson. It is often helpful to provide a description of the activities in which they will participate before the activities actually begin.
- When manipulative materials are to be used, give clear and complete directions about their use.
- Solicit responses from children during the instructional process, using these responses as an evaluative device to modify the lesson.
- Use multisensory instructional techniques. Information is acquired through a variety of senses.
- When new vocabulary is being associated with a model, display a written form of the word, identify how the word is pronounced, and have the children pronounce the vocabulary. For example, when the word "sphere" is introduced for the first time, the word would be written or displayed, and the teacher could say, "This word is pronounced 'sphere.' Say the word 'sphere' with me."
- Associate the use of a model with the development of an abstract expression. For example, if you are using a place-value chart to show regrouping in addition, after the regrouping with the model, show the same step with the symbols.
- Give positive recognition for correct responses and try to find some correct aspect of a wrong answer that can be used in the instructional process. Reward correct answers with praise and try to acknowledge that an answer is incorrect without condemnation. Remember that incorrect answers are a normal part of the learning process and don't become a problem until the errors are habituated.
- Strive to promote a good learning environment. Good learning environments are present when all students can be actively involved in the learning process.
- Be prepared during the instructional process to help students who need special assistance.
- Let group leaders or individual students provide summaries of the concepts being developed. This is especially important when a rule, generalization, property, or process is being developed. Summaries can be oral or written.
- Use methods that require the student to interact with the learning process and other students. Questions bring students into the learning process. A series of well-constructed questions, leading students to see "why" or "how," is a better technique than simply telling. Responses to questions not only hold students' attention, but allow the teacher to determine whether students understand what is being presented. Many activities function like questions in the teaching process. For example, problem-solving activities, discovery activities with patterns or properties, and manipulative activities with models are activities that involve the student and give evidence that the child is attaining the concept.
- Provide practice that closely parallels the way the concepts were developed. Practice activities should proceed from the simplest to the most difficult exercises. Practice exercises should provide for a wide range of abilities. Learning-disabled children can use special algorithms or augment their skill level with tables, charts, or technological devices. Alternate exercises may present a challenge to a gifted student.
- Include opportunities for children to communicate mathematical ideas. For example, outside of the classroom, mathematics serves

as a vehicle for communicating with others. Even when a solution to a problem is found, it often is only the first step in applying that solution. Others must be convinced of the "appropriateness" of the solution before they are willing to accept the solution. These skills are only developed in an environment which permits pupils to communicate mathematical ideas to other students. Problem-solving efforts in the work world may involve teams of people, such as environmental groups, industrial workers, engineers, scientists, etc. Helping pupils gain an appreciation for the use of mathematics in society, its flexibility, and the connections between mathematical ideas is best nurtured by involving children in cooperative team projects and team problem-solving efforts.

- Include opportunities for children to work independently of others. There are some goals that are best achieved in a setting where the pupil may control the independent learning environment. For example, individuals need research skills, independent study skills, and opportunities to investigate applications of mathematics that reflect individual interests. Some skills, such as number sense, are best

nurtured when the pupil is engaged in an independent exploration or study activity that permits reflective thinking.

1.6 LONG-RANGE MAINTENANCE AND EXTENSION OF TEACHING SKILLS

Because mathematics is a dynamic science and ongoing research in teaching is constantly adding to our knowledge of how pupils learn, there is an ever-present need for teachers to be aware of the changes in mathematics and teaching.

Teaching is different each day, each week, and each year. Last year's plan is never just right for this year's group of students. The pupils in a classroom are different—their backgrounds are different. This is not to say that teachers can't profit by their previous teaching experiences; teachers combine techniques and skills acquired from previous teaching experiences with new techniques and skills. Teachers grow in skill by seeking out and applying new ideas and techniques learned from interacting with fellow teachers, attending inservice meetings, consulting with mathematics spe-

Resources for Maintaining and Improving Mathematics Teaching Skills

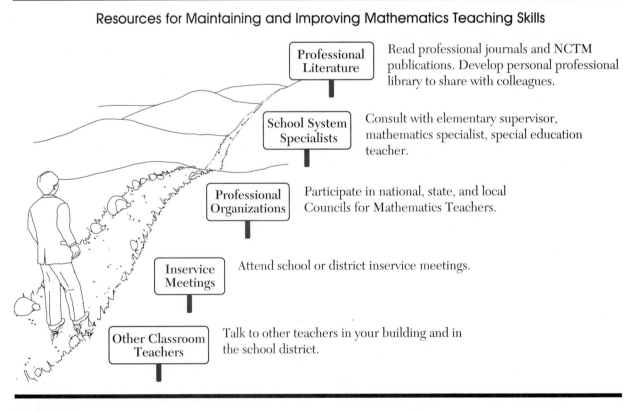

Professional Literature — Read professional journals and NCTM publications. Develop personal professional library to share with colleagues.

School System Specialists — Consult with elementary supervisor, mathematics specialist, special education teacher.

Professional Organizations — Participate in national, state, and local Councils for Mathematics Teachers.

Inservice Meetings — Attend school or district inservice meetings.

Other Classroom Teachers — Talk to other teachers in your building and in the school district.

FIGURE 1.3

cialists and curriculum supervisors, participating in professional organizations, and reading professional literature. Figure 1.3 illustrates some of the resources available which assist teachers in improving their teaching skills.

1.7 SUMMARY

The American elementary school mathematics curriculum has been in a constant state of evolution since the colonial period when boys were trained as "keepers of the stores." Each new curriculum movement promoted changes in the mathematics curriculum based on the reformers' perception of the best way to teach children mathematics.

The current movement, which has as its goal preparing students to use and apply mathematics in the twenty-first century, is unique in that it was funded and developed by mathematics educators belonging to the National Council of Mathematics. The document *Curriculum and Evaluation Standards for School Mathematics* sets out its recommendations for reforming the mathematics curriculum.

In addition to the *Standards*, there are continuing trends in mathematics education that are compatible with the recommendations of those *Standards*. The mathematics curriculum still must consider the use of technological devices, multistructured learning environments, cooperative learning groups, individualized learning activities, and greater use of mathematical applications.

To become efficient when teaching elementary school mathematics, a teacher must have a deep understanding of the

> **M**athematics content and concepts taught in elementary school.
>
> **A**ttributes of children and how to adjust for these attributes.
>
> **T**echniques that a skilled teacher uses to teach mathematics.
>
> **H**euristics, or general learning structures, including the concept of unit plans and lesson plans.

To maintain and enhance their skills teachers must seek professional renewal through interacting with other teachers, attending inservice meetings, seeking advice from curriculum specialists, participating in professional organizations, and reading professional literature.

EXERCISES

1. Identify three factors that continually generate a need to update the elementary school mathematics curriculum.
2. Identify two results of the National Assessment of Educational Progress that have influenced the current movement towards revising the mathematics curriculum.
3. How has the availability of handheld calculators and computers impacted on the need to revise the mathematics curriculum?
4. Describe seven assumptions of the *Curriculum and Evaluation Standards for School Mathematics*.
5. Describe the *Standards'* recommendations for each of the following:
   a. Problem solving as a process
   b. Communicating mathematical ideas
   c. Mathematics as a process for reasoning
   d. Making mathematical connections
   e. Extensive estimation activities
   f. Number sense and numeration
   g. Whole-number operations and concepts

   h. Developing fraction and decimal concepts in the lower grades
   i. Developing computation and estimation in the upper grades for whole numbers, integers, fractions, decimals, and rational numbers
   j. Developing geometry concepts and spatial sense
   k. Measurement
   l. Statistics and probability
   m. Development of patterns, relations, and functions
   n. Algebraic explorations
6. Describe five continuing trends in American education that tend to reinforce the recommendations of the *Standards*.
7. Identify five characteristics of the expert teacher.
8. Identify four knowledges that a teacher must have before he or she can plan a mathematics lesson.
9. In this text, what does each letter in the

acronym MATH stand for?

10. Identify the types of attributes of children that must be provided for when planning instruction.

11. Contrast how different types of lessons within a unit are developed. What elements are common to each type of lesson? Identify the components of each type of lesson plan.

12. Identify one mathematics skill that is best developed by groups of children interacting

with each other.

13. Identify one mathematics skill that is best developed by a child in an independent learning activity.

14. Describe several considerations that must be taken into account in executing a lesson plan.

15. Describe four ways that teachers maintain and improve their teaching skills during their careers.

REFERENCES

Baroody, A. J. "The Value of Informal Approaches to Mathematics Instruction and Remediation." *Arithmetic Teacher* 33 (January 1986): 14–18.

Bright, G. W. *Microcomputer Applications in the Elementary Classroom, a Guide for Teachers.* Newton, Mass.: Allyn & Bacon, 1987.

Brownell, W. A. "When is Arithmetic Meaningful?" *Journal of Educational Research* 38 (March 1945): 481–498.

Bruner, J. S. *Toward a Theory of Instruction.* Cambridge, Mass.: Harvard University Press, 1960.

Burns, M. "The Role of Questioning." *Arithmetic Teacher* 35 (February 1985): 14–16.

Callahan L. G., and V. J. Glennon. *Elementary School Mathematics: A Guide to Current Research.* 4th ed. Washington, D.C.: Association for Supervision and Curriculum Development, 1975. Pp. 4–5.

Carpenter, T. P. et al. "Results of the Fourth NAEP Assessment of Mathematics: Trends and Conclusions." *Arithmetic Teacher* 36 (December 1988): 38–41.

Clements, D. H. "Computers and Problem Solving." Edited by J. A. Van de Walle. *Arithmetic Teacher* 35 (December 1987): 26–27.

Cremin, L. A. *The Transformation of the School.* New York: Alfred A. Knopf, 1961. P. 128.

D'Augustine, C. H. "What Collegiate Business Students Need From Secondary Schools." *Mathematics Teacher* 82 (March 1989): 163–165.

Davis, E. J. et al. "Training Elementary School Teachers to use Computers—with Emphasis on Logo." *Arithmetic Teacher* 32 (October 1984): 18–25.

Dossey, J. A. et al. *The Mathematics Report Card: Are We Measuring Up?* Princeton, N.J.: Educational Testing Service, 1988.

Dossey, J. A. "Learning, Teaching, and Standards." *Arithmetic Teacher* 35 (April 1988): 20–21.

Edward, N., and H. G. Richey. *The School in the American Social Order.* Boston: Houghton Mifflin, 1947. Pp. 765–767.

Kilpatrick, W. H. *The Dutch Schools of New Netherlands and Colonial New York.* U.S. Department of the Interior, Bureau of Education, Washington, D.C.: U.S. Government Printing Office, Bulletin 12, 1917.

Leinhardt, G., and R. R. Putnam. "Profile of Expertise in Elementary School Mathematics Teaching." Edited by L. G. Callahan. *Arithmetic Teacher* 34 (December 1986): 28–29.

Monroe, W. S. *Development of Arithmetic as a School Subject.* U.S. Department of the Interior, Bureau of Education, Washington, D.C.: U.S. Government Printing Office, Bulletin 10, 1917.

Moyer, M. B., and J. C. Moyer. "Ensuring That Practice Makes Perfect: Implications for Children with Learning Disabilities." *Arithmetic Teacher* 33 (September 1985): 40–42.

National Commission on Excellence in Education. *A Nation at Risk: The Imperative for Educational Reform.* Washington, D.C.: U.S. Government Printing Office, 1983.

National Research Council. *Everybody Counts: A Report to the Nation on the Future of Mathematics Education—Summary Document.* Washington, D.C.: National Academy Press, 1989.

National Science Board Commission on Precollege Education in Mathematics, Science and Technology. *Educating Americans for the 21st Century.* Washington, D.C.: National Science Foundation, 1983.

NCTM. *An Agenda for Action: Recommendations for School Mathematics for the 1980s.* Reston, Va.: National Council of Teachers of Mathematics. 1980.

NCTM Committee on Standards. *Curriculum and Evaluation Standards for School Mathematics.* Reston, Va.: National Council of Teachers of Mathematics. 1989.

Piaget, J. "How Children Form Mathematical Concepts." *Scientific American* 189 (No. 3, 1953): 74–79.

Polya, G. *How to Solve It.* Princeton, N.J.: Princeton University Press, 1957.

Reys, B. J., and R. E. Reys. "Mental Computation and Computational Estimation—Their Time Has Come." *Arithmetic Teacher* 33 (March 1986): 4–5.

Reys, R. E. "Estimation." *Arithmetic Teacher* 32 (February 1985): 37–41.

Riedesel, C. A. *Guiding Discovery in Elementary School Mathematics.* New York: Appleton-Century Crofts, 1967. Pp. 16–20.

Roberts, L. et al. *Integrating Computers into the Elementary and Middle School.* Englewood Cliffs, N.J.: Prentice-Hall, 1988.

Smith, D. E., and J. Ginsburg. *A History of Mathematics in America Before 1900.* Chicago: The Mathematical Association of America, 1934.

"The Impact of Computing Technology on School Mathematics: Report of an NCTM Conference." Compiled and edited by M. K. Corbitt. *Arithmetic Teacher* 32 (April 1985): 14–18.

Thorndike, E. L. *The Psychology of Arithmetic.* New York: Macmillan, 1922. Pp. 141–155.

Van de Walle, J., and C. S. Thompson. "Promoting Mathematical Thinking." *Arithmetic Teacher* 32 (February 1985): 17–23.

VanEngen, H.; M. L. Hartung; and J. E. Stochl. *Foundations of Elementary School Arithmetic.* Chicago: Scott, Foresman, 1965.

Wiebe, J. "Calculators and the Mathematics Curriculum." *Arithmetic Teacher* 34 (February 1987): 57–60.

CHAPTER 2

EVALUATING PUPILS, INSTRUCTION, AND CURRICULUM

INTRODUCTION

At first glance one might think that evaluating pupils, instruction, and curriculum represents three nonrelated types of evaluations. In fact, the manner in which the elementary school mathematics curriculum is stated will direct how a topic will be presented—thus determining both the evaluation of the instruction and the pupil. For example, if a primary goal is developing problem-solving skills, then students will be examined to determine if they have acquired these skills and the effectiveness of the instructional program will be evaluated.

In a sense, evaluation must always be concerned with simultaneously evaluating pupils, instruction, and the curriculum. Ideally, such an evaluation would reveal that students (through well-designed and well-executed instruction) are mastering the objectives selected by the school system to prepare its pupils to function in a technological society. In the *worst scenario*, children might master curriculum skills that ill prepare them for the future, or might not master curriculum skills which would prepare them for a technological society.

While evaluation of each of the elements (pupils, instruction, and curriculum) will be developed in separate sections of this chapter, the reader should recognize that evaluation of each evaluative segment must be done **only** in relation to the other two factors.

2.1 EVALUATING STUDENTS

The broad nature of mathematics curriculum goals necessitates the use of a wide variety of evaluative procedures with students. The contemporary goals of mathematics instruction include being able to: communicate mathematical ideas, identify prob-

lems and utilize a wide variety of strategies in solving problems, utilize estimation concepts, recognize applications of mathematics (ranging from number to probability), utilize technological devices (such as the calculator and computer), understand the meaning of a wide variety of mathematical processes, create and utilize mathematical models, etc.

Therefore, methods of evaluating whether students are meeting these goals require a broad spectrum of techniques.

Evaluation might be compared to one's perspective when observing a glass containing water. If a teacher sees the glass as "half full" he/she concentrates upon how much more is needed to fill it up; if the glass is viewed as "half-empty," the teacher focuses upon what is missing. Expert teachers look at *both* where the child *will* be and where the child currently *is*—not toward what is missing.

Error analysis and diagnostic activities play an important role in a contemporary mathematics program, but they should be perceived as giving the teacher insights into how to facilitate the child's mastery of mathematical concepts, not as a failure of the child. (Caution! Non-habituated or careless errors are a normal part of the learning and problem-solving process, and as such may evoke no special instructional needs.) Diagnosis can be conducted informally by analyzing the errors students are making in their daily work or during a pupil-teacher conference. At times it is necessary to conduct a more formal diagnosis using tests, such as the *Stanford Diagnostic Test*. Suggestions in this text are designed to aid the teacher in informally diagnosing and using the results to help pupils overcome handicaps. (Teachers who are interested in more formal diagnostic procedures should examine the references at the end of this chapter.)

Evaluative techniques can be classified into five general categories:

1. Evaluation that takes place before instruction. (Preassessment)
Preassessing the skills and concepts students bring to a learning experience is essential when planning efficient uses of instructional time. In chapters 4 through 14 illustrative lesson fragments identify prerequisite skills and concepts (listed under the "H" part of the MATH acronym). Prior to instruction, teachers must carefully evaluate those prerequisites to determine whether pupils possess these skills.

2. Evaluation that takes place during the interactive teaching process.
Good teaching incorporates evaluation during instruction. Sensitivity to the way pupils respond to questions and their body language can help a teacher judge whether students understand a concept. Every-pupil response techniques are but one way of evaluating during the lesson. At other times, teachers may test student understanding by requiring use of concrete materials to verify answers. Student re-

sponses to specific questions during the instructional process also provide valuable data on how well pupils are following the lesson's development.

During the instructional process teachers may identify children who distinguish themselves during the lesson (discover creative solutions, have special insights, or exhibit conceptual misunderstandings). The teacher can record these observations in anecdotal records or onto special checklists following the lesson.

3. Evaluation that occurs as a part of non–teacher-guided learning activities.
This type of evaluation generally takes place in two settings: children working alone and children interacting with other children as a part of group activities. When children work by themselves teachers make inferences about their learning from their behaviors (intense concentration, disinterest, expressions of puzzlement, etc.). As students are working the teacher may wish to intrude on the child's thinking process with statements such as, "That looks like a very interesting way to do that. Do you want to tell me about it?"

Insights may also be gained from observing students interact with their peers. The quality and/or quantity of discussion that takes place within a group can reveal how deeply those students understand the concepts. The roles pupils take within a group can also identify students who are logical thinkers, creative problem solvers, data gatherers, or experimenters.

4. Evaluation that uses products incidental to the learning process.
As students practice skills that were taught in a lesson they produce materials which may be used in the evaluation process. These materials can be worksheets, performance on a sorting task completed at a learning station, or project displays following an experiment. The nature of the product dictates the type of evaluation. Care should be taken in evaluating products. For example, if a language arts activity is used to judge a pupil's ability to communicate, it may not present an accurate picture of the student's mathematical understanding since the pupil's mathematical understanding may be obscured by his/her limited writing or speaking skills.

5. Evaluation that compares a pupil to established standards or other students.
Teachers often must report the achievement or progress of an individual student to school

authorities and parents. These "grades" are generally determined by comparing the pupil's accomplishments with an established criterion. On other occasions, the teacher may determine "grades" by comparing the pupil's progress with the progress of other children in the class.

Student progress is also evaluated by comparing performance on local, state, or national tests with other students who have taken the same tests, or comparing with established standards. Such tests may be criterion-based or norm-based. When a student's performance is based on national norms, the student's performance is really being compared to the sample of students used to norm the test. Some published tests provide national, state, and local norms to aid the teacher. When tests are criterion-based, pupil performance is compared to a predetermined criterion to determine if mastery of an objective is demonstrated—for example, "the pupil will correctly answer three out of four problems."

Teachers tend to rely primarily upon WRITTEN tests since those instruments provide gradebook documentation and seem to be more OBJECTIVE. However, evaluation may be done in many different ways—not just with paper and pencil. Pupil mastery of concepts and understanding may be more effectively measured by observing pupils as they model an operation. Observations of pupil performances, widely used in music and physical education, is equally valid when evaluating students' understandings in mathematics.

Teacher observations become more objective when an efficient record-keeping procedure is employed. Observation checklists are one way of both reducing the amount of writing required and focusing the teacher's attention on specific objectives to be observed. It is not necessary to complete ALL observations in a single sitting or on a single day. Observation of a particular objective MAY extend over several days or even all year. Pupil performance objectives occasionally direct teachers to evaluate over a period of time as in the following example, "On three different occasions the pupil will draw a picture to model the solution to a problem."

In addition to evaluating children's understanding and mastery of mathematical concepts, skills, and processes, teachers also assess pupil **attitudes** toward mathematics and its applications. When pupils have positive attitudes toward mathematics they are more likely to do much more than the minimal requirements. Assessment of pupil attitudes requires the teacher to use techniques that differ from those used when evaluating a pupil's mastery of specific mathematical concepts, skills, and processes. Teachers can use children's comments or children's lists of favorite subjects and least favorite subjects as an indicator of the children's attitudes. Attitudes may also be judged by how many children participate in recreational activities that require mathematical skills. A pupil's attitude towards mathematics may also be determined by observing whether a pupil chooses to extend his/her mathematical skills once the basic requirements have been met.

2.2 EVALUATING INSTRUCTION

Just as pupils are evaluated to determine mastery of a given skill, instruction is evaluated to determine its effectiveness. To judge the effectiveness of an instructional procedure, the teacher must first identify the purpose for which the evaluation is to be used. Evaluation might be directed toward:

1. Modifying instruction during the teaching of the lesson.
Evaluation is an inherent part of instruction. When a teacher works with pupils, it is their feedback which gives direction to the lesson. When students follow a lesson as it develops, the teacher may proceed without major variations from the way the lesson was originally planned. However, if pupils seem to be having difficulty as the lesson progresses, then the teacher must depart from the plan, searching for ways to make the instruction more comprehensible.

2. Planning follow-up instruction for pupils.
After a lesson is taught a teacher must determine which objectives need further development. Sometimes a teacher recognizes that the students had not sufficiently mastered prerequisite skills so follow-up instruction must include development of these skills.

3. Determining the appropriateness of what was taught.
Occasionally a teacher may discover that the instruction did not develop the identified concept in the school's scope and sequence. On other occasions the procedure may not be appropriate for the objectives chosen for the lesson plan. This may occur when a teacher follows an adopted textbook only to discover after the lesson that the pages developed something

quite unrelated to the objectives specified by the school's system.

Teachers must associate instruction with the objectives in the school system's mathematics curriculum guide. In planning instruction, the teacher may ask, "Is the planned lesson conducive to meeting the objectives as specified in the curriculum guide? Does what is being taught match the curriculum objectives of what should be taught?" For example, if the objective specifies that children will be taught a variety of problem-solving strategies, are the children only being taught to solve problems by drawing pictures to determine which operations to use? If the goal of the mathematics curriculum is to develop the child's communication skills, then instruction should not be a text-oriented lesson conducted in a noninteractive mode.

4. Identifying other areas in the curriculum where the concepts being developed can be applied or further developed.

As teachers examine the instructional process, a conscious effort must be made to identify curriculum areas in which the concepts can be applied or developed. When studying measurement, teachers may use measurement concepts in a science unit on plant growth, an art lesson, or during physical education.

5. Locating effective/ineffective aspects of the lesson for future lesson planning.

As the teacher looks back at the lesson taught, he/she should jot down notes about those aspects of the lesson that proved effective and those that need to be improved. The next time a similar lesson is planned, these notes in the margin will provide guidance for improving instruction.

6. Determining adjustments to long-range (or yearly) plans.

Frequently, an evaluation of the teaching procedure will reveal a need to make changes in the long-range plans. If a unit takes twice as long as anticipated, future units may need to be shortened accordingly. When a unit is completed more quickly than anticipated, it may be possible to explore an enrichment topic. When pupils have difficulty attaining the desired degree of mastery, a teacher may need to reschedule future units requiring these prerequisites.

7. Improving one's own teaching skills.

Evaluation of instruction provides the teacher with valuable insights into how his or her own teaching skills may be improved. Looking back upon a lesson a teacher should ask, "How could I have improved the presentation or development? Would more hands-on manipulative materials make the lesson more effective? What other problem situations would be appropriate for introducing this concept? What other ways might I better motivate the students? What additional resources might be used? Could the lesson have been more effectively developed using cooperative learning groups or independent study activities?" Answering these questions serves to hone one's own teaching skills.

Much of the aforementioned evaluation takes place as the teacher examines the teaching process. Instruction may also be evaluated by examining the product produced by pupils. Product evaluation is usually identified in lesson plans as a test at the end of the unit, a culminating project, a research paper, an oral report, or group summary of solutions. Examining how pupils complete their assignments is a traditional means of determining the effectiveness of the lesson. While most written exercises are primarily designed to evaluate individual pupil growth, teachers may also examine the overall class performance to determine how effective the lesson is in accomplishing the objectives. Satisfactory performance by students suggests that the lesson was successful.

Even when the teacher has carefully matched his or her instructional techniques to the curriculum objectives, instruction may prove ineffective when evaluated against how well children are attaining objectives. Evaluation must be judged in the context of the curriculum objectives and how well the teacher is adjusting instruction to the nature of the material being taught and the attributes of the children being taught.

Children need opportunities to explain their thought process.

2.3 EVALUATING THE ELEMENTARY SCHOOL MATHEMATICS CURRICULUM

While pupils and instruction are evaluated in terms of the objectives of the school's curriculum, the curriculum itself must <u>also</u> be constantly examined to determine whether the **stated objectives** effectively direct the education of pupils toward <u>competencies needed now and in the future</u>. The elementary school mathematics curriculum is not a static body of skills. Changes in society and technology force schools to **constantly** reexamine their curriculums to determine if they are **still** appropriate. If curriculums did not change then pupils would still be computing with Roman numerals!

Most states require that local school systems review their curriculum guides periodically (every three to five years). Teacher committees review the curriculum to determine **if**: (1) new objectives are needed, (2) any objectives can be eliminated, (3) the sequence (grade placement) is appropriate, and (4) the guide meets the minimum standards set by the state department of education.

At some point in every elementary teacher's career he/she will be assigned to a school's committee to evaluate the curriculum. While beginning teachers often wish to be excused from this assignment, their input is important. Beginners, through their teacher preparation program, have a perspective toward the curriculum and current trends that veteran teachers may lack. Since the school system objectives will be used to select textbooks, direct instruction, and evaluate instruction, ALL teachers need to participate in the process of examining the curriculum.

How is a Curriculum Evaluated?

In each school system, evaluation of the curriculum starts by examining the objectives of that system. Objectives may be evaluated from a variety of perspectives. Consider the following questions:

1. Is the objective obsolete due to contemporary or future applications of the skill or knowledge? If not obsolete, does the objective receive too much (or too little) emphasis?

An objective should identify an understanding, concept, or skill that would contribute to the future of the student. For example, suppose an objective specifies that a student will be able to multiply two factors, each of which have four digits (using paper and pencil). Question: In an age of inexpensive calculators, should this skill be de-emphasized

and the skill of finding the product with a calculator and estimating the answer be emphasized? (Notice the word <u>de-emphasized</u> has been used. Why might a <u>school system's</u> curriculum guide specify that pupils should have a reasonable skill level in paper-and-pencil computational skills, rather than specifying that children should attain a high skill level?)

2. Is the objective clearly stated? If not clearly stated, what clarifying information is needed?

An objective should guide teachers when planning instruction. It should also provide a means to determine whether children are meeting the objective. For example, an objective might state, "The curriculum will develop each student's ability to solve problems." No one would quarrel with this as a goal for mathematics instruction. However, is this objective stated specifically enough to give direction in planning instructional strategies or for determining whether a child has met the objective? For example, should children be able to do multistep problems from a wide variety of applications, using a variety of strategies? Should children be able to find a solution, find multiple paths to the solution, identify that something is a problem, work as a member of a team in solving problems, etc.? A curriculum objective may need several subskill objectives (and examples) to give a teacher sufficient guidance in meeting a broadly stated objective.

3. Has consideration been given to recommendations of professional organizations (i.e., NCTM's *Standards*) and state guidelines?

Recommendations from professional organizations (like NCTM and MAA) represent a general agreement of leaders in the field. In making their suggestions, they consider the changes in the subject (mathematics), research in the teaching of the subject, and the future needs of society. Such organizations recognize that communities differ. Some schools will easily be able to incorporate all of their recommendations. Others will adopt the standards more slowly.

4. Is the placement of an objective in the proper sequence? Are prerequisite skills developed at previous grade levels?

Textbook series are usually carefully designed to ensure that prerequisite skills are developed before they are needed for new concepts. Committees that design their own scope and sequences may overlook this aspect when evaluating a curriculum. In addition to examining textbooks and their sequences, curriculum committees also ask teachers for input on appropriate sequences for topics.

5. Are the curriculum and the testing program compatible?

One way to judge the effectiveness of the curriculum is to examine how pupils perform on tests. While the best tests for evaluating the effectiveness of the curriculum would be a criterion-referenced test, many school systems use the performance of their pupils on standardized achievement tests. Achievement tests are only useful when they evaluate the same skills as those being taught. If the skills evaluated by a standardized test correspond to the school's curriculum, then instruction might be judged effective or not effective in terms of scores on those tests. However, if the test and the curriculum are not compatible then the evaluation is inappropriate. Schools must examine their chosen standardized test to determine whether the school curriculum and skills tested are compatible.

Testing companies are currently reviewing curriculum changes, and are adjusting their tests to meet these changes. Technological changes (calculators and computers), changes in instructional approaches (cooperative learning and individualized and teacher-guided interactive learning activities), and changes in the skills being emphasized (communication, estimation, and problem-solving skills) may require new modes for evaluating achievement.

2.4 SUMMARY

Evaluation must always be concerned with simultaneously evaluating pupils, instruction, and the curriculum. Evaluation should reveal whether students are mastering the objectives specified by the school system, as well as providing information on instructional effectiveness. Evaluation should also reveal insight into the strengths and weaknesses of the curriculum.

Evaluation should be conducted using a wide variety of techniques (observations, interviews, examination of seatwork, tests, achievements of students, achievement tests, etc.).

While evaluation should focus on the positive aspects of what a student has attained, there is a place for diagnosis that gives the teacher insight into how to help the child grow.

EXERCISES

1. Identify and describe four general categories of evaluating students. Give examples for each category of evaluation.

2. Identify seven reasons for evaluating instruction.

3. Identify four criteria for evaluating a mathematics curriculum.

4. Look at a school system curriculum guide and compare its objectives to:

a. The skills developed in a textbook series.

b. The skills tested on a textbook "end-of-the-year test."

c. The skills tested on a standardized test.

5. Discuss how a teacher would evaluate "communication skills" in mathematics.

RELEVANT COMPUTER SOFTWARE

Math Assistant I and II: Error Analysis in Addition and Subtraction; Multiplication and Division. Apple II. New York: Scholastic Inc. Software Sales, 1985.

REFERENCES

Ashlock, R. B. *Error Patterns in Computation: A Semi-programmed Approach.* 4th ed. Columbus, Oh.: Charles E. Merrill, 1986.

Braswell, J. S., and A. A. Dodd. *Mathematics Tests Available in the United States and Canada.* Reston, Va.: National Council of Teachers of Mathematics, 1988.

Brumfield, R. D., and B. D. Moore. "Problems with the Basic Facts May Not Be the Problem." *Arithmetic Teacher* 33 (November 1985): 17–18.

Chambers, D. L. "Calculating the Influence of Tests on Instruction." *Arithmetic Teacher* 36 (May 1989): 10–11.

Dossey, J. A. et al. *The Mathematics Report Card: Are We Measuring Up?* Princeton, N.J.: Educational Testing Service, 1988.

Learning by Doing. National Assessment of Educational Progress. Princeton, N.J.: NAEP, 1987.

Liedtke, W. "Diagnosis in Mathematics: The Advantages of an Interview." *Arithmetic Teacher* 36 (November 1988): 26–29.

Lindquist, M. M. "Assessing through Questioning." Edited by A. McAloon and G. E. Robinson. *Arithmetic Teacher* 35 (January 1988): 16–17.

Loef, M. M. et al. "Integrating Assessment and Instruction." *Arithmetic Teacher* 36 (November 1988): 53–55.

McClintic, S. V. "Conservation—a Meaningful Gauge for Assessment." *Arithmetic Teacher* 35 (February 1988): 12–14.

McKillip, W. D., and G. M. Stanic. "Putting the Value Back into Evaluation." Edited by A. McAloon and G. E. Robinson. *Arithmetic Teacher* 35 (February 1988): 37–38.

O'Daffer, P. G., and R. I. Charles. "Asking Questions to Evaluate Problem Solving." *Arithmetic Teacher* 35 (January 1988): 26–27.

Richardson, K. "Assessing Understanding." *Arithmetic Teacher* 35 (February 1988): 39–41.

Trafton, P. "Tests—A Tool for Improving Instruction." Edited by A. McAloon and G. E. Robinson. *Arithmetic Teacher* 35 (October 1987): 17–18.

Williams, D. E. "Using Calculators in Assessing Mathematics Achievement." Edited by A. McAloon and G. E. Robinson. *Arithmetic Teacher* 35 (December 1987): 21–23.

CHAPTER 3

TEACHING PROBLEM SOLVING

INTRODUCTION

In 1980, the National Council of Teachers of Mathematics published *An Agenda for Action*, listing ten recommendations for school mathematics. The first goal of that *Agenda* was problem solving. During that same year NCTM advertised its current yearbook, *Problem Solving in School Mathematics* (1980), emphasizing that:

> Problem solving is the reason for teaching mathematics. This skill—one that students must use throughout their lives—is a skill that can be taught and must be taught. (*Arithmetic Teacher*, 1980)

NCTM's 1989 landmark publication, *The Curriculum and Evaluations Standards for School Mathematics* emphasizes **problem solving as the major goal of school mathematics**. First and foremost in the *Standards'* five general goals for students was that of helping students "**become mathematical problem solvers**." The *Standards* STRONGLY restates the goal that NCTM had identified eight years earlier in its *An Agenda for Action* (NCTM, 1980).

Problem solving is not a new topic in the mathematics curriculum. During the early colonial period of our country, special schools were organized for training in "ciphering" because the Dutch West India Company needed "keepers of the stores." In the 1800s Warren Colburn (*An Arithmetic on the Plan of Pestalozzi*, 1821) proposed "problems that were to be reasoned out, often orally, rather than solved by direct application of rules" (NCTM, 1970). In the early 1900s, Robert Morton, a prolific author of children's arithmetic textbooks and teacher-education texts, wrote, "We teach arithmetic in order that our pupils may be able to solve the problems which they encounter in their school days and in their post-school experiences" (Morton, 1927).

If problem solving has always been a part of the elementary school mathematics curriculum, why is everyone concerned now? Although of recognized importance in the child's everyday life and future career, problem solving remains one of those skills that children seem to have difficulty acquiring. From 1972 to 1973 the mathematics performance of pupils was tested in the National Assessment of Educational Progress (NAEP). On that assessment, solving problems was **identified as an area of weakness in each of the four tested groups** (9-year-olds, 13-year-olds, 17-year-olds, and adults 26–35). Later assessments had similar findings. An analysis of the second NAEP in *Arithmetic Teacher* concluded:

> At all levels, and in virtually every content area, performance was extremely low on exercises requiring problem-solving or applications of mathematical skills. In general, respondents demonstrated a lack of even the most basic problem-solving skills. (Carpenter, 1980)

The following mathematics assessment (NAEP, 1982) showed no substantial change in the problem-solving ability of school-aged children. Mathematics educators found that:

> . . . performance changed very little in topics that are relatively difficult to teach, such as non-routine problem solving. . . . Changes at the higher cognitive levels will occur only when higher cognitive activity becomes a curricula and instructional focus. (Lindquist, 1983)

The fourth National Assessment (NAEP, 1986) reported that nearly all students have mastered simple arithmetic facts, but many do not understand the more complex applications (Carpenter, 1988). This assessment found that simple (one-step) problems could be solved by only one-fifth of the 9-year-olds, and nearly three-fourths of the 13-year-olds. When multistep problems were presented, however, it was a more sobering picture. NAEP reported less than five out of a thousand 13-year-olds could work these multistep problems successfully! (Dossey, 1988). Most alarming was that the problems were not really that hard! Writers of articles for popular magazines, such as *Time Magazine* (June 20, 1988) were appalled when children were unable to answer such "top level" questions as "Suppose you have ten coins and have at least one each of a quarter, a dime, a nickel, and a penny. What is the least amount of money you could have?"

3.1 WHAT IS PROBLEM SOLVING?

Children begin to solve problems by trial and error a few months after birth. By the time children enter school they have solved a variety of problems ranging from mastering their eating utensils to constructing a building with toy blocks.

Teaching activities—such as finding the sum of 48 + 96—are sometimes called "problems." These computational exercises are not problems. A problem occurs when someone desires to reach a goal, but cannot immediately perceive how to reach the goal. Problem solving then becomes the process both of striving to reach the goal and reaching that goal.

Each act of problem solving uses a process. The primary focus in developing problem solvers should be the teaching of a process and not on finding a solution (which is only the end product in the problem-solving process). The solutions children pursue in their elementary school mathematics prob-lem-solving activities are only transient bits of information. However, the **process** children use in solving these problems can, if nurtured, become strategies that will be used throughout their lives.

The computational skills which children develop throughout elementary school are simply TOOLS that are used in the problem-solving process. Such skills are best introduced when used in the context of problem solving. Indeed, the motivation for learning how to compute should originate from the context of a problem. The application of computational skills—especially as a tool for solving problems—must remain the focus of study throughout the development of computational skills. If a child becomes a computational wizard but can't use those skills to solve problems, then the child has learned little of practical value. On the other hand, if a child acquires a wide variety of strategies to solve problems, but has difficulty computing, that child can augment computational skills with a calculator or microcomputer program.

Problem solving is the primary reason to study noncomputational mathematical concepts. The study of number, geometry, measurement, and other areas in mathematics should be taught in the context of problem solving, because children become motivated to explore ideas when they see how these concepts help them solve problems.

Let us examine a problem and observe the problem-solving process used in its solution:

Problem

We notice in the paper that there is a yard sale at 16 Hizzhonor Street. We want to go to the sale, but don't have any idea where this street is located. (We have a goal, but do not immediately perceive how to reach that goal.)

Process

Strategies we have used in the past to solve similar types of problems:

1. When we didn't know how to get to a place in the past, we have asked someone how to get there. Once they gave us directions, we followed their instructions to get to our destination.
2. If we had a map available we looked up the location on the map and then used the map to get to the location.

In this situation we choose to look it up on a map. (See Figure 3.1.)

Previously-Learned Skills We Needed to Solve This Problem Were

1. Ability to use the map's index.
2. Ability to locate the street using the coordinates mentioned in the map's index.
3. Ability to read the map from our location to the location of the street we want.
4. Ability to drive our car to the location indicated on the map.

Utilizing these skills we arrive at our goal, thus the problem is solved.

Later in the month when we desire to go to Hizzhonor Street again we remember how we got there before. Now getting there is not a problem. However, once we start out on our trip, we find that the thruway which we used before is closed for repair. At this point, because the situation has been modified slightly and we don't immediately know how to get to our goal—we have a new problem situation.

Problem solving is developed in a manner quite similar to the previous example, with the teacher

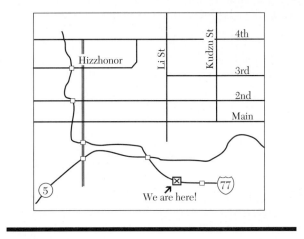

FIGURE 3.1

slowly building a child's ability to solve problems. In this process the teacher proceeds from simple problems to more complex problems, building the complexity of the problems by adding new wrinkles to previously solved problems and by combining elements of previously solved problems to form structures which represent new problems. When working with children, teachers often must shape nonproblem situations into problem situations to help children adjust to new conditions and strengthen skills. For example, Mrs. Washington's kindergarten class has been sitting in pairs at small tables. Over the weekend Mrs. Washington rearranged the room so that there would be six to a table. Pupils can no longer come up and get a carton of milk for themselves and their partner. A new plan for milk distribution must be decided upon.

Because each child brings his or her own unique past problem-solving experiences to each new problem (as well as any of the skills he or she has attained that can be applied to the new problem), individual children may select various strategies resulting in different paths to the solution of the problem. In the previous street location example, if you didn't have map-reading skills, you may have asked someone how to get to the street, or if you couldn't drive a car, you might have asked a friend to drive you to the yard sale.

Good problems for children will have many available alternative paths for their solution. Good problems not only allow each child to use his or her unique problem-solving experiences and skills, but also permit the child to profit from being exposed to alternate paths that other children may employ in solving the same problem.

The three main responsibilities of the teacher

when nurturing children's problem-solving abilities are to

1. Help children develop a repertoire of problem-solving strategies.
2. Assist children in mastering the mathematical concepts, techniques, and computational skills needed to solve problems.
3. Provide children with an opportunity to utilize these strategies in a wide variety of settings.

3.2 GUIDELINES FOR DEVELOPING PROBLEM-SOLVING STRATEGIES

If everyone faced the same problems in life, then all problems to be faced could be categorized. If there were only a limited number of possible problems, then children could be taught to solve problems by applying set response patterns. However, not only are the categories of problems almost unlimited, but our rapidly expanding technological society creates problems for tomorrow that have not yet been identified. Therefore, the teacher must pursue a program which will develop skills broadly applicable to problem solving.

George Polya, in his book, *How to Solve It* (1957), analyzed the problem-solving process and described a GENERAL structure for solving problems. His model—when simplified—had four basic steps: (1) **LOOK** at the problem (and try to understand it); (2) **PLAN** how to attack the problem; (3) **USE** your plan; and (4) **CHECK** back to see if your plan worked. Some textbook publishers who incorporate this approach in their textbook series use the four words "Read—Plan—Do—Check"; others expand the list to "Read, Think, Make a Plan, Carry Out the Plan, Check Your Work."

While Polya's general structure provides a good foundation for attacking problems, most children need more specific help. Before exploring how the teacher can develop specific problem-solving strategies, it might be useful to examine a few general guidelines. The teacher should:

1. Encourage children to create their own problems. An important aspect of becoming a good problem solver is to recognize when a problem exists. This is really the "LOOK and understand the problem" in Polya's model. Much of the mathematics curriculum concentrates on building skills to solve problems that already have been identified. Therefore, teachers must find opportunities that allow children to **create and identify problems**. Sources

can employ data (or nondata) from classroom activities in nonmathematical curriculum areas such as science, health, music, language arts, social studies, the children's nonschool activities, simulations, vocational and recreational fields, the media. As a matter of fact, all aspects of human existence can serve as sources for creating and identifying problems.
2. Present problems that require children to select appropriate data from among relevant and irrelevant data. (Caution: Initially introduce children to problem solving with relevant data only. Then add the "wrinkle" of irrelevant data as the previous situations cease to be a challenge.)
3. Allow children sufficient time to engage fully in the problem-solving process. Allow time for children to discuss the processes and strategies they used to get their answers—not just the answers themselves.
4. Give children opportunities to estimate and check their guesses. Estimation plays a crucial role in many problem-solving situations.
5. Encourage children to generalize from patterns and examples, and to test their generalizations.
6. Present problems that challenge but do not overly frustrate. By definition, a problem does

Teachers can evaluate students' understanding by listening to explanations.

not exist until an individual is frustrated in perceiving an immediate path to a goal, so problem solving can sometimes cause a high level of anxiety. The teacher often must mediate the frustration by providing clues or guided questions. The teacher must match the difficulty of the problems with the capabilities of the children, so children do not develop negative attitudes toward the problem-solving process. Solving problems as part of a cooperative group can reduce the frustration level of some students.

7. Acknowledge the worth of different paths and lead all children to a similar recognition. Children need to observe alternative paths to a solution. They gain greatly by analyzing paths for efficiency of effort and creativity. To some extent, problem solving is a creative effort allowing each child to express his/her individuality. The different paths chosen should be valued by the teacher and shared with the rest of the class. **Gifted children** often may find very imaginative strategies and need to be recognized for their creativity or uniqueness. The **learning-disabled** child may need manipulatives or technological devices when solving problems. The teacher must also commend these techniques, by pointing out that everyone uses manipulatives and technological devices in some problem-solving situations.

8. Instruct children to check their solutions against the requirements of the problem and to interpret the implications of the solution. Generally, children are eager to find a solution to a problem. However, this eagerness frequently does not transfer to the task of checking a solution.

9. Encourage children to use calculators in problem-solving activities. The availability of inexpensive calculators for the elementary school classroom makes possible a more thorough development of problem solving skills. Calculators allow instruction to focus upon the process rather than the computations leading to the solution. Previously, the computational skill level of pupils kept teachers from developing complex, realistic problem skills consistent with children's needs and interests. Calculators now make it more possible for teachers to include real problems from the daily life of the child. Pupils ALSO complete more problems in the same period of time when calculators are used. Even the learning-disabled child can solve problems when not restrained by the lack of computational skills.

3.3 WHAT ARE PROBLEM-SOLVING STRATEGIES?

Each day you face a wide variety of problems. Many problems are handled quickly because you have dealt with that kind of problem before. You have a strategy for solving each of those problems. Some problems at first appear too difficult to solve, but you make them easier to solve by modifying some technique you previously have used to solve problems. In these cases, you have a strategy, but it may take you a while to find out just how to apply the technique. However, sometimes you will try many different ways that you have used in the past to solve problems, but nothing works. You cannot find an appropriate strategy.

For example, suppose you wake up in the morning, go to your closet, and can't get the door open. All your clean clothes are in that closet. **You have a problem.** You think, this door has been stuck before and it just required a little more "pull"—so you give the door a yank. **It doesn't move.** You speculate—if I pull harder, it will move. So you ask a friend to help: Together you pull, and still it will not budge. Then you decide to attack the problem in another manner. You remember that when your dresser at home was stuck, you pried it open with a screwdriver. You look around the room, but there is no screwdriver. You remember that you saw a friend hit the bottom of her kitchen cabinet and then the upper corner popped open. You pound—and the door becomes more stuck! You give up, finally going to the hamper and putting on the clothes you wore yesterday. You vow to attack the problem later in the day. Throughout the day you pose the problem to a number of your acquaintances. Everyone has a suggestion for solving the problem. Some suggestions are ridiculous, some you have already tried; some seem like they **might** work; and one in particular sounds like a very creative way to solve the problem. When you return that evening—with a friend to assist you—you remove the pins from the hinges and swing the door out from the side opposite the latch. Eureka! The problem is solved!

The **process** described above goes on in **every** problem-solving situation. You are confronted with a problem. You attack that problem by using techniques (**strategies**) that you think will work. If your first try is unsuccessful, you modify that technique. If that doesn't work, you think over OTHER approaches that you have used and try to imagine if they might be successful. If you eventually solve the problem using a technique that is different from those used before, you add this new approach to your "bag of strategies" for future use.

Teachers must help children develop their own "bag of tricks." We call this bag of tricks **problem-solving strategies**. The strategies are used in the PLAN step of the Polya model. The list of strategies can be lengthy and broken into many subdivisions or shortened and classified into categories. In a two-book set entitled *Problem Solving—a Basic Mathematics Goal*, S. P. Meiring describes 16 basic strategies and five "Looking-Back" strategies (Meiring, 1980). In the list below these strategies are placed into five categories.

Modeling Strategies

- Act it out
- Make a model
- Make a drawing or diagram

Organizing-Data Strategies

- Construct a table or graph
- Look for a pattern
- Account for all possibilities

Analysis Strategies

- Restate the problem
- Write an open sentence
- Select appropriate notation
- Look for a subgoal
- Identify wanted, given, and needed information
- Check for hidden assumptions

Approach Strategies

- Solve a simpler problem
- Guess and Check
- Change your point of view
- Work backwards

Looking-Back Strategies

- Find another way to solve it
- Find another solution
- Check the solution
- Study the solution process
- Generalize

Some texts identify even more strategies—often subdividing these listed strategies into substrategies. Others group several of the strategies together under "modeling" or "analyzing."

3.4 DEVELOPING CHILDREN'S ABILITY TO USE PROBLEM-SOLVING STRATEGIES

Before examining how a teacher can help children develop problem-solving skills, let's first look at the task as seen by the child. Think back to when YOU were in grade school. Do you remember an incident like this?

> The teacher assigns page 147 for "practice in solving problems." You start on the first problem and immediately become frustrated. You raise your hand to get the teacher's help. What was her first suggestion? "Read the problem to me." Of course, you have already read it five times, but you dutifully read the problem aloud to the teacher. You look up expectantly, hoping for advice from your teacher. Then she says, "What does the problem ask you to do?" Dumbfounded, you sit there and think—if I knew what to do, I would not have raised my hand! However, you answer, "I don't know." Your teacher then turns and walks away, saying, "Well, you just think about it and I'm sure you will figure it out."

In terms of the Polya model, the child SAW the problem, but could not PLAN what to do. The teacher's advice—to "think about it"—did not provide the child with any direction for attacking the problem. While the teacher must be careful not to work the problem FOR the child, suggesting one or two "strategies" may get the pupil started. A teacher who asks, "Do you think drawing a picture would help?" or "Why don't you try smaller numbers?" will lead the child to try similar strategies when facing new problems.

Many problem-solving skills are best developed in a group situation. One of the advantages of cooperative learning groups is that the shared insights of members of the group helps each child learn to construct a PLAN for attacking problems. In cooperative learning groups children share their strategies, in much the same way the teacher will share one or two strategies to get the student started. However, an added advantage of cooperative learning is that frequently members will analyze the practicality of strategies being suggested by others in the group, before actually putting the strategies to use. This type of interplay of ideas is valuable in helping each pupil refine both communication skills and reasoning skills.

In the section which follows, each of the five major categories—Modeling Strategies, Organizing-

Data Strategies, Approach Strategies, Analysis Strategies, and Looking-Back Strategies—will be explored. Since some of the **subcategories** overlap, not all of them will be presented in this chapter. Throughout the chapters that follow, other examples of how children learn to use the strategies will be presented. This section examines the general role the teacher plays in developing a child's problem-solving skills.

Using Modeling Strategies

Children begin solving problems using manipulatives (models in the form of toys or mobiles) even before the age of one. Preschool children engage in many problem-solving activities during play time **(individual learning activities)**. These skills develop informally as the preschooler builds with a set of wooden blocks or constructs roads and tunnels in a sand pile. When a tunnel in the sand causes the road to collapse, the child may take a board and make a bridge. When the child builds a <u>new</u> bridge in the sand this new technique is incorporated into his/her "road-building strategies."

Teachers reinforce and extend the problem-solving skills children possessed before entering school and help children develop new approaches to solve problems. For example, the teacher helps the students develop a more formal strategy of "using models" instead of actually acting the problem out. Pupils may be asked to **draw a picture** to illustrate what's happening in a problem situation. This, in turn, may help students uncover clues to solve the problem. Children may **construct a model** of the situation, so that a solution might be visualized. (Models and drawings frequently are employed by architects, engineers, and scientists as an intermediate strategy for solving problems.)

Act-it-out Strategy

Suppose Maria (before being formally introduced to division) is playing "grocery store." Her turn as clerk is over and she must share her "profits" of $21 with the two other clerks. Realizing that two ten-dollar bills and a one-dollar bill cannot be shared fairly as tens and ones, she solves the problem by trading in two tens for 20 ones and then deals the 21 single dollar bills out into three piles (see Figure 3.2).

Maria was acting out the problem situation. This approach, known as the **act-it-out strategy**, is a problem-solving approach that a child uses many times before formally entering school. Preschoolers often are observed playing with their toys

Maria has 21 dollars to share with 2 friends.

She can trade 2 tens for 20 ones.

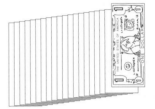

Now she can put the ones into 3 equal-sized piles.

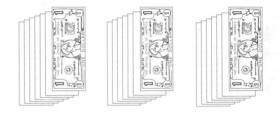

Each person will get 7 dollars!

FIGURE 3.2

and acting out a situation they have seen Mother or Father confront. Primary teachers, when introducing a new operation (addition, subtraction, etc.), will bring children to the front of the room to "act out" a problem. The teacher's use of this technique may help children see the value of the strategy and lead them to incorporate modified forms of this approach into their own problem-solving repertoire.

Using Organizing-Data Strategies

As pupils grow in their ability to use models, the teacher employs more sophisticated models for organizing data—going from tables to graphs and to mathematical models called formulas. Figures 3.3 through 3.6 illustrate how students might "act out" the problem (Figure 3.3), use a model (Figure 3.4), construct a graph (Figure 3.5), or use a formula (Figure 3.6) in solving a lemonade-stand problem.

Developing Problem-Solving Strategies

Act It Out

City License—$2.00

Cost of ingredients per glass—5¢

Revenue per glass—15¢

How many glasses must be sold to break even?

FIGURE 3.3

Developing Problem-Solving Strategies

Make a Model

Each ball = 5 cents
40 balls = license fee

For each lemonade sold—
put 3 balls in revenue pan
and 1 ball in cost pan.

Cost will balance revenue after 20 lemonades!

FIGURE 3.4

Developing Problem-Solving Strategies

Make a Graph

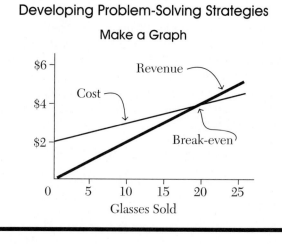

FIGURE 3.5

Developing Problem-Solving Strategies

Equation Strategy

Revenue = Cost
Selling price per unit = s
Units sold = n
License fee = F
Cost of ingredients per unit = c

$$sn = cn + F$$

FIGURE 3.6

Children use different ways of organizing data to be used in solving problems. As early as pre-school and kindergarten the child learns to recognize a pattern when stringing beads or participating in a clapping rhythm activity. When the pupil counts by fives, he/she "hears" a pattern. In approaching a problem, a student will often look for a pattern—if the pattern does not garner a solution, it may provide clues which will lead to the solution of a problem. This approach, called the **looking-for-a-pattern strategy**, is one of the first "Organizing Data" processes used by children (see Figure 3.7).

As students learn to use patterns, the teacher introduces ever more subtle patterns and encourages the development of generalizations from the discovered patterns. Thus, the children learn to use "look for a pattern" as a way of organizing data to use in solving a problem (see Figure 3.8).

Once pupils learn to symbolize mathematical concepts they are ready to place those symbols into a format which might aid in solving problems. When the symbols are numerical, they may be organized into a list, into a table, or onto a number line (see Figure 3.9). When the symbolism is geometrical, the pupil may utilize spatial organization to attack the problem.

Sometimes it is easier to solve a problem by trying out all solutions! When children first start working with simple jigsaw puzzles they just pick up different pieces and try them out. Later, children become more organized and systematically try out each piece until a "fit" is found. When solving problems, a similar approach can be used. Some books call this technique "**accounting for all possibilities.**" In Figure 3.10 the problem posed might be solved by trying out each combination of tricycles and wagons until the correct combination is found. Many children attack a problem with this strategy. Then after three or four possibilities are tried, they find a **pattern** which can be used to omit some of the "trials."

In the tricycle/wagon problem, it is also possible to "draw a picture" to show the possibilities. Simplified sticks and rings are used by children to show wagons and wheels. Drawing the pictures is also a way of accounting for all possibilities, but in a picture rather than a chart format.

As children learn to solve problems from data organized in lists, tables, and formulas, a logical reasoning (or analysis) strategy is incorporated into their organizational structures (see Figure 3.11).

Using Prealgebra (Analysis) Strategies

As operations are developed, children learn to express these operations in open-number sentences (equations). Once able to associate an operation with an appropriate number sentence, pupils are ready to use these **open-number sentences** (or **equations**) as tools for analyzing problems. Open-number sentences (equations) provide the pupil with a step-by-step "map" of procedures to be used with a calculator. The open-number sentence will be used as a "blueprint" by a computer to "decide" what to do at each step in solving problems. The open-number sentence is one of the most powerful and versatile of the problem-solving strategies. (Using a number sentence will be explored in more detail later in this chapter.)

Sometimes the nature of the problem is so complex that a problem must be broken down into a

---

Independent Learning Activity

Look for a Pattern

What is next?

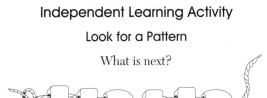

Kindergarten activity of stringing beads
to follow teacher's pattern.

FIGURE 3.7

Independent Learning Activity

Look for a Pattern

Area = s × s = 3 × 3 = 9 sq. units

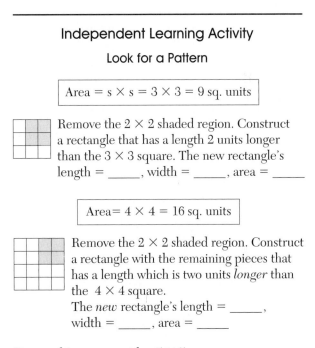

Remove the 2 × 2 shaded region. Construct a rectangle that has a length 2 units longer than the 3 × 3 square. The new rectangle's length = _____, width = _____, area = _____

Area = 4 × 4 = 16 sq. units

Remove the 2 × 2 shaded region. Construct a rectangle with the remaining pieces that has a length which is two units *longer* than the 4 × 4 square.
The *new* rectangle's length = _____, width = _____, area = _____

Repeat this process with a 5 × 5 square, a 6 × 6 square, and a 7 × 7 square.

Can you find a pattern?

FIGURE 3.8

---

sequence of simpler problems in order to solve a more complex problem. This strategy is developed over an extended period of time, beginning in the elementary school and continuing into the secondary program and beyond. Development usually begins with "2-step" problems requiring the use of intermediate steps to reach a solution (see Figure 3.12). Getting pupils to the point where they can identify separate subgoals within a problem is difficult to accomplish. However, because many of the problems that people encounter are multistep problems and **looking for subgoals** is a very powerful problem-solving strategy, every effort must be made to develop this skill.

Using Approach Strategies

Before entering school, children already have learned some ways of approaching problems. They have used trial-and-error countless times before kindergarten and first grade. This strategy, which is more formally called "**guess and check**," enables the young child to get cookies out of a cabinet or devise a way to get out of the crib. Guess and check is one strategy that everyone continues to use throughout life. As we grow in conceptual knowledge and experiences, the process of solving a problem is shortened because we gain better insight into some trials not to take, and our guesses (estimates) become more than random efforts. We end up having to make fewer checks of our estimates.

Small Group Learning Activities

Make a Table

The largest number of coins needed to make any amount within each range has already been identified. Can *you* identify the kind and number of each type of coin that would be needed?

Hint: You would need at least 1 dime, 1 nickel, and 4 pennies to make *any* amount from 1 cent to 19 cents.

Use only pennies, nickels, and dimes.

Range	Most number of coins	Types and number of each type
.01–.04	4	*4 pennies*
.01–.09	5	
.01–.19	6	
.01–.29	7	
.01–.39	8	
.01–.99	14	

FIGURE 3.9

Independent Learning Activity

Account for All Possibilities

Eleven children came to Billy's party. Some rode their tricycles and some came in their wagons. Billy counted 40 wheels. How many came in tricycles and how many came in wagons?

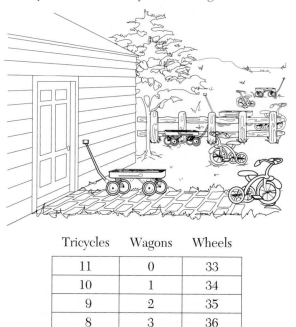

Tricycles	Wagons	Wheels
11	0	33
10	1	34
9	2	35
8	3	36
4	7	40

FIGURE 3.10

One responsibility of the teacher in developing the guess-and-check strategy is emphasizing the "check" part of the strategy. When one guesses, that "guess" must be examined to first decide if it is a "good" guess. Even a guess that does not result in the correct solution can be a "good" guess. Children should learn that guesses may be an intermediate step. Guesses give clues which can help when solving the problem. In Figure 3.13 there are several geometric shapes that can be formed into a square. As the shapes are moved around the child will be making guesses. Some of the guesses help the child see how part of the shape can be assembled. For example, IF you put triangle shapes "4" and "5" together to make half of the square—then you can see that the other four pieces can be used

Small-Group Learning Activity

It's Halloween and everyone is wearing costumes and masks. See if you can unmask the person sitting across from Lisa.

Tim sits across from Cindy. Char sits to the right of Tim. Lisa sits between Jeff and Char. Ali sits on Cindy's right. Ann sits between Al and Ali.

Strategy
Use a logic table for analysis.

Yes = ▨   No = ☐

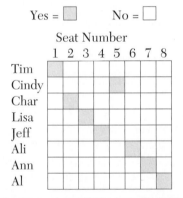

FIGURE 3.11

to make the other half of the square. Figure 3.14 illustrates a successful trial at making the square.

As children mature, their guesses get better and better, requiring fewer adjustments for errors. At some point—with the teacher's assistance—students will formalize this strategy. The guesses will eventually become "**hypotheses**" and the trials become "**experiments**."

Using Looking-Back Strategies

Perhaps the most neglected of all the problem-solving skills are those which require the child to reexamine the **process** used. After a child solves a problem, the motivating force—finding the answer—is removed. Indeed, many pupils don't even check to see if their answer is appropriate! Consider the problem: "There are going to be four relay teams in Mrs. Jones' fifth grade. If there are 25 pupils in the class, how many will be on each team?" Some children, after dividing 25 by 4, will write the answer as "$6\frac{1}{4}$ pupils." The fact that it would be impossible to have $\frac{1}{4}$ of a pupil is not even considered!

The teacher must encourage children to always check the solution for appropriateness and reasonableness. The computation—as in the problem above—may be correct, but is it appropriate in light of the question? Children need to ask themselves, "Is the answer reasonable?" This means that the teacher should get children in the habit of inquiring, "Does the answer make sense?" Evaluation should focus on such questions as "How do you know it is reasonable?"

In the Polya problem-solving model, the checking step is far more than just seeing if the answer is appropriate. The "CHECK" in problem solving looks back at the process to gain new problem-solving skills from every problem solved! Helping children study the solution process is an important, but often neglected, task of the teacher. Discussions of the processes being used to solve

Development of Multistep Problem-Solving Skills

Trinni has been saving to buy a bicycle to use on her paper route. She has saved 35 dollars. The bike cost 95 dollars. She will have to pay an additional 5.5% sales tax. How much more money will she have to save?

The steps that Jason's group used:

Step 1. Find the cost of the bicycle including the tax.
Step 2. Find the difference between the cost of the bicycle and what Trinni has saved.

FIGURE 3.12

Independent Learning Activity

Guess and Check

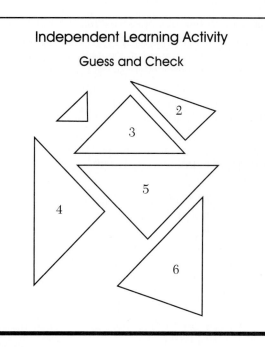

FIGURE 3.13

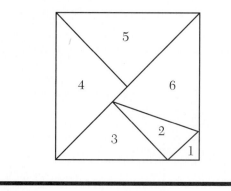

FIGURE 3.14

problems—whether those discussions are done in team, cooperative group, or total class environments—encourage participants to examine and try new strategies. Evaluation questions such as, "How did you decide on that process?" are much more valuable than asking, "What is the answer?" Some teachers find that children can be encouraged to explain their thought processes if a question is posed in this manner—"Pretend you are trying to help some younger children solve this problem. How would you help them?"

For pupils to learn more efficient processes, they must examine different paths which lead to a solution. To encourage students to **find another way to solve a problem**, the teacher may REQUIRE them to "prove" their answers by finding a different way to solve the problem. (Solving problems as a part of a cooperative learning team also encourages children to share strategies.)

The problems that confront children in textbooks generally have a single solution. Most **real-life** problems have more than one solution. This means that the teacher must search out problem situations where more than one solution is appropriate. Looking for the best way to walk from the classroom to the library might present opportunities to find another solution. "If we wanted the 'most' direct route to the library, would it be the most scenic? Suppose they were painting the hall and we could not use the 'most direct' route—what other ways are possible?"

In the preceding section an overview of problem-solving strategies was presented. A teacher may choose to devote several lessons specifically to developing pupil skills using strategies; however, problem-solving should be incorporated into ALL mathematics units since one of the primary goals of instruction is to teach children to solve problems using mathematics. As concepts related to operations, number, geometry, measurement, statistics, and probability are developed in the remaining chapters of this text, additional problem-solving strategies will be illustrated.

3.5 UTILIZING TEXTBOOK STORY PROBLEMS

All children's mathematics texts contain "story" problems. However, these problems have a number of shortcomings that must be considered and overcome if they are to be used effectively in the classroom. Some significant limitations are:

1. Many "story" problems are not "problems," simply because the child is familiar with the path to the goal even before the story problem is examined. Textbooks persistently include story problems that require the exact computational skills developed on the text's preceding pages. Children do not utilize problem-solving strategies to attack the problem. Instead, they simply apply these newly learned computational skills using the numbers from the story problems. A child thinks, "We've been studying two-digit division—so these problems must require division. Here is a two-digit number, so I will use this number as my divisor and the other number for my dividend."

Implication: Mix your story problems so that

a variety of paths are represented by the problems given to the children. Instead of using ALL the story problems on a textbook page—SAVE some of the problems to be used later when exploring a different operation. (For example, save some subtraction story problems to use when working with division.)

2. A child may not be able to solve a story problem because he/she can't read the words or comprehend what is being read. Not every fifth-grade child will be able to read the problems in a fifth-grade mathematics text.

Implication: Story problems must be written at a level commensurate with the child's ability to read. The teacher may use alternate ways of presenting the problems other than reading. For example, "story" problems can be recorded on audio tapes so children with reading or visual deficits can listen to the problems. In primary grades, pictures or "rebus" stories may be used to compensate for reading deficiencies.

3. A diet of story problems from the text is a poor substitute for "real" problems. They do not develop the broad skills that an individual needs to become a functional problem solver. Story problems rarely have children create problems from actual data. They seldom contain extraneous information or require a number of steps to arrive at a solution. Most do not allow a variety of paths to the solution—they simply require pupils to select the best path under the circumstances.

Implication: Supplement story problems with real-world problems where the children have to extract the data that will be needed to solve the problem and several paths that will lead to a solution. Give children opportunities to identify problems that might be generated from data and situations.

If teachers recognize the limitations of textbook story problems and provide other problem-solving experiences to make up for these limitations, textbook "story" problems can serve many useful functions in the development of children's problem-solving skills. Textbook story problems can serve:

Application functions. Solving story problems helps children develop insight into a wide variety of problem-solving situations. Story problems can serve as examples of circumstances where specific problem-solving skills and strategies can be used. Children can see immediate uses for mathematics.

Computational practice functions. While not their primary function, story problems DO allow children to practice their computational skills in a problem-solving environment.

Practice functions. In addition to the computational practice, finding an answer allows pupils to practice strategies such as modeling, translating to equation format as an intermediate solution strategy, developing intermediate questions, setting up tables, graphs, or drawings, acting out the problem, guessing and checking, trial and error, and pattern searches.

Skills functions. Story problems help students organize their problem-solving attack skills.

Reference base functions. Having a repertoire of solved story problems gives children a reference base when they encounter new but similar problems.

Textbook problems serve as one tool that may be used by the teacher in developing problem-solving skills. From this base the teacher can extend the child's problem-solving skills, using nonstory, real-life problem situations.

Examining Two Approaches to Story Problems

Let us examine two approaches for using story problems in the classroom: the **match-to-model approach** and the **prealgebra (analysis) approach**. Remember, the final goal of any approach is to help pupils learn to use a wide variety of problem-solving strategies. Therefore, teachers should constantly be on the lookout for ways that "story" problems can be used to introduce children to new problem-solving strategies.

The first approach examined will be that of matching the activity of a story problem back to a model for an operation. There are from 25 to 40 or more models in elementary mathematics texts that can be associated with the activities in whole number and fractional (common and decimal) operations. The variance in the number of models is due more to the way subclasses are defined than to any fundamental difference between texts. (Basic models commonly associated with operations will be developed in later chapters.)

Match-to-Model Approach

In a **match-to-model approach**, the students read or listen to a "story" problem. Pupils then attempt to match the activity of the story problem to a previously learned model, such as one of the models for addition, subtraction, multiplication, or division. After deciding which model matches the activity of the story problem, an **open-number sentence (equation)** is written and the computation is completed to solve the problem. The reasonableness of the answer is checked against the requirements of the problem.

Aspects to consider when using the **match-to-model approach**:

1. The pupil must develop a sense of the activity taking place in the story problem to employ this strategy successfully. Not every word in the problem is essential to understanding the gist of the activity taking place.

2. Matching to a model is much like "acting it out" and is less abstract than the **prealgebra (analysis) approach** (which is developed later in this section). Since matching to a model is less abstract, it meets the needs of a learning disabled child better than a prealgebra (analysis) strategy.

3. Reducing a problem to a simplified model is a strategy that everyone uses throughout his or her life. Thus, it should be included in every child's repertoire of problem-solving strategies.

Teacher-Guided Interactive Learning Activity

Let us examine a fragment of a lesson that assists children in developing this strategy.

LESSON FRAGMENT

M: Matching a "story" problem to a model

A: Small group of children, some of whom have reading comprehension problems

T: Modeling strategy

H: Children have previously learned the four models that are being used in this lesson

The teacher places the four models on the board. The story problem is placed on the board and a student reads it. (Caution: The story should be read before the method is applied.)

Mary unpacked four cups.
She found one of them broken.
How many were not broken?

Teacher-Guided Interactive Learning Activity

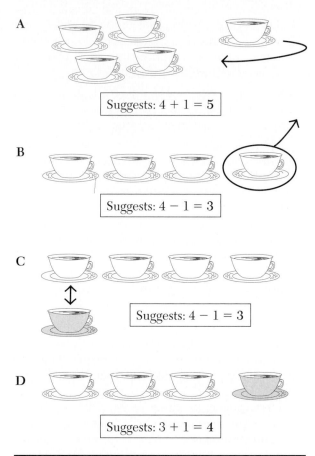

A   Suggests: 4 + 1 = 5

B   Suggests: 4 − 1 = 3

C   Suggests: 4 − 1 = 3

D   Suggests: 3 + 1 = 4

FIGURE 3.15

Teacher: Are two sets of cups being put together and do we want to know **the total number** of cups we have? (POINTS TO MODEL "A" AS THIS IS SAID.) (SEE FIGURE 3.15 THAT THE TEACHER HAS MADE FOR THIS LESSON. IN ACTUALITY, THE MODELS ARE ONLY MATCHED FOR SIMILAR ACTIVITIES AND THE NUMBER OF OBJECTS AND TYPES OF OBJECTS MAY NOT BE THE SAME, BECAUSE THE SAME SET OF MODELS ARE USED AS REFERENTS FOR ALL "STORY" PROBLEMS ONCE THEY HAVE BEEN DEVELOPED. IT IS THE "COMMON" ACTIVITY THAT LEADS TO EITHER AN ADDITION OR SUBTRACTION EQUATION THAT IS THE CRITICAL FACTOR, NOT THE NUMBERS IN THE "STORY" PROBLEM.)

Teacher: Are part of the cups being removed and do we want to know how many cups **are left**? (POINTS TO MODEL "B.")

Teacher: Is one set of cups being **compared to another set** of cups, and do we want to know how many more or less one set has than another set? (POINTS TO "C.")

Teacher: Do we know something about the whole set of cups and part of the set of cups and do we want to find out something about **the rest of the set**? (POINTS TO "D.") THE TEACHER REREADS THE PROBLEM.

Teacher: Write the letter of the model you think fits the situation onto a piece of paper. When I say go, show me your answer. Go!

(CHILDREN'S ANSWERS WILL VARY, DEPENDING ON WHETHER THEY THOUGHT OF THE BROKEN CUPS AS BEING PART OF A SET OF WHOLE CUPS, OR THOUGHT THAT THE BROKEN CUPS WERE REMOVED FROM THE SET. BUT NOTICE THAT BOTH PATHS WILL GET THE CHILD TO THE SOLUTION.) THE TEACHER LISTENS TO THE REASONS WHY DIFFERENT CHILDREN SELECTED DIFFERENT MODELS AND REACTS. (NOTICE HOW THIS APPROACH HELPS CLARIFY THE CHILDREN'S THINKING AND PROVIDES **EVALUATION** DATA TO THE TEACHER.)

Individual Learning Activity

Many subskills of the match-to-model approach can be developed and/or practiced in individual learning activities. For example, with "story" problems placed on individual cards, children visit a learning station to complete tasks of constructing models (or drawings) that represent activities in the "story" problem. Students might *match* story problem cards to other cards depicting models of the activities being suggested by the "story" problem cards. Other subskills, such as constructing equations from models and estimating the reasonableness of answers, also lend themselves to learning-station activities.

Cooperative Learning Groups

The **match-to-model** approach lends itself to use in **cooperative learning settings** because the model being selected frequently will depend on how an individual perceives the activity of the story. Different perceptions will generate different models and hence promote discussions among children relating to why one model seems to fit the activity better than another model. (In this text operations are presented in a problem context. The problem is developed by matching activities to models to assist students in making associations between real-world problems, activities with models, and mathematical expressions and equations.)

Prealgebra (Analysis) Approach

A second approach is the **prealgebra (analysis)** strategy. While this is more structured than the **match-to-model approach**, some students thrive on it. This strategy requires students to have both good reading-comprehension skills and good analytical skills. It assists in the development of the major problem-solving strategy of analysis.

The **prealgebra (analysis) approach** requires the student to read the "story" problem carefully. Words and phrases of the "story" are "translated" into expressions that are chained together to form an equation.

Aspects to consider when using this approach are:

1. Good reading comprehension is required for its successful use.

2. The order in which numerals and operations signs appear in translated equations is determined by convention and sometimes does not readily fit the order in which they appear in the problem.

3. This is a difficult strategy to employ with those learning-disabled children who have visual memory deficits. For these children, the teacher may wish to supplement the instruction with audio and technological devices when using this approach.

4. The analytical skills utilized in this approach are fundamental skills that play a vital role in both later mathematics skills and current problem-solving strategies.

Let us examine a fragment of a lesson that uses this approach.

Teacher-Guided Interactive Learning Activity

LESSON FRAGMENT

M: Translating a "story" problem into an equation

A: Small group of children with good reading-comprehension skills

T: Analysis strategy

H: Introductory activity

In the lesson fragment above (Figure 3.16), background knowledge must be applied once the open sentence is written. The child may think,

"The SUM is known so I won't add to get the answer. I must 'undo' the addition. Subtraction will 'undo' addition, so I'll subtract to find the number of cookies. Nine minus three is SIX. So the answer must be six cookies."

In some elementary mathematics series the students are given a list of steps to follow when using the **prealgebra (analysis) approach**. Directions contain the following elements:

1. What question is to be answered?
2. Find the essential information.
3. Decide on the appropriate operation(s).
4. Write the equation(s).
5. Solve the equation(s).
6. Put the answer(s) into an English sentence.
7. Check the answer(s) against the question(s) asked.

Notice that the rules do not instruct the child in "how" to choose the operation. In both the **match-to-model approach** and the **prealgebra (analysis) approach**, success is dependent on the child associating the activity within the story with the models for the mathematical operations. In other words, the child must be able to see the relationship between activities in the real world and the associations that the teacher has established between models, mathematical expressions, and equations.

3.6 PROBLEM SOLVING BEYOND STORY PROBLEMS

Because problems in real life rarely come prepackaged and preidentified, story problems should be supplemented with activities that match the essence of the types of problems that children will encounter in everyday life. To accomplish this, the teacher must establish an environment conducive to solving problems. This environment must contain materials that permit children to utilize a variety of strategies to solve problems (materials for models, drawings, etc.), work space that will permit problem-solving projects to be worked on over a period of time and areas for small groups to meet and discuss strategies to be used when solving problems.

Let us examine how a teacher might establish an environment conducive to building students' problem-solving skills and strategies. A four-step simplified model of Polya's process will be used as

Developing Equation-Building Skills

Story Problem Translation	Analysis
Meg has some cookies. (☐ stands for the number of cookies Meg has.)	☐
Joe gives Meg 3 more cookies. (Give is really like putting together or forming the union—thus + is linked with 3.)	☐ + 3
Meg now has 9 cookies. (What she started with and what Joe gave her equals a total of 9.)	☐ + 3 = 9
How many cookies did Meg start out with?	6 + 3 = 9

FIGURE 3.16

a framework for structuring the problem-solving activity.

A student has proposed that the class hold its annual picnic at a nearby park instead of on the playground. Everyone liked the idea. (A **goal** has been identified.) At this point, however, the class has not perceived that there are problems which must be surmounted in order to reach this goal. The teacher then structures the problem into a four-step simplified model of the Polya-type process.

1. **Understanding what the problems are.**

Teacher: What are some of the problems we will have to solve before we can have our class picnic at the park?

Children's questions and suggestions:

- When will we go?
- How will we get to the park?
- Do we need the city's O.K. to use the park?
- Will the principal let us have the picnic off the school grounds?
- What type of food should we take to the picnic?
- How will we get food and drinks to the park?
- How much food and drink should we take?
- Will parents need to go along with us?
- What games can we play in the park?

Teacher adds:

- Does the school's liability insurance cover everyone while they are at the park?

- What hazards exist at the park that we must be prepared for?
- Are rest rooms available at the park?
- Is water available at the park?
- Will any of the special teachers (art, physical education, music, librarian) want to go with us?

Let us assume that all the questions have been answered satisfactorily except for the question of how we are going to get the class and the food and drinks to the park.

2. Devising a plan.

A committee is established to devise a plan to get to the park. They suggest a variety of ideas **(alternate paths)**—walking, using a school bus, having parents drive groups of children to the park and back. The pros and cons of each alternative are discussed.

The committee decides to use parents, recognizing that parents can take the students home when the picnic is over. Problems occur in getting enough parents to volunteer to drive children to the park, but the problem is resolved when a parent from another class volunteers.

3. Carrying out the plan.

The day of the picnic comes and the children have their picnic.

4. Looking back (check the solution).

The day following the picnic the teacher and the class see if there were any things about the planning that could have been improved. Some of the suggestions were:

- There were too many people in each car. We needed more cars or a school bus.
- We didn't have enough ice cream for everyone. (We forgot to include the parents in the people who would be eating ice cream.)
- We had a lot of potato salad left over. Not everyone liked potato salad.
- Next time we need to find out who will be eating the food we bring. Someone suggested that we should have taken a survey.
- We should have planned to get there an hour earlier, because we ended up eating an hour later than we usually eat.
- We didn't have enough places to sit to eat. Next time we will need to take chairs.

Notice what a rich complexity of problems and skills were represented in the simple activity of planning and carrying out a picnic. Also note how the experience of **looking back** served the purpose of assisting children grow in their problem-solving skills. If a new site is chosen next year by this same group of children, new problems will occur, but each similar previous experience can, if carefully exploited by the next teacher, assist the children in becoming better problem solvers than they were in the past.

A creative teacher will draw upon the many activities occurring in the classroom to provide settings where children can identify when problems exist; then devise and execute plans for solving those problems. Once the goal is reached the teacher will provide an opportunity for the children to reexamine their plans and suggest ways that the planning and execution could have been modified so that they could reach their goal more efficiently.

3.7 PROBLEM SOLVING AT THE PRIMARY LEVEL

Children begin solving problems long before they enter the primary grades. Some problems faced by preprimary children require sophisticated problem-solving skills. By the time children enter the primary level, children have developed their own personal approaches and strategies for solving these complex problems. It is the primary teacher's responsibility to assist children in extending, refining and adding to their problem-solving approaches and strategies.

Even at the primary level, problem solving should be the focus of almost all mathematics instruction the child will encounter. Computational skills are taught so they can be used as tools in the problem-solving process.

In the past, some schools taught problem solving by exposing children to problems and hoping that somehow—after working many problems—the children would automatically develop into problem solvers. Such programs had children solve "problems" that used addition, division, fractions, etc. Today's approach utilizes the results of research on how children learn to solve problem. Students are systematically involved in examining various problem-solving approaches—called strategies—which can be used in a wide variety of problem-solving situations. When encountering problems the pupil will draw upon these strategies. For example, when the young child encounters a problem he might think, "I'm not sure what to do—so maybe I can draw a picture to help me see what is happening. Maybe I could use simpler numbers and see how that might help."

To insure that problem-solving skills are systematically developed, the responsibility for formally exploring a particular strategy in the problem-solving strand may be delegated to a specific grade level. This insures that the pupil will, before leaving the elementary program, become acquainted with a wide variety of approaches that can be utilized when solving problems. This does not mean that the child may not use a specific strategy before it is designated for development. On the contrary, teachers should let the nature of the problems dictate the introduction of new strategies.

The strategies commonly delegated to the primary level are:

- **Act it out.** Teachers in kindergarten and first grade use this approach when developing models for addition and subtraction. Rebus problems, which use pictures to convey words, are used as a basis for children physically "acting out" a problem.
- **Draw a picture.** Children's textbooks use drawings and pictures throughout the early development of mathematical concepts, as well as beginning problem-solving exercises. However, teachers must design activities that encourage children to use this skill.
- **Use a model.** As early as kindergarten, teachers will be using representations on the flannel-board or magnetic board to illustrate addition and subtraction situations. Children also should have opportunities to use their own sets of materials (at their desks) to "act out" the problem using counters or number lines.
- **Collect and organize data.** Children start making simple, teacher-directed graphs as early as kindergarten. By second grade they should be constructing bar graphs and getting information from tables.
- **Look for a pattern.** Bead-stringing, paper chains, and rhythm activities used in kindergarten lay a foundation for this strategy. Children start identifying patterns with pictures or symbols in the first grade. By the third grade, students will extend these skills to include numerical patterns (odd/even numbers, multiples of fives, etc.).
- **Guess and check.** Children begin "guessing" even before the teacher introduces this skill! Before a pupil can become very skillful with this strategy, some number and measurement skills must be developed. The teacher SHOULD be building **estimation skills** as children work with whole numbers, operations, and measurement so children will have a fairly good foundation in estimation skills before the third grade.

Responsibility for developing the above strategies generally is specified in each school system's curriculum guide. Because of this the authors have not specifically indicated a grade level. In general, school systems follow this order (from "Act It Out" to "Guess and Check"). However, as problems present themselves, teachers should seize the opportunity to introduce appropriate strategies, even though the responsibility to formally develop these strategies may be assigned to a later grade level.

3.8 PROBLEM SOLVING AT THE INTERMEDIATE LEVEL

Children enter the intermediate grade levels with many problem-solving skills. They have number and measurement skills and some skill in the four operations—addition, subtraction, multiplication, and division. Of course, the intermediate-level teacher will be extending students' skills with number, numeration, measurement, geometry, probability, and statistics. The intermediate teacher will again look at models suggested by problems, especially problems involving operations. Since many of the problem-solving strategies explored at the intermediate level rely upon the child's ability to relate a physical action to a mathematical operation, a review of models associated with each type of activity is helpful.

At the intermediate level, students will confront problems which are much more complex. Textbook story problems may include too much information or not include enough information. Some problems will require multisteps before students can arrive at a solution. As students learn to work with fractions and decimals, they will solve problems that use these numbers. Likewise, the study of ratio, percent, interest, and negative numbers will incorporate these numbers into problem-solving situations.

In addition to strategies that were developed at the primary level, students at the intermediate level will explore new strategies such as:

- **Write an open-number sentence.** The skill of writing open-number sentences, as related to action in a problem, is explored in the primary grades. At the intermediate level, the teacher will be spending much more time to develop this skill.
- **Make a table, diagram, or chart.** The ability to read a table, chart, or diagram is developed in the primary grades. The child will learn to make a table, chart, or diagram as a

tool to solve problems early in the intermediate program.

- **Identify subgoals.** One outcome from using "two-step" problems is that pupils become more skillful in identifying subgoals. Multistep problems provide a more formal approach which forces the child to break the problem into subgoals. Of course, many everyday problems do not have subgoals that are as easily identified.

- **Systematically find all possible solutions.** Most students must be formally introduced to this technique. Since it seems to be time-consuming, children often feel that it has little value as a problem-solving strategy.

- **Solve by working it backwards.** Most activities require one to start at the beginning and work to the end. It is difficult for a child to see any other way than beginning at "start." Careful selection of problems can present situations where the child will see the value of starting at the end and working it backwards.

- **Solve a simpler problem.** When working with fractions, students can make the problem easier to understand if whole numbers are used in place of the fractions. Once the operation (addition, subtraction, etc.) is identified with whole numbers, then the fractions can be returned to the problem. (Caution: When this approach is used students need to be aware that multiplication does not always result in a larger number, and division does not always result in a smaller number, or they may ignore the information gained through the application of the simpler problem and apply the wrong operation to get the larger (or smaller) number they perceive they should be getting.)

- **Use formulas to solve problems.** Problems that involve finding the area of a field, the volume of a can, etc., require the use of formulas. Pupils must be taught to recognize when such notation is appropriate.

- **Check for hidden assumptions—change your point of view.** Most textbook problems, since they are designed for children, do not present "hidden assumptions." In real-life situations, however, we often are frustrated because we face the problem with an assumption that may not be true. Children perceive hidden assumption problems as "trick problems" that do not really occur in life. The problem—"I have two coins whose total value is 15 cents. One of the coins is not a nickel. What are the coins?"—has many assumptions. Are the coins U.S. coins? Could the "other" coin be a nickel? Is this a coin collection in which "value" means worth of the coins?

- **State the problem in your own words.** This really is the first step in Polya's model—"Understand the Problem." When you state the problem in your own words, you must absorb and understand what is asked—and what is needed.

- **Identify wanted/given information.** This formal technique is first used in textbook story problems. Children look at the problem to find out "What is needed? What information is given?" Problems that have too little information or too much information also are used to build skill.

Sometimes when solving problems, children should recognize that SEVERAL strategies may need to be employed. In the problem below, a pupil might first draw a picture of the chart—BUT make the chart only to 25 ("make the problem simpler").

> Tommy liked to play with his computer. One day he decided to tell his computer—using BASIC computer language, of course—to make a chart which counted to 500. He then told the computer, "Place a ring around every number. If the number is a multiple of 2, take the ring OFF." He had the computer go through every multiple for 3, 4, 5, 6, etc., until EVERY NUMBER through 500 had been processed using the rule, <u>IF it has NO ring, draw one. IF it has a ring from a previous multiple, erase it.</u> When the computer finished, which numbers had rings around them?

After drawing a simple picture, the child might **then** draw (and erase) rings around the numerals ("act it out") hoping to "find a pattern" **before** reaching 25!

3.9 SUMMARY

Problem solving has long been important as a part of the elementary mathematics curriculum. However, in recent years, national tests have shown that children are **not** very good problem solvers. Concerned mathematics educators have made problem solving a focus of the 1980s to 1990s mathematics curriculum. Problem solving will remain a major goal of mathematics instruction into the twenty-first century.

Problem solving is a <u>process</u> of striving to reach a goal and then reaching that goal. This chapter has examined methods that teachers use to develop children's problem-solving processing skills. Some of the processing approaches that were discussed were: modeling strategies, organizing-data strate- gies, approach strategies, analysis strategies, and looking-back strategies.

Two methods of using "story" problems in de- veloping problem-solving processing skills (match- to-model approach and prealgebra (analysis) ap- proach) were discussed.

EXERCISES

1. What is meant by the statement, "A problem for one child may not be a problem for an- other child"?
2. Describe how each of the following strategies could be used to develop the following prob- lem with children:

   Zack is going to sell Zappers for 75 cents a Zap- per. Each Zapper costs 50 cents. The monthly rental on the place where Zappers are to be sold is $100. How many Zappers must be sold each month to make $500 profit after expenses?

   a. Using an act-it-out strategy
   b. Using a make-a-model strategy
   c. Using a construct-a-graph strategy
3. Describe how the following problem could be developed using a pattern strategy:

   How many squares are represented in the follow- ing figure? (*Hint:* Work the largest square toward the smallest squares.)

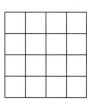

FIGURE 3.17

4. Describe how the following problem could be developed using
   a. An account-for-all-possibilities strategy
   b. Guess-and-check strategy

   You have seven coins; some are nickels, some are dimes, and some are quarters. The total value is 85 cents. What are the coins?

5. Suppose a child says an answer to a problem is 6.25 people. How does the looking-back strategy help avoid unreasonable answers?
6. Which strategy can be implemented when using a team approach to problem solving? (*Hint:* Several people will produce several paths.)
7. Identify four functions of "story" problems.
8. Identify two approaches for developing prob- lem solving.
9. Which approach in exercise eight would re- quire the child to have a higher competency in reading?
10. Which approach in exercise eight would have direct application in translating alge- braic story problems into equations?

RELEVANT COMPUTER SOFTWARE

Adventure Alpha and the Islands of Beta. 1984. Apple II family. Milliken Publishing Co., 1100 Research Bou- levard, P.O. Box 21579, St. Louis, Miss. 63132.

Math Blaster Mystery. 1989. Apple II family. Davidson and Associates, 3135 Kashiwa Street, Torrance, Calif. 90505.

Math Story Solvers. 1985. Apple II family. Imperial Inter- national Learning Corporation, P.O. Box 548, Kan- kakee, Ill. 60901.

Problem Solving Strategies. 1983. Apple. MECC Distri- bution Center, 3490 Lexington Ave. N., St. Paul, Minn. 55112.

Strategies in Problem Solving: Dinosaurs and Squids. 1985. Apple II. Scott, Foresman, 1900 East Lake Avenue, Glenview, Ill. 60025.

Winkler's World of Patterns. Apple II family. Sunburst Communication, 39 Washington Avenue, Pleasantville, N.Y. 10570.

REFERENCES

Bowen, E. "Flunking Grade in Math." *Time,* June 20, 1988, p. 79.

Bush, W. S., and A. Fiala. Problem Stories: A New Twist on Problem Posing." *Arithmetic Teacher* 34 (December 1986): 6–9.

Carpenter, T. P. et al. "Results and Implications of the Second NAEP Mathematics Assessment: Elementary School." *Arithmetic Teacher* 27 (April 1980): 47.

Carpenter, T. P. et al. "Results of the Fourth NAEP Assessment of Mathematics: Trends and Conclusions." *Arithmetic Teacher* 36 (December 1988): 38–41.

Charles, R. I. "The Role of Problem Solving." *Arithmetic Teacher* 32 (February 1985): 48–50.

Clements, D. H. "Computers and Problem Solving." Edited by J. A. Van de Walle. *Arithmetic Teacher* 35 (December 1987): 26–27.

Cobb, P. et al. "Creating a Problem-Solving Atmosphere." Edited by J. Sowder and L. Sowder. *Arithmetic Teacher* 36 (September 1988): 46–47.

Dossey, J. A. et al. *The Mathematics Report Card: Are We Measuring Up?* Princeton, N.J.: Educational Testing Service, 1988.

Easterday, K. E., and C. A. Clothiaux. "Problem-solving Opportunities." *Arithmetic Teacher* 32 (January 1985): 18–20.

Gilbert-Macmillan, K., and S. J. Leitz. "Cooperative Small Groups: A Method for Teaching Problem Solving." *Arithmetic Teacher* 33 (March 1986): 9–11.

Grouws, D. A., and T. L. Good. "Issues in Problem-solving Instruction." Edited by J. Sowder and L. Sowder. *Arithmetic Teacher* 36 (April 1989): 134–35.

Hosmer, P. C. "Students Can Write Their Own Problems." *Arithmetic Teacher* 34 (December 1986): 10–11.

Krulik, S., and J. A. Rudnick. "Reduction." Edited by P. G. O'Daffer. *Arithmetic Teacher* 33 (December 1985): 38–39.

Lester, H. K. "Research on Mathematical Problem Solving." Edited by R. J. Shumway. *Research in Mathematics Education.* Reston, Va.: NCTM, 1980.

Leutzinger, L. P. "Asking Intermediate Questions." Edited by P. G. O'Daffer. *Arithmetic Teacher* 33 (October 1985): 34–35.

Lindquist, M. M. et al. "The Third National Mathematics Assessment: Results and Implications for Elementary and Middle Schools." *Arithmetic Teacher* 31 (December 1983): 19.

Martin, H. "The 12.7 cm Hot Dog Corporation." *Arithmetic Teacher* 36 (January 1989): 12–13.

Meiring, S. P. *Problem Solving—A Basic Mathematics Goal.* Columbus, Oh.: Ohio Department of Education, 1980.

Morton, R. L. *Teaching Arithmetic in the Intermediate Grades.* New York: Silver Burdett, 1927.

National Council of Teachers of Mathematics. *A History of Mathematics Education in the United States and Canada. 32nd Yearbook.* Washington, D. C.: The National Council of Teachers of Mathematics, 1970.

———. *Arithmetic Teacher.* (April 1980). Back Cover.

———. *An Agenda for Action: Recommendations for School Mathematics, Grades K–12.* Reston, Va.: NCTM, 1980.

O'Daffer, P. G. *Problem Solving: Tips for Teachers.* Reston, Va.: NCTM, 1988.

O'Daffer, P. G. "Solve a Simpler Problem." *Arithmetic Teacher* 32 (March 1985): 34–35.

O'Daffer, P. G. "Find a Pattern." *Arithmetic Teacher* 32 (January 1985): 34–35.

Polya, G. *How to Solve It.* Princeton, N.J.: Princeton University Press, 1945.

———. *How to Solve It.* 2nd ed. Princeton, N.J.: Princeton University Press, 1957.

Schaaf, O. "Computation Problems—Choosing Strategy Sequences." Edited by P. G. O'Daffer. *Arithmetic Teacher* 33 (January 1986): 38–39.

Souviney, R. "Conducting Experiments." Edited by P. G. O'Daffer. *Arithmetic Teacher* 33 (February 1986): 56–57.

Sowder, L. "Story Problems and Student's Strategies." Edited by J. Sowder and L. Sowder. *Arithmetic Teacher* 36 (May 1989): 25–26.

Stimpson, V. C. "Using Diagrams to Solve Problems." *Mathematics Teacher* 82 (March 1989): 194–200.

Talton, C. F. "Let's Solve the Problem Before We Find the Answer." *Arithmetic Teacher* 36 (September 1988): 40–45.

Thiessen, D. "Helping Students Approach a Problem." Edited by J. A. Van de Walle. *Arithmetic Teacher* 35 (April 1988): 58–59.

CHAPTER 4

TEACHING NUMBER AND NUMERATION CONCEPTS

INTRODUCTION

Parents throughout the world begin teaching children number concepts long before their children begin any formal schooling. Many cultures teach number rhymes and poems to their children at a very early age. Children hear number words and concepts being used frequently by others as they go through their daily activities.

This chapter will examine the teaching of whole-number concepts and the many ways of naming whole numbers. Some aspects of teaching numeration (exploring ancient numeration systems, exponential notation, scientific notation, etc.) are developed in later chapters.

In the kindergarten and primary grades, extensive time is devoted to teaching number and numeration concepts through hands-on explorations using manipulative materials. This development emphasizes the nature of number, one-to-one correspondence, less than and greater than, and positional or place value. In addition, children learn to estimate number and read and write names for numbers (numerals).

At the intermediate level, students' conceptual understanding of number and numeration is extended through a more formal analysis of the decimal system. Also, enrichment explorations into nondecimal numeration systems (other number bases developed in a later chapter) provide some students with a better appreciation and understanding of their own base-ten system. By the time a student finishes the intermediate grades, he/she will have explored whole numbers and their names, learned a variety of applications of whole-number concepts, and expressed whole numbers in a variety of forms (for example, the student will be able to express 4,900 as four thousand nine hundred; forty-nine hundreds; four hundred ninety tens, etc.).

While the topics included in this chapter <u>could</u> appear in many different places in the elementary school mathematics programs, generally they are placed in a "number and numeration" **strand.** Some programs also include fractions (positive rational numbers), decimals, and integers in the number and numeration strand. Since the choice of when and where various topics are taught depends upon the perceived needs of each school system (or textbook publisher), the following sequence of topics may differ from a particular sequence found in a school or textbooks.

The primary-level section of this chapter will look at whole number and numeration skills **typically** found in primary programs. Since the kindergarten is responsible for so many beginning number skills, the kindergarten will be listed separately from grade one. The following illustrates a typical sequence for teaching number and numeration in the primary grades:

Kindergarten

Prenumber Concepts
- Classification
- Comparison (more, less)
- One-to-one correspondence
- Ordering (seriation)
- Rote counting

Number Concepts
- Rational counting to 30
- Number recognition through ten
- Numeral recognition through ten
- Number/numeral matching through ten
- Ordinal numbers through third
- Writing numerals through ten

Grade 1

Number Concepts
- Rote and rational counting through 99
- Read and write 2-digit numerals
- Order and compare numbers through 99
- Greater than and less than symbols
- Odd and even numbers
- Count by tens, fives, and twos
- Ordinals through tenth

Grade 2

Number Concepts
- Rote and rational counting through 999
- Read and write 3-digit numerals
- Order and compare numbers through 999
- Count by hundreds
- Ordinals through twentieth

Grade 3

Number Concepts
- Rote and rational counting through 99,999
- Read and write 5-digit numerals
- Order and compare numbers through 99,999
- Count by thousands
- Count by 25s to 100
- Rounding to nearest ten or hundred

4.1 INTRODUCING NUMBER IN THE KINDERGARTEN AND PRIMARY GRADES

Prenumber Explorations

When many 5-year-olds enter kindergarten they are still operating at the level which Piaget calls the preoperational level. One of the distinguishing features of this level is that the child cannot conserve number. That is to say, if two rows of blocks were lined up and matched, the child would recognize that they have the same number. BUT if one of the rows is spread apart (see Figure 4.1) most children would believe that there are more blocks in the stretched-out row, because it is longer.

Before children can really understand number operations, they must be able to conserve number. Therefore, most kindergarten programs include activities to assess a child's ability to conserve and provide opportunities to build these skills. Concepts which serve as foundations for working with number are called **prenumber concepts.**

Children enter kindergarten with mastery of some of the prenumber concepts. For example, children have longed ceased calling every male "daddy," or every animal "doggy," and they have refined their ability to classify things to the point that they differentiate between dogs, cats, horses, people, etc. Children also can make some comparisons with respect to many, few, etc. They are aware of some elemental ordering; knowing, for example, socks go on before shoes, and shirts or blouses before coats. Parents or nursery school teachers will have taught some children to rote count (saying the counting words without matching the words to objects). Most children entering kindergarten will not have had experiences in matching sets in a one-to-one correspondence.

Let us examine some ways that children's prenumber concepts are extended.

Explorations with Classification

All kindergarten classes are filled with activities that can be used to strengthen a child's conceptual understanding of classification. For example, after playtime, balls must be put back in the ball box, blocks onto the block shelf, resting pads into the storeroom, tricycles parked beside the storeroom, sand pails put into the "pail box," jackets hung on pegs, tempera brushes placed in the brush can, etc. In addition, many of the card games played and enjoyed by kindergarten children require matching (classification) like things; for example, "Go Fish" and "Old Maid."

Evaluation

An inability to conserve number.

FIGURE 4.1

To increase the range of items being classified beyond those found in commercially available materials, teachers frequently design their own materials. For example, the teacher-constructed game "Do You Have?" uses a series of 3-by-5 cards with pictures of houses, shoes, coins, fish, and other items, pasted on the backs. There are four or more cards of each type (four different houses, four different fish, etc.). Each child is dealt four cards. The object of the game is to match all of the cards and have none left. The first player, if he or she has no matching cards, asks the second player, "Do you have a—(house, dog, shoe, etc.)?" If that player has the object, it is given to the first person, who puts the matched pair on the table and asks another question. If an object card is requested, but the other player does not have that card, the player then must take a card from the deck. If no match is made, then the other player repeats the process (see Figure 4.2).

Children enjoy sorting objects. Activities that require sorting can develop out of natural situations, such as the need to sort scissors and crayons after an art activity, the need to put silverware in one bucket and empty milk cartons in the garbage can after mid-morning snacks, or the need to put wooden blocks into similar groups for stacking on shelves.

Children often must ignore one characteristic of an object and concentrate on a second characteristic (or attribute). When children sort out a set of yellow, red, and blue blocks they find there are

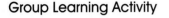

Group Learning Activity

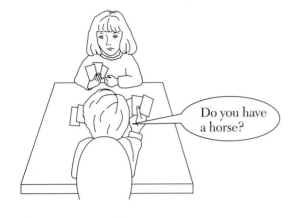

Do you have a horse?

FIGURE 4.2

squares, triangles, circles, and rectangles of different sizes. Sometimes they are asked to "Put all of the red blocks together." To do this, children must ignore the shape and size and concentrate only on color. On other occasions children may be asked to sort out all of the circles, disregarding the color and size (see Figure 4.3).

Even before studying number, children can sort cards which have identical patterns of one, two, three, and four dots. (When dot arrangements are identical, the child does not need a counting skill in order to classify the cards.)

Explorations with Comparison of Sets

Before children can develop an understanding of number, they must be able to look at two sets that differ significantly in amount and recognize that one set has more than the other. If a child cannot tell that two sets differ in amount, it is inappropriate to confront the child with the task of learning to distinguish between sets of three, four, and five! Until the child has developed the concept of one-to-one matching, the comparison of sets should be restricted to comparing sets grossly different in number where visual differences are clear. During these comparison activities vocabulary such as "more," "less," and "fewer" is emphasized. The teacher has a chance to emphasize these concepts as children identify what they want to do during their free time, because situations will occur when "more" people want to participate in an activity than can be accommodated.

Most children enter kindergarten with the word "more" as a part of their oral vocabulary. Therefore, the teacher is just reinforcing this understanding

and expanding that knowledge to new situations. The words "less" and "fewer" are much more difficult for children because they seldom use the words when talking to their peers. They use the word "more" to serve a double function. A child will say, "I have more candy than you" or "You have more candy than me." A child rarely says, "I have less candy than you."

The teacher must ensure that the child hears these words (more, less, fewer) in activities throughout the day. When eight youngsters want to ride the tricycles and the class only has three tricycles, the teacher could explain, "We have fewer tricycles than we have pupils who want to ride." The teacher at times will use both "more" and "less" in order to contrast the meanings. When showing the amount of paint left after an art activity, the teacher might say, "We have far less red paint left than yellow. See, we have much more yellow paint."

Explorations with One-to-One Correspondence

When the members of one set can be matched with the members of another set (placed in one-to-one correspondence with each other), it is said that the two sets have the same number property. For example, if we say we have two eyes, then all the sets in the world that can be matched one-to-one with our eyes will also have the property we call twoness. Thus, the task, in teaching children the concept of number, is to identify the number property of various sets and help a child to understand that all the

Individual Learning Activity

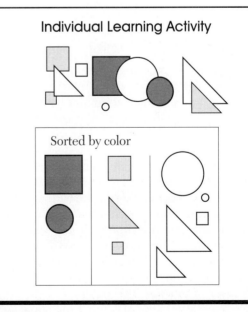

Sorted by color

FIGURE 4.3

sets that have members that will match the members in this set in one-to-one correspondence will have the same number property. **Comment:** When a child learns to count, he/she will use the counting words to match one-to-one with members of a set to determine the number. The last word the child says in matching the counting words with the objects will identify the number of the set. The concept of one-to-one correspondence also permits the child to make fine comparison between sets, ordering sets differing in number by only one object.

There are many informal activities that occur in kindergarten that give the teacher an opportunity to focus on developing **one-to-one correspondence** skills. Having children in the class pair up when walking down the hall permits the teacher to comment on the inequality of the matching by statements such as: "I see we have one person who does not have a partner" or "Today, everybody has a partner." Having children pass out objects, straws, paper plates, napkins, sheets of paper, allows individuals to develop one-to-one correspondence skills.

Some play activities, designed primarily to develop children's eye/hand coordination and ability to control small and large muscles, can also be used to develop one-to-one correspondence skills. Figure 4.4 shows an activity that requires a child to use one-to-one matching. The teacher should make a conscious effort to elicit from the children whether they found there were more, less (fewer), or the same amount of objects by their one-to-one matching. Sometimes the teacher may wish to have the children **estimate** if there will be more, less, or the same number, <u>before</u> beginning the one-to-one matching task.

Explorations with Ordering

Like comparison, ordering (or seriation) of sets is most easily accomplished when there are gross differences in amount; or in terms of measurement, easily visualized differences in length. Many seriation activities take place before the child has learned to match sets in a one-to-one correspondence. Before reaching kindergarten, the child may have to help mother or dad put cans on the shelf, with the smaller cans on top of the larger cans. The child may have to put books back onto a shelf, arranging them from the shortest to the tallest book. In the classroom, teachers may use structured play materials to help build this skill. For example, Figure 4.5 shows how a child arranged rods into a "staircase" to practice ordering.

When children line up before lunch, to get onto

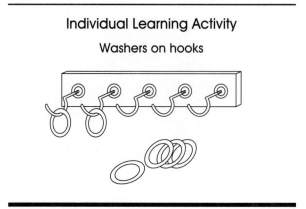

Individual Learning Activity
Washers on hooks

FIGURE 4.4

the bus, or other activities, the teacher has an opportunity to develop the vocabulary associated with ordering—first, last, and next. "Rita, you can go first," "Ken, you can be next." Once a child has mastered skills associated with one-to-one correspondence, then sets can be ordered differing by only one number. Children can identify the set with the fewest members and the set with the most members. Figure 4.6 illustrates a hanger type of activity where a child orders a set of beads from smallest to largest by using the matching lines as a guide.

Teaching Rote Counting

Rote counting is simply saying the number words in order (one, two, three, etc.) without associating those words with objects. While rote counting is not "counting" in the sense of determining the number of objects in a set, it is an important prerequisite to rational counting (counting objects). Without the rote counting skill, children inevitably "miscount" a set of objects because one word of the number sequence is missing. If a child says, "One, two, three, five, six, seven," when counting a set of objects, the set will be misnamed.

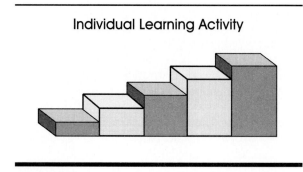

Individual Learning Activity

FIGURE 4.5

While many children enter school with skill in rote counting, the teacher must continue to build this skill. Number songs and rhymes generally are used to build skill in rote counting. Many of the rhymes can be used in conjunction with physical movements (see Figure 4.7).

Songs such as "One little, two little, three little Indians" also are helpful in developing the child's rote counting skills. In choosing rhymes and songs, the teacher should select those which contain fewer and fewer noncounting words as the child progresses in rote counting skills. For example, "One, two, three, four, five, I opened up the hive. Six, seven, eight, nine, ten, I closed it up again" uses sequences of five counting words, before including noncounting words. The repeating lyrics, "One, two, three, four, five, six, seven, eight, nine, ten, I'll start it all again," puts the first ten counting numbers in order before adding noncounting words.

Some kindergarten programs teach a child to rote count to twenty. Typically, this counting is performed after the child has participated in many rational counting activities with sets of ten or less. When kindergarten children are taught to count to 20 it usually is done in stages, counting to 13 and then to 16 and finally to 20.

Early Explorations with Number

While children can be taught number concepts in the absence of the prenumber concepts developed in the previous section, these prenumber concepts

Individual Learning Activity

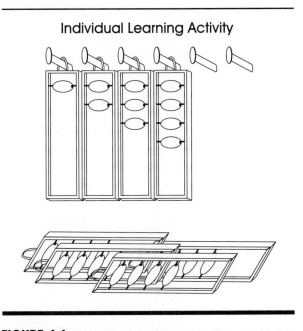

FIGURE 4.6

Group Learning Activity

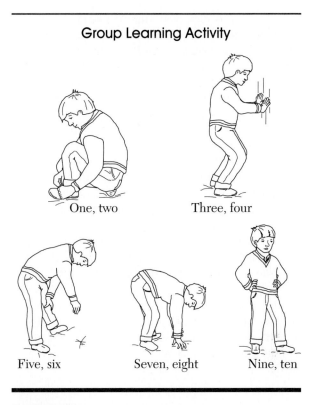

One, two   Three, four

Five, six   Seven, eight   Nine, ten

FIGURE 4.7

greatly facilitate the learning of number. With prenumber concepts established, a teacher has a choice of strategies for developing children's conceptual understanding of number. The teacher may start with some common sets of two, three, four, and five and have children find other sets which match using one-to-one correspondence. The teacher may proceed directly to a rational counting approach and begin developing the number of sets through counting. In actual practice many teachers intermingle these two strategies, because both strategies are needed to give a child a full understanding of number concepts.

This text will begin with a counting approach and then develop sets from a model-set approach. This is not to imply that starting with a counting approach is necessarily any better than starting with a models approach. In some cases a situation may arise during school activities that will dictate which strategies is used first.

Developing Rational-Counting Skills

To understand rational counting, a child must be able to:

1. Match each counting word to one and only one object. (Adults often take this skill for granted, but if a child who has not yet learned this skill is observed, one will hear the counting words pouring from the child in an uncoordinated rush as each object is touched.)

2. Recognize that the last counting word said tells the total objects counted. (For example, after counting out five objects a child may pick up the last object and incorrectly call it "five.")

3. Manage the set for counting. This may involve arranging the set in a line before counting it, and removing or marking off items in the set as they are counted. Children who do not have this skill may count objects more than once, because a systematic way of counting has not been developed.

4. Construct a set by counting out a set from a larger set. (This is a **more difficult skill for the teacher to facilitate** than simply counting the number of objects in a set. In this activity, the child must consciously remember the stopping number during the counting process, rather than just counting until every member of the set has been named.)

Initial Activities in Rational Counting: Touch Counting

Instruction in rational counting begins by teaching a coordination skill. Pupils must learn to speak and touch simultaneously. Initial activities require the child to pause after each counting word before moving on to the next object. At first these pauses are exaggerated. As the child develops the coordination skill, the pauses become shorter and shorter. When first developing this skill, the teacher will stop the child after each object is counted and wait for a short pause. This activity might be called "stop counting." The children might be told to count orally as the teacher touches the desk of each child in the row. They are directed to "Say the number word only when my hand touches the desk." Figure 4.8 illustrates an activity where "stop counting" is being employed.

Another form of "stop counting" occurs when a child is asked to count a set of objects by sliding the object as the number word is said. This process of sliding the object prevents the child from starting the next number word until the object has been moved and the next object is touched.

Teaching a child to count a set of objects is taught mainly by example. The teacher could illustrate how to line up a set before counting, saying, "You start counting at this end and continue until you get to the other end." Likewise, when teaching a child to count a pile of objects, it is sufficient to show the child how to move an object from the pile

as it is counted so it won't be counted twice. In showing a child how to mark off a set of objects pictured on a piece of paper, the teacher may wish to give the child some guidance about starting at the top and working his/her way to the bottom of the paper. The teacher should also remind pupils to look when they are finished to see that they have marked all objects to be counted.

Teachers can help children to recognize that the last number name used in counting is the number of the set. Placing a number of crayons on the desk, the teacher may have a child count the set and then pick up the entire set of objects. The child then holds the set of objects and says, "I have six crayons in my hand." If a child continues to have difficulty recognizing that the last-used counting word names the number of the whole set, an error correction method may be used. For example, if the child only picks up the last item when told to pick up the six items he/she has just counted the teacher might say, "No, put all six into your hand. Six is the number of the whole set."

Teaching a child to count out a fixed number of objects from a larger set is complicated because it requires two mental skills—memory and task perseveration. A child may forget the target number once the counting process is undertaken. Each individual (even adults) probably has some limit beyond which he or she would forget the target number. A second limitation is that some children tend

---

Teacher-Guided Interactive Learning Activity

Teacher and class choral count: One, two, three

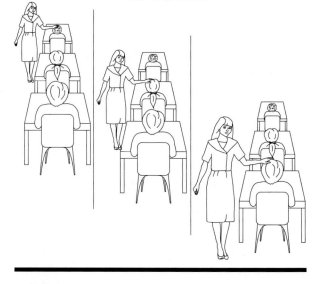

FIGURE 4.8

to perseverate a task to such an extent that it becomes an automatic unthinking act. This is much the same as some individuals who have difficulty carrying on a conversation while they are driving without forgetting where they are going and missing some street where they planned to turn. In other words they perseverate the task of driving the car to the extent that they fail to remember to turn at a certain street which they had been consciously remembering until someone engaged them in conversation.

Within the limits previously described, children are taught to count objects from a set by example and practice. Early experiences should be restricted to counting just a few objects. As children gain experience with this task the number of objects is increased. Memory-deficit problems (when recognized by the teacher) can be accommodated by engaging the child in counting a fixed number from a set that is within the memory capabilities of the child. Perseveration problems require a task environment that provides for the fewest distractions and also provides for varied practice activities that minimize perseveration.

Extending the Child's Rational Counting Skills: Visual Counting

While initial rational counting activities require touching the object, the child will eventually count by just looking at the objects without touching them. When visually counting, the child looks at the object and mentally says the number name. In early activities, many children softly verbalize the words as they look at the objects. Later they nod their heads as they look at the objects and mentally count them.

When the number of objects to be counted visually exceeds four or five, children sometimes find it difficult to keep track of the objects already counted. The task becomes even more taxing when the objects are arranged in a random order. When preparing materials to be counted visually, objects should be arranged so there are defined places where the eye can "pause." In Figure 4.9 objects are illustrated in two ways—a random arrangement and a patterned arrangement. Children can visually miscount either arrangement, but the patterned illustration is counted correctly far more often than the random arrangement.

In addition to visually counting a set of objects, children also may learn to count sounds. If a teacher claps his/her hands five times, the child can listen to each sound and mentally count the claps. A teacher may vary this activity by playing "Secret Number." The teacher will announce that

Curriculum should actively involve children in doing mathematics.

the "secret number" for today is "six," and then start clapping her hands. The pupils silently count along, but at some point (say after four claps), the teacher will stop and point to a child. That child must continue the clapping to reach six claps (including the teacher's four).

Children often use rational counting when involved in a play activity—keeping track of the number of times a pupil "runs around the ring" or "pops" a balloon. One activity enjoyed by youngsters is the "Bouncing Ball" game. Pupils take turns bouncing a ball the number of times directed by the teacher. The teacher may say, "Tommy, bounce the ball <u>four</u> times." When Tommy is finished, and the ball is passed on to the next pupil, the teacher will say, "Mary, bounce the ball <u>seven</u> times!" (Each pupil in the game mentally counts as the ball hits the ground—combining both the counting of "sound" and the watching of an event.)

Children need many rational counting activities to firmly establish this skill. Counting the number of children present each day by touching each desk is one activity that is often used to provide daily practice in counting through 25 or 35 (depending upon the number of children enrolled). Counting days on the room calendar is another activity which gives children an opportunity to rationally count

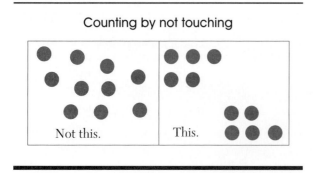

Counting by not touching

Not this.   This.

FIGURE 4.9

through 30. Many kindergarten programs expect entering first-grade pupils to be able to rationally count through 30. When the number required by the school system is larger (50 to 100), teachers must be creative in finding meaningful activities that allow pupils to count such large amounts daily!

In those kindergarten programs that teach a child to rote and rational count to 30, the rational counting skills just described have been well developed by extensive counting experiences before the child begins to learn to rational count from ten to 20. Once the child learns to rote count to 20 it is a simple matter to transfer his/her rational counting skills relating to counting sets of ten or less to sets of 20 or less. Frequently, rational counting parallels the manner in which the rote counting is being developed. For example, if the child is taught to rote count to 13 and then to rote count to 16, then he/she is taught to rational count to 13 and then rational count to 16, etc.

Developing Number Recognition from Common Patterns and Model Sets

Children frequently enter kindergarten knowing the number of common sets. They know that they have two eyes, two ears, two hands, etc. Even when they are not aware of a particular number (for example, they might not know that a dog has "four" legs, or that a tricycle has "three" wheels), when shown a dog with a leg missing or a tricycle with a wheel missing, they sense the need for fourness or threeness with these common things and recognize that a leg or a wheel is missing. The teacher can capitalize on the children's conceptual understandings of number associated with common items by extending the twoness, threeness, or fourness of these common sets to other sets. For example, children can be given two cards—each of which contains a picture of an eye—and be told to find other

sets of two by matching one-to-one the pictures of the eyes and members of another set.

If the children have rational counting skills, then counting can be used to verify the threeness of the set. The teacher might say, "Let's count our sets to check that we have three. One, two, three."

Using common patterns—stoplight for three, eyes for two, legs on a table for four—is one way of using a model set to establish number recognition. Use of a model set requires the child to be able to put sets in one-to-one correspondence. To determine the number of objects in a set, the child may match those objects with a set he/she already knows. If the child recognizes that a pattern card contains five dots, he/she can match a penny to each dot on the card and get a set of five pennies.

Some children find it difficult to match a model to other sets—especially the sets illustrated as pictures on a page. In such a situation, the child cannot move the pictured objects to match the set. Teachers may overcome this deficiency by using buttons, which the child places upon the model set. The child can then move the buttons to the pictured set and see if the two sets match (see Figure 4.10). At some point the teacher may wish to include common patterns associated with sets of a certain number (domino patterns or rectangular models) as part of the one-to-one matching activities.

Individual Learning Activity

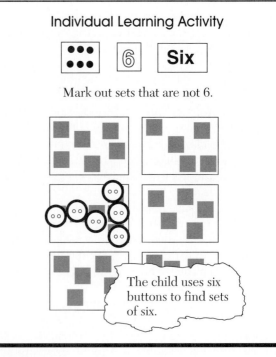

Mark out sets that are not 6.

The child uses six buttons to find sets of six.

FIGURE 4.10

To help children recognize numbers (and later to associate those sets with numerals), teachers generally display models of numbers already developed in the classroom. Children come to recognize the number associated with sets as they see the models displayed. When models for numbers greater than five are presented, the teacher should carefully examine the manner in which the objects are placed within the model set. Most children eventually recognize the number of a set as large as five without counting. However, when more than five objects are displayed in a random manner, the child will usually need to count the objects. When those model sets are placed on the wall, the child will not be able to touch and count each object. Teachers can overcome this problem by making sure that the objects in the model set are grouped into subsets with five or fewer members in the group. Allow the child to have a distinct stopping point when visually counting.

Using the One-More Approach to Teaching Number

When teaching children the numbers from one through ten, a readiness for other number skills can be established. The one-more approach for introducing new numbers provides a strong foundation for addition and helps many children master the basic addition combinations that include the number one as an addend. The one-more approach also strengthens previously developed numbers since it builds a new number by relating it to a previously learned number.

The lesson fragment below describes a lesson with a group of kindergarten children who are learning the number eight.

Teacher-Guided Interactive Learning Activity

LESSON FRAGMENT

M: Number eight

A: Group of kindergarten children

T: Modeling

H: One-to-one correspondence, model sets

Teacher: Today, boys and girls, I have placed some stars on the flannel-board. Who can tell me how many stars there are? Mike?

Mike: Seven!

Teacher: Very good, Mike. Now who can come up and make a set of apples that will match this set?

FIGURE 4.11

Beatrice, would you like to do that? (BEATRICE COMES TO THE FLANNEL-BOARD AND PLACES SEVEN APPLES BENEATH THE SET OF STARS. SHE MATCHES EACH STAR WITH AN APPLE. (SEE FIGURE 4.11.)

Teacher: Excellent, Beatrice. Now we have seven apples because they match with our set of stars and we already know that there are seven stars. (THE TEACHER PLACES ONE MORE APPLE AT THE END OF THE LINE. IT IS UNMATCHED AND "HANGS OVER" THE LINE OF STARS.) Now, boys and girls, I put one more apple with the other apples. Do we still have seven? Gertie?

Gertie: No, teacher. It doesn't match anymore so it can't be seven!

Teacher: That is a very good observation, Gertie. It doesn't match so it can't be seven. If it can't be seven it must be some other number. We are going to call this NEW number "eight." Eight is one more than seven. As I point to each apple, I want everyone to count with me. (THE TEACHER POINTS TO EACH APPLE AND LEADS THE GROUP TO RATIONALLY COUNT THE NEW SET.) One, two, three, four, five, six, seven, eight!

The concept of zero needs to be given special attention. Zero is generally not a part of the children's vocabulary, and will not have been encountered in counting situations. However, pupils will understand some aspect of the zero concept in their vocabulary. For example, before learning the number word zero, children recognize related concepts such as "empty," "none left," "they are all gone," etc. Teachers can relate these understandings to the concept of "zero" things. For example, when a child requests another cookie during mid-morning snack, the teacher might say, "They are all gone. We have zero cookies left." Teachers should take advantage of opportunities for using zero in the everyday course of kindergarten events. Simply calling the children's attention to the fact that there is a number name called zero is sufficient; it tells the children that they don't have any of a particular object. Occasionally the teacher may wish to ask the children, "What is the number name we use to tell us we don't have any?" Most kindergartens develop the concepts of zero through ten as part of their mathematics program.

Developing Numeral Recognition

After children understand the concept of oneness, twoness, etc., of various sets and can identify the number associated with a set, they are ready to learn numerals (names for numbers). Before children begin this skill, they recognize their printed names and other children's names. Children's names are often posted for chores, free-time activities, or special recognition. The teacher can capitalize on pupil knowledge of names by using this idea to develop the names for numbers. Figure 4.12 illustrates a kindergarten teacher using the idea of a child and a child's name to introduce the concept of a number and a number's name (numeral).

To read and write names for numbers there will be several skills that child must master. The pupil must be able to:

1. Orally state the name when presented with a numeral.
2. Associate the numeral with a set containing that many objects.
3. Read the word name for a number.
4. To associate the word name with a set containing that many objects.
5. Write a specified numeral.
6. Write a numeral naming a number when given a set containing a certain number of objects.
7. Construct a set containing a certain number of objects when given a numeral or word name for a number.

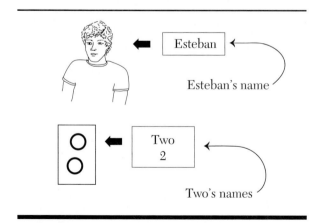

FIGURE 4.12

Children enter kindergarten with some knowledge of numerals. Many recognize the local television channel numerals. They know their favorite channel is "4," "10," "13," or even "31." If a numeral "10" is displayed, the child might readily announce that it is "ten" (or perhaps "channel ten"). However, if shown the numeral, that same child would not be able to assemble a set of ten objects. In this case, the child recognizes the numeral ten, but cannot <u>match (or associate) that numeral with a number</u>. Entering kindergarten children generally do not recognize all of the numerals from 0 through 10 and most cannot write the numerals.

When **evaluating** which numerals are recognized by the child, a teacher must be careful in drawing a conclusion based on a single question. If a teacher holds up a numeral 8 and asks a child for its name, a child may not be able to give an answer. However, if the teacher lays numeral cards on a table and asks the same child to pick up the "eight," the child might be able to perform that task. In this example, the child may recognize the numeral, but not have the oral word as a part of his/her vocabulary. Before deciding whether a child can recognize a given numeral, the teacher must check BOTH ways of asking the question. That is to say, if shown the symbol (numeral), the child should give its name, AND if given the name, the pupil should be able to identify (not write) the symbol.

When teaching recognition of the numerals, the symbol is usually presented in conjunction with a set model to associate the numeral with its corresponding number. Each time children identify the number of a set, the teacher interjects ". . . and this is its name," displaying the numeral. For example, suppose children have been working with three objects. The teacher shows them a numeral "3" and says that this tells them they are talking about three objects.

When teaching, numerals are usually taught in conjunction with number. However, for a pupil to match a numeral to a number (number/numeral matching) requires mastery of two different prerequisite skills—numeral recognition and number recognition. To match the numeral and number five, a pupil must first recognize that the set has five members and that the symbol (numeral) is read as 5. The child must then employ a new skill—that of associating the numeral with the amount. Teachers must be careful in assessing pupil mastery of a skill. A child who cannot match a "5" with a set containing five members may have one of the subskills but not the other. The student may have <u>both</u> skills, but not be able to associate the two.

Figure 4.13 illustrates a few of the many excellent commercial games and puzzles that are designed to help the child learn to recognize the numeral in association with the number concept. One of the more difficult aspects of teaching a child to <u>read</u> numerals is the wide variety and style of these numerals. One way to develop the ability to read different variations of the same numeral is to have the child sort numerals as illustrated in Figure 4.14.

Written word names for numbers are taught in a similar manner, with the teacher first identifying the word name for a particular number. The child learns to associate this name with the number of a set. The matching activities are the same as with numerals, with the child learning to match the written word to a set of that number and to construct sets of a specified number when given the written word.

Writing the Numerals

Since young children have limited control of the small muscles required to hold a pencil and direct its movement, the writing of numerals is often delayed until children enter first grade. However, some kindergarten programs introduce the formation of the numerals in kindergarten, especially to those children who demonstrate a readiness for this skill. Regardless of the grade level at which the writing of numerals is introduced, children will need many experiences in which they see numerals before they are required to write them.

Number/numeral matching activities allow the child to move the numeral to match the set, but do not require writing the digit. Through this and similar activities, the child becomes familiar with the general shape of the symbol. When the child begins writing the numeral, it is this awareness which helps the child recognize when the numeral is incorrectly formed. Young children, especially those who have limited experiences with numerals, tend to focus upon a single attribute of a numeral. For example, the child notices that the numeral 3 has two "humps." When writing the numeral 3, the child may draw the two curved sections of the numeral, but may have them facing the wrong direction. When children have had many experiences with numerals before writing them, they tend to recognize that "something is wrong" with their numeral (see Figure 4.15).

When helping a child learn to write numerals the teacher goes through various stages. In the first stage, the student is taught to trace numerals in the air and to walk through numerals pasted on the

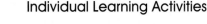

Individual Learning Activities

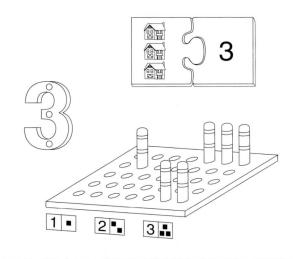

FIGURE 4.13

Individual Learning Activity

Numeral Sorting Task

FIGURE 4.14

A child may focus on a single attribute.

A three has two humps.

FIGURE 4.15

Teacher-Guided Interactive Learning Activity

FIGURE 4.16

floor to get a kinesthetic feel for how the numerals are formed. Figure 4.16 illustrates a teacher setting up an air-tracing activity for the numeral 5.

Another method of helping a child develop a kinesthetic feel for how numerals are formed is to tape 5- or 6-foot numerals on the floor and direct the child to "walk the numeral path." In constructing the material, the teacher should carefully identify the starting point for the numeral and the direction which the child should follow. Figure 4.17 shows a child walking through the numeral 8 to develop a kinesthetic feel for the numeral. Note that the starting point is identified with a star and that there are arrows on the path of the numeral to show the child the proper direction.

Having a child trace sandpaper numerals (or large paper numerals) with the index finger of his/her writing hand is another technique to develop the kinesthetic feel for how numerals are written. Commercial materials that have the child place his/her finger or pencil in a groove and follow the path are also available.

After kinesthetic-development activities, children practice making the numerals on a surface

(chalkboard, unlined paper, etc.), referring to an illustration that shows the proper starting point and direction. These activities may have the child use fingerpaint or tempera to draw the numerals. Teachers also have children use chalk to make LARGE numerals on the chalkboard. On a sunny day, a teacher may have children use paintbrushes and water to "paint" the numerals on the playground surface. Of course, children also are allowed to write the numerals with pencils or crayons onto sheets of unlined paper. The activity illustrated uses a tempera brush that makes use of the child's large muscles (which develop ahead of the child's small muscles); the numerals will be later written within lined paper. Figure 4.18 illustrates one form for making the numerals 0 through 9.

In most schools children learn to form the numerals in accordance with their adopted writing system, so there will be no conflict between the form of the numeral used when working mathematics and when working handwriting exercises. The way a writing system chooses to form the numeral (or letter) usually is based upon legibility studies which examine the effect on a numeral when an individual is hurried, careless, etc. For example, the numeral 8 is taught as a continuous path rather than two separate "circles" (snowman "8") as found in printed material. When children hurry, the numeral 78 can become 700 if using the separate circle eight (see Figure 4.19).

Before writing numerals on lined paper, the child will need many experiences with making the numerals on unlined paper, with tempera, fingerpaints, crayons, and kindergarten-type pencils. Fig-

Individual Learning Activity

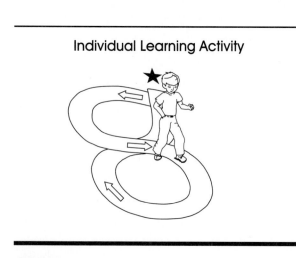

FIGURE 4.17

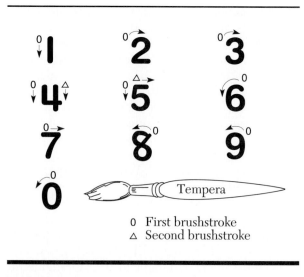

o First brushstroke
△ Second brushstroke

FIGURE 4.18

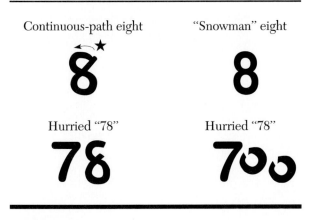

Continuous-path eight

"Snowman" eight

Hurried "78"

Hurried "78"

FIGURE 4.19

ure 4.20 illustrates some of the many commercial materials that prepare the child to work on lined paper.

4.2 EXTENDING THE CONCEPT OF CARDINAL NUMBER

A teacher should assess children's conceptual understanding of cardinal number when they enter first grade. Some children enter the first grade with a strong foundation in the skills identified in the scope and sequence chart as typical skills developed in a kindergarten program. For a variety of reasons, not all children who enter the first grade will be well founded in these skills. For this reason one of the first tasks of a first-grade teacher is to assess each child's entering skill level with prenumber and number concepts. The curriculum guide will frequently give guidance on how each

skill can best be assessed. For example, if the curriculum objective for the kindergarten states that given a set of ten objects the child will be able to count a specified number from the set, then the teacher will have to make provisions for this type of assessment activity. When children are found deficient in the types of skills developed in section 4.1, then the teacher will have to make provisions for developing the skills of children found with these skill deficits.

When children demonstrate that these skills are present, then **maintenance activities** are desirable. While some maintenance can be accomplished at the primary level using paper-and-pencil activities, such as the one illustrated in Figure 4.21, manipulative activities are highly desirable at the primary level.

For example, maintenance activities might include having children pass out items to the class (juice at mid-morning snack time, paper, booklets, etc.) where the number furnished is equal to, greater than, or less than the number needed. Having the children discover that they <u>need more</u>, they have <u>too many</u>, or they <u>have just enough</u> will **apply their skills to real problem-solving situations.**

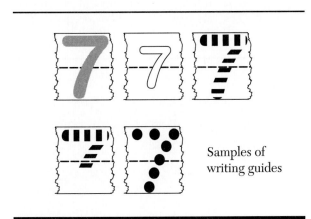

Samples of writing guides

FIGURE 4.20

Independent Learning Activities

Logical matching activities with paper and pencil

Symbolic matching activities are more difficult

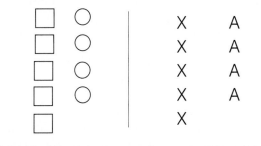

FIGURE 4.21

One concept maintained and extended in the first grade is that of being able to determine when one set has more, less (fewer), or the same number of objects as another set. Shortly after the concepts of equal and not equal are reviewed (or retaught) the **symbols** are introduced. Concepts and symbols associated with inequalities generally are taught at the same times as equality. While the development of most concepts at the primary grades will begin using the language of children, the symbols for equal and not equal are so fundamental to the development of many mathematical concepts as to warrant a more formal approach in their development.

Let's examine a fragment of a lesson that introduces the symbol for **greater than** in an analogy.

Teacher-Guided Interactive Learning Activity

**LESSON
FRAGMENT**

M: Symbol for greater than

A: Group of first-graders

T: Analogy, models, involvement

H: Concepts of sets equal in number, not equal in number, fewer members, and more members

Teacher: Today I'm going to tell you a story which will help us when we work with numbers. We all know that birds like to eat worms. Once there was a bird that saw a lot of worms crawling around. The bird flew down and by chance landed **between** two sets of worms. Let's put our bird on the flannel-board. He looked to his left and there were five worms—see them on the flannel-board? He looked to his right and there were two worms. He did not know where to start; this would be a feast! Well, this was a greedy bird and he **always** wanted to start with the most worms. Which set of worms should we have our greedy bird facing? (**NOTICE THE TEACHER HAS USED AN ANALOGY TO REDUCE THE LEVEL OF ABSTRACTION FOR THE CHILDREN.**)

Instructional Group: Toward the five worms! (SEE FIGURE 4.22)

Teacher: Yes, he's going to open his big mouth and face the group with the greatest number of worms. (SEE FIGURE 4.23)

Teacher: Now we can use numerals to show this. We have a 5 and a 2. (THE TEACHER PLACES THE NUMERALS "5" AND "2" ON THE CHALK-BOARD.) To show the greedy bird, we will use just the outline of his mouth—see how it opens wide?

Using an Analogy to Reduce Level of Abstractness

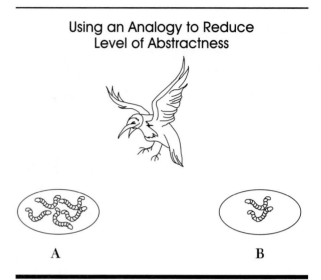

A   B

FIGURE 4.22

(THE TEACHER SHOWS THE SYMBOL FOR GREATER THAN.) Now, which direction do you suppose we should have the mouth facing?

Group: Put the big part facing the 5.

Teacher: Good! I'll place the **greater than** symbol between the 5 and 2. Now let us read the sentence: "5 is greater than 2." Read this with me.

Group: 5 is greater than 2. (SEE FIGURE 4.24)

While children can readily remember the direction the greater-than/less-than symbol faces when they associate it with an open mouth (of an alligator, Pacman™, duck, etc.). Many children experience great difficulty **reading** the symbols. Rather than always reading left-to-right, many children read both symbols, ">" and "<", as "greater than," and read the sentence right-to-left. For instance, they read "2 < 5" as: "Five is greater than two," rather than "Two is less than five." In this case, the child understands the concept of comparison, but does not read the symbol properly. The

A   B

FIGURE 4.23

$$5 > 2$$

FIGURE 4.24

teacher will need to provide children with many opportunities to <u>hear</u> the symbol read correctly. The "does not equal," "is not less than," and "is not greater than" symbols should be introduced only after equality and inequality symbols are mastered.

Common dot-number patterns that a child brings to first grade are extended in the primary grades. When the child can recognize the number of objects present by its pattern, the teacher can eliminate the time-consuming process of having sets of objects counted, before developing other concepts with number such as place value and operations. Figure 4.25 illustrates some of the more common patterns taught. What would you expect would be another benefit of having a child be able to recognize a pattern of three and five as a pattern

Patterns for six through ten are made by combining patterns of one through five.

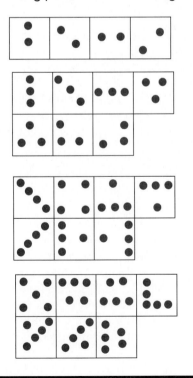

FIGURE 4.25

for eight? When teachers review patterns, they should emphasize the identification of the number without counting.

Maintenance and Extension of Counting Skills

While children may come to the first grade having mastered the counting skills identified in the scope and sequence for kindergarten, there are still many counting skills and concepts to be mastered. The following material discusses some of the methods for teaching these skills:

- Counting by ones beyond ten (to 20 if not taught or learned in kindergarten, and to 100)
- Counting by tens (and hundreds)
- Counting by multiples and ones (tens and ones; hundreds, tens and ones)
- Counting backward
- Counting by multiples (fives and twos)

Figure 4.26 shows one sequence for teaching the counting skills. Other sequences are also used frequently. For example, counting by twos, fives, and other single-digit numbers is often deferred and used concurrently with the development of multiplication as a readiness activity for introducing multiplication facts. Some teachers prefer to go directly from counting by ones to 20 to teaching a child to count by ones to 100. While most kindergarten programs will teach a child to count to 20, other programs defer counting beyond ten until place value is to be developed. This delay allows the teens with their corresponding numerals to be

1 Rote counting to ten prerequisite to . . .
  Rational counting to ten.

2 Rote counting to 20 prerequisite to . . .
  Rational counting to 20.

3 Counting by tens to 100 prerequisite to
  Counting by tens and ones to 100 prerequisite to
  Counting by ones to 100.

4 Counting by twos, fives, etc., to 100.

5 Counting by hundreds.
  Counting by hundreds, tens, and ones.

■ Anytime after Step 1—Counting backwards.

FIGURE 4.26

developed concurrently with the development of the positional value of each digit.

Many teachers prefer to teach children to count by tens to 100 soon after the child has mastered counting by ones to ten. There are several distinct advantages in using this particular sequence. One obvious advantage is that it reinforces the child's understanding of the digits 1 through 9. In working with the tens the children first learn to count the number of objects in the group, finding that there are TEN in each group. Once pupils recognize that there are ten in **each** set, the teacher will have them count the number of sets, emphasizing that there are ten objects in each set by saying "one *ten*, two *tens*, three *tens*, four *tens*," etc. When children can recognize sets of ten and count sets of tens, the teacher can introduce the **words** that go with multiples of tens, counting "ten, twenty, thirty, forty," etc.

Besides emphasizing the importance of ten, teaching counting by tens to 100 before counting by ones to 100 provides a useful reference when children must bridge from one decade to the next decade. Generally children have little difficulty counting **within** a decade. In counting the twenties, the child readily calls out 21, 22, and so on until 29 is reached. Then the child must recall what multiple of ten comes after 20. When a child has learned to count by tens, he/she can readily recall that 30 follows 20. Once "thirty" is announced, the pattern of adding the numbers words—thirty-one, thirty-two, thirty-three, thirty-four, thirty-five, thirty-six, thirty-seven, thirty-eight, and thirty-nine—is a simple task.

Let us examine a fragment of a lesson that tackles a rational counting approach to counting by tens.

Teacher-Guided Interactive Learning Activity

LESSON FRAGMENT

M: Rational counting by tens to 30

A: A group of children who have average auditory memory and recall abilities

T: Modeling and involvement— (choral counting)

H: Children can count, read, and write numerals to 20

Teacher: You have three bundles of ten on your desk. I have placed three bundles of ten just like yours

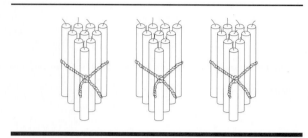

FIGURE 4.27

on the board. Listen to me count these bundles by ten. Then we will all orally count our bundles of ten together. Ten, twenty, thirty. Now let's count our bundles together. (See Figure 4.27)

Instructional Group: Ten, twenty, thirty.

By adding three and four more tens to each counting lesson, the children can be taught to count to 100 by tens.

After children learn to count by tens, they are ready to count by tens **and** ones. Learning to count by ones to 100 serves a dual purpose: it reinforces the place-value concept used when developing 2-digit numerals, and requires a shorter time for counting sets of 99 or less.

Let us examine a fragment of a lesson that incorporates the skill of counting by tens when teaching a child to count by tens and ones.

Teacher-Guided Interactive Learning Activity

LESSON FRAGMENT

M: Counting by tens and ones

A: A group of first-graders who have average auditory memory and recall abilities

T: Modeling and involvement (choral counting)

H: Children can count by tens to 100

Teacher: Today we are going to learn to count by tens and ones. Listen to me count these sets on my flannel-board. Then we will count them together. (POINTING TO EACH SET AS IT IS COUNTED.) Ten, twenty, thirty, thirty-one, thirty-two. Now count them with me. (SEE FIGURE 4.28)

Group: Ten, twenty, thirty, thirty-one, thirty-two.

In a similar manner, counting by tens and ones could be developed for numbers between 20 and 100.

Ten, twenty, thirty,
thirty-one, thirty-two!

FIGURE 4.28

The skill of being able to count by tens and ones greatly facilitates the rapid development of teaching numeral concepts for numbers between 20 and 100. It also is useful when helping children with auditory memory deficits count large sets. (Rather than attempt to count large sets by ones, these children should first group the set into as many tens as they can, and then count the sets by tens and ones.)

Teaching a child to count by ones to 100 could be taught after teaching a child to count by tens, concurrently with counting by tens and ones, or after teaching a child to count by tens and ones. No matter which sequence the teacher chooses, utilizing the previously learned skill of counting by tens will facilitate this process.

Let us examine a fragment of a lesson which utilizes the skill of counting by tens to develop the skill of counting by ones to 100.

Teacher-Guided Interactive Learning Activity

LESSON
FRAGMENT

M: Counting by ones to 100

A: A group of first-grade children who do not have auditory memory deficits

T: Involvement, using a pattern

H: Prerequisite skills: counting by ones to 20, counting by tens to 100

Teacher: Listen to me count. As soon as you pick up the pattern I am using, then count aloud **with** me. When I say *stop,* stop counting. Then I'll start an-

other pattern. When you pick up the pattern, start counting with me until again I say stop. All right. Listen as I start counting. Twenty-one, twenty-two, twenty-three, . . . (AT THIS POINT SOME OF THE CHILDREN PICK UP THE PATTERN AND JOIN IN.)

Group: . . . twenty-four, twenty-five, twenty-six, . . . (WHEN THE GROUP GETS TO TWENTY-NINE THE TEACHER SAYS **STOP!**)

Teacher: Ten, twenty, what comes next?

Group: Thirty. (THE TEACHER PICKS UP THE COUNTING AT THIRTY-ONE JUST AFTER THE CHILDREN SAY THIRTY.)

Teacher: Thirty-one, thirty-two, thirty-three. (AT THIS POINT SOME OF THE CHILDREN PICK UP THE PATTERN AND JOIN IN.)

Group: Thirty-four, thirty-five, . . . thirty-nine.

Teacher: **Stop!** Ten, twenty, thirty, what comes next?

Group: Forty.

Teacher: Forty-one, forty-two, etc.

Once children have learned to read and write numerals associated with the numbers from one through 99, numeral patterns can be used to teach counting by multiples of twos, fives, etc.

Let us examine a fragment of a lesson that uses numeral patterns to count by fives. Children are given a sheet of paper with a **hundred board** on it similar to the one in Figure 4.29.

Teacher-Guided Interactive Learning Activity

LESSON
FRAGMENT

M: Counting by fives

A: Group of children

T: Using patterns, a model, and involvement (choral counting)

H: Children can count by ones to 100 and can read and write numerals to 100

Teacher: Start at one and mark every fifth numeral. (FIGURE 4.30 SHOWS THE RESULTS OF ONE CHILD'S EFFORT.)

Teacher: You have marked out the multiples of five just like counting by fives. Does anyone notice a pattern in the ones place for the numerals you marked out?

Child: It looks like striped wallpaper!

Teacher: Good. Do you see anything else?

Child: There is a five in the ones place.

Teacher: Is that all?

Child: There is also a zero.

1	2	3	4	5	6	7	8	9	10
11	12	13	14	15	16	17	18	19	20
21	22	23	24	25	26	27	28	29	30
31	32	33	34	35	36	37	38	39	40
41	42	43	44	45	46	47	48	49	50
51	52	53	54	55	56	57	58	59	60
61	62	63	64	65	66	67	68	69	70
71	72	73	74	75	76	77	78	79	80
81	82	83	84	85	86	87	88	89	90
91	92	93	94	95	96	97	98	99	100

FIGURE 4.29

Teacher: We find either a five or a zero in the ones place when the number is a multiple of five. Let's count by fives by reading in order the numerals you crossed out. I'll point to the numerals on my large chart on the front board as we count.

Group: Five, ten, fifteen, twenty, twenty-five, etc.

Counting by fives, twos, etc., also can be taught by just using the auditory pattern that develops as the counting words are said. However, the use of both visual and auditory patterns helps when memorizing these patterns, especially if a child has either a visual or auditory memory deficit.

The skill of counting backward can be taught at any time after a child can count forward. Let us examine a fragment of a lesson in counting backward that uses an analogy:

Teacher-Guided Interactive Learning Activity

LESSON FRAGMENT

M: Counting backward from ten to one

A: Children with good auditory memory and recall

T: Analogy, a model, and choral counting

H: Children can count from one to ten

Teacher: Here we have a model of a rocket ship. When a rocket ship is launched there is a count-down to tell the ship when to take off. They say, "Ten, nine, eight, seven, six, five, four, three, two, one, ignition, blast-off." I've placed a picture of a

Teacher-Guided Interactive Learning Activity

1	2	3	4	5	6	7	8	9	10
11	12	13	14	15	16	17	18	19	20
21	22	23	24	25	26	27	28	29	30
31	32	33	34	35	36	37	38	39	40
41	42	43	44	45	46	47	48	49	50
51	52	53	54	55	56	57	58	59	60
61	62	63	64	65	66	67	68	69	70
71	72	73	74	75	76	77	78	79	80
81	82	83	84	85	86	87	88	89	90
91	92	93	94	95	96	97	98	99	100

FIGURE 4.30

rocket on the flannel-board. We can pretend we are "launching" our rocket. Let us practice saying the countdown so the rocket can take off. (SEE FIGURE 4.31)

Group and teacher: Ten, nine, eight, seven, six, . . .

Counting backward is an important skill that should be developed as the child learns to count to larger numbers. It is useful when developing subtraction skills and it provides a useful bridge when developing place value involving tens, hundreds, thousands, etc.

Teaching children to count **beyond** 100 almost always is taught with the objects grouped into

Relating Skill to Application

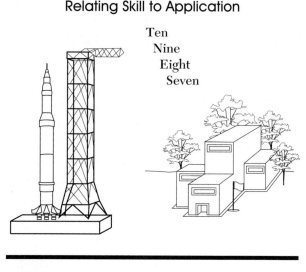

Ten
Nine
Eight
Seven

FIGURE 4.31

hundreds, tens, and ones, or thousands, hundreds, tens, and ones.

For example, in counting two hundreds, three tens, and four ones, a child would first count the hundreds (one hundred, two hundred) and finally pick up the counting on the tens (two hundred ten, two hundred twenty, two hundred thirty) and then pick up the counting on the ones (two hundred thirty-one, two hundred thirty-two, two hundred thirty-three, two hundred thirty-four).

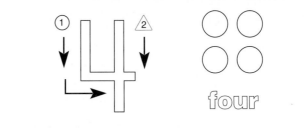

FIGURE 4.32

4.3 MAINTENANCE AND EXTENSION OF NUMERATION CONCEPTS

A teacher will want to assess the numeration skills a child brings to the primary program. The teacher can expect the average child who has completed a kindergarten program to read and write numerals 1 through 10, and recognize the written word names for one through ten. Also, given a set of objects with ten members or less, a child should also be able to associate the proper numeral and also be able to construct a set of objects if given a numeral 1 through 10. When the teacher identifies children who are lacking any of these skills, individual programs must be planned to overcome these deficiencies. (See **Section 4.1** for activities to promote the development of numeration skills involving numerals 1 through 10 and sight association of word names for one through ten.)

Some kindergarten programs do not teach children to write numerals. Children from such programs will be able to identify the numerals and sometimes will have learned to copy the digits, but the child will have had no formal instruction in the proper formation of the numeral. Therefore, first-grade teachers must spend some time developing skill in the writing of each numeral from 0 through 10. Since the teacher will review each number to ensure pupils' familiarity with those digits, the writing of the numerals is also taught at that time.

Teaching how to write each numeral usually begins by showing the proper formation, using large arm movements (see **Section 4.1**). The child will start writing numerals by tracing large examples that have the starting point and direction clearly identified. Later the child will use lined paper with a midlined dash mark to proportion the numerals. Finally the child will be able to write smaller, carefully- and quickly-formed numerals without this midline guide.

Throughout the period when children are learn-

ing the proper formation of the numerals, charts (that show the beginning point and direction of the path) should be prominently displayed. Children who forget how a numeral is formed can refer to the display and recall its formation (see Figure 4.32). The teacher should always make sure that the children are forming the numerals with the proper movements, and correct any children who are forming their digits incorrectly.

After a brief maintenance review of the digits one through ten, the teacher introduces place value and 2-digit numerals. By the time a child finishes the second grade, he/she should meet the following objectives:

- When given a 2- or 3-digit numeral, the child is able to identify the place value associated with each digit in the numeral.
- When given objects grouped by tens and ones, or hundreds, tens, and ones, the child is able to write a numeral (or number word name) reflecting the grouping.
- When given a 2- or 3-digit numeral (or word naming a number less than 1,000), the child is able to construct models that reflect the number named.

By the time the child finishes the third grade he/she should be proficient with the same skills through the thousands.

Teaching Place Value and 2-Digit Numerals

The introduction of 2-digit numerals requires the integration of the children's previously learned skills of reading and writing 1-digit numerals together with advanced counting skills.

Let us examine a fragment of a lesson that introduces place value and the naming of sets that have been grouped into tens and ones.

Teacher-Guided Interactive Learning Activity

LESSON FRAGMENT

M: Tens and ones place value

A: A group of first-graders

T: Models, involvement

H: Children can count by tens and ones, and can identify common dot patterns of ones and tens

Teacher: When I say go, show me with your fingers how many tens I have. Go! (CHILDREN SHOW THREE FINGERS.) (SEE FIGURE 4.33)

Teacher: Good! Let us record the three under the tens name to show we have three tens. (SEE FIGURE 4.34)

Teacher: When I say go, show me with your fingers how many ones I have here. Go! (TEACHER POINTS TO THE TWO ONES. CHILDREN SHOW TWO FINGERS.)

Teacher: Good! Let us record the two under the ones name to show we have two ones. Now let us count the sets by tens and ones to see when we have three tens and two ones how many we have.

Group: Ten, twenty, thirty, thirty-one, thirty-two.

Teacher: The last thing we counted was thirty-two, so when we have three tens and two ones we have thirty-two.

Many similar types of activities are conducted. When the teacher feels that the children have practiced with the frame long enough to develop a kinesthetic feel that tens are on the left and ones are on the right in the numeral, he/she will encourage the children to write the numerals without a frame. Some children may need to use the frame longer than other children. If some children reverse the tens digit with the ones digit, the teacher may re-

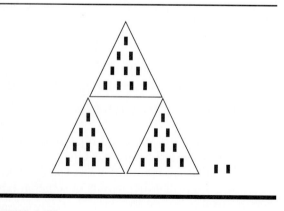

FIGURE 4.33

Developing Kinesthetic Feel for Location of Tens and Ones Digits

Tens	Ones
3	

Tens	Ones
3	**2**

FIGURE 4.34

quire them to return to the developmental form by using the frame.

When developing 2-digit numerals, particular attention must be given to those cases which have a zero in the ones place.

The following types of activities are needed to maintain 2-digit place-value skills:

Activities where the child

- Identifies the tens and ones digit.
- Writes a numeral associated with things grouped into tens and ones.
- Writes the 2-digit numeral that identifies the number of objects in a set.
- Constructs a set of a number named by a 2-digit numeral.

Teaching 3-Digit Numeration

The development of hundreds, tens, and ones proceeds in a manner similar to the development of tens and ones. Before learning to read and write 3-digit numerals the child is taught to count by hundreds to 1,000. This is a comparatively easy skill to teach since the child can transfer skill in counting 1 through 9 to counting sets of 100 through 900. In beginning activities the child may say ten hundreds (instead of one thousand since the word "thousand" has not been introduced). The teacher will present "one thousand" as another name for ten hundred. The child later will need to be aware that ten tens is another name for one hundred and ten hundreds is another name for one thousand.

Let us examine a fragment of a lesson used to introduce place value and the reading of 3-digit numerals:

Teacher-Guided Interactive Learning Activity

LESSON FRAGMENT

M: Counting hundreds and reading 3-digit numerals

A: Group of second-graders

T: Models, involvement

H: All 2-digit numeration skills, counting by hundreds to 1,000

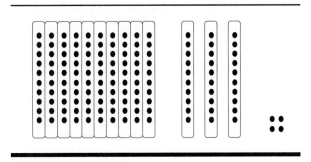

FIGURE 4.35

Teacher: Look at the beansticks I placed on the board. (SEE FIGURE 4.35) Write on your place-value frame the number of hundreds, tens, and ones that you see displayed. Hold up your frame to show me your answers. (THE CHILDREN DISPLAY THEIR ANSWERS.)

Teacher: Listen to me count the beans as I touch them. (POINTING AT EACH GROUP AS IT IS COUNTED.) One hundred, one hundred ten, one hundred twenty, one hundred thirty, one hundred thirty-one, one hundred thirty-two, one hundred thirty-three, one hundred thirty-four. Now let's count the beans in unison as I touch the beans.

Group: One hundred . . . one hundred thirty-four.

Teacher: What was the last thing we said when we were counting?

Child: One hundred thirty-four.

Teacher: So we have counted one hundred thirty-four things. When we have one hundred, three tens, and four ones, we have how many beans?

Child: One hundred thirty-four.

In developing hundreds the teacher also will need to develop cases in which there are zero ones (for example, 230), and zero tens (for example, 609), and cases where there are zeros in both the tens and ones place (for example, 700).

Teaching Numeration Involving Thousands

Thousands are frequently developed in the third grade. While thousands are introduced in the primary grades, a complete development of the concept of period names is deferred to the intermediate grades. Once the child becomes proficient with reading and writing 3-digit numerals, teaching a child to read thousands involves helping the child transfer previously learned skills to thousands. Figure 4.36 illustrates a coverup activity that promotes this type of transfer.

Teaching the Written Words for 2- and 3-Digit Numerals

Teaching words for 2- and 3-digit numbers usually takes place in a multidisciplinary context. Their development can be found in reading, spelling, writing, and mathematics lessons. However, their initial introduction is found in the context of learning other number names for numbers and their development follows the same sequence as that of numerals; that is, the child is first taught to read the number names and then to write them.

Some of the basic rules for teaching the number words are:

1. From 20 to 100 the number words formed by a tens name and a ones name are hyphenated (for example, seventy-five).

2. The word "and" is reserved for use in identifying a decimal when saying a number name.

Teacher-Guided Interactive Learning Activity

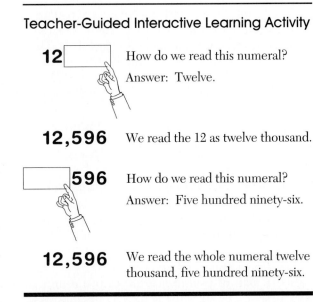

12 How do we read this numeral?
Answer: Twelve.

12,596 We read the 12 as twelve thousand.

596 How do we read this numeral?
Answer: Five hundred ninety-six.

12,596 We read the whole numeral twelve thousand, five hundred ninety-six.

FIGURE 4.36

For example, 5.7 is read five and seven-tenths. The numeral 247 is read as "two hundred forty-seven," not "two hundred and forty-seven."

4.4 TEACHING ORDINAL NUMBERS

Ordinal number names are frequently used in everyday activities, even in kindergarten. Children talk about their fifth birthday, visiting the first grade, playing with the third-graders, etc. Teachers build ordinal number concepts when they have children line up and call for one child to be first, another to be second, etc.

Ordinals are used to designate position in a designated order, while cardinal numbers identify how many are in a set. Ordinals come with a vocabulary distinctively different than the number words for cardinal numbers. The ordinals of first, second, third, and fifth are quite distinctive and seem to have little in common with the number names for cardinal numbers (one, two, three, and five). The ordinals of fourth, sixth, seventh, and so on are easily developed, using their cardinal counterparts as a basis for instruction.

Some of the concepts which must be developed when teaching ordinal numbers are:

1. Ordinal numbers tell us which one in a line or sequence of events we are talking about.
2. Ordinal numbers help us find locations when the locations have been given ordinal designations. For example, if we are looking for 17 Home Street, and we have passed houses 1, 2, 3, then we know if we continue down the street, we will come to 17 Home Street. Or if we are looking for 6th Street and we have passed 2nd and 3rd Streets, we know if we continue in the same direction, we will come to 6th Street.
3. Except for first, second, and third, we can establish that someone is talking about an ordinal number by the *th* at the end of the number word they use.
4. Sometimes a cardinal number word is used in an ordinal sense. For example, some sports fans may say, "My team is number one," when they mean that their team is in first place.

Let us examine a fragment of a lesson that uses the skill of counting to develop the ordinal numbers.

Teacher-Guided Interactive Learning Activity

LESSON FRAGMENT

M: Ordinals fourth, fifth, and sixth
A: Group of first-graders
T: Models, involvement
H: Rational counting to ten

Teacher: Let's have all of the pupils from the back table come to the front of the room and line up facing me. (SIX CHILDREN COME TO THE FRONT.) Now I'm going to give you each a number card and I want you to line up according to your number. (CHILDREN ARRANGE THEMSELVES IN A LINE WITH THE FIRST CHILD HOLDING THE "1" CARD. THE CHILDREN WITH 2, 3, 4, 5, AND 6 LINE UP IN ORDER BEHIND "1.")

Teacher: Hold your cards so everyone in the room can see that you are in order. Now let's turn our cards over. We see that there are words written on the back of the cards. Number one, your name is "first." The one who begins the line is called the first person. What do you think we call the person who is next in line? Tommy?

Tommy: Second!

Teacher: Billy, will you turn over your card so we can see that your name is "second"? What name should we give to the person who comes next? Mary?

Mary: Third—because that person is the third person in line.

Teacher: Very good, Mary. Will the "third person" turn over the card? This is the word we use for third. Now, all of the other people in the line turn over their cards. Let's see if we can identify their positions. Let's start at the first person and read the cards together. "First, second, third, fourth, fifth, sixth."

The teacher continues the lesson by having the second person trade places with the fifth person, making sure that the children trade ordinal cards. The teacher may alter the activity by calling upon various other pupils in the room to take the place of the sixth person, etc. Before the activity is completed, the teacher may have the entire line turn around and face the opposite direction. Children should then change their cards, since the last person has now become the first person—and the others in the line must check to ensure that their labels are proper for their positions.

Just as the word names for cardinal numbers are taught in many subject areas (reading, language arts, spelling, mathematics), so are the words for ordinal numbers. However, except for first, second, third, and fifth, teaching the word names for ordinal numbers is simply a matter of showing the child how to convert cardinal names to ordinal names by adding the *th*.

4.5 TEACHING NUMBER AND NUMERATION IN THE INTERMEDIATE GRADES

For the intermediate teacher to extend a student's conceptual development of numeration beyond 3-digit numerals, the pupil must have a sound foundation. Before working with large numbers the teacher should determine if the pupil can read and write 3-digit numerals and recognize the place value associated with position. If a pupil does not possess a strong understanding of 3-digit numerals, then work with thousands, millions, billions, and trillions should be delayed.

The following illustrates the whole number and numeration skills typically developed at the intermediate level.

Grade 4

Read and write amounts to millions

Read and write amounts in expanded notation

Round to the nearest thousand

Grade 5

Read and write amounts to billions

Write amounts in expanded form using powers of ten

Round to the nearest ten thousand

Grade 6

Read and write amounts to trillions

Read and write amounts in expanded form using powers of ten and exponents

Grades 7 and 8

Read and write amounts in expanded notation using positive and negative exponents

Read and write amounts using scientific notation

Recognize the significant digits in a numeral

4.6 MAINTENANCE AND EXTENSION OF NUMBER AND NUMERATION

The maintenance of skills taught in the primary grades is an integral part of almost every number and operation activity performed at the intermediate level. For example, addition, subtraction, multiplication, and division operations use place value, and "story" problems continually review the reading of numerals and word names for numbers. However, it is a good practice to review numeration concepts periodically at every grade level.

The foundation the pupil develops in the primary level makes the extension of number concepts a matter of expanding and extending previously acquired skills. The pupil recognizes new skills as being similar to the concepts already learned. For example, the rounding of numbers to thousands is very similar to rounding to the nearest ten or hundred; learning to read the period names (billions, millions, etc.) uses concepts developed to read 1-, 2- and 3-digit numerals.

Reading Large Numerals

Once pupils can read and write 3-digit numerals, the next step is to teach *period* names. At one point in American education students learned the period names for as many as twenty periods. While a teacher may wish to explore the names for numerals with as many as 63 digits, teaching the names through trillions will make the pupil functionally literate with most numerals encountered in everyday life. (Most numbers greater than trillions are expressed in scientific notation. Discussion of scientific notation is developed in Chapter 10—Decimals.)

While it is not difficult to illustrate ones, tens, hundreds, and even a thousand, finding examples to use as illustrations of ten thousand, hundred thousand, million, and billion is quite challenging. Teachers may point to the federal budget requiring millions, billions, and trillions of dollars, but students cannot actually visualize these amounts. Therefore the teacher must depend upon the pupils' ability to visualize hundreds and thousands to bring meaning to larger amounts. The lesson fragment below describes one teacher's development of a million using physical representations.

Teacher-Guided Interactive Learning Activity

LESSON FRAGMENT

M: Representing one million
A: Fourth-grade group
T: Physical modeling
H: Ability to read and write 3-digit numerals

Teacher: Yesterday Tommy said that he had about a "million" baseball cards. Now you didn't really count every one to arrive at that number, did you, Tommy?

Tommy: Well, I didn't exactly count them—but I have lots of stacks.

Teacher: And I imagine that it must *seem* like a million when you are putting them away. But let's spend some time today trying to determine how big a million really is. I brought in some paper from the office to use to **represent** Tommy's cards. Here is one sheet of paper. It is not very thick, is it! Here, Tommy, lift it up to see if it weighs about as much as one of your cards.

Tommy: It's lighter than one of my cards.

Teacher: Here we have a stack of ten sheets. Is it as thick as ten baseball cards, Tommy?

Tommy: No, the cards are thicker.

Teacher: Here are *ten* of those stacks of ten—or 100 sheets of paper. They are a little heavier than just one stack of ten—and the stack is thicker, too. Now if I wanted to show 1,000 sheets of paper, how many of the stacks of a hundred would I need?

Marianne: Ten, because it takes ten hundreds to make 1,000.

Teacher: Good, Marianne. And here is 1,000 sheets of paper. (TEACHER DISPLAYS TWO REAMS OF PAPER.) Here, Tommy, can you lift these?

Tommy: (LIFTING THE TWO REAMS OF PAPER WITH EFFORT.) I can lift them, but they sure are heavy!

Teacher: Since I couldn't get much paper from the office, we are going to use a strip of paper to show how thick the stack of ten thousand would be. Hold the thousand sheets while I measure them, Tommy. Here would be the mark for 1,000—here would be 2,000—here would be 3,000—(THE TEACHER MEASURES OUT TEN MARKS ON A STRIP OF

ADDING MACHINE PAPER. THE TOTAL LENGTH ENDS UP TO BE NEARLY A METER LONG.) So here we have a model of <u>ten thousand</u> sheets of paper. This is how thick the sheets would be. Tommy, pass the stack of 1,000 sheets around so the rest can see how much they weigh. Do you think you would be able to lift 10,000 sheets, Burt?

Burt: Hey, just 1,000 is heavy—I don't want to carry ten of them!

Teacher: Now let's see how much <u>one hundred thousand</u> would be. Since we don't have a ladder to measure the stack going up, let's imagine putting them on their sides and stretching them along the wall. How many of these strips representing 10,000 will we need in order to show 100,000? Jeanie?

Jeanie: We will need ten of the ten thousands. I bet it is going to take a lot of room!

Teacher: Let's see. (THE TEACHER—WITH THE HELP OF PUPILS—MEASURE OUT 10 OF THE STRIPS OF PAPER ALONG THE WALL. <u>IT REACHES THE ENTIRE LENGTH OF THE CLASSROOM.</u>) So the thickness of 100,000 sheets of paper would reach the length of the classroom!

Tommy: I don't think my baseball cards would reach that far—so I guess I don't have a million—or even a hundred thousand—but I still have a lot.

Teacher: I'm sure you do, Tommy. Does anyone have a guess about how far <u>one million</u> thicknesses of paper would reach?

Jeanie: Well, it would be ten classrooms—and the principal's office is only five classrooms away so it would be about the same as going five classrooms past the principal's office.

From the lesson fragment above, students begin to see that one million is a large amount. The teacher might follow up such a lesson by having Tommy bring in 100 cards and finding out how far one million cards would reach. The class may wish to make a model on the playground that would remind them of the lesson and help them see how much one million is. A teacher may use calculators to help students see how long it would take to draw one million dots, read one million words, or walk one million steps.

Students learn to read thousands in the primary grades. Numbers larger than 10,000 are best taught using period names. Many teachers introduce the names for billion, million, and thousand in the initial introduction of period names, even though they plan to concentrate only on reading amounts in the millions. Let us examine a fragment of a lesson that introduces the concept of periods and uses the students' ability to read 3-digit numerals.

Teacher-Guided Interactive Learning Activity

LESSON FRAGMENT

M: Period names and commas

A: Fourth-grade group

T: Analogy and involvement (choral response)

H: Ability to read 3-digit numerals

Teacher: Today we are going to learn to read a numeral with as many as 12 digits. I have written a 12-digit numeral on the chalkboard. Let us see if we can read PART of the numeral. I've placed the last three digits in a show-me holder. (THE TEACHER SHOWS 326 IN HOLDER.) Who can read this? Maria?

Maria: That's easy. It's three hundred twenty-six.

Teacher: Good. You see we already have one of the most important skills in reading large amounts. Now I am going to put all of these digits in the holders and we can see that they all are the same "three hundred twenty-six." The only difference is where the digits appear in a large numeral. Maria has more than her first name—she has a family name. She is Maria Santos. We can think of numbers also having "family" names. Of course, we don't call them family names—we call them "*periods*." On the chalk tray I am going to place four houses. You can see that they are named billion, million, thousand, and there isn't a name on the last house. That last house is called the units or ones. These house names show the family name or period for each group of digits. I am going to place a numeral holder in each house to help us read the numeral. (SEE FIGURE 4.37)

Teacher: I am going to read the numeral, using the house names. (THE TEACHER POINTS TO THE 3-DIGIT NUMERAL AND READS ITS NAME.) "Three hundred twenty-six (THEN THE TEACHER POINTS TO THE HOUSE NAME.) **billion**, three hundred twenty-six (THEN POINTING TO THE HOUSE NAME) **million**, three hundred twenty-six (THEN POINTING TO THE HOUSE NAME) **thousand**, three hundred twenty-six." Now that you have heard me read it, let's use the house names to help us read it together.

Instructional group: Three hundred twenty-six *billion*, three hundred twenty-six *million*, three hundred twenty-six *thousand*, three hundred twenty-six. (THE TEACHER WOULD WORK WITH SEVERAL EXAMPLES USING 3-DIGIT NUMERALS IN THE HOLDERS. ADDITIONAL INSTRUCTION WILL BE NEEDED TO EXPLAIN THE USE OF THE ZERO WHEN 2- AND 1-DIGIT NUMERALS ARE PLACED IN THE POCKET HOLDERS.)

Following the introduction of periods, the teacher will need to work on special problem cases. The manner in which zero is read in 2- and 3-digit numerals has been established before the pupil starts reading larger amounts. For example, "30," "320," and "300" have already been taught prior to the introduction of period names. However, the teacher will need to help students understand each of the following zero situations when they appear in larger numerals:

> Zero in the hundreds place—
> **,017,** is read just like 17 and **,020,** is read just like 20

> Zeros in the hundreds and tens place—
> **,005,** is read just like 5

> Zeros in the hundreds, tens, and ones place—
> **,000,** the period is skipped (silent)

Concurrent with teaching a pupil to read numerals in the trillions, billions, millions, etc., the place value within a period is reviewed. For example, within the billions period, one digit is in the hundred billions place, a second digit in the ten billions place, and another digit in the one billions place.

Multiple Names for Digits Within a Period

Some situations in life require a person to think of 40¢ as 40 pennies and also as four dimes. When speaking of years, we read 1492 as "fourteen hundred ninety-two" rather than "one thousand

---

The amount—326326326326   units house name not read

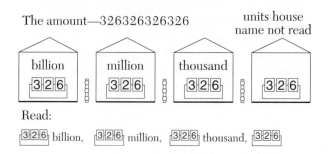

Read:

When *writing* the amount—start at the *units* and count to the left in groups of three. Use *commas* for fences.

326,326,326,326

FIGURE 4.37

four hundred ninety-two." Likewise, there are situations in mathematics which require a person to think of numbers named in different ways. For example, if one wants to subtract nine from 400 it is more efficient to think of changing one of the 40 tens into ten ones when performing the subtraction algorithm, rather than regrouping one of the four hundreds into ten tens, and *then* regrouping one of the ten tens into ten ones.

Figure 4.38 illustrates an independent activity device for developing multiple ways of thinking about place value. The strip is pulled through a slot exposing a variety of ways of looking at the place value associated with 5,235.

Rounding Numbers

By the time students finish the intermediate grades they must be able to round numbers in a variety of ways. There are two elements of this skill. First a pupil must be able to identify the digits that will remain after the rounding. That is, if the number 2,523 were to be rounded to the nearest hundred, the pupil must identify that the 5 is in the hundreds place so there are 25 hundreds. Then the pupil must look at the digit to the right of the identified position and decide whether to round DOWN

or round UP. The digits 0, 1, 2, 3, 4 suggest rounding DOWN and the digits 5, 6, 7, 8, 9 suggest rounding UP. Since "5" is the halfway point, it really does not matter whether it suggests rounding up or down. The lesson fragment below shows a teacher developing rounding to the nearest thousand.

Teacher-Guided Interactive Learning Activity

LESSON FRAGMENT

M: Rounding to nearest thousand

A: Group of fourth-grade pupils

T: Analogy

H: Identify thousands position in numeral

Teacher: (POINTING TO ILLUSTRATION—FIGURE 4.39) Here we have a number line that shows a "service station" at each thousand. If we need gasoline for our car, we could stop at any of these stations. Suppose we were riding along in a car—like this—(THE TEACHER PLACES A PICTURE OF A CAR AT A SPOT WHICH WOULD REPRESENT 4,784 AND WRITES THE NUMERAL ON THE CHALKBOARD.) and we ran out of gas at the 4,784-kilometer marker. Which station would be closer, Gertrude?

Gertrude: It would be closer to go to the station at 5,000 than the one at 4,000. It is a lot closer.

Teacher: Yes, it is closer, isn't it. Suppose I moved the car to 3,293. (THE TEACHER PLACES THE CAR AT APPROXIMATELY 3,293 AND WRITES THE NUMERAL ON THE CHALKBOARD.) Now which station is closer? Bill?

Bill: The car is closer to 3,000 than to 4,000.

Teacher: Yes, it would be a lot closer to go back to 3,000 than to go to 4,000. Suppose we ran out of gas at 4,500. Which station would you go to? Katrina?

Katrina: It wouldn't make any difference—they are both the same distance away.

Teacher: When we round a number we are going to the closest specified multiple that lies between the number we are rounding. For example, if we are rounding to thousands, 3,293 lies between 3,000 and 4,000, but it is closer to 3,000, therefore we round 3,293 to 3,000.

Teacher-Guided Interactive Learning Activity

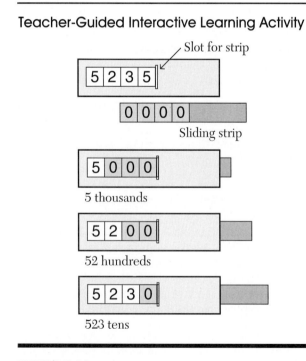

Slot for strip

5 2 3 5

0 0 0 0

Sliding strip

5 0 0 0

5 thousands

5 2 0 0

52 hundreds

5 2 3 0

523 tens

FIGURE 4.38

Using an Analogy to Reduce Level of Abstractness

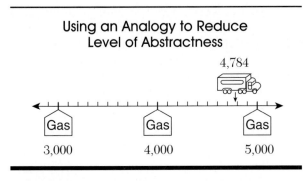

FIGURE 4.39

Device for Independent Learning Activity

Rounding Verifier

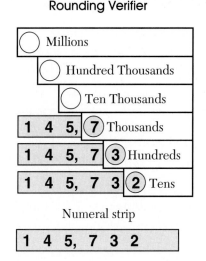

Numeral strip

Example: To round to thousands the strip is placed under the thousands, exposing 145. To see if the number should be rounded *up* or *down* the digit in the ring is examined. In this case it is a seven, so the number 145,732 is rounded *up* to 146 thousand.

FIGURE 4.40

A useful device for developing rounding skills is the *Rounding Verifier* device illustrated in Figure 4.40. To use this device, students make a series of numeral strips. For example, suppose they were told at a learning station to round 6,234,789 to the nearest million. They would place the strip under the millions section so that just the 6 extends beyond the frame. Then to decide if the numeral should be rounded up or down, they would look at the digit which appears in the "hole." Seeing a "2," the number is rounded to six million. If rounding to thousands, they would put the strip under the thousands section so that the 6,234 showed. In the "hole" a "7" appears, so the number is rounded UP to 6,235 thousands.

Multiple Names for Numbers

Different expanded notations for numerals are employed in intermediate grade levels to help students develop a better understanding of the structure of the decimal numeration system. Some formats stress the place value of the digits, others help the pupil understand different algorithms, and some serve as precursors for the development of decimal notation. The choice of a visual aid to represent the form will depend to a large extent on the nature of the expanded notation being developed. For example, the 20-bead abacus is a good device when place value is being emphasized, whereas a chart may be better when one wishes to emphasize that ten tens are equal to one hundred and ten hundreds are equal to one thousand, etc.

Some expanded forms are a combination of words and numerals, while others use both the operation of addition and multiplication. There are expanded notation forms which emphasize the nature of tenness being associated with the place value, while others use exponential notation. The following illustrates twelve thousand three hundred thirty-six using a wide variety of formats.

$12{,}336 =$ (1) 12 thousand, 336
(2) $10{,}000 + 2{,}000 + 300 + 30 + 6$
(3) 1 ten thousand + 2 thousands + 3 hundreds + 3 tens + 6 ones
(4) $(1 \times 10{,}000) + (2 \times 2000) + (3 \times 100) + (3 \times 10) + 6$
(5) $(1 \times 10 \times 10 \times 10 \times 10) + (2 \times 10 \times 10 \times 10) + (3 \times 10 \times 10) + (3 \times 10) + 6$
(6) $(1 \times 10^4) + (2 \times 10^3) + (3 \times 10^2) + (3 \times 10^1) + 6$
1.2336×10^4 (The use of scientific notation and negative exponents is developed in a later chapter.)

While the first three notations listed above can be used before multiplication is fully developed, notations (4) and (5) require that students understand multiplication, and notation (6) requires the pupil to understand exponents.

Using a Calculator to Develop Numeration and Number Concepts

Calculators are used to not only *develop* an understanding numeration, but also to provide *practice* for these concepts. Teachers may find that these devices also provide a way of remediating misconceptions.

Calculators are an excellent tool to help students associate a numeral with *counting*. If a pupil enters "96" and then "+1," pressing the "=" will let the pupil see the next number. Each time the "=" is pressed, the next counting number will appear. When the pupil reaches "99" and presses "=," the "100" will appear. At the intermediate level, similar activities are helpful to show the pupil that the next number after 199 is not a thousand and the number that follows 20,999 is 21,000, not 30,000.

Counting by amounts other than one are also easily accomplished with the calculator. Students often use the calculator in first grade to count by 2s and by 5s. Counting by tens (enter "10 + =") helps a pupil see the pattern of tens. Students generally recognize (without teacher assistance) that counting by tens (when starting at a multiple of ten) always ends with a zero! A little more advanced activity would be counting by ten—but starting at some number other than ten. For example, if a pupil started at 7 and counted by ten (enter 7 + 10 =), then the calculator would display 17, 27, 37, 47, 57, 67, etc.

Calculators are good *verifiers* for expanded notation. For example, to verify that 600 + 20 + 3 really is "six hundred twenty-three" the pupil simply enters the 600 + 200 + 3, and presses "=," and the amount is verified. Similarly, the teacher can show that 360 is really 36 tens by showing 36 × 10 and then pressing "=." Similar activities can be used to determine how to write "37 hundred" (37 × 100 =) and even "37 ten thousands" (37 × 10,000 =).

To practice positional value, students enter a large amount—such as 4,236,189—and try to change the "3" to a "0" by pressing the operation key "−" and then an amount. The moment the pupil enters the "3," the original numeral disappears from the screen so the pupil must remember the positional value of the "3." To change JUST the "3" to a "0," the amount "30,000" must be entered since the "3" needs to be in the "ten thousands" place. This activity is even more effective when one pupil gives an *oral direction* to the calculator operator; for example: "subtract three ten-thousands" or "subtract thirty thousand." Directions such as "subtract a three with four zeros" would not be an acceptable direction.

4.7 COMPUTERS

Using BASIC (computer language), teachers can easily design a wide variety of programs for developing number and numeration concepts. For example, a simple program can be written where one pupil inputs a "secret number" and a second pupil tries to guess the number on the computer. The computer would be programmed to respond by telling them whether the guess was "higher" or "lower" than the secret number. This activity develops the pupil's **number sense** (less than and greater than) and **estimation skills**. Computers also can be programmed for practice in sequence skills. For example, the computer can display a number from one to 1,000 and then ask for the *next* number (or ten greater, etc.). Of course, the program also can ask the pupil for place-value information, period names, or many other number or numeration ideas.

Let us examine a generic BASIC program for the numeration guessing game. (Because the exact instructions that would be written would depend on the type of computer system being used, only a general description of the types of commands is being given.)

1. Tell the computer to PRINT the following types of information:
The name you wish given to the game, the instructions for playing the game, and directions that the player is to clear the screen after the instructions are read.
2. Tell the computer to PRINT: "What is the number you want guessed?"
3. Tell the computer what this "input" will be called. (Let's assume you designate the input as X.)
4. Tell the computer to PRINT: "Make a guess."
5. Tell the computer what this new "input" will be called. (Let's assume you designate this new input as Y.)
6. Tell the computer if X = Y, go to step ten.
7. Tell the computer if Y > X to PRINT: "The guess is too high."

8. Tell the computer if Y < X to PRINT: "The guess is too low."

9. Tell the computer to go back to step two.

10. Tell the computer to PRINT: "You've got it."

If a teacher has not yet mastered programming using BASIC, this should not deter the teacher from incorporating computer programs into the elementary mathematics curriculum. There are many public-domain computer programs in professional journals (*Arithmetic Teacher*, etc.) that only require that the teacher enter them into the computer. There are also many commercial programs available as software, so that only a disk is inserted into the computer.

4.8 EVALUATION AND INTERVENTION

When evaluating a pupil's understanding of number and numeration the teacher must determine not only ability to *record* numerals, but also the pupil's understanding of *place value* and his/her ability to *count* by various sequences.

Some assessment/diagnosis of whole-number skills occurs as a teacher examines the pupil's performance on **practice worksheets**. Assessment of a pupil's ability to read and write numerals and his/her understanding of place value can effectively be accomplished in this manner. Evaluation of counting skill (such as the ability to count across transit points) may require the teacher to observe <u>oral</u> counting activities.

The teacher can expect some errors to occur commonly in the learning process. Many will be eliminated as the pupil becomes more familiar with the materials. Some errors, however, reflect a pupil's lack of understanding of essential concepts of numeration. These errors should direct the teacher to remedial procedures which will help the pupil overcome this deficiency. Some typical errors are listed below, along with suggested remedial procedures.

1. Error: Incorrect numeral form.
Remediation: Have pupil use template-guided letters.
Comment: These errors should be corrected early in the instructional process before the pupil establishes improper habits.
2. Error: Value of digits improperly identified. Pupil cannot identify tens or hundreds position in numeral.
Remediation: Have students record objects grouped in a specific place into hundreds, tens, and ones in a frame which identifies hundreds, tens, and ones.
3. Error: Oral counting (rote or rational) errors when counting between tens or at 100—pupil says "twenty-nine, twenty-ten."
Remediation: Practice counting by tens to make sure pupil is fluent. Read sets of numerals that go through transition points. For example, 98, 99, 100, 101, etc.

4.9 MEETING SPECIAL NEEDS

Students with special needs can be classified into two categories. At one end of the spectrum the teacher will find students who have quickly mastered skills and concepts normally taught at a given grade level. This rapid mastery may be due to the fact that a pupil has high natural ability (gifted), or because the student had an unusually strong background in the topics being developed. At the other end of the spectrum, students will be found who are experiencing an inordinate amount of difficulty in mastering concepts due to a particular learning deficit (learning disabled), or motivational/experiential factors. With the more advanced student the teacher will wish to "extend" or "enrich" the student's conceptual understanding of the topics mastered. When working with the slower student, the teacher will wish to find ways to help the pupil master those skills essential for living in today's society.

Students who have mastered whole-number concepts might be assigned an **individual research project** by posing the question "How are very large numbers named, for example 1,000,000,000,000,000,000,000?" Calculators will let the gifted pupil and the pupil with extensive mastery of whole-number concepts explore ways of illustrating large numbers. For example, to illustrate a million—a pupil might find how much room it would take to store a million bottle caps. Another pupil may find the number of pages in a newspaper that would be filled with a million letters. Using the calculator, the gifted pupil may wish to find out how long it would take to reach one million if the calculator was used to "add one" every time the " = " was pressed.

Newspapers are an excellent medium for extending and enriching students' appreciation of numbers. All students can find examples of numbers in the newspaper. Construction of a bulletin board that displays applications of large numbers found in newspapers and magazines is an excellent **small-group learning activity**.

A learning-disabled pupil may engage in the process of trying to learn numeration handicapped with visual perception problems that make it difficult for him/her to orient the numerals properly, handicapped by poor kinesthetic and haptic memory, or poor motor coordination skills that make writing well-formed numerals difficult if not impossible. Deficits of these types require the teacher to provide learning structures that will facilitate the learning or restructure the curriculum by delaying when a topic is to be mastered. In some instances the teacher may eliminate a specific curriculum requirement. A particular ability may be developmentally *delayed* for a pupil; for example, the inability to sense that the tens are on the left and the ones are on the right in a numeral. In such a case, restructuring numeral-writing activities to permit the pupil use of frames which denote where the tens and ones belong when recording 2- and 3-digit numerals may be quite appropriate. This activity may extend into work with the addition and subtraction algorithm.

Sometimes a difficulty may represent a permanent learning disability, and curriculum restructuring may become a permanent accommodation for the pupil. For example, a spastic muscle condition may prevent a pupil from being able to use a pencil, pen, crayon, or other similar writing device. Under these circumstances, a calculator becomes the pupil's main form of communicating mathematical information to others and requires a major adjustment in the pupil's mathematics curriculum.

When a handicap is related to *small muscle control*, the teacher may permit the pupil to write his/her numerals with broad strokes, or to use a calculator or paste-on numerals (see Figure 4.41). In many instances, large numerals will present fewer problems than small numerals. It will be necessary for some students to use primary-lined paper longer than others. Special adapters are made that convert a regular pencil into a primary-grade thickness for those students who have small muscle control deficits.

Large numerals are appropriate for some *visual deficit* situations. Large symbols are easier to read and write. Special magnifying lenses may be used to augment students' visual ability when they are learning to read and write numerals.

Bypassing Strategies

Child is unable to make well-formed numerals using a pencil.

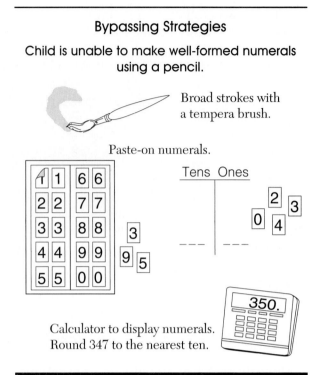

Broad strokes with a tempera brush.

Paste-on numerals.

Calculator to display numerals. Round 347 to the nearest ten.

FIGURE 4.41

4.10 SUMMARY

Most students enter kindergarten and the primary grades with rote counting skills. Some have learned to rational count sets to ten or more, recognize the number of some sets without counting, and are able to write their numerals up to 10.

The first task of the primary-grade teacher is to assess the skills that the pupil brings to the primary grades and then to build on these skills. In the primary grades the pupil learns number and numeration concepts through hundreds. The skills and concepts are introduced through hands-on explorations.

By the end of the primary grades, children can count by ones and various multiples (2s, 5s, 10s, 100s, etc.); they can write numerals and word names for numbers to 1,000; and understand place value associated with each digit in 4-digit numerals. He/she can compare and order numbers.

In the intermediate grades skills are extended to include period names (millions, billions, etc.). Students learn multiple names for numbers (four hundreds, 40 tens, 400 ones) and can round to the nearest ten and hundred. Place-value concepts are extended for digits within periods.

EXERCISES

1. There are five prenumber concepts identified in the chapter. Name each one and then describe an activity which could be used by a teacher to build each concept.
2. Number recognition skills may be taught using different approaches. Suggest an activity which might be used by a teacher to teach the number six using
   a. Model sets
   b. One-more approach
   c. Rational counting
3. Describe an activity that might be used to strengthen pupil skill in
   a. Numeral recognition
   b. Number/numeral matching
   c. Writing the digit 5
4. How might a teacher introduce the greater than and less than symbols so that a pupil will remember how to construct the symbols correctly?
5. When teaching pupils to read and write 2- and 3-digit numerals, the use of manipulative materials is essential. Describe a lesson that might be used to develop 3-digit numeral skills in which
   a. The learning is a teacher-guided interactive activity.
   b. The learning is facilitated by an independent activity.
   c. The learning is facilitated by a cooperative group activity.
6. Suggest essential components of a lesson which would build pupil understanding of the ordinals 1–10.
7. Describe a teacher-guided interactive activity which helps pupils
   a. Recognize and visualize large numbers (millions, billions, etc.).
   b. Read numerals with more than six digits.
   c. Round numbers to the nearest ten, hundred, thousand, or ten thousand.
8. Show how to strengthen pupil understanding of place value using a calculator.

RELEVANT COMPUTER SOFTWARE

Number Sea Hunt, TRS-80 and Commodore 64. Gamco Industries, P.O. Box 1911, Big Spring, Tex. 79720.

Place Value, 1985. Apple II family. Educational Materials & Equipment Co. P.O. Box 17, Pelham, N.Y. 10803.

REFERENCES

Carlow, C. D. "Early Focus on Number Awareness." Edited by R. E. Reys and B. J. Reys. *Arithmetic Teacher* 34 (December 1986): 16.

Demi, *Count the Animals One—Two—Three*. New York: Putnam Publishing Group, 1986.

Flexer, R. J. "The Power of Five." *Arithmetic Teacher* 34 (November 1986): 5–9.

Sawada, D. "Computer Power in Primary Grades: Mathematics with Big Trak.®" *Arithmetic Teacher* 32 (October 1984): 14–17.

Singer, R. "Estimation and Counting in the Block Corner." *Arithmetic Teacher* 36 (January 1988): 10–14.

Turkel, S., and C. M. Newman. "What's Your Number? Developing Number Sense." *Arithmetic Teacher* 35 (February 1988): 53–55.

Van de Walle, J. A. "The Early Development of Number Relations." *Arithmetic Teacher* 35 (February 1988): 15–21.

CHAPTER 5

TEACHING ADDITION OF WHOLE NUMBERS

INTRODUCTION

The nature of addition skills individuals need in today's society are decidedly different from the skills required in the pretechnology age. There is little need to be able rapidly to add columns of figures manually today. Long columns of figures are routinely computed using a calculator or computer. However, the pervasive use of these technological devices requires teachers to place greater emphasis on helping children **understand** the addition operation and its properties, to apply addition in **solving problems**, and to give children **reasonable** proficiency in paper-and-pencil type addition algorithms. Children will need to recognize **when** to use addition and **what** addition will do, much more than they need to be able to speedily add long columns of figures. Of course, in order to **estimate efficiently**, children must have some skill in addition. A child should be able to add a column of figures, even though calculators are available. We use computational devices because they are efficient—not because we have no other way of getting a sum.

Children enter school with an intuitive concept of addition. This understanding develops from experiences they have had playing with their toys; interaction with their parents, siblings, and with other children in the neighborhood; and participation in activities in preschool settings. The **school mathematics program** extends each child's understanding by:

- using concrete materials to develop a deeper understanding of addition;
- helping the child discover properties of the operation;
- developing the child's skill in using algorithmic and equational forms for adding;
- promoting use of those skills in problem-solving situations; and
- encouraging the child to apply those skills in his/her everyday life.

This chapter will look at the addition skills **typically** found in the whole number addition strand of the elementary school mathematics curriculum.

5.1 TEACHING ADDITION IN THE KINDERGARTEN AND PRIMARY GRADES

While counting activities prepare children for addition, a more organized effort is desirable when readying children for the formal exploration of addition and subtraction found in the primary grades. The readiness activities used in kindergarten are usually not designed to develop the formal vocabulary and symbolism that will be used later. Addition explorations will grow out of the children's desire to find the total number when sets are put together.

Preschool children and kindergarten children engage in many activities that acquaint them with introductory addition concepts. For example, parents say, "Jenny, you can have only one more cookie. You have already had two and if you have more than three it will spoil your supper." Parents also introduce the child to some of the initial addition concept vocabulary. For example, words such as "and," "is," and "are" are a part of the child's vocabulary before he/she enters first grade. The teacher will use the vocabulary the child brings to school when using manipulative materials. For example, when the child puts one block with two blocks the teacher may say: "Good! One **and** two **is** three," or "Good! One block **and** two blocks **are** three blocks."

Most kindergarten programs include a "readiness" for addition as an objective. When children enter first grade the teacher uses that background to develop the addition operation. Children first see addition as **putting things together** (the union of disjoint sets). They learn to record what happens by writing a mathematical sentence (**equation**). During this process children develop a "hearing vocabulary" for addition. They associate the plus symbol (+) with "and," and learn the word and symbol for "equals." Children will use concrete materials to "act out" addition sentences and write a sentence when observing an action.

Later, children will learn that addition can be used to describe things that have <u>already</u> been "put together"—associating addition with **describing subsets within a set**. It is important for the teacher to develop BOTH models for addition. Many programs also introduce a formal vocabulary for addition, naming each subset as an **addend** and the entire set as the **sum** (see Figure 5.1). (At one time some elementary programs made a distinction between the first addend and the amount being added to that addend. This "added amount" was called the **augmend**. Contemporary programs do not make this distinction.)

Remember: Early communications are conducted within the children's structure of language

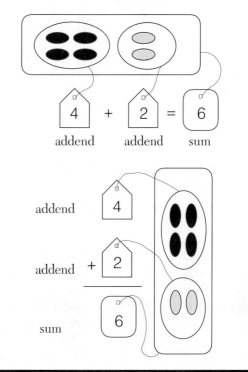

FIGURE 5.1

Early work in the primary grades concentrates on developing the meaning of addition, its properties, and its applications in problem-solving situations. As children become familiar with the operation, strategies for organizing basic combinations ("sum families," "counting on," "make-a-ten," "near doubles," "sharing numbers," and "related facts") are explored. These strategies deepen children's understanding of the operation and help them master the basic combinations more efficiently.

As the child progresses through first, second, and third grades, algorithms for using the basic facts to add 2-, 3-, and 4-digit numbers are introduced. During this time some algorithms are employed that deepen the child's understanding of the operation, rather than increase his/her efficiency in adding. It is important for the teacher to understand the purpose of these **developmental algorithms** and the role they play in the instructional program. For example, the developmental algorithm in Figure 5.2 (expanded notation using words) reinforces the understanding of place value, forces the pupil to recognize that 35 is really 3 tens and 5 ones, and requires that the ones be put with the ones and the tens with the tens.

The addition skills that are developed at the primary level are the foundation upon which later skills are built. It is imperative that pupil understanding not be sacrificed simply for greater efficiency in computing. Indeed, the teacher may, at times, postpone the introduction of more efficient algorithms in order to develop depth of understanding.

The following presents a **general overview** of the addition skills introduced at the primary level:

Kindergarten

Development of addition concepts
- using hands-on explorations

Grade 1

Meaning of addition
- putting groups together
- describing a set

Exploration of addition properties
- commutative property
- identity
- associative property

Introduction of addition vocabulary
- plus, add, equals, addend, sum

Adding 1-digit addends
- explore all basic facts
- counting-on strategy introduced
- mastery of facts with sums through 12
- explore adding three addends

Adding 2-digit numbers with no regrouping

Grade 2

Strengthen previously introduced skills

Adding 1-digit addends
- missing addends
- strategies for exploring basic facts (make-a-ten, near doubles, sharing numbers)
- mastery of basic facts sums through 18

Adding 2- and 3-digit addends
- without regrouping
- with regrouping
- using column addition (three addends)
- using decade facts

Checking by estimation

Grade 3

Strengthen previously introduced skills

Adding 3- and 4-digit addends
- (with and without regrouping)
- column addition

Checking with the inverse (subtraction)

Developmental Algorithm

Tens	Ones
3	5
+ 4	3
7	8

Developmental Algorithm

$$35 = \underline{3} \text{ tens and } \underline{5} \text{ ones}$$
$$+ \ 43 = \underline{4} \text{ tens and } \underline{3} \text{ ones}$$
$$\underline{7} \text{ tens and } \underline{8} \text{ ones}$$

FIGURE 5.2

5.2 DEVELOPING THE MEANING OF ADDITION

Children need many hands-on experiences with addition before the technical vocabulary associated with addition is introduced. (For example, terms such as addition, add, plus, equals, addends, and sum should be delayed until the child has modeled addition using informal terms such as **"and," "is,"** and **"are."**)

After readiness activities the teacher must provide a more comprehensive and organized development of the addition operation. How these early experiences are constructed is determined by the number skills mastered by the child. If the child only has rational counting skills, then only activities using those counting skills can be used. On the other hand, if the pupil can count and recognize the number of a set when organized into various common patterns, then the teacher can utilize both skills. Let us first examine a lesson in which children have rational counting skills, but do not yet associate common patterns with number concepts.

Teacher-Guided Interactive Learning Activity

LESSON FRAGMENT

M: Associating addition with putting two sets together and determining number of the resulting set. (The terms "add" and "addition" have not been introduced at this point.)

A: Group of first graders

T: involvement (physical)

H: Number and numeration

PROBLEM-SOLVING SITUATION:

OVER THE WEEKEND THE TEACHER BOUGHT THREE NEW FISH FOR THE CLASS AQUARIUM, WHICH ALREADY HAD TWO FISH. BECAUSE THE FISH WERE MOVING AROUND, IN AND OUT OF THE AQUATIC PLANTS, THEY COULD NOT BE COUNTED. ONE CHILD SAID THERE WERE FOUR FISH WHILE ANOTHER WAS CERTAIN THAT THERE WERE AT LEAST SEVEN. TO SOLVE THE PROBLEM, THE TEACHER SUGGESTED THAT THEY COULD USE PAPER PLATES AND BLOCKS TO **REPRESENT** THE FISH. THEN EACH CHILD COULD "MAKE A MODEL OF THE SITUATION." (SEE FIGURE 5.3 FOR THE ACTIVITY THAT MOTIVATED THE PROBLEM-SOLVING SITUATION.)

Teacher: Let's have everyone use two blocks to show the fish we had last Friday. Put the blocks on the colored plate. Now let's count out three more blocks and put them in your other plate. (SEE FIGURE 5.4.)

To help us remember how many we have—take your numeral cards and place the numeral 2 under the plate that has two blocks. How many blocks do we have in the other plate? (THREE) Let's put the numeral 3 under the plate with three blocks.

We are going to put the three blocks with the two blocks in the colored plate just as I put the three

Involvement and Evaluation

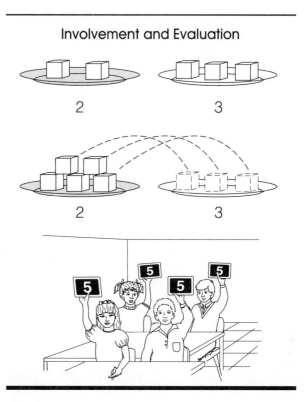

FIGURE 5.4

Computation Introduced Through Problem-Solving Situations

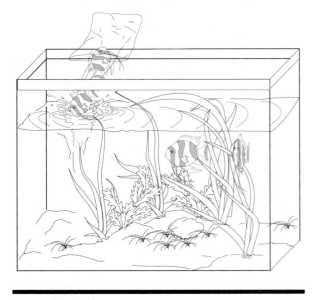

FIGURE 5.3

fish with our two fish this morning. When we put two numbers together we ADD them.

Now count to see how many blocks you get when you add two and three. Find a numeral card that tells how many blocks you have when you put three blocks with two blocks. When I say go, hold up your card to show me your numeral. Go! (THE CHILDREN DISPLAY THE NUMERAL "5" TO THE TEACHER, WHO CHECKS EACH CHILD'S EFFORT.)

Teacher: Good work! Yes, we now have five fish!

In the "lesson fragment" children used a hands-on activity to learn that addition can be associated with putting two sets of known amount together to find the number associated with the resulting set. The teacher took the problem from a classroom event. As a foundation for a later development of the problem-solving strategy "modeling," the teacher used "blocks" to represent the fish in the problem. Later, the teacher will wish to associate this kind of physical action with an equation ($2 + 3 = 5$). This association is made by using terminology already in the child's vocabulary: "two **and** three is five." Gradually, a more formal language is used when reading the equation ("2 **plus** 3 **is** 5," "2 **plus** 3 **equals** 5," etc.).

5.3 INTRODUCING THE BASIC ADDITION FACTS

Once children associate addition with **putting two sets together**, the number sentence (equation) is introduced as a way of recording what was done physically with blocks. This will be the child's first experience with the addition "**basic facts**." (Basic addition facts are defined as those addition cases in which both addends are one digit. For example, $3 + 9 = 12$ is a basic fact because the addends 3 and 9 are single digits. The sum, in this case 12, may or may not be a single digit.)

Many beginning activities using basic facts are designed to explore the properties of addition. Presentation of basic facts may be organized in a variety of ways. While each activity can be used to build the child's understanding of a property, a strategy, or pattern, it is possible that many children will actually memorize the facts during that period of time. Later, when memorizing the basic fact becomes the goal (AFTER building an understanding of the operation), memory enhancement activities will be employed.

Initial experiences with the basic combinations are designed to strengthen the child's understanding of the operation. During these activities the child learns to write a number sentence that "records" what is happening when two blocks are pushed together. Some situations should be designed that require the child's use of models (blocks, sticks, etc.) to illustrate an equation such as "$3 + 4 = $."

First activities illustrate addition as the ACTION of putting things together, but the child will also need to recognize that addition is also associated with naming a set that has already been put together. Showing four girls and two boys sitting at a table, the teacher can "identify" that table as "$4 + 2 = 6$." This may help pupils recognize that we do not always see the action—sometimes we only see two subsets that are already joined.

Developing Addition Facts When "1" Is An Addend (One-More Facts)

Children find some facts easier to recall than others. Those facts which have a "1" as an addend fall into the "easy" category. Children intuitively recognize that finding the next number is adding one. Indeed, one of the techniques used when helping young children learn number concepts is called the

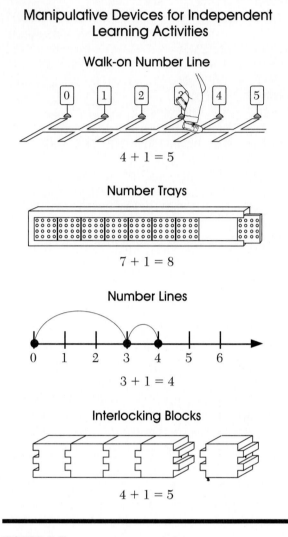

Manipulative Devices for Independent Learning Activities

Walk-on Number Line

$4 + 1 = 5$

Number Trays

$7 + 1 = 8$

Number Lines

$3 + 1 = 4$

Interlocking Blocks

$4 + 1 = 5$

FIGURE 5.5

"one-more approach." Using this method, a teacher first directs the child to construct a set, and give the name for that set. Once the amount is identified the teacher will put **one more** with the set and point out that the new set is more than the original. The child will then be asked to name the new set—the set that is one more than the first amount. The child thinks, "I had five. I put one more with it, so it can't be five anymore. It must be a new number. That number is six."

Many manipulative aids encourage the child to add one or to count one more. Figure 5.5 illustrates some of the devices that permit a child to explore addition concepts independently using counting.

Calculator Activities

Calculators can help children discover the relationship between counting and "adding one more." To direct such an activity, the teacher would direct the child to enter a number such as 7, press the operation key for addition ($+$), and then the number 1. When the the equal key ($=$) is pressed, the next number (8) appears. Children soon recognize that it is faster and easier to add "1" in their heads than to use the calculator.

Using Sum Families To Organize the Basic Facts

When first exploring basic addition combinations it is more important for pupils to learn about the addition operation and its properties than to memorize sums. Sum families provide an opportunity for children to work in small groups to discover that a number can have many different names. To find the **"Sum Family"** for SIX, a team would count out a set of six objects. Using that set, they would find ALL of the two-addend arrangements that equal six. Six can be $5 + 1$, or it can be $2 + 4$, etc.

While finding sum families the pupil is, of course, learning the basic facts that add to six (see Figure 5.6). While exploring basic facts that have a sum of six, children will also discover many interrelationships among the addition facts—that $2 + 4$ is really just $4 + 2$ turned around; that 6 is really one more than 5; that taking away something from one addend and putting it with the other addend does not change the sum.

Not only do sum families help children organize the exploration of the addition facts, the activity also lets pupils use one set of manipulative materials. The basic addition fact matrix (Figure 5.7) illustrates the combinations that would be studied for the sum family of six.

Let us examine a fragment of a lesson that uses a "sum family" approach in a more guided exploration.

Teacher-Guided Interactive Learning Activity

LESSON
FRAGMENT

M: Sum family of four

A: A group of first-graders

T: Models

H: Children know the meaning of addition and the vocabulary associated with the addition equation

PROBLEM-SOLVING SITUATION:
THE TEACHER INTRODUCED THE LESSON BY SHOWING THAT THERE WERE DIFFERENT ARRANGEMENTS OF A QUANTITY. SHE HAD 3 BOYS AND A GIRL COME TO THE FRONT OF THE ROOM AND NOTED THAT THERE WERE 4 PU-

Small-Group Learning Activity

Use the six lima beans to find all the pairs of numbers that will give a sum of 6.

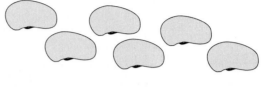

FIGURE 5.6

PILS IN THE GROUP. SHE WROTE ON THE BOARD $3 + 1 = 4$. SHE HAD ONE BOY SIT DOWN AND A GIRL TAKE HIS PLACE. SHE WROTE ON THE BOARD $2 + 2 = 4$. SHE ASKED IF THERE WERE OTHER ARRANGEMENTS THAT COULD ALSO GIVE 4. WHEN THE PUPILS GAVE A FEW MORE, THE TEACHER SUGGESTED THEY USE THEIR COUNTING DISKS TO MODEL WHAT HAD HAPPENED WITH THE GROUP.

Teacher: Put two paper plates on your desk. Take out four counting disks and put them in one of the plates. Let's put the numeral "4" card under your plate with four disks. Now, how many disks do you have in the other plate?

Child: None.

Teacher: That's right, you have **zero** disks on the plate. Let's put the numeral "0" under your disk with zero disks. We are going to put our two plates together. What symbol should we use between our "4" and "0" to show we put the sets together?

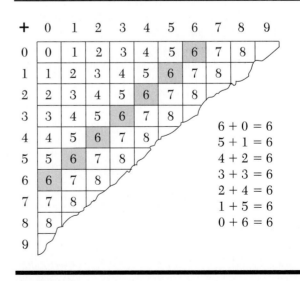

+	0	1	2	3	4	5	6	7	8	9
0	0	1	2	3	4	5	6	7	8	
1	1	2	3	4	5	6	7	8		
2	2	3	4	5	6	7	8			
3	3	4	5	6	7	8				
4	4	5	6	7	8					
5	5	6	7	8						
6	6	7	8							
7	7	8								
8	8									
9										

$6 + 0 = 6$
$5 + 1 = 6$
$4 + 2 = 6$
$3 + 3 = 6$
$2 + 4 = 6$
$1 + 5 = 6$
$0 + 6 = 6$

FIGURE 5.7

Child: Plus sign.
Teacher: Right! Now put your plus sign between the numerals and put the two plates together. How many disks do we have in all? (SEE FIGURE 5.8.)
Child: Four.
Teacher: Place the equal sign and a "4" to make your equation. Let's see if we can find some other arrangements for four. (ONE DISK IS NOW SHIFTED TO THE OTHER PLATE AND THE PROCESS IS CONTINUED BY DEVELOPING 3 + 1 = 4. IN A SIMILAR MANNER THE WHOLE SUM FAMILY OF FOUR IS DEVELOPED. WHEN ALL THE NAMES FOR FOUR WERE FOUND, THE TEACHER SUGGESTED THAT EACH PUPIL INDEPENDENTLY FIND ALL OF THE NAMES FOR SIX.)

Note that in this development, a number sentence is being developed to correspond with the action, giving meaning to each part of the equation. The sum family is an early exploratory approach and is not normally used when sums are greater than ten. If used with larger sums, children would encounter combinations that are not basic facts as in 15 = 12 + 3. Developing the addition facts around the sum families is but one approach and must be supplemented by a variety of other approaches to fully develop the addition facts.

Using the Order (Commutative) Property to Explore the Basic Facts

As meaning, related symbolism, and vocabulary for addition are developed, children explore the effect of changing the order of two addends. Using manipulative materials, pupils find that changing the order of the addends does not change the sum. When the child is older he/she will be taught that the formal name for this concept is the **commutative property** for addition.

When developing understanding of the addition operation, the teacher will include numerous references to the order property of addition. For example, after the child has put a set of three with a set of two and determined that there are five things, the teacher will reverse the process and put a set of two with a set of three. To emphasize the relationship the teacher will ask, "Did we get the **same amount** when we put 3 with 2 as when we put 2 with 3?" Children may also see this same relationship if they use the walk-on number line—starting at 3 and then taking two more steps to verify that he/she will end at the same spot as starting at 2 and taking three steps.

Once a child understands the commutative property of addition, then manipulation of physical objects will be used less often to verify sums. When the child discovers with blocks that three and two equals five, the teacher can then generate a new fact by asking, "If 3 and 2 is 5, what will we get if we add 2 and 3?" (See Figure 5.9.)

Later the child will be encouraged to apply the property to larger numbers. Showing a box with seven blocks and four blocks, the teacher might ask, "If I told you that 7 plus 4 is eleven—what do you think 4 plus 7 would be?" (Change the order of the boxes to illustrate.) "Now let's use our imaginations a little—suppose we had 30 blocks in the red box and 20 blocks in the blue box. If I emptied the blue box on the table first and then added the red box, would that be the same number of blocks as emptying the red box first and then the blue?"

The 100 basic addition combinations that the child is required to master are illustrated in a matrix format in Figure 5.10. The sums that are shaded are facts that do not need extensive practice—if the pupil understands the commutative property. When the child understands and uses the commutative property, the number of independent facts to be practiced is reduced from 100 to 55! (Notice that the sums on the diagonal result from 0 + 0, 1 + 1, 2 + 2, etc. and have no other fact related by the commutative property. There are ten of these "doubles," leaving 90 basic facts. Half of the 90—45 basic facts—can be mastered by using the commutative property!)

Using the Identity Property to Develop Addition Facts

In an earlier example an addition fact with zero as an addend was developed as a member of a sum family. However, some pupils fail to recognize the identity generalization when it is embedded in a sum family. For these pupils it will be necessary to develop the property using several situations in which zero is an addend. The lesson fragment below uses examples to lead to a generalization (but

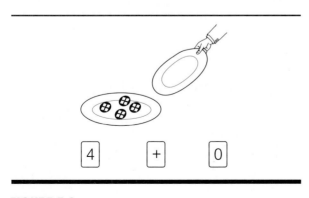

FIGURE 5.8

Horizontal Format

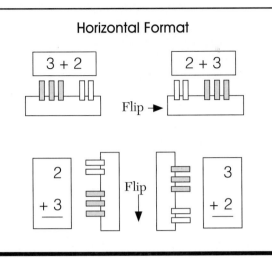

FIGURE 5.9

does not use specific terminology, which is deferred until the child is older).

Teacher-Guided Interactive Learning Activity

LESSON FRAGMENT

M: Identity concept, but not the terminology

A: First-grade group

T: Models, examples, discovery

H: The meaning of addition, some addition facts, and the ability to read and write numerals through 99

Teacher: I placed some of the addition facts on the board. We worked these with our blocks. I'm going to give you a new fact with a zero in it that we have not used our blocks to find. (TEACHER SHOWS A BOX WITH NINE BLOCKS AND AN EMPTY BOX. SHE WRITES "9 + 0 =" ON THE BOARD.) Who thinks they can give me the sum? (CHILD RAISES HER HAND.)

Child: Nine.

Teacher: Good! (TEACHER WRITES THE "9" IN THE EQUATION ON THE BOARD.) Can you explain how you got the sum so easily?

Child: You had nine and you put nothing with it so it stayed nine!

Teacher: What would you get if you added zero to 45? (NOTICE THAT THE TEACHER HAS USED AN EXAMPLE THAT IS NOT A BASIC FACT. THIS IS FREQUENTLY DONE WHEN WORKING TOWARD A GENERALIZATION.)

Child: Forty-five.

Teacher: Suppose we had a box and there was an amount we called "lottsa" in the box. We took another box that had zero things in it and we added it to the first box. What do you think you would get for a sum?

Group: A "lottsa." (SEE FIGURE 5.11.)

It does not take long for youngsters to realize that adding zero to an addend results in a sum equal to the original number (in mathematical terms, $n + 0 = n$ and $0 + n = n$ when the child uses the commutative property). Children say, "Adding zero doesn't change anything!"

An understanding of **identity** also reduces the number of basic facts that must be practiced! Zero facts should be practiced as a generalization. The matrix Figure 5.12 identifies 19 facts that have zero as one of the addends. (The encircled numerals indicate the sums of 19 basic facts that have zero as an addend.) If one were to place ALL 100 of the basic addition facts onto flash cards and put them into a stack, about $\frac{1}{5}$ of that stack could be thrown away **if** the child understood identity! Of course, teachers should recognize that children MAY need the identity concept of addition reinforced AFTER multiplication is introduced. Some children get $4 + 0 = 4$ and $4 \times 0 = 0$ confused when they are practicing multiplication facts and then return to an addition algorithm.

Using Counting-on as a Strategy for Discovering Sums

When a teacher first presents the basic addition facts (with sums through ten) the major emphasis is upon developing the child's **understanding** of the addition operation. As these facts are explored,

+	0	1	2	3	4	5	6	7	8	9
0	0	1	2	3	4	5	6	7	8	9
1	1	2	3	4	5	6	7	8	9	10
2	2	3	4	5	6	7	8	9	10	11
3	3	4	5	6	7	8	9	10	11	12
4	4	5	6	7	8	9	10	11	12	13
5	5	6	7	8	9	10	11	12	13	14
6	6	7	8	9	10	11	12	13	14	15
7	7	8	9	10	11	12	13	14	15	16
8	8	9	10	11	12	13	14	15	16	17
9	9	10	11	12	13	14	15	16	17	18

FIGURE 5.10

Beyond Manipulations to Generalizations

$$2 + 0 = 2$$
$$3 + 0 = 3$$
$$5 + 0 = 5$$
$$6 + 0 = 6$$

⇩

$$9 + 0 = 9$$

⇩

Lottsa + 0 = Lottsa

FIGURE 5.11

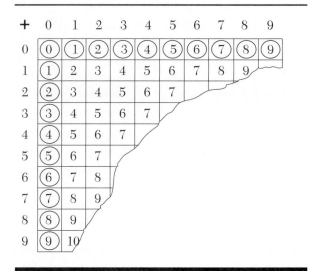

FIGURE 5.12

the teacher emphasizes "pushing two sets together," thereby associating the action with the operation. As the teacher continues, the child learns that the order in which two sets are put together does not affect the sum (**commutative property**) and that adding zero does not change the first addend (**identity**). Throughout most of this development, the teacher may allow the child to count the members of the first set; the members of the second set; and then, after pushing the two sets together—count the members of the joined set. These counting activities are valuable in the beginning because the teacher is building the concept of addition while strengthening the child's rational counting skill.

Once the child understands the addition operation, more efficient ways of finding sums must be introduced or the child will remain at this immature "counting" stage. One of the first techniques introduced by the teacher is counting-on. **Counting-on** is a skill that is used even in adult life. When we pick up a quarter and three pennies saying, "25, 26, 27, 28" and when we read 3:17 on the clock counting by fives and then by ones, we are using counting-on skills. Sometimes we even add 386 and 3 by saying "387, 388, 389."

The child first learns to count-on in kindergarten. There she/he practices counting (by ones) from numbers other than one. To teach this skill, the kindergarten teacher may say, "Today let's start counting at a different spot. I'm going to say a number and then we will count-on—by ones—until we reach 20. All right, let us start at five and count together. 'Five, six, seven, ...' "

The teacher must lead children to use **"counting-on"** when working with basic facts. If the teacher displays a set of five and a set of three and asks a child to give the sum, the child will first count the

set of five (even though the teacher said there were five). So now it is obvious that the child knows that there are five things in the first set. But when asked to give the sum, the child <u>invariably</u> will count the first set again and continue counting "six, seven, eight."

<u>To prevent immature counting from occurring, the teacher must design the activity so the child cannot count the first five objects.</u> In Figure 5.13 the teacher first displayed the set of five and the set of three. Then the five stars are covered with a card on which the numeral "5" has been written. The teacher will point to the numeral saying "five" and then to each of the remaining stars saying, "six, seven, eight. Five plus three is eight."

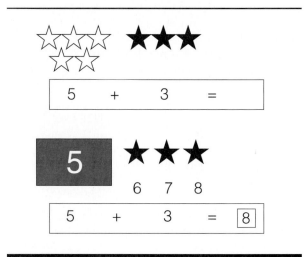

FIGURE 5.13

Introducing the Facts with Sums Greater than Ten

Most children understand addition as "putting together" by the time addition combinations with sums greater than ten are introduced. Exercises that required the child to "put two sets together and count" were effective when first building understanding of the operation. Continuing to illustrate addition simply as "putting sets together and counting" when working with sums greater than ten will contribute <u>little</u> to the child's growth. It is now time for the teacher to deepen the child's understanding of the operation by introducing different strategies that utilize the facts already mastered. These strategies not only provide the child with new insights into the operation, but also provide more efficient ways of remembering the combinations.

The following section will describe techniques for developing the child's understanding of (1) the **associative property**, (2) the **"make-a-ten" strategy**, (3) the **"nines pattern,"** (4) the **"near doubles" strategy**, and (5) the **"sharing numbers" strategy**. (Other strategies are explored in section 5.6, Addition at the Intermediate Grade level.)

Using the Associative Property for Facts with Sums of 11 through 18

Just as changing the order of the addend does not change the sum, changing the grouping also will not affect the sum. Children discover this as they put sets of objects together. Of course, when this action is recorded in a mathematical sentence, most children do not recognize it. To ensure that pupils associate the action with the mathematical property, it may be necessary for the teacher to structure activities in which pupils put three sets of objects together. Children should recognize that when you have three addends you will get the same sum if you add the first two addends and then add the third, **or** if you add the second and third addends and then add the first. Pupils should first recognize the action, then the recording of the action, and finally recognize that this property holds true with all whole numbers. The name "associative property" may be used with the action, but primary pupils are not expected to use this term. [Mathematically the associative property is stated as $(n + m) + t = n + (m + t)$.]

Let us examine a fragment of a lesson that uses an analogy to help the child understand the associative property of addition.

Teacher-Guided Interactive Learning Activity

LESSON FRAGMENT

M: Concept of associative property of addition; vocabulary not introduced

A: Group of first-graders

T: Analogy

H: Concept of addition, terminology, and symbolism associated with addition; sums through ten

Teacher: Beth has left her toys throughout the house. She is outside playing and her mother calls her in to pick up her toys. Her mother knows there are nine toys to be picked up, because she counted them. Beth comes in the front door and picks up the toys in the first and second room. Her mother asks her, "How many toys have you picked up?" Beth says, "Five," and then goes in the other room and picks up four more toys.

Let's show what Beth did by writing an addition sentence on the board. We put these parentheses around the 2 + 3 to show Beth picked up the two and three first to get five and then added the four to the five. (SEE FIGURE 5.14A.)

Suppose Beth had come in the side door and picked up the toys in the second and third room when her mother asked her how many she had picked up. How many would she say she had picked up?

Child: Seven.

Teacher: Then she would go into the front room and pick up the other two toys. (SEE FIGURE 5.14B.) Let's write an addition equation to describe what she did the second time. We put the parentheses around the 3 and 4 to show she picked up the toys in the second and third room first and then picked up the two toys.

Did we get the <u>same sum</u> whether we added the 2 and 3 first and then the 4, as when we added the 3 and 4 first and then the 2? (MORE EXAMPLES ARE GIVEN, AND THE CHILDREN ARE ASKED TO WORK SIMILAR PAIRED EQUATIONS WITH MISSING SUMS.)

Using Make-a-Ten as a Strategy

Once children recognize the associative property, they can use this grouping property to find the sums between 11 and 18. In a fact such as 7 + 7, the pupil can take three from one of the sevens to **"make-a-ten"** and then have four left over. Mathematically, the pupil has <u>renamed</u> one of the sevens as 3 + 4 and <u>grouped</u> the three with the other first seven to make ten or 7 + 7 = 7 + (3 + 4) = (7 + 3) + 4 = 10 + 4 = 14. After children have

been given instructions to make a ten in the process of finding a sum they can engage in independent learning activities exploring facts that lend themselves to this strategy (see Figure 5.15).

Once children learn "make-a-ten" as a strategy, they abandon the manipulative materials (or developmental steps) and shorten the procedure to a simple thinking process. In 8 + 8, the child would think "8 and 2 make ten"—writing "8 + 8 = **1**"; then the child would think—"taking 2 from 8 leaves six"—completing the sum "8 + 8 = **16**."

Using the Doubles to Find other Sums

Organizing the study of the addition facts around the doubles (0 + 0, 1 + 1, 2 + 2, . . . , 9 + 9) serves several purposes. The doubles are recognized by children even before they begin their formal study of addition, so they come to formal instruction with a readiness for these facts. For example, many of the doubles facts can be associated with parts of your body—four fingers on each hand, five "fingers" if you count the thumb, etc.

Once pupils master the doubles, they can use these to find the sums of facts that are <u>close</u> to doubles. For example, 4 + 3, 3 + 4, 5 + 6, 6 + 5, 7 + 8, 8 + 7, 8 + 9, and 9 + 8 are <u>nearly</u> doubles. The addends are only one apart (see Figure 5.16). This means that the sum will be one number away from the sum of the double. This is

A

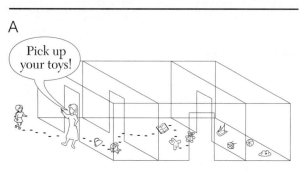

2 + 3

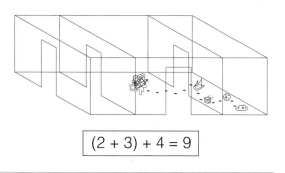

$$(2 + 3) + 4 = 9$$

B

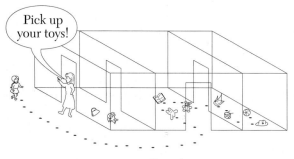

3 + 4

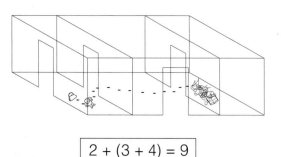

$$2 + (3 + 4) = 9$$

FIGURE 5.14

Independent Learning Activity
MAKE-A-TEN Strategy

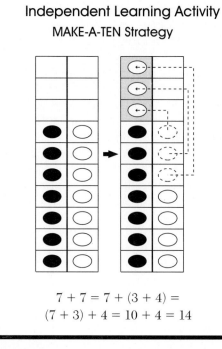

$$7 + 7 = 7 + (3 + 4) =$$
$$(7 + 3) + 4 = 10 + 4 = 14$$

FIGURE 5.15

Independent Learning Activity
Near Doubles Strategy

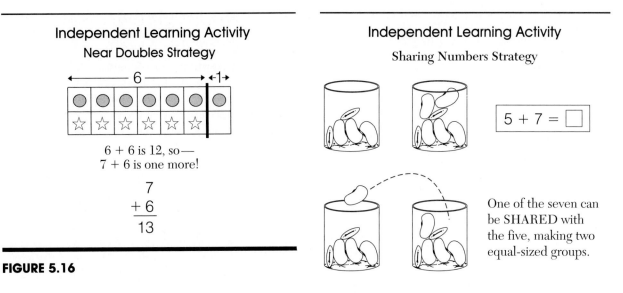

6 + 6 is 12, so—
7 + 6 is one more!

$$\begin{array}{r} 7 \\ + 6 \\ \hline 13 \end{array}$$

FIGURE 5.16

an easy concept to develop using models. Facts that are one away from the doubles are commonly called the "**near doubles**."

Another way the doubles are used to help pupils master the basic facts is through "sharing." **Sharing numbers** are two apart. If you take one away from "the big addend" and give it to "the little addend," you'll get a double. For example, if one is taken from the 8 in "8 + 6" and shared with the 6, then the fact would become 7 + 7! Let us examine a fragment of a lesson in which children learn to use "sharing" numbers.

Teacher-Guided Interactive Learning Activity

LESSON FRAGMENT

M: Strategies—sharing numbers

A: Group of first-graders

T: Modeling

H: Meaning of addition, terminology, symbolism, and doubles have been developed

Teacher: Today we are going to learn about addition facts using sharing numbers. Each **team** has been given two cups and some beans. Put your two cups for holding your lima beans on your desk. Set up your beans for working this problem . . . 5 + 7 = _____, but don't put the beans together yet. First, let's see if we can share one of the beans from the seven cup with the other cup holding five beans. How many beans will you <u>now</u> have in each cup? (SEE FIGURE 5.17.)

Children: Six.

Teacher: Do we still have the same number of beans in all that we had before we shared?

Independent Learning Activity
Sharing Numbers Strategy

$$5 + 7 = \boxed{}$$

One of the seven can be SHARED with the five, making two equal-sized groups.

$$6 + 6 = 12$$

FIGURE 5.17

Children: Yes.

Teacher: What kind of number fact is it when both addends are the same?

Children: The doubles!

Teacher: Since we know 6 and 6 is twelve, what must 5 and 7 be?

Child: Twelve.

(TEAMS ARE GIVEN SEVERAL EXAMPLES TO EXPLORE. THEY ARE TO KEEP A RECORD OF THE FACTS THEY DISCOVER THAT CAN USE THIS SHARING STRATEGY. LATER THE TEAMS LIST ON THE BOARD THE 16 FACTS WITH SHARING NUMBERS THEY HAVE DISCOVERED.)

Figure 5.18 illustrates which facts are developed as **doubles**, **near doubles**, and **sharing numbers**.

Practicing Facts for Mastery

Some basic facts may be mastered when children explore a strategy for organizing facts. For example, when introducing the sum family of six, the teacher may find that children have already memorized 6 + 0 = 6, 5 + 1 = 6, 3 + 3 = 6, 0 + 6 = 6, and 1 + 5 = 6 (the doubles, identity, and one-more facts). This would mean that only 2 + 4 = 6 and 4 + 2 = 6 are left to be mastered. With only two

+	0	1	2	3	4	5	6	7	8	9
0	0	1	2	3						
1	1	2	3	4	5					
2	2	3	4	5	6	7				
3	3	4	5	6	7	8	9			
4		5	6	7	8	9	10	11		
5			7	8	9	10	11	12	13	
6				9	10	11	12	13	14	15
7					11	12	13	14	15	16
8						13	14	15	16	17
9							15	16	17	18

■ Doubles

□ Sharing

□ Near Doubles

FIGURE 5.18

facts to learn it is a fairly simple matter to incorporate an **auditory experience** into the everyday activities to help children recall that 2 + 4 = 6 and 4 + 2 = 6. For example, small groups of children can play a game called "**Password.**" Whenever a child from a group leaves the room the "password" must be given. Some child in the group (or the teacher) is appointed the "**Fact Captain.**" As a child prepares to leave the room, the Fact Captain will ask that child, "2 + 4 equals what?" (See Figure 5.19.) The child must give the correct "password" (answer). If the child "forgets" the password he/she must ask another member of the group for the password and then repeat the password to exit from the class.

The teacher can also participate in the process by establishing a password for exiting for lunch or recess. Before children line up the teacher will REPEAT the combination. As children move up in the line they can be heard softly "repeating" the fact over and over to make sure they know the "password." When this activity is used, a group of children will have "heard" a given fact many times in a single day. Depending upon the difficulty children have recalling the fact, teachers may wish to change the "password" during the week—or even use a different password in the morning than in the afternoon.

Another interesting method of promoting mastery is to pin a different fact on each child in the class. This becomes the child's "name" for the day. Any time the teacher wishes to call upon a child that day the child's <u>fact name</u> will be used. For example, instead of saying, "Irving, would you read

the next paragraph?" the teacher would say, "6 + 4 = 10, would you read the next paragraph?" (See Figure 5.20.)

Small learning groups permit children to play matching games to practice facts. In one activity pupils use two sets of cards—one containing **sums** and the other **facts**. To play the game each child turns over two cards in his turn. If the player can "**Match Em**" the pair can be kept and the player chooses again. If the pair does not match, the next player takes a turn. The pupil with the most cards at the end wins. (This game will be "self-checking" because other players in the game make sure the match is correct. If a child doesn't "match em," he can ask another player what the sum is so next time he'll know the proper sum. In this way the child will remember the combination until it is his turn again.)

Flash cards have long been used as a device for developing speed of recall (hence the name flash cards). They do not work well, however, when the child knows only a few facts. The teacher may assemble several flash cards, but include just two or three facts that the children in a team have not mastered. The children can **team up** to practice the facts using the flash cards. Keeping the unknown facts to a small number reduces the level of frustration during the learning process. Other techniques for helping children memorize basic facts are described in Chapters 6, 7, and 8.

Small-Group Learning Activity

Password to leave the room.

Fact Captain   2+4 equals what?   6

FIGURE 5.19

Each child is given a facts name for the day.

FIGURE 5.20

5.4 DEVELOPMENT OF COMPUTATIONAL SKILLS

Concurrent with the development of the basic facts, children will learn to add numbers with two and three digits. Soon after the basic addition facts are introduced, the parallel concept of adding tens to tens (and when hundreds are introduced, adding hundreds to hundreds) is explored.

Let us examine a fragment of a lesson that uses manipulative materials to explore the concept of adding tens to tens.

Teacher-Guided Interactive Learning Activity

LESSON
FRAGMENT

M: Addition of tens to tens

A: First-graders

T: Models (toy money)

H: Children understand addition facts

Teacher: Take out your toy money and place one pile of two tens on your desk and another pile of three tens. Put the numeral "20" under your two tens and the numeral "30" under your three tens. We are going to put the three tens with the two tens and find the total number of tens. What operation

is suggested when we **put together** two sets and want to find the total number? (NOTE THE TEACHER REVIEWING THE MEANING OF ADDITION.) (SEE FIGURE 5.21.)

Children: Addition.

Teacher: Let's put a "+" sign between the two numerals to show we are adding. Now put three tens with your two tens. How many tens do you get?

Children: Five tens.

Teacher: Notice this is just like our basic fact where we add two and three and get a five. What is another name for five tens?

Children: Fifty.

Teacher: Put " = 50" down to complete the equation.

Teachers may use a developmental algorithm (see Figure 5.22) when adding tens to tens. Once a child recognizes the pattern in adding tens to tens, addition of hundreds to hundreds, thousands to thousands, or even millions to millions is easily learned.

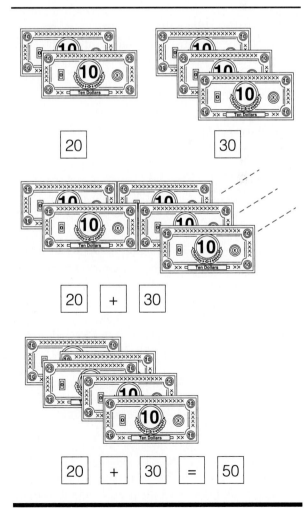

FIGURE 5.21

Using Developmental Algorithms to Introduce Addition with no Regrouping

Soon after children recognize positional value and master some of the basic addition facts (with sums less than ten), problem situations which require the addition of two 2-digit amounts (with no regrouping) will be explored. Traditionally, this occurs during the first grade. Using a developmental algorithm that emphasizes place value, the adding of 2-digit numbers strengthens the child's mastery of place value AND helps the child recognize the value of memorizing the basic combinations. There are several algorithms that can be utilized in early development. Regardless of which is used, ALL algorithms should be taught in conjunction with the use of manipulative materials. The **place-value chart** is an effective instructional tool that can be used by the teacher when introducing addition of 2-digit addends. When using the place-value chart, the teacher may call upon one child to illustrate the 2-digit amount with concrete materials— deepening that child's understanding of place value. Another child may be used to "put the ones together"—reinforcing that child's understanding of the addition operation. The lesson fragment below illustrates the use of a developmental algorithm to record the action taken on the place-value chart.

Teacher-Guided Interactive Learning Activity

LESSON FRAGMENT

M: Adding two 2-digit addends, no regrouping

A: First-grade class

T: Modeling

H: Children understand 2-digit place value and basic facts with sums to ten

PROBLEM-SOLVING SITUATION:
TO INTRODUCE ADDITION, THE TEACHER HAS ARRANGED FOR ANOTHER GROUP TO JOIN HER CLASS AT RECESS. THIS PRESENTS A SITUATION WHERE TWO 2-DIGIT AMOUNTS WILL BE ADDED AND WHERE PUPILS MAY SEE THE APPLICATION OF THE ADDITION SKILL.

Teacher: Mrs. Brown's class will be joining us on the playground today. We have 23 pupils in our class and she has 16 pupils present today. How many pupils will there be on the playground? Who has a guess?

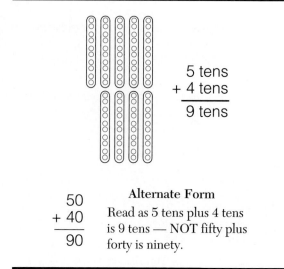

$$5 \text{ tens}$$
$$+ 4 \text{ tens}$$
$$9 \text{ tens}$$

$$50$$
$$+ 40$$
$$90$$

Alternate Form
Read as 5 tens plus 4 tens is 9 tens — NOT fifty plus forty is ninety.

FIGURE 5.22

Tommy: I'll bet that will be close to a hundred.

Mary: No—that can't be right because there are less than 30 in each class, so that would be less than sixty.

Teacher: You have some good estimates. I'll write both of those down and then let's see if we can find the exact amount using the place-value chart to help us. Tommy, can you come to the chart and use the tags to represent the number of pupils in our class? (TOMMY WAS CHOSEN BECAUSE HE COULD USE THE PRACTICE IN PLACE VALUE. HE PLACES TWO TAGS IN THE TENS COLUMN AND THREE TAGS IN THE UNITS COLUMN.) (SEE FIGURE 5.23A.)

Teacher: I'm going to write that amount on the chalkboard. Now, Mary, can you illustrate the 16 pupils in Mrs. Brown's class using the tags? (ON THE LINE BENEATH THE 23, MARY PLACES ONE TEN AND SIX ONES—FIGURE 5.23B.) I'll record the amount on the board.

Teacher: We are going to put the two groups together, so we will record a **plus** to indicate addition. Who would like to come and put our ones together? Manuel? (WHILE MANUEL PUTS THE ONES TOGETHER, THE TEACHER TURNS TO THE CLASS AND ASKS:) How many tags do you <u>think</u> Manuel will have in the ones when they are all together? (AFTER THE RESPONSE OF NINE IS GIVEN, THE TEACHER HAS MANUEL **VERIFY** THIS BY COUNTING THE TAGS. THE TEACHER RECORDS THAT AMOUNT, POINTING TO THE 3 AND THEN THE 6 SAYING) Three **plus** six is nine. (THE TEACHER WRITES THE "9."— FIGURE 5.23C.)

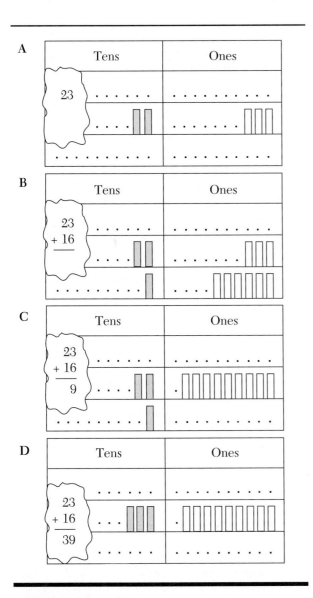

FIGURE 5.23

Teacher: Now, who can come and put the tens together? Betty? (AFTER BETTY PUTS THE TENS TOGETHER, THE TEACHER POINTS TO THE TWO TENS AND THE ONE TEN AND SAYS:) Two tens **plus** one ten is three tens. (THE TEACHER WRITES THE "3."—FIGURE 5.23D.) So if our class of 23 plays with Mrs. Brown's class of 16 there will be 39 pupils on the playground.

Introducing Addition with Regrouping

After children master addition of 1-, 2-, and 3-digit numbers in nonregrouping situations, they are ready for **regrouping**. The term "regroup" describes the process used when the sum in any column is <u>ten or more</u>. Years ago teachers called this process "carrying"—but that word does not reflect the "trading in of ten things for one of a greater value" that actually occurs when the pupil uses concrete materials. While no great harm is done when the word "carry" is used instead of "regroup," the word "carry" adds nothing to the child's <u>understanding</u> of the addition operation. Therefore, it is recommended that the teacher make a conscious effort to use **regroup** or **trade** instead of "carry" when a sum is ten or more and it "flows over" into the next column.

Regrouping traditionally is introduced in the second grade while children are mastering the basic facts with sums from 11 through 18. Pupils need a strong background in place value when first exploring regrouping. Exercises can be planned that require children to regroup bundles of sticks, pop beads, interlocking blocks, etc. Extra time should be taken to firmly demonstrate the trading of ten ones for one ten since this regrouping will be used in all operations (addition, subtraction, multiplication, and division).

Developmental algorithms generally allow the child to write the sum of each column as a 2-digit numeral, regrouping **after** all addition is completed. (In the conventional algorithm, regrouping takes place after all digits of <u>each column</u> have been added.) Figure 5.24 shows <u>several developmental</u> algorithms that lead to the conventional algorithm. Developmental algorithms require the use of manipulative materials to reinforce the meaning of the algorithm. The purpose of a developmental algorithm is to <u>build an understanding of the algorithm</u>. It is not designed to be the most efficient way of finding a sum. Teachers may lead their pupils through several developmental algorithms as they build an understanding of adding 2- and 3-digit addends. **A developmental algorithm should be abandoned when it no longer strengthens the child's understanding of the addition process.** Some pupils continue to use developmental algorithms long after the process is understood. It is the teacher's responsibility to <u>lead</u> the pupil to more efficient ways of adding by encouraging the child to abandon unneeded steps in the algorithm. (Of course, individuals occasionally return to a developmental algorithm because they have confidence in that algorithm. Many adults **still** use the "conventional algorithm with helper numeral"—when they are capable of remembering and adding the regrouped number **without** writing it down.)

Let us examine a fragment of a lesson that uses a place-value chart to introduce the child to addition with regrouping.

Developmental Algorithms

Expanded Notation Using Words

28 = 2 tens 8 ones
+ 57 = 5 tens 7 ones
      7 tens 15 ones = 8 tens 5 ones

Expanded Notation Using Numerals

28 = 20 + 8
+ 57 = 50 + 7
      70 + 15 = 70 + (10 + 5)
              = (70 + 10) + 5
              = 80 + 5 = 85

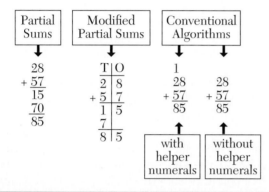

Partial Sums	Modified Partial Sums	Conventional Algorithms

Partial Sums:

28
+ 57
15
70
85

Modified Partial Sums:

T | O
2 | 8
+ 5 | 7
1 | 5
7 |
8 | 5

Conventional Algorithms:

1
28
+ 57
85

with helper numerals

28
+ 57
85

without helper numerals

FIGURE 5.24

Teacher-Guided Interactive Learning Activity

LESSON FRAGMENT

M: Addition with regrouping—conventional algorithm with helper

A: Group of second-graders

T: Model (place-value chart)

H: Basic addition facts, addition of ones to tens and ones without regrouping

PROBLEM-SOLVING SITUATION:
THE CLASS HAS BEEN MAKING A PAPER CHAIN FOR AN UPCOMING PARTY. RECOGNIZING THAT THIS WAS AN OPPORTUNITY TO INTRODUCE REGROUPING, THE TEACHER MADE SURE THAT THE AMOUNT OF LINKS MADE TODAY WOULD CREATE A NEED FOR REGROUPING.

Teacher: Today we made 28 more links for the paper chain for our party. We made 57 yesterday. So we

Children need time to think through problem-solving strategies.

are going to **put them together** or **add**. I have used tags on the place-value chart to represent the paper links. (THE TEACHER POINTS TO THE FIVE TENS AND SEVEN ONES AND ASKS) What number does this represent?

Children: Fifty-seven. (THE TEACHER WRITES 57 ON THE BOARD.)

Teacher: The second line on the place-value chart represents the chain we completed yesterday. How many does it show?

Children: Twenty-eight. (THE TEACHER WRITES "28" IN THE ALGORITHM.)

Teacher: We are going to put these together so we will write a plus to remind us to add. Remember that our rows on the place-value chart will only hold **ten tags**. If I put seven ones with eight ones will I get more than ten? (SEE FIGURE 5.25.)

Children: Yes.

Teacher: Let's have Georgio put the tags together for us. How many will we get?

Children: Fifteen.

Teacher: (GEORGIO PUTS THE ONES TOGETHER AND VERIFIES THAT THERE ARE 15.) Yes, we have 15 ones. We can see on the chart that we have filled one line and we have five left over. We can think of 15 as being ten ones and five ones so let us trade the ten ones for one ten. Georgio, take the row of ten ones out of the chart and give them to Mary. She will trade you one ten for ten ones.

Teacher: Put the regrouped ten in the tens column, Georgio, but let's put it in the top line so we won't get it mixed up with the other addends. How many ones do you have left?

Georgio: Five.

Teacher: Let me **record** what Georgio has done so far. (POINTING TO THE 7 AND THEN THE 8 THE TEACHER CONTINUES.) When we added seven and eight the sum was 15. We **kept** the five (THE TEACHER RECORDS "5" IN THE ONES COLUMN) and we traded in ten ones for . . . (POINTING TO THE REGROUPED TEN IN THE TOP LINE) . . . one ten. (THE TEACHER RECORDS A "1" AT THE TOP OF THE TENS COLUMN.)

Teacher: Now let us work with the tens. Georgio, put the regrouped ten with the five tens—that makes six tens. Now put the six tens with the two tens. That will make how much, class?

Children: Eight tens.

Teacher: Let me record what Georgio did. (POINT-ING FIRST TO THE REGROUPED TEN AND THEN THE FIVE TENS) We added our regrouped ten to the five tens, making six tens. Then (POINTING TO THE "2") we added two tens, making eight tens. (THE TEACHER RECORDS THE "8" IN THE TENS COLUMN.) Our answer is eight tens and five ones. So how many links will we have in our chain now, class?

Children: Eighty-five.

Introducing Addition of Three Addends

Adding three numbers with a sum of ten or less is generally introduced in the first grade. The emphasis is upon understanding the associative property. It is essential for a pupil to understand the associative property so that it may be used as a strategy for mastering the basic combinations. When introducing column addition care must be taken that the first two addends do not add to a sum greater than ten. (If the first two addends add to a sum greater than ten, then the child is required to utilize a different skill.) In the problem "4 + 3 + 8," the child will say "4 + 3 equals 7 and 7 + 8 is 15." In this problem, the child used only basic facts. If the problem had been 8 + 4 + 3, the child—if adding in order—would first get 12 and then would need to add 12 + 3! This combination is **not** a basic fact! It is a 1-digit number that will be added to a 2-digit number. Such combinations, when done as a mental operation, are called **decade facts** (also called "adding by endings" or "upper-decade facts").

"Basic facts" are 1-digit numbers added to 1-digit numbers. Children are expected to readily recall the sums of any two 1-digit addends. If a child cannot recall the sum and must "count," then the child has not "mastered the basic fact." (There are 100 basic facts that a child will memorize.) When adding only two addends, basic facts are generally sufficient to ensure a proper sum. When adding three numbers or more, as in column addition, however, the child may encounter combinations in which one of the addends is greater than ten while the other addend is a one-digit number. Children who do not possess "decade fact skills" generally find the sum by counting on their fingers. Some children look for other combinations in the column so they will not be required to use decade facts. For example, a child may see that the problem "7 + 8 + 3" can be solved by adding the 7 + 3 to get 10 and **then** adding the 8 (using place value). While this is a way of **compensating** for a skill not possessed, children will need decade facts in multiplication and division, so it is important that teachers help children gain this skill.

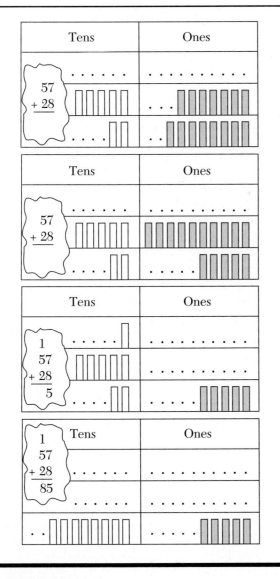

FIGURE 5.25

Decade facts are usually introduced in the second grade since pupils are beginning to work with column addition and regrouping at this time. Before a child can become skillful, he/she must recognize that the basic facts can be used to make the mastery of decade facts easier. In early explorations, the teacher will use manipulative materials to help the pupil picture the role played by the basic fact.

A variety of manipulative materials can be employed when helping a child understand the relationship between the basic combinations and the decade facts. (The terms "basic facts" and "decade facts" are terms used by the teacher to describe a technical skill—children are not expected to use this vocabulary.) A number track and interlocking blocks (Unifix Blocks®, etc.) are useful as a demonstration device. Placing a 5-bar in the number track so that it starts at the 4 will show that the bar ends at 9. When the teacher moves the bar to 14, the child notices that the bar still ends at a "9" but that this "9" is in the **teens**. As the teacher slides the bar along the track, the child recognizes that the 4-bar will **always** end at the "9"—if starting at 24 it ends at 29; at 34 it ends at 39; at 44 it ends at 49; etc. (See Figure 5.26.)

A hundred board may also be used to develop decade facts. The child begins by using a counting-on technique: for example, in "33 + 4" the child places his/her finger on 33 and counts—with the other hand—four more spaces. The child sees that

Individual Learning Activity

1	2	③	4	5	6	⑦	8	9	10
11	12	⑬	14	15	16	⑰	18	19	20
21	22	㉓	24	25	26	㉗	28	29	30
31	32	33	34	35	36	37	38	39	40
	42	43	44	45	46	47	48		

Use your hundred chart to check your answers!

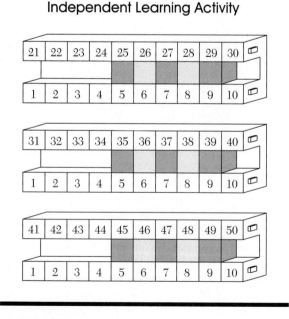

3	13	33	53	83
+4	+4	+4	+4	+4

8	28	48	58	88
+6	+6	+6	+6	+6

9	39	49	69	99
+1	+1	+1	+1	+1

FIGURE 5.27

33 + 4 = 37. The teacher can extend this understanding by having the child try 3 + 4; 13 + 4; 23 + 4; 43 + 4; 53 + 4; etc. By holding one finger on the starting point and the other hand on the ending point, the child quickly recognizes that he/she will always end up in the "7 column." A child would say, "I just slide my fingers up and down the columns. If I start with something in the 3 column and add 4—I'm gonna end up in the 7 column." Figure 5.27 illustrates an independent learning activity involving this example.

Once children recognize how basic facts and decade facts work together, opportunities must be provided for pupils to practice their newly acquired skills. When practicing, the teacher must construct the activity so the child uses basic facts rather than counting-on. Using "chain addition" in which a group tries to keep adding 1-digit amounts to an accumulated amount provides an interesting drill for youngsters. To start the chain the first student will give an amount—for instance, 23, and then suggest a 1-digit number. The next player must give the sum and then suggest a 1-digit number for the next player in the "chain." Everyone tries to keep the chain "unbroken" as they keep adding 1-digit numbers.

Independent Learning Activity

21	22	23	24	25	26	27	28	29	30
1	2	3	4	5	6	7	8	9	10

31	32	33	34	35	36	37	38	39	40
1	2	3	4	5	6	7	8	9	10

41	42	43	44	45	46	47	48	49	50
1	2	3	4	5	6	7	8	9	10

FIGURE 5.26

Calculators may also be used to reinforce decade fact skills. Two players can play "chain addition" by passing one calculator back and forth between them. After entering a 2-digit amount, the first player will then enter a "+" and a 1-digit number. The opponent must remember the 2-digit amount because only the 1-digit figure will appear on the screen. Now the second player must give the sum BEFORE pushing the "+" sign. (When the "+" is entered, the total will appear so the pupil can verify the response.) If correct, the second player now enters another 1-digit number onto the screen and passes the calculator back to the first player for his/her response.

Teaching Children to Check Addition

Children use manipulative materials to verify sums when they first explore the algorithm. As children mature in the use of the algorithm, these manipulative materials are abandoned and results are checked by **adding up the column** (commutative and associative properties) or by **estimation**. When working with more than two addends, adding up the column requires the child to use different combinations than adding down the column. Figure 5.28 illustrates how adding down the column gives the child the combinations of 9 + 4 and then 13 + 3, while when adding up the column the child will use 3 + 4 and then 7 + 9.

Another checking technique introduced in the primary grades is the use of **upper and lower boundaries**. This is an initial estimating procedure that will be refined in later use to get more accurate estimates. Upper and lower boundaries not only help children learn to estimate; they also give practice in **rounding**. In the problem in Figure 5.29, children find a lower boundary by rounding the addends <u>down</u> to the nearest ten. They find the upper boundaries by rounding <u>up</u> to the next ten. Teachers can help a child by saying "36 is

Estimating the Correctness of Sums

Lower Boundary		Upper Boundary
↓		↓
30	36	40
20	21	30
+ 40	+ 48	+ 50
90	105	120

Sum must be between 90 and 120.

FIGURE 5.29

BETWEEN 30 and 40—it is more than 30 and less than 40." Once the boundaries are written, the child adds the lower amounts to find the "lowest possible answer" and the upper boundaries to find the "highest possible answer." The SUM must be BETWEEN these two boundaries. Later, children will be rounding to the <u>nearest</u> ten (or hundred or thousand) in a refinement of this method.

Using Calculators with Larger Numbers

The calculators used in classrooms are generally the "nonprinting" variety (no tape record of entries) so no record is kept of errors made **entering** the addends. Since the calculator can **quickly** add the figures, children "re-add" to check (verify) the sum.

Pupils can learn the value of clearly enunciating amounts when placed in teams that must use calculators to add columns of figures. One team member may be selected as the "reader" while the other team members enter the amounts they hear into the calculators. Both the reader and the other team members must pay careful attention in order to enter the figures correctly. BEFORE the amount is tabulated, each team should **estimate** the sum of each example.

5.5 TEACHING ADDITION IN THE INTERMEDIATE GRADES

Intermediate-level teachers will need to assess which addition skills identified in the curriculum guide for mastery in the primary grades have not yet been attained by entering intermediate-level students. As deficiencies are found, provisions for remediating these deficiencies should be made. Students seldom need to return to a developmental

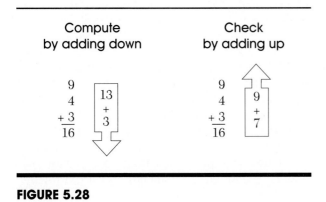

Compute by adding down		Check by adding up	
9		9	
4	13	4	9
+ 3	+ 3	+ 3	+ 7
16		16	

FIGURE 5.28

algorithm, but may benefit from examining the process used within the algorithm and **analyzing** each step in terms of the properties used. Such an activity is not designed to increase an individual's computational efficiency, but rather to serve as a review of the process, deepening the student's understanding of the addition operation and building a foundation for later work in algebra.

When examining the skills normally developed at the intermediate level, teachers should recognize that "maintaining skills" generally varies depending upon the individual pupil. Teachers should also realize that a review of addition skills will also occur when adding fractions and decimals. The following is a typical scope and sequence of topics developed at the intermediate level.

Grade 4

Maintain and recall addition facts
Use addition to check subtraction
Solve problems involving addition using
  - paper-and-pencil
  - calculator
  - computer
Compute
  - with 2- through 4-digit addends
  - columns with three and four addends
Check using
  - rounding to estimate sums
  - adding up column

Grade 5

Solve multistep problems involving addition
  - paper-and-pencil
  - calculator
  - computer
Compute using
  - 2- through 5-digit addends
  - columns with 4 and 5 addends
Check using
  - estimation
  - casting out nines

Grade 6

Solve multistep problems involving addition using
  - paper-and-pencil
  - calculator
  - computer spreadsheets
Compute
  - with 2- through 6-digit addends
  - column addition

Check using
  - estimation
  - casting out nines

Grades 7 and 8

Maintain addition skills
Use of computer spreadsheets with tabular data

5.6 MAINTENANCE OF ADDITION SKILLS

Though most students enter the intermediate grade level understanding the addition operation, not all have mastered their basic addition facts. In truth, many have become "fast counters." They have not memorized their facts—they simply count quickly to find the sum. While this counting will give pupils a sum, it is not very efficient. Students find it difficult to estimate when they do not know the basic addition facts. Therefore, the intermediate teacher must develop individual programs to aid those individuals who are deficient in this skill.

Intermediate-level pupils are introduced to an additional strategy used to organize the study of basic facts. While exploring this new strategy students will not only work to master specific addition combinations, but they will also explore the addition operation and discover a generalization. The **odd/even generalization** is an interesting exploration since students discover what happens when even and odd numbers are added—and may apply this information to numbers greater than the basic facts.

There are many different materials that can be used by pupils to explore this topic. **Structured regions** are particularly effective since they allow the pupils to visualize the process and see how the generalization can apply to ALL odd and even numbers. Such an exploration with the addition operation also builds a firm foundation for later explorations with the other operations (subtraction, multiplication, and division). In using structured regions, even numbers are pictured as 2-by-n arrays (see Figure 5.30) and odd numbers in a similar pattern but with the odd region "hanging over." By moving the regions around, students see that even amounts ALWAYS will stay "smooth" on the end. An odd region and an even region (or even and odd) will ALWAYS have a "piece hanging over." Students will then find when they move two odd regions around, the pieces that "hang over" will match up and make a "smooth" (even) number.

Calculator Explorations

Calculators may also be used to explore the odd/even generalization. Students can discover the odd/even generalization as they work with basic facts, but the calculator will allow them to try out large numbers to verify the generalization. Figure 5.31 illustrates how a student might use a calculator to explore odd and even numbers.

Students need encouragement to memorize the facts instead of "counting on." The calculator is again a good tool to help students see the value of knowing the combinations. A "race" may be arranged between a student **with** a calculator and a student without a calculator. If the teacher displays a basic addition flash card to the two "competitors" (with the stipulation that the student with the calculator MUST use the calculator), the student **without** the calculator should be faster in calling out the sum than the student with the calculator. Students are challenged by the fact that they CAN recall a fact faster than their opponent can get the result with a machine.

There are also many mechanical and electronic "practice devices" that allow an individual student to become more proficient with the basic facts. These devices usually pit the pupil against the machine and are, in that respect, motivating for many. **Computer programs** can present facts in a game format that students find very interesting. Indeed, many pupils who do not need the practice can be found in front of the computer—playing the game. An interesting feature of some programs is the record-keeping function that provides the teacher with a record of the problems missed by each pupil.

Reviewing the Arithmetic Algorithm

Students who enter the intermediate grades can add multidigit addends, but the skill is perfected at this level. When reviewing multidigit addition, teachers will still use manipulative materials to **demonstrate** the process of adding in the addition algorithm, but it is not essential for every student to use these materials. The manner in which the material is used should **require** the student to look at each action with the material as it relates to the algorithm.

Base ten blocks—since they help the pupil visualize the structure of the base ten numeration system—are a commonly used material used to illustrate regrouping. By placing ten unit blocks beside a rod, pupils can see that ten units can be traded for one ten. Pupils can also see that ten rods (ten tens) will fit atop one flat (hundred) and that ten

---

Independent Learning Activity
Structured Regions

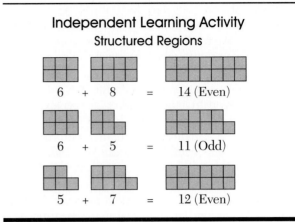

6 + 8 = 14 (Even)

6 + 5 = 11 (Odd)

5 + 7 = 12 (Even)

FIGURE 5.30

Independent Learning Activity

Learning Station

Use the calculators at this LEARNING STATION to find the sum of each pair of numbers. CHECK whether the sum is ODD or EVEN.

	Answer	Odd	Even
7 + 5	_____	☐	✔
8 + 6	_____	☐	☐
3 + 4	_____	☐	☐

After you finish the exercise above — pick a pair of ODD numbers less than 1000. BEFORE you enter the numbers into the calculator, ESTIMATE whether the sum will be ODD or EVEN. Then use the calculator to check estimate.

FIGURE 5.31

flats (ten hundreds) may be traded for one cube (thousand). (See Figure 5.32.) Activities in which the blocks are used to demonstrate regrouping may continue as the materials are used to illustrate addition of 3- and 4-digit amounts.

The 20-bead computing **abacus** is another useful device for developing addition at this level. The teacher can hold the abacus and write on the chalkboard while maintaining eye contact with the class. Clothespins are used to separate the addends on the abacus. As the beads are combined, the clothespins are removed.

The following lesson fragment uses the 20-bead abacus to explore addition of hundreds, tens, and ones with regrouping.

Teacher-Guided Interactive Learning Activity

LESSON FRAGMENT

M: Addition of 3-digit addends with regrouping

A: Fourth-grade group

T: Modeling (The teacher uses a 20-bead abacus)

H: Addition of tens to tens, and ones to tens, and ones, with regrouping

PROBLEM-SOLVING SITUATION:
A LOCAL GROCERY CHAIN HAS A PROJECT TO GIVE SCHOOLS COMPUTERS IF THEY COLLECT RECEIPTS FROM PURCHASES MADE AT THEIR STORE. THE CLASS STARTED BRINGING IN RECEIPTS AND THE TEACHER IS GOING TO USE THIS SITUATION TO REINFORCE ADDITION WITH REGROUPING SKILLS.

Teacher: We had 385 dollars worth of receipts and now Gertrude brought in 267 dollars' worth that her mother totaled for us. About how much do you think this will make us?

Gertrude: It will be more than 500 dollars and less than 700 dollars.

Gus: I think it will be close to 650.

Teacher: Good estimates—I'll write them on the board. To help us find the sum, I have set up my 20-bead abacus to show the problem on the board. I've used clothespins to separate the addends. (FIGURE 5.33A.)

Teacher: First we will add our ones. I will remove the pin to put the ones together. How many ones do we have? (FIGURE 5.33B.)

Students: Twelve.

Teacher: Since we have more than ten we will need

Regrouping using base ten blocks

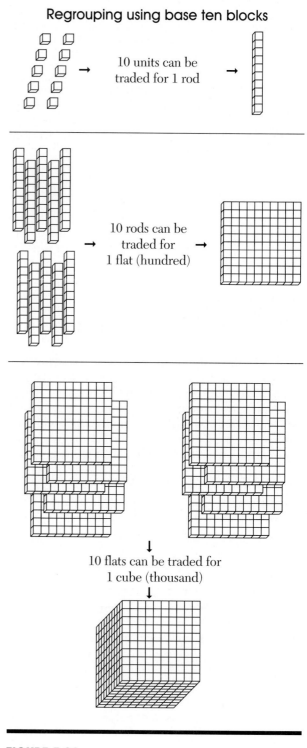

10 units can be traded for 1 rod

10 rods can be traded for 1 flat (hundred)

10 flats can be traded for 1 cube (thousand)

FIGURE 5.32

to trade ten ones in . . . (TEACHER FLIPS TEN ONES OVER TO THE BACK) . . . for one ten. (TEACHER BRINGS ONE TEN OVER FROM THE BACK AND SEPARATES THIS FROM THE OTHER TWO ADDENDS WITH A PIN.) Let's record that on the chalkboard. (TEACHER POINTS TO THE 5 AND THEN THE 7, SAYING)—we added 5 and 7 to get 12. We <u>kept</u> the 2 (TEACHER RECORDS "2" IN THE ONES COLUMN) and traded ten ones for one ten. (TEACHER RECORDS "REMINDER NUMERAL" AT TOP OF TENS COLUMN—FIGURE 5.33C.)

Teacher: Now what will we do, class?

Students: Add the tens.

Teacher: Fine. We'll start by adding the regrouped ten (REMOVING THE PIN BETWEEN THE 1 AND 8) to the eight tens, making nine tens. Now we add the six tens (REMOVING THE PIN BETWEEN THE 9 AND 6) to make 15 tens. Again we need to regroup, this time to the hundreds column. If we regroup ten tens for one hundred, how many tens will be left, Marty? (FIGURE 5.34A.)

Marty: You'll have five tens because you took 10 from the 15.

Teacher: (AFTER MOVING TEN TENS TO THE BACK OF THE ABACUS AND BRINGING ONE HUNDRED OVER TO THE FRONT, THE TEACHER CONTINUES) I'll record what happened. (POINTING TO THE REGROUPED "1" AND THEN THE "8") . . . We added 1 and 8 to make 9 and then 6 more made 15. We kept the 5 (TEACHER RECORDS "5" IN THE TENS COLUMN) and regrouped ten tens for one hundred. (TEACHER RECORDS THE "REMINDER NUMERAL "1" IN THE HUNDREDS.) Now what will we do, Cliff? (FIGURE 5.34B.)

Cliff: We need to add the hundreds.

Teacher: Very good—let's do that. We'll put the regrouped hundred with the three hundreds. Those four will go with the two hundreds to make six hundreds. (TEACHER PULLS PINS WHILE TALKING.) I'll record that on the algorithm—adding the hundreds, I have one plus three is four and four plus two is six. (TEACHER RECORDS "6" AT BOTTOM OF HUNDREDS COLUMN.) (FIGURE 5.34C.) It looks like the sum is very close to the estimate that Gus gave us!

Teacher: I have some more tapes that a friend has given me. I'm going to give each group a few tapes to total for us. Each group will work together to VERIFY that each sum is correct. Now send your group leader to pick up your tapes.

While many addition skills are maintained in the intermediate grades by systematically providing problems that require addition with whole numbers, addition skills will also receive extensive use as the student explores the multiplication algorithm, adds rational numbers (common fractions and decimals), etc. Figure 5.35 illustrates a variety

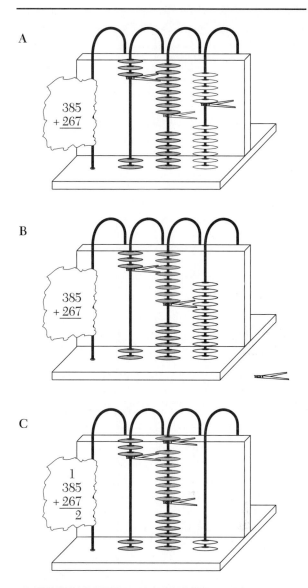

FIGURE 5.33

of intermediate-grade situations in which addition skills are utilized.

Refining Skills in Adding Columns of Figures

While students do not have to attain the skill level of precomputer and precalculator days, they <u>still</u> must develop a <u>reasonable proficiency</u> in adding columns of figures. When reviewing column addition, the teacher may wish to involve other aspects that broaden student skills. Students should explore alternate ways of grouping within the algorithm, estimating, and checking—in the context of column addition.

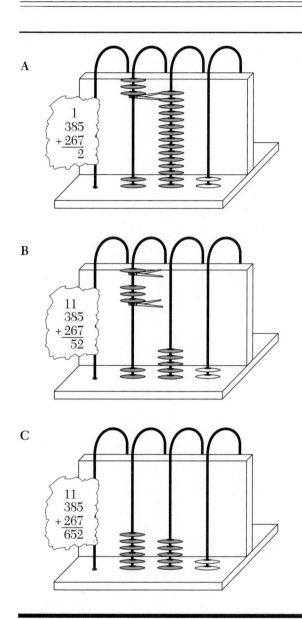

A

$$\begin{array}{r} 1 \\ 385 \\ +267 \\ \hline 2 \end{array}$$

B

$$\begin{array}{r} 11 \\ 385 \\ +267 \\ \hline 52 \end{array}$$

C

$$\begin{array}{r} 11 \\ 385 \\ +267 \\ \hline 652 \end{array}$$

FIGURE 5.34

While the most efficient way of adding a column of figures is to add systematically down the column, students may look for ways to group addends in a column to make the combinations easier to handle. This is especially true for the student who has not mastered the decade facts and therefore cannot add 17 + 6 without counting-on. This student may "look for tens" within the column and then come back to pick up the "leftover" numbers. In Figure 5.36 a student worked problem "A" by putting the 2 and 8 together to make 10 and then found a 6 and 4 to make another ten. This left 9 to be put with the two tens—29. In this case the student was able to use place value and simple combinations to avoid the use of the decade facts. When adding

Addition Maintenance

Addition involving decimals	Addition involving multiplication algorithm

$$\begin{array}{r} 3.46 \\ 7.67 \\ 8.99 \\ 3.55 \\ + 3.67 \\ \hline 27.34 \end{array}$$

$$\begin{array}{r} 34 \\ \times 78 \\ \hline 272 \\ 238 \\ \hline 2652 \end{array}$$

Addition of positive rational numbers

$$\frac{35}{100} + \frac{27}{100} = \frac{62}{100}$$

Addition of integers

$$^{-}13 + {}^{-}62 = {}^{-}75$$

FIGURE 5.35

problem "B," the student used multiplication (3 × 7 = 21) and then grouped the 9 to make 30. Now all the student had to do was add the leftover "8" to make 38.

Students must be cautioned that when one skips around in a column a number MAY inadvertently be omitted, resulting in an incorrect sum. The importance of checking must be emphasized. The traditional check—add back up the column—is not very effective when one "groups within a column" since the same combinations will be used. Teachers may, at this time, wish to introduce an alternate checking technique called **cast-out nines** (sometimes called the "excess-of-nines" check). This technique will not catch all of the errors made in addition, but it is a quick check that

Developing Number Sense

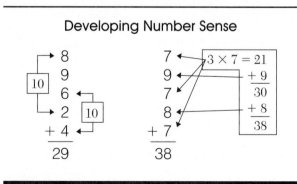

FIGURE 5.36

Cast-out nines check for addition

$$842 \rightarrow 8+4+2 \rightarrow \quad 14 \rightarrow 5$$
$$635 \rightarrow 6+3+5 \rightarrow 0+5 \rightarrow 5$$
$$423 \rightarrow 4+2+3 \rightarrow \quad 9 \rightarrow 0$$
$$+168 \rightarrow 1+6+8 \rightarrow 6+0 \rightarrow 6$$

$$2068 \qquad\qquad\qquad 16 \rightarrow 1+6 \rightarrow 7$$
$$2+0+6+8 \rightarrow 16 \rightarrow 1+6 \rightarrow 7$$

Same — answer probably right

FIGURE 5.37

students seem to enjoy. In checking addition, the cast-out nines technique may not save a great deal of time. However, since all sums are simplified to single digits, students find it easier. (The cast-out nines check is also used in multiplication and division.)

Figure 5.37 illustrates the use of the cast-out nines check in a column addition problem. To "cast out the nines," one adds the digits ACROSS the numeral. If the sum is 2-digit, these are added until a single digit is reached. In "842," $8 + 4 + 2 = 14$, so now the 1 and 4 are added to get "5." In "635" a shortcut can be taken. Since $6 + 3 = 9$, the nine can be "cast out," leaving zero. Now zero and 5 are added together to make 5. (If all digits are added—$6 + 3 + 5$—then the sum would be 14, which would equal 5 when the nines are cast out.) When all addends have been reduced to a single digit, these digits are added together (and reduced to a single digit by casting out nines). This "sum" MUST be the same as the cast-out-nine digit of the original sum. If the two digits differ— then the answer is incorrect. If the digits are the same—the answer is **probably** correct. (Note: Cast-out nines compares the **remainders** after a number is divided by nine. It does not compare the quotients. The check cannot distinguish between numbers such as 345 and 543 since they both add to the same single digit.)

Refining Column Addition Skills in Multistep Problems

In the intermediate grades students solve problems that involve more than one step. Many of those multistep problems are found in situations that require column addition—student book orders, inventories for the school store, schoolwide col-

lections of promotional labels for playground equipment, etc.

To help students understand how to tackle these multistep problems, the teacher may guide them through the problem with a series of questions. These questions break the problem down into manageable parts and help the students develop another **problem-solving strategy**.

Column addition is often required in real-life situations, but seldom is an adult required to add long columns of figures without the use of an adding machine or calculator. Students need to be taught to use these computational tools efficiently once they understand column addition. After students have learned the fundamentals of computation, calculators can be employed routinely to do these types of computations.

The following lesson fragment examines alternate paths students use to solve problems. Some of these paths will require repeated use of addition.

Teacher-Guided Interactive Learning Activity

LESSON FRAGMENT

M: Multistep problem solving

A: Group of fifth-grade students

T: Tables, calculators

H: Students are able to work single-operation type problems

PROBLEM-SOLVING SITUATION:
THE FIFTH AND SIXTH GRADES HAVE BEEN COLLECTING ALUMINUM CANS FOR RECYCLING. EACH DAY THE CANS ARE COUNTED FOR EACH CLASS AND RECORDED IN A TABLE. THE TEACHER IS GOING TO USE THIS TABLE TO PRESENT A PROBLEM TO THE CLASS.

Teacher: Each day we have <u>recorded</u> the number of cans collected in a table. Our table shows us how many cans were collected each day by each class, during the first week. Let's use our calculators and find out how many cans were collected in all. I'm going to let you work in your groups, but I'll be asking for a report from each group. (SEVERAL STUDENTS ARE ASKED TO PUT THEIR SOLUTIONS ON THE BOARD. THE FOLLOWING ARE THE TEACHER'S COMMENTS ON EACH SOLUTION. NOTICE THE ACCEPTANCE OF DIFFERENT PATHS TO THE SOLUTION AND THE ANALYSIS OF THE EFFICIENCY OF EACH METHOD.)

Teacher: Let's look at Cheryl's approach. She added

across each line. This would be an efficient way to find our answer when we also want to know which day the most cans were collected. (SEE FIGURE 5.38.)

Teacher: Zack added **down** each column. This would be an efficient way to find our answer when we want to find out which class brought in the most cans.

Teacher: Joy used her calculator to find the total of cans collected. This is the most efficient way to solve the problem when you only want to find out the **total number.** Joy, I noticed you were one of the last people to finish; did you have trouble getting the answer by your method?

Joy: I kept forgetting where I was and had to start over. I had to add it three times before I got the same answer twice.

Teacher: Sue, you have an interesting way to work the problem. Why did you work it that way?

Sue: My mother is an accountant and she told me she adds across and down, so she has a way of checking if she made a mistake. If her final two totals are the same, she knows that is the correct answer.

Calculator Explorations

The problem-solving activity illustrated in Figure 5.39 represents an independent learning activity, but it could just as easily be structured for a small-group learning activity. In structuring the activity as a small-group learning activity, the teacher would wish to add factors to increase the complexity of the problem and hence increase the development of communication skills. For example, "What other factors might Mrs. Kim wish to consider, besides population, in establishing the location for her business?"

5.7 EXPLORING THE PROPERTIES AND PATTERNS OF ADDITION

In the primary grades, children used the identity, commutative, and associative properties while exploring the basic addition facts. In the intermediate grades teachers should reexplore these properties with a goal of deepening the child's understanding and appreciation of the properties. Students at this level may formally name properties and explore their use in **prealgebra** (analytical) settings. Such a development strengthens the student's understanding of the computational process and prepares the pupil for later application in algebraic proofs.

Multi-step Multi-path Problem Solving

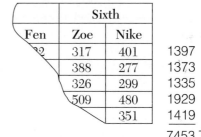

	Fifth		Sixth	
	Dil	Fen	Zoe	Nike
Mon	357	322	317	401
Tue	297	411	388	277
Wed	399	311	326	299
Th	460	480	509	480
Fri	363	342	363	351

Cheryl's path to the goal

	Sixth		
Fen	Zoe	Nike	
22	317	401	1397
	388	277	1373
	326	299	1335
	509	480	1929
		351	1419
			7453 Total

Zack's path to the goal

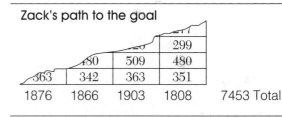

299
480
509 480
80 509 363 351
363 342 363 351
1876 1866 1903 1808   7453 Total

Joy's path to the goal

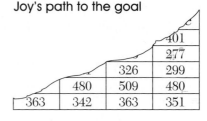

401
277
326 299
480 509 480
363 342 363 351

7453 Total

Sue's path to the goal

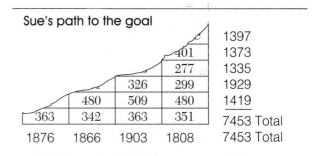

401   1397
277   1373
326 299   1335
480 509 480 1929
363 342 363 351 1419
                 7453 Total
1876 1866 1903 1808 7453 Total

FIGURE 5.38

Using Calculators to Explore Properties

A teacher may employ calculators to explore the properties of addition. Students may enter different numbers into their calculators, trying to **invalidate** a generalization. This approach is limited by the number of digits that can be represented by a sum on the calculator. (While this approach will not validate the generalization, it will convey a strong impression to the student of the truth of the generalization.)

Exploring the identity property requires a different strategy than that used for the commutative and associative properties. A series of single equation explorations (using the calculator) will suggest to students the generalization that "$n + 0 = n$." For example, after different students use calculators and their "favorite number" in the equations $\Delta + 0 = ?$, have them share equations along with numbers such as $46,679,254 + 0 = 46,679,254$ and $888,777,666 + 0 = 888,777,666$. The teacher may then help students generalize: "For all n, $n + 0 = n$."

The commutative and associative properties may require pairs of equations. Let us examine a fragment of a lesson that uses pairs of equations and **calculators** to develop the commutative property.

Teacher-Guided Interactive Learning Activity

LESSON FRAGMENT

M: Formal exploration of commutative property

A: Fourth grade

T: Calculators, tables

H: Students have had exploratory activities with commutative property in the primary grades

Teacher: Today we are going to add pairs of numbers with our calculators. I am going to let each of you pick the pair of numbers you wish to add. We'll call one of your numbers "N" and the other number "M." When I call on you, I am going to ask first for your "N" number and then your "M" number. I will then record it in our chart. (EACH STUDENT IS ASKED FOR THEIR "N" NUMBER AND THEIR "M" NUMBER AND THESE ARE RECORDED IN THE CHART.) (SEE FIGURE 5.40.) (UNCOVERING THE RIGHT SIDE OF THE TABLE, THE TEACHER ASKS EACH STUDENT TO IDENTIFY THE SUM THAT GOES WITH THEIR PAIR OF NUMBERS, AND THE SUMS ARE RECORDED IN THE TABLE. THE TEACHER THEN UNCOVERS ANOTHER PART OF THE TABLE AND ASKS THE STUDENTS TO FIND THE SUM

WHEN N IS ADDED TO M. THESE SUMS ARE RECORDED.)

Teacher: What do we notice when we get the sum of "N" and "M" and the sum of "M" and "N"?

Students: We get the same sum.

Teacher: This is called the commutative property, and we say for all numbers n and m that $N + M = M + N$.

Independent Learning Activity

Using Calculators in Problem-Solving Activities

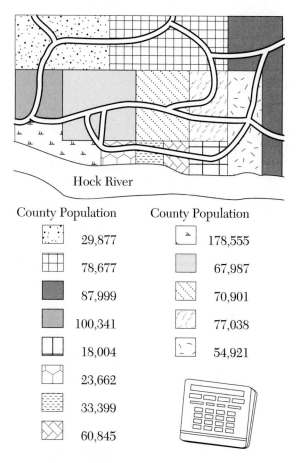

Hock River

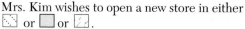

County Population		County Population	
	29,877		178,555
	78,677		67,987
	87,999		70,901
	100,341		77,038
	18,004		54,921
	23,662		
	33,399		
	60,845		

Mrs. Kim wishes to open a new store in either ⬚ or ⬚ or ⬚.

She will make her decision based on the following: She will put up her store in the county that has the greatest combined population of that county and the adjacent counties serviced by a road directly into that county.

Which county should she choose? Use your calculators to work the problem. Record your work.

FIGURE 5.39

Calculator Explorations

n	m
23,459	47,155
387	4100
71,888	6
5228	2162

n	m	n + m
23,459	47,155	70,614
387	4100	4487
71,888	6	71,894
5228	2162	7390

n	m	n + m	m + n
23,459	47,155	70,614	70,614
387	4100	4487	4487
71,888	6	71,894	71,894
5228	2162	7390	7390

FIGURE 5.40

The associative property may be similarly developed by a series of paired activities resulting in the generalization that for all numbers N, M, and T that $(N + M) + T = N + (M + T)$. To explore the grouping without altering the order of the addends, the left side of the equation may be entered directly, since the calculator will add N and M first—showing the sum before adding M. However, to show $N + (M + T)$ students may need to use the "memory capacity" of the calculator. To maintain the order of the addends, students may enter "N" into the memory (M+) and clear the display. Then the student might enter M + T and find the sum. Once the sum is displayed, that amount may be added to N by pressing "M+". This will add the sum to the number in the memory. By pressing the RM (Recall Memory), the sum of the three numbers will then be displayed.

Student understanding of these properties is maintained at the intermediate level by the use of checking procedures for the addition algorithm (add up), and by examining their use in different number systems (integers, rationals, etc.). By the time students begin working with algebraic proof these properties will be very familiar. Figure 5.41 illustrates some questions that are answered by intermediate-grade students as they explore why various processes and procedures work as they do.

Many of the step-by-step analytical processes explored in the intermediate grades establish a readiness for later mathematical proofs. There are some pupils who are not yet ready for this kind of mathematical thought. For those students, it may be necessary to delay this form of exploration until they are more mature. Figure 5.42 shows a step-by-step analysis with whole numbers and its corresponding counterpart in algebra.

5.8 COMPUTERS

In business and industry, routine addition of long columns of numerical data is generally handled by computer programs (or by using a calculator). One user-friendly computer program used to handle this task goes under the generic name of "spreadsheet." Software such as Lotus 1-2-3™, Excel™, Appleworks™, and MicroSoft Works™ are some of the more commonly used spreadsheets. Elementary teachers will find these spreadsheet programs useful in collecting, organizing, and computing data for pupil records.

In addition to their administrative functions, spreadsheet programs can also be used to create interesting and realistic addition problems for stu-

What PROPERTY is being used?

```
   Add
   3 ↓        3 ↑
   5 ↓        5 ↑
 + 7 ↓      + 7 ↑
  _____    _____
             Check
```

$$
\begin{array}{c}
48 \\
+ \ 2569
\end{array}
\rightarrow
\begin{array}{c}
2569 \\
+ \ \ 48
\end{array}
$$

$$34 + 5 = (30 + 4) + 5 =$$
$$30 + (4 + 5) = 30 + 9 =$$
$$39$$

FIGURE 5.41

Addition Analysis

$$34 + 21 = \text{(Rename)}$$

$$
\begin{aligned}
(30 + 4) + (20 + 1) &= \text{(Associative Property)}\\
30 + (4 + 20) + 1 &= \text{(Commutative Property)}\\
30 + (20 + 4) + 1 &= \text{(Associative Property)}\\
(30 + 20) + (4 + 1) &= \text{(Addition)}\\
50 + 5 &= \text{(Addition)}\\
55
\end{aligned}
$$

Algebraic Parallel

Prove:

$$(n + m) + (r + s) = (n + r) + (m + s)$$

$$
\begin{aligned}
(n + m) + (r + s)\\
n + (m + r) + s &= \text{(Associative Property)}\\
n + (r + m) + s &= \text{(Commutative Property)}\\
(n + r) + (m + s) &= \text{(Associative Property)}
\end{aligned}
$$

FIGURE 5.42

dents. The only skills an elementary student needs to know to use these spreadsheet programs for addition activities is how to record each number in its individual box (cell) and how to tell the computer to find the sum of the numbers in the boxes. Figures 5.43 and 5.44 explain some of the concepts a teacher would find valuable when using spreadsheets with students or for managing student records.

5.9 EVALUATION AND INTERVENTION

Evaluation, diagnoses, and remediation are on-going processes. They begin as soon as the student enters formal instruction in mathematics. The assessment process begins when concepts are introduced as a means of determining if the instruction has been effective and whether more emphasis needs to be placed on conceptual development. In Chapter 2 **general principles** were presented that guide teachers when evaluating children, instruction, and the curriculum. This section will look at specific and/or unique problems that occur in the teaching of addition.

Too often only a pupil's ability to calculate a correct sum is assessed. Evaluation of the understanding that undergirds that process is often neglected. To assess student understanding the teacher will normally provide manipulative materials so the pupil can demonstrate the concept or

General Information On Spreadsheets

Spreadsheets are organized by CELLS, which are designated by coordinates. For example, the shaded cell identified as B2.

Within a cell you can write words, formulas, or numerical data. For numerical data, you may specify HOW you wish the data to appear—for example: money notation, decimal notation, percent, etc.

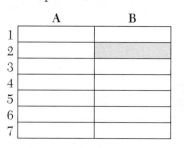

FIGURE 5.43

process. For instance, the teacher may ask a student to use <u>bean sticks</u> to work the problem 38 + 26. When the student trades in ten of the 14 ones for a ten stick, the teacher can determine how well that student understands the regrouping process.

There are some skills that teachers can anticipate as areas that will be difficult for students. Students typically have trouble memorizing the basic combinations; regrouping; working with decade facts; and dealing with column addition with ragged columns. As concepts, these take more instructional time and occur more often as errors when assessing pupil strengths and weaknesses.

Teachers must recognize that students will misunderstand—even when good teaching has taken place. Students can "understand" how to regroup immediately following an instructional lesson and then "forget" a few days later. Students will be at different levels of readiness. Some students in the class readily understand regrouping—on the first presentation. Others will need to see the same idea expressed <u>many times</u>, perhaps with different materials. Therefore, the teacher must carefully examine pupil work to determine if a return to manipulative materials is required.

Evaluating a student's ability to solve problems takes place in a variety of settings. Observations of

Computer Spreadsheets

After recording data in each cell, tell the computer what to do with the data. Example: When you request a function for a sum (along with the range in which the addends are to be found), the computer will enter the sum in the cell where the function was originally placed.

	A	B
1	2999	
2	34666	
3	984	
4	35100	
5	98211	
6	76777	
7		

By typing SUM (A1:A6)

and then striking the RETURN key, the computer—

—is told to put the SUM of the addends A1 through A6—

	A	B
1	2999	
2	34666	
3	984	
4	35100	
5	98211	
6	76777	
7		Sum (A1:A6)

	A	B
1	2999	
2	34666	
3	984	
4	35100	
5	98211	
6	76777	
7		248737

—into the CELL that is called B7.

FIGURE 5.44

small groups interacting can reveal students with particularly creative approaches to solving problems that would require addition. Observations also reveal students who resort to ineffective or improper procedures and students who have worked (or failed to work) problems involving several steps. Personal interviews with students can provide insight into the strategies being used, as well as identifying how well the child uses estimation in the problem-solving process.

5.10 MEETING SPECIAL NEEDS

The teacher will have many ways of extending addition concepts for both the gifted students and students who quickly achieve the core objectives. Two

kinds of activities are particularly effective in extending student understanding of addition concepts: explorations with nonconventional addition algorithms in base ten and activities that encourage pupils to create their own computational algorithm for addition. This section will examine only nonconventional algorithms.

Explorations for the Gifted and Students with Strong Foundation Skills

Sometimes in order to truly appreciate the manmade nature of the various computational algorithms, it is helpful to examine, if only briefly, computational schemes that can be created by varying the basic rules. For example, instead of adding columns from right to left, would it be possible to compute from left to right? If we did, what "new" rules would we have to invent? Figure 5.45 illustrates one way rules **could be** structured for a left-to-right addition algorithm. Can you think of other ways?

Explorations with only slight variations of the standard algorithm may be sufficient to promote a better understanding of the addition algorithm. For example, if we were to use a right-to-left algorithm where partial sums are recorded similar to Figure 5.45, but in a right-to-left manner, the nature of the abstract regrouping process is better highlighted than in the process of simply recording the "regrouped" number at the top of the column away from the other part of the sum obtained by adding the column. For example, in Figure 5.46 the partial sums algorithm is contrasted with the develop-

Gifted Student Explorations of Non-standard Algorithm

Can you find a way to add this column of figures starting on the right instead of the left?

$$
\begin{array}{r}
678 \\
544 \\
875 \\
+\ 552 \\
\hline
\end{array}
$$

Procedure identified by one student.

1. Add left to right.
2. Find partial sums.
3. Keep re-adding until there is a single digit in each column.
4. Write down the standard numeral.

$$
\begin{array}{r}
24 \\
23 \\
19 \\
2 \\
6 \\
4 \\
9 \\
\hline
2649
\end{array}
$$

FIGURE 5.45

mental addition algorithm that records the "regrouped" number at the top of the column.

Explorations with nonconventional algorithms are not intended for mastery. Their primary function is to provide the student with a greater understanding of the nature of addition. It is possible, however, that some students **may** find a given algorithm interesting enough to continue to use in recreational activities.

Providing for the Learning-Disabled Child

The teacher of the learning-disabled student can choose from a variety of algorithms that develop the student's understanding of addition computational algorithms, before this student begins full-scale use of a calculator. The two algorithms that follow represent two extremes of learning disability. Both algorithms are **"low stress"** algorithms in that they allow the student to record intermediate steps. Writing these intermediate steps relieves the student of the task of "remembering" partial sums (an especially difficult task for a student with a short-term memory deficit). The first algorithm is normally used with a student who has difficulty counting beyond ten, but has some mastery of place value and understands numbers less than 100. The second algorithm is more appropriate for the student who has mastered the basic facts and understands regrouping but has not learned to use the higher decade facts.

The algorithm for the more disabled student could be called the "**counting addition algorithm**." Figures 5.47 through 5.49 show how the student uses the "counting addition algorithm."

The second algorithm is used with the slightly disabled student. This algorithm could be called a **"basic facts addition algorithm."** This algorithm permits the development of column addition for those learning-disabled students who cannot use the higher decade facts (which are required as a prerequisite for mastery of column addition using the conventional algorithm). In the "basic facts addition algorithm" the student records each fact while adding down the column, writing the ones to the right of the ones column and recording the tens to the left of the ones column when a fact of ten or greater is obtained. (In each succeeding column a

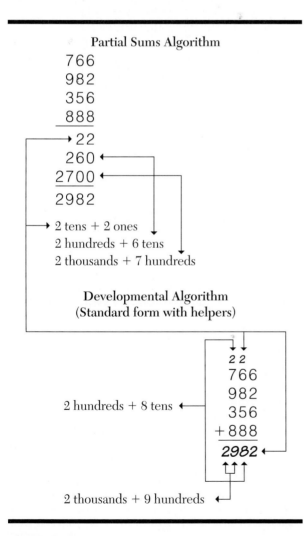

FIGURE 5.46

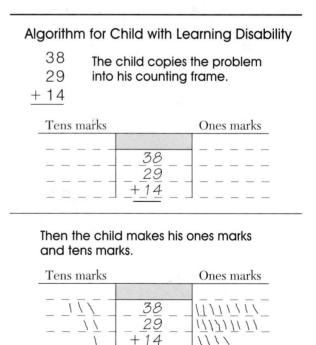

FIGURE 5.47

The child then proceeds to count and mark off the ones marks. When he gets to ten, he draws a *ring* around them and starts counting to ten again. Every ten counted gets a *ring*. When the child can no longer get a group of ten, he counts the *rings* and makes a tally for each group of ten—in the tens column. The child counts the number of ones *left over* and records this amount in the ones column. Once the ones are recorded, the child counts and marks the tens—recording the amount in the tens column.

Tens marks		Ones marks
_ \ \ \	38	\\\\\\\\
_ \ \	29	\\\\\\\\\\
_ \	+14	\\\\\

Tens marks		Ones marks
_ \ \ \	38	(\\\\\\\\)
_ \ \	29	(\\\\\\\\\\)
_ \	+14	\\\\\

FIGURE 5.48

similar process is used.) Figure 5.50 illustrates the thought process that a student goes through in using this algorithm.

A modified algorithm form of this algorithm is illustrated in Figure 5.51. This algorithm (sometimes called **"scratch addition"**) speeds up the column addition of the basic facts algorithm by

Tens marks		Ones marks
_ \ \		
_ \ \ \	38	(\\\\\\\\)
_ \ \	29	(\\\\\\\\\\)
_ \	+14	\\\\\
	1	

Tens marks		Ones marks
_ ⅄ ⅄		
_ ⅄ ⅄ ⅄	38	(\\\\\\\\)
_ ⅄ ⅄	29	(\\\\\\\\\\)
_ ⅄	+14	\\\\\
	81	

This algorithm may be used by the learning disabled pupils when a calculator is not available.

FIGURE 5.49

Pre-calculator algorithm for learning-disabled child.

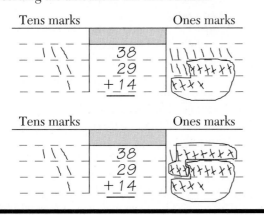

Child's Thinking Process for "Basic Facts Addition Algorithm"

"Nine and eight is seventeen." (She records '1' on the tens and '7' on the ones side.

Looking only at the ones side she says, "Seven and nine is sixteen." (She records the '1' on the tens side and a '6' on the ones side. She then copies the '6' in the sum.)

"I have 2 tens to regroup (counting the tens which are indicated with the '1's") so I write the '2' at the top of the tens column. I add the regrouped 2 and 2 to get 4. (Write '4'.) Add 4 and 1 to get five. (Write '5'.) Now add 4 and 5 to get nine. (Write '9'.) Now I copy the 9 in the tens place of the sum."

FIGURE 5.50

eliminating some of the writing that is a part of a "low stress" algorithm. The algorithm requires the pupil to remember SOME figures in his/her head while working with the addition. Only the "ten" is written down—by "scratching" through one of the digits. The excess of ten is "remembered" and added to the next digit. Anytime ten or more is reached, a "scratch" is made to remind the pupil of the ten. When the column is completed, the pupil counts the "scratches" and uses this as the regrouped "reminder" numeral.

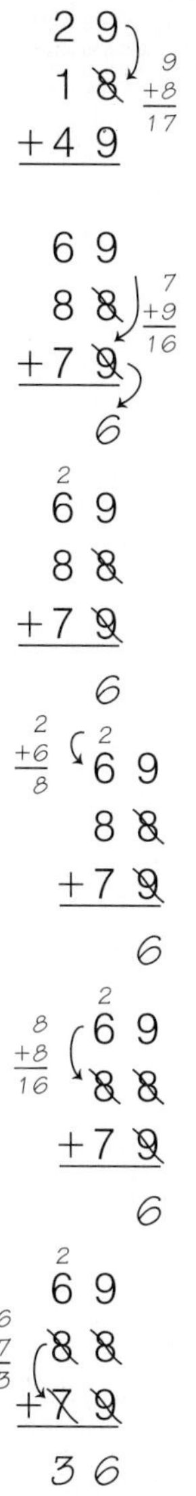

Child's Thinking Process for Scratch Addition.

"Nine and eight is seventeen." The child scratches through the 8 and remembers the '7'.

"Seven and nine is sixteen." (The child scratches through the '9' and remembers the '6'. A '6' is written in the sum.)

Count the scratches and use these as the "regrouped" figure. "I'll write the '2' at the top of the tens column and then add down the tens. Eight plus eight is sixteen. I'll scratch the '8' for the ten part and remember the six."

"Six plus seven is thirteen, so I'll scratch the seven for the ten part and write down the '3'. Now I'll count up the scratches in the tens column and that will give me 2 hundreds—so I'll write a '2' in the hundreds place of the sum."

"My answer is 236."

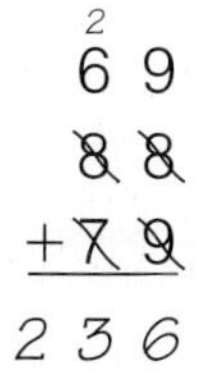

FIGURE 5.51

5.11 SUMMARY

A good foundation in addition skills is the cornerstone for the development of all future computational skills. This foundation is, for the most part, completed by the time the student finishes the primary grades.

By the end of the third grade the average student will recognize addition as putting sets together or describing subsets. The student will have used concrete materials to discover the commutative, associative, and identity properties. Strategies for mastering the basic addition facts will have been introduced and most students will have mastered (memorized) the 100 basic combinations. The student will be proficient, although not necessarily speedy, when adding 2- and 3-digit addends (both with and without regrouping). The student will be able to use such technological devices as the calculator and microcomputer to perform lengthy and involved computation involving whole numbers. The student will be able to solve simple problems where addition is used in arriving at the solution.

At the intermediate level the addition skills the student brings from the primary grades will be maintained and extended. This will involve teaching the student special techniques for improving his/her skill with column addition, such as the use of higher decade facts and special groupings (making tens and using multiples). Properties of addition that were explored at the primary level are formally developed at the intermediate level and used in analysis to give the student a greater understanding of addition concepts and to serve as readiness for the study of algebra.

Activities with the calculator and microcomputer are extended at the intermediate level to involve multistep problem-solving activities and computer programs that use addition operations, such as "spreadsheet" programs.

EXERCISES

1. Choose a manipulative device and describe how it would be used to illustrate the basic fact 4 + 5.
2. Describe how a teacher could use manipulative materials to develop each of the following:
   a. Addition as the union of two disjoint sets
   b. The identity element for addition
   c. The commutative property for addition
   d. The associative property for addition
3. Describe how each of the basic fact strategies listed below would be developed:
   a. Counting-on
   b. Make-a-ten
   c. Near doubles
   d. Sharing numbers
   e. Odd/even generalization
4. Listed below are several basic addition facts.

Choose the best strategy for developing each fact.

a. 4 + 0 **b.** 6 + 6 **c.** 7 + 1
d. 8 + 3 **e.** 7 + 6 **f.** 8 + 6

5. Work the problems below using the algorithms indicated.
   a. 23 + 35 (expanded notation using words)
   b. 47 + 36 (expanded notation using numerals)
   c. 385 + 269 (partial sums)

6. Use a place-value chart (or modern computing abacus) to develop the conventional algorithm with helper for the example 283 + 469.

7. Describe how a teacher could use a manipulative device (hundred chart or Unifix™ track) to illustrate how basic facts can be used to find sums for decade facts. Use the basic fact 3 + 6 and the decade facts 13 + 6 and 23 + 6.

8. Work the problems below using the conventional algorithm, then check with the technique indicated.
   a. 38 + 42 + 52 (check with upper/lower boundaries)
   b. 386 + 332 + 128 (check with cast-out nines)

9. Work the following example using one of the nonconventional algorithms described in the chapter (left-to-right addition; counting addition; basic facts addition; scratch addition): 384 + 293 + 598 + 769.

10. Describe a classroom situation that could be used by a teacher to introduce:
    a. The commutative property of addition
    b. The sum family
    c. Regrouping in addition

11. Examine each of the computational errors illustrated below. Describe how the student arrived at the sum and then suggest a procedure to help the pupil overcome this difficulty.
    Tommy: 54 + 29 = 713
    Annie: 467 + 296 = 653
    Betty: 427 + 276 = 811
    Joe: 455 + 27 = 682

12. Examine a scope and sequence from a currently published elementary school mathematics textbook series. How does the sequence differ from the sample presented in this chapter?

13. Examine G. W. Bright's article "Mathematics and Spreadsheets" (see References). After reading his article, choose one of the articles suggested in his bibliography and examine other applications of spreadsheets.

RELEVANT COMPUTER SOFTWARE

Highrise Math. Joe Calabrese, 1986. Apple II family. Word Associates, 3096 Summit Avenue, Highland Park, Ill. 60035.

Basic Math Facts. Doug Sapen and Gail Newell. 1986, Apple II family. Houghton Mifflin Co., 12 East Lake Street, Suite 104, Bloomington, Ill. 60108.

Strategies in Problem Solving: Dinosaurs and Squids. Mary Grace Kantowski, Scott McFadden, and Kenneth Vas. Apple II. Scott, Foresman & Co., 1900 East Lake Avenue, Glenview, Ill. 60025.

REFERENCES

Bright, G. W. "Mathematics and Spreadsheets." *Arithmetic Teacher* 36 (April 1989): 52–53.

Cruickshank, D. E., and L. J. Sheffield. *Teaching Mathematics to Elementary School Children.* Columbus, Oh.: Merrill Publishing Company, 1988. Pp. 110–112.

Kamii, C., and L. Joseph. "Teaching Place Value and Double-Column Addition." *Arithmetic Teacher* 35 (February 1988): 48–52.

Kennedy, L. M., and S. Tipps. *Guiding Children's Learning of Mathematics.* Belmont, Calif.: Wadworth Publishing Company, 1988. Pp. 319–321.

Reys, R. E.; M. N. Suydam; and M. M. Lindquist. *Helping Children Learn Mathematics.* Englewood Cliffs, N.J.: Prentice-Hall, 1984. Pp. 116–123.

Riedesel, C. A. *Teaching Elementary School Mathematics.* Englewood Cliffs, N.J.: Prentice-Hall, 1985. Pp. 128–133.

Smith, D. E. *Number Stories of Long Ago.* Washington, D.C.: National Council of Teachers of Mathematics, 1975.

Sovchik, R. J. *Teaching Mathematics to Children.* New York: Harper & Row, 1989. Pp. 199–204.

Stanic, G. M., and W. D. McKillip. "Developmental Algorithms Have a Place in Elementary School Mathematics Instruction." *Arithmetic Teacher* 36 (January 1989): 14–15.

Tucker, B. F. "Seeing Addition: A Diagnosis-Remediation Case Study." *Arithmetic Teacher* 36 (January 1989): 710–711.

CHAPTER 6

TEACHING SUBTRACTION OF WHOLE NUMBERS

INTRODUCTION

Subtraction, like addition, is used throughout life to solve everyday problems. When we keep a checkbook balance, make change, compare prices, and even when we want to know how much farther we must travel to reach our destination—we are using subtraction. Subtraction also plays a major role in the development of other mathematical skills.

Like addition, many subtraction transactions are completed using electronic devices. For example, finding the difference between the amount of money tendered and the cost of items purchased is now routinely calculated by automated cash registers. Though calculators may be used for many of the subtraction calculations individuals once completed using paper-and-pencil subtraction algorithms, individuals still need to understand the subtraction process and be reasonably proficient with paper-and-pencil subtraction algorithms.

When teaching subtraction, emphasis must be placed on **understanding** the operation, its properties, and being able to apply the operation to problem solving. Children must recognize when to use subtraction and what subtraction will do. They will use this understanding much more often than they will use high-level computational skills. It is essential for children to understand subtraction well enough to **estimate** the reasonableness of a difference displayed on a computer or calculator screen.

Children seem to have more difficulty learning subtraction than addition. They do not enter the formal study of subtraction at the same level of readiness as addition. While extensive activities involving counting and putting sets together provide good readiness experiences for the study of addition, few children enter school having had extensive experiences counting backwards; removing part of a set to determine how much is left; and seeing how much more one set has than a second set. A second factor that makes the study of subtraction more difficult than addition is the variety of situations that suggest subtraction. When pupils explore addition they learn to associate the operation with two models—putting sets together or describing the subsets of an "already assembled" set. When studying subtraction they must recognize four situations—removing objects from a set, comparing sets, subset situations, and putting a set of unknown number with another set.

6.1 TEACHING SUBTRACTION IN THE PRIMARY GRADES

Preschool and kindergarten children do have some experiences that may be used as a foundation for a systematic development of subtraction concepts. Parents informally communicate "subtractive" situations to children. For example, parental statements such as "Betty, you **lost** one of your mittens . . . Two of the bulbs are **burnt out** . . . I wonder how much **taller** you are **than** your brother? . . . or . . . You have **fewer** cookies than your sister"—provide an intuitive understanding of subtraction. However, subtraction's many guises require the primary teacher to use discretion in using an entering student's <u>intuitive</u> understanding of subtraction. Initially instruction examines each subtraction situation in isolation from the others; a teacher can bring coherence to the learning structure for the children.

Kindergarten programs sometimes develop a readiness for subtraction; however, in first grade a teacher must still engage children in more exploratory activities for subtraction than for addition. Children first will associate subtraction with <u>taking away</u> objects from a set. They'll learn to write what happens in a mathematical sentence (equation). While doing this the child develops a listening vocabulary to associate with subtraction. The minus symbol ($-$) is associated with "less," or "take away," and meaning for "equals" ($=$) is extended. Children use many concrete materials to "act out" a subtraction situation, then write a sentence when observing an action.

After associating subtraction with taking away, children learn to associate the operation with finding how many more items one set has than another; finding the number of a subset of a set (when the number of a set and part of a set is known); and finding a missing addend when the sum and one of the addends are known. By the time the child finishes the primary grades all four subtraction models will have been explored.

When first exploring subtraction the teacher will use the child's vocabulary. As the subtraction models are developed, the appropriate mathematical vocabulary is gradually developed. In the early part of the century, the mathematical terms "minuend" and "subtrahend" were used to describe parts of the subtraction algorithm. These terms may be used to describe (in a teaching objective) a skill to be taught as in, "The child will be able to find the difference when the minuend has three digits and the subtrahend has one digit." Children find it much more meaningful to use terms such as "**sum**," "**known addend**," and "**missing ad-**

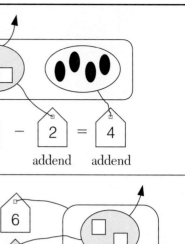

sum   addend   addend

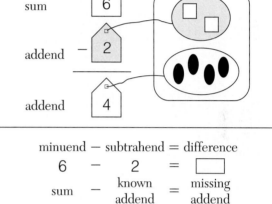

minuend $-$ subtrahend $=$ difference

6 $-$ 2 $=$ ▢

$\underset{\text{sum}}{6}$ $-$ $\underset{\substack{\text{known} \\ \text{addend}}}{2}$ $=$ $\underset{\substack{\text{missing} \\ \text{addend}}}{}$

FIGURE 6.1

dend." The "missing" addend is also referred to as the "**difference**." (See Figure 6.1.)

Early work in the primary grades emphasizes the development of the meanings of subtraction and the patterns associated with it. Children later will explore strategies that will help them organize the basic combinations—related facts, compensation, $N - N = 0$ facts, $N - 0 = N$ facts, $N - 1$ facts, and bridging-to-ten facts. These strategies help the child master the basic combinations more efficiently. More importantly they strengthen the child's understanding of the subtraction operation.

As the child progresses through first, second, and third grades, algorithms for using the basic facts to subtract 2-, 3-, and 4-digit numbers are introduced. As with addition, teachers use developmental algorithms to deepen the child's understanding of subtraction. The developmental algorithms illustrated in Figure 6.2 strengthen understanding of place value by forcing the child to write a number as tens and ones. The algorithms further require the child to subtract ones from the ones and tens from the tens.

The primary purpose of developmental algorithms is to build understanding, not to make children "superefficient" when subtracting. No

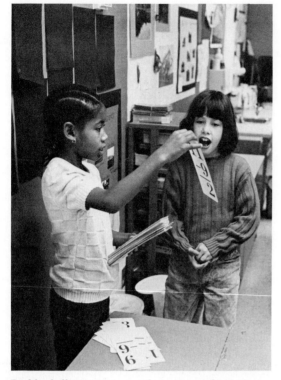

Buddy drills motivate pupils to master basic facts.

Developmental Algorithm

$$\begin{array}{r|r} \text{Tens} & \text{Ones} \\ \hline 4 & 6 \\ -2 & 1 \\ \hline 2 & 5 \end{array}$$

Developmental Algorithm

$$\begin{array}{l} 46 = 4 \text{ tens and } 6 \text{ ones} \\ -\ \underline{21 = 2 \text{ tens and } 1 \text{ one}} \\ 2 \text{ tens and } 5 \text{ ones} \end{array}$$

FIGURE 6.2

amount of practice can make the child as efficient as a calculator, but without understanding the child will not be able to use these technological devices effectively. There are times when subtraction must be done with paper and pencil—often because a calculator is not readily available. Because of this, the standard subtraction algorithm must be developed.

A **general overview** of the subtraction skills introduced at the primary level in a typical curriculum guide are shown below.

Grade 1

Meaning of subtraction
  • develop take-away concept
  • develop inverse of addition concept
Subtraction vocabulary
  • missing addend, difference
Subtracting 1-digit addends
  • all combinations introduced
  • sums to 12 mastered
Subtracting 2-digit numbers with no regrouping

Grade 2

Meaning of subtraction
  • strengthen take-away concept
  • develop comparison concept

  • develop missing addend concept
Subtracting 1-digit addends
  • mastery of facts with sums through 18
  • basic facts strategies explored
      related facts
      compensation patterns
      bridge-back-to-ten patterns
      nines facts
Subtracting 2- and 3-digit numbers
  • without regrouping
  • with regrouping
Checking addition
  • by estimation
  • by inverse operation (adding)

Grade 3

Meaning of subtraction
  • maintain take-away, comparison, and missing addend concept
  • develop subset concept
Subtracting 1-digit addends
  • maintain skill in all basic facts
Subtracting 2-, 3-, and 4-digit addends
  • with and without regrouping
  • zeros in subtraction
Checking by inverse and estimation

6.2 DEVELOPING THE MEANINGS OF SUBTRACTION

Children need hands-on experience with subtraction to understand the operation. Most elementary mathematics programs initially <u>introduce</u> subtraction through **take-away** situations; then introduce other types of situations, one at a time. By the end of the primary grades children are familiar with four models commonly associated with subtraction—take-away, comparison, additive, and subset.

Take-away Model for Subtraction

Before children reach kindergarten they have taken things away. They may have eaten two pieces of candy leaving only three pieces, or have been playing with a group when one or two of the other children went home. By introducing subtraction in terms of the **"take-away" model**, teachers utilize the child's experiential background. The take-away model is easy for pupils to understand—the child removes objects and simply counts the amount that is left to find the answer.

It is the teacher's responsibility to expand these initial experiences so the child also associates the take-away action with **"undoing"** addition. Children learn to "push things together" when they add and "take them back apart" when they subtract. (In mathematical terms subtraction is said to be the **inverse** of addition. In children's terms, subtracting will "undo" addition.)

In the following lesson fragment a take-away subtraction lesson is being developed.

Teacher-Guided Interactive Learning Activity

LESSON FRAGMENT

M: Associating subtraction with removing part of a set and determining the number of the remaining set. (The terminology of "subtract" and "subtraction" has not been introduced at this point.)

A: Group of first-graders.

T: Involvement (physical), hands-on work with models.

H: Children are able to rationally count to ten.

PROBLEM-SOLVING SITUATION:

PARENTS HAD MADE NINE CAKES TO SELL AT THE SCHOOL CARNIVAL. THE CAKES WERE PLACED ALONG THE WINDOW LEDGE SO THEY WOULD BE OUT OF THE WAY UNTIL THE START OF THE CARNIVAL. WHEN THE CUSTODIAN OPENED THE WINDOW TO REMOVE A BLIND CORD, THREE OF THE CAKES WERE RUINED. THE RUINED CAKES WERE THROWN OUT AND THE REST OF THE CAKES WERE TAKEN TO THE CARNIVAL. IN THE MORNING

THE STUDENTS WERE TOLD WHAT HAD HAPPENED. THEY WANTED TO KNOW HOW MANY CAKES WERE TAKEN TO THE CARNIVAL. THE TEACHER SUGGESTED THAT THEY COULD USE THEIR COUNTERS TO **REPRESENT** THE CAKES, THEN EACH CHILD COULD "MAKE A MODEL OF THE SITUATION" TO SOLVE THE PROBLEM. (SEE FIGURE 6.3.)

Teacher: Everyone place nine of your counting disks in a row to show the cakes sitting on the window ledge. To help us remember how many we have, take your numeral cards and place the "9" on the left side of your desk. (SEE FIGURE 6.4.) How many cakes were ruined when the window was lowered? (THREE) Let's put the numeral "3" to the right of the nine. Now we are going to remove three of our disks. To suggest with numbers what we are going to do, place this symbol between the 9 and the 3. (THE TEACHER HOLDS UP A "MINUS"

Concept Introduced from Problem Situation

Take-away Subtraction Model

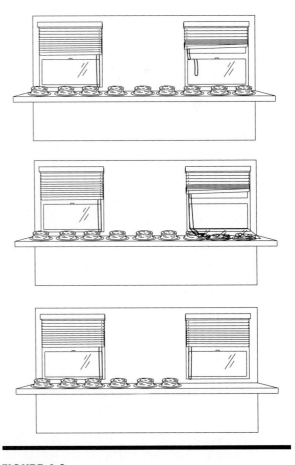

FIGURE 6.3

Equation Building and Evaluation

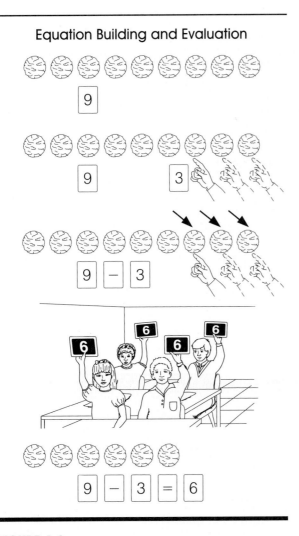

FIGURE 6.4

SIGN.) We are going to **subtract** our numbers. Remove three of your disks. When I say go, show me with your numeral cards how many disks you have left. Go! (THE CHILDREN DISPLAY THE NUMERAL "6" TO THE TEACHER, WHO CHECKS EACH CHILD'S EFFORT.)

Teacher: Good! Place your equal sign and a six after your three. Listen to me read this equation: Nine minus three is six. Or we could read it nine subtract three equals six. (THE TEACHER LEADS THE CLASS TO WORK TWO OR THREE MORE EXAMPLES.)

Teacher: Today I want us to work in our teams to explore subtraction. When each team is ready with their counters at their table, you may send your team leader to get your assignment sheets. Now let's move into our groups. (AS PUPILS WORK IN SMALL GROUPS THE TEACHER WILL CIRCULATE AROUND THE ROOM—OBSERVING PROGRESS AND PROVIDING ADDITIONAL INSTRUCTION IF NEEDED.)

Comparison Model for Subtraction

After children understand subtraction as it relates to take-away situations, the teacher will introduce the **comparison** model. While comparison subtraction is similar to take-away, nothing is removed in comparison. To compare two groups, the objects in one set are **matched** to the objects in a second set. The **unmatched** members are counted to find the **difference**. (In "take-away subtraction" those that **remained** were counted.) The more-than-or-less-than idea is emphasized with the comparison model.

Teachers can help children see the relationship to take-away by showing that "matching off" is somewhat like "taking the objects away" even though the objects are never **really** removed.

The following lesson fragment develops children's understanding of the **comparison** model of subtraction.

Teacher-Guided Interactive Learning Activity

LESSON FRAGMENT

M: Subtraction suggested by comparing how much longer or shorter one set is than another

A: Second-grade class

T: Models, involvement

H: Children understand subtraction suggested by take-away situations

PROBLEM-SOLVING SITUATION:

ZANA BROUGHT IN A PICTURE SHOWING HER AND HER MOTHER EACH HOLDING UP A FISH THAT THEY CAUGHT DURING SUMMER VACATION. ZANA SAID HER FISH WAS 13 INCHES LONG AND HER MOTHER'S FISH WAS NINE INCHES LONG. (SEE FIGURE 6.5.) SOMEONE ASKED HOW MUCH LONGER ZANA'S FISH WAS THAN HER MOTHER'S FISH. THE TEACHER SUGGESTED THEY USE THEIR **COLORED RODS** TO REPRESENT THE FISH.

Teacher: Let's use colored rods to represent Zana's fish. (EVERYONE HAD PREVIOUSLY LEARNED TO PLACE A ROD REPRESENTING TEN AND A ROD REPRESENTING THREE TOGETHER TO REPRESENT 13.) (SEE FIGURE 6.6.) Place your numeral card for 13 below your rods to record this amount. Now let's place a second rod beside the rods you are using for Zana's fish to show her moth-

Concept Introduced from Problem Situation

Comparison Subtraction Model

FIGURE 6.5

Equation Building

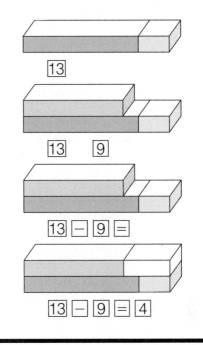

FIGURE 6.6

er's fish. Place the numeral card for nine to the right of the 13.

We are going to **compare** 13 inches to nine inches. To show comparison, we use a minus sign to show we are going to match one set to the other set to find the difference. Place a **minus sign** between the 13 and 9, because this is another way we use subtraction.

Let's use our rods to find out how much longer 13 is than 9. We can record this difference by placing an equal sign in the number sentence. Now let's find how much longer Zana's fish was than her mother's. Show me your answer by putting the proper card in your number sentence.

(THE TEACHER WALKS AROUND THE ROOM AND CHECKS EACH CHILD'S WORK.)

Additive Model for Subtraction

As children learn to add (putting sets together) they also encounter **additive subtraction** situations. Suppose that Tommy puts out three blocks. When Mary puts a few more blocks with Tommy's they find they <u>now</u> have eight blocks. To discover how many blocks were added to the set, Tommy will want to **undo** the addition. If the teacher were to write the number sentence to show the action that <u>originally</u> took place, it would be written "**3 + N = 8.**" In this case, the sum is known because the blocks have already been put together. Tommy must take his three blocks back to find out how many Mary put with them. The "undoing" to find

the missing addend is much like "taking away." In fact, children generally remark—when they see the action of putting together and then reversing the action—that they are taking away (subtracting).

In Figure 6.7, the action of putting together (adding) <u>has already taken place</u>. Children must be led (through discussion and use of manipulative materials) to see that this action must be <u>undone</u>. This is an excellent opportunity for the teacher to help the child recognize the relationship between addition and subtraction.

Additive subtraction **also** occurs in situations where "counting-on" is used. If Mike had four jelly beans and his mother told him he could have ten in all, he would start at four and <u>count-on</u> until he reached ten. To represent this in a number sentence one would write "**4 + N = 10.**" Teachers "act out" the situation using concrete materials— counting-on to reach ten. Then, <u>to help children see that this is really a subtraction situation</u>, the teacher will **take back** the original jelly beans to show how subtraction can undo addition.

Some children use their fingers and "count-on" to answer a problem such as 8 − 5 = N, saying "five," then raising a finger for each number until eight is reached. The fingers that are "up" are then counted to see how many were "added" to get to eight.

Additive subtraction may require the teacher to

Relating Subtraction to Addition

Additive Subtraction Model

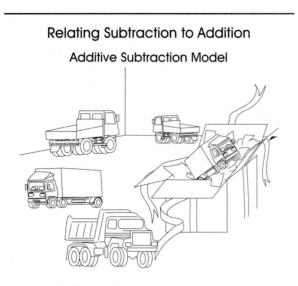

I had 2 trucks. I got some more trucks
for my birthday! Now I have 5. How
many trucks did I get as gifts?

FIGURE 6.7

create a problem situation to develop this model for
subtraction. The teacher may suggest a problem
when returning reading books to a classroom shelf.
If a child has placed seven books on the shelf and
then finds there are a total of 15 books on the shelf,
the teacher may ask the class to determine how
many books were originally on the shelf.

Subset Model for Subtraction

The subset model for subtraction is developed at
some point after the additive subtraction model. It
is a little more difficult for children to see this situation as subtraction because **no action is taking
place**. Objects are **not** taken away—they are **not**
compared—they are **not** added on. A set is simply
being **described**. For example, a set has five members, three of the members are red, how many are
not red is a description that can be expressed in
equation form as "$5 = 3 + \Delta$."

Sometimes a child recognizes that the sum is
given and that the sentence calls for a **missing
addend**; then the use of subtraction is easily
understood. If the child needs the manipulation of
concrete materials the teacher can illustrate the
model in two ways. The teacher may cover a set of
five objects and then allow the class to see three of
the objects, pointing out that the rest are "still hidden." Some children may perceive this as "taking
the two from the five" and associate this with take-
away subtraction. Some children may look at the

model and determine that they can "count on" to
determine the number of hidden objects.

Subset models in natural problems will occur
less frequently than the "take-away" and "comparison" situations. Thus it may be necessary for
the teacher to create a situation leading to the development of this type of concept. One naturally
occurring situation is a class itself. If one child
counts the total number of children in the class and
another child counts the girls, the question can be
posed, "How many boys do we have in the room?"
Another commonly occurring situation is determining the number of children absent each morning
by using the total number of children enrolled and
the number of children present.

While all four models for subtraction can be developed using basic facts, situations that include
larger numbers also can be used. When larger
amounts are used, the teacher may utilize the situation to help children learn to use the problem-
solving strategy of **using simpler numbers** to
model solutions for problems. It is appropriate—
even desirable—for the teacher to model this
strategy in all grade levels. To use a "basic fact" in
the former example (the class was going to determine the number of boys) the teacher could say,
"To see how we work this type of problem, let us
pretend we have only nine people in our class and
there are only four girls. We can use our counters
to help us work this "easier" problem. Later we can
use the same technique with larger numbers, but
perhaps we will not need counters then."

The lesson fragment below illustrates how the
teacher uses counting disks that have different
colors on each side.

Teacher-Guided Interactive Learning Activity

UTILIZING MODELS WITH SIMPLER
NUMBERS TO SOLVE PROBLEMS

LESSON
FRAGMENT

M: Subset model

A: Second-grade class

T: Models

H: Children understand three of
four meanings of subtraction

PROBLEM-SOLVING SITUATION:
THE PUPILS HAVE BEEN KEEPING TRACK OF
ABSENCES EACH DAY AND YESTERDAY THEY
FOUND IT DIFFICULT TO FIND OUT HOW
MANY BOYS WERE ABSENT WITHOUT WRITING
DOWN ALL OF THE NAMES AND MARKING OFF

THOSE WHO WERE NOT THERE. THE TEACHER POINTS OUT THAT SOME OF THE BOYS ARE NOT HERE TODAY, BUT POSES THE QUESTION—"HOW MANY BOYS ARE THERE IN THE CLASS?"

Teacher: Before we work with the larger number of 27 in the class, let's work with a smaller number. Take out nine disks and place them on your desk—white side up. These disks will represent the nine pupils in our **"pretend"** class. (THE CHILDREN TAKE OUT NINE DISKS TO SHOW THE NUMBER OF PUPILS IN THE CLASS.) Let us place our numeral card for 9 under this set. Now, how many pupils in this set did we say were girls?

Maxine: Four.

Teacher: All right, let us turn over four of the disks to represent the girls in the class. (THE CHILDREN TURN OVER FOUR DISKS, EXPOSING THE RED SIDE OF THE DISKS.) We can describe this set in our number sentence by first placing an **equal sign**. Now let us describe the set we see, "**9 = 4 + N.**" We are going to use a box to represent the number of boys because we really do not know this amount until we count them. How can we find the missing number?

Maxine: There must be five, because 4 + 5 = 9.

Teacher: Good, Maxine, but suppose we had larger numbers and we did not KNOW the basic combination—what could we do?

Darlyne: We turned the four counters over when we said four girls and to me that LOOKED like taking them away. We have 27 in our class and 13 are girls—so if we took the 13 girls away from the 27 we would be left with the boys. There would be 14 boys.

Teacher: Darlyne is suggesting that we could subtract to find the missing addend in the number sentence. Why do you suppose that would work, Dick?

Dick: That's easy. We have the sum so we will need to UNDO the adding. We can subtract to undo addition.

In the next section we will examine how basic facts and properties of subtraction are developed through manipulative and exploratory activities.

6.3 TEACHING THE BASIC SUBTRACTION FACTS

Shortly after the take-away concept of subtraction is first introduced, children will explore the basic subtraction facts. Early work will emphasize the relationship between addition and subtraction. When children put two sets together they will write the addition sentence that corresponds with the action. The teacher can then have children take back from the collection the amount that was added—writing the subtraction equation for the action. For example, when three things are added to five things the sentence 5 + 3 = 8 is written. Then when the three things are taken back from the eight, the sentence 8 − 3 = 5 is written. From this the children recognize that subtraction will **undo** the addition. (In mathematical terms, each addition fact has a corresponding subtraction fact that represents the **inverse**.)

One way of organizing the subtraction facts is to teach the subtraction facts along with addition facts. This has a distinct advantage in that learning the subtraction facts **reinforces** the learning of the addition facts and vice versa. If a teacher uses this approach, shortly after a set of addition facts are introduced, the **related** subtraction facts are introduced. In some instances, after introducing the meaning of addition and subtraction, the facts may be introduced concurrently with "doing," then "undoing" activities.

Using Related Facts and the Addition Table to Teach Subtraction Facts

Some teachers get double usage from the addition matrix by using it to teach **both** addition and subtraction facts. When this is done, teachers organize the teaching of basic facts around groups of **related facts**. For example, for the numbers 9, 6, and 3 the addition table could be used to explore the related facts: 3 + 6 = 9, 6 + 3 = 9, 9 − 3 = 6, and 9 − 6 = 3. Of course, the use of any table must be preceded by extensive hands-on manipulative activities.

Subtracting One from a Number (the n − 1 facts)

Once children learn to count backwards from ten the teacher can use this skill to develop subtraction of one from a number. Or, concurrent with the development of **adding** one to a number, children can examine the result of **"undoing"** the object just added to a set. Figure 6.8 illustrates a few of the manipulative materials that can be used for concurrent instruction with addition, or for teaching subtraction in nonrelated facts activities.

Using Patterns to Explore the Basic Facts

There are several subtraction patterns that facilitate the teaching of the subtraction facts. Two com-

Manipulative Devices for Independent Learning Activities

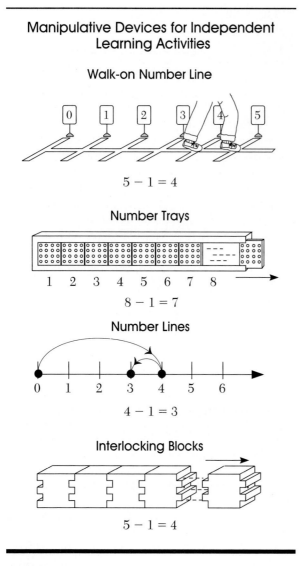

Walk-on Number Line

$$5 - 1 = 4$$

Number Trays

$$8 - 1 = 7$$

Number Lines

$$4 - 1 = 3$$

Interlocking Blocks

$$5 - 1 = 4$$

FIGURE 6.8

mon patterns involve zero. The following lesson fragment uses **guided discovery** to elicit the pattern for "**n − n = 0**."

Teacher-Guided Interactive Learning Activity

USING PATTERNS TO DEVELOP GENERALIZATIONS

LESSON FRAGMENT

M: Pattern $n - n = 0$

A: First-grade class

T: Discovery, models, involvement

H: Subtraction associated with take-away situations, subtraction equations, terminology

Teacher: Place three disks on your desk. Put the three disks away. How many disks do you have left, Ron?

Ron: Zero.

Teacher: Everyone write an equation suggested by our activity. When I say go, hold up your answers and show me. Go! (THE CHILDREN DISPLAY "3 − 3 = 0." THE PROCESS IS REPEATED WITH FOUR, THEN SIX, THEN SEVEN DISKS.)

Teacher: Who thinks they see a subtraction pattern? (SEVERAL CHILDREN RAISE THEIR HANDS. THE TEACHER CALLS ON A CHILD AND TESTS HER UNDERSTANDING BY GIVING HER A NEW SUBTRACTION FACT.)

Teacher: Eretha, what does nine minus nine equal?

Eretha: Zero.

Teacher: Good, Eretha has the pattern! Who else would like to see if they have discovered a pattern?

A second pattern involving zero is "**n − 0 = n**." The language for its development is a little awkward, because one usually does not say one is taking "zero things" away. The teacher can build the idea by having a bag of eight blocks and asking pupils to reach in to take out different amounts. When instructing the child the teacher may say, "Bill, reach in and get ZERO blocks—how many blocks will be left?" Some pupils see the generalization when it is presented as a pattern of subtraction facts culminating with taking away zero. The pupils are directed to write an equation for each story:

> Three birds on a fence, <u>three</u> fly away. How many birds are left? (3 − 3 = 0)

> Three birds on a fence, <u>two</u> fly away. How many birds are left? (3 − 2 = 1)

> Three birds on a fence, <u>one</u> flies away. How many birds are left? (3 − 1 = 2)

> Three birds on a fence, <u>zero</u> birds fly away. How many birds are left? (3 − 0 = 3)

Subtracting 1 Using a Calculator

Calculators may be used to explore the subtraction of 1 from any number allowing pupils to use large numbers as well as small numbers. The teacher may wish to <u>begin</u> with the simple activity of entering a number; the minus sign; "1"; and finally an "=" sign. Pupils completing this activity find the number that comes <u>just before</u> the number entered always appears. Later, the teacher will want to use the "repeated operation function" of the calculator to show how subtracting one is really counting backwards. Figure 6.9 illustrates one way an

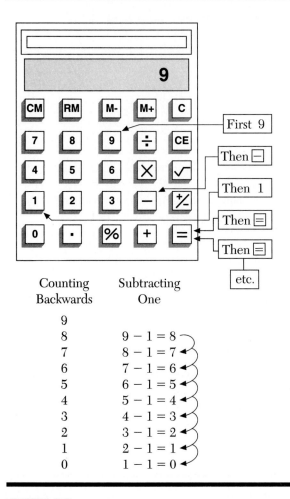

Counting   Subtracting
Backwards   One

9
8   9 − 1 = 8
7   8 − 1 = 7
6   7 − 1 = 6
5   6 − 1 = 5
4   5 − 1 = 4
3   4 − 1 = 3
2   3 − 1 = 2
1   2 − 1 = 1
0   1 − 1 = 0

FIGURE 6.9

activity can be structured using the calculator to discover this relationship.

Counting-on as a Strategy for Exploring the Facts

Just as pupils use a "counting-on strategy" when exploring the addition facts, the additive model of subtraction makes it possible to use a "counting-on" strategy to explore a whole range of subtraction facts. Figure 6.10 illustrates how a child can use a walk-on number line to see how many steps it would take to get from one number to another.

Building-to-Ten (minuends 11 through 18)

One independent exploration that promotes an understanding of the basic facts with minuends of 11 through 18 is to have children build to sets of ten and then from ten to the minuend to get the difference. For example, in finding the difference of 13 and six the child would use four to get a set of

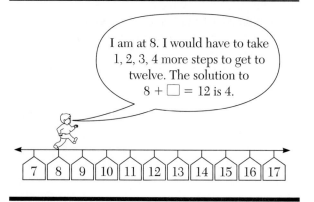

FIGURE 6.10

ten and then three more to get the 13. (See Figure 6.11.)

Memorization of the Basic Facts

Only after a child understands the take-away concept of subtraction should basic facts be practiced with the intent of memorizing differences. Understanding can be checked by having a sentence such as "7 − 3 = N" demonstrated by a child using manipulative materials. The child also should be able to write the number sentence that would be suggested by the action of removing three from a set of seven. It is not necessary that a child understand all <u>four</u> meanings associated with subtraction before systematically promoting memorization of the basic subtraction facts. (A teacher may find that

---

Individual Learning Activity

The child thinks, "it takes 4 to go from 6 to ten and

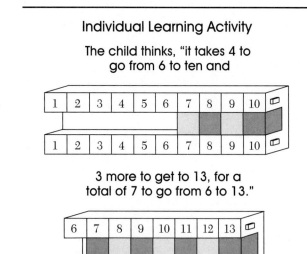

3 more to get to 13, for a total of 7 to go from 6 to 13."

FIGURE 6.11

children can already recall some of the basic subtraction facts <u>before</u> the teacher begins this systematic process. They can remember <u>some</u> facts as a byproduct of the manipulative exploratory activities they have had with subtraction.)

The principles for mastering the addition facts (described in Chapter 5) are equally applicable when working with the subtraction facts. Figure 6.12 summarizes these principles.

To aid the pupil in mastering subtraction facts, the teacher may organize the combinations in a variety of ways. The subtraction facts may be grouped with their related addition facts (7 + 4, 4 + 7, 11 − 4, and 11 − 7) and practiced together. Another organization may relate the subtraction facts to sum families (6 − 0 = 6, 6 − 1 = 5, 6 − 2 = 4, 6 − 3 = 3, 6 − 4 = 2, 6 − 5 = 1, and 6 − 6 = 0).

FIGURE 6.12

Small-Group Learning Activity

Some beans are placed in one hand—in this case six beans are used.

The player puts both hands together, shakes the beans, and shifts SOME beans to the other hand. BOTH hands are clenched and presented to the other player.

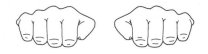

One hand is chosen and then opened, revealing SOME of the beans. The player then must guess how many are in the CLOSED HAND.

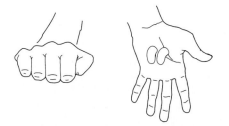

FIGURE 6.13

Practice Activities for Memorizing Facts

Gamelike activities may be selected by the teacher to practice the subtraction facts. "How Many in THIS Hand?" is a game that is self-checking. One asset of this game is that it helps children recognize that there are many different combinations that will have the same sum (numbers have many different names). Figure 6.13 illustrates how this game is played.

Subtraction facts may also be organized around common differences. For example, all the facts that have a <u>difference</u> of seven might be practiced. A variation of the Fact Captain activity (Chapter 5) can be useful when working with "common differences." In this case the child must use a subtraction "password" that was not used by the previous child. (See Figure 6.14.)

After children have mastered many of the subtraction facts, teachers may find a group game

Small-Group Learning Activity

FIGURE 6.14

Individual Learning Activity

Delivering the Mail

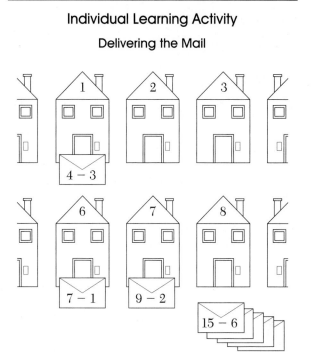

FIGURE 6.15

called "Deliver the Mail" to be an effective practice procedure. Children are given a set of fact cards (without the differences). Each child selects two or three cards (letters) to be "delivered" to the proper addresses—houses that have been placed along the chalk tray. (See Figure 6.15.) When all letters have been delivered, the class (directed by the teacher) will "check" to see if the letters reached their proper destination. This checking process allows the teacher to <u>review</u> all of the combinations that were placed on the chalk tray.

When quick recall of differences is the goal, the group activity "Sponge Ball" may be employed. Figure 6.16 illustrates how this activity is used to drill a class on a set of subtraction facts. To ensure the maximum benefit from the activity, the leader must make <u>each</u> child believe that the ball MAY be thrown in his/her direction. Leaders may make the game more challenging by (a) looking in one direction but throwing in another; (b) throwing the ball back to an individual who just gave an answer; or (c) cutting down on the reaction time for quicker pupils by tossing the ball as the combination is said. Since pupils must concentrate upon catching the ball, they do not have time to find the answer by counting on their fingers.

Flash cards have historically been used to practice basic facts. When using flash cards in group settings, the leader can keep children alert by saying the pupil's name <u>after</u> displaying the card. This way all children must be <u>ready</u> to answer—keeping everybody on their toes.

(Additional techniques to practice basic combinations are presented in other chapters. Each of the practice activities presented in the whole number operation chapters of this text may be <u>adapted</u> to use with addition, subtraction, multiplication, or division facts.)

6.4 TEACHING SUBTRACTION ALGORITHMS

Even while the subtraction facts are being explored, children <u>begin</u> 2- and 3-digit subtraction (without regrouping). Subtracting tens from tens is introduced soon after the children begin learning their basic facts. Learning that five <u>tens</u> minus two <u>tens</u> equals three <u>tens</u> reinforces the understanding of $5 - 2 = 3$. When hundreds are introduced children also are taught to subtract two <u>hundreds</u> from five <u>hundreds</u>.

The lesson fragment that follows uses manipulative materials to introduce the concept of subtracting tens from tens.

Small-Group Learning Activity

The tosser will try to make every child believe that the ball will be tossed in his/her direction. A child must respond as the ball is caught. No time is allowed to "count" to get the answer. This activity builds immediate recall of the basic fact.

Sponge Ball

FIGURE 6.16

Teacher-Guided Interactive Learning Activity

LESSON FRAGMENT

M: Subtracting tens from tens

A: First-graders

T: Models (toy money)

H: Children have mastered the parallel subtraction facts

PROBLEM-SOLVING SITUATION:

THE CLASS HAS BEEN STUDYING MONEY— IDENTIFYING AND COUNTING DIMES, NICK- ELS, AND PENNIES. TODAY THE CLASS IS GOING TO OPEN A "PLAY STORE" IN WHICH PLAY MATERIAL CAN BE "BOUGHT" USING PLAY MONEY. THE GAMES MAY BE USED DUR- ING FREE PLAY.

Teacher: Today we are going to open our store and we will be purchasing games and toys to use during free play. We need to make sure that the clerks in our store handle the money correctly and give us the correct change. To practice subtracting tens, we are going to take out our toy dimes and place a pile of five dimes on your desk. Put the numeral 50 un- der your five dimes to show that this is 50 cents. We are going to <u>take away</u> two of the dimes, or 20 cents. What operation is suggested when we take away part of the set and want to find the remaining part? (NOTICE THAT THE TEACHER IS REIN- FORCING THE CHILDREN'S UNDERSTAND- ING OF THE TAKE-AWAY MODEL OF SUB- TRACTION.)

Children: Subtraction.

Teacher: Put a minus sign and a 20 down to show that we are going to take two tens or twenty cents away. (SEE FIGURE 6.17.) Remove two tens. How many tens are left?

Children: Three tens.

Teacher: Notice it is just like our basic fact when we subtract two from five and get three. What is an- other name for three tens?

Children: Thirty.

Teacher: Use your equal sign and numeral card for thirty to complete the equation. (SEE FIGURE 6.18.) Today, our groups are going to explore sub- tracting tens. Go to your team tables and then your team leader may get the assignment sheet. (PU- PILS WORK IN GROUPS USING PLAY COINS TO COMPLETE THE ASSIGNMENT.)

Teachers often use developmental algorithms to help children understand subtraction of tens from tens. (See Figure 6.19.) Once a child recognizes the pattern in subtracting tens from tens, subtraction of hundreds from hundreds, thousands from thou- sands, or even millions from millions, is easily learned.

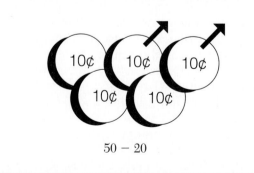

50 − 20

FIGURE 6.17

Using Developmental Algorithms to Introduce Subtraction with no Regrouping

Just as when developing addition skills, as soon as children recognize positional notation and master some of the basic subtraction facts (minuends less than ten), the teacher will present problem situations that require the subtraction of 2-digit amounts (with no regrouping). Such exploration traditionally occurs in the first grade. The use of a developmental algorithm during this introductory phase strengthens the child's skill in place value AND helps the child recognize the value of memorizing the basic combinations. The teacher may select from several developmental algorithms. Whichever algorithm is chosen, it should be used only in conjunction with manipulative materials.

Bean sticks are effective when introducing subtraction of 2-digit minuends and subtrahends. (Ten beans are glued on each tongue depressor or popsicle stick to show sets of tens. Children use loose beans to represent ones. Bean sticks are inexpensive and allow each child to have his/her own set of manipulative materials.)

The lesson fragment below illustrates the use of a developmental algorithm to record the action taken on the place-value chart.

Teacher-Guided Interactive Learning Activity

LESSON FRAGMENT

M: Subtracting a 2-digit subtrahend from a 2-digit minuend (no regrouping)

A: First-grade class

T: Modeling

H: Children understand 2-digit place value and basic subtraction facts with minuends through nine

PROBLEM-SOLVING SITUATION:
ANOTHER TEACHER BORROWED SOME CHAIRS FROM THE STOREROOM FOR A PROGRAM. THE PUPILS ARE EXCITED ABOUT THE ACTIVITY THAT HAS BEEN GOING ON FOR THE LAST TWO DAYS. THE TEACHER USES THIS INTEREST TO INTRODUCE SUBTRACTION WITHOUT REGROUPING.

Teacher: Mr. Krosnoski's class borrowed 23 of the 76 chairs in our storeroom. How many chairs are left? We can find an answer using materials, but before

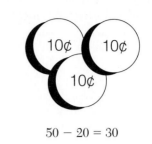

$$50 - 20 = 30$$

FIGURE 6.18

we do—let's ESTIMATE what our answer will be. When you give me a "guess" you must tell me WHY you guessed that number.

Mary: About 50—because 23 is close to 25 or a quarter. If I had a quarter it would take 50¢ to make 75¢.

Teacher: Very good, Mary. Now, let's use our bean sticks to help us solve this problem. I'm going to have each cooperative group work together and then we will share what we found. (THE TEACHER WALKS AROUND AS PUPILS WORK IN GROUPS TO FIND AN ANSWER—NOTING THE DIFFERENT WAYS GROUPS APPROACH THE PROBLEM.)

Teacher: Now that we all have an answer, I'm going to ask a few groups to share what they found. Remember that EVERYBODY in each group should

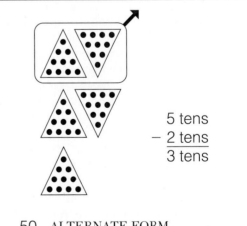

5 tens
− 2 tens
3 tens

50   ALTERNATE FORM
− 20   Read as "5 tens less 2 tens is 3 tens"—
30   not fifty less twenty is thirty.

FIGURE 6.19

have taken part in the activity so I can call on ANY-ONE in the group to explain what happened. I saw Mike's group working very hard at the task. Billy, can you tell us what you did?

Billy: We took out 76 beans and took away 23. We had 53 left.

Teacher: Good, Billy. There were some other groups that worked it in a different way. Marialice's group had an interesting way. Jeff, can you explain your group's work?

Jeff: We used our tens sticks and showed seven sticks and six singles. Then we took away three singles—leaving three loose beans. We took two bean sticks and that left five sticks—so our answer was 53, too. Of course, we don't have beans all over the place.

Teacher: Yes, Jeff, your way does seem to be efficient. Let's work that problem again using the technique Jeff described and I will RECORD what we do after each step. (SEE FIGURE 6.20.) (THE GROUPS WORK THROUGH THE PROBLEM—LED BY THE TEACHER. AS EACH STEP IS TAKEN THE TEACHER RECORDS THAT IN THE ALGO-RITHM.) Now that we worked a problem together, I'm going to ask all groups to practice using this technique—but this time let's pretend that there were 79 chairs in the storeroom and Mr. Krosnoski's class borrowed 35. Make sure you RECORD what happens as I did on the chalkboard.

Introducing Subtraction with Regrouping

Once the child learns to subtract 2- (and 3-) digit numbers in nonregrouping situations (and while the child is learning the basic facts with minuends of ten through 18), the child is ready for **regroup-ing.** Teachers in the 1930–1940s taught subtrac-tion using a different algorithm (equal addition) and this process was called "borrowing." When teachers started teaching the regrouping algorithm (decomposition subtraction) the term "borrow" did not describe the trading-in process, so the term "re-group" was adopted for use with children. Unfor-tunately, some teachers still retain the language of the earlier algorithm even though it no longer fits the algorithm that they teach. "Regroup" or "trade" are the preferred words to use when de-scribing the action taking place.

Regrouping traditionally is introduced in the second grade. As with addition, children need a good background in place value when first explor-ing subtraction with regrouping. Activities should be planned that require children to unbundle groups of sticks, pop beads, interlocking blocks; trade bean sticks or base ten rods for singles, etc.

Teachers can anticipate that pupils may have

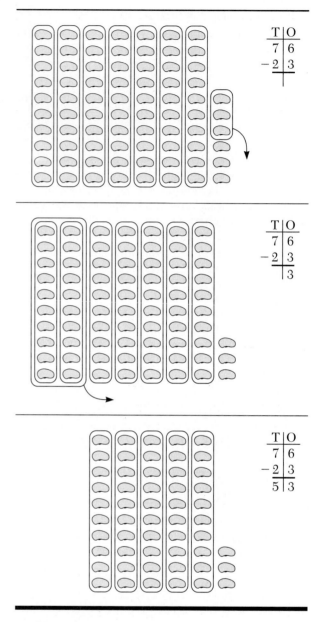

FIGURE 6.20

difficulty with the regrouping concept. It is essen-tial that pupils have a firm understanding of this process BEFORE extensive development of the subtraction algorithm. Once pupils start writing in the algorithm—using helping numerals—they often forget what the little marks beside the nu-merals really mean. Teachers should return to the regrouping concept many times during the year—encouraging pupils to DEMONSTRATE the proc-ess using concrete materials to justify their proce-dure.

Figure 6.21 shows several developmental algo-rithms that lead to the conventional algorithm. De-velopmental algorithms require the use of manipulative materials to reinforce the meaning of the algorithm. The purpose of the developmental algorithm is to build an understanding of the algorithm, so teachers should not hastily abandon it. Teachers may lead their pupils through several developmental algorithms as they strive to build pupil understanding of subtracting 2- and 3-digit minuends and subtrahends. Since a developmental algorithm is used to build understanding it should be abandoned when it no longer effectively performs this function. When a pupil routinely copies amounts into a developmental algorithm without thinking about their meaning, the teacher should consider moving to a more efficient algorithm.

Let us examine a fragment of a lesson in which the teacher uses a place-value chart and the pupils use bean sticks when introducing subtraction with regrouping.

Teacher-Guided Interactive Learning Activity

LESSON FRAGMENT

M: Subtraction with regrouping; conventional algorithm with helper

A: Group of second-graders

T: Model (place-value chart and base ten blocks)

H: Basic subtraction facts; subtraction of tens and ones from tens and ones without regrouping

PROBLEM-SOLVING SITUATION:

THE TEACHER HAS ORDERED 76 WRITING PADS FOR THE CLASS. THE PADS HAVE ARRIVED AND THE TEACHER IS READY TO DISTRIBUTE THEM TO THE CLASS.

Teacher: I ordered 76 writing pads for the class. Each of you—28 pupils—will get one pad. How many pads will we put in the storeroom for later use? Before we start, let's ESTIMATE how many there will be left. When you make your guess—you should have a reason for the estimate. I'll call on one of you to share your guess—but you must tell WHY you have that amount. Douglas?

Douglas: I think it will be around forty—because 28 is near 30 and 76 is near 70.

Teacher: Very good, Douglas. I know some of you have other guesses—you write them down and we'll look at them later. Let us use our bean sticks to help us solve our problem. I will be using the place-

Developmental Algorithms

Expanded Notation (Using Words)

$$
\begin{array}{rcl}
61 &=& 6 \text{ tens } 1 \text{ one } = 5 \text{ tens } 11 \text{ ones} \\
-\,25 &=& 2 \text{ tens } 5 \text{ ones } = 2 \text{ tens } 5 \text{ ones} \\
\hline
&& 3 \text{ tens } 6 \text{ ones}
\end{array}
$$

Expanded Notation Using Numerals	Place Value

$$
\begin{array}{rcl}
61 &=& 60 + 1 \;=\; 50 + 11 \\
-\,25 &=& -(20 + 5) = -(20 + 5) \\
\hline
&& 30 + 6
\end{array}
\qquad
\begin{array}{c|c}
\text{T} & 0 \\
6 & 9 \\
-\,2 & 5 \\
\hline
4 & 4
\end{array}
$$

Conventional algorithm with "helpers"	Conventional algorithm
$\begin{array}{r} {}^{5\;11}\!\!\not{6}\,\not{1} \\ -\,2\,5 \\ \hline 3\,6 \end{array}$	$\begin{array}{r} 6\,1 \\ -\,2\,5 \\ \hline 3\,6 \end{array}$

FIGURE 6.21

value chart to show your actions with your base ten blocks. Will someone come up and represent the 76 on our place-value chart while the rest of you show 76 with your bean sticks? Martin?

Martin: I'll put seven tags in the tens place and six tags in the ones place.

Teacher: Everyone set up your rods and units to show 76. (THE TEACHER WALKS AROUND THE GROUP AND CHECKS EACH CHILD'S WORK.) We are going to be taking 28 away. What operation does this suggest, Billy Jo?

Billy Jo: Subtraction.

Teacher: I'll write our problem on the board while you write the problem on your scrap paper. (SEE FIGURE 6.22.) How many ones will we remove? Sherry?

Sherry: Eight.

Teacher: Do we have enough ones to remove eight of them?

Sherry: No.

Teacher: What could we trade in to get more ones? Rebecca?

Rebecca: We could trade in one ten and get ten more ones. (REBECCA COMES TO THE CHALKBOARD AND TRADES ONE TEN FOR TEN ONES ON THE PLACE-VALUE CHART.)

Teacher: Thank you, Rebecca. You can take your seat while we record what has happened so far. We traded in one ten leaving six tens. (TEACHER CROSSES THROUGH "7" ON ALGORITHM AND WRITES THE REMINDER NUMERAL "6".) Now how many ones do we have, George?

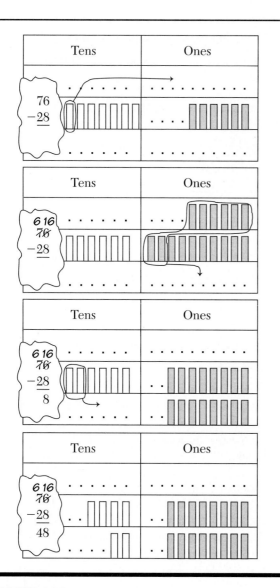

FIGURE 6.22

George: Sixteen.

Teacher: Let's record that on our problem. (TEACHER CROSSES THROUGH THE "6" ONES AND WRITES "16" AS A REMINDER NUMERAL.) Now who can come up to remove our ones for us? Cela?

Cela: I'll take eight ones from 16 ones and I have eight ones left.

Teacher: Good, Cela. Now class, you remove your eight ones. You, too, should have eight single beans left. Let's record that on our problem. (POINTING TO THE "16" THE TEACHER SAYS) 16 minus eight (POINTING TO THE "8" IN THE SUBTRAHEND) is eight. (THE TEACHER WRITES THE "8".)

Teacher: Now, Cela, let's take two tens from the six

tens. Class, you remove two of your bean sticks. How many ten sticks do you have left?

Instructional Group: Four.

Teacher: Cela, how many do we have left on the place-value chart?

Cela: Four.

Teacher: While Cela is taking her seat, let's record what happened. We had six tens—remember we traded in one ten—(TEACHER POINTS TO THE "6" IN THE MINUEND) and we want to subtract two tens (TEACHER POINTS TO THE "2" IN THE SUBTRAHEND), which leaves four tens. (THE TEACHER WRITES "4" IN THE TENS PLACE.) Now, who can tell me how many writing pads we will have left in our storeroom after we have passed out 28 pads? Dirk?

Dirk: Forty-eight pads.

Teacher: I'm going to let you use your rods and units at your desks to complete the problems on the sheets I am passing out. Some of you MAY wish to work in your groups, but you may work independently if you wish.

6.5 TEACHING SUBTRACTION IN THE INTERMEDIATE GRADES

Students come to the intermediate grades with many subtraction skills. In the primary grades they learned the meanings of subtraction; the basic subtraction facts; and subtraction involving 2- and 3-digit minuends—including regrouping. Just as with addition, some students will not have completely mastered subtraction skills from previous grade levels. Intermediate-level teachers must assess each individual's skill in whole number subtraction and provide help in overcoming any deficiencies.

The following illustrates the subtraction skills generally developed at the intermediate level.

Grade 4

Meaning of subtraction
   • maintain take-away, comparison concepts
   • reinforce additive and subset concepts
Subtracting 1-digit addends
   • maintain skill in basic facts
Subtracting with 2- through 5-digit addends
   • with and without regrouping
   • zeros in subtraction
Checking by inverse and estimation
Utilize calculator for multidigit subtraction
Solve problems using subtraction

Grades 5 and 6

Maintain subtraction skills with multidigit addends
Compare properties of addition to those of subtraction
Utilize memory-subtract function on calculator
Explore alternate algorithms for subtraction

Grades 7 and 8

Maintain subtraction skills

6.6 MAINTENANCE OF SUBTRACTION SKILLS

Most students entering the intermediate grades will recognize subtraction when it occurs in take-away and comparison situations, but many will still encounter difficulty when subtraction occurs in additive or subset situations. Not all pupils will have mastered the basic subtraction facts. Some will have developed some *inefficient habits* (such as counting on their fingers) rather than committing the subtraction facts to memory. Estimation is difficult when one has not mastered the facts. Therefore, the intermediate teacher must develop individual programs to aid those students who are deficient in this skill.

Students explore new strategies for organizing basic facts in the intermediate grades. These strategies allow pupils to develop generalizations about the subtraction operation. The strategies commonly developed at this level are the **odd/even generalization,** the **nines' pattern,** and the **compensation pattern.**

The Odd/Even Generalization

In the addition chapter, structured regions were used to develop the odd/even generalization. In a similar fashion, structured regions may be used to develop an odd/even generalization for subtraction. Starting with the sum, the students would take away an odd (or even) addend to determine whether the other addend would be odd or even. Such a practice not only helps students develop an odd/even generalization for finding differences, but it reinforces a student's understanding of the inverse relationship of subtraction and addition.

The calculator also may be used to explore the odd/even generalization for subtraction. While basic facts **may** be used to explore the relationship

Independent Learning Activities

Learning Station

Use your calculator to find the difference between each pair of numbers. Check whether your answer is odd or even.

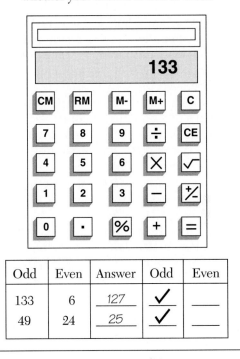

Odd	Even	Answer	Odd	Even
133	6	127	✓	___
49	24	25	✓	___

Pick an odd number and an even number so that the odd number is greater than the even number. Subtract the even number from the odd number using your calculator. Did you get an even number or an odd number?   *Make up a rule!*

Now try the same activity using—
—an even number which is larger—
—two even numbers—
—two odd numbers—

FIGURE 6.23

of adding odd and even numbers, the calculator allows the student to try out much larger numbers to explore the generalization. Figure 6.23 illustrates how a student might use a calculator to subtract odd and even numbers. While the illustration only shows subtracting odd numbers from even numbers, a full development would involve odd from odd, even from odd, and even from even to complete the generalization.

The Nines' Pattern for Subtraction Facts

The pattern when the subtrahend is a nine is particularly interesting. Some students discover this pattern without any teacher guidance. This discovery comes more readily if they utilize a "make-a-ten" strategy when exploring the addition facts. In examining a problem such as 13 − 9, the student may think, "If I start at 9 and **add** 1, that will make 10. Now I have 3 more and so that makes 4. I added 1 and 3 just like the 1 and 3 in the minuend! If you want to subtract 9 from any teen number you can just add the digits of the minuend and you'll get the difference."

Students who discover this simple pattern (adding the digits of the minuend), often do not rationalize **why** the pattern works. The teacher's responsibility in exploring the nines' pattern is to help students understand why adding the digits works with nine as a subtrahend, but does not work when other numbers are used as subtrahends. A wide variety of devices, such as the number line, Unifix™ blocks, and the calculator, may be used to help students explore this relationship. Students discover that subtracting nine from a teen number gives a difference that is **one more** than the units digit in the minuend. Some may discover that when subtracting **eight,** the difference is **two more** than the units digit in the minuend if one is subtracting from ones. Even with manipulative materials some students may not fully understand or appreciate the underlying principles that make the nines' pattern work. They do benefit, however, from seeing a "shortcut" that will help them remember the subtraction facts for the nines. Figure 6.24 illustrates an exploration that employs number lines with the nines' pattern.

The Compensation Pattern for Subtraction Facts

Like the odd/even pattern and nines' pattern, the compensation pattern is introduced to assist students when memorizing the basic subtraction combinations. Compensation **also** is useful when pupils explore alternate algorithms as an intermediate-grade enrichment activity. The compensation pattern, $(N + C) − (M + C) = N − M$, is one of the more interesting subtraction patterns. Its existence permits an organization around families of differences. The following lesson fragment leads to the discovery of this pattern.

Teacher-Guided Interactive Learning Activity

LESSON FRAGMENT

M: Compensation pattern of subtraction

A: Fourth grade

T: Discovery, models

H: Understanding of the meanings of subtraction, subtraction algorithm

PROBLEM-SOLVING SITUATION:

TO INTRODUCE THE COMPENSATION PATTERN THE TEACHER POINTS OUT TO THE CLASS THAT THERE ARE EIGHT BOOKS ON THE TOP SHELF AND ONLY TWO ON THE SECOND SHELF. THE PUPILS ARE ASKED, "HOW MANY MORE BOOKS ARE ON THE TOP SHELF?" AFTER THE RESPONSE OF "SIX" IS GIVEN, THE TEACHER PUTS FIVE MORE BOOKS ON BOTH THE TOP AND SECOND SHELVES—POINTING OUT THAT THERE ARE NOW 13 BOOKS ON THE TOP SHELF AND SEVEN ON THE SECOND SHELF. SHE STANDS IN FRONT OF THE BOOKS SO THE PUPILS CANNOT COUNT THEM AND ASKS, "NOW HOW MANY MORE ARE ON THE TOP SHELF THAN THE SECOND SHELF?" THERE ARE DIFFERING ANSWERS BUT SOME OF THE PUPILS RECOGNIZE THAT THE DIFFERENCE HAS NOT CHANGED.

Exploring Patterns

Do you see the pattern when you subtract nines?

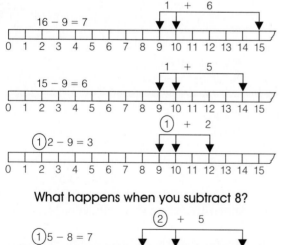

What happens when you subtract 8?

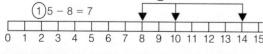

FIGURE 6.24

Teacher: Now suppose I placed more books on each shelf—do you think the difference between the two amounts will change? (ANSWERS DIFFER.) We are going to find out more about what is happening when this sort of thing occurs. Let's use our counters to represent the books and we can act out what is happening to see if we can discover a pattern. Place a row of five counters on your desk and under that row put a row of two counters. (SEE FIGURE 6.25.) What equation is suggested if we want to find out how many more counters there are in the set of five than in the set of two?

Student: Five minus two equals box. (THE TEACHER WRITES THIS EQUATION ON THE BOARD.)

Teacher: What is the difference?

Student: Three.

Teacher: Now place three more counters in your row of five and three more counters in your row of two. Since we put the three with the five and the three with the two, the equation suggested by our activity would be $(5 + 3) - (2 + 3) =$. (THE TEACHER WRITES THIS NEW EQUATION BELOW THE OTHER EQUATION.) What is the solution to this new equation?

Student: Three, the same as before.

Teacher: Now let's see how this might help us on more difficult combinations. Suppose we use $13 - 7$. What would we need to add to seven to get us to ten, Martinez?

Martinez: Three.

Teacher: Now let's use that three to make the fact easier. Let's add three to the seven **and** to the 13. I'm going to write that on the chalkboard. (TEACHER WRITES $(13 + 3) - (7 + 3)$ ON THE CHALKBOARD.) Thirteen plus three is 16 and

Application of Compensation Pattern

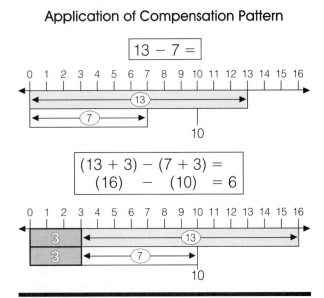

FIGURE 6.26

seven plus three is ten so we REALLY have $16 - 10$. What is the difference between 16 and 10, class?

Class: Six. (SEE FIGURE 6.26.)

Teacher: So, $13 - 7 = 6$. Who can tell us how we can use this procedure to help us find the difference in $15 - 8$? Betty?

Betty: Well, eight and two make ten, so I'll add two to 15, getting 17. The difference between 17 and ten is seven, so $15 - 8$ is 7.

Teacher: Good, Betty. Now let's just see how this might help us with a really big problem. Suppose we had $163 - 98$. Who can get a difference? Burt?

Burt: If you add two to 98, you'll get 100. So I'll compensate by adding two to 163, making it 165. The difference between 100 and 165 is 65!

Teacher: Excellent, Burt! Later on we may wish to explore how this procedure, "compensation," can be used with larger numbers. However, now we might want to use "compensation" to help us with any of those basic combinations that are still giving us trouble.

Practicing the Basic Subtraction Facts

Previously described strategies for mastering facts can also be used at the intermediate level when working with the subtraction facts. Since students at the intermediate level often will be working on specific fact combinations that are different from facts other students are working on, it is difficult to organize facts around group activities. When possible, it is desirable that instructional activities

Compensation Pattern Exploration

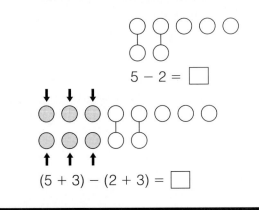

FIGURE 6.25

involving mastery of facts be **student specific.** That is, each student will practice the set of facts that he/she failed to master in the primary grades. Such a procedure requires that some devices be used that not only give the student immediate feedback on responses, but also focus on facts not yet mastered.

There are computer programs, such as those listed in the "Related Computer Software" section at the end of the chapter, and electronic practice devices that teachers can use to provide individual practice. Nonelectronic devices, while less sophisticated than their electronic counterparts, are nonetheless effective in providing the student with immediate feedback for facts not yet mastered. Many of these simple devices can be purchased through school supply stores or can be made by the teacher. Figure 6.27 illustrates one such device, the **Holey Card,** which is made with an index card and a hole punch. Facts that have been missed by a student are copied onto the "Holey" card as those that the individual has not yet mastered. The student practices his/her "demon combinations" using a partner. The partner places the pencil through one of the holes, indicating the basic fact for which the pupil is to give a response. The partner—looking at the correct response on the back of the card—affirms or denies the response.

The Holey Card allows the student to participate in a "**Buddy Drill**"—quickly reviewing those facts that have been identified as needing practice. Such drills must be short and rapidly paced to encourage immediate recall and to maintain interest. Practice sessions should be limited to a one- or two-minute duration. Buddies can change cards and work on the other's demons. Of course, this form of practice also needs to be followed by an oral or written assessment of the student's mastery of the facts.

Checking by Addition

Subtraction is commonly checked by its inverse operation—addition. Teaching the student to check in this manner serves two purposes. Adding to check helps <u>maintain</u> addition skills and is self-checking in that the "sum" must equal the minuend. Even more importantly, such a check reinforces the pupil's understanding of the inverse relationship of the two operations. (Students may have learned an alternate checking technique called "casting out nines" when working with addition. While it is **possible** to check subtraction using this technique, casting out nines is NOT less time-consuming, as it was in addition. Since casting out nines will not detect every kind of error, it is not practical to use this technique with subtraction problems—although more advanced students may wish to explore its use.) Figure 6.28 illustrates the addition-checking process to be taught.

Refining the Subtraction Algorithm

Students enter the intermediate grades with most of the essential subtraction skills developed. There is one situation in the subtraction algorithm introduced in the primary grades that needs more exploration in the intermediate grades. Subtraction where there are **zeros in the minuend** is one kind of regrouping that continues to give students difficulty even into the sixth and seventh grades. Students who can otherwise subtract when there are multiple regroupings struggle with problems such as $500 - 238$. Development of this special case of regrouping in subtraction is commonly found in the third and fourth grades. At these grade levels the teacher is extending an understanding of the algorithm, so helper numerals still will be used.

Small-Group Learning Activity

Holey Practice Card

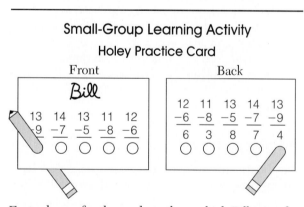

Facts chosen for the card are those which Bill missed on earlier practice sheets. The practice is individualized to meet Bill's practice needs.

FIGURE 6.27

Using Addition to Check Subtraction

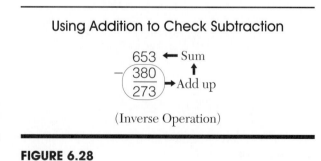

(Inverse Operation)

FIGURE 6.28

Let us examine a fragment of a lesson where this concept is developed at the intermediate level. While it is possible to use a place-value chart, base ten blocks, or bean sticks to develop the algorithm, the teacher has chosen to use the 20-bead abacus. The abacus is held and the beads are manipulated by the teacher. This allows the teacher to direct the group's attention to each step as the beads are moved. The exchange of one bead for ten beads on the abacus is quickly accomplished, thereby allowing the lesson to progress smoothly.

Teacher-Guided Interactive Learning Activity

LESSON FRAGMENT

M: Subtraction algorithm with zero cases

A: Group of fourth-graders

T: Model

H: Subtraction algorithm with regrouping

PROBLEM-SOLVING SITUATION:

THE PREVIOUS DAY THE CLASS HAD BEEN INVOLVED IN AN ART PROJECT USING CONSTRUCTION PAPER. THOUGH THERE ARE MANY SCRAPS WHICH CAN BE USED FOR OTHER PROJECTS, THE TEACHER SEES THE USE OF 129 SHEETS AS AN OPPORTUNITY TO WORK WITH SUBTRACTION WHERE THERE ARE ZEROS IN THE MINUEND.

Teacher: Yesterday we had a stack of 400 sheets of construction paper. We used 129 of them for our art project. How many sheets do we have left? Let's first ESTIMATE to get an idea of what a REASONABLE response might be. Each of you write down your own guess and I will call on two students—but each person must tell WHY the guess was chosen.

Vaughn: Between 200 and 300 sheets—because we used more than 100 sheets and less than 200 sheets.

Andrea: Close to 275—because 129 is close to a dollar and a quarter. If I spent that much from $4, I would have two dollars and three quarters left.

Teacher: Good guesses; now let's use the 20-bead abacus to help us see what happens when we work this problem. I will write the problem on the board. (SEE FIGURE 6.29.) We want to remove nine ones but we do not have any ones. We will need to regroup from the tens. Since we don't have any beads in the tens to regroup to ones, what will we have to do to get some tens? Paco?

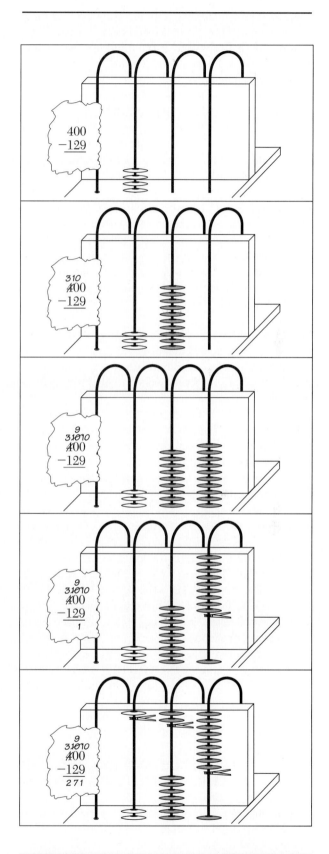

FIGURE 6.29

Paco: You can take one from the hundreds and trade it for tens.

Teacher: If I trade one of the hundreds, how many hundreds will I have left? Revetta?

Revetta: Three hundreds.

Teacher: (ONE OF THE HUNDREDS IS PUSHED TO THE BACK OF THE ABACUS.) I'm going to **record** that on the algorithm by crossing out the 4 and writing a "3" to show that we **now** have three hundreds. How many tens can I get for my one hundred? Nick?

Nick: Ten.

Teacher: (10 TENS ARE BROUGHT FORWARD.) I'm going to record that the tens column is no longer empty—I have ten tens. So I will **write** a "10" to show this.

Teacher: Now I have some tens. If I trade in one of my tens for ten ones, how many tens will I have left? Quince?

Quince: Nine.

Teacher: (MOVES ONE TEN BEAD TO THE BACK.) I'm going to record that by crossing out the ten and writing that we **now** have **nine** tens. How many ones will we get for our one ten? Al?

Al: Ten.

Teacher: (THE TEACHER BRINGS TEN UNIT BEADS TO THE FRONT OF THE ABACUS.) I will **write** "ten" in the units column to indicate we now have ten ones.

Teacher: Julia, how many ones will we have left if we subtract nine ones?

Julia: One one.

Teacher: (PUSHES UP THE NINE ONES AND HOLDS THEM IN PLACE WITH A PIN. THESE ARE LEFT ON THE FRONT OF THE ABACUS SO THE PUPILS CAN SEE THE AMOUNT TAKEN AWAY AND THE AMOUNT REMAINING.) We'll **record** the one one in our algorithm.

Teacher: Barbara, how many tens will be left if we subtract two tens?

Barbara: Seven tens.

Teacher: (PUSHES UP TWO TENS AND PLACES A CLIP TO HOLD THEM.) We'll now **record** our seven tens.

Teacher: Cindy, how many hundreds will be left, if we subtract 100 from 200?

Cindy: One hundred.

Teacher: (PUSHES UP ONE HUNDRED AND PLACES A CLIP TO HOLD IT.) We'll now **record** our two hundreds.

Teacher: How much construction paper will we have left if we used 129 of 400 sheets? Raff?

Raff: Two hundred seventy-one.

Andrea: I was really close, wasn't I, teacher!

(WHEN THE PROBLEM IS COMPLETED, THE PUPILS WILL SEE THAT SUBTRACTION SEPARATES A SUM INTO TWO ADDENDS—THE KNOWN ADDEND IS ON THE TOP AND THE MISSING ADDEND REMAINS ON THE BOTTOM. THE PROBLEM CAN BE CHECKED BY <u>PUTTING THE SETS TOGETHER OR UNDOING THE SUBTRACTION</u>.)

Teacher: Now we are going to work in our groups using our base ten blocks. Each leader will pick up an assignment sheet. You can take turns using the BLOCKS to verify the answers.

After students understand the regrouping that takes place when there are zeros in the minuend, the teacher will help students become more efficient in this kind of subtraction situation. Later (sometimes in the next grade level) the algorithm is shortened to bypass the step-by-step regrouping in favor of a single regrouping act. Figure 6.30 illustrates how the skills developed with place value are implemented in the shortcut method of dealing with zero cases.

Maintenance of Subtraction Skills in Other Areas

As with addition, some maintenance of subtraction skills will occur during the normal development of work in other areas. Subtraction of fractional numbers (positive rationals) and decimals contribute to maintaining subtraction skills. The division algorithm, which is usually developed in the fourth, fifth, and sixth grades, also requires proficiency in subtraction. (See Figure 6.31.)

Using place value skills to become more efficient when subtracting with zeros in the minuend.

zeros in the minuend	Regrouping each column	More advanced thinking
400 −129	$\overset{9}{\cancel{3}}\,\overset{}{\cancel{10}}\,\overset{}{10}$ 400 −129	$3\;9\;10$ 400 −129 271

Instead of looking at the tens column and thinking there is nothing in the tens column — the child thinks — "I have forty tens. If I regroup one ten it will leave 39 tens."

FIGURE 6.30

Subtraction Skills Maintained Incidental to the Development of More Advanced Skills

Fractional Numbers

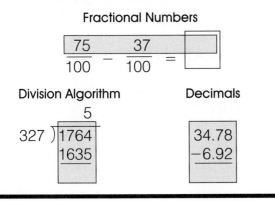

$$\frac{75}{100} - \frac{37}{100} = \boxed{}$$

Division Algorithm

$$327 \overline{)\begin{array}{c} 5 \\ 1764 \\ \underline{1635} \end{array}}$$

Decimals

$$\begin{array}{r} 34.78 \\ -6.92 \\ \hline \end{array}$$

FIGURE 6.31

Using a Calculator in Multistep Problem Solving

When children have access to calculators they conduct many more explorations with subtraction than when calculators are not available. Without a calculator, children spend much of their time calculating with paper and pencil—not developing problem-solving skills. **When calculators are available, children spend most of their time analyzing the problem and choosing the operation—not practicing calculation skills.** Problem-solving concepts can be developed almost independent of the child's ability to compute manually, provided the child understands the meaning of the operation being undertaken on the calculator. The teacher's decision to make calculators available to pupils should be based upon the purpose (objective) of the lesson. If the lesson objective is practicing computational skills in a setting that allows the child to see an application of the skill in typical situations, then perhaps calculators should not be used. If the objective of the lesson is one of building problem-solving skills, then making calculators available is an appropriate choice.

Teachers must carefully analyze the school setting to provide opportunities for pupils to USE subtraction in meaningful situations. Some schools allow individual classes to operate a room or school store. Pupils can use a calculator to accurately maintain a balance. As a part of operating a store, the class treasurer should report the daily balance in the class' **school supply account** after "posting" each day's expenses. Figure 6.32 illustrates the account book used by the student and some of the expenses that must be entered. The student is

Multistep Problem Solving Using a Calculator

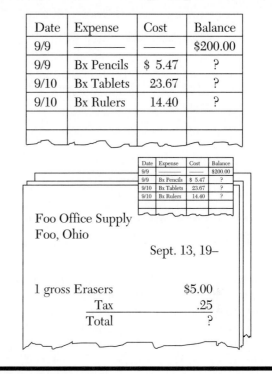

Date	Expense	Cost	Balance
9/9	———	———	$200.00
9/9	Bx Pencils	$ 5.47	?
9/10	Bx Tablets	23.67	?
9/10	Bx Rulers	14.40	?

Foo Office Supply
Foo, Ohio

Sept. 13, 19–

1 gross Erasers	$5.00
Tax	.25
Total	?

FIGURE 6.32

required to record the date, the type of item, the cost of the item, and the balance in the account after each item is recorded. The activity illustrated occurs at the beginning of the year and all of the expenses for stocking the class school supply account must be "posted." (The beginning balance is the amount placed into the account from the school activity fund.)

6.7 EXPLORING SUBTRACTION PATTERNS AND PROPERTIES

While the commutative and associative properties do not exist for the subtraction operation with whole numbers, children may still learn a great deal from the explorations that lead to this discovery. Children can easily discover that the commutative property does not hold for subtraction. Figure 6.33 illustrates a learning-station card that may lead a child to this discovery.

One does not have to resort to models to demonstrate effectively that the associative property does not hold for subtraction. Having the student independently study carefully selected pairs of

Learning-Station Card

How many do we have left if we take 2 from 5?

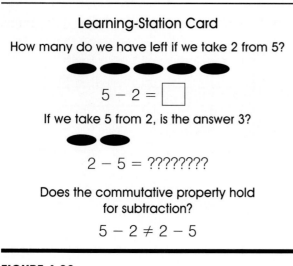

$$5 - 2 = \square$$

If we take 5 from 2, is the answer 3?

$$2 - 5 = ????????$$

Does the commutative property hold
for subtraction?

$$5 - 2 \neq 2 - 5$$

FIGURE 6.33

equations will quickly demonstrate this fact to the student. For example, the following illustrates one such pair of equations that can be used to demonstrate that the associative property does not hold for subtraction: Is "N" the same in BOTH equations? (a) **(7 − 4) − 3 = N** (b) **7 − (4 − 3) = N**

Patterns such as "n − 0 = n" and "n − n = 0" should be reviewed in the intermediate grades. Review of other patterns, such as the compensation pattern for subtraction, occurs in the natural course of instruction and enrichment activities.

6.8 COMPUTERS

The task of balancing a checkbook is an excellent multistep problem-solving activity. The description below describes how the spreadsheet program, introduced in Chapter 5, can be used for this task. (A calculator could also be used for this task.) During the "accounting process" children will be using both subtraction and addition. Figure 6.34 describes the components required for setting up the problem on a spreadsheet. Figure 6.35 summarizes the process of reconciling the "books" with the bank statement, after the conceptual understanding of the process has been developed.

When the activity (described above) uses a computer, individual pupils are permitted to work through the problem as time allows. When calculators are used, the teacher may wish to make the balancing of the books a class activity with all children using their calculators to check the records—comparing their results at the end of the period.

If recording errors (misrecorded checks and/or

deposits) do not occur naturally, the teacher may wish to present data with "errors" for the class to find. Determining how to make adjustments for errors extends the child's problem-solving skills.

6.9 EVALUATION AND INTERVENTION

In assessing the child's understanding of subtraction, teachers must remember there are different models that a child needs to be able to associate with subtraction (take-away, comparison, subset, and additive) in order to be successful problem solvers. Many children need help recognizing sub-

Multistep Problem Solving
Using Spreadsheet Programs

Setting up a Spreadsheet for Bank Statement/Checkbook Reconciliation

FIRST	THEN
1. Designate a cell for this month's bank statement balance.	Record Data
2. Designate enough cells to record all deposits not recorded on bank statement.	Record Data
3. Designate a cell to hold a function that will add 1 and 2.	Specify Function
4. Designate enough cells to record all the checks that have not come to the bank yet.	Record Data
5. Designate a cell to hold a function to add data in 4.	Specify Function
6. Designate a cell to hold a function to subtract 5 from 3.	Specify Function
– Designate a cell next to this cell labeled "Adjusted Bank Balance."	Label
7. Designate a cell to record checkbook balance.	Record Data
8. Designate a cell to record service charge.	Record Data
9. Designate a cell to hold a function to subtract 8 from 7.	Specify Function
– Label this cell "adjusted checkbook balance."	Label

COMPARE TWO ADJUSTED BALANCES

FIGURE 6.34

Simplified Reconciliation Form

1. Write end-of-the-month bank balance here. . . . . _____

2. Write total of deposits that are not in the bank statement here. . . . . _____

3. Total of 1 and 2 . . . . _____

4. Sum of checks which have not reached the bank yet here. . . . . . . _____

⑤ Subtract 4 form 3. This is your adjusted balance . . . . . [____]

6. Write your checkbook balance here . . . . _____

7. Write the service charge (what the bank charges for its service). . . _____

8. Subtract 7 from 8. This is your adjusted checkbook balance . . . . . [____]

⑨ The amount in 5 and 8 should be the same! Is it?

FIGURE 6.35

traction, especially when it appears in additive and subset situations—even in the fifth through eighth grades. A few children, primarily those in the third and fourth grades, also experience difficulty relating comparison to subtraction. Children seldom encounter difficulty associating subtraction with take-away. Indeed, many children read the equation "8 − 3" as "eight take-away three."

The assessment/diagnosis of subtraction computational skills is a part of evaluating the child's daily practice worksheets. The focus should be to determine if a pupil's understanding of the operations is deficient, or if the child has habituated some type of error that needs to be remediated. Figure 6.36 illustrates three of the more common types of **habituated** errors that pupils make with subtraction.

6.10 MEETING SPECIAL NEEDS

Once students have a sound foundation in subtraction concepts, a teacher may extend understanding of subtraction in many ways. One way of deepening understanding is for students to explore nonconventional algorithms in base ten and student-created subtraction algorithms. In this section

Typical Computational Errors in Subtraction

$$\begin{array}{r} 9\overset{7\ 13}{\cancel{8}3} \\ -257 \\ \hline 625 \end{array}$$

Type of error:
Basic fact error

REMEDIATION FOCUS—

Pupil regroups properly. Basic facts 9 − 2 and 13 − 7 are not yet mastered. Manipulative materials would not generally be needed.

$$\begin{array}{r} 82 \\ -19 \\ \hline 77 \end{array}$$

Type of error:
Subtracts smaller digit from larger digit

REMEDIATION FOCUS—

Understanding of the subtraction operation and algorithm.

$$\begin{array}{r} 4\overset{1}{6} \\ -7 \\ \hline 49 \end{array}$$

Type of error:
Does not reduce the traded in digit

REMEDIATION FOCUS—

Regrouping process—return to using manipulative materials to establish reason "4" is changed to "3" in the algorithm.

FIGURE 6.36

nonconventional algorithms are examined as devices for extending the child's understanding of subtraction.

The subtraction regrouping (decomposition) algorithm is commonly used in mathematics programs today. It is not the only algorithm for subtraction. Forty to fifty years ago American schools taught children using the equal addition algorithm. The algorithm is still used by some adults, and occasionally teachers will find a child who was taught this algorithm by his/her grandparents. The equal addition algorithm utilizes the understanding that equal amounts can be added to the minuend and subtrahend without changing the difference (compensation). Figure 6.37 illustrates the algorithm and the rationale for each step.

Sometimes a student will ask the question, "Can you subtract from left to right?" Such questions provide an excellent opportunity to examine a left-to-right algorithm (Figure 6.38) as an enrichment activity. After using this algorithm children will recognize why a right-to-left algorithm is normally used, especially when a neatly written difference is desired.

Enrichment Exploration

Equal-Addition Algorithm (Compensation)

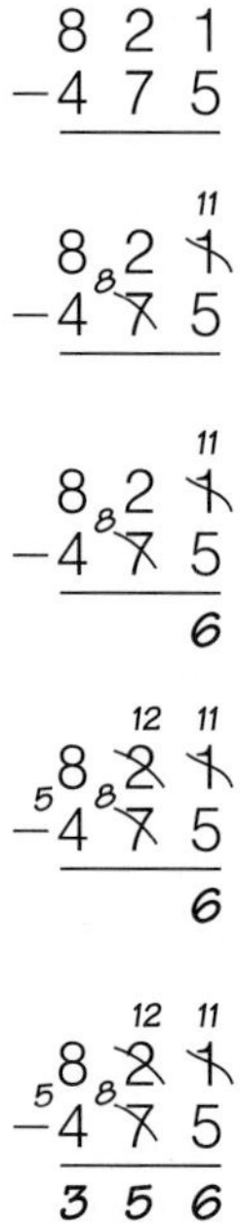

$$
\begin{array}{r}
8\ 2\ 1 \\
-4\ 7\ 5 \\
\end{array}
$$

STEP 1
"Borrow" ten ones in the minuend and "pay back" by adding 1 ten in the minuend.

$$
\begin{array}{r}
8\ {}_{8}2\ \overset{11}{\cancel{1}} \\
-4\ \cancel{7}\ 5 \\
\end{array}
$$

STEP 2
Subtract 5 ones from 11 ones.

$$
\begin{array}{r}
8\ {}_{8}2\ \overset{11}{\cancel{1}} \\
-4\ {}^{8}\cancel{7}\ 5 \\
\hline
6
\end{array}
$$

STEP 3
"Borrow" 10 tens in the minuend and "pay back" 1 hundred in the subtrahend.

$$
\begin{array}{r}
8\ {}_{8}\overset{12}{\cancel{2}}\ \overset{11}{\cancel{1}} \\
-{}_{5}4\ \cancel{7}\ 5 \\
\hline
6
\end{array}
$$

STEPS 4 & 5
Subtract 8 tens from 12 tens. Then subtract 5 hundreds from 8 hundreds.

$$
\begin{array}{r}
8\ {}_{8}\overset{12}{\cancel{2}}\ \overset{11}{\cancel{1}} \\
-{}_{5}4\ \cancel{7}\ 5 \\
\hline
3\ 5\ 6
\end{array}
$$

FIGURE 6.37

Enrichment Exploration

Front-End Subtraction (Left to Right Algorithm)

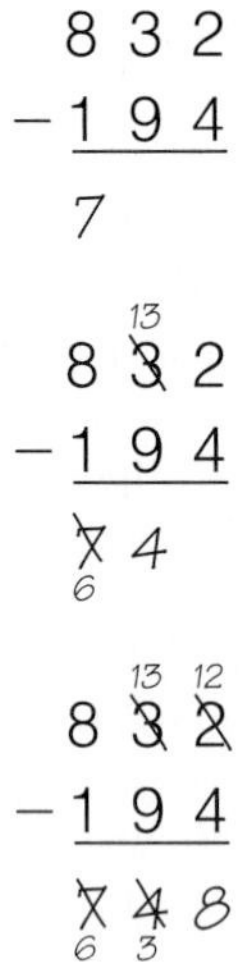

$$
\begin{array}{r}
8\ 3\ 2 \\
-1\ 9\ 4 \\
\hline
7
\end{array}
$$

Subtract the 1 hundred from the 8 hundreds.

$$
\begin{array}{r}
8\ \overset{13}{\cancel{3}}\ 2 \\
-1\ 9\ 4 \\
\hline
\underset{6}{\cancel{7}}\ 4
\end{array}
$$

• Regroup 1 hundred from the 7 in the *difference* and trade for 10 tens. *Change* the 3 to 13 tens and subtract 9 from 13 to get 4 tens.

$$
\begin{array}{r}
8\ \overset{13}{\cancel{3}}\ \overset{12}{\cancel{2}} \\
-1\ 9\ 4 \\
\hline
\underset{6}{\cancel{7}}\ \underset{3}{\cancel{4}}\ 8
\end{array}
$$

• Regroup 1 ten from the 4 tens in the *difference* and trade it for 10 ones. *Change* the 2 ones to 12 ones and subtract 4 ones to get 8 ones.

FIGURE 6.38

Providing for the Learning Disabled

Learning-disabled children benefit from being able to use a calculator when solving computational

Algorithm for Learning-Disabled Student

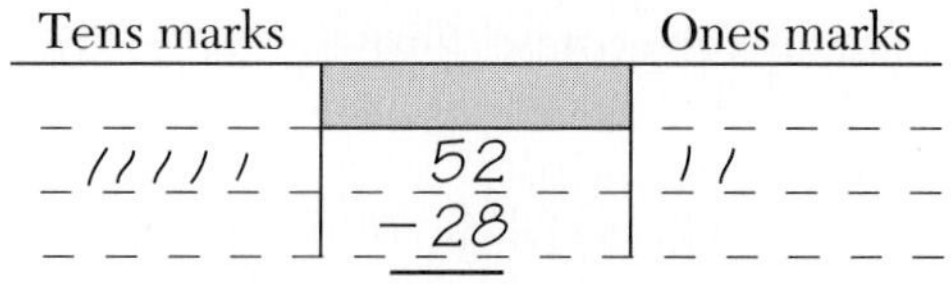

The child copies the problem to the counting frame, making his tens marks and ones marks. He counts his ones to see if he can remove 8 ones.

Child renames 1 ten to 10 ones.

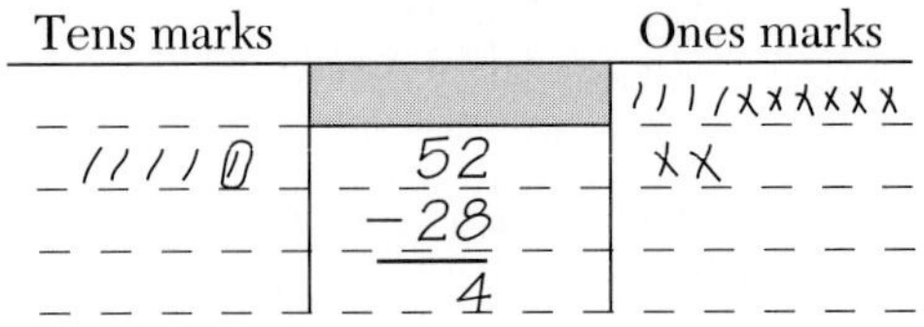

The child then proceeds to mark off 8 ones and records the 4 ones that are left. He now sees that he can take 2 tens from 4 tens.

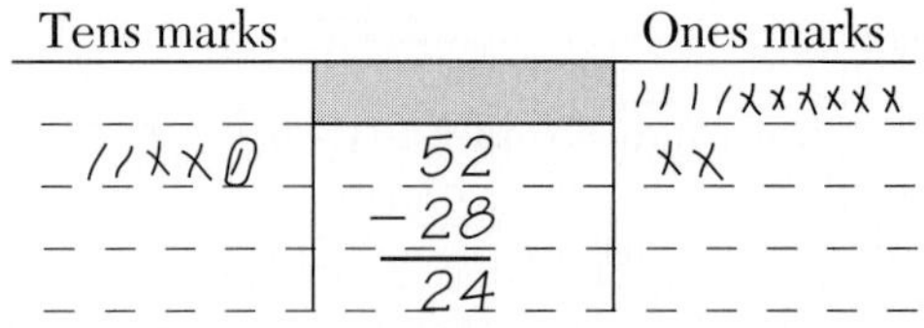

FIGURE 6.39

problems. However, before using calculators regularly, learning-disabled children must first understand subtraction—its models and its algorithm. There are several nonstandard algorithms that may be used by the teacher to develop the child's understanding of subtraction computational algorithms.

This section presents two algorithms that teachers of learning-disabled children may find useful. To use the first algorithm (the **counting subtraction algorithm**) a child must be skillful with place value, counting, and the take-away meaning of subtraction (see Figure 6.39). The second algorithm (**dribble subtraction algorithm**) requires the child to be functional with basic facts through minuends of ten (see Figure 6.40).

Algorithm for Learning-Disabled Student

Child's Thinking Process for Dribble Subtraction Algorithm

$$\begin{array}{r} 82 \\ -\ 37 \\ \hline \end{array}$$

I can't subtract 7 from 2. I'll trade 1 ten for 10 ones.

$$\begin{array}{r} {}^{7\ 10} \\ 8\!\!\!/2 \\ -\ 37 \\ \hline 5 \end{array}$$

I'll subtract 7 from ten and get 3. Then I'll put the 3 with the 2 that I had, making 5 ones.

$$\begin{array}{r} {}^{7\ 10} \\ 8\!\!\!/2 \\ -\ 37 \\ \hline 45 \end{array}$$

Now I'll take 3 tens from 7 tens, leaving 4 tens.

FIGURE 6.40

Algorithm for More Able Student

Compensation

$$\begin{array}{r} 7845 \\ -\ 2997 \\ \hline \end{array}$$

The child thinks:
⟵———— If I add 3 to 2997 it will become 3000.

$$\begin{array}{r} 7845 + 3 \\ -\ 2997 + 3 \\ \hline \end{array}$$

So I'll add 3 to the 7845 to *compensate*.

$$\begin{array}{r} 7848 \\ -\ 3000 \\ \hline 848 \end{array}$$

7848 is 4,848 more than 3000!

FIGURE 6.41

Providing for the Gifted Student

Like learning-disabled children, gifted children have special needs that are addressed either by horizontal enrichment or vertical enrichment. Each school system determines which of these approaches will be used. With horizontal enrichment the teacher provides material that will broaden the child's understanding of those skills being taught to all children. The teacher may make the gifted child aware of the historical development of the subtraction algorithm and how terms such as "borrow" became a part of the language of subtraction. A teacher could examine some of the "shortcut" subtraction algorithms that would utilize a gifted child's ability to remember data as he/she is processing an algorithm—for example, pointing out how the compensation property can be used when the subtrahend is close to but less than a multiple of hundreds, or thousands, or ten thousands. Such a process permits the student with good memory faculties to bypass the conventional paper-and-pencil regrouping algorithm and mentally compute the answer. Figure 6.41 illustrates the thought process of using the compensation process when encountering one of these special subtrahends.

6.11 SUMMARY

For the most part the foundation for subtraction skills is completed by the time the child finishes the primary grades. By the end of the third grade the average child will recognize four subtraction models—removing part of a set (take-away); matching sets to determine which set has more or less than the other set (comparison); finding a part of a larger set (subset); and putting together sets where the number of one of the sets was known (additive). Strategies for mastering the basic subtraction facts are introduced and most children will have mastered (memorized) the 100 basic combinations—though some still count to get a difference. The child will be proficient, although not necessarily efficient, in subtracting with 2- and 3-digit minuends and subtrahends (both with and without regrouping), although problems with zeros in tens, hundreds, and thousands may not be mastered by the end of the third grade. The child will be able to use technological devices such as the calculator and computer to do lengthy and involved subtraction involving whole numbers.

At the intermediate level the subtraction skills the pupil brings from the primary grades will be maintained and extended. A major emphasis at this level is on working problems that require multiple regroupings—especially those with zero in the minuend. Activities with the calculator and computer become much more extensive at the intermediate level, including activities with multistep problem solving and the use of "spreadsheet" programs.

EXERCISES

1. Illustrate with drawing and/or materials 10 − 3 using:
   a. The take-away subtraction model.
   b. The comparison subtraction model.
   c. The additive subtraction model.
   d. The subset subtraction model.
2. Describe how a teacher would develop each of the listed approaches to exploring the basic facts:
   a. Counting-on strategy
   b. Build-to-ten
   c. Related facts strategy
   d. Odd/even generalization strategy
   e. Nines pattern
   f. Compensation pattern
3. For each of the strategies or patterns above, describe an activity that could be arranged by a teacher to develop an understanding of the concept.
4. Examine the "story problems" below. Tell which subtraction model would be appropriate when illustrating the problem and write an open number sentence that follows the action of the problem.
   a. Mrs. Ball had 228 records. She gave some of them to Jim. She then had 175 records. How many records did she give to Jim?
   b. Ellen saved $4.75 and Kay saved $7.00. Ellen saved how much less money than Kay?
   c. Carol saved some spools. She used 88 of them to make dolls. Then she had 174 spools. How many spools had Carol saved?
   d. Sue wants to buy a set of dolls that costs $3.45. She has $.98. How much more money does Sue need before she can buy the set of dolls?
   e. A clerk has large balloons and small balloons. He has 78 balloons in all. Thirty-two of the balloons were small—how many were large?
   f. Bill got nine new train cars. He then had 36 train cars in all. Bill had how many train cars before he got the nine new cars?
   g. Mike is 53 inches tall. That makes him eight inches taller than his younger brother. How tall is his younger brother?
5. Examine a current textbook series. Look at the "story problems" that require subtraction. Decide which subtraction model would be most appropriate for each example.
6. Use a place-value chart or base ten blocks to associate each step of the conventional subtraction algorithm with a physical action using the materials. Use the problems illustrated below.
   a. 87 − 25   b. 72 − 38   c. 342 − 169
   d. 700 − 436
7. The set of exercises below show how three different pupils worked a given problem.
   a. Examine each problem and speculate upon how the pupil arrived at the answer.
   b. Suggest an instructional procedure which might be used to overcome the misunderstanding.

   TOM: 832 − 246 = 614
   533 − 217 = 324
   728 − 385 = 463

   BILL: 832 − 246 = 597
   533 − 217 = 317
   728 − 385 = 353

   ANN: 832 − 246 = 696
   533 − 217 = 326
   728 − 385 = 443

8. When possible, new skills should be introduced in a meaningful situation. Suggest a classroom situation that could be used to introduce regrouping. (Use 2-digit numbers.)
9. Work the problems below using the algorithms suggested.
   a. 58 − 26 (developmental algorithm—using expanded notation with words)
   b. 83 − 47 (developmental algorithm—using expanded notation with numerals)
   c. 843 − 285 (conventional algorithm—using helper numerals)
   d. 500 − 238 (conventional algorithm with helpers—shortened version)
   e. 736 − 158 (enrichment algorithm—front-end subtraction)
   f. 437 − 248 (enrichment algorithm—equal addition algorithm)
   g. 8354 − 1628 (enrichment algorithm—dribble subtraction)
10. Read and summarize—"Modelling Subtraction Situations" by Thompson and Van De Walle (see References).
11. Identify two concept areas that present problems when teaching subtraction.
12. In assessing a student's ability to solve prob-

lems involving subtraction you notice that one student attempts to solve additive subtraction situations by addition because he is using only the "putting together" as his clue for solving the problem. Identify a teaching strategy you would use to help this student make the proper association with the correct subtraction model.

RELEVANT COMPUTER SOFTWARE

Educalc. Apple II family. Grolier Electronic Publishing, Sherman Turnpike, Danbury, Conn. 06816. (A tutorial on spreadsheets—provides interactive practice and a simple spreadsheet.)

Math Amazing. Apple II family. 1986. Light 8, 3915 Third Avenue, San Diego, Calif. 92103.

Minus Mission. (Available for various computers.) Developmental Learning Materials, One DLM Park, P.O. Box 4000, Allen, Tex. 75002. (Practices subtraction in an arcade game format—variable speeds.)

Subtraction Defenders. Apple II family. 1985. Gamco Industries, Box 1911, Big Spring, Tex. 79720.

Whole Numbers. (Available for various computers.) Control Data Publishing Co., P.O. Box 261127, San Diego, Calif. 92126. (Practice in basic facts in a game format.)

REFERENCES

Balka, D. *Polyhedra Dice Games for Grades K to 6.* Palo Alto, Calif.: Creative Publications, 1978. Pp. 16–18.

Hiatt, A. A. "Activities for Calculators." *Arithmetic Teacher* 34 (February 1987): 38–43.

Hiebert, J. "The Struggle to Link Written Symbols with Understandings." *Arithmetic Teacher* 36 (March 1989): 38–43.

Moser, J. M. "Arithmetic Operations on Whole Numbers: Addition and Subtraction." Edited by T. R. Post. Chapter 5 in *Teaching Mathematics in Grades K–8: Research Based Methods.* Boston: Allyn and Bacon, 1988.

Reys, R. E.; M. N. Suydam; and M. M. Lindquist. *Helping Children Learn Mathematics.* Englewood Cliffs, N.J.: Prentice-Hall, 1989. Pp. 137–140.

Riedesel, C. A. Chapter 7 in *Teaching Elementary School Mathematics.* Englewood Cliffs, N.J.: Prentice-Hall, 1984.

Thompson, C. S., and J. Van De Walle. "Modelling Subtraction Situations." *Arithmetic Teacher* 32 (October 1984): 8–12.

Thornton, C. A. " 'Look Ahead' Activities Spark Success in Addition and Subtraction Number-Fact Learning." *Arithmetic Teacher* 36 (April 1989): 8–11.

Thornton, C. A., and P. J. Smith. "Action Research: Strategies for Learning Subtraction Facts." *Arithmetic Teacher* 35 (April 1988): 8–12.

CHAPTER 7

TEACHING MULTIPLICATION OF WHOLE NUMBERS AND FACTORS, MULTIPLES, PRIMES, AND EXPONENTS

INTRODUCTION

Multiplication plays a major role in many everyday problem-solving activities. Each time multiple items are purchased multiplication plays a role in finding the total cost. The purchase prices of electrical energy, gas, gasoline, and water are computed by multiplying rate per unit and the units purchased. In addition, many items are purchased by the carton, box, dozen, or other multiples, and multiplication is used to determine the total cost number when more than one unit is involved.

A thorough understanding of multiplication concepts also serves as a foundation for success with a wide variety of other mathematical processes. Mastery of the division algorithm, fractional number operations, least common multiple, greatest common factor, equivalent fractions, powers, roots, factoring, etc., requires multiplication skills.

Technological devices are commonly used by store clerks, accountants, engineers, and homemakers when they need to find the product of two numbers. Most adults use a calculator to multiply large numbers. Calculators or computers are the most efficient means of multiplying two numbers (except for basic fact combinations), but a good understanding of the operation, its properties, and its applications is essential when using these technological devices. This under-standing must be the primary focus when multiplication is taught.

There are a variety of activities that suggest multiplication. Putting together equivalent sets and determining the total; finding the total number associated with equal sets; finding the number associated with an array, or finding the number associated with the cross-product of two sets all suggest multiplication.

In contrast to addition and subtraction, which are extensively developed in the primary grades, most exploration of the multiplication operation takes place in the intermediate grades. Pupils find that a good foundation in addition helps when learning the multiplication facts. Additions skills are extensively employed in multiplication algorithms, when partial products are added to find the product.

While it may be difficult to physically count the number associated with many products, multiplication offers a variety of patterns that can be used to promote memorization of basic facts. These patterns add interest to the study of basic multiplication facts and provide readiness experiences for basic algebraic equations.

7.1 TEACHING MULTIPLICATION IN THE PRIMARY GRADES

Children enter the primary grades with very limited experience with multiplication concepts. For the most part, those experiences are limited to an awareness of ideas such as two sets of five fingers is the same as ten fingers, and two sets of two is four. Children also are aware that one set of objects has a certain number associated with it, which is later formalized as "1 × N = N." In contrast to the vocabulary they brought to the primary grades for addition and subtraction, children do not bring to the primary grades the type of vocabulary that can immediately be utilized by the teacher to develop multiplication. Because of children's limited experience with multiplication concepts and vocabulary, the teacher must bridge from addition concepts to multiplication and must provide extensive development of the vocabulary associated with multiplication as well as multiplication concepts.

Children first associate multiplication with finding the total number of objects associated with a number of equivalent sets. Before introducing terminology such as times, multiplier, factor, and product, the teacher must stress finding the number associated with N sets of M (for example, 2 sets of 4 equals 8). Gradually, as the models are explored, a formal vocabulary is developed. Years ago, terminology such as multiplier and multiplicand were used. These terms have generally been supplanted by the term "factor," which has later applications in the study of fractional numbers, primes, etc. (see Figure 7.1).

In the latter part of the primary grades, a teacher will use the child's ability to count by ones, twos, and fives to develop the ones, twos, and fives multiplication facts. Some properties and patterns of multiplication will be explored.

In some third-grade programs the multiplication algorithm will be explored with 1-digit multipliers and 2-digit multiplicands. Just as with other oper-

Three sets of two equal 6.

Multiplier	Multiplicand	Product
3	× 2	= 6
Factor	Factor	Product

Factor	2	Multiplicand
Factor	× 3	Multiplier
Product	6	Product

FIGURE 7.1

ations, a developmental algorithm is used to build understanding. The developmental algorithms in Figure 7.2 strengthen the child's understanding of place value and the use of the distributive property.

The study of multiplication is generally found in the "Whole Number Operations" **strand** of the elementary school curriculum. The scope and sequence that follows may vary from a given program in the timing of the introduction of the multiplication algorithm. Some programs introduce this topic in the third grade and other programs in the fourth grade. This text places exploration of the algorithm in the third grade, but limits these activities to the multiplication facts families that have been introduced in that grade level. As calculators become a more established part of the elementary curriculum it is quite likely that schools will choose to examine the multiplication algorithm much earlier than they presently do.

Grade 1

Readiness for multiplication
• skip counting by twos, fives, and tens

Developmental Algorithms
Expanded-Notation Algorithm

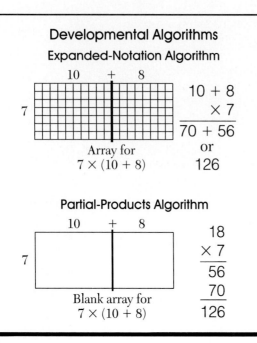

Array for
$7 \times (10 + 8)$

$$\begin{array}{r} 10 + 8 \\ \times\ 7 \\ \hline 70 + 56 \end{array}$$
or
126

Partial-Products Algorithm

10   +   8

7

Blank array for
$7 \times (10 + 8)$

$$\begin{array}{r} 18 \\ \times\ 7 \\ \hline 56 \\ 70 \\ \hline 126 \end{array}$$

FIGURE 7.2

Grade 2

Develop meaning of multiplication
- develop equivalent sets concept and equal measures concepts

Develop multiplication vocabulary
- factor, product, times

Explore basic facts
- explore ones, twos, fives

Examine properties and patterns
- explore identity property; commutative property
- explore twos and fives pattern

Grade 3

Develop meaning of multiplication
- strengthen equivalent sets and equal measure concept
- develop array concept

Multiply 1-digit factors
- master zeros, ones, twos, fives
- explore with threes, fours, sixes, sevens, eights, and nines

Examine properties and patterns
- maintain commutative and identity properties
- explore with associative and distributive properties
- examine zeros, twos, fours, fives, and nines patterns

Multiply ones times tens
Multiply 1-digit times 2-digit (teens)

7.2 DEVELOPING THE MEANINGS OF MULTIPLICATION

Children need many hands-on experiences with multiplication to understand the operation. The first model used to introduce children to multiplication will involve situations using **equivalent sets** (sets that have the same amount). By introducing multiplication using set models, a teacher takes advantage of the children's familiarity and extensive work with set models before encountering the concepts of multiplication. Other models for multiplication are explored in the intermediate grades.

The Equivalent-Sets Model for Multiplication

By the time a child begins formal study of multiplication, he/she will have several skills that can be used in its study. One of these skills is "skip counting." The pupil's ability to count by twos and fives will prepare the child for studying multiplication with twos and fives facts. While the number of objects represented by the product can be determined by ones, the use of skip counting is more efficient in developing teaching lessons. It not only cuts the amount of time spent in counting, but has direct benefit later when the child memorizes the facts.

Let us examine a fragment of an equal-sets multiplication lesson being developed from the following problem situation.

Teacher-Guided Interactive Learning Activity

LESSON
FRAGMENT

M: Associating multiplication with the activity of finding the total number of objects in a number of sets equal in number

A: Group of second-graders

T: Involvement (choral), hands-on work with models

H: Children can skip count by twos

PROBLEM-SOLVING SITUATION:
THE STUDENTS HAVE BEEN INVOLVED IN A CLASS PROJECT—COLLECTING CANS OF FOOD

TO DONATE TO A LOCAL FOOD PANTRY. YES-TERDAY NINE CHILDREN EACH BROUGHT IN TWO CANS. THE TEACHER POSED THE QUESTION, "DOES ANYONE KNOW HOW MANY CANS THEY BROUGHT IN ALL?" FROM THIS PROBLEM THE FOLLOWING LESSON DEVELOPS.

Teacher: Yesterday nine of you brought in cans of food. We wanted to find out how many cans we had in all and many suggested just counting them. Before our groups get started today we are going to explore other ways of finding out how many in all when each person has the same amount. I would like for each person in your group to put six sets of two counters on your desk. We are going to use this to represent six sets of two cans. I am going to place a numeral "6" card on the chalk tray to tell the number of groups and a "2" card to tell how many cans in each group. Put <u>cards</u> under your set as I am doing. (CHILDREN PLACE THEIR SETS AND NUMERAL CARDS ON THEIR DESKS.) (SEE FIGURE 7.3.)

Teacher: (HOLDS UP A TIMES SIGN.) This is called a <u>times</u> sign. It tells us we are going to find the total number of objects when we have equivalent sets. Put the times sign between the 6 and 2, as I am doing.

Teacher: Let's count together—by twos—to find the total number when we have six groups with two in each group.

Instructional group: Two, four, six, eight, ten, twelve.

Teacher: Six groups of two is how many, Bess?

Bess: Twelve.

Teacher: We can put "equals twelve" after our "six times two." Everyone do this. (THE GROUP PLACES "= 12" ON THEIR DESKS.) We read this multiplication equation "Six times two equals twelve." Let's read it together.

Instructional group: Six times two equals twelve.

Teacher: Today our groups are going to explore "putting equal-sized groups together." Each team leader can pick up a picture sheet of some of the equal-sized groups we have seen. Work together in your groups—using your counters to act out the situation and then use your numeral cards to build a number sentence. REMEMBER—we want EVERYONE in your group to be able to demonstrate this new way of writing number sentences. When ALL in your group agree that the number sentence is correct, your Recorder can copy your sentence onto the sheet. (FIGURE 7.4.)

The Array Model for Multiplication

Sets are found in everyday situations in a special type of arrangement called an **array**. Food items

Teacher-Guided Interactive Learning Activity and Evaluations

FIGURE 7.3

are packaged in arrays for convenience of stacking, fruit trees are planted in arrays for ease of cultivation, stamps are sold in sheets, etc.

The array offers an efficient model for generating models for multiplication facts. A large array can be reproduced and then with the use of scissors, quickly cut to the desired model or models for the multiplication facts or use in teaching the multiplication algorithm.

When using arrays to explore basic facts, commutative property, identity, and the distributive properties, it is best to establish a <u>consistent</u> way of describing arrays. In mathematical arrays the rows run left-to-right, such as marked seats in a ballpark or auditorium. The vertical arrangement of elements in the array is called columns.

The following lesson fragment uses arrays:

Teacher-Guided Interactive Learning Activity

LESSON FRAGMENT

M: Associating multiplication with finding the number associated with an array

A: Group of third-graders

T: Hands-on work with models; make a model problem-solving strategy

H: Children understand the sets model for multiplication and the ones, twos, and fives facts

PROBLEM-SOLVING SITUATION:
JASON BROUGHT A BOX OF DINNER ROLLS TO SCHOOL FOR THE SPECIAL CLASS LUNCH. IT WAS PUT IN THE LUNCHROOM COOLER, BUT THE CHILDREN SAW THAT THE CARTON HAD FOUR ROWS, WITH SIX ROLLS IN EACH ROW.

Teacher: Let's think back about the rolls Jason brought today. I want us to work in our groups to find out how many rolls were in the package. When we finish we want to be able to draw a picture to <u>verify</u> our response. In your groups you may use your counting tiles to make a MODEL of the package. Remember that there were four rows with six rolls in each row. (SEE FIGURE 7.5.) I'll be coming around to look at your work. Make sure that EVERYONE in your group makes the model and constructs a sentence to describe that model. (TEACHER CIRCULATES AMONG THE GROUPS.)

Teacher: I see that most of you remembered Jason's package of rolls. Mary Alice—how many rolls did your group find?

Mary Alice: We found there were four groups of six, or 24. We wrote it as a multiplication sentence: $4 \times 6 = 24$.

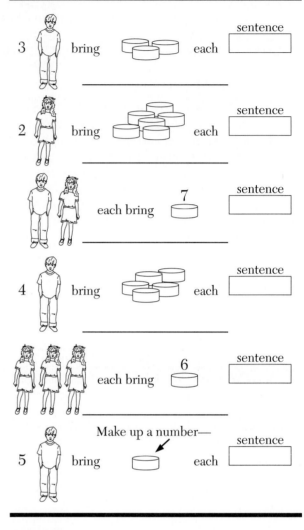

FIGURE 7.4

Teacher: Your group did good work, Mary Alice. Now I would like for our groups to EXPLORE putting objects into rows and columns and then writing sentences to describe their picture. The arrangement we are using—putting things into rows and columns—is called an ARRAY. In each group—take your counters and make different ARRAYS. As you assemble an array—write the sentence that describes it. When ALL in your group agree that the array and sentence agree—have one team member draw a picture of the array and copy the sentence. Let's see if we can find at least ten different arrays.

Using Number Lines to Develop the Basic Facts

The number line—which is used to develop understanding for the addition and subtraction operations—can also be used when exploring the basic

Teacher-Guided Interactive Learning Activity and Evaluation

FIGURE 7.5

multiplication facts. When picturing multiplication on the number line the teacher will illustrate "3 × 4" as three <u>jumps</u> the size of four spaces. By allowing the multiplier to represent the number of jumps, pupils can recognize a parallel to the set model that shows 3 × 4 as three <u>sets</u> of four. Since

number lines have been used to illustrate addition, pupils will find that the number sentences 4 + 4 + 4 = 12 and 3 × 4 = 12 BOTH will describe the drawing. (Some texts present moves on the number line as "vectors." Figure 7.6 shows BOTH jumps and vector illustrations.)

Teachers should emphasize moving in EQUAL-SIZED JUMPS from zero when modeling multiplication on the number line. Such an activity builds a foundation that is used when examining the relationship between multiplication and division. (Division will be illustrated as jumps in the <u>opposite</u> direction, <u>undoing</u> the multiplication.)

7.3 TEACHING THE BASIC MULTIPLICATION FACTS

Pupils explore all of the basic multiplication combinations before leaving the primary grades. First experiences with the basic facts emphasize the concept of multiplication, explore the properties, and identify patterns in the multiples. During this early work—usually in the second grade—facts with <u>factors of five or less</u> are commonly used since the student has already worked with these numbers. The multiples of two and five have been introduced as skip counting in the first grade. These multiples have many applications that give their development a high priority early in the primary program. The twos are used in reading thermometers and fives are used both for telling time and counting money.

Relating the Multiplication Facts to Addition

In the early 1900s multiplication was taught as "a special case of addition." While this "definition" of multiplication generally works in the set of counting numbers, when pupils reach multiplication of rationals, addition cannot be used to illustrate problems such as $\frac{2}{3} \times \frac{3}{4}$. Therefore, care should be taken when multiplication may be perceived only as "repeated" addition. Multiplication should be viewed as an activity associated with finding the total number associated with equivalent sets. Even though early modeling activities may "push equal-sized sets together," it is not necessary to join these sets to make the association with multiplication.

Teachers may point out that looking at equivalent sets is "much like" adding. Pupils will see that the number line picture of 3 × 4 looks like 4 + 4 + 4. Calculator explorations also help pupils see

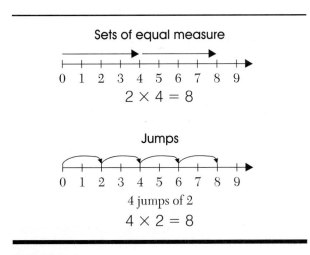

FIGURE 7.6

the similarity of the two operations. Figure 7.7 shows how a pupil can enter a four, press the plus sign, and by pressing the "=" the number of times to be added, 3 × 4 can be illustrated.

Exploring the Identity Property for Multiplication

The identity property, 1 × N = N, is easily discovered by children. This property may first be explored by working with single sets of various numbered objects (one set of six, one set of three, etc.) and then extended by using other materials. The concept is also developed on the number line when pupils are directed to look at a <u>single</u> jump of given lengths. Pupils may then use the calculator to <u>check</u> their observation of "If we took <u>one</u> jump of 6,543—<u>where</u> would we be on the number line?" Figure 7.8 illustrates a series of initial explorations in the development of 1 × N = N.

Exploring the Zero Generalization

The zero generalization is easily understood by children. After showing pupils how things can be stored in boxes, the teacher may show that putting

Individual Learning Activity

Exploring Multiplication Facts with a Calculator

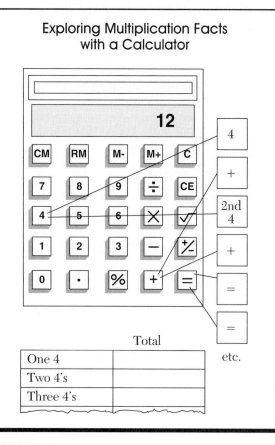

FIGURE 7.7

Individual Learning Activity

1 × N = N Explorations

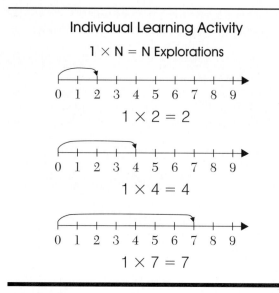

$1 \times 2 = 2$

$1 \times 4 = 4$

$1 \times 7 = 7$

FIGURE 7.8

two things in three boxes could be written as 3 × 2 and the product would be six. Continuing with the same exploration the teacher would show three boxes with one thing and finally three empty boxes—writing the sentence 3 × 0 =. Pupils have no difficulty recognizing that there would be nothing in the boxes so the product would be zero. Even when confronted with a "large number problem" of 384 × 0, the pupil recognizes that the product will be zero!

At the same time the teacher may wish to explore a number sentence that has zero as its first factor. Using the box example from above, the pupils may illustrate 3 × 2 as three boxes of two blocks, 2 × 2 as two boxes of two, 1 × 2 as one box of two, and finally they discover that 0 × 2 would be NO boxes at all—so there would be zero blocks! To verify their discovery, pupils can try out different numbers on their calculators—even entering large numbers to be multiplied by zero. Though pupils may use different ways of "making up a rule," they should recognize that multiplication sentence that has zero as one of its factors will ALWAYS have a product of zero.

While pupils quickly comprehend the effect of having zero as a factor, they <u>do</u>—on occasion—give a SUM instead of a product (or, when given an addition sentence with zero as one of the addends, give the product—zero). If the child REREADS the equation, generally the error is detected without any help from the teacher. However, the teacher should recognize that this error may occur—even though the pupil <u>understands the concept</u>.

Using the Commutative Property to Explore the Basic Facts

Shortly after the meaning, related symbolism, and vocabulary for multiplication are developed, children should explore the effect of changing the order of the two multiplication factors (**commutative law**). Using manipulative materials (sets or arrays), pupils see that changing the order of the factors will not change the product. It is not critical in the early stages that the children know that this concept is called the "commutative property of multiplication"—the concept is explored first and the formal vocabulary is developed later.

The teacher should use this property whenever a new fact is explored. For example, after pupils have determined the product of three sets of four, the teacher will have the children determine the number associated with four sets of three. The teacher will ask, "Did we get the same amount for three sets of four as we got for four sets of three?" Figure 7.9 illustrates how arrays might be used to facilitate explorations with this concept. A pupil may also be directed to "take three jumps of four," then have his friend take four jumps of three, to verify BOTH end at 12.

When the child understands the commutative property of multipliction, fewer illustrations with

concrete materials will be needed to verify products. If the child uses counters to discover that three times four equals 12, then a new fact can be generated by using the commutative property. "If three times four equals 12, what will we get for a product for four times three?" Later activities may encourage the pupil to apply the property to larger numbers. Showing the children an 8-by-7 array, the teacher might ask, "If I told you that 8 times 7 is 56, what do you think 7 times 8 would be?" (Turn the array to suggest 7 times 8.) "Suppose we had an 800 by 700 array that equals 560,000. Would the same product be suggested if I turned the array so it illustrated 700 times 800?" To follow this activity, pairs of equations with commuted factors in one pair can be practiced on calculators.

It is important that the pupil learn to use the commutative property to reduce the number of basic combinations that must be practiced. The 100 basic multiplication combinations that the child needs to master are illustrated in a matrix format in Figure 7.10. If the pupil understands the commutative property, only the shaded products are facts that need development. When the child understands and uses the commutative property, the number of independent facts to be practiced is reduced from 100 to 55! (Notice that the products on the diagonal result from 0×0, 1×1, 2×2, etc., and have no other fact related by the commutative property. There are ten "squares," leaving 90 basic facts. Half of the 90 can be mastered by using the commutative property.) If a child uses all three properties—identity, commutative law, and the zero generalization—only 36 facts need to be practiced instead of 100! (See Figure 7.11.)

Learning-Station Activity Card

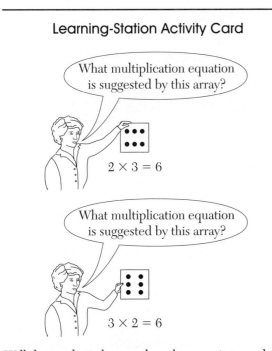

What multiplication equation is suggested by this array?

$2 \times 3 = 6$

What multiplication equation is suggested by this array?

$3 \times 2 = 6$

Will the product change when the array is turned on its side?

FIGURE 7.9

×	0	1	2	3	4	5	6	7	8	9
0	0	0	0	0	0	0	0	0	0	0
1	0	1	2	3	4	5	6	7	8	9
2	0	2	4	6	8	10	12	14	16	18
3	0	3	6	9	12	15	18	21	24	27
4	0	4	8	12	16	20	24	28	32	36
5	0	5	10	15	20	25	30	35	40	45
6	0	6	12	18	24	30	36	42	48	54
7	0	7	14	21	28	35	42	49	56	63
8	0	8	16	24	32	40	48	56	64	72
9	0	9	18	27	36	45	54	63	72	81

FIGURE 7.10

×	0	1	2	3	4	5	6	7	8	9
0	0	0	0	0	0	0	0	0	0	0
1	0	1	2	3	4	5	6	7	8	9
2	0	2	4	6	8	10	12	14	16	18
3	0	3	6	9	12	15	18	21	24	27
4	0	4	8	12	16	20	24	28	32	36
5	0	5	10	15	20	25	30	35	40	45
6	0	6	12	18	24	30	36	42	48	54
7	0	7	14	21	28	35	42	49	56	63
8	0	8	16	24	32	40	48	56	64	72
9	0	9	18	27	36	45	54	63	72	81

36 facts (white) remain to be practiced after identity, zero generalization, and commutative property have been developed.

FIGURE 7.11

Learning the Doubles

The doubles (or twos) multiplication facts are among the easiest to teach, because children come to the multiplication experience having learned to add doubles: $1 + 1, 2 + 2, 3 + 3$, through $9 + 9$. When studying the twos facts the teacher should relate 2×3 to the addition fact $3 + 3$. When pupils see this relationship they quickly recognize that they ALREADY know the products for the twos facts!

Using Patterns to Learn the Fives Facts

Most children can count by fives before they study the fives facts. Childhood games such as "hide-and-seek" and counting nickels have laid the foundation for easy mastery of the fives facts. When children tell time they learn to associate the numerals on the clock with the multiples of five. When the long hand is on the "6," it is 30 minutes past. When reading facts such as 8×5, a student may look at a clock face and remember that the time would be 40 minutes past. Looking at the pattern associated with multiplying a number by five further facilitates the child's mastery of the "5" facts. An easily recognized pattern is that the products always end in five or zero. (See Figure 7.12.)

Using the Distributive Property to Explore New Facts

Once pupils learn their twos and fives, the teacher can use the distributive property to explore facts that have a second factor of four, six, or seven. The fact 4×6 can be examined as $4 \times (5 + 1)$ since the pupils will know $4 \times 5 = 20$. Using both the commutative and distributive properties will allow pupils to discover the fours, sixes, and sevens facts. Figure 7.13 illustrates how 3×4 can be developed as $3 \times (2 + 2) = 3 \times 2 + 3 \times 2$. Since $6 + 6$ is a double that pupils already know, $3 \times 4 = 12$ can be discovered.

Independent Learning Activity

Pattern Exploration

EVEN NUMBERS TIMES FIVE

Zero sets of five = ____ $0 \times 5 = $ ____

Two sets of five = ____ $2 \times 5 = $ ____

Four sets of five = ____ $4 \times 5 = $ ____

Six sets of five = ____ $6 \times 5 = $ ____

Eight sets of five = ____ $8 \times 5 = $ ____

ODD NUMBERS TIMES FIVE

One set of five = ____ $1 \times 5 = $ ____

Three sets of five = ____ $3 \times 5 = $ ____

Five sets of five = ____ $5 \times 5 = $ ____

Seven sets of five = ____ $7 \times 5 = $ ____

Nine sets of five = ____ $9 \times 5 = $ ____

FIGURE 7.12

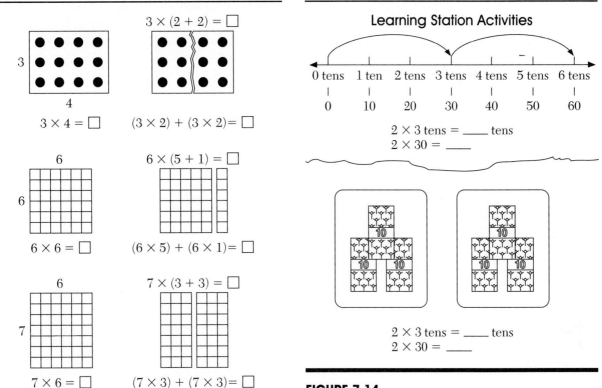

FIGURE 7.13

Learning Station Activities

2×3 tens = _____ tens
2×30 = _____

2×3 tens = _____ tens
2×30 = _____

FIGURE 7.14

7.4 INTRODUCING THE MULTIPLICATION ALGORITHM

The multiplication algorithm, when studied in the primary grades, is introduced in a very limited way. In all cases problems are limited to 1-digit times 2-digits. Usually the algorithm is introduced with teen numbers representing the 2-digit multiplicand since such problems do not require the pupil to work with multiples of ten (20s, 30s, etc.). When the two digits represented are greater than the tens, pupils are taught to relate the multiplication to the basic facts. Figure 7.14 illustrates two ways teachers illustrate units times tens.

Once the basic facts, distributive property, and multiplication of tens have been explored students have the necessary prerequisite skills to begin learning to work with the multiplication algorithm. Initial exposure to the algorithm is accomplished using one of the developmental algorithms to help pupils understand the application of the distributive property to the algorithm.

The lesson fragment that follows introduces the developmental form of the multiplication algorithm from a problem situation:

Teacher-Guided Interactive Learning Activity

LESSON FRAGMENT

M: Multiplication of ones times tens and ones

A: Group of third-graders

T: Hands-on model, involvement, make a drawing of problem-solving strategy

H: Basic facts and multiplication of ones and tens

PROBLEM-SOLVING SITUATION:
ON THE PREVIOUS WEEK THE CLASS VISITED A FARM. CHILDREN WERE ABLE TO RIDE ON A HAY WAGON THROUGH THE FARMER'S ORCHARD. THEY SAW THAT HE PLANTED SOME OF HIS TREES IN ROWS ON EITHER SIDE OF A ROAD. TODAY THE TEACHER IS GOING TO USE THAT EXPERIENCE TO DEVELOP THE MULTIPLICATION ALGORITHM. (SEE FIGURE 7.15A.)

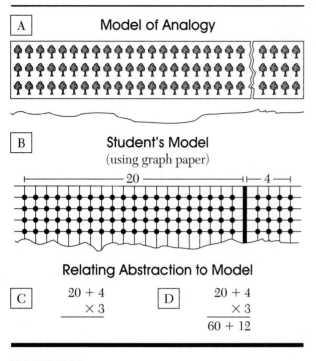

FIGURE 7.15

Teacher: When we visited the farm last week we saw that Mr. Brown had his apple trees planted in nice rows—extending across the road. I did not count all of the trees, but I remember he had three rows of trees. Near the barn there were four trees in each row and on the other side of the road he had 20 trees in each row. Today we are going to work in our groups to find out how many trees he had in all. Your group can use graph paper to make a dot array to show the trees in the orchard. Draw a mark between the rows of 20 and the rows of ones to represent the road. (SEE FIGURE 7.15B.)

Teacher: (THE TEACHER CIRCULATES AROUND THE GROUPS, ASSISTING WHERE NEEDED. AFTER ALL HAVE DRAWN PICTURES THE TEACHER DIRECTS THE GROUP TO AN ALGORITHM.) I see that all groups were able to count and find that there were 72 trees. Today we are going to learn how to use multiplication to help us work with numbers larger than ten. Let's write down what we did in our graph drawing. We had 20 trees in a row and then we had four trees in a row near the barn. I will write that as two tens plus four ones. Now let us look at how many rows we had. Jules, how many did you show?

Jules: Three.

Teacher: Since there is the same amount in each group this suggests MULTIPLICATION. I am going to write <u>times three</u> underneath the 20 and

the 4, because we are trying to find the total associated with three sets of 24. (SEE FIGURE 7.15C.) If we have three rows of four trees, how many trees will be in this part, Pearl?

Pearl: $3 \times 4 = 12$.

Teacher: How many trees will we have in the 3×20 section? AnnaBelle?

AnnaBelle: $3 \times 20 = 60$.

Teacher: We will want to <u>put together</u> the two parts of the orchard. What operation should we use with the 60 and 12? Velma?

Velma: Addition.

Teacher: Good! I will write a plus between the 60 and the 12. (SEE FIGURE 7.15D.)

Teacher: When we add the 60 and the 12, what will be the sum, Michael?

Michael: Seventy-two.

Teacher: Our algorithm now shows 72 just as our drawings did. To become more skillful in this new way of working with larger numbers, I have a sheet of several other arrangements that Mr. Brown **could** have used when planting his trees. In each group I want you to use this new technique to find the total number of trees for each new arrangement. When you complete your algorithm—draw a graph array to check your work.

7.5 TEACHING MULTIPLICATION IN THE INTERMEDIATE GRADES

Since the primary grades concentrate on addition and subtraction skills, students will enter the intermediate level with limited skill in multiplication. Pupils who complete the primary curriculum can recognize a set or array model for multipliction, recall many of the basic multiplication facts, find the product of 1-digit times 2-digit numbers, and will have had some experience applying multiplication to problem-solving situations. Of course, not ALL children will have this basic foundation.

To insure that each pupil has a sound foundation, the intermediate teacher thoroughly reviews previously presented meanings of multiplication and designs activities that will promote mastery of multiplication facts. The ability to recall multiplication facts plays an important role not only in the development of multiplication skills, but also in skills related to estimation, operations with fractional numbers, and the long-division algorithm.

In the intermediate grades the students become proficient using multiplication in multistep problem-solving situations and develop reasonable proficiency with the conventional multiplication algorithm when both factors contain several digits. **Reasonable proficiency** is generally accomplished by working with factors which contain no more than three digits. While occasionally a student may explore the algorithm with larger numbers, individuals typically use calculators or computers when working with large numbers.

While learning to multiply, students also learn to <u>rename</u> numbers as <u>factor expressions</u>. For example, students learn that 1, 2, 3, 4, 6, and 12 are factors of 12 and that $2 \times 2 \times 3$ is the <u>prime factor expression</u> for 12. Students will explore <u>multiples</u> of numbers as part of the process of learning multiplication skills. For example, students learn that 12, 24, 36, 48, etc., are multiples of 12. By exploring factors, prime factor expressions, and multiples concurrently with multiplication skills students develop these skills prior to their use with fractional numbers.

Multiplication skills typically developed at the intermediate level are as follows:

Grade 4

Reinforce meanings associated with multiplication
  • equal sets, arrays, linear measure
Explore cross-product model
Reinforce skills in multiplying with 1-digit factor
  • basic facts
  • multiplication algorithm (1-digit multiplier)
Extend multiplication algorithm (2-digit multiplier)
Check multiplication with commutative property
Explore factors and multiples
  • multiples of ten
  • powers of ten
Utilize calculator for multidigit multiplication
Apply skills to solve problems

Grade 5

Maintain understanding of multiplication concepts
Extend multiplication algorithm (3-digit multiplier)
Check multiplication using division
Explore factors, multiples, and exponents
  • sets of factors
  • multiples
  • common multiples
  • prime factorization
  • factor trees
  • exponents
Solve multistep problems with addition, subtraction, and multiplication

Grade 6

Maintain and extend multiplication skills
Explore alternate algorithms

Grades 7 and 8

Maintain multiplication skills

7.6 MAINTENANCE AND EXTENSION OF MULTIPLICATION FACTS

When reviewing basic facts with intermediate-level students, a teacher must reinforce the meanings associated with multiplication. In addition to the equivalent sets, number line, and array models for multiplication, teachers will extend student understanding to include the cross-product model. In the **cross-product model** one attempts to find all the ways elements of two different sets can be paired. For example, if a man had three pairs of slacks (black, brown, and gray) and two shirts (white and blue) he could wear the white shirt with each of the different-colored pairs of slacks to make three distinct outfits. Then he could wear the blue shirt with each of the pairs of slacks to make three different outfits. In all—with three pairs of slacks and two shirts (3×2)—he could show up on six separate days wearing a "different" outfit each day. Figure 7.16 shows an example of 3×2, using four different models (including the cross-product model).

Promoting Facts Mastery Through Patterns and Properties

There are many patterns that are explored when reviewing the basic multiplication facts. Some patterns were introduced in the primary grades—for example, the zero generalization ($n \times 0 = 0$). The teacher will also examine the patterns found in the various multiplication tables, either when reviewing the basic facts or when exploring multiples of numbers. One distinct pattern that is useful in helping students master the basic facts is the "nines pattern." When pupils recognize this pattern, the mastery of the nines facts becomes less of a chore. These patterns also provide an opportunity for individuals to discover some mathematical relationships that will prove useful in later mathematics explorations.

The fact that the nines facts have a distinct pattern can easily be observed when pupils use a

Multiplication Models for 3 × 2

Equivalent Sets

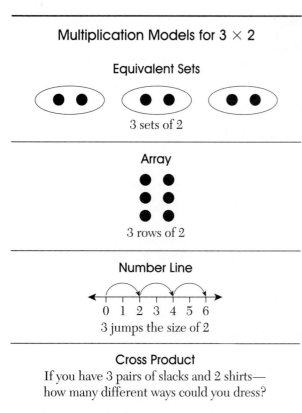

3 sets of 2

Array

3 rows of 2

Number Line

3 jumps the size of 2

Cross Product

If you have 3 pairs of slacks and 2 shirts—
how many different ways could you dress?

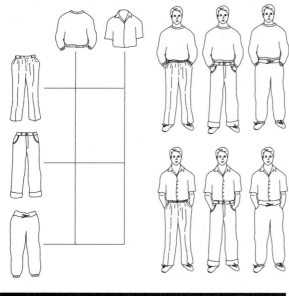

FIGURE 7.16

hundred chart. After directing students to count nine spaces and mark out the number (9, 18, 27, 36, etc.), the teacher can point out the "diagonal" pattern on the chart (see Figure 7.17). Students also will see that for each decade the marked-out numeral is one less than the previous decade. Some students may note that the first mark—representing 1 × 9—is one less than ten. The second mark

(2 × 9) is 2 less than 2 tens, the third mark (3 × 9) is 3 less than 3 tens, etc. With more advanced pupils, an exploration of the distributive property (N × 9 = N × [10 − 1] = [N × 10] − [N × 1]) becomes an interesting extension of this pattern. When pupils first explore the nines table, however, simple recognition of a pattern (though it is not as apparent as the fives, tens, or twos) is appropriate.

Once students recognize there is a pattern for the nines table, a teacher may encourage them to find a "hidden pattern" by looking at the multiples of nine (9, 18, 27, 36, 45, 54, 63, 72, and 81). Unlike the multiples of five (which end in a five or zero) one cannot tell if a number is a multiple of nine just by looking at the units digit. Some pupils, however, discover that adding the two digits always results in a sum of nine. (The recognition of this pattern is an important foundation for later work with "divisibility." Some teachers introduce the divisibility rule for nines and fives at this time.) The fact that the tens digit will be one less than the non-nines factor (for basic facts) makes the nines facts easy to remember. For example, to find the product of 8 × 9, a student could make the tens digit "one less than eight" (which would be 7) and then decide that two is added to seven to make nine (2). The pupil then writes 8 × 9 = 72.

When reviewing basic facts, the teacher may demonstrate how the distributive property can be used. For instance, 8 × 6 can be illustrated as 8 × (5 + 1) or 40 + 8. Since facts with factors of five seem to be easy for students, renaming one of the factors to include a five tends to make the fact easier. If the fact 6 × 6 is renamed as 6 × (5 + 1),

1	2	3	4	5	6	7	8		10
11	12	13	14	15	16	17		19	20
21	22	23	24	25	26		28	29	30
31	32	33	34	35		37	38	39	40
41	42	43	44		46	47	48	49	50
51	52	53		55	56	57	58	59	60
61	62		64	65	66	67	68	69	70
71		73	74	75	76	77	78	79	80
	82	83	84	85	86	87	88	89	90
91	92	93	94	95	96	97	98	99	100

FIGURE 7.17

then the pupil may think $6 \times 5 = 30$ and $6 \times 1 = 6$; so $6 \times 6 = 36$. Any fact can be renamed to use the distributive property, but sometimes the mental operation of adding two 2-digit numbers is too burdensome [as in $7 \times 7 = 7 \times (5 + 2) = 35 + 14 = 49$]. Even though teaching pupils to use the distributive law with basic combinations takes additional time, it is well worth the effort for it provides both a review of the basic combinations and prepares pupils for the use of this property in the multiplication algorithm.

The facts that produce products that are square numbers ($n \times n = n^2$) provide an interesting exploration. Pupils may use calculators to find the product of $n \times n$ (even when the factors are not 1-digit numbers). These products can then be compared to the product of a combination that has a factor that is <u>one less</u> and a factor that is <u>one more</u> (7×7 compared to 6×8). This pattern (called the down-up-down pattern by pupils) not only is an interesting exploration using the basic facts, but it also provides readiness for a later algebraic generalization [$(n - 1) \times (n + 1) = n^2 - 1$]. Notice how this pattern is developed in the learning-station activity illustrated in Figure 7.18. The teacher may wish to have the children explore other patterns related to the square numbers, for instance, $(n - 2) \times (n + 2) = n \times n - 4$.

Learning Station Activity

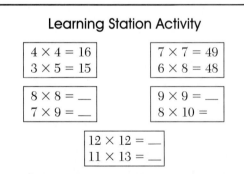

Can you discover the pattern that exists between the pairs of equations?

Use the calculator to find the products of A and B.

After finding the products test your pattern by filling in the blanks.

A	B
$15 \times 15 =$	$20 \times 20 =$
$\_ \times \_ =$	$\_ \times \_ =$

Make up 10 "pairs" to test your discovery.

FIGURE 7.18

Promoting Mastery of the Multiplication Facts

Basic multiplication facts are used extensively when working with the multiplication algorithm, division algorithm, and when estimating products/quotients. Therefore, children should be encouraged to become familiar enough with the combinations so they can readily recall the products. Most students recognize the need to remember the multiplication facts. Unlike addition facts—which can be quickly found by counting on one's fingers—the multiplication facts are difficult to "rediscover." Therefore, pupils are more amenable to practice activities that promote speedy recall.

If a student recognizes a few of the combinations, flash cards are one way of encouraging students to speed up response time. Commercial computer software programs (which can be adjusted for response time) usually utilize game elements that encourage quick response. When facts are missed, computer programs immediately display the correct responses. Many programs <u>also</u> record the facts missed by an individual child, so a teacher may prescribe specific remedial activities.

Speed tests may be used to promote speedy recall. Such a procedure encourages students to abandon inefficient methods used to rediscover a product and just remember it. To administer a speed test, the teacher places a sheet of basic facts face-down on each student's desk. When the signal is given, each pupil turns the test over and begins. When the time is up the teacher instructs the children to turn their papers over. A record is kept both of the number of correct responses and the total number of responses. Some pupils become tense when taking speed tests. To ease the pressure, the teacher should encourage each pupil to work against his/her own past recall record. For example, a student who started out being able to answer 39 facts, who can now answer 62 facts in the same time, has made considerable improvement over his/her own benchmark.

7.7 EXPLORING THE PATTERNS AND PROPERTIES OF MULTIPLICATION

Most students entering the intermediate grades recognize that one times any number produces that number (**identity property**) and that the order in which factors appear in an equation does not change the product (**commutative property**). They also know that zero times any number gives a product of zero (**zero property**). They have been exposed to the distributive property when exploring basic facts and when 1-digit times 2-digit numbers were examined. The **associative property of multiplication**, however, is generally a new concept for the intermediate-level pupil. Some primary children may have discovered the concept with their calculators, but they do not associate this concept with the formal property name.

A sheet of stamps can be used to illustrate the associative property. The teacher may wish to use a postal rate increase from 25¢ to 29¢ as a practical situation for introducing the stamp model (see Figure 7.19). To use up "old" 25¢ stamps, one would need to buy a few 4¢ stamps. When the teacher shows the 2×3 array of stamps, students can be asked to determine the cost of the 4¢ stamps. Once the amount (24¢) is determined, pupils should be asked to describe how they worked the problem. Some pupils will describe the array as having 6 stamps since there were 2 rows of 3. Since stamps cost 4¢, they may multiply—$(2 \times 3) \times 4$ or $\underline{6} \times 4$. Other students may indicate that they first found that each <u>row</u> was worth 12¢ and then multiplied by 2 because there were 2 rows—$2 \times (3 \times 4)$ or $2 \times \underline{12}$.

Pupils can easily explore the associative property by using calculators. For example, let pupils pick any three numbers as factors in the equation $\mathbf{P \times K \times T = N}$. Instruct half of the class to group the first two factors, then multiply them to get a total before using the other factor. Write the equation $\mathbf{(P \times K) \times T = N}$. The rest of the class should work the problem by grouping the last two factors and finding their product before multiplying by the first factor. Show this in an equation as $\mathbf{P \times (K \times T) = N}$. The class should then inspect the products to see if changing the grouping (association) of the factors changes the product. Since the calculator can perform the task quickly, efficiently, and with little labor many examples can be explored.

While the associative property COULD be used to help pupils master specific basic facts ($4 \times 4 = [2 \times 2] \times 4 = 2 \times [2 \times 4] = 2 \times 8$), it usually is not very efficient. However, when students learn to multiply 1s × 10s; 10s × 10s; 10s × 100s—the associative property is quite useful. For example, $6 \times 20 = 6 \times (2 \times 10) = (6 \times 2) \times 10 = 12 \times 10$, shows that six times two tens = 12 tens or 120.

The **distributive property** is reviewed with arrays similar to those used at the primary level. When preparing an array to illustrate large numbers such as 8×34, teachers generally use graph paper rather than drawing 272 separate units. Once students are familiar with the array model, "blank arrays" (where the dimensions are given but individual dots do not appear) may be used. For example, to illustrate 8×34, a blank rectangular region should be drawn to <u>represent</u> eight rows of thirty-four. Students might suggest "folding" the array by renaming 34 as three tens and four ones, which would be written as "$8 \times (30 + 4)$." (See Figure 7.20.) The teacher could then point to each side of the fold and show that one side would be eight rows of 30 and the other side would contain eight rows of four. This would be written as (8×30) and (8×4). The teacher would remind pupils that the whole array was composed of the two parts, so the two parts would be added <u>together</u> to show 8×24. The teacher would then write the "+" between the (8×30) and (8×6), resulting in (8×30) + (8×6).

Since students are more mature at the intermediate level, properties can be formally introduced by name. Awareness of mathematical properties and their names are useful when exploring larger numbers. For example, in each of the following steps, students could identify the property that permits one to take the step:

Exploring Properties using Problem-Solving Situations

$2 \times 3 \times 4$

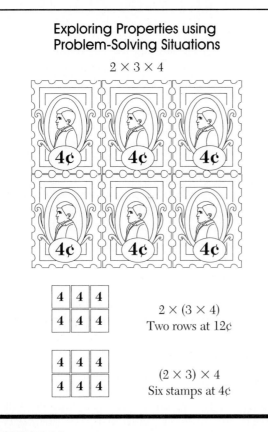

$2 \times (3 \times 4)$
Two rows at 12¢

$(2 \times 3) \times 4$
Six stamps at 4¢

FIGURE 7.19

6601   We change the order of the   5678
×5678   factors to make the problem   ×6601
        easier to compute. What
        property allows us to do this?

- Since we did not memorize our 6601 × 5678 fact as we did our basic facts, we are going to break apart 6601 into 6000 + 600 + 0 + 1 and multiply by each part. What property allows us to do this?
- We think 1 × 5678 and write the 5678 down. (What property is being used?)
- We do not need to multiply by zero. Why? (What property is being used?)

Formally incorporating the properties of multiplication into the development of mathematical concepts serves a twofold purpose: it helps the child remember how an algorithm works and also provides readiness for algebraic proofs that may be explored in the latter part of the intermediate program.

7.8 TEACHING MULTIPLES, FACTORS, AND EXPONENTS

Students enter the intermediate level familiar with some multiples. For example, pupils can count by twos, fives, and tens. Some may recognize multiples of nine. However, most multiples, such as the threes, fours, sixes, sevens, and eights, need special attention since students do little with these multiples in the primary grades.

To develop multiples, some teachers prefer to employ a **counting approach** similar to the way the twos and fives were developed. Children are taught to count by threes and fours, as a way of promoting their understanding of multiples. Other teachers use a **pattern approach**. For example, using the hundred chart in Figure 7.21, the pupil places a bean on every third number to locate the multiples of three. Once the beans are in place, the student may note that there is a "diagonal" pattern on the chart. As a follow-up to this activity the child records the multiples of three—3, 6, 9, 12, 15, 18, 21, 24, 27, 30, 33, 36, 39, 42, etc. Unlike the twos, fives, and tens there is no distinct pattern in the units position when working with the multiples of three. Because of the distinct visual pattern on the hundred chart many students suspect there must be a "hidden pattern." Some may discover that adding the digits of the multiples (until they reach

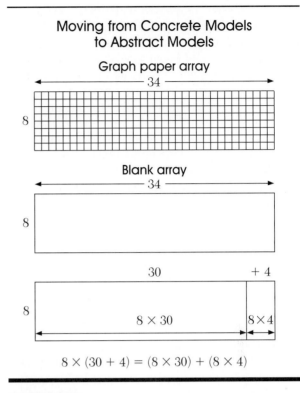

Moving from Concrete Models to Abstract Models

Graph paper array

8 × (30 + 4) = (8 × 30) + (8 × 4)

FIGURE 7.20

a single digit) will **always** give a sum of 3, 6, or 9! (Students later learn that this is the "divisibility rule" for three.)

Using a hundred chart allows students to discover many patterns and to recognize the relationship of one multiple to another. By examining two different sets of multiples pupils may discover relationships between the two sets. For example, if

1	2		4	5		7	8		10
11		13	14		16	17		19	20
	22	23		25	26		28	29	
31	32		34	35		37	38		40
41		43	44		46	47		49	50
	52	53		55	56		58	59	
61	62		64	65		67	68		70
71		73	74		76	77		79	80
	82	83		85	86		88	89	
91	92		94	95		97	98		100

FIGURE 7.21

multiples of two are marked with a red crayon and multiples of four are marked with a blue crayon, students discover that multiples of four always appear on a red square! Many will discover the pattern that multiples of four are "every other multiple of two." Similar activities for the twos and eights or the fours and eights are interesting explorations. Comparing the multiples of three and six, pupils find out that every multiple of six is also found in the set of multiples of three. Actually, multiples of six are multiples of <u>both</u> two and three, so they are even numbers that are multiples of three.

When students first explored multiplication a few basic terms were introduced. Pupils learned that in $3 \times 4 = 12$ the number 12 was the "product of 3×4." Twelve also is a **multiple** of three and a **multiple** of four. They learned that three and four are called factors of 12. This familiarity with terms becomes useful when students explore naming a number as a factor expression.

When children first learned to rename numbers they renamed them as addends (12 could be renamed as $10 + 2$ or $7 + 5$, etc.). At the intermediate level students learn to rename 12 using <u>factors</u>, as in 1×12, 2×6, and 3×4. Examining these expressions, students may be requested to list the <u>set of factors</u> for 12 (1, 2, 3, 4, 6, and 12). Initial activities with factors simply have students rename a number in a "two-factor expression." In later activities pupils systematically find ALL of the whole

Set of factors for 18

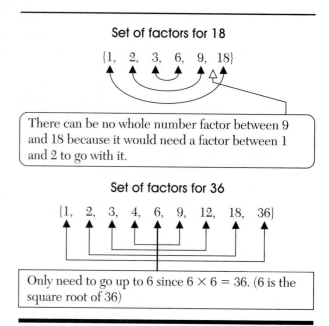

$\{1, \quad 2, \quad 3, \quad 6, \quad 9, \quad 18\}$

There can be no whole number factor between 9 and 18 because it would need a factor between 1 and 2 to go with it.

Set of factors for 36

$\{1, \quad 2, \quad 3, \quad 4, \quad 6, \quad 9, \quad 12, \quad 18, \quad 36\}$

Only need to go up to 6 since $6 \times 6 = 36$. (6 is the square root of 36)

FIGURE 7.23

number factors for a number by starting at one and then finding the "other" factor needed for a product of 12. Figure 7.22 illustrates how a student might put factors written on index cards into a factor-expression holder and then develop the set of factors with that material.

Students may also explore renaming numbers as the product of <u>three or more whole number factors</u>. It does not take students long to discover that a number can be named as the product of several factors—especially if they use the number "1" many times. For example, six can be named as 2×3 using two factors, but by including the number one, it is possible to have a factor expression with several factors—$1 \times 1 \times 1 \times 1 \times 1 \times 2 \times 3 = 6$. Of course, many numbers can be named with three, four, five, and more factors <u>without</u> using the number one. Among several product expressions for 36, 4×9 **and** $4 \times 3 \times 3$ **and** $2 \times 2 \times 3 \times 3$ will be found by students.

When the teacher asks the class to find factor expressions <u>without</u> using "1" as a factor, students find that some numbers cannot be named. Such an activity provides a <u>readiness</u> for learning **prime numbers**. Students may be encouraged to find the sets of factors for the numbers zero through 25 and to look for "special numbers." Children should be encouraged to work from the "ends to the middle" (Figure 7.23). This process helps pupils recognize that they do not need to test numbers beyond the "middle factor" (square root) since they are matching a large factor with each smaller number tested. Completing a chart similar to that found in Figure

Individual Learning Activity

Factor Expression

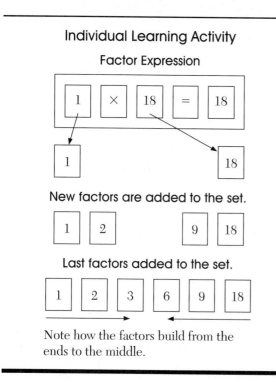

| 1 | × | 18 | = | 18 |

New factors are added to the set.

| 1 | 2 | | 9 | 18 |

Last factors added to the set.

| 1 | 2 | 3 | 6 | 9 | 18 |

Note how the factors build from the ends to the middle.

FIGURE 7.22

7.24, students will find that only one number—zero—has EVERY number as a factor. They also find that the number one has only one factor. Of course, there are several other observations that students will make as they explore sets of factors:

- all numbers have one as a factor
- all numbers have themselves as a factor
- all even numbers have two as a factor
- multiples of five have five as a factor
- some numbers have an odd number of factors (square numbers)
- some numbers have only two factors—one and themselves.

It is this last observation—"Some numbers have only two factors"—that the teacher will wish to stress, for it can be used as a definition for **prime numbers**.

When exploring prime numbers the hundred chart is very effective. The chart allows students to eliminate those numbers that are not prime by marking out multiples of numbers through multiples of seven. This sorting or sifting process is called the "Sieve of Eratosthenes." In this activity the student first crosses out the number one "be-

cause it only has one factor." Using colored crayons or pencils, the pupil will draw a ring around the first prime—"2"—and then mark out every multiple of two "because those will have more than two factors." Once all the multiples of two (greater than two itself) are eliminated, the pupil finds the next unmarked numeral (3). Choosing a different color, the student will draw a ring around the "3" and proceed to mark out all other multiples of three. Since pupils do not easily recognize all of the multiples of three, it is a good practice to have the child count three places (reaching the six) marking out every third numeral (9, 12, 15, 18, through 99). A similar process is repeated with the 5, using a new color to show its multiples. Finally, the pupil selects a color for seven and draws a ring around the "7" since it is prime. Then every seventh numeral (14, 21, 28, through 98) will be marked out. As the child continues to use the chart he/she finds that the 8, 9, and 10 are already marked out because they were multiples of previous primes. The first unmarked number will be 11, but there will be no unmarked multiples of 11 since all of the multiples of 11 through 110 (10 × 11) have been marked out by factors less than 11. So any number remaining unmarked on the hundred chart will be prime. For example, the number 83 remains unmarked on the chart, so it is a prime number.

In later work, students will not use a hundred chart to find prime numbers, but they will be using the process. To determine whether a number (less than 121) is prime, one checks to see if it is evenly divisible by two, three, five, or seven. If it is evenly divisible, the number cannot be prime (since it is a multiple of a prime number and would have at least three factors). To determine if any number—no matter how large—is prime, the same sifting process of the Sieve is used. The student first finds the "middle factor" (square root) of the number to determine the largest prime that must be used in the sifting process. Then the number is checked to see if it is evenly divisible by any prime smaller than its square root. If it is divisible, then it is "marked off the chart" since it would not be prime. If it is not evenly divisible, the number would have remained unmarked on the chart, so it is a prime number. Figure 7.25 illustrates the sifting activity that has identified the prime numbers less than 100.

Pupils also enjoy examining the completed Sieve of Eratosthenes to discover other interesting things about particular numbers, such as, "What numbers are multiples of both two and five? . . . Multiples of five and seven? . . . Multiples of two, five and seven?", etc.

Individual Learning Activity

No.	Set of factors	No.	Set of factors
0	{0,1,2,3,4,...}	13	{1,13}
1	{1}	14	{1,2,7,14}
2	{1,2}	15	{1,3,5,15}
3	{1,3}	16	{1,2,4,8,16}
4	{1,2,4}	17	{1,17}
5	{1,5}	18	{1,2,3,6,9,18}
6	{1,2,3,6}	19	{1,19}
7	{1,7}	20	{1,2,4,5,10,20}
8	{1,2,4,8}	21	{1,3,7,21}
9	{1,3,9}	22	{1,2,11,22}
10	{1,2,5,10}	23	{1,23}
11	{1,11}	24	{1,2,3,4,6,8,12,24}
12	{1,2,3,4,6,12}	25	{1,5,25}

- Which numbers have only one factor?

- Which number appears most often as a factor? Why?

- Which numbers have 2 as a factor?

- Which numbers have 3 as a factor?

- Which numbers have only 2 factors?

FIGURE 7.24

Individual Learning Activity

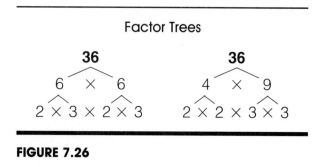

— Multiples of 2 greater than 2.

| Multiples of 3 greater than 3.

\ Multiples of 5 greater than 5.

/ Multiples of 7 greater than 7.

FIGURE 7.25

A logical <u>extension</u> of primes and multiples is studying factoring numbers into prime factor expressions. Constructing factor trees is an interesting way of helping students express a number as prime factors. Students construct the tree using a variety of approaches. One student may first take a number such as 36 and decide it can be expressed as 6 × 6, then factor each 6 into the prime factors 2 × 3. Another student may remember that 4 × 9 = 36 and use this as the first step in factoring the number, then changing 4 into the prime expression 2 × 2 and 9 into the prime expression 3 × 3 (see Figure 7.26). Regardless of how the student begins—the prime factor expression will be the same, except for the order of the prime factors (fundamental theorem of arithmetic).

The teacher must keep in mind that the factor tree itself is not the goal of the activity. The goal is

Factor Trees

36

6 × 6

2 × 3 × 2 × 3

36

4 × 9

2 × 2 × 3 × 3

FIGURE 7.26

Initial procedure renaming each line as a name for 48 until only prime factors are used

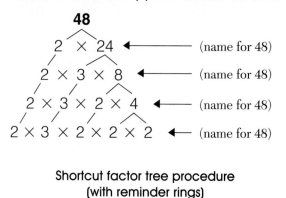

48

2 × 24 ◄——— (name for 48)

2 × 3 × 8 ◄——— (name for 48)

2 × 3 × 2 × 4 ◄——— (name for 48)

2 × 3 × 2 × 2 × 2 ◄——— (name for 48)

Shortcut factor tree procedure (with reminder rings)

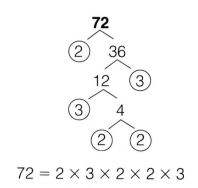

72

② 36

12 ③

③ 4

② ②

72 = 2 × 3 × 2 × 2 × 3

FIGURE 7.27

for students to recognize that a number can be named many ways and to visualize the process of naming a number when using only prime factors. Eventually students will be able to rename a number into its prime factors as a mental process only—without using a tree. Mindful of this goal, teachers may wish to first construct trees so that each step in the tree represents a complete name for the number (Figure 7.27). Later, students may wish to use "shortcuts," stopping each branch of the tree when it ends with a prime. Teachers should be careful about introducing such an algorithm since students who use it often "rewrite" the final expression and neglect to include <u>all</u> of the discovered factors. Teachers may discourage such mistakes by requiring students to "draw a ring" around each prime as it is written in the tree. Then, when a student looks back at the tree, he/she includes all the "ringed" factors.

When developing the final "mental process" for renaming numbers into prime factors, students will use one of two procedures (or a combination of both). One process—"peeling"—finds all of the factors of two in the number, then the factors of three, etc., until all the prime factors are discovered. A second prime factor technique called "splitting" finds a pair of composite numbers with the selected product and then renames each of those composites into primes. Figure 7.28 illustrates each "technique" in a prime factor tree for 180. Notice that each "branch" ends with a prime, so students could use all of the ends of the branches to make the prime factor expression.

Naming numbers in prime factor expressions presents an excellent opportunity for the teacher to introduce the concept of exponents. Exponent notation may be introduced by using a sets model. For example, six sets of "six sets of six" could be written as $6 \times (6 \times 6)$ or $6 \times 6 \times 6$ or 6^3 (read "six to the third power" or more commonly as "six cubed"). This approach usually involves using blocks made into square shapes when the factor is used twice (for example, 4×4 is represented by a four-by-four square array). When the factor is used three times, as in $5 \times 5 \times 5$, the number is represented by a $5 \times 5 \times 5$ **cube**. This approach is especially useful when building the vocabulary of "four squared" and "five cubed," but it is limited when introducing powers greater than three.

Some teachers prefer to use "factor cards" when introducing exponents. Index cards representing factors are used to construct a factor

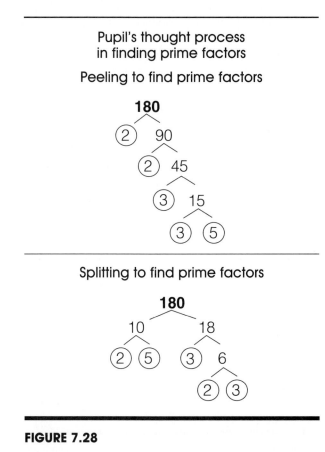

Pupil's thought process in finding prime factors

Peeling to find prime factors

180

Splitting to find prime factors

180

FIGURE 7.28

144

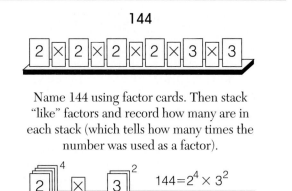

Name 144 using factor cards. Then stack "like" factors and record how many are in each stack (which tells how many times the number was used as a factor).

$144 = 2^4 \times 3^2$

FIGURE 7.29

expression. For instance, 144 would be shown as $2 \times 2 \times 2 \times 2 \times 3 \times 3$ by placing on the chalk tray four index cards with "2" written on them and two cards marked "3" (see Figure 7.29). To "simplify" the expression, the teacher would gather up all of the 2s and place them into a single stack and then place all of the 3s in a second stack. (The extra times signs would be removed.) Then to "remind" students of the quantity of 2s in the stack, a small numeral would be written slightly above each factor stack. This small numeral (exponent) reminds pupils of the times the 2 and 3 were used as factors. When using such a technique, teachers should make sure students work both ways—collecting the index cards and putting them into a stack, and taking the stack and expanding it into a full expression by replacing the times sign.

Exponents of zero and one are difficult to explain at the intermediate level since pupils have not yet explored operations with exponents. The concept of a number to the first power can be illustrated as a single grouping. By convention, when an exponent is not exhibited for a number, it is understood that the exponent for that number is the number one. The zero power could be interpreted as having the intent of grouping by a number, but the grouping has not yet taken place; therefore the objects are ungrouped in ones. For example, 3×10^0 could be interpreted as the "intent" to group by tens; but since we only have three objects, we are unable to group yet and the three objects are ungrouped.

Some pupils may have difficulty following the logic of the "intent to group" development. Those pupils may more easily follow the development in the context of the place-value system (see Figure 7.30). Constructing a chart to show that a million is really $10 \times 10 \times 10 \times 10 \times 10 \times 10$ or 10^6,

10,000	1,000	100	10	Units
$10 \times 10 \times 10 \times 10$	$10 \times 10 \times 10$	10×10		
10^4	10^3	10^2	$10^?$	$10^?$

FIGURE 7.30

or that a hundred thousand is 10^5, will help a child see that each position to the right is one power less than its neighbor to the left. Therefore, the tens place must be one power less than a hundred (10^2) and must be written 10^1. Since the ones are immediately to the right of the tens, the power must be 10^0. An advantage of this approach is that it allows students to <u>speculate</u> on exponent names for tenths (10^{-1}), <u>hundredths</u> (10^{-2}), thousandths (10^{-3}), etc. Once exponents have been developed, naming numbers using expanded notation can provide practice in using exponents.

7.9 MAINTENANCE AND EXTENSION OF THE MULTIPLICATION ALGORITHM

While the multiplication algorithm may be *introduced* in primary programs, its full development is deferred until the intermediate level. By the end of the intermediate level the student will be able to multiply when both the multiplier and multiplicand contain several digits. (For problems that require multiplication beyond 3-digit multipliers the student will <u>generally</u> be using either a calculator or computer.)

Building Skill with Multiples of Tens and Hundreds

Multiplying a multiple of ten and a hundred by a 1-digit multiplier was explored in the primary grades, but it must be reviewed at the intermediate level. Since the intermediate-level pupil is more mature, use of multiplication properties may provide new insight into the process. For example, consider the following explanation by the teacher illustrated in Figure 7.31. By a similar explanation ones times hundreds could be developed using base tens blocks or properties. For example,

6 × 4 hundreds
6 × 400 = 6 × (4 × 100)   Why?
6 × (4 × 100) = (6 × 4) × 100   Why?
(6 × 4) × 100 = 24 × 100   Why?
24 × 100 = 24 hundreds = 2400   Why?

Building the Multiplication Algorithm

Pupils in the intermediate grades will reexplore multiplying 2-digit multiplicands by 1-digit multipliers. It is valuable for pupils to see the algorithm modeled using a variety of materials. At the primary level, pupils may use a place-value chart to develop the algorithm. In the intermediate grades, pupils may illustrate the operation with base ten blocks or the teacher may use a 20-bead abacus. The lesson fragment that follows utilizes the child's mastery of the basic facts and his/her understanding of ones times tens and hundreds to develop the algorithm for multiplying with a 1-digit multiplier and a 3-digit multiplicand.

Teacher-Guided Interactive Learning Activity

LESSON
FRAGMENT

M: One digit times three digits
A: Fourth-grade class
T: Model (abacus)
H: Multiplication facts, ones times tens, ones times hundreds

PROBLEM-SOLVING SITUATION:
LAST WEEK TOMMY WAS SENT TO THE STOREROOM TO REPLENISH THE SUPPLY OF

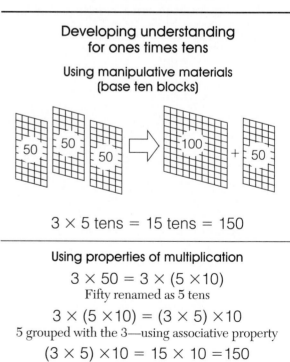

Developing understanding for ones times tens

Using manipulative materials (base ten blocks)

3 × 5 tens = 15 tens = 150

Using properties of multiplication

3 × 50 = 3 × (5 × 10)
Fifty renamed as 5 tens

3 × (5 × 10) = (3 × 5) × 10
5 grouped with the 3—using associative property

(3 × 5) × 10 = 15 × 10 = 150
finding the product

FIGURE 7.31

PENCILS. THERE WERE 144 PENCILS IN EACH BOX AND TOMMY BROUGHT BACK THREE BOXES. THIS WEEK THE TEACHER IS USING THAT SITUATION TO EXTEND PUPIL UNDERSTANDING OF THE MULTIPLICATION ALGORITHM.

Teacher: Last Friday Tommy brought our pencils from the storeroom. Does anyone know how many pencils he got for us?

Melissa: He had three boxes—but I don't know how many were in a box.

Teacher: I can look at the label on the box and see that each box holds 144 pencils. How many would you ESTIMATE that to be?

Melissa: It is going to be more than 300—and since 144 is close to 150 it probably will be between 400 and 500.

Teacher: Very good, Melissa. I'm going to write that amount on the board and then ask each math learning group to find out exactly how many pencils there would be. For this activity, I'm going to ask that you not use your calculators—but you can use any manipulative materials back on the math table. (AS THE PUPILS MOVE TO THEIR GROUPS AND DISCUSS THE PROBLEM THE TEACHER MOVES AROUND THE ROOM—POSING A QUESTION TO A GROUP IF IT HAS DIFFICULTY GETTING STARTED. WHEN ONE OR TWO OF THE GROUPS FINISH EARLY, THE TEACHER SUGGESTS THAT THE GROUP FIND ANOTHER WAY TO VERIFY ITS FIRST RESPONSE.)

Teacher: As I visited your groups I found many different ways of solving the problem. Bertrand's group used the box of centimeter blocks and counted out three groups of 144. Then they counted all of them. Lester's group used base ten blocks and set up three groups with one flat, four rods, and four units in each group. Melissa's group used play money and they were using dollars to represent the hundreds, dimes to represent the tens, and pennies to represent the ones. These were all good ways of finding exactly how many pencils there were. You used different ways to model the problem. Today I'm going to use a 20-bead abacus to model the same problem and together we will see if we can develop a way of solving this problem using paper and pencil. (THE TEACHER WRITES THREE TIMES 144 ON THE BOARD AND SETS UP THE ABACUS TO SHOW THREE SETS OF 144 AS ILLUSTRATED IN FIGURE 7.32A.)

Teacher: Let's work first with our ones by putting our three sets of four ones together. We'll remove the pins. (TEACHER REMOVES THE THREE PINS ON THE UNITS WIRE SHOWING 12 BEADS.)

How many ones do we get? Sue?

Sue: Twelve ones.

Teacher: We can trade in ten of our units for one ten. (THE TEACHER PUSHES TEN OF THE UNIT BEADS TO THE BACK AND BRINGS ONE TENS BEAD FROM THE BACK. THE TEACHER PLACES A PIN TO SEPARATE IT FROM THE THREE SETS OF FOUR TENS.) Let's record on the algorithm what we have done thus far. We put three groups of four together and got 12. We **kept** two (TEACHER RECORDS "2" IN THE PROD-

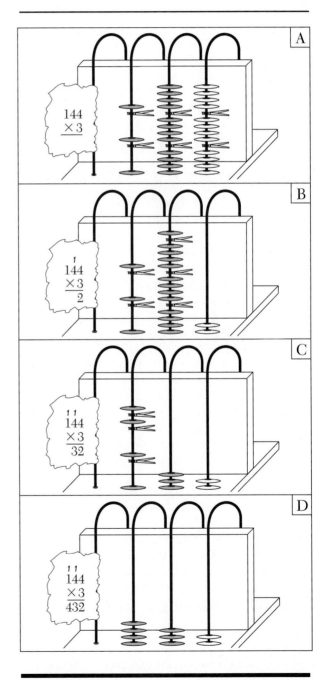

FIGURE 7.32

UCT) and traded ten units for one ten so let's put a small "1" to remind us of the regrouped ten. (THE TEACHER WRITES A SMALL "1" OVER THE FOUR TENS.) (SEE FIGURE 7.32B.)

Teacher: Now we have three sets of four tens to be put together. (THE TEACHER RELEASES THE PINS HOLDING THE THREE SETS OF FOUR TENS APART AND SHOWS THAT WE NOW HAVE 12 TENS.) We still have our regrouped ten up here, so let's put it with the 12 tens making 13 tens. (THE TEACHER PULLS THE PIN HOLDING THE REGROUPED TEN.) Since we have 13 tens, we can trade ten of our tens for one hundred, leaving us three tens. (THE TEACHER MOVES TEN TENS TO THE BACK OF THE ABACUS AND PULLS ONE HUNDRED TO THE FRONT—SEPARATED WITH A PIN FROM THE THREE SETS OF 100.) Now let's show on the algorithm what we did with our abacus. We multiplied 3 × 4 tens and got 12 tens, THEN we added the regrouped ten making 13 tens. We kept three of the tens (THE TEACHER WRITES A "3" IN THE TENS PLACE OF THE PRODUCT) and traded ten tens for 100. (THE TEACHER WRITES A SMALL "1" ABOVE THE NUMERAL 1 IN THE MULTIPLICAND.) (SEE FIGURE 7.32C.) Now we have three sets of 100 (TEACHER PULLS THE PINS SEPARATING THE THREE SETS OF 100) and one more hundred. (TEACHER PULLS THE LAST PIN.) How many hundreds do we have, Al?

Al: Four hundreds.

Teacher: Good. Let's record this step. We multiply 3 × 1 to get 3 and then we add this regrouped hundred to make our 400. (SEE FIGURE 7.32D.) So our three boxes of pencils with 144 pencils in each box give us a total of 432 pencils—which is very close to Melissa's estimate.

Teacher: We'll practice one or two problems together and then I am going to ask you to work in your groups to become more skillful with this algorithm. You can use your materials to verify your product— but we will want everyone in our groups to learn how to use this algorithm. (WHEN PUPILS GO TO THEIR GROUPS, ALL—INCLUDING BERTRAND'S GROUP—DECIDE TO USE BASE TEN BLOCKS OR MONEY AS MODELS RATHER THAN COUNTING OUT LARGE SETS OF SINGLES.)

Refining Skills with 1-digit Multipliers

When using the conventional multiplication algorithm students must utilize the basic multiplication facts, the distributive property, and regrouping. In addition there is another skill that will need review

if students are to become proficient with the algorithm. **Decade facts**, first used by the child in column addition, will also be used in the multiplication algorithm. For instance, when multiplying 7 × 48, the student will first think of 48 as four tens and eight ones. Then, using a basic fact, the pupil finds that 7 × 8 = 56. Keeping the 6, the pupil regroups the 50 ones into five tens. The student will then multiply 7 × 4 tens to get 28 tens. The 5 must be added to the 28—a decade fact!

If the combination 28 + 5 were written in an algorithm form, the pupil could easily add the 8 and 5, regroup and easily find the sum. But in the multiplication algorithm, the student is required to mentally add the 5 and 28—without writing it down. When students are not proficient with decade facts, they count-on using their fingers, saying "29, 30, 31, 32, 33." While such a process will find the answer, it is not an efficient way of working problems.

Since students need this skill not only when using 1-digit multipliers, but also when working with multidigit multipliers, multidigit divisors, and column addition, it is appropriate to devote some time to helping pupils become skillful using decade facts. Activities that help pupils understand how their knowledge of the basic addition combinations can be used in decade facts are described in Chapter 5 (addition) and the teacher may wish to use those activities when reviewing decade facts.

Since students will be using their decade facts with multiplication, many teachers combine practice of the decade facts with practice of basic multiplication facts. For example, the teacher might ask the class to show their responses to (4 × 7) + **8** using "show-me cards" or "slates." A calculator can also be used when practicing decade facts. Using a buddy drill, the teacher might have one pupil read the problem and work it on the calculator, while his/her buddy responds orally. During these practice activities, the emphasis should be upon the mental computation—no paper or pencil should be used. The teacher may wish to incorporate a timed component to discourage pupils from counting-on to get the answer.

Developing the Ability to Multiply Tens by Tens

Before working with 2-digit multipliers the pupils will need to understand the concept of tens times tens. One way of helping a child see that tens times tens results in hundreds is to use blank arrays partitioned into ten-by-ten regions. A child might picture 20 × 30 seeing that it would be 2 tens × 3 tens. The student can then determine the number of blocks in each 10 by 10 region. (If a child needs help seeing that there are really 100 blocks in each 10 × 10 region, the teacher may use graph paper cut into 10 × 10 regions and place these into each of the regions on the 20 × 30 blank array.) An alternate approach appropriate for this level is to show that tens times tens equals hundreds by a step-by-step <u>analytical</u> approach reviewing the properties of <u>multiplication</u> and their use in such problems (see Figure 7.33). While some pupils enjoy this step-by-step development, not all students are ready for this analytic style of thinking.

Once students can reason through a problem, the teacher may extend that skill to include problems such as 30 × 400 and 400 × 600. When working problems such as 30 × 400 at the abstract level, the pupil should think "3 × 4 is 12 and 10 times 100 is 1,000, so the product is 12 <u>thousand</u>." Teachers should also help students see that it is possible to use the commutative property (change the order) and multiply 400 × 600 by thinking, "hundreds times hundreds would be <u>ten thousands</u> so I'll write four zeros (_0,000) putting the product into the ten thousands <u>place</u>. Now I'll multiply 4 × 6 to get 24, so my answer will be 24 ten thousands or <u>24</u>0,000."

Using Multidigit Multipliers

To calculate efficiently when using multidigit numbers, the student must first be able to find products using a 1-digit multiplier. In addition to understanding the 1-digit multiplication algorithm, the pupil must be able to multiply by tens. Most teachers review these skills prior to introducing 2-digit multipliers. When a student understands how the algorithm develops, multiplication by 3-, 4-, 5-, or many digit multipliers is easily mastered. Of course, the more steps in calculation, the greater the possibility of careless errors. So the teacher can anticipate that pupils will make more errors in multidigit multiplication than when using a 1-digit multiplier.

To develop the algorithm for multiplying by a 2-digit multiplier, the teacher may use a blank array to show how a multiplier such as 38 (in 38 × 47) can be renamed. While BOTH the multiplier *and* the multiplicand **can** be renamed, the algorithm would follow such a development differently than the standard algorithm so many teachers use that as an enrichment activity.

Developing understanding for tens times tens

20 × 30 (or 2 tens × 3 tens)

Using manipulative materials

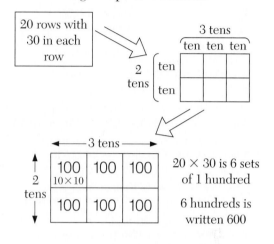

Using properties of multiplication

20 × 30 = (2 × 10) × (3 × 10)
tens renamed as 2 tens and 3 tens

= 2 × (10 × 3) × 10
grouping changed—associative property

= 2 × (3 × 10) × 10
order changed—commutative property

= (2 × 3) × (10 × 10)
grouping changed—associative property

= 6 × 100 = 600
multiplication and renaming

FIGURE 7.33

Once students can multiply using a 1-digit multiplier, it is possible to develop the multidigit algorithm abstractly, without relating it to the array. Using the array, however, strengthens the pupils' understanding of the distributive property and builds a strong foundation for both the multiplication algorithm and later work with algebraic equations.

When introducing the multiplication algorithm using a multidigit multiplier, the teacher will use materials that will help the student build a <u>mental image</u> of each step in the algorithm. The <u>lesson</u> fragment below shows how a teacher uses expanded notation cards to associate the algorithm with representative materials.

Teacher-Guided Interactive Learning Activity

LESSON FRAGMENT

M: 2-digit multiplier

A: Fourth-grade class

T: Blank array and expanded notation cards

H: Multiplication algorithm for 1-digit multipliers

PROBLEM-SOLVING SITUATION:

YESTERDAY THE CLASS DECIDED TO MAKE A MAY DAY CHAIN FOR THE CAFETERIA TO PROVIDE A MORE FESTIVE ATMOSPHERE AT LUNCH. THEY DECIDED THAT EACH PERSON WOULD MAKE A CHAIN OF 48 LINKS AND THAT LATER THOSE WOULD BE JOINED TO MAKE A LONG CHAIN. RECOGNIZING THE PUPIL INTEREST IN THE PROJECT, THE TEACHER DECIDED TO USE THIS SITUATION TO INTRODUCE 2-DIGIT MULTIPLIERS.

Teacher: We decided yesterday that each of us would make 48 links in our May Day chain for the cafeteria. There are going to be 28 of us so that will make a very long chain. How many links do you suppose will be in the long chain? Lincoln?

Lincoln: About 500.

Teacher: Tell me how you got that amount, Lincoln.

Lincoln: Well, 48 is close to 50—so ten of us would make about 500. Wait—it's going to be more than 500—it would be close to three times that amount, or 1500. I only estimated for 10 of us!

Teacher: Good work—you can adjust your estimate. I'll write that amount on the board and today we will learn how to find exactly how many links by multiplying 28 × 48 to find the product. I know you can find a product when there is a 1-digit multiplier, but this problem has a 2-digit multiplier. To demonstrate exactly what is happening, I have cut out an array using graph paper that will show 28 rows of 48. We can use this to help us. (THE TEACHER DISPLAYS A 28 × 48 ARRAY.) Now, who knows their 28 multiplication facts? Tommy?

Tommy: We only learned up through our tens, teacher.

Teacher: True! We learned that to multiply something like 8 × 28 we could break the 28 apart and deal with just part of the number at a time. Could we do that on this problem, Maria?

Maria: We don't have to break up the whole thing—we already know how to work 8 × 48.

Teacher: That's right, Maria, so we need not rename the 48. Perhaps we could rename the 28 by folding the array into eight rows and then 20 rows. (THE

TEACHER SHOWS THE FOLD ON THE ARRAY AND LABELS THE ARRAY. THE TEACHER ALSO WRITES THE ALGORITHM ON THE CHALKBOARD—SEE FIGURE 7.34A.)

Teacher: Now let's look at the algorithm. We have 28 rows of 48, which we renamed as 20 + 8. (THE TEACHER SHOWS 28 AS AN EXPANDED NOTATION CARD. THE "8" IS PLACED AS THE MULTIPLIER AND THE "20" IS PLACED IN THE CHALK TRAY.) Maria, you pointed out that we know how to multiply 8 × 48, so will you come to the board and do that part of the problem for us? (MARIA WRITES THE PRODUCT 384—SEE FIGURE 7.34B.)

Teacher: Very good work, Maria. I'm going to write that amount on our array. Now we need to find the product for 20 × 48. So let us put the "8" in the chalk tray and work with the "20." (THE TEACHER PLACES THE "20" PART OF THE EXPANDED NOTATION CARD AS THE MULTIPLIER IN THE PROBLEM.) We know that 20 ×

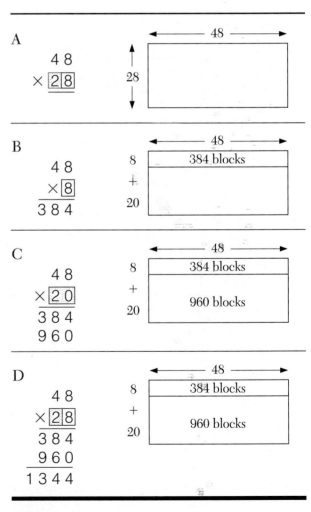

FIGURE 7.34

48 is **really** two sets of ten times 48—so let's multiply by the ten <u>first</u>. (THE TEACHER WRITES A ZERO IN THE TENS PLACE OF THE SECOND PARTIAL PRODUCT.) We can show tens by writing a zero in the ones position—this moves us into the tens place. Now we can multiply 48 by the 2, giving us 96 of the tens. (THE TEACHER WRITES 96 TO THE LEFT OF THE ZERO TO MAKE 960—SEE FIGURE 7.34C.)

Teacher: I'll write that amount on our array to show the number of blocks in the 20 × 48 section of the array. To find out the number of blocks in the entire array what must we do, Gracie?

Gracie: We will put the two parts together.

Teacher: Yes, Gracie, we will **add** the two partial products together to find the total. (THE TEACHER ADDS THE TWO PARTIAL PRODUCTS ON THE ALGORITHM TO GET 1344—SEE FIGURE 7.34D.) So we can see that we will have 1344 links in our chain if each of the 28 people make 48 links. Rather than work in our groups today, I think we will work two or three more problems together and then I'll let each of you work a few at your seat so that you can practice this new skill.

Using a similar process as described above, a teacher can develop the algorithm for using a multiplier with 2-, 3-, 4- or more digits. In the case of 354 × 826 the teacher may provide an expanded notation card to show 4, 50, and 300 and develop the algorithm in a similar fashion. After students have worked several problems, the teacher can abandon the array and use only the expanded notation cards. (Occasionally, the teacher may wish to return to the array to help the student continue to see how the distributive property is being used within the algorithm.) As pupils become proficient in using multidigit multipliers they may wish to shorten the algorithm—placing the partial product for the tens <u>in the tens place</u> rather than using a "0" to hold the tens position. The teacher must be careful to build understanding before suggesting a "rule" of moving over one place to the left for the tens and two places to the left for the hundreds.

Zeros in the Multiplier

Multiplication when a zero occurs in the multiplier is a case that requires special attention by the teacher. Children who simply "follow a rule" will unnecessarily write a whole row of zeros when the multiplier has a zero. For example, in 304 × 422, the more efficient way to handle the zero is to skip it entirely and go directly to the hundreds. Students

should be encouraged to think, "I have 0 in the tens place. Zero times <u>any</u> number is zero, so I can go directly to the hundreds." The following shows how a student might work the example using an inefficient algorithm and then a more efficient algorithm.

Inefficient Algorithm	More Efficient Algorithm
422	422
×304	×304
1688	1688
000	1266
1266	128288
128288	

When there are a series of zeros in the multiplier, with a zero starting in the ones place, it is convenient to shift the multiplier to line up the first nonzero digit of the multiplier with the ones column of the multiplicand. The examples below illustrate this shift for multiplying. In a problem such as 3000 × 2423 students would first be encouraged to think, "I am multiplying by three <u>thousand</u> so I can write three zeros to show the thousands place and now I can multiply by the 3. (Later, pupils may devise a "rule" of "bringing down the zeros before multiplying by the rest of the number." Even when pupils have developed their own "rule," occasional checks should be made to ensure that the pupil understands **why** the zeros are "brought down.")

Modified Algorithms

2423	86	362
×3000	×70	×4800
7269000	6020	289600
		1448
		1737600

Estimating and Checking Multiplication

One of the first estimation techniques used in addition—upper and lower boundaries—is a good beginning algorithm for checking multiplication. In 7 × 384 the student would think, "384 is **between** 300 and 400. Seven times 300 is 2100. Seven times 400 is 2800. So my answer must be somewhere between 2100 and 2800." Later, pupils recognize that the product <u>should</u> be closer to 2800, since 384 is closer to 400 than 300.

Lower Boundary		Upper Boundary
300	384	400
× 7	× 7	× 7
2100	2688	2800

Lower Boundary		Upper Boundary
600	683	700
×400	×472	×500
240000	322376	350000

Example: Check by Inverse Check

```
 384         384
×  6      6)2304
 2304        18
             50
             48
             24
             24
```

Example: Commutative Property

```
  683          472
 ×472         ×683
 1366         1416
 4781         3776
 2732         2832
322376       322376
```

While using "boundaries" with multidigit multipliers gives a general estimate, the boundaries tend to be large. When estimating 427 × 683, rounding both factors down (400 × 600) gives 240,000 while rounding up (500 × 700) gives 350,000. This difference of 110,000 is a satisfactory "ballpark" figure, but most pupils feel uncomfortable with such a wide difference. When this occurs, pupils find that "rounding to the nearest multiple" (of ten, hundred, or thousand) is a better technique.

After working with rounding in numeration, students will recognize that 472 could be rounded to 47 tens or five hundreds. While estimates using "47 tens" would be more accurate than estimates using five hundreds, pupils are not proficient in their "basic facts for 47," so 472 is usually rounded to 500 for estimating purposes. The number 683 is rounded to 700. To mentally compute 500 × 700, the pupil should think, "5 × 7 is 35 and hundreds times hundreds is ten thousands. So my estimate would be 35 ten thousands, but probably less since both numbers were rounded up. Now, is the product close to 350,000? Yes, when I compute I get 322,376, so the product is close to my estimate."

For more accurate results, students are encouraged to **check** their computation by using either the commutative property (multiply 683 × 472 instead of 472 × 683) or by the inverse (divide 322,376 by 472). When multiplying by 1-digit multipliers, students generally use the inverse operation (division) to check the product, since the commutative property seems inappropriate. But when checking multidigit products, students tend to use the commutative property since their division skills with 2- and 3-digit divisors generally are not as well developed as their multiplication skills.

Since multidigit multiplication is generally computed by using a calculator, skill in estimating products will be needed by students. Errors made when using calculators generally occur because the wrong keys were pressed. When students examine the display, their estimates will reveal unreasonable answers. Since the calculator performs the operation quickly and effortlessly, students may check by inverse operation or by reentering the problem using the commutative property.

Without access to computers or calculators, checking (of multidigit multipliers) becomes a chore dreaded by most pupils. Estimation may help pupils detect some errors, but many basic fact errors cannot be revealed by this technique. To provide still another quick checking process, some teachers introduce students to checking multiplication by casting out nines. Casting out nines is not as accurate as the commutative property or inverse check and it does not identify every incorrect prod-

Children need opportunities to develop number sense.

uct, but it does allow the student to examine a product quickly without writing out an algorithm.

When using the casting-out-nines check, the digits of the multiplier are added together and eventually a single digit is reached. (See the development of the casting-out-nines check for addition in Chapter 5.) The same is done for the multiplier. Since the operation is multiplication, the two single-digit numbers are <u>multiplied</u>. The product is reduced to a single di<u>git</u> by "casting out nines." The student then checks his/her answer by casting out the nines in the product. If the single digit products agree, the answer is <u>probably</u> correct. If the digits are not the same, the answer is <u>wrong</u>. (The student should recognize that a reversal of digits in a product cannot be identified when using casting out nines, and therefore the check will not catch every mistake.)

Cast-Out-Nines Check

$$
\begin{array}{ll}
148 & (1 + 4 + 8 = 13; 1 + 3) \qquad 4 \\
\times 233 & (2 + 2 + 3 = 8) \qquad\qquad \times 8 \\
\hline
34484 & \text{(Correct answer)} \qquad\quad 32 \; (2 + 3 = 5)
\end{array}
$$

$(3 + 4 + 4 + 8 + 4 = 23; 2 + 3 = 5)$

$$
\begin{array}{l}
148 \\
\times 233 \\
\hline
33484 \quad \text{(Incorrect answer)}
\end{array}
$$

$(3 + 3 + 4 + 8 + 4 = 31; 3 + 1 = 4)$

Using a Calculator to Extend Multiplication Skills

The calculator is an especially useful device in broadening students' conceptual understanding of multiplication as well as extending students' problem-solving abilities. Calculators make it possible to quickly generate a series of products, patterns, and multiples, thus helping the teacher make efficient use of the limited amount of time available for the teaching of mathematics. A calculator is also an efficient device for checking multiplication seatwork.

One of the earliest uses of the calculator in multiplication is in the generation of lists of multiples. For example, 1×3, 2×3, 3×3, etc., can generate the multiples of three on the calculator. Students also can see the relationship of multiplication to addition by use of the repeated function key. On many calculators, the multiples of three can be generated by pressing the "3" key, the "+" key, and then the "=" key. Thereafter, each time the "=" key is pressed the next multiple of three appears.

To become skillful in the use of decade facts, the student must concentrate on the mental process—not perform computational operations with paper and pencil. Since a calculator can handle a string of operations quickly, it can be used to verify oral responses. A teacher may group three students into a **"buddy group"** to practice the skill. One pupil reads the problem $(6 \times 7) + 2$ from a sheet of exercises provided by the teacher. The other two students "compete" to see who can say the answer first. One student enters the entire problem into the calculator, but is not allowed to say the answer until it appears in the display window. The other student works the problem mentally. The individual who answers first gets a point. With each new problem the three "buddies" change roles—with the calculator competitor becoming the "teacher," the mental competitor becoming the calculator player, and the "teacher" becoming the mental competitor.

The calculator is also used when students explore multiples of tens, hundreds, and thousands. While a place-value analysis will help some students see that ten hundreds is the same as one thousand, verifying this fact through the use of the calculator strengthens insight into the relationship. Students can see a pattern when multiplying *any* number by a hundred (or a multiple of a hundred). When a pupil multiplies 8, 39, or 534 by 100, the answer will be in the hundreds (as indicated by the two zeros that appear in the ones and tens place in the display window). Hundreds (with two zeros) times thousands (with three zeros) will give hundred thousands (with five zeros). Such explorations can be made even more effective if the teacher requires the student to **predict** how many zeros will be in the product before using the calculator to see if his/her prediction is correct, thus developing **estimation skills**.

To help an intermediate-level student understand the "moving over" process with the standard multiplication algorithm, a calculator with a memory function might be used. An example, such as 386×497, is written in the standard algorithm format. The student is instructed to use the calculator to find each partial product. As the student finds the first partial product (6×497), he/she is instructed to copy it in the algorithm and to enter that number into the memory $(M+)$. Then the second and third partial products are found using the calculator, written into the algorithm, and added to the memory. The student is then instructed to add the partial products in the algorithm. The student can check the result with the sum that is stored in the memory by pressing the "recall memory" (RM) key. The two sums should agree. Often the student will find that the calculator response is not the true product (verified by multiplying 386×497 on the calculator). This occurs when the student uses the calculator to find the product of $(6 \times 497) + (8 \times 497) + (3 \times 497)$ <u>instead of</u> $(6 \times 497) + (\textbf{80} \times 497) + (\textbf{300} \times 497)$. At this point the teacher should question the student about the "moving over" process in the algorithm: "How do you tell the *calculator* to "move over" when multiplying by the 8, or by the 3, in the example?"

Calculators can be used when studying exponents to quickly transform a number such as 8^4 into 4096 by entering $8 \times 8 \times 8 \times 8$. Some students discover that their calculator has a repeat function, allowing the user to enter "8" and "x"; then each time the "=" is pressed the number is raised a power. (Note: Pupils should recognize that the first time the "=" is pressed, the display will show 64 since it multiplied the "8" by 8. This would mean that pressing the "=" displays 8^2 and that the next time the "=" key is pressed, 8 raised to the third power will appear.) This type of activity is especially beneficial because it makes the child transform the exponent form to factor form for working. Some students interpret the number 6^4 as 6×4 rather than $6 \times 6 \times 6 \times 6$. Using the calculator can quickly illustrate that the products are not the same.

Factor trees can be generated by using a calculator. To find the prime factors of 48, a pupil may enter 48 and then test to see if 2 is a factor by dividing by 2. Since the quotient (24) comes out without a remainder, then 2 is the first factor. Now the student would test 2 again and find that the quotient is 12, so 2 is a second factor. Then the student would divide by 2 again—getting a quotient of 6—and again, getting a quotient of 3. Taking these numbers the pupil would write $2 \times 2 \times 2 \times 2 \times 3$. If a number, such as 73, does not divide evenly by 2, then the pupil would test 3, 5, and 7. To check the prime factor expression, the pupil can multiply the factors to see if the original number reappears.

While the hundred chart is an excellent device to illustrate <u>how</u> the Sieve of Eratosthenes works, the calculator is a far more effective tool when determining if an individual number is a prime or a composite. On calculators with a memory function, the pupil can enter a number to be tested. If the number 293 is entered into the memory, the pupil would test that number for its square root (17.117 . . .). This helps the student decide which primes must be used in the Sieve. The last prime less than 17.117 is "17," so the number 293 would be tested by the primes 2, 3, 5, 7, 11, 13, and 17. By recalling the number (293) from the memory and dividing by each of the primes, the student will find that none of the primes divide evenly, so the number 293 must be a prime. When using the calculator, the student lets the machine do the "sifting."

Problem-solving activities can be greatly expanded when a calculator is used, rather than having to use time-consuming paper-and-pencil algorithmic methods. This additional time can be utilized to let students create their own problems from data, and tackle problems involving multiplication that would normally be too time-consuming if paper-and-pencil methods were employed.

7.10 COMPUTERS

Many commercial-software and public-domain programs are available that motivate students to practice multiplication facts. Such programs allow the teacher to adjust the pupil response time from slow to fast, making the activity more challenging for individuals. (Programs also are available which check the ability of a child to find the factors or multiples of a number, work through a problem with the standard algorithm, find prime numbers, etc.) Most keyboard pads on computers now resemble a calculator and can be used in a similar fashion. There are many software programs that present multistep story problems in gamelike environments complete with fascinating graphics and sound effects.

Some commercial software not only allows the pupil to practice multiplication skills, but also keeps a record so the teacher can assess the competency of a child. When a child is experiencing difficulty, his/her record can be analyzed by the teacher to determine which skill needs reinforcing and to plan instruction to overcome the deficiency.

7.11 EVALUATION AND INTERVENTION

Evaluating students' conceptual understandings in multiplication is more complex than evaluating their attainments in either addition or subtraction.

For example, when a child fails to obtain a reasonable proficiency with the multiplication algorithm, failure may be due to one or more of the following factors: lack of understanding of the meaning of multiplication, lack of mastery of multiplication facts, the inability to place partial products properly, lack of understanding of decade facts, inability to use addition facts within the algorithm, and the inability to apply the addition algorithm within the multiplication algorithm.

Five typical types of errors associated with multiplication are listed below. Following each error are some general strategies for remediation.

ERROR: Child chooses the wrong operation to solve a problem.

Remedial Strategy: Teacher reviews the meanings associated with multiplication and the meaning associated with the operation used. (The teacher should be aware that some errors associated with "story" problems may result from faulty reading comprehension rather than an inability to understand a meaning associated with multiplication.)

ERROR: A child records an incorrect multiplication fact.

Remedial strategy: Teacher will identify the specific fact or facts not mastered and provide individualized practice on those combinations.

ERROR: A child incorrectly handles the regrouped part of the product in the algorithm.

Remedial strategy: Teacher first has child show process using concrete materials. If understanding is demonstrated, then the child should orally describe each step when working the algorithm.

ERROR: Pupil records improperly within the algorithm.

Remedial strategy: Pupil may need more work on tens times hundreds, etc. Errors MAY occur because of improper use of algorithm format.

ERROR: A child makes errors doing the addition within the multiplication algorithm.

Remedial strategy: Difficulty may be a due to lack of skill in decade facts. However, the teacher will wish to identify this specifically as the problem error through an interview with the pupil.

Since classroom time is limited, most errors are diagnosed from seatwork turned in to the teacher. However, there will be times when the error a child is making cannot be determined without the teacher either observing the child as he/she works, or interviewing the child. This is especially true with respect to evaluating a student's competence in the area of problem solving.

When an interview is appropriate, the teacher should work with the student in a secluded part of the room. The student is then encouraged to talk his/her way through the multiplication algorithm or the problem-solving strategy he/she has used. Since the student must feel comfortable in order to share the process with the teacher, care must be taken to protect his/her feelings. Even when an error is made, the teacher *may* need to refrain from correcting it at that time, for some students will feel threatened by such an intrusion. If the child makes several types of errors, the teacher then must select which one needs to be handled first. In general, priority should be given first to meaning errors (operation and problem solving). (Comment: If a child understands the process associated with multiplication, calculators can be used to continue the student's development of further curriculum concepts, while time is set aside for remediating other types of errors.) Basic combinations errors (needed for later conceptual understandings) and then errors with the algorithm are examined. While overcoming basic fact errors, a pupil may need to use a sheet containing the basic combinations while learning to properly use the algorithm. Basic fact practice can be scheduled at a different time. When both addition and multiplication mistakes are being made, the addition errors should be tackled before the multiplication errors.

7.12 MEETING SPECIAL NEEDS

Multiplication is rich with activities that lend themselves to extending the conceptual understandings of both the student with strong foundations in multiplication skills and the gifted student. These activities range from examining multiplication algorithms that others have used in the past to examining the effect of changing the rules for the multiplication algorithm.

Students generally are interested in other cultures—both foreign and historical. One of the more interesting historical explorations in mathematical computation is the Russian Peasant multiplication algorithm. This algorithm is based on representing numbers as sums of powers of two. For example,

37 is equal to $32 + 4 + 1$ or $(2^5 + 2^2 + 2^0)$. **Any** number can be written as the sum of powers of two. The **Russian Peasant** method requires no multiplication fact greater than two. For example, if we want to multiply 276 by 37, we could multiply 276 by $(1 + 4 + 32)$ using the distributive property and get the correct product. However, one does not need to rename 37 into powers of two in advance—the algorithm will do this "automatically."

To work the problem 37×276, one factor (usually the larger number) is DOUBLED while the other factor (the smaller number) is cut in half—throwing away any fractional parts. When the "half" column reaches 1, the "double" column products that are opposite "odd numbers" in the "half" column are selected to be added. Let's examine this process:

	Half	Double	
Take half of 37—$18\frac{1}{2}$	37	276	(1×276)
Throw away the $\frac{1}{2}$; double the 276	18	552	(2×276)
Half of 18 is 9; double the 552	9	1104	(4×276)
Half of 9 is 4 (throw away $\frac{1}{2}$); double the 1104	4	2208	(8×276)
Half of 4 is 2; double the 2208	2	4416	(16×276)
Half of 2 is 1; double the 4416	1	8832	(32×276)

To find the product, add the numbers in the *doubles* column that are <u>next to odd numbers in the *half* column</u>. Why the odd numbers? Hint: 1×276, 4×276, 32×276. Children enjoy exploring this unusual algorithm and determining, "What skills would a person need to have to use this method? Would they have to know multiplication facts? Could this process be used if one ONLY knows how to add? Why might this algorithm be appropriate for people who have had little schooling?"

Students at the intermediate level enjoy exploring <u>patterns</u> that occur in multiplication. Using pattern exploration as a paper-and-pencil activity provides practice for pupils in using the standard algorithm as well as pattern identification. Using a **calculator** to explore these patterns eliminates the

---

Individual Learning Activity

Can you find the pattern in each set of problems below?

$$(9 \times 9) + 7 = 88$$
$$(98 \times 9) + 6 = 888$$
$$(987 \times 9) + 5 = ????$$

$$66 \times 3367 = 222222$$
$$99 \times 3367 = 333333$$
$$132 \times 3367 = ??????$$

$$11 \times 11 = 121$$
$$111 \times 111 = 12321$$
$$1111 \times 1111 = ?????$$

$$999999 \times 4 = 3999996$$
$$999999 \times 7 = 6999993$$
$$999999 \times 3 = 2??????$$

$$2 \times 37037 \times 3 = 222222$$
$$7 \times 37037 \times 3 = 777777$$
$$5 \times 37037 \times 3 = ??????$$

$$9 \times 12345679 = 111111111$$
$$18 \times 12345679 = 222222222$$
$$27 \times 12345679 = ?????????$$

Can you discover why the pattern works?

FIGURE 7.35

"practice" aspect and focuses attention upon identifying the pattern. Several patterns are illustrated in Figure 7.35. Teachers may wish to explore mathematics enrichment books for other patterns that may be appropriate for the entire class or for gifted pupils.

When exploring the prime factors, many teachers encourage students to search through the primes to discover "special" kinds of primes. It does not take students long to discover that "2" is the only <u>even</u> prime number. With a little guidance, pupils also recognize that there is only one multiple of three that is a prime and one multiple of five, etc. Other primes of interest are those which are separated only by a single number, such as 11 and 13. These numbers are called <u>prime "twins."</u> Once students find all of the "twins" between one and 100, many will want to find out if there are other twins beyond 100. There is one special set of primes—3, 5, 7—that is called "triplets." Pupils sometimes look through the primes to see if there are any other triplets, but they will not be able to find any.

Providing for the Gifted Student

A teacher can select from a wide range of multiplication skills to challenge **gifted** children. Pupils might find products associated with **sequential powers** of a specific number. For example, 6^0, 6^1, 6^2 are equal to 1, 6, 36. Other students are challenged by solving **Diophantine application equations**. For example the question, "You have twenty coins made up of quarters, dimes, and nickels, and the total amount is valued at $3.65. What coins do you have?"

Gifted children are interested in finding "easier" or more efficient ways to find products, and are particularly interested in those which can be done without paper and pencil. Finding a product when one of the factors is 11 is an interesting exploration. When multiplying 11×53, pupils find that they can write down "53" and then write the sum of the two digits $(5 + 3)$ and place it between the 5 and 3. Having students explore what happens when the sum of the two digits is greater than nine, or develop a "rule" for multiplying 11 times a 3- or 4-digit number, provides an irresistible challenge for many.

Gifted students can discover another interesting "rule" by finding the product of any 2-digit numbers whose units digits have a sum of ten and the tens digits are the same, as in 47×43—the tens digits (4) are the same; the units digits (7 and 3) have a sum of ten.

$$47 \times 43 = 2021 \qquad 82 \times 88 = 7216$$
$$35 \times 35 = 1225 \qquad 51 \times 59 = 3009$$

In the problems above a student will discover that the last two digits of the answer is the product of the units numbers. (For example, in 47×43, the last two digits of the answer are 21 or 7×3.) The first two digits in the answer are the product of the tens digits times the next consecutive number. (For example, in 47×43, the first two digits are 20 or 4×5). Those who wish to see why the rule works may explore by using the distributive property.

The gifted students may wish to design multiplication algorithms that use just the associative property, or where an algorithm is worked left-to-right, rather than from right to left. When the gifted student associates the algorithm with an array drawing, many explorations are available. Once the pupil recognizes that $23 \times 37 = (20 + 3) \times (30 + 7) = (20 \times 30) + (20 \times 7) + (3 \times 30) + (3 \times 7)$ (see Figure 7.36), then the same drawing can be applied to mixed numbers (fractions) and even algebraic expressions such as $(a + b)^2$.

Multiples common to several numbers can be challenging when the numbers do not have factors in common. For example, finding the smallest multiple common to 35, 51, and 38 allows pupils to explore the use of prime factor expressions as a way of constructing the least common multiple.

Magic squares challenge the child's ability to organize factors in generating common products. For example, arrange 2, 4, 8, 16, 32, 64, 128, 256, and 512 in a 3-by-3 matrix (three rows with three boxes in each row) so that if the numbers are multiplied across each row, one will obtain the same product as when the numbers are multiplied down each column. Such an activity is much more readily explored if pupils have access to calculators.

Providing for the Learning-Disabled Student

While there are aspects of multiplication that challenge the gifted student, multiplication presents almost insurmountable learning obstacles for many learning-disabled pupils. Previous operations (addition and subtraction) could be completed by counting (even though this may be an inefficient method). However, the size of the products ($8 \times 7 = 56$; $9 \times 9 = 81$, etc.) makes counting too burdensome for most learning-disabled pupils.

It is important for the teacher to stress the meaning of multiplication as when working with the learning-disabled pupil. Early work on basic combinations should focus on the concept of "putting together equal-sized groups," relating multiplication to addition. This early work—since it in-

---

Learning-Station Enrichment Activity

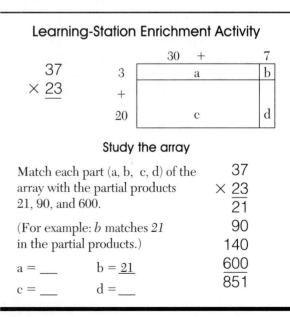

Study the array

Match each part (a, b, c, d) of the array with the partial products 21, 90, and 600.

(For example: b matches 21 in the partial products.)

a = ___   b = 21

c = ___   d = ___

$$\begin{array}{r} 37 \\ \times\ 23 \\ \hline 21 \\ 90 \\ 140 \\ 600 \\ \hline 851 \end{array}$$

FIGURE 7.36

Individual Learning Activity

Enrichment Algorithm
Lattice Multiplication

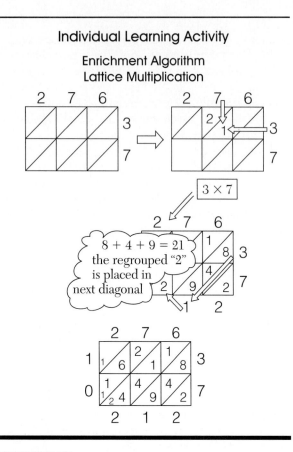

FIGURE 7.37

volves the use of manipulative materials such as sets of objects, arrays, and the number line—is easily managed by learning-disabled children. Emphasis upon the use of the distributive property (breaking a number apart, multiplying each part, and putting the parts back together) also is important for the pupil to comprehend.

Problem-solving applications must concentrate on making learning-disabled students functionally literate with the kinds of multiplication problems they will encounter in daily living situations—for example, finding the cost of multiple purchases (using a calculator).

When developing the multiplication algorithm, the teacher must recognize that a handicapped child with memory deficits will have difficulty remembering the basic combinations. Therefore, it would be appropriate to allow such students to use fact cards or tables when working with multidigit multiplicands or multipliers. Such aids focus the pupil's attention upon the way the algorithm functions and removes the handicap of limited skill with the basic facts. Some basic understanding of the algorithm is necessary to be able to fully utilize a calculator in problem-solving applications.

If the standard algorithm is too difficult for the child, the teacher may wish to introduce a different

algorithm. A ancient algorithm—Gelocia multiplication—can be used effectively with some children. This algorithm uses a "lattice" to structure the basic combinations and is sometimes called "lattice multiplication." Since lattice multiplication does not require users to be proficient in decade facts, and somewhat ignores place value, it is particularly suitable for pupils who have a reasonable proficiency with the basic facts. In fact, many students—even the gifted—<u>prefer</u> to use lattice multiplication rather than the standard algorithm. This algorithm is often found in fifth- and sixth-grade texts as an enrichment exploration. One of the side benefits of the algorithm is that errors in basic facts can be quickly identified by the teacher. Let us examine the exercise, 37 × 276, using the lattice method. The 276 and 37 are placed as shown in Figure 7.37. Then the child writes the facts for 7 × 6, 7 × 7, 7 × 2, 3 × 6, 3 × 7, and 3 × 2 in the corresponding boxes with the tens part above the diagonal and the ones part below the diagonal. Then the digits are added <u>on the diagonal</u> to find the product.

After learning-disabled children understand the meanings associated with multiplication, have worked on their facts, and have developed a reasonable understanding of the multiplication algorithm, the teacher should allow them to use calculators to find products.

7.13 SUMMARY

In the primary grades children learn three meanings associated with multiplication (equivalent sets, arrays, and linear measure) and explore some of the properties (zero generalization, commutative and distributive properties, and identity). The multiplication facts are introduced at the primary-grade level, and many elementary programs explore the multiplication algorithm for a 1-digit multiplier. Most multiplication concepts and skills, however, are developed in the intermediate grades.

The intermediate-level student adds the cross-product model for multiplication to those meanings introduced in the primary level. The pupil learns to recall the multiplication facts quickly and develops reasonable proficiency in multiplying with 1-, 2-, and 3-digit multipliers. The student learns to estimate and check products, find multiples and sets of factors, and write numbers in prime number expressions and exponential notation. The student learns to use the calculator and computer to work problems that use multiplication to arrive at a solution. By the end of the intermediate grades the child can solve multistep problems that require multiplication as one of the steps.

EXERCISES

1. Illustrate with drawing and/or materials the problem 4 × 6:
   a. Using the union of equivalent sets model
   b. Using the cross-product model
   c. On a number line
   d. Using an array model
   e. Relating multiplication to repeated addition using a calculator
2. Describe how a teacher could use manipulative materials to develop each of the following:
   a. Identity
   b. The zero generalization
   c. The commutative property of multiplication
   d. The associative property of multiplication
   e. The distributive property of multiplication
3. Describe how a teacher would develop each of the listed approaches to exploring the basic facts:
   a. Identity
   b. Zero generalization
   c. Doubles
   d. Patterns (fives, nines)
   e. Distributive property
4. Use an array to show how the distributive property is used in developing an algorithm for finding the product of 7 × 18.
5. Use a manipulative material (place-value chart, computing abacus, or base ten blocks) to show the development of the conventional algorithm (with helpers) for 7 × 387.
6. Associate the conventional algorithm for 47 × 53 with an array picture.
7. Find the sets of factors for the numbers from 26 through 50 (as illustrated in Figure 7.23).
8. Use a factor tree to find the prime factor expression for the numbers listed below. Rewrite each expression using exponents.
   a. 16   b. 30   c. 56   d. 81   e. 144
9. Construct a chart from 101 to 200. Use a Sieve of Eratosthenes to find the prime numbers.

RELEVANT COMPUTER SOFTWARE

Math Maze. 1983. Apple II family. Designware, 185 Berry Street, San Francisco, Calif. 94107.

Meteor Multiplication. Acorn, Apple, Atari, Commodore 64, IBM PC. Developmental Learning Materials, One DLM Park, P.O. Box 4000, Allen, Tex. 75002. (Arcade game format—builds multiplication skills.)

Numbers of Fortune, Whole Number Edition. 198. Apple IIe and IIc. Fortune Software, 70 Sierra Road, Boston, Mass. 02136.

REFERENCES

Fendel, D. M. *Understanding the Structure of Elementary School Mathematics.* Boston: Allyn and Bacon, 1987. Pp. 163–167.

Hazekamp, D. W. "Components of Mental Multiplying." In *Estimation and Mental Computation: NCTM Yearbook.* Reston, Va.: National Council of Teachers of Mathematics, 1986. Pp. 116–126.

Henrickson, A. D. "Verbal Multiplication and Division Problems: Some Difficulties and Some Solutions." *Arithmetic Teacher* 33 (April 1986): 26–33.

Jensen, R. J. "Common Multiples: Activities On and Off the Computer." *Arithmetic Teacher* 35 (December 1987): 35–37.

Katterns, B., and K. Carr. "Talking with Young Children about Multiplication." *Arithmetic Teacher* 33 (April 1986): 18–21.

Meyer, R. A., and J. E. Riley. "Multiplication Games." *Arithmetic Teacher* 33 (April 1986): 22–25.

Quintero, A. H. "Children's Understanding of Situations Involving Multiplication." *Arithmetic Teacher* 33 (January 1986): 34–37.

Ryoti, D. E. "Investigating Growth and the Powers of Two with the Computer." *Arithmetic Teacher* 34 (December 1986): 34–35.

CHAPTER 8

TEACHING DIVISION OF WHOLE NUMBERS

INTRODUCTION

Division occurs often in everyday situations, though children may not be called upon to use this skill as often as adults. Pupils "divvy up" candy, making sure each gets the same amount, but they do not associate this activity with division. Division also plays an important role in understanding rational numbers, rational number operations, decimal operations, percent, ratio, and average.

Today, the use of calculators and microcomputer programs to perform long division has almost entirely replaced the act of manually finding a quotient of two large whole numbers. It still is necessary, however, for a child to understand both how to find a quotient manually, and also to have a **reasonable** level of proficiency with the paper-and-pencil algorithm. This skill is used to evaluate the reasonableness of an answer obtained by a technological device. It is also used to perform computations when manual computation would be the more efficient procedure for obtaining the quotient (either because the computation is simple or because a technological device is not readily available).

Crucial to teaching division concepts is the development of the child's ability to use the operation in appropriate problem-solving situations. This means the teacher must develop the child's ability to recognize when the operation of division is required by the problem solution. Like other operations, the development of meaning is established when the child participates in extensive and varied problem-solving situations that require division.

Since children need addition, subtraction, and multiplication skills to be able to complete the division algorithm, full development of the conventional long-division algorithm is deferred until the intermediate grades. Primary-grade lessons focus upon the development of meanings for the operation; discovery of the relationship of division to multiplication; exploration of common division patterns; and exploration of the basic division facts and algorithm. The intermediate level develops mastery of the basic division combinations; builds skill with the division algorithm; extends problem-solving skills to include multistep problems; estimation and checking; and relates division to fractions.

8.1 TEACHING DIVISION IN THE PRIMARY GRADES

Children come to the primary grades with a very limited background in division. Of course, children know that four can be put into two sets of two. They also recognize that ten is two fives since they have two hands with five fingers on each hand. While they may have used terms like "let's divide the cookies" when they shared their treats, most children entering the first grade have little understanding of division as an operation.

Understanding the terminology used with division is complicated by the many guises in which it will be taught. For example, sometimes division results in quotients with <u>no</u> remainder (where the elements of the division equation can be related to the factors and a product in a multiplication equation). On other occasions, division results in quo-

tients <u>with</u> remainders. When remainders occur, multiplication terminology (known factor, missing factor, and product) is not appropriate. (See Figure 8.1.)

Children explore the easy division facts only **after** multiplication facts are explored. While a <u>complete</u> mastery of the multiplication facts is not a prerequisite to division facts, an understanding of multiplication and facility with the simpler basic facts are essential. In the primary grades development of the division algorithm is usually limited to 1-digit divisors.

Children first associate division with finding the number of equal-sized sets that can be formed from a set (measurement). Later, pupils associate division with sorting objects to form equal-sized sets similar to the way cookies or cards would be passed out one at a time (partition).

Which meaning of division is explored first by the teacher may depend upon the problem situation that generates the need for division. Before words such as "dividend," "divisor," "quotient," "product," "known factor," and "unknown (or missing) factor" are introduced, the child must have activities that require finding either the number **of** equal-sized sets that can be **measured** out of a given set, or the number **in** each set when a set has been **partitioned** into a given number of sets.

As with other operations, developmental algorithms can also be used to deepen the child's understanding of division. The developmental algorithms such as those in Figure 8.2 strengthen the child's understanding of place value, particularly with the use of the measurement illustration for division. The standard algorithm may be developed effectively by using it in a partition illustration.

Terminology without remainder

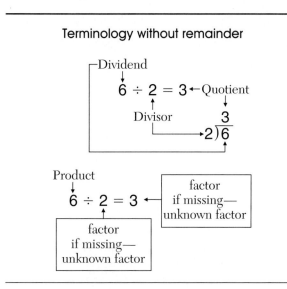

Terminology with remainder

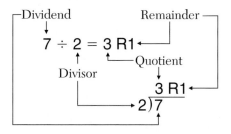

Multiplication terminology is not appropriate when a remainder is present.

FIGURE 8.1

Developmental Algorithms

```
          3                    3
         20                   100
        100
    2)246                2)246
      200 | 100            200
       46 |                 46
       40 | 20              40
        6 |                  6
        6 |  3               6
        0 |                  0
```

FIGURE 8.2

A general overview of the division skills introduced at the primary level is listed below.

Grade 1

Incidental explorations with division

Grade 2

Develop meaning of division
- measurement concept
- partition concept

Understand division vocabulary
- known factor, unknown factor, product
- divisor, dividend, quotient

Recall easy basic facts
- ones, twos, fives

Explore patterns and properties
- division by one
- n divided by n equals one
- division as the inverse of multiplication

Problem-solving activities

Grade 3

Develop meaning of division
- strengthen measurement concept
- strengthen partition concept

Explore division facts
- mastery of easy division facts
- explorations with harder division facts

Examine properties and patterns
- explorations with properties and patterns

Explore 1-digit divisors, 2- and 3-digit dividends

Problem-solving activities

8.2 DEVELOPING THE MEANINGS OF DIVISION

Division concepts (similar to meanings associated with addition, subtraction, and multiplication) are developed through hands-on experiences. The **measurement** meaning of division is generally developed first because teachers want to associate division with the equivalent sets meaning of multiplication. However, children encounter the **partition** meaning of division in the course of play activities, when someone must "make sure" that each child gets his/her fair share of a set (cookies, candy, toy blocks, etc.). To accomplish this, a child "deals" out the objects <u>one at a time</u>, until the set is exhausted. Pupils should become familiar with BOTH models for division. The terms (partition

and measurement) are not terms children will be expected to use when describing division. These terms will be employed by the teacher when defining objectives for a lesson.

Introducing the Measurement Model for Division

In the second-grade classroom, there are many times when objects are "packaged" (stacked, put into piles, arranged, grouped, boxed, etc.) into equal-sized sets. These situations present an excellent opportunity for the teacher to develop the measurement concept of division.

In the following lesson fragment, the teacher used pupil interest in a spring carnival to explore the measurement model for division.

Teacher-Guided Interactive Learning Activity

LESSON FRAGMENT

M: Associating division with the activity of finding the number of sets formed when measuring out sets equal in number

A: Group of second-graders

T: Hands-on work with models, involvement

H: Children have had explorations with equal sets involving multiplication

PROBLEM-SOLVING SITUATION:
THE CLASS IS MAKING CLOWN DOLLS FOR PRIZES AT THE SPRING CARNIVAL. STUDENTS ARE TO PUT TWO BUTTONS ON THE FRONT OF EACH CLOWN. A NOTE WAS SENT TO PARENTS ASKING THEM TO DONATE ANY SPARE BUTTONS. MRS. WITKOSKI SENT 12 BUTTONS. THE TEACHER POSED THE QUESTION, "HOW CAN WE FIND THE TOTAL NUMBER OF CLOWNS WE CAN MAKE USING MRS. WITKOSKI'S BUTTONS?" OUT OF THIS PROBLEM THE FOLLOWING LESSON WAS DEVELOPED.

Teacher: Before we start working to find an answer to this question—let's first see if we have any "guesses." Terry?

Terry: There will be fewer than 12 because there is going to be more than one button on each clown.

Teacher: Right, Terry. To help us find a more exact answer we are going to work at our desks and use our counters. Everyone take out a set of 12 counting disks and put them on your desk to represent the

12 buttons. I'll put <u>my</u> set of buttons on the flannelboard. To keep a record, place your numeral card for 12 under the set to show how many buttons we have. (SEE FIGURE 8.3A.)

Teacher: We will need two buttons for each clown, so place the numeral "2" to the right of the "12" to remind us to take out groups of two. To show the

Teacher-Guided Interactive Learning Activity Measurement Model

FIGURE 8.3

operation, we are going to use this sign. (THE TEACHER HOLDS UP A "÷" CARD.) It tells us to divide. Find <u>your</u> division sign and place it <u>between</u> the 12 and 2. (SEE FIGURE 8.3B.)

Teacher: Now take out as many sets of two as you can. When I say "Go," show me the card that tells you how many sets of two are in 12. Go! (SEE FIGURE 8.3C.)

Teacher: Very good. All of you found that you could get six sets of two. Place the equal sign and "6" to complete the equation. We read this equation, "Twelve divided by two equals six." Let's read the equation *together*. (SEE FIGURE 8.3D.)

Instructional group and teacher: (AS THE TEACHER POINTS TO EACH PART OF THE EQUATION, THE GROUP READS.) Twelve divided by two equals six.

When pupils break a group into equal-sized sets, the teacher must associate the action with division—writing either the equation or the algorithm form. Many different objects—counters, blocks, pieces of paper, children—are commonly used when division of a set of objects is desired. Unifix™ blocks, commonly found in kindergarten and first grade, are an excellent material to be used in second and third grades to provide hands-on exploration with division concepts. The blocks, since they can be used either as a set of separate blocks or connected into rods to show a **linear model**, are a versatile manipulative material. A rod of 12 blocks could be used to illustrate 12 ÷ 3. Children can measure off a rod of three and then use that rod to <u>measure</u> other rods of three from the remaining 9-rod. Children find that a 12-rod can be broken into four rods measuring three blocks each. (See Figure 8.4.)

The number line is another way of illustrating measurement division. A <u>walk-on number line</u> allows pupils to act out problems by taking "trips" along the line. When using a walk-on number line, the teacher will tape or draw a number line on the classroom floor. To illustrate 12 ÷ 4, a child is directed to stand on 12 and take "trips" or "jumps" the size of four. The class counts to see how many "trips" it takes to get back to zero. (See Figure 8.5.) Once the operation has been acted out several times on the walk-on number line, the teacher should illustrate the action on a number line <u>drawn</u> on the chalkboard. Such explorations provide a good foundation for later experiences children will have with number-line drawings that appear in textbooks.

When using the measurement model to develop the <u>division equation</u>, the first number (dividend)

Individual Learning Activity

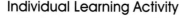

$$12 \div 3 =$$

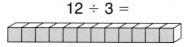

How many rods of 3 can you make from a 12-rod? Take off 3 rods and use them to measure other rods of 3. Keep taking off rods of 3.

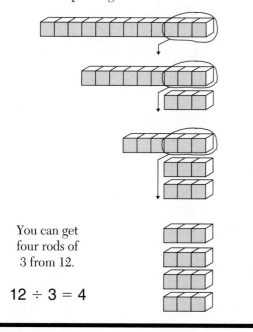

You can get
four rods of
3 from 12.

$$12 \div 3 = 4$$

FIGURE 8.4

represents the beginning amount—whether roses, bottles, counters, blocks, starting point on the number line, etc. In the equation $18 \div 3 = 6$, the divisor (3) represents the number to be placed **in** each group (or the size of a jump on the number line). The quotient (6) shows the number **of** groups (or jumps).

Introducing the Partition Model for Division

The 1960s textbooks introduced division in measurement situations with the divisor associated with the number IN each set and the quotient representing the number OF sets. (If we had 12 things and we took out groups the size of 3, how many groups would we have?—$12 \div 3 = \Delta$.) When partition division was introduced, to be consistent and retain the same structure the "missing part" occurred as the divisor. (We have 12 things and we want to distribute them equally among four people—how many would each person get?—$12 \div \Delta = 4$.) Today, this distinction is no longer main-

Walk-on Number Line

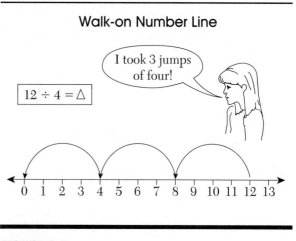

I took 3 jumps of four!

$$12 \div 4 = \Delta$$

FIGURE 8.5

tained—both measurement AND partition division situations are written with missing quotients ($12 \div 3 = \Delta$ and $12 \div 4 = \Delta$). Most children do not seem to be disturbed by this inconsistency in the equation, but teachers must recognize that individual pupils MAY be confused.

The "partition" model for division occurs when the number of groups into which the original amount will be distributed is known, but the number **in** each set is <u>not</u> known. Children encounter the concept of division in many of the games they play. Card and board games typically begin with each player receiving the <u>same number</u> of cards (or amounts of money). Distribution is accomplished by "dealing" the cards (or money) out, <u>one at a time</u>. Any time a set is distributed "evenly" among a fixed number of sets (boxes, bags, cartons, strips, etc.), the operation of division is suggested.

Figure 8.6 illustrates a child exploring a partition division situation involving an independent learning activity. The child has been given a set of directions that state, "Sort sets of 6, 12, 18, 24, and 27 counters into three equal-sized piles. First record the action you will be undertaking in a division sentence." For example, $18 \div 3$ tells the child to distribute a set of 18 into three equal piles and then record the number of objects he finds in each of the three piles.

Working with Remainders

Since development of skills grows from problem-solving situations, division with a remainder may be explored early in the development of the division operation. Using manipulative materials, children can remove groups of a designated number (measurement division) and <u>discover</u> that sometimes there are objects left over (remainders). When il-

Independent Learning Activity

Partition Model

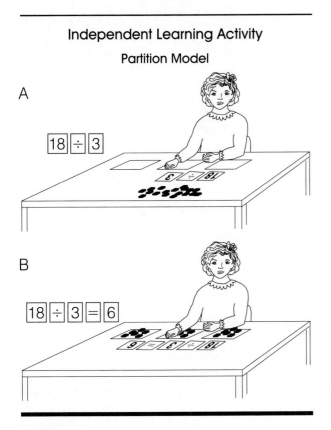

FIGURE 8.6

Division with Remainder

Partition Model

Distribute 7 blocks so that each person will get the same number of blocks.

Give one to each person.

Give another to each person.

Each person now has 2 blocks and there is one block left. This is called the remainder.

FIGURE 8.7

lustrating partition division, children find that giving seven marbles to two pupils results in each child getting three marbles, but there is one marble left over.

When working with remainders, it is suggested that the teacher use the algorithm form—3)7— rather than the equation form, $7 \div 3 = \Delta$. Use of the algorithm will allow children to subtract in a <u>familiar</u> format. Since the standard division algorithm develops easily when using a partition approach, many teachers introduce remainders in a partition rather than a measurement situation (see Figure 8.7).

8.3 TEACHING BASIC DIVISION FACTS

Since division is the inverse operation of multiplication, teachers may organize the teaching of division facts much as they do the teaching of the multiplication facts. For example, after students explore multiplication facts with a factor of two, they learn the division facts with a divisor of two. By the end of the third grade, children will have explored all of the division facts through $81 \div 9$. (Note: In a division fact, the divisor and quotient are 1-digit numbers.)

Organizing the Division Facts for Exploration

Multiplication and division facts can be explored together. Such a procedure helps children understand the inverse relationship of the two operations. After putting three sets of two together to illustrate $3 \times 2 = 6$, the teacher may direct the child to take sets the size of two from six ($6 \div 2 = 3$). From such explorations, the child recognizes that division will <u>undo</u> multiplication. Figure 8.8 illustrates a variety of visual aids that can be used when relating division to multiplication (measurement model).

Relating Repeated Subtractions to Division Facts

When the division facts are illustrated as repeated subtraction, it serves a dual purpose. Not only does it provide another means of exploring the basic division facts, but the insight gained through these explorations can be transferred to algorithms in which subtraction is used to find the quotient. Figure 8.9 shows a child finding a series of differences by repeatedly subtracting three. In the final step the child transfers the information gained by the activity with manipulative materials to the task of finding the quotient.

Using the Calculator to Explore Division Facts

The calculator can be used to demonstrate how division is related to repeated subtraction. After entering 45, children may be asked to enter a "minus" and a five. The pupils then press the equal sign and keep subtracting five until they reach zero. Since the purpose is to find how many fives can be subtracted, pupils must count as each five is subtracted. Using the calculator, students can try many different combinations, discovering that the quotient is always the number of subtractions it takes to reach zero.

Since the calculator will allow children to easily divide many problems (even those with large numbers), it is an excellent tool to be used when examining patterns in division. Looking at $N \div 1 = N$, $N \div N = 1$, $0 \div N = 0$ ($N \neq 0$), and division by fives and nines allows pupils opportunities to discover patterns which occur when dividing. Figure 8.10 shows how the calculator keys are manipulated to perform division. Notice that the calculator follows the same order as the division equation.

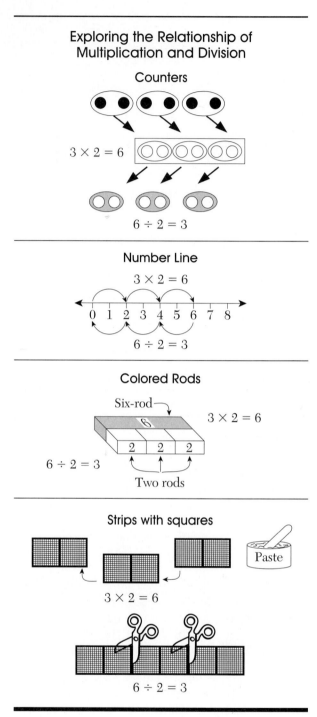

Exploring the Relationship of Multiplication and Division

Counters

$3 \times 2 = 6$

$6 \div 2 = 3$

Number Line

$3 \times 2 = 6$

$6 \div 2 = 3$

Colored Rods

Six-rod

$3 \times 2 = 6$

$6 \div 2 = 3$

Two rods

Strips with squares

Paste

$3 \times 2 = 6$

$6 \div 2 = 3$

FIGURE 8.8

Organizing Instruction around Division Patterns

Dividing by one (the n ÷ 1 facts) is introduced soon after the meaning of division is established and some other facts have been developed. While the fact can be developed using either a measurement

Independent Learning Activity

A

$12 \div 3$

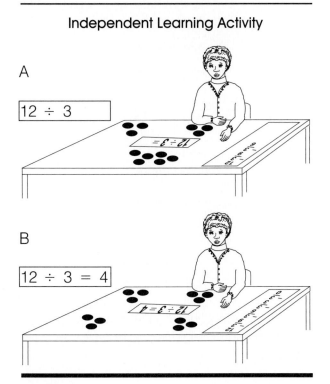

B

$12 \div 3 = 4$

FIGURE 8.9

Exploring Relationships

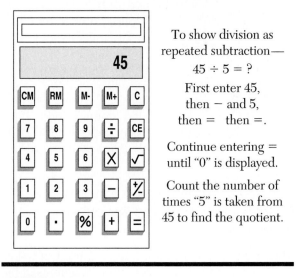

To show division as repeated subtraction—

$45 \div 5 = ?$

First enter 45, then $-$ and 5, then $=$ then $=$.

Continue entering $=$ until "0" is displayed.

Count the number of times "5" is taken from 45 to find the quotient.

FIGURE 8.10

Exploring Patterns

$n \div 1$ facts

Exploring with a number line

$4 \div 1 = \square$

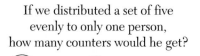

How many jumps the size of one will it take to return to zero?

Exploring with Counters

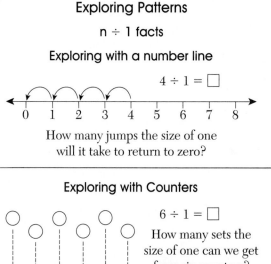

$6 \div 1 = \square$

How many sets the size of one can we get from six counters?

If we distributed a set of five evenly to only one person, how many counters would he get?

$5 \div 1 = \square$

FIGURE 8.11

or a partition approach, it is probably better to use measurement. When using a measurement approach the key question becomes, "If we are at six (for example) and we take jumps the size of one, how many jumps will we take?"

Sets of objects may also be used to help pupils realize that n ÷ 1 = n. Starting with six counters, the pupils are asked to take groups the size of one from the original six counters. When they finish, they find that there are six groups of one in six. (See Figure 8.11.)

Another way of exploring this generalization is to relate N ÷ 1 to the identity property for multiplication. For example, the equation $\Delta \times 1 = 7$ asks, "What number times one would equal seven?" Pupils can be asked to find the <u>related</u> division equation for this multiplication equation ($7 \div 1 = \Delta$). At the primary level, however, it perhaps is better to develop generalizations from hands-on explorations rather than from abstract mathematical sentences.

Dividing a number by itself The N ÷ N = 1 (N ≠ 0) facts can be explored using a measurement approach. For example, "Take out four objects. How many sets of four can you get out of this group?" When this activity is repeated with sets of different numbers it is followed by writing the division equation suggested by the activity. Children soon see that N ÷ N = 1. (See Figure 8.12.)

Zero as a dividend   The facts 0 ÷ N = 0 (where N ≠ 0) are more difficult to develop, but seem easy for the child to learn. Some of the difficulty is caused by the awkwardness of trying to talk about measuring out a certain number of objects when the set has <u>zero</u> members. (See Figure 8.13.) Even partitioning a set of zero members into a certain number of sets is awkward. Another option available is the use of related multiplication equations using zero. (This option must be used with care, however, to avoid giving the impression that division by zero is possible.)

Using Related Facts and the Multiplication Matrix to Teach Division Facts

The multiplication matrix (table) is used not only to show multiplication facts; it can also be used for the division facts. To find a quotient (18 ÷ 3 = Δ) the pupil locates the factor (3) and goes <u>across</u> the table until the product (18) is reached. The pupil then runs his/her finger <u>up</u> the column—reading the factor at the top. When division facts are taught with the corresponding multiplication facts, the group of facts are called the "related facts" (for example, 3 × 6 = 18; 18 ÷ 6 = 3; 6 × 3 = 18; 18 ÷ 3 = 6). (Extensive activities with hands-on manipulative activities must precede any use of the matrix.) Figure 8.14 illustrates a variety of related sentences, involving the numbers 18, 6, and 3.

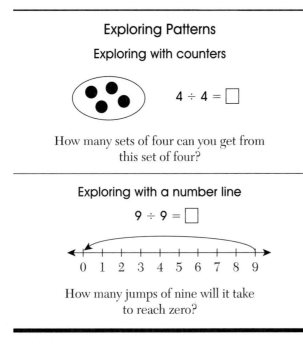

Exploring Patterns

Exploring with counters

4 ÷ 4 = ☐

How many sets of four can you get from this set of four?

Exploring with a number line

9 ÷ 9 = ☐

How many jumps of nine will it take to reach zero?

FIGURE 8.12

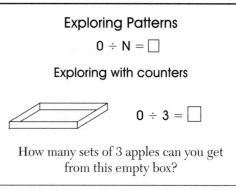

Exploring Patterns

0 ÷ N = ☐

Exploring with counters

0 ÷ 3 = ☐

How many sets of 3 apples can you get from this empty box?

Exploring with a number line

Start here!   0 ÷ 3 = ☐

0 1 2 3 4 5 6 7 8

How many jumps the size of three will it take to reach zero—if you start at zero?

FIGURE 8.13

Properties that Don't Exist for Division

Since the commutative and associative properties do not hold for division, there is a tendency by teachers to ignore them. However, it is valuable for children to explore these properties in division. Using manipulative materials, children can see a difference between, for example, 1 ÷ 4 and 4 ÷ 1. The teacher may wish to use the partitioning meaning to emphasize this difference, showing that when one whole is partitioned into four equal sets, there is $\frac{1}{4}$ in each set. When four is sorted into one set, there is one set of four. Having children work pairs of equations such as "(16 ÷ 4) ÷ 2 = Δ" and "16 ÷ (4 ÷ 2) = N" clearly demonstrates that the associative property does not hold for division. Calculators may also be used to examine the effect of changing the order—or the grouping. Remember that such work is <u>exploratory</u> and use of the words "commutative" and "associative" is inappropriate.

Memorizing the Basic Facts

Drills to memorize division facts should be postponed until a child understands the meaning of division. Understanding may be checked by having a child <u>demonstrate</u> the sentence (8 ÷ 2 = N) using manipulative materials. The child should also be asked to write the number sentence suggested by a division activity demonstrated by the

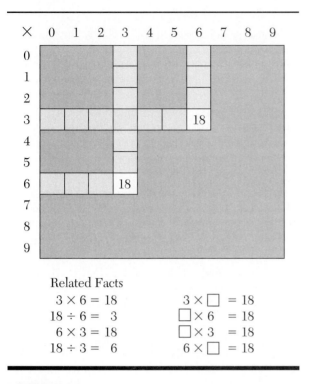

×	0	1	2	3	4	5	6	7	8	9
0										
1										
2										
3							18			
4										
5										
6				18						
7										
8										
9										

Related Facts

$3 \times 6 = 18$	$3 \times \square = 18$
$18 \div 6 = 3$	$\square \times 6 = 18$
$6 \times 3 = 18$	$\square \times 3 = 18$
$18 \div 3 = 6$	$6 \times \square = 18$

FIGURE 8.14

teacher. (It is not necessary that the child demonstrate <u>both</u> meanings associated with division before beginning to practice the basic facts. Children may have mastered <u>some</u> facts as a byproduct of their exploratory activities.)

The principles for mastering division facts are similar to those used when working with addition, subtraction, and multiplication facts. (These principles, as well as activities, can be found by reviewing the appropriate chapters.)

There are many ways to help children memorize the division facts. One technique matches the division facts with corresponding multiplication facts in a gamelike activity. For example, when the teacher works on $2 \times 5 = 10$ and $5 \times 2 = 10$, children also practice $10 \div 2 = 5$ and $10 \div 5 = 2$. Children can take sets of multiplication and division facts and sort them into "teams" of related facts.

There are also group activities that help pupils practice the multiplication and division facts and strengthen pupil recognition of the relationship between the two operations. "Related Fact Teams" is a gamelike activity that allows each student to play the "role" of a division or multiplication fact. Facts—written on index cards—are passed out so that each pupil has one card. The leader (or teacher) then chooses one or two pupils to come to the front of the room and hold their cards high in

the air. The rest of the class examine their cards to see if they belong to the two identified teams. Pupils who belong to the "team" (related fact team) race to join their leader. In early practice activities, the pupils representing multiplication facts (commutative law) quickly recognize that they should join the team. Those pupils who represent the "inverse members" (division facts) of the team are generally slower to recognize their affiliation with the group. Teachers may vary the activity by selecting the division facts as the "leader." (See Figure 8.15.)

Of course, as children begin practicing the division facts, they will discover that some of these facts have already been learned through previous activities. Many facts will be mastered by relating the division to a "missing factor" in multiplication. For example, the problem $24 \div 6 = \Delta$ can be written as $\Delta \times 6 = 24$. The child then thinks, "What number times six will give me 24?"

8.4 INTRODUCTION OF THE DIVISION ALGORITHM

The division algorithm is introduced only in a limited way—if at all—in the primary grades. When the algorithm is introduced, situations are limited to 1-digit divisors and 2- and 3-digit dividends. Problems generally have no remainder—although some primary programs will explore quotients with remainders. For example, a problem such as 43 divided by three, which gives a quotient of 14 and a

Group Practice Activities

Related Fact Teams

FIGURE 8.15

remainder of one, may be developed as an extension of hands-on activities with basic division facts.

This section will examine how the division algorithm might be developed using a partition model. A partition approach is used because the model effectively illustrates EACH step of the conventional division algorithm. However, since some textbook series may explore developmental algorithms based on a measurement approach before introducing the standard algorithm with the partition approach, a teacher may wish to examine the measurement algorithm developed in Section 8.11, "Meeting Special Needs."

Introducing the Division Algorithm

Once the pupil has learned to record quotients and remainders using simple situations involving single-digit quotients, the transition to larger quotients using a single divisor is a matter of getting the student to understand the role of place value in the division algorithm.

The lesson fragment which follows extends the child's understanding of the division to 1-digit divisors and 2-digit quotients:

Teacher-Guided Interactive Learning Activity

LESSON FRAGMENT

M: Division algorithm with 1-digit divisor and 2-digit quotient, no remainder

A: Group of above-average third-graders

T: Involvement, models

H: Children can work problems with 1-digit divisors and 1-digit quotients (with and without remainders)

PROBLEM-SOLVING SITUATION:
THREE THIRD-GRADE CLASSES JOINED TO OPERATE A RING-TOSS BOOTH AT THEIR SCHOOL'S SPRING FESTIVAL TO RAISE MONEY FOR NEW SPORTS EQUIPMENT. THE BOOTH MADE $84 AFTER EXPENSES. THE TEACHER POSES THE QUESTION, "HOW MUCH MONEY SHOULD EACH CLASS RECEIVE AS ITS FAIR SHARE?"

Teacher: Before we use materials to get an accurate amount—who can give us an estimate? Remember, when we give our estimate we are going to share

with the class WHY we believe it is a good estimate.

Melody: It'll be more than 25 because three quarters would be 75¢ and 84 is more than 75.

Teacher: All right, I'll write that down and now we can go to our groups to see if we can determine the amount. (THE TEACHER CIRCULATES AND HELPS FIND MATERIALS WHEN THEY ARE NEEDED. IF A GROUP GETS AN ANSWER QUICKLY, ANOTHER AMOUNT IS SUBSTITUTED FOR THE 84 SO THE PUPILS CAN "VERIFY THEIR APPROACH.")

Teacher: I see that most of you found $28 to be an answer. Let's work the problem TOGETHER on the place-value chart. We'll place three "doors" on the side of the place-value chart rows to represent the rooms. I am going to record our problem on the chalkboard as we work. (SEE FIGURE 8.16A.)

Teacher: Lee, can you come up and share the tens with our three rooms. (SEE FIGURE 8.16B.) While Lee shows this on the chart—can we "guess" how many tens each room will get? Show me with your fingers. (EACH MEMBER OF THE GROUP DISPLAYS TWO FINGERS.)

Teacher: Good—Lee gave each room two tens. Let's record that. We'll write the 2 in the tens place to show that each of the three rooms is going to get two tens. That took care of six tens. We took those

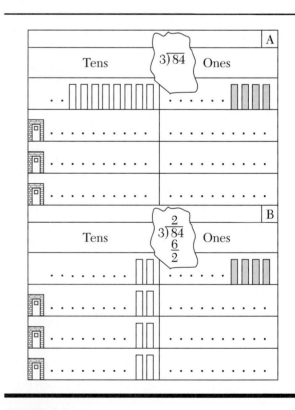

FIGURE 8.16

from the eight tens and there were two tens left. We'll write 6 under the eight tens because three sets of two is six, and then we took six tens from eight tens—so we will subtract and record the two tens left. (SEE FIGURE 8.16B.)

Teacher: Could we trade for each of our tens, Lee?

Lee: Yes—we could trade one ten for ten ones so two tens would give us 20 ones.

Teacher: I see that you put the 20 ones with the four ones, making 24 ones. I'm going to record that on the chalkboard. We can take our four and put it with the two tens to show the 24 ones that we have on the chart. Thank you, Lee—you can take your seat and we will let Buffie help us for a while. Buffie, can you distribute the 24 ones evenly to the three rooms? (SEE FIGURE 8.17A.)

Buffie: I know there are going to be eight in each group, because 24 divided by three is eight.

Teacher: Good, Buffie. Now why don't you put the tags in the chart to verify that each room will get eight ones. I'll write the eight in the ones place to show what Buffie is doing. Since there are three sets of eight that will take care of all of the 24, so we can write our 24 to show how many were used up. We can subtract to verify that there would be no ones left. (SEE FIGURE 8.17B.)

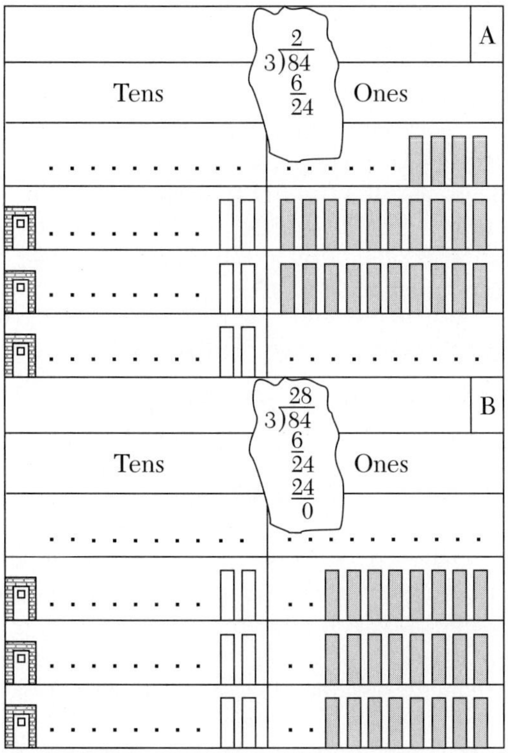

FIGURE 8.17

Teacher: Each room should get two tens and eight ones, or $28. So Melody's estimate of a little over 25 was pretty close, wasn't it? Now I would like each group to continue working to develop skill in dividing. I will write some other amounts on the chalkboard—money we MIGHT have made at the ring toss. Work in your group using paper and pencil. When each has found an answer—select a team member to use materials to verify your quotient.

8.5 TEACHING DIVISION IN THE INTERMEDIATE GRADES

Division and its problem-solving applications are introduced at the primary level. Children master some of the division facts. The standard division algorithm may have been introduced, but because of its complex nature, mastery is deferred until the intermediate level. One of the difficulties in learning to use the division algorithm is the number of different concepts and subskills that must be employed before the algorithm can be mastered. To use the division algorithm effectively, the child must be able to recall division facts; have good subtraction skills; be able to multiply with 1-digit multipliers; be able to round numbers, estimate factors, and adjust trial quotients (when partial products are too large or too small). Adding to this complexity is the fact that quotients that do not come out evenly may be treated in various ways (as a whole-number remainder, as a fractional number, and as either a terminating or repeating decimal).

Just as multiples were taught concurrently with multiplication concepts, divisibility rules are explored while working on division concepts. Some divisibility rules (divisible by six, eleven, etc.) are used as enrichment activities, but most pupils will learn the rules for divisibility for two, four, five, and nine as part of the regular intermediate program.

The following illustrates the division topics normally developed at the intermediate level:

Grade 4

Review division facts
Examine properties
- N divided by 1
- N divided by N (N ≠ 0)
- 0 divided by N (N ≠ 0)
- (NXM) divided by (RXM) = N divided by R

Introduce multiples of 10 as a divisor
Explore division algorithm
- 1-digit divisors; 2- and 3-digit quotients

- 2-digit divisors; 1- and 2-digit quotients
- remainders and mixed numeral quotients

Adjust quotients
Estimate and check quotients
Problem-solving activities

Grade 5

Maintain basic fact skills
Extend skill in algorithm
- multiples of ten as divisor
- zeros in dividend
- zeros in quotient
- remainders, mixed numerals, and decimal quotients

Estimate and check quotients
Problem-solving activities

Grade 6

Explore rules of divisibility
Extend algorithm skills
- 2- and 3-digit divisors; 1-, 2- and 3-digit quotients
- zeros in quotient
- remainders and mixed numerals
- decimal quotients with terminating and non-terminating decimals

Estimate and check quotients
Problem-solving activities

Grades 7 and 8

Maintain division algorithm skills
Extend rules of divisibility
Estimate and check quotients
Problem-solving activities

8.6 MAINTENANCE AND EXTENSION OF BASIC FACTS

Many students do not master the division facts until they reach the intermediate grades. Hands-on explorations similar to those used in the primary grades are employed by teachers when reviewing division. Children explore both measurement and partition situations, using sets of objects and linear models (number-line models).

Since division is the inverse of multiplication, many teachers organize practice activities around the related facts, thus emphasizing the relationship of the operations. For example, the basic multiplication facts $4 \times 6 = 24$ and $6 \times 4 = 24$ are

Children should explore strategies when learning basic facts.

reviewed with $24 \div 6 = 4$ and $24 \div 4 = 6$. To further strengthen this relationship, teachers may ask pupils to write a division sentence ($24 \div 4 = \Delta$) as a multiplication sentence ($\Delta \times 4 = 24$). (When a sentence is written $\Delta \times 4 = 24$, the measurement concept of division is being reinforced since the size of the set is known and the number of sets is missing. Writing the sentence as $4 \times \Delta = 24$ would show the partition concept, since the student knows that there are four sets, but does not know the amount in each set.)

The related facts method is but one way of organizing the basic division facts. Some teachers prefer to group practice activities so common-divisor families are emphasized. For example, all the facts with divisors of 2, as in $2 \div 2$, $4 \div 2$, $6 \div 2$, etc., can be studied as a block of facts. This organizational pattern is commonly associated with learning the division tables.

Practicing the Basic Division Facts

When organizing practice of basic division facts, the teacher may notice that there are some facts that are better reviewed focusing pupil attention upon a pattern or generalization. For example, any number divided by "1" will result in the original number ($N \div 1 = N$). Another set of combinations best mastered by recognizing the pattern associated with the quotient would be $N \div N = 1$.

Facts such as $0 \div N = \Delta$ (where $N \neq 0$) are best explored by changing the sentence into a corresponding multiplication sentence, such as $\Delta \times N = 0$. Pupils quickly recognize that zero is the only number that can replace Δ, so that the product would be zero. Such a development provides an avenue for the teacher to explore why "N ÷ 0" (where N ≠ 0) and "0 ÷ 0" are not reasonable expressions. When "N ÷ 0 = Δ" is rewritten as "Δ × 0 = N," students will find that no number can be found to replace "Δ." When "0 ÷ 0 = Δ" is rewritten as "Δ × 0 = 0," students see that any number can be used for "Δ."

Not all students master division facts at the same time, so the teacher must organize facts differently for individual pupils. There are commercial and public-domain computer programs that offer systematic ways to individualize the study of basic facts, including division facts. Teacher-directed activities, such as buddy drills with "Holey Cards" (Chapter 6) and class activities like "Fact Captain" (Chapter 5) also are effective.

When a child lacks only a few basic division facts, the teacher can design practice activities in the context of music. Such an approach is a "memory enhancement technique," which utilizes the association of the elements of the equation in an auditory pattern rather than a mathematical analysis. Such memory techniques are effective when an individual wants to remember specific facts or data. When using this memory enhancement technique the teacher should first make sure the student understands the mathematical concept. Then, if a basic fact such as 42 ÷ 6 = 7 is identified as a combination that needs practice, the teacher may record that fact on an audiotape cassette as a "radio commercial" song or even a "rap" jingle. The teacher first repeats the fact, "42 divided by 6 is 7," two or three times to establish the tune or rhythm. Then the teacher would record "42 divided by 6 is (tone)"—the answer is not given; just a tone is recorded for the "seven." When the child listens to the tape and repeats the phrase two or three times, his/her brain will supply the "7" at the tone. If this rhythmic cycle is repeated several times, the student soon finds him/herself singing the fact to the music.

Tile-sorting activities are another way of practicing division facts. (Tile sorting can be modified to help students practicing addition or subtraction facts.) The tiles commonly used in such an activity are simply basic combinations written onto oaktag or posterboard and cut into 1-inch square regions. A student is given a set of the tiles and ten envelopes. On each envelope is written a different 1-digit quotient (0, 1, 2, 3, 4, 5, 6, 7, 8, and 9). The pupil is then instructed take the tiles and sort them into their proper envelopes. For example, the tile with 18 ÷ 3 would be placed in the "6" envelope along with 54 ÷ 9; 42 ÷ 7; etc. (See Figure 8.18.)

Familiar games like checkers, tic-tac-toe, etc.,

Individual Learning Activity
Tile-Sort Activity

Put the tile into its proper quotient envelope.

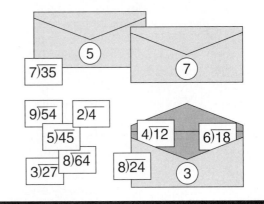

FIGURE 8.18

may be modified to serve as interesting practice activities. Checkerboards, for example, can have division facts pasted onto the jump squares. The game would be played just like checkers, except that a player can move a checker piece to any square only when the quotient of the fact listed on that square is given. Figure 8.19 illustrates part of a modified checkerboard.

8.7 MAINTENANCE AND EXTENSION OF THE DIVISION ALGORITHM

Due to its complexity the division algorithm requires the intermediate-grade teacher to organize instruction into a sequence of carefully measured

Small Group Learning Activity

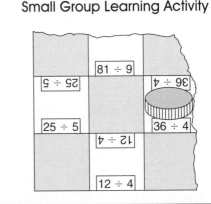

FIGURE 8.19

steps. Appropriate prerequisites must be developed before proceeding to the next step. For example, before beginning division with 2-digit divisors, students should be familiar with 1-digit divisors (long-division algorithm); be able to round numbers (both up and down); and be able to use multiples of ten as divisors. One typical sequence for working with 1-digit divisors is listed below. In general, examples with remainders are taught immediately following each problem type (after $64 \div 2 = 32$; $64 \div 3 = 21$ R1 would be explored); problems that require regrouping follow those with no regrouping.

(a) $64 \div 2$	**(b)** $72 \div 6$
(no regrouping)	**(regrouping)**
(c) $124 \div 4$	**(d)** $232 \div 8$
(renaming)	**(renaming and regrouping)**

Extending the Division Algorithm

Though the standard 1-digit divisor algorithm is introduced in many primary programs, it is explored with much greater depth at the intermediate level. The following lesson fragment reviews the 1-digit long-division algorithm, extending it to include 3-digit dividends:

Teacher-Guided Interactive Learning Activity

LESSON FRAGMENT

M: One-digit divisor, 3-digit dividend

A: Fourth-grade class

T: Model (place-value chart)

H: Basic division facts, place value, subtraction skills

PROBLEM-SOLVING SITUATION:

THE SCHOOL-SPONSORED YARD SALE WAS A BIG SUCCESS LAST WEEK AND THE PUPILS ARE STILL SPECULATING ON HOW MUCH PROFIT THEIR ROOM WILL MAKE. FINAL FIGURES ARE NOT YET AVAILABLE, BUT THE PARENT/TEACHER SPONSORS HAVE INDICATED THAT THERE WILL BE OVER $400 FOR THE THREE FOURTH-GRADE CLASSROOMS TO SHARE. DUE TO THIS INTEREST, THE TEACHER HAS POSED A QUESTION—SPECULATING ON "POSSIBLE" PROFITS.

Teacher: I have been informed that we will get over $400 from the school yard sale. Of course—we must share it among the three classes. So that we can have a better idea of what OUR share will be, today

we are going to "speculate" on different amounts. Suppose we earned $431. ABOUT how much would our share be for our picnic? Vanessa?

Vanessa: We'll get over $100—because 431 is more than 300. And we'll get less than $200 because $600 would be $200 for each.

Teacher: Very good, Vanessa. Often we don't need an exact answer—your guesses gave us a boundary for our answer. Now suppose we wanted to know exactly how much each class would get. How could we find out?

Vanessa: Since we want to share equally, we could divide $431 into three equal groups.

Teacher: Good. I wonder if you could set up this problem for us on the place-value chart. (AS THE STUDENT PLACES FOUR TAGS IN THE HUNDREDS, THREE TAGS IN THE TENS, AND ONE TAG IN THE UNITS, THE TEACHER WRITES THE DIVISION PROBLEM IN ALGORITHMIC FORM.) (SEE FIGURE 8.20A.) As Vanessa helps us with the place-value chart, I will record these steps on the board. If we gave each class an equal amount of hundreds, how much would each get?

Vanessa: (PLACES ONE TAG BY EACH FIGURE AND LEAVES ONE TAG IN THE UPPER POCKET.) I gave each class one hundred and there is one hundred left.

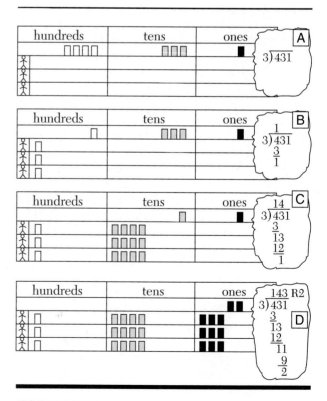

FIGURE 8.20

Teacher: I'll record what Vanessa did. Each class got one hundred, so we'll write a "1" in the <u>hundreds place</u>. Three groups of 1 hundred would make 3 hundreds. We can **record** the "3" under the "4" hundreds, designating the hundreds we used. Since we took the 3 hundreds from the 4 hundreds, we will subtract the "3" from the "4" in the algorithm and show that we have 1 hundred left. (SEE FIGURE 8.20B.) Now since we want to distribute the amount evenly, what are we going to do with this extra hundred? Norman?

Norman: We can trade in our 1 hundred for ten tens. (VANESSA TRADES IN THE ONE TAG FROM THE HUNDREDS FOR TEN TAGS TO PLACE IN THE TENS.)

Teacher: How many tens do we have altogether— when we put the ten tens with the three tens that we already had? Shirley?

Shirley: Thirteen tens.

Teacher: To show this in the algorithm, I'm going to bring down our 3 and place it beside the 1 that was left in the hundreds. Remember that we traded 1 hundred for ten tens and we put it with our three tens to make <u>13 tens</u>. Now that we have 13 tens, we can give them to three classes. Before Vanessa does this on the chart, who can tell me how many tens each person will get? Burt?

Burt: Each person will get four tens and there will be one ten left over.

Teacher: Can you tell us how you came up with that number, Burt?

Burt: Well, I know that $12 \div 3 = 4$, so $13 \div 3$ must give us a remainder of 1.

Teacher: Very good! Let's see if that is what Vanessa gets when she distributes the tags. (VANESSA GIVES EACH FIGURE ONE TEN AT A TIME AND FINDS THAT EACH RECEIVED FOUR TENS WITH ONE LEFT OVER JUST AS BURT SUGGESTED.) Since our chart shows the same thing, let us record this on our algorithm. Each class received four tens, so we write down a "4" in the tens place. We distributed three sets of four tens, or 12 tens. We can show the 12 tens by multiplying three times four and recording the 12 under the 13 tens. By subtracting the 12 from the 13 we can show the one ten that remains. (SEE FIGURE 8.20C.) Now we have one ten left over. What can we do with the ten? Ruth?

Ruth: We can trade one ten for ten ones. (THE TEACHER DIRECTS VANESSA TO TRADE IN ONE TEN FOR TEN ONES ON THE PLACE-VALUE CHART.)

Teacher: How many ones do you have altogether, Vanessa?

Vanessa: Eleven ones.

Teacher: So now I can bring down our one and write it beside the one ten to show that we now have 11 ones. How many ones will each of the three classes get? Charles?

Charles: Each will get three ones, but we will have two ones left. (THE TEACHER DIRECTS VANESSA TO MAKE THE DISTRIBUTION TO VERIFY THE RESPONSE.)

Teacher: Good, Charles! We did have two left! Let's record what Vanessa did. Each class received three ones, so we write a "**3**" in the units place. Since we passed out three sets of three, this took nine ones. We can show this by multiplying three times three and then writing our "**9**" beneath the 11 ones. We took the nine ones from the 11 ones so we can subtract in our algorithm to show that we have two left. (THE TEACHER RECORDS EACH NUMBER ACCORDINGLY.) So we have a <u>remainder</u> of two. We can record this by writing "**R 2**." (SEE FIGURE 8.20D.) So our quotient is 143. Since it falls BETWEEN 100 and 200, as Vanessa suggested, the answer is reasonable.

Teacher: We are going to try a few more amounts— working together. Then I am going to have each of you work in your group to practice this skill. When EACH team member gets a quotient, select someone in your group to use their base ten blocks to see if the answer is reasonable.

Extending Place-Value Skills in the Division Algorithm

When first exploring 1-digit divisors and the division algorithm, students work problems that have an equivalent number of digits in both the dividend and the divisor. For example, in $72 \div 6 = 12$ the dividend (72) and the quotient (12) both have two digits, and in $948 \div 3 = 316$ the dividend and quotient both have three digits. Such problems require pupils to recognize the positional value of the digits (hundreds, tens, and ones) and may require regrouping.

When pupils encounter problems in which the quotient has <u>fewer</u> digits than the dividend ($138 \div 6 = 23$), a different understanding of the positional value system is required. Before pupils can become proficient with these problems the teacher must <u>extend</u> student understanding of positional value so they recognize that numbers can be <u>interpreted</u> in a variety of ways. Most students recall from the primary grades that the number 138 could be interpreted as "138 ones" or "one hundred, three tens, and eight ones." Many students, however, are not yet comfortable thinking of 138 as **13 tens** and eight ones. To be efficient in working the problem

138 ÷ 6, a student must first recognize that the amount (138) will be distributed into six equal-sized groups. Then the pupil must recognize that there are not enough hundreds to give each of the six a hundred. If the amount (138) is reexamined, the student may then recognize that there are 13 tens and eight ones. Each of the six groups could get at least one ten and probably two tens.

Zeros in the Quotient

As students become more skillful dividing with 1-digit divisors, they find some problems more difficult than others. Almost universally, quotients that include zeros are more often incorrectly calculated than any other kind of problem. Most teachers plan special lessons to help pupils overcome this difficulty. The place-value chart, computing abacus, and base ten blocks are all effective materials to illustrate why a zero appears in the quotient. When working with these concrete models, pupils typically have little difficulty. They see that there are no tags, beads, or blocks in a given position, and record a "0" to show this.

When students abandon the manipulative materials and compute quotients with paper and pencil, algorithmic errors are more likely to occur. Pupils "forget" to record a zero in the quotient (see Figure 8.21A). Even though a teacher may remind the class to make sure that each step in the algorithm is carefully recorded, pupils forget after a few examples and mistakes recur.

To reduce this kind of error, teachers should stress that the first step in using the algorithm is estimating the size of the quotient. In the problem 4248 ÷ 6, pupils recognize that each of six "people" could not get a thousand, since there are only **four** thousands. Each of the six "people" could get at least one hundred since there are **42** hundreds. Once it is determined that the quotient will be less than 1000 and at least 100, a "dash" may be placed in the hundreds, tens, and ones position of the quotient (see Figure 8.21B). Students should be encouraged to think of the "dashes" as placeholders upon which the digits of the quotient will be recorded. When a digit (such as zero) is omitted in the quotient, an empty "dash" reminds the pupil that the quotient must have three digits (see Figures 8.21C and D).

A technique such as the one described above should be used as a developmental algorithm and abandoned as individual students become more proficient. While the technique is useful in helping individuals overcome a particular kind of computational error, the greatest value of the algorithm is that it encourages students to **estimate** quotients **before** computing.

Multiples of Ten as Divisors

Dividing by multiples of ten (10, 20, 30, 40, etc., through 90) or one hundred (100, 200, 300, 400, . . ., 900) requires fewer prerequisite skills than dividing by 2-digit or 3-digit numbers such as 37 and 428. Therefore, multiples-of-ten divisors are typically the first 2-digit divisors explored by students. When using these numbers, teachers can concentrate upon developing the algorithm and estimation skills, while allowing additional time for pupils to master the division facts.

Since the partition model for division works so well when developing the long-division algorithm using 1-digit divisors, the teacher may wish to continue to use this approach when introducing divisors that are multiples of ten. Using play money (tens and ones) or base blocks (rods, units), the teacher may suggest that an amount (80) is to be distributed evenly to 20 class members. (See Figure 8.22A.) When a student is chosen to distribute the tens, everyone will quickly see that only eight pupils could get a ten-rod. The rods must be traded in single units. (See Figure 8.22B.) When the eight rods are changed into 80 singles, **then** the single units may be distributed among the 20 pupils. Each student would get four rods. (See Figure 8.22C.)

The "acting out" of the problem is but a beginning step in helping students understand the division algorithm with 2-digit divisors. Its value lies

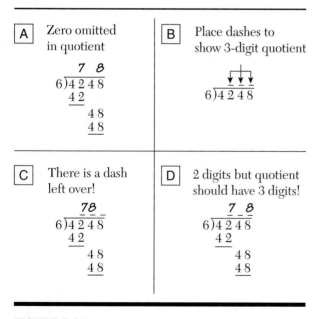

FIGURE 8.21

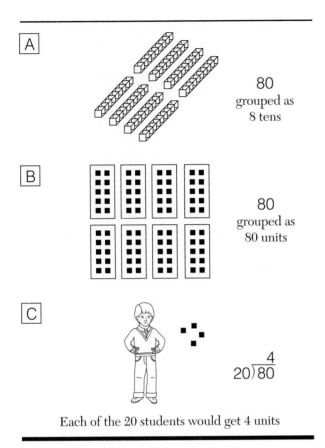

A

80
grouped as
8 tens

B

80
grouped as
80 units

C

$$\begin{array}{r} 4 \\ 20\overline{)80} \end{array}$$

Each of the 20 students would get 4 units

FIGURE 8.22

in its effectiveness in guiding pupils to recognize that the same process used with 1-digit divisors is employed when 2-, 3-, or multidigit numbers are used as divisors. Once students associate the algorithm with the model, the teacher may wish to use an <u>analytical</u> approach to extend their understanding.

While it is possible to partition 120 objects into 20 sets to demonstrate that $120 \div 20$ would result in **six** objects in each of the 20 sets, it extends pupil understanding if the teacher restates the division equation as $\Delta \times 20 = 120$, or "what number times two <u>tens</u> would give you 12 <u>tens</u>?" Looking at 120 and 20 as 12 tens and two tens allows students to utilize knowledge of the properties of multiplication to help them understand division.

Stated as Inverse	Stated as Division
$\Delta \times 20 = 120$	$120 \div 20 = \Delta$
$\Delta \times 2$ tens $= 12$ tens	12 tens $\div 2$ tens $= \Delta$
6 $\times 2$ tens $= 12$ tens	12 tens $\div 2$ tens $= $ **6**

The calculator is another way students can explore division by multiples of ten. Using the cal-

culator to find the quotient for problems that have multiples of ten allows pupils to observe certain patterns and to speculate on why they occur. Since the calculator completes a division operation using a decimal notation when quotients are not evenly divisible, teachers should provide students with carefully designed sets of problems so that the pattern is easily discernable. A sample of such a problem list (with quotients) is listed below:

$8\underline{0} \div 2\underline{0} = 4$	$24\underline{0} \div 8\underline{0} = 3$
$42\underline{0} \div 6\underline{0} = 7$	$25\underline{0} \div 5\underline{0} = 5$
$72\underline{0} \div 9\underline{0} = 8$	$24\underline{0} \div 4\underline{0} = 6$
$120\underline{0} \div 3\underline{0} = 40$	$560\underline{0} \div 7\underline{0} = 80$

Although a measurement approach to develop the standard division algorithm is not common, it may be useful to develop some division by multiples of ten. In the previous example, $120 \div 20$, the 12 *tens* would be measured out into sets of two *tens*, giving exactly six sets. For some students this illustration is more meaningful than the partition illustration. The measurement model, using multiples of ten, also may reinforce pupil understanding of this meaning for division since problem solving takes place in both partition and measurement situations.

Most students find dividing by multiples of ten in situations without remainders easier than those that have remainders, so those problems are explored first. However, the teacher must remember to extend pupil skills to include division with remainders. For example, $125 \div 20 = 6$ R5. At this stage pupils are taught to examine the possible range of numbers that might occur as a remainder. For example, when dividing by 20 the remainder could range from 0 to 19.

Teaching Division with 2-, 3-, and Multidigit Divisors

The development of skills necessary when dividing with multidigit divisors is based upon the pupil's understanding of division with 1-digit divisors. There are some major differences in the development, however. While division with multidigit divisors can still be effectively developed using a partition model, the size of the multidigit divisor and dividend often make use of models unwieldy. Most problems must be <u>reasoned</u> through and the use of mathematical understandings and subskills employed. When a pupil is deficient in any of the understandings or subskills, then successful completion of the algorithm is restricted. It should not be surprising that division is one of the most difficult operations for students to master.

Extending the Division Algorithm Using a Problem-Solving Situation

To help students become proficient in the use of the algorithm, teachers often break the development into smaller steps—limiting the number of subskills or concepts required by the pupils. One approach provides the pupil with divisor tables, thus limiting the necessity of estimating and multiplying while focusing upon the development of the algorithm. When using the tables, the teacher concentrates on helping pupils estimate the quotient (Is the quotient in the thousands? hundreds? tens?) and on the internal steps of the algorithm. In the lesson fragment below, a teacher uses tables, but does not require pupils to round the divisor or multiply by the partial quotient.

Teacher-Guided Interactive Learning Activity

LESSON FRAGMENT

M: 2-digit divisor algorithm

A: Fifth-grade class

T: Analysis; use of tables

H: Division of 1-digit divisors and multiples of ten

PROBLEM-SOLVING SITUATION:
THE SCHOOL IS PREPARING FOR ITS ANNUAL FAIR. THE CLASS WILL AGAIN BE SPONSORING THE "GO FISHING" BOOTH. SINCE THE NUMBERS ARE LARGE AND THE INTEREST IN THE FAIR IS HIGH, THE TEACHER HAS CHOSEN THIS SITUATION TO INTRODUCE DIVISION WITH 2-DIGIT DIVISORS.

Teacher: The School Fair Committee has given us 48 packages with 144 bags in each package for our "Go Fishing" booth. This means that we have 6,912 bags. Each of us will take an equal number of bags to fill with prizes and candy. We have several days to complete the job, but we want to share the task equally. So that means the 27 of us will sort out the 6,912 bags so we each have the same number. Who can tell me what operation can be used to tell us how many each will get? Mike?

Mike: We could pass the bags out one at a time.

Teacher: Wouldn't that take a long time?

Mike: Yeah, I guess it would. It would be easier if each person came up and counted out their share.

Teacher: How can we determine how many that will be, Mike?

Mike: Since we are going to share equally, I guess that would be division.

Teacher: Very good, Mike! (THE TEACHER WRITES THE PROBLEM 6912 ÷ 27 ON THE BOARD IN AN ALGORITHM FORM.) Before we start with the division—who has an estimate of the quotient—and remember, share with us WHY you made this particular guess. Betsy?

Betsy: About 3000, because two will go into six three times. No—wait—that's not right because if each person got 3000 that would only be two people. Twenty seven is close to 30 and 30 × 100 would be 3000—so I guess it would be a little more than 200.

Teacher: I'm glad to see you rethinking and revising your estimates. Now let's see if we can get started on the algorithm to get a more accurate answer. If there are 27 of us, would each of us get a thousand? Betsy?

Betsy: No, teacher, we only have 6000. But each of us would get *at least* one hundred because there are 69 hundreds in 6,912.

Teacher: Excellent! I'm going to put a dash over the hundreds, tens, and ones places so we will remember that Betsy told us that our answer would be in the hundreds. Now how many of you have learned your 27 tables? (NO STUDENT VOLUNTEERS.)

Betsy: Do we have to learn them to work the problem, teacher?

Teacher: No, Betsy. I know that we have not yet learned how to work with 2-digit divisors, so I have prepared a table to help us work the problem. (THE TEACHER DISPLAYS THE MULTIPLE CHART FOR 27. SEE FIGURE 8.23.) Let's use this to help us find the quotient. Who can suggest a trial quotient for the number of hundreds we each will get? Zeke?

Zeke: Looks like three would be too much since 3 × 27 is 81 and we only have 69 hundreds. So we should try two hundreds.

Teacher: I will write that in the quotient and then multiply two times 27. We can see from the chart that it will equal 54. Now we can subtract the 54 hundreds from the 69 hundreds to see how much

$$27\overline{)6912}$$

Basic facts for 27			
0	0	5	135
1	27	6	162
2	54	7	189
3	81	8	216
4	108	9	243

FIGURE 8.23

we have left. (TEACHER RECORDS ON THE CHALKBOARD, SHOWING THAT IT WOULD LEAVE 15.) Now what should be done? Nida?

Nida: Well, we can bring down the one.

Teacher: Nida, I know you know what "bringing down" means, but if someone wanted to know **why** you bring it down, could you explain it?

Nida: I'm really trading in the 15 hundreds for tens—giving us 150 tens and then I'm going to have you put the one ten with it to make 151 tens.

Teacher: Thank you, Nida. Now how many tens would we each get? You want to try again, Zeke?

Zeke: The chart shows that 5 × 27 is 135 and 6 × 27 is 162, so I think we should try the five.

Teacher: Good, Zeke. (TEACHER WRITES THE "5" AND SAYS) Five times 27 is 135, so I'll write 135 in the tens place and subtract that from the 151 tens, leaving 16 tens. What shall I do now, Burt?

Burt: You'll trade the 16 tens in for ones and put the other two ones with it to make 162 ones. That means you can "bring down" the 2 and write it with the 16.

Teacher: Thank you, Burt, for such a complete answer. (TEACHER BRINGS DOWN THE 2.) Now how many ones will we get? Phyllis?

Phyllis: The chart says that 6 × 27 equals 162, so it looks like we are going to come out even.

Teacher: It does look that way, doesn't it. (THE TEACHER COMPLETES THE ALGORITHM.)

To strengthen the concept and the pupils' understanding of the algorithm, the teacher would continue the lesson trying other amounts, but using 27 as the divisor. Pupils would use the chart to complete follow-up exercises. The teacher may wish to show other multidigit divisors **using charts of multiples**. (With such an approach, students can explore division with 2-, 3-, and even 4-digit divisors without being handicapped by limited multiplication or rounding skills.)

Becoming Skillful with Multidigit Divisors

Adults seldom compute multidigit divisor problems without the assistance of a calculator or computer, but there are occasions when individuals find paper-and-pencil calculation to be more convenient than searching out such technological devices. Division with 2-, 3-, and even 4-digit divisors is **explored** at the intermediate level. However, the degree of proficiency in the use of the algorithm is somewhat less than that which pupils will achieve with 1-digit divisors. The development of 2-, 3-, and 4-digit divisor skills should emphasize the

estimation skills employed in the algorithm since those same skills are used whether the student computes with paper and pencil or with a calculator.

As indicated earlier, students may be introduced to the multidigit divisor algorithm with tables. Once students become familiar with the procedure as it applies to the algorithm, they will abandon the tables and use rounding to help choose a trial quotient. At this point teachers will again need to remind pupils **why** they round the divisor. When a table is available, rounding is unnecessary since it is apparent what the multiples of the divisor would be. With no table, rounding is used, along with basic facts to help determine the trial quotient. When using a rounded divisor, the best trial quotient is not always chosen.

To show how rounding is used in an algorithm, let us examine the first few steps in the problem "3,358 ÷ 73." First we will determine how many digits will be in the quotient. We have 3358 to be distributed to 73 people. Each person will not be able to get a thousand since we have only three thousands. Each person will not be able to get a hundred since we have only 33 hundreds. We know, however, that 3,358 can be arranged as 335 tens and eight ones, so it would appear that each person will get **at least** one ten. Once we have identified that the quotient will have two digits, we need to know how many tens each person will get. Since we do not know our 73 tables, we'll round 73. While 73 is seven away from 80, it is only three away from 70, so we'll round 73 down to 70.

Now, we can use our rounded divisor—70 (or seven tens)—to find a trial quotient. We know that Δ tens × 7 tens (rounded divisor) must give us about 3300 (33 hundreds). Since 10 × 10 gives hundreds, we need to look at the 33 to find Δ times 7 will give us that number, or if we cannot get a product equal to 33, then a smaller product must not differ from 33 by more than 6 (7 − 1). Our basic facts tell us that 4 × 7 = 28 and 5 × 7 = 35. Thirty-five would be too much, so we'll try 4 as the first trial quotient. When we multiply 4 (tens) × 73 we get 292 (tens). When this is subtracted from 335 tens we find that 43 tens are left, so our trial quotient was effective.

In this example, the rounded divisor led to the best trial quotient. In a problem such as 2,179 ÷ 34, rounding 34 down to 30 will give a trial quotient of seven tens, which would be too large. Teachers must help pupils understand that the rounded divisor is not the actual divisor, so the trial quotient **may** be too large or too small.

Teaching Students to Round the Divisor

As observed in an earlier lesson fragment, students who are proficient with 1-digit divisors could work with 2- and even 3-digit divisors if they knew the multiplication facts for the multidigit divisors. However, it would be absurd to memorize combinations for all 2- and 3-digit numbers. Instead of attempting this overwhelming task, students are taught to **round** the divisor and use the rounded number to find a trial quotient.

It is important in the early explorations with 2- and 3-digit divisors for students to recognize that the rounding of the divisor is a way of avoiding the mastery of unwieldy multiplication tables for 2- and 3-digit divisors. A rounded divisor is not the actual divisor; it simply gives the pupil a **trial quotient**. When pupils understand why the divisor is rounded they are not nearly as frustrated when they find their trial quotient is "too small" or "too large." Even an occasional poor guess is more desirable then memorization of all of the multiples of a 2-digit divisor. (**Note:** If a large number of problems had the same divisor, it probably would be practical for an individual to construct a table—as in the previous exploratory lesson. But since we do not often use the same divisor in problems, using a rounded divisor is a more practical approach.)

Prior to extensive development of multidigit divisor skills, the student should have experiences with rounding 2- and 3-digit numbers to the next higher (and lower) multiple of ten or a hundred. In division, the purpose of rounding is to allow the pupil to utilize knowledge of the basic facts. Therefore, 2-digit numbers are rounded to multiples of ten, while 3-digit numbers are rounded to multiples of a hundred (rather than multiples of ten).

In the standard algorithm the student is taught to round to the nearest multiple of ten or a hundred. Teachers should help students recognize that the closer a number is to a multiple, the more likely the trial quotient will be successful. When developing this skill, pupils are generally instructed to round the digit (in the position to the right of the desired power of ten) down when it is a 1, 2, 3, or 4, and to round up when it is a 5, 6, 7, 8, or 9. Pupils sometimes question the appropriateness of rounding "up" when the digit is a "5." With 2-digit numbers, five is the midpoint and it really would not make a difference. However, when rounding to hundreds, a "5" in the tens place is followed by digits in the units place, which usually would make the number past the midpoint (the exception would be when the five is followed by a zero). When working with 3-digit divisors, pupils should round "0"

down (since it generally is followed by a digit greater than 0). If the last two digits of a 3-digit number are zeros, then the pupil does not need to round at all.

Teachers should help students recognize that the selection of a trial quotient which was too large (or too small) is not a wasted effort. Much can be learned from this "guess." Students should be led to see that:

a. When a divisor is **rounded down** to estimate the trial quotient, an amount that is too large may occur and a smaller trial quotient (usually 1 less) should be chosen for the next trial.

b. When a divisor is **rounded up** to estimate the trial quotient, an amount that is too small may occur and a larger trial quotient (usually 1 more) should be chosen for the next trial.

In the following lesson fragment students learn the thought process required for successful mastery of the division algorithm:

Teacher-Guided Interactive Learning Activity

LESSON FRAGMENT

M: Multidigit divisors

A: Fifth-grade class

T: Step-by-step analysis and examples

H: Basic division facts, rounding, division by multiples of ten

PROBLEM-SOLVING SITUATION:
THE CLASS HAS BEEN STUDYING LIVING CREATURES OF THE SEA. YESTERDAY A CHILD BROUGHT IN SOME OF HIS SHELL COLLECTION. THERE WAS A GREAT DEAL OF DISCUSSION ABOUT THE COLLECTION SO THE TEACHER DECIDED TO USE THIS AS A BASIS FOR EXPLORING MULTIDIGIT DIVISORS.

Teacher: (THE TEACHER WRITES 17,167 ÷ 365 IN ALGORITHMIC FORM ON THE BOARD.) Yesterday, Tom told us he had been collecting shells from the beach for the last year and that now he has 17,167 shells! Many of the shells are very small and some are large. We know that on some days he collects more than others, but suppose he collected the same amount each day. How many would he need to find each day to end up with 17,167 shells? I've written the problem on the chalkboard as a division problem so we can work through it together.

What is the first thing that we are going to do? Nisha?

Nisha: We need to find the number of digits in the quotient. If each day had the same amount each day, it wouldn't be 10,000 because there is only one ten thousand and it wouldn't be one thousand since there are only 17 thousands. I guess it wouldn't be a hundred either, since there would only be 171 hundreds and there are 365 days. So I guess we need to show that it is a 2-digit quotient.

Teacher: (THE TEACHER PLACES A DASH ABOVE THE "6" AND THE "0" OF THE DIVIDEND.) Good, Nisha. Now let's see what we can do next. Since we do not know our 365 combinations, we will need to **round** our divisor and find a trial quotient. What number should 365 be rounded to? Biddie?

Biddie: It's a lot closer to 400 than 300, so it would be better to round up.

Teacher: I think that's a good idea, Biddie. Now, we need to decide upon a first trial quotient. (TEACHER POINTS TO THE DASH IN THE TENS PLACE OF THE QUOTIENT.) We'll be working with tens times hundreds, so our answer will be in the thousands. How many thousands do we have in our problem, Zen?

Zen: We have 17 thousands.

Teacher: Since we rounded to four hundreds, what number times four will give us about 17? Zen?

Zen: I'd try four since 4 × 4 is 16.

Teacher: Good. Let's try it out. Four times 365 is 1460—that's less than 1716. (TEACHER WRITES 1716 IN ALGORITHM.) Now let's subtract to see how many tens are left. (TEACHER SUBTRACTS AND WRITES 256.) So our trial quotient was a good estimate since 256 is less than 365. We can't work with the tens anymore so we can change the 256 tens to ones and put the "7" ones with it to make 2567. (THE TEACHER "BRINGS DOWN" THE 2.) We will need to find another trial quotient. Phil, what would you suggest?

Phil: Well, we have 2567 left. Ones times hundreds will give us hundreds and we have 25 hundreds. I guess we ought to try six because six times the four hundreds would give us 24 hundreds.

Teacher: Okay, Phil, I'll write our trial quotient in the ones and multiply. Six times 365 is 2190. Let's subtract to see how good our guess was. (TEACHER WRITES 2190 IN THE ALGORITHM. WHEN THE SUBTRACTION IS COMPLETED THE NUMBER "377" APPEARS IN THE ALGORITHM.)

Phil: We have too much left, teacher. I guess seven would have been a better guess.

Teacher: Very good. Phil rounded up and sometimes when we round up we get a trial quotient that is

too small. But, as Phil pointed out, we **know** now that the quotient will need to be one number higher so we can erase this trial quotient and use the seven as he suggested. (THE TEACHER ERASES THE TRIAL QUOTIENT AND REWORKS THE PROBLEM TO END WITH THE ANSWER 47 R12.)

Checking Division Using Multiplication

Just like subtraction, division is checked by the inverse operation. When the quotient has no remainder, multiplying the quotient by the divisor will easily verify the accuracy of the calculation since multiplication will "undo" division. However, some modification must be made when there is a remainder. There are various ways of dealing with remainders. Students generally can make adjustments when working with remainders, but they experience difficulty interpreting how to express the "remainder." Each new way of processing the remainder (whole number, fraction form, terminating decimal, repeating decimal, etc.) requires the teacher to revise the form for checking answers.

The commonly used form for checking quotients with remainders is to translate the division sentence into an equation format before checking. For example, $17,167 \div 365 = 47$ R12 can be written as the equation $(47 \times 365) + 12 = 17,167$ for checking purposes. To check the correctness of the division the child would multiply 47 and 365, then add 12 to the product. The answer is correct if the result is the same as the dividend.

Even when calculators are used for computation, students must understand the way quotients and remainders translate into equations for checking. Division with paper and pencil may result in a remainder, but when the same problem is computed using a calculator, the resulting quotient is seen in decimal form rather than as a quotient and whole number remainder. Even if the remainder were expressed as a fraction in manual computation, there might not be a direct correspondence to the answer on the calculator since calculators tend to "round" a nonterminating decimal to fit the display window. While this may present some difficulty when checking division **before** decimals have been developed, once the student understands decimal operations, the calculator proves of great help in building the relationship between multiplication and division.

Some teachers shorten the conventional paper-and-pencil check for division by showing students how to use "cast-out nines." Indeed, once students become proficient in the use of this check, it can be done quickly and without using paper and pen-

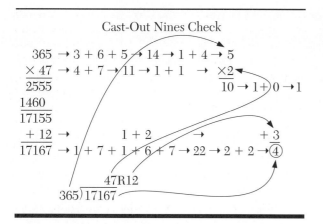

Cast-Out Nines Check

FIGURE 8.24

cil. When first exploring the cast-out nines division check, teachers generally point out the relationship to the standard "multiply and add the remainder" check. Students later can use the numbers as they appear in the division algorithm <u>without</u> rewriting them into a multiplication format (see Figure 8.24).

Using a Calculator with Division Activities

Since the conventional calculator does not lend itself easily to finding quotients when there is a <u>remainder</u>, the value of the calculator may be somewhat restricted until working with decimals. There are several **teacher-guided learning activities** that can be used to help pupils understand the division operation, the algorithm, estimating, and checking.

Exploring the division operation by comparing it to other operations is an insightful activity for intermediate-level pupils. When students use the calculator to <u>multiply</u> two numbers (for example, 38×67), they will find that <u>dividing the product</u> by one of the factors (either 38 or 67) results in the <u>other</u> factor. After a few problems most pupils recognize that division will **undo** multiplication and that multiplication will **undo** division. The teacher may wish to add to this understanding by pointing out that multiplication and division are inverse operations. (Teachers may also wish to review the relationship between addition and subtraction to reinforce that these two operations have a similar relationship.)

Calculators that employ a repeat-operation function can be used to illustrate that division can be viewed as repeated subtraction. One way of checking to see if a calculator has this ability would be to enter a number and an operation $(4, +)$ and then press the equal $(=)$ key two or three times. If the display keeps adding four to the previous number, then the calculator will easily show the repeated subtraction concept of division. (Some calculators handle this "constant" in a different manner. The instruction manual for the calculator should describe how this can be done.) To use the repeat function to illustrate the relationship between subtraction and division, the pupils are directed to enter a number such as 48, press the minus key $(-)$, then the "6" key. Each time the equal key $(=)$ is activated, six is subtracted from the number in the display. If pupils count the number of sixes subtracted—until "0" appears on the screen—they can tell how many sixes can be taken from 48. (If students start with a number that is not evenly divisible, the teacher may suggest that the display window must be constantly <u>monitored</u> to make sure that there is still enough left so the "6" can be subtracted. If pupils inadvertently subtract too much, ending with a negative number, they may be directed to use the inverse operation (addition) and undo the last subtraction by <u>adding the 6 back</u>. The number then displayed will be the remainder.

With guidance, pupils can build skill in estimating quotients using calculators. Exercises should first direct students to estimate a quotient—but not work the problem with paper and pencil. Pupils then divide, using the calculator, to verify their estimate. When working with remainders, teachers may direct students to ignore the digits to the right of the decimal since they are verifying estimates and not quotients. Some teachers present the activity in a gamelike situation, awarding one point if the estimate is the right number of digits; two points if the estimate is within ten (2-digit quotient); or within a hundred (3-digit quotients).

Once a student learns how to check quotients manually using the inverse operation, then using a calculator strengthens his/her insight into the process. When students become proficient in working problems that result in a quotient <u>and a remainder</u>, then the procedure used to check division must be adjusted to "<u>first</u> find the product of the divisor and quotient and <u>then</u> add the remainder." For example, in $16{,}842 \div 37 = 455$ R7 the pupil would check to see if multiplying 455×37 and then adding 7 would result in the 16,842 (the dividend).

Calculators can be used to find a remainder, but simply pressing the divide key generally will not display the remainder. The calculator will continue dividing the number as a decimal and eventually round if there is not enough room in the display window. (Most calculators will only display a maximum of eight digits.) While it is possible to multiply the divisor by the "digits to the right of the decimal" to find the remainder, students who are beginning division with remainders typically do not have the background necessary to interpret the result since often the number must be rounded to obtain a whole number.

Students can find the whole-number remainder on the calculator by using a series of steps. To display a whole-number remainder, the student would first divide to find the quotient—discarding the digits to the right of the decimal point. The whole number quotient is then multiplied by the divisor and the product is <u>subtracted</u> from the divisor. When the calculator **memory keys** are used a problem can be done with a limited number of steps. For example, to divide 16,842 by 37 one would enter 16,842 into the memory; find the quotient; reduce the quotient to a whole number; multiply the quotient by the divisor; then subtract the product from the divisor (which is stored in the memory). The sequence written below indicates each key (or number) by enclosing it within parentheses. By following the sequence from left to right, the remainder will be displayed in the window. Of course, some calculators may operate in a different manner, so the teacher may need to adapt the sequence for his/her particular brand.

(16,841) (M+) (÷) (37) (=)—(Keep the whole number quotient—or clear and reenter the whole number quotient) (×) (37) (=) (M−) (RM)

Since the sequence above involves subtraction rather than the traditional addition used in checking division, students should be queried as to <u>why</u> the subtraction is appropriate.

Calculators also may be used to help a pupil find the error he/she has made in written computation. Once the student completes a set of exercises, calculators may be employed to verify the quotient. When an incorrect quotient is found, the calculator would be used to check each step taken manually. When checking the steps in the previous problem the student must think about the value of each digit in the quotient. To find the first partial dividend, the pupil enters 16,842 into the memory and then multiplies 37 by **400** since the 4 in 455 is in the hundreds place. When the product is found it is checked against the written work to see if the error occurred in multiplying. (Students must recognize that in the standard algorithm the two zeros are not written since the hundreds are shown by the po<u>si</u>tion.) If no error is found, the student would press the subtract from the memory (M−) key and then recall the memory (MR). The resulting partial div-

idend should correspond with the number written by the student, <u>except</u> the calculator also displays ALL of the "bring-down" numbers. Such an exploration helps students recognize that the written algorithm takes some "shortcuts" that are not appropriate when using the calculator. For instance, in the algorithm the 400 of the quotient is written as a "4" in the hundreds place. The calculator must be **told** that the 4 represents a hundred <u>by entering two zeros after the 4.</u>

8.8 EXPLORING THE PROPERTIES AND PATTERNS OF DIVISION

Children explore properties and patterns of division when the facts are first explored. They have used manipulative materials to discover that changing the order (commutative property) or the grouping (associative property) do not work in this operation. When the intermediate-level teacher helps pupils reexamine the operation of division, it is taught with a much more formal approach—even using the formal terminology. The purpose of this exploration is more than development of division skills— it builds a foundation that will be used when exploring fractions ($\frac{0}{n} = 0 \div n$, etc.) and when exploring algebraic ideas.

Exploring Patterns with the Calculator

Since pupils have already explored division and its properties with manipulative materials, they are much more ready to use a **calculator** to reexamine the operation. Even though pupils have little difficulty understanding <u>why</u> the identity property ($N \div 1 = N$) holds in division, calculators allow pupils to explore much larger numbers divided by 1—finding that the same results still hold. Dividing a number by itself ($N \div N = 1$) may also be explored using large numbers. On most calculators division by zero will cause an error message to be displayed on the screen—encouraging pupils to reexamine *why* zero is not used as a divisor. Other properties—such as the commutative and associative properties—may also be explored. Since the calculator can process large as well as small numbers, students can readily explore the effect of changing the order or the grouping, finding many examples that would show the quotients to differ. A teacher may propose a more challenging activity by asking students to find specific examples where changing the order or grouping does <u>NOT</u> affect the quotient.

The right distributive property of division, (M + R) ÷ N = (M ÷ N) + (R ÷ N), is used extensively when teaching the division algorithm at the intermediate level. Positional notation used within the division algorithm obscures the use of this property, so most students are not aware of its existence. To focus attention upon the property, the teacher may suggest that students explore the relationship between pairs of equations similar to those in the exercise which follows.

Find the answers to each pair of equations.

Is quotient (**a**) the same as quotient (**b**)?

1. (**a**) (20 + 8) ÷ 4 = _____
   (**b**) (20 ÷ 4) + (8 ÷ 4) = _____
2. (**a**) (35 + 15) ÷ 5 = _____
   (**b**) (35 ÷ 5) + (15 ÷ 5) = _____
3. (**a**) 24 ÷ (8 + 4) = _____
   (**b**) (24 ÷ 8) + (24 ÷ 4) = _____

When are quotients (**a**) and (**b**) the same? Is there a pattern? When doesn't the pattern work? Now try to *predict* whether quotients (**a**) and (**b**) will be the same on the following problems.

4. (**a**) 54 ÷ (6 + 3) = _____
   (**b**) (54 ÷ 6) + (54 ÷ 3) = _____
5. (**a**) 30 ÷ (1 + 2) = _____
   (**b**) (30 ÷ 1) + (30 ÷ 2) = _____
6. (**a**) (20 + 4) ÷ 4 = _____
   (**b**) (20 ÷ 4) + (4 ÷ 4) = _____

Most pupils in the intermediate grades can explore the properties of division at the abstract level, but some may need to see it more concretely. To show that the commutative property does not hold for division a teacher may have pupils use the "acting it out strategy" (problem solving) to see if distributing 12 apples to six people (12 ÷ 6) is the same as sharing six apples between 12 people (6 ÷ 12). Identity (N ÷ 1) and dividing a number by itself (N ÷ N) may be similarly illustrated.

Exploring Patterns for Divisibility Rules

As students work with divisors they begin to recognize patterns. Recognition of patterns initially occurs as simple observations. Later, pupils develop formal "rules for divisibility." Knowledge of such rules have multiple uses in the elementary school mathematics curriculum.When students represent fractions in lowest terms, understanding rules of divisibility will help minimize the use of trial and error as an approach. A knowledge of divisibility also aids the pupil when factoring numbers, con-

structing factor trees, and finding the least common multiple of two numbers. A side benefit of the explorations is that the very activity of verifying whether a number is divisible by another number provides good division and/or factorization practice.

One of the first patterns recognized is that even numbers are evenly divisible by two and that numerals with a zero or a five in the ones place represent numbers that are evenly divisible by five. Other rules of divisibility may not be quite so obvious. Calculator exploration help pupils recognize that hundreds and thousands are ALWAYS evenly divisible by four. Pupils may also recognize that hundreds and thousands end in zero. However, it may take some teacher guidance to help pupils understand WHY these multiples are always divisible by four. The teacher may structure an activity that requires pupils to use analysis to help them discover some rules. One way of helping children analyze numbers using factors is demonstrated below. From such an exercise, pupils <u>may</u> discover that hundreds are evenly divisible by $\overline{2, 4}$, 5, 10 (which is 2 × 5), 25 (which is 5 × 5), 20 (which is 2 × 2 × 5) and 50 (which is 2 × 5 × 5)!

$$300 = 3 \times 10 \times 10 = 3 \times (5 \times \mathbf{2}) \times (\mathbf{2} \times 5)$$
$$= 3 \times 5 (\mathbf{2} \times \mathbf{2}) \times 5 = 3 \times 5 \times \mathbf{4} \times 5$$
$$7000 = 7 \times 10 \times 10 \times 10 = 7 \times 10 \times (5 \times$$
$$\mathbf{2}) \times (\mathbf{2} \times 5) = 7 \times 10 \times 5 \times (\mathbf{2} \times$$
$$\mathbf{2}) \times 5 = 7 \times 10 \times 5 \times \mathbf{4} \times 5$$

Explorations with multiples of ten may lead children to see that even multiples of tens (20, 40, 60, etc.) are divisible by four, but the odd multiples of ten—when divided by four—result in a remainder of two. This information, coupled with the fact that the units digits 0, 4, and 8 are evenly divisible by four, while the units digits 2 and 6 give a remainder of two, provide a basis for developing a rule for dividing by four. Figure 8.25 illustrates a less formal approach in which pupils may work with sets of objects to discover a rule for identifying numbers that are divisible by four. As different examples are examined, the teacher may lead students to focus on the tens and ones digits to see if they can use these digits to make up a rule for numbers that are divisible by four. Several observations that pupils may contribute are listed below:

— All numbers that are divisible by 4 are even numbers.

— If the tens digit is even (0, 2, 4, 6, 8)—then the units digit must be a 0, 4, or 8

— If the tens digit is odd (1, 3, 5, 7, 9)—then the units digit must be a 2 or 6.

Exploring Patterns

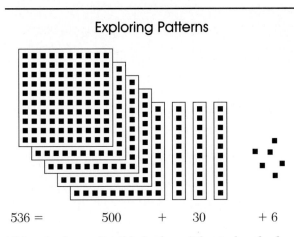

$$536 = \qquad 500 \quad + \quad 30 \quad + 6$$

All hundreds are divisible by four. (That is, hundreds can be grouped into sets of four without remainders.)

Thirty is an odd number of tens. (That means that 30 will leave a remainder of two when grouped into sets of four.)

Six will leave a remainder of two when grouped into sets of four.

The two remainder sets of two can be grouped into one set of four. Therefore, 536 is divisible by four.

FIGURE 8.25

Students who use the cast-out nines check already have a foundation for understanding the divisibility rule for nines. The multiples of nine have a distinctive pattern (as discovered by looking for multiples on the hundred chart) even though the units can display any digit. Explorations with the multiples of nine can lead pupils to see that adding the digits of the multiple (until a single digit is obtained) will always give a sum of "9." Some students will also recognize that if the sum of the digits is a number other than nine, then that digit is really the remainder.

Many advanced pupils wish to explore why adding the digits of a multiple of nine always results in the remainder. Using an expanded notation form and renaming each position to show divisibility by nine not only aids the more advanced pupils to understand the cast-out nines check and divisibility rules for nine, but also develops analytical skill and deepens their understanding of the right distributive property of division. For example, a pupil may investigate divisibility of the number 2,453 in the following manner: $2453 \div 9 = 2000 + 400 + 50 + 3 = [2 \times (999 + 1) + 4 \times (99 + 1) + 5 \times (9 + 1) + (3 \times 1)] \div 9$. Now the student can distribute the divisor to show: $[(2 \times 999) + (2 \times 1)] + [(4 \times 99) + (4 \times 1)] + [(5 \times 99) + (5 \times 1)] \div 9 = [(\mathbf{2 \times 999}) \div 9 + (2 \times 1) \div 9] + [(\mathbf{4 \times 99}) \div 9 + (4 \times 1) \div 9] + [(\mathbf{5 \times 9}) \div 9 + (5 \times 1) \div 9] + [(3 \times 1) \div 9]$. By examining this development the pupil finds that all **boldface** parts of the equation are evenly divisible by nine since they have a factor of nine. This leaves only $[(2 \times 1) + (4 \times 1) + (5 \times 1) + (3 \times 1)] \div 9$. The dividend in the problem $(2 + 4 + 5 + 3) \div 9$ is composed of the same digits as appeared in the original number 2,453! When the sum of digits in the original number (2,453) is divided by nine, then the remainder (6) will be the same as the remainder when the original number is divided by nine $(2453 \div 9)$.

8.9 COMPUTERS

Computer programs offer a variety of ways to develop division skills. Some commercial software encourages students to practice simple skills such as basic division facts. More complex programs tackle tasks such as developing skills in the use of the division algorithm. The teacher can construct highly specific programs to focus on some skills required for mastery of the division algorithm. For example, a program can be written using BASIC that requests a pupil to estimate a trial quotient. The student is then told when the estimate is too high or too low and is given an opportunity to estimate again. It is also possible to construct the program so the student is not given the "too high/too low" information, but rather is given a rule for deciding whether to estimate higher or lower when the first trial quotient fails. Any number of variations can be developed by a teacher skilled in writing in BASIC. (See computer software lists at the end of the chapter.)

8.10 EVALUATION AND INTERVENTION

Both models for division (partition and measurement) should be included when evaluating a pupil's understanding of division. Observation of students working with the models, examination of the student's seatwork, and interviews may all be necessary to give the teacher a complete picture of how well students understand division concepts and how they apply that understanding in problem-solving situations.

The division process requires the pupil to utilize many separate subskills as he/she works through the standard algorithm. Incomplete mastery of any of these subskills results in incorrect quotients. Since many subskills are employed, it is important for the teacher to identify the particular skill that is deficient, isolate that skill to provide remediation, and then help the pupil reapply that skill into the division algorithm. Children may be unable to master the algorithm successfully because they have not mastered one or more of the following skills:

1. Basic division facts
2. Rounding numbers
3. Estimating quotients using multiples of tens, hundreds, etc.
4. Adjusting for an incorrect trial quotient
5. Multiplication (including basic facts, regrouping, and decade facts)
6. Format for multiplying quotient and divisor. (It does not appear in the standard vertical format.)
7. Subtraction (basic facts, regrouping)
8. Placement of zeros in the trial quotient
9. Place value
10. Format of division algorithm

Frequently children exhibit more than one kind of error when working division problems. The teacher must determine which error to attack first. As a general rule the choice of which error to remediate follows the sequence of the development of the concepts in the curriculum. For example, errors with place value would be remediated before errors with multiplication because place value is taught before multiplication, because place-value skills have an applicability to areas other than division, and because multiplication proficiency is affected by the student's skill in place value.

Some examples of children's errors are illustrated in Figure 8.26. While the error—"does not line up columns"—may also occur in addition, subtraction, and multiplication, its effect is particularly harmful within the division algorithm. Students learn to write their trial quotient directly over a digit in the dividend—or learn to "bring down" the next digit in the algorithm. Since the partial dividends generally do not terminate in the units column, students often lose track of positional value. Sometimes a teacher can remind a pupil to "carefully line up the figures" so frequently that it borders on "nagging"—and errors still occur. At that point the teacher may provide grid paper so the student will have guide columns and lines to aid in the structure of the algorithm.

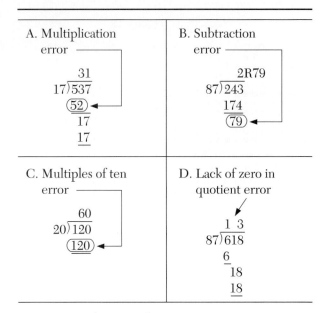

FIGURE 8.26

8.11 MEETING SPECIAL NEEDS

Explorations with alternate division algorithms offer excellent opportunities to extend conceptual understandings of division for most students. One alternate algorithm, widely used in the 1960s, is an adaptation of a technique used in an early American textbook by Isaac Greenwood. Because the algorithm places partial quotients along the right of the problem rather than on the top, it looks much like a carpenter's scaffold for a building—so pupils call this technique "scaffolding" division. Scaffolding division uses a <u>measurement</u> model in its development, rather than the partition explanation used in the conventional division algorithm. The divisor represents the number of objects in a set and groups of these sets are subtracted from the dividend. (Some literature will refer to this tech-

Enrichment Algorithm
Scaffolding Division Algorithm

We can get at least 100 sets of 72 from 34,343.	72)34,343 __ 00	A
Round 72 to 80. What times 8 is about 34? (4) Try 400.	72)34,343 28 800 | 4 00 5 543	B
We can't get any more hundreds, but there are 554 tens. We'll indicate "tens" with one zero.	72)34,343 28 800 | 4 00 5 543 __ 0	C
We'll multiply tens times tens to get hundreds. We have 55 hundreds. What times 8 is about 55? (6) Try 60.	72)34,343 28 800 | 4 00 5 543 4 320 | 6 0 1 223	D
Since we have 122 tens left we'll need to take ten more 72s, leaving 503. We can't get ten sets of 72 so we'll try a multiple of one. One times tens will give tens. We have 55 tens. We'll try 6 because 6 × 8 tens is 48 tens.	72)34,343 28 800 | 4 00 5 543 4 320 | 6 0 1 223 720 | 10 503 432 | 6 71 | 476	E

FIGURE 8.27

nique as a "subtractive" form rather than the "distributive" form used in the conventional algorithm.)

The scaffolding algorithm is particularly useful with weaker students who are poor "estimators." The technique allows the student to continue work as long as the trial quotient produces a number that is less than the dividend and/or partial dividend. Students are forced to erase work when estimates are too large. When working with multidigit divisors, students estimate with a divisor that is always rounded up. Rounding up is justified by suggesting that a number, such as 32, may be closer to 30 than 40—BUT using 30 as an estimate **may** produce a number that is greater than the dividend, requiring the work to be erased. If the number is rounded up, the number obtained from the trial quotient will never be too large. (The number obtained may be too small, but the algorithm will allow the pupil to continue without erasing previous work.) Pupils generally reach the rounding process by thinking, "Thirty-two is between 30 and 40. If I can take out groups the size of 40, then I know I'll be able to get groups the size of 32." For weaker students, this single "rounding-up rule" is much easier to remember and apply than the conventional rounding rule.

Figure 8.27 illustrates the scaffolding algorithm using a 2-digit divisor and a 5-digit dividend. At the intermediate level the enrichment activity would begin with 1-digit divisors since the estimation of trial quotients would be easier.

There are other activities for division, besides alternate division algorithms, that can be used to extend conceptual development for the student with strong foundations skills with division. For example, properties that are not a regular part of the elementary school mathematics curriculum may be explored as enrichment activities. The right distributive property of division over subtraction is just such a property. Unlike the right distributive property of division over addition, which plays an integral role in the standard division algorithm, enrichment explorations with the right distributive property of division over subtraction is used in non–paper-and-pencil mental computation and also serves as readiness for algebraic skills that use this property. Enrichment activities might have students discover this property through working paired equations (see Figure 8.28).

Providing for the Learning-Disabled Student

While the division algorithm may not be very challenging for a gifted student, it presents an almost insurmountable obstacle for some learning-disabled students. One adjustment for the learning-disabled is to permit the child to use the calculator whenever division is required. Such an adjustment is complicated by the fact the typical curriculum first develops division with remainders before working with quotients expressed in decimal notation. In addition, the quotient displayed in the calculator window will generally need to be rounded, a skill that is somewhat deficient in many learning-disabled students.

Before learning-disabled students can successfully employ calculators, it is essential that they have a good understanding of the concepts of division—both partition and measurement—and problem-solving applications. While the machine

---

Individual Learning Activity

Learning Center

Use your calculator to solve the following pairs of equations:

a. $(180 - 24) \div 6 =$ ____
   and $(180 \div 6) - (24 \div 6) =$ ____

b. $(300 - 60) \div 10 =$ ____
   and $(300 \div 10) - (60 \div 10) =$ ____

c. $(100 - 4) \div 4 =$ ____
   and $(100 \div 4) - (4 \div 4) =$ ____

What did you discover?

Could this property help you find the quotient of $196 \div 4$ without using the calculator?

Select 5 of the problems listed at this station and try out this new pattern. Try to find the quotient without using the calculator! (You may verify with the calculator.)

FIGURE 8.28

can efficiently calculate the quotient, the student who presses the keys must understand the problem sufficiently to be able to select the correct operation. The student must also be able to interpret the results of the calculation and apply them to the problem.

Some pupils are not as handicapped as others. Many students can successfully work through division when there is a 1-digit divisor. When 2- or 3-digit divisors are introduced many students—not just those with a learning handicap—experience difficulty. Since 2- and 3-digit divisors require the pupil to round and work with "trial" quotients, weaker students must erase much more frequently than those who are more efficient "estimators." The scaffolding (Greenwood) algorithm employs a single rule—rounding up—and allows a pupil to continue when a guess is too small, so teachers sometimes use this algorithm with handicapped pupils.

Some of the strengths of the scaffolding algorithm can be incorporated into a modified form of the standard algorithm. This **modified algorithm** is not only useful for learning-disabled pupils but can be used by any student who experiences frustration learning the conventional algorithm and its "round to the nearest" (round-up/round down) technique for estimating. (Figure 8.29 shows a development of $34{,}458 \div 54$. Note that the algorithm

starts in the conventional manner with the student locating the number of digits in the quotient. The next step in the algorithm differs from the standard algorithm. Instead of rounding down (where a trial might be larger than the dividend) the student **rounds up** as in the scaffolding algorithm. Now the trial figure **may** be too small, but it will never be too large. Using 60 as an estimation figure, a trial quotient of 5 is selected and the multiplication completed. After subtracting and recording 74, the student sees that the trial quotient should be larger. In **this** algorithm, the student crosses through the "5", writes "6," and then takes one more group of "54" away leaving 20 as in Figure 8.29A. This "crossing out and continuing" relieves the pupil of

---

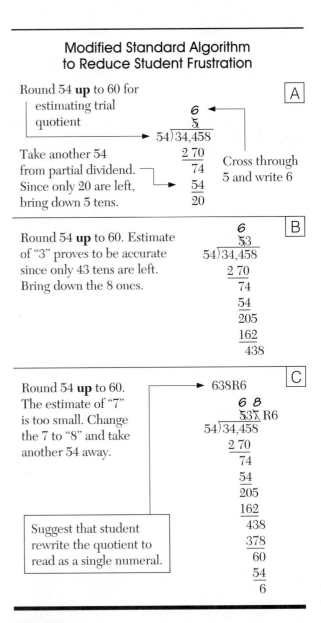

Modified Standard Algorithm to Reduce Student Frustration

Round 54 **up** to 60 for estimating trial quotient

Take another 54 from partial dividend. Since only 20 are left, bring down 5 tens.

Cross through 5 and write 6

Round 54 **up** to 60. Estimate of "3" proves to be accurate since only 43 tens are left. Bring down the 8 ones.

Round 54 **up** to 60. The estimate of "7" is too small. Change the 7 to "8" and take another 54 away.

Suggest that student rewrite the quotient to read as a single numeral.

FIGURE 8.29

erasing and then multiplying with a larger number. This makes the computation within the algorithm much more tolerable. Note that in Figure 8.29B rounding-up gave a much better trial quotient than the traditional "round to the nearest multiple of ten." When the student selects a trial quotient for the units, the rounding-up again gives a number that is too small. However, changing the "7" to "8" and subtracting another "54" quickly resolves the problem as illustrated in Figure 8.29C.

(One should recognize that the divisor used in Figure 8.29 is a number that would be traditionally rounded down. Therefore there will be more opportunities for an incorrect trial quotient to occur. Numbers that end in the digits 5 through 9 would usually be rounded up in either algorithm.)

Providing for the Gifted

Explorations of either the **modified algorithm** or the **scaffolding algorithm** are both interesting topics for the gifted student. Being quite capable with the standard algorithm the bright pupil is less likely to adopt a new algorithm since neither is as efficient as the standard algorithm. However, such students welcome the opportunity to explore different ways of performing operations and find new or historical algorithms fascinating. The "galley method" used at the time of Columbus is described in the NCTM publication *Number Stories of Long Ago* by David Eugene Smith. This book was first printed in 1919. Written for intermediate-level students with good reading skills, the book describes historical number systems, ancient algorithms, and includes some fascinating "number puzzles" like the one shown below. In the puzzles below, students are asked to substitute a digit for each letter. Once a letter is given a digit, it must keep that digit throughout both problems.

Explorations into quick and easy mental computation using division are also enjoyed by gifted students. To divide by 25, one can easily understand that multiplying by 100 and then dividing by four can be done mentally while dividing by 25 may require a written algorithm. Divisibility rules also offer many avenues for exploration. Once pupils learn the divisibility rules for 2, 4, 5, 9, and 10, many will want to find out whether similar rules exist for 3, 6, 7, 8, and 11.

Investigating how one would divide in other systems—other number bases, modulo systems, and even historical numeration systems (see Chapter 13) such as Roman or Egyptian provide a challenge for the talented in mathematics. For example, students might be asked to see if they can design a system for dividing using Roman numerals—or base four numerals.

8.12 SUMMARY

The concepts of division are only briefly introduced at the primary level. Children explore measurement and partition models for division; do hands-on explorations with the division facts; examine division with single-digit divisors; find quotients that also have a remainder; and informally examine properties and patterns of division. In some primary programs the child uses the standard division algorithm to find 1- and 2-digit quotients when there is a 1-digit divisor. In the primary grades the child is encouraged to explore division in problem-solving situations.

A major goal of the intermediate-level teacher is assisting students in becoming proficient when using the standard division algorithm. Development of the pupil's skill is complicated by the fact that mastery of the algorithm is dependent on the student being proficient in a wide variety of prerequisite skills including multiplication, subtraction, estimation, rounding, decade facts, etc.

At the intermediate level the student formally explores patterns and properties of division such as $N \div 1$; $N \div N$; $0 \div N$; $N \div R = M$ is equivalent to $N = M \times R$; $(N + M) \div R = (N \div R) + (M \div R)$; and $N \div M = (N \div R) + (M \div R) = (N \times R) \div (M \times R)$. While there is some application of these properties to the mastery of division facts, the exploration is more directed toward building readiness for later work in algebra. While exploring patterns, the pupil discovers some of the rules of divisibility that play such a major role in the development of fractional numbers. In addition to applying the division operation to problem-solving situations, intermediate students will also use division when solving multistep problems.

EXERCISES

1. Illustrate with drawings and/or materials the problem 12 ÷ 2:
   a. using the measurement model
   b. using the partition model
   c. relating division to repeated subtraction using a calculator
   d. developing its related facts using pennies as counters
2. Use a manipulative material (place-value chart, computing abacus, or base ten blocks) to show the development of the conventional algorithm for 763 ÷ 3.
3. Show how a teacher might develop the conventional algorithm for 1,478 ÷ 23 using a chart of multiples for 23.
4. When teaching pupils to round a divisor, the teacher should help pupils recognize the effect the rounding would have on the trial quotient.
   a. What is the effect of rounding up on the trial quotient?
   b. What is the effect of rounding down on the trial quotient?
5. Use a calculator to find the quotient and remainder for the example 1,478 ÷ 23. Check the answer by cast-out nines.
6. Work the problems below using the algorithms suggested.
   a. 175,780 ÷ 323 (enrichment algorithm—scaffolding division)
   b. 26,416 ÷ 43 (modified standard algorithm)
7. When possible, new skills should be introduced in a meaningful situation. Suggest a classroom situation that could be used to introduce:
   a. division in a measurement situation
   b. division in a partition situation
   c. a 1-digit divisor with a remainder
   d. a 2-digit divisor with a remainder
8. Examine the errors made in the computational exercises below. Determine the probable cause of the error and suggest an instructional procedure that might be used to help the student.
   Megan: 1,205 ÷ 17 = 65
   Bob: 22,385 ÷ 37 = 65
9. Select a currently published elementary school mathematics series. Look through the books to determine the grade level in which:
   a. measurement division is introduced
   b. partition division is introduced
   c. division with a remainder is introduced
   d. the division facts are mastered
   e. rounding of the divisor is introduced
   f. the division algorithm with a 2-digit quotient is introduced. What manipulative materials are suggested?
   g. estimation and checking procedures for division are explored
10. Look through a current mathematics textbook for fifth or sixth grade. Choose several story problems and decide how each should be illustrated using concrete materials. Which problems require a measurement illustration? Which problems require a partition illustration?
11. Choose one of the articles in the References section. After reading the article, write down three ideas that might be shared with a fellow teacher.

RELEVANT COMPUTER SOFTWARE

Quotient Quest. Gail Hanka et al. Apple II. MECC, 3490 Lexington Avenue N., St. Paul, Minn. 55126.

The Great Number Chase. Apple II family. Milliken Publishing Co., 1100 Research Boulevard, P.O. Box 21579, St. Louis, Mo. 63132.

REFERENCES

Bright, G. W. "Estimating Numbers and Measurements." *Arithmetic Teacher* 36 (September 1988): 48–49.

Duea, J., and Ockenga, E. "Using a Calculator." Edited by P. G. O'Daffer. *Arithmetic Teacher* 34 (February 1987): 44–45.

Henrickson, A. D. "Verbal Multiplication and Division Problems: Some Difficulties and Some Solutions." *Arithmetic Teacher* 33 (April 1986): 26–33.

Jensen, R. J. "Division in the Early Grades." *Arithmetic Teacher* 35 (October 1987): 50–51.

Overholdt, J. L.; J. B. Rincon; and C. A. Ryan. *Math Problem Solving for Grades 4 through 8.* Boston: Allyn and Bacon, 1984. Pp. 405–406.

Reys, R. E.; M. N. Suydam; and M. M. Lindquist. *Helping Children Learn Mathematics.* Englewood Cliffs, N.J.: Prentice Hall, 1984. Pp. 133–137.

Souviney, R. J. *Learning to Teach Mathematics.* Columbus, OH: Merrill Publishing Company, 1989. Pp. 379–385.

Van de Walle, J., and C. S. Thompson. "Partitioning Sets for Number Concepts, Place Value, and Long Division." *Arithmetic Teacher* 32 (January 1985): 6–11.

CHAPTER 9

TEACHING FRACTIONAL NUMBERS AND OPERATIONS

INTRODUCTION

Today, children and adults primarily use common fractions in measurement, but as our society slowly embraces the metric system, the use of fractions is expected to diminish. Fractional numbers, however, are <u>still</u> widely used in our society—for example, kitchen recipes frequently specify $\frac{1}{4}$ teaspoon, $\frac{1}{2}$ cup, etc. A change in the quantity for the recipe (cutting by half, or increasing it to feed a crowd) necessitates being able to perform operations with fractional numbers. Trade workers such as carpenters, electricians, and plumbers often are required to perform operations with fractional numbers. Most professions require individuals to be skilled in working with fractional numbers.

Fractional number concepts are repeatedly encountered in the routine of daily living. Children watch their parents pour milk from a half-gallon container; fill up a tank that is $\frac{1}{4}$ full with gas costing .98 and $\frac{9}{10}$ cents per gallon; stop at the deli for a quarter-pound of lunch meat and half a dozen donuts; come home from work at half past the hour; heat lunch in the microwave for $1\frac{1}{4}$ minutes; and brag about a newborn weighing $9\frac{1}{2}$ pounds. The day is filled with fractional number concepts.

As with most concepts developed at the elementary school level, the primary instructional focus of studying fractional numbers is to facilitate children's ability to apply these numbers in problem-solving situations.

9.1 TEACHING FRACTIONAL NUMBERS AND THEIR NAMES IN THE PRIMARY GRADES

Children enter the primary grades with misconceptions about fractional numbers. Some of these misconceptions stem from the way fractions are used in everyday language. For example, when a parent says, "Hand me the half gallon of milk," the container usually does not contain one-half gallon of milk. The parent is asking for the half-gallon <u>container</u> that has some milk in it. While such expressions often elicit the desired response, they blur the mathematical concept for the child. Likewise, when a child says he ate half an apple, it generally only means he did not eat <u>all</u> of the apple. For the child entering first grade, "half" commonly means "a part of something"—not the mathematical idea of one of two <u>equal-sized parts</u> of a whole.

212

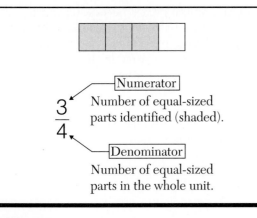

FIGURE 9.1

The primary teacher helps children build an understanding of fractional numbers through **hands-on explorations.** The teacher also helps children understand how these fractional numbers are applied in daily **problem-solving activities.** Fraction names (half, third, etc.) and terminology (numerator, denominator, etc.) are developed concurrently with children's understanding of fractional number concepts (see Figure 9.1). Explorations with operations on fractional numbers, when they occur at the primary level, are limited to readiness activities for addition and subtraction of fractional numbers with like denominators.

Most primary programs formally introduce the fraction and its meaning in the first grade, restricting examples to **unit fractions** (a fraction with a numerator of one). In grade two this understanding expands to include numerators other than one, and children compare two fractions (using models) to determine which is greater. By the end of the third grade, pupils will have explored the relationship of fractional numbers to sets and will use manipulative materials to find equivalent fractions. The scope and sequence below shows a typical primary program.

Grade 1

Explore fractional parts of whole regions (unit fractions) $\frac{1}{2}$, $\frac{1}{3}$, $\frac{1}{4}$
Compare fractions ($\frac{1}{2}$, $\frac{1}{3}$, $\frac{1}{4}$)
Use fractions in classroom situations

Grade 2

Examine fractional parts of a whole region
Compare $\frac{1}{2}$, $\frac{1}{3}$, $\frac{1}{4}$, $\frac{2}{3}$, $\frac{3}{4}$
Find fractional parts of a set
Use fractions in solving problems

Grade 3

Determine fractional parts of a whole (a/b)
Examine fractional parts of a set
Compare to find equivalent fractions ($\frac{1}{2} = \frac{2}{4}$, etc.)
Use fractions in problem-solving situations

9.2 DEVELOPING MEANINGS FOR FRACTIONAL NUMBERS

Only two of the meanings associated with fractional numbers are formally explored in the primary grades. Children learn to associate fractional numbers with part of a whole and part of a set. Two more meanings (ratios and the specialized ratio called percent) are introduced at the intermediate level.

Fractional Parts of a Region

For a child to understand the fractional number concepts associated with **parts of a whole** the child must understand each of the following:

- Fractional numbers are associated with a whole unit separated into equal-sized parts. Figure 9.2 provides an illustration of whole

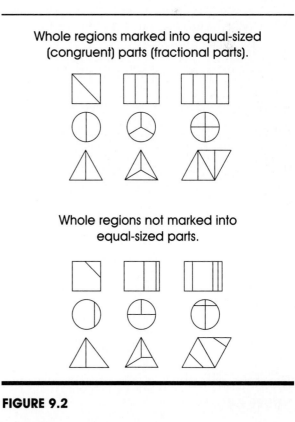

Whole regions marked into equal-sized (congruent) parts (fractional parts).

Whole regions not marked into equal-sized parts.

FIGURE 9.2

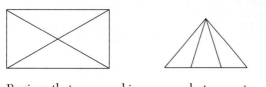

Regions that are equal in measure but are <u>not</u> congruent. The child would not be able to place one part on top of another to compare size. These drawings are generally inappropriate for introductory lessons.

FIGURE 9.3

regions marked to show congruent parts and whole regions cut into unequal-sized parts.

- Children verify that parts are equal-sized <u>by placing one on top of the other</u>. If one piece "hangs over" or does not fit "exactly," children feel that the shape is not cut into "equal-sized" pieces. Therefore, the primary teacher should <u>always</u> strive to illustrate regions by cutting them into **congruent** parts. Figure 9.3 shows some shapes in which the region has been cut so that areas are equal but shapes are not congruent. <u>Such illustrations would not be appropriate for young children.</u>
- When a whole has been divided into two equal-sized parts those parts are called halves; with three equal-sized parts the parts are called thirds; etc. (See Figure 9.4.)
- Once the names of the parts have been established, then a part is identified by linking

one and the **part's name.** For example, if a whole unit has been divided into thirds, then one of these parts is referred to as <u>one</u>-third. Similarly if two parts are being named, then these parts would be called <u>two</u>-thirds, etc. (See Figure 9.5.)

As the teacher develops each fractional number with models, pupils should explore the combinations for a particular type of fraction. For example, when using the model of fourths, pupils should examine one-fourth, two-fourths, three-fourths, **and** four-fourths during the same set of explorations. The teacher should point out that four-fourths is one whole cut into four equal-sized pieces.

The name of the fractional number (**fraction**) is developed concurrently with the use of the models. Figure 9.1 (shown earlier) illustrates the relationships between the numerator, the denominator, and the models being explored. With the exceptions of "halves," the denominator is read using the ordinal name (third, fourth, fifth, etc.). The numerator (which identifies how many are being considered) always uses the cardinal-number name.

Fractional Parts of a Set

Fractional numbers may also be modeled using **parts of a set.** The set model pictures objects—some of which are shaded comparing a selected subset to the entire set. The quantity of the entire set is used as the <u>denominator</u> and the quantity selected as a subset is associated with the <u>numerator</u>. For example, there are five mittens. Two mit-

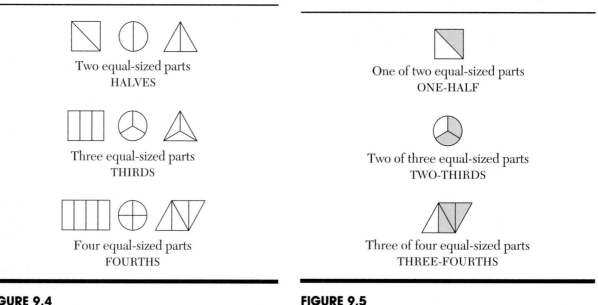

Two equal-sized parts
HALVES

Three equal-sized parts
THIRDS

Four equal-sized parts
FOURTHS

One of two equal-sized parts
ONE-HALF

Two of three equal-sized parts
TWO-THIRDS

Three of four equal-sized parts
THREE-FOURTHS

FIGURE 9.4   **FIGURE 9.5**

tens are red and three are green. The pupil would identify that $\frac{2}{5}$ of the mittens are red and $\frac{3}{5}$ of the set is green.

To select a fractional part of a set when given a set of objects, the pupil must sort the objects into groups with the same amount in each (equivalent subsets). If the objects are sorted into three equivalent groups, then each group would be $\frac{1}{3}$ of the set; two of the groups would be $\frac{2}{3}$; and all three subsets would be $\frac{3}{3}$. (See Figure 9.6.)

When first exploring this model, the teacher may help pupils recognize that $\frac{3}{4}$ of 8 and $\frac{6}{8}$ of 8 are the same amount. Since pupils are more familiar with region models for fractions, they may find it easier to recognize that $\frac{3}{4}$ and $\frac{6}{8}$ are equivalent if the objects are arranged into an array (see Figure 9.7) and equal-sized sections partitioned off.

9.3 EXPLORATIONS WITH FRACTIONAL NUMBERS

Children need many experiences using both parts-of-a-whole models and parts-of-a-set models before they are comfortable with the concept and notation system. While it is important to acquaint the child with a **variety** of geometric shapes for parts of a whole, it is best to restrict the child's initial representations to shapes that can be easily folded to

Fractional Part of a Set Model

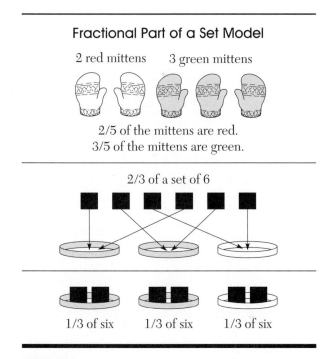

2 red mittens   3 green mittens

2/5 of the mittens are red.
3/5 of the mittens are green.

2/3 of a set of 6

1/3 of six   1/3 of six   1/3 of six

FIGURE 9.6

Find 3/4 of 8

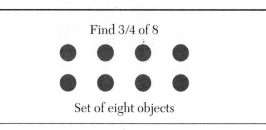

Set of eight objects

Set is partitioned into four equivalent subsets

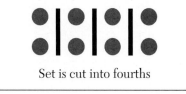

Set is cut into fourths

3 of the subsets are identified

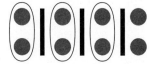

Three-fourths of the set have been marked with loops

The set could also have been partitioned in a different manner

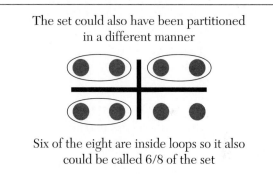

Six of the eight are inside loops so it also could be called 6/8 of the set

3/4 of 8 = 6/8 of 8

FIGURE 9.7

divide the whole into equal-sized (congruent) parts. For example, a rectangular sheet of paper can be easily folded into halves, fourths, and eighths. Using a secretarial fold, a sheet of paper also can be divided into thirds which, in turn, can be folded into sixths (see Figure 9.8). A circular shape can be folded into halves, fourths, and eighths, but it is difficult to fold a circular region into thirds without using a protractor.

It also is advisable to use models for parts of a whole that are **congruent** (same shape and size) because, following the development of fractional numbers, the teacher may wish to develop the concept of equivalent fractions using the same models.

Let's examine a fragment of a lesson that develops the concept of three-fourths and its name.

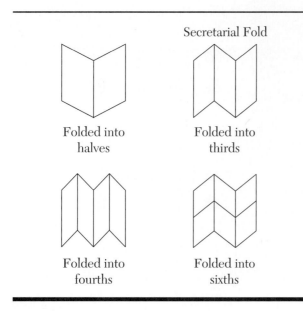

Secretarial Fold

Folded into
halves

Folded into
thirds

Folded into
fourths

Folded into
sixths

FIGURE 9.8

(With whole numbers the "name" for a number is called a **numeral**. When using fractional numbers, the "name" is called a **fraction**.)

Teacher-Guided Interactive Learning Activity

LESSON
FRAGMENT

M: The fractional number three-fourths and the fraction $\frac{3}{4}$

A: Second-grade class

T: Models, involvement

H: Children have explored parts of a whole for halves and thirds

PROBLEM-SOLVING SITUATION:

THE TEACHER HAS ARRANGED TO MAKE JACK-O-LANTERNS FOR ROOM DECORATIONS. THE DECORATIONS WILL BE MADE FROM CONSTRUCTION PAPER AND THE LESSON HAS BEEN DESIGNED SO 3 PIECES OF PAPER—$\frac{1}{4}$ OF A SHEET IN SIZE—WILL BE NEEDED BY EACH PUPIL.

Teacher: To prepare for our art project this afternoon, I am going to give each group three pieces of orange paper. We will be making jack-o-lanterns for our bulletin board. I want each of you to have the same amount of paper.

Marion: But there are four people in our groups, teacher—we'll need another sheet.

Teacher: You won't need a full sheet, Marion. In fact,

you can use smaller pieces because each is going to make more than one jack-o-lantern.

Marion: Can we cut the paper?

Teacher: Yes—but EACH person MUST have the same amount. You talk about it in your groups. You may wish to draw a picture or use small pieces of scrap paper to test your ideas. When you are SURE you have a way to share equally, call me to your group and I will see if you are ready for your orange sheets.

AFTER SEVERAL GROUPS HAVE WORKED WITH DRAWINGS AND FOUND A WAY, THE GROUPS ARE ALLOWED TO CUT THEIR SHEETS.

Teacher: Most of you found good ways of sharing your paper. We will use them later this afternoon, but NOW I would like for Misty's group to share how they did their paper. I'll give you a black sheet to use to follow Misty's directions.

Misty: Well, we took a sheet of paper and folded it so one part fit exactly on top of the other part. (CHILDREN FOLLOW MISTY'S EXAMPLE AND FOLD THE PAPER IN HALF.) Now let's fold it over again so that one part will again fit on top of the other—just as I am doing. (CHILDREN FOLLOW MISTY'S EXAMPLE AND FOLD THE FOLDED PAPER IN HALF.) Open your folded papers and hold them up to see if they look like mine. (THE CHILDREN DISPLAY THEIR PAPERS SO MISTY AND THE TEACHER CAN CHECK THEIR WORK.) Now we can cut along the fold lines—this will give us four equal-sized pieces. In our group we each took three of these and we all had the same amount.

Teacher-Guided Interactive Learning

Activity & Evaluation

FIGURE 9.9

Teacher: Good, but we don't have a full sheet of paper, do we?

Misty: No, we have three parts—but we cut the sheets into four equal parts.

Teacher: Very good—let's use our numerals to show this amount. Into how many equal-sized parts was the paper folded? Hold up your numeral! (SEE FIGURE 9.9A.) Place your numeral on your desk. Now pick up a bar strip that looks like this (THE TEACHER HOLDS UP A FRACTION BAR) and let's place it over the 4. Good, I see that everyone has placed their bar over the 4. (SEE FIGURE 9.9B.) Now let us show the three pieces we have. (SEE FIGURE 9.9C.)

Teacher: To show that we have three, place your numeral 3 **over** the bar. This shows that we have **three of the four equal-sized parts.** We read this fraction "three-fourths." Read it with me as I touch the numerals. (THE CHILDREN, IN CHORUS, READ THE THREE-FOURTHS WITH THE TEACHER.) (SEE FIGURE 9.9D.)

Comparison of Fractions

As children work with fractional models they will learn that $\frac{1}{2}$ of a sheet of paper is larger than $\frac{1}{3}$ or $\frac{1}{4}$ of that same sheet of paper. For some children this concept is difficult to grasp. They have learned that three is greater than two, and now—when written in a fractional numeral—the three indicates something that is smaller. The teacher must always stress that the denominator indicates the number of congruent pieces into which the **whole unit** was cut. The child needs many experiences comparing the cut pieces with the original whole unit.

Care also must be taken that comparison of models for fractions ($\frac{1}{2}$, $\frac{1}{3}$, $\frac{1}{4}$, etc.) always use the **same whole region.** If children compare $\frac{1}{3}$ of a pizza to $\frac{1}{2}$ of a soda cracker they may come to the conclusion that $\frac{1}{3}$ is greater than $\frac{1}{2}$. (See Figure 9.10.)

Children again may encounter difficulty comparing fractions when unit fractions (those with numerators of one) are <u>not</u> used. Children in the first grade learn that $\frac{1}{2}$ is greater than $\frac{1}{3}$, but in second grade they find that **2**/3 is more than **1**/2! Children will need many experiences with models so they can compare and verify that two of the "smaller" pieces ($\frac{2}{3}$) when combined are larger than one of the larger pieces ($\frac{1}{2}$).

9.4 TEACHING EQUIVALENCE OF FRACTIONS

Children explore equivalent fractions in the primary grades. Since rectangular regions are easily folded into congruent parts, these regions are commonly used to develop equivalence of fractional numbers—especially when pupils construct their own materials. <u>Precut</u> circular shapes are also effective when illustrating equivalent fractions.

When illustrating equivalence the teacher should stress that two fractions are equivalent when one fits **exactly** on top of the other. Figure 9.11 shows equivalence being established between the fractions $\frac{2}{3}$ and $\frac{4}{6}$ by placing the region used to represent $\frac{2}{3}$ on top of the region representing $\frac{4}{6}$.

9.5 TEACHING FRACTIONAL NUMBERS IN THE INTERMEDIATE GRADES

At the intermediate level, students continue to use concrete representations to explore equivalence and nonequivalence when expressing fractions in simplest terms and naming fractions in higher terms. Pupils will order fractional numbers and apply fractional number concepts to solve problems. The concept of a fractional number being represented as parts of a region and set are strengthened and extended to include representations of ratios, equivalent ratios, and rates.

Intermediate students learn to add, subtract, multiply, and divide fractional numbers. To ensure meaningful learning problem situations are still used to introduce the operations—especially addition and subtraction of fractional numbers. Since addition and subtraction operations with like denominators are easier for pupils, these are explored

---

When comparing two fractions make sure the same whole unit is used for both fractions.

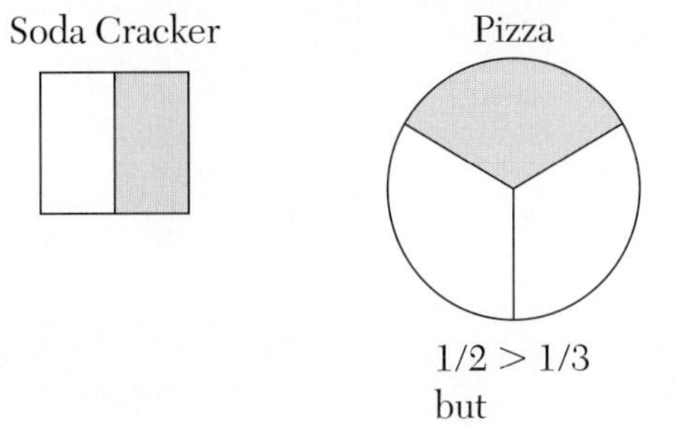

Soda Cracker   Pizza

1/2 > 1/3
but
1/3 of a pizza is much more than 1/2 of a soda cracker!

FIGURE 9.10

Independent Learning Activity

Use the fraction strips to find fractions that are the same size. Cut shaded parts and find which factions are congruent.

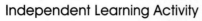

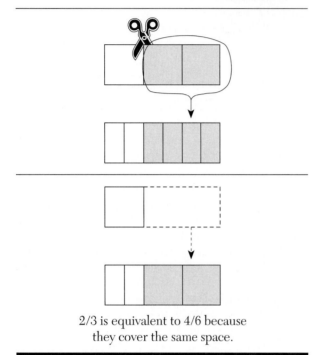

2/3 is equivalent to 4/6 because they cover the same space.

FIGURE 9.11

first. Fractions with unlike denominators require the pupil to apply skills related to multiples and factorization of numbers, so these topics are reviewed prior to working with these numbers. With the metric system (using decimal notation) becoming more widely used, situations in which fractions would normally be needed are diminishing. Since the need to multiply and divide fractions occurs less often in everyday problems (outside of more advanced mathematics), it may be much more difficult to find problem situations where these operations can be introduced.

The fractional number skills typically developed at the intermediate level are as follows:

Grade 4

Maintain understanding of fractional number concepts
- part-of-a-region concept
- part-of-set concept
- equivalence of fractions

Explore additional fractional number concepts
- compare fractions
- examine fractions as indicated division
- order fractions
- simplify fractions
- change to higher terms
- state as proper, improper, and mixed numerals
- find common denominators

Explore algorithms for addition and subtraction
- <u>like</u> denominators, with and without regrouping
- <u>unlike</u> denominators, with and without regrouping

Use fractions in problem-solving activities

Grade 5

Maintain previously explored fractional number concepts

Examine ratio concept
- equivalent ratios
- proportions
- scale drawings

Explore percent concepts

Maintain and extend skills in addition/subtraction of fractions
- with and without regrouping

Explore multiplication of fractional numbers

Apply fractional number operations to problem-solving situations

Manipulative materials help develop fractional number sense.

Grade 6

Maintain understanding of fractional number concepts

Maintain skill in adding and subtracting fractional numbers

Extend skill in multiplying fractional numbers

Explore division of fractional numbers

Extend understanding of ratio concepts

Use ratio and fractional number skills in problem-solving situations

Grades 7 and 8

Maintain understanding of previously introduced fractional number concepts

Maintain skill in fractional operations (addition, subtraction, multiplication, and division)

Extend understanding of ratio and proportion

Use skills to solve problems

9.6 MAINTENANCE AND EXTENSION OF FRACTIONAL NUMBER CONCEPTS

The concepts of fractional numbers have a wider application in everyday use than do the operations with fractional numbers. Fractional parts of whole regions, as well as fractional parts of sets, ratios, rates, and percentages, permeate our daily activities. We use fractions in activities ranging from cooking in the kitchen and making purchases in stores to using fractional number measurements for a do-it-yourself construction project. When maintaining and extending student understanding of fractional number concepts, teachers must seek out problems that require the application of fractional numbers.

Reviewing Fractional Number Concepts

Even though students explored fractions in the primary grades, the intermediate teacher still needs to use manipulative materials when reviewing the part-of-a-whole region and part-of-a-set concepts for fractional numbers. Teachers may wish to relate familiar uses of fractional numbers when reviewing those topics, for example: a half dollar is $\frac{1}{2}$ the value of a dollar, the coin called a quarter is $\frac{1}{4}$ the value of a dollar, the minute hand has traveled $\frac{1}{2}$ way around the clock face when the time is half past, etc. Fractional measurements in science or art projects also are used to maintain and extend pupil skill in fractional number concepts.

Since students will be using region models and number-line models when exploring fractional number operations, the teacher should review their use before introducing addition and subtraction. These explorations allow pupils to compare fractions, recognize the relationship of the numerator and denominator to the model, and build readiness for addition and subtraction of fractional numbers. Pupils may cut a piece of paper and label each part with a "4" to indicate that it was cut into four **equal-sized** regions—relating the parts to the denominator of the fraction. Writing a "1" with a bar beneath it (to separate the "1" from the "4") helps the pupil see there is only "one" of those four pieces. When students **collect** three of the $\frac{1}{4}$s and put them together, they should write "$\frac{3}{4}$"—associating the action with $\frac{1}{4} + \frac{1}{4} + \frac{1}{4} = \frac{3}{4}$.

Most students recognize fractions as parts-of-a-whole region, but some still have difficulty associating fractions with parts of a set. The fact that red jelly beans in a pile of three reds and one green is $\frac{3}{4}$ of the pile is readily comprehensible. However, some individuals have difficulty reconciling the fact that "$\frac{3}{4}$ is less than one" since there are three jelly beans, which would be MORE than ONE jelly bean. In this case the teacher must direct focus to the SET as the whole unit and emphasize that the individual jelly beans are "parts of the whole," as in parts of a region.

Fractions as Indicated Division

At the intermediate level students extend their understanding to recognize that a fraction can be used to indicate division. For example, $12 \div 4$ could be written as $\frac{12}{4}$ and $3 \div 4$ could be written as $\frac{3}{4}$. To help students recognize that $\frac{12}{4}$ and $12 \div 4$ result in the same number, the teacher may direct part of the class to take 12 pieces of paper and partition them into four groups while the rest of the class cuts enough paper to show 12 pieces the size of $\frac{1}{4}$. When the results are compared, the two groups of students will see that each process resulted in "3." The example $3 \div 4$ and $\frac{3}{4}$ might be a little more perplexing, especially when pupils see that there are not enough units in three to put a whole unit in each of four groups. Once the group recognizes that each of the whole units could be cut into four equal-sized pieces and then distributed, the task is easily completed. Of course, the half of the class which cut paper into four parts, keeping three ($\frac{3}{4}$), would have an equal amount in their stack as the group which looked at four groups and found that each group had $\frac{3}{4}$ of a sheet of paper.

Once pupils discover that a fraction can be used to express a division problem, then the operation with whole numbers which resulted in quotients

Concept Introduced from Problem-Solving Situation

Fractions as implied division

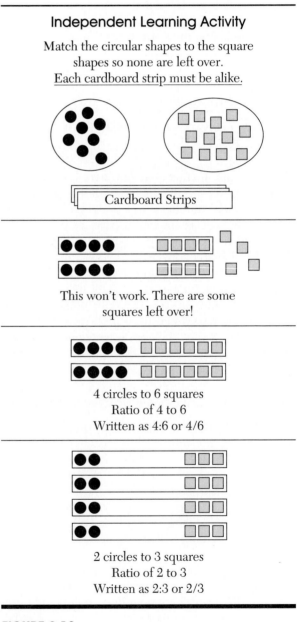

Divide 1 piece of paper between 2 people.
Each person will get 1/2 of that piece of paper.

FIGURE 9.12

and <u>remainders</u> can be extended to show fractional parts. For example, suppose a problem involves passing out seven sheets of wrapping material so that each person gets the same amount. Dividing 7 by 2 results in a quotient of 3 and a remainder of 1. The distributor can show that the "one" piece remaining can be cut into two halves, so that each person ends up getting $3\frac{1}{2}$ sheets. The quotient is therefore $3\frac{1}{2}$. (See Figure 9.12.)

Teaching Rate Pairs, Ratio, and Percent

While school programs formally introduce the concept of rate pairs in the intermediate level, pupils already have experienced many-to-many matchings involving measurement components early in the elementary school curriculum. In the primary grades they matched two pints to one quart, ten dimes to one dollar, three feet to 36 inches, and used terms such as "cents per pound" and "miles per hour."

The ratio concept of fractional numbers is one of the last fractional number concepts to be developed at the intermediate level. Ratio behaves differently from other fractional number concepts, so special care must be used in developing ratios, particularly the special type of ratio called <u>percent</u>. (Ratios can't be added, subtracted, multiplied, or divided.) To say that a ratio exists between two sets means that a many-to-many matching can be made between sets <u>that will leave no members unmatched in either set</u> after the matching activity has been completed. For example, suppose we have two sets, one of which has 40 members and the other of which has 60 members. If we matched pairs of two members in the first set with groups of three members in the second set, there would be

no members unmatched in either set when we were through, thus establishing a 2-to-3 ratio between the members of the first set and the members of the second set. Of course, this is not the only ratio that could be established between the two sets. Other ratios might be 4 to 6; 10 to 15; 20 to 30; and 40 to 60.

The first concept developed by a teacher is that <u>ratios represent relationships</u> between two sets or two collections of sets. If for every two apples in Set A there are three bananas in Set B, one can say that there is a ratio of 2 to 3 between the apples in Set A and bananas in Set B. Initial activities with ratio encourage students to find different ratios be-

Independent Learning Activity

Match the circular shapes to the square shapes so none are left over.
<u>Each cardboard strip must be alike.</u>

FIGURE 9.13

tween two sets. Figure 9.13 identifies two ratios that pupils identified between the circular shapes and the square shapes.

Intermediate-level students are mature enough to formally define equivalence of rate pairs (or ratios). Two rate pairs (or ratios) **a/b** and **c/d** are said to be equivalent "if and only if **a × d = b × c**." (In the case of the proportion "a : b :: c : d," one may say the product of the extremes [a × d] is equal to the product of the means [b × c].) Equivalence is important in applying ratios, rate pairs, or percents in problem situations. For example, suppose three cans of corn cost 89 cents. How much would twelve cans cost? The definition of rate pairs provides a clue as to how to approach the problem. "Three is to 89 as nine is to what?" becomes the question, or written in equation format it becomes $\frac{3}{89} = \frac{9}{N}$. By using the cross-product we get $3 \times N = 9 \times 89$ or $3 \times N = 801$. Therefore N equals 267 cents or $2.67. Students who have explored the "cross-product" method for finding equivalent fractions see the process of finding equivalent ratios simply as an application of a previously learned skill. (Use of cross-products to find equivalents is developed later with comparison of fractions.)

Many programs introduce percent as a special application of ratio. Percents are seen in comparison to 100 (*percent* means per hundred). Explorations with the percent concept will direct the pupil to determine the number of objects in the first set when the second set has 100. In Figure 9.14 the student would identify that there were five SHADED regions compared to the 100 of the whole region. When 100 units are not illustrated (as in three compared to 25), the student writes the ratio as a fraction and then converts the fraction to an equivalent form in which the <u>denominator</u> is a hundred. Once the fraction is written as a hundredth, it may be expressed as a percent.

(The concept of percent is developed more extensively in Chapter 10—Decimals. Inclusion of percent in this section is only intended to show its relationship to the concept of ratio.)

Teaching Comparison of Fractions

When students explored fractional numbers in the primary grades, they learned how to write the numeral (fraction) as related to its model and found that $\frac{1}{2}$ was larger than $\frac{1}{3}$ using manipulative materials. As the teacher works with these concepts at the intermediate level, emphasis will be placed upon comparison, ordering, and construction of sets of equivalent fractions.

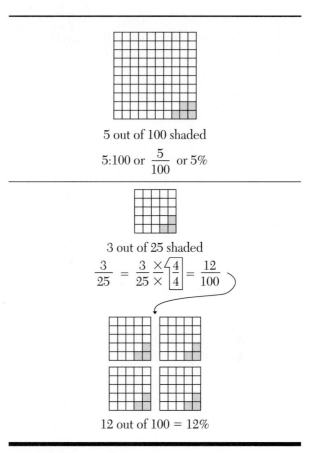

5 out of 100 shaded

5:100 or $\frac{5}{100}$ or 5%

3 out of 25 shaded

$$\frac{3}{25} = \frac{3 \times \boxed{4}}{25 \times \boxed{4}} = \frac{12}{100}$$

12 out of 100 = 12%

FIGURE 9.14

When reviewing concepts developed at the primary level, the intermediate-level teacher will still need to use concrete representations to help students become ready for a more analytical approach. To establish that $\frac{2}{3}$ is less than $\frac{3}{4}$ a student may take a cut-out model that is $\frac{2}{3}$ of a region and place it over another cut-out that is $\frac{3}{4}$ of a region. Another student might <u>reason</u> that $\frac{2}{3}$ is really a whole region with $\frac{1}{3}$ removed and that $\frac{3}{4}$ is a whole region with $\frac{1}{4}$ removed. Since $\frac{1}{4}$ is smaller than $\frac{1}{3}$, then the remaining part ($\frac{3}{4}$) must be larger than $\frac{2}{3}$. Still another pupil might decide that $\frac{3}{4}$ could be changed to $\frac{9}{12}$ and that $\frac{2}{3}$ could be changed to $\frac{8}{12}$, thus discovering that nine of the twelfths would be greater than eight of the twelfths.

Students who can change fractions that have unlike denominators to fractions with common denominators for the purpose of comparing two fractions have already developed a skill that will be utilized often when they begin learning how to add and subtract fractional numbers. Most pupils begin comparing fractions by using concrete representations (regions or number lines). After using the materials on several occasions <u>some</u> of the equivalent fractions will be recalled. Unfortunately, such remembering is not systematically organized and pupils cannot recall every equivalent fraction name that will be needed. To compare fractions by changing fractions to names with common denominators requires students to develop a more systematic means for generating equivalent fractions.

If a student has not yet learned to generate equivalent fractions (via the multiplicative identity) the teacher may use fraction bars or multiple number lines partitioned into fractional parts to generate sets of equivalent fractions or to compare fractions. Figure 9.15 illustrates an exercise that uses multiple-fractional number lines as a means for finding equivalent fractions. The second exercise uses these number lines to compare fractions. For example, a pupil could determine that $\frac{5}{12}$ is less than $\frac{3}{6}$ by comparing where the fractions appear on the number lines.

Exploring Mixed Numerals, Proper Fractions, and Improper Fractions

With the use of manipulative materials (fractional regions and number lines) students encounter situations in which the number is greater than one. When pupils count out five fractional pieces, each labeled as $\frac{1}{4}$ of the original whole unit, they find they have five-fourths. When writing this as a fraction ($\frac{5}{4}$), students see that the numerator is greater than the denominator. Since a whole unit is only four fourths, pupils also see that $\frac{5}{4}$ is $\frac{1}{4}$ greater than one whole unit—or $1\frac{1}{4}$. Situations in which the fraction represents a number greater than one will occur frequently as students work with fractional number operations and the teacher will need to devote some time to exploring these fractional numbers.

Fractions that have a numerator representing a number smaller than the denominator are called **proper fractions.** If the numerator of a fraction is equal to or greater than the denominator ($\frac{3}{3}$ or $\frac{4}{3}$, for example) the fraction is called an **improper fraction.** When a numeral contains both a whole number name and a fraction, it is called a **mixed numeral.** Some programs use the more traditional term, "mixed number," to describe amounts that contain both a whole number and a fraction. However, "mixed number" may convey to the student that the number—rather than the manner in which it is written—is mixed. Regardless of which term is used, the teacher must make sure students recognize that the method used to write the number's name (mixed numeral or improper fraction) does not change the number itself.

When pupils explore mixed numerals, proper fractions, and improper fractions, the teacher must keep in mind the twofold purpose of the activity. Both the concept of writing names for numbers in different forms and the vocabulary used to describe these forms must be stressed. Since people recognize a number more readily when it is expressed as a whole number or mixed numeral (rather than an improper fraction), students should realize why it is inappropriate to leave a number as an improper fraction.

When working with manipulative materials to represent fractional numbers greater than one, pupils should be encouraged to assemble groups that are equivalent to one from the total amount, and **exchange** those for whole units. When using region models, students can place the fractional pieces on top of the whole unit to "cover" the unit and make an equal exchange. Activities with manipulative materials allow the students to recognize the similarity of the process when changing from improper fractions to mixed numerals and from mixed numerals to improper fractions.

While the actual exchange of fractional regions for whole units is a valuable exploratory activity,

---

Independent Learning Activity

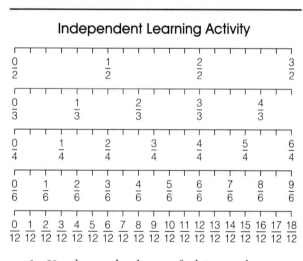

1. Use the number lines to find 4 equivalent names for each of the following fractions:

   a. $\frac{2}{4}$ c. 1

   b. 0   d. $1\frac{1}{2}$

2. Place the proper symbol (=, <, >) between each pair of fractions.

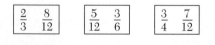

FIGURE 9.15

the number-line model for fractions may also be used, especially when reviewing the concept. The number line shows both the fractional names <u>and</u> the whole number names for marks on the line. Students **see** (rather than exchange) that an improper fraction, such as $\frac{9}{4}$, is that point $\frac{1}{4}$ farther along the line than the mark indicating the whole number "2." Using this visual recognition technique, students name the point ($\frac{9}{4}$) as 2 and $\frac{1}{4}$. Changing from a mixed numeral, such as $2\frac{1}{4}$, students would find that point which is $\frac{1}{4}$ unit beyond the "2" and see that it also is named $\frac{9}{4}$. (See Figure 9.16.)

Throughout these early activities, the teacher must make certain students understand how the process of changing from one name to another is related to the model **before** introducing mathematical properties to change from one name to another. When a pupil reaches a point when changing from improper fractions to mixed numerals must be done quickly and efficiently, the teacher will introduce the process of "dividing the denominator into the numerator." Students should see this "division" as a process of taking groups from the numerator to make whole units. For example, in the

fraction $\frac{19}{8}$, the pupil would envision $19 \div 8$ as taking out groups the size of $\frac{8}{8}$, and would understand that dividing by the denominator (8) tells that there are two groups of $\frac{8}{8}$ and three of the eighths left, or $2\frac{3}{8}$.

Changing from a mixed numeral to an improper fraction is presented as exchanging the whole number for fractional parts. So, for the mixed numeral $3\frac{1}{6}$, students envision exchanging each of the three whole units for $\frac{6}{6}$ and then putting the $\frac{18}{6}$ with the $\frac{1}{6}$ to make $\frac{19}{6}$. As a shortcut, pupils can multiply the whole number by the denominator and add that to the numerator. After students start using the shortcut, the teacher may wish to check their understanding by asking "<u>why</u>" questions: "<u>Why</u> are you multiplying the whole number and then <u>adding</u> to the numerator? Use this fractional-parts kit to <u>show</u> <u>me</u> what you are doing."

Comparing Fractions Using Cross-Multiplication

Once pupils can find equivalent fractions using models, teachers may use patterns to introduce the cross-multiplication technique for comparing two fractions. One interesting pattern students can discover with pairs of <u>equivalent</u> fractions is that the products are equal <u>when</u> multiplying the denominator of one fraction by the numerator of the other fraction (if a/b = c/d then, a × d = b × c). For example, if the two fractions $\frac{3}{4}$ and $\frac{6}{8}$ are equivalent, then 8×3 and 4×6 are equal.

After students work with this pattern, many will see that it can be used to <u>compare</u> fractions. They recognize that if the two <u>products</u> are <u>not</u> equal, then the fractions are <u>not</u> equivalent. With a little guidance, students learn to recognize <u>which</u> of the fractions represents the greater number by simply comparing the products. In the example in Figure 9.17 the two fractions $\frac{3}{8}$ and $\frac{4}{9}$ are compared by cross-multiplying. Emphasis should be placed upon the fact that multiplying the numerator **by** the denominator will give the new <u>numerator</u>. So, in the example, 9×3 will change the numerator for the fraction $\frac{3}{8}$ into 27, and 8×4 will change the <u>numerator</u> for $\frac{4}{9}$ into 32. When these numerators are compared, 27 is less than 32, so $\frac{3}{8}$ is less than $\frac{4}{9}$.

Many students will not be ready to go beyond recognizing the pattern involved in cross-multiplying and using it when comparing fractions. A few pupils, however, will be ready to discover why this pattern works. As illustrated in Figure 9.17, the <u>denominators</u> for both fractions $\frac{3}{8}$ and $\frac{4}{9}$ would be changed to 72nds if the "shortcut" of cross-multiplication had not been used. Multiplying $\frac{3}{8}$ by $\frac{9}{9}$ (a name for

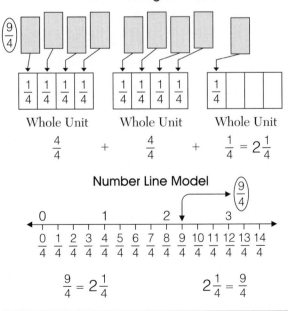

Improper Fractions	Proper Fractions	Mixed Numerals
$\frac{9}{5}$ $\frac{4}{4}$ $\frac{7}{2}$	$\frac{2}{5}$ $\frac{1}{4}$ $\frac{7}{9}$	$1\frac{3}{4}$ $5\frac{5}{9}$

Fractional Regions Model

$\frac{4}{4}$ + $\frac{4}{4}$ + $\frac{1}{4}$ = $2\frac{1}{4}$

Whole Unit   Whole Unit   Whole Unit

Number Line Model

$\frac{9}{4} = 2\frac{1}{4}$ $2\frac{1}{4} = \frac{9}{4}$

FIGURE 9.16

Equivalent Fractions—Cross-Products

$$\frac{3}{4} \times \frac{6}{8}$$

$$\begin{array}{l} 8 \times 3 = 24 \\ 4 \times 6 = 24 \end{array}$$

$$\frac{5}{6} \times \frac{20}{24}$$

$$\begin{array}{l} 24 \times 5 = 120 \\ 6 \times 20 = 120 \end{array}$$

Comparing non-equivalent fractions

$$\overset{(27)}{\frac{3}{8}} \times \overset{(32)}{\frac{4}{9}}$$

$$\begin{array}{l} 9 \times 3 = 27 \\ 8 \times 4 = 32 \end{array}$$

Explanation: We are really multiplying 3/8 by 9/9 and 4/9 by 8/8. Both denominators will be 9×8 or 72. If both denominators are the same, we can compare numerators.

$$\frac{\boxed{1\frac{9}{9}} \times \frac{3}{8} = \frac{27}{\boxed{72}}} \qquad \boxed{1\frac{8}{8}} \times \frac{4}{9} = \frac{32}{\boxed{72}}$$

FIGURE 9.17

identity) would result in $\frac{27}{72}$, and multiplying $\frac{4}{9}$ by $\frac{8}{8}$ (identity) would produce $\frac{32}{72}$. Since we <u>know</u> the denominators will be the <u>same</u>, we usually just use shortcut and only multiply the numerators.

Generating Sets of Equivalent Fractions Using Identity

While concrete materials such as number lines, number bars, and shaded regions (circular shapes, square shapes, etc.) help build a foundation for finding equivalent fractions, students must be encouraged to abandon such materials and develop a more systematic approach. Some students discover new names for fractional numbers through the use of patterns. They recognize that $\frac{6}{8}$ can be generated by "doubling the numerator and denominator" in $\frac{3}{4}$. By "tripling" both parts of the fraction $\frac{3}{4}$, they can make $\frac{9}{12}$, which they know is another name for $\frac{3}{4}$. However, most students must be guided by the teacher to adopt a more mature approach.

Before the 1950s some books taught students to change fractions to "higher" terms by using a <u>rule</u> called "the golden rule of fractions." Pupils learned to "do unto the numerator as you would do unto the denominator." (They would multiply the numerator and denominator by the same number, thus generating a fraction which was equivalent to

the original number.) While such rules work—and pupils can apply them effectively—just applying rules does not help students learn basic principles of mathematics. Contemporary mathematics programs use the <u>identity property</u> and the <u>renaming of the number "1"</u>—upon which the "golden rule" was based—to generate new fractional names.

To help pupils understand how identity is used in renaming a fraction, teachers begin by using shaded rectangular regions. Folding a representation for the fraction $\frac{3}{4}$, for example, students can see that $\frac{3}{4}$ does not change <u>size</u> when the new name $\frac{6}{8}$ is used. Pupils can count to see that now they have <u>two times</u> as many shaded parts and <u>two times</u> as many total regions. Writing this in a multiplication sentence, the teacher can show that $\frac{2}{2} \times \frac{3}{4} = \frac{6}{8}$ uses $\frac{2}{2}$ which is a name for 1. Reminding pupils that multiplying <u>any</u> number by one does not

---

Independent Learning Activity
Equivalent Fractions Using Identity

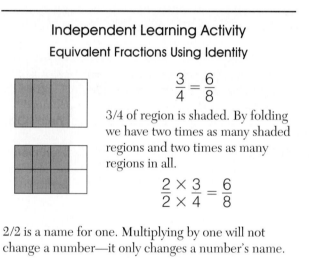

$$\frac{3}{4} = \frac{6}{8}$$

3/4 of region is shaded. By folding we have two times as many shaded regions and two times as many regions in all.

$$\frac{2 \times 3}{2 \times 4} = \frac{6}{8}$$

2/2 is a name for one. Multiplying by one will not change a number—it only changes a number's name.

$$\boxed{1} \quad \boxed{\frac{2}{2}} \quad \boxed{\frac{3}{3}} \quad \boxed{\frac{4}{4}} \quad \boxed{\frac{5}{5}} \quad \boxed{\frac{6}{6}} \quad \boxed{\frac{7}{7}} \quad \boxed{\frac{8}{8}}$$

We can collect many names for one and put them into a book. We can find new names for a fraction by multiplying by the different names.

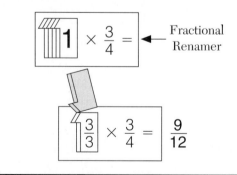

$$\boxed{1} \times \frac{3}{4} = \qquad \leftarrow \text{Fractional Renamer}$$

$$\boxed{\frac{3}{3}} \times \frac{3}{4} = \frac{9}{12}$$

FIGURE 9.18

change that number ($n \times 1 = n$), the teacher may suggest using other names for one such as $\frac{3}{3}$, $\frac{4}{4}$, $\frac{5}{5}$, etc. Each new name can be illustrated by showing folding a region model of $\frac{3}{4}$, just as $\frac{2}{2} \times \frac{3}{4} = \frac{6}{8}$ was illustrated. (See Figure 9.18.)

Once students see the role of different names for one using a region model, the teacher can show how a **Fractional Renamer** can be used to generate new names for a fraction. The Renamer shows the numeral ONE as a "book of names for one," which include $\frac{2}{2}$, $\frac{3}{3}$, $\frac{4}{4}$ through $\frac{n}{n}$. Multiplying the numerator and denominator of the fraction—just as one would "fold the region"—will generate a new name for the fraction. Students readily see that any name for one could be used—$\frac{100}{100} \times \frac{3}{4} = \frac{300}{400}$.

One valuable application of the Renamer occurs when students want to change a fraction so it will have a specific denominator. For example, if pupils want to change $\frac{3}{8}$ to 24ths, they use the Renamer with the book of names for ONE "closed." They write the denominator, 24, and then decide which name for one would be used to change the denominator (8) to 24. Once the pupils decide the number would be three, the book of names for one is opened to find a name that contains a three in the denominator. When the page containing $\frac{3}{3}$ is opened, students then see that the product for the denominator (3×8) is already written. The students then multiply the numerator by three to get $\frac{9}{24}$. (See Figure 9.19.)

Introducing Greatest Common Factors (GCF) and Least Common Multiples (LCM)

Before students can become proficient with operations using the set of fractional numbers, two skills—finding greatest common factors (GCF) and least common multiples (LCM) must be developed. A background for these skills is established when students first explore multiplication of whole numbers. The term **factor** is used by the teacher when describing the parts of a multiplication sentence. The concept of multiples begins early when first grade children learn to count by fives, but the word "**multiples**" generally is not used until the third or fourth grade, and so it may seem to be a new concept to pupils. Both greatest common factor and least common multiple play an important role in simplification of fractions and in addition and subtraction of fractions with unlike denominators.

Although the GCF and LCM are used when working with fractions, they are generally explored

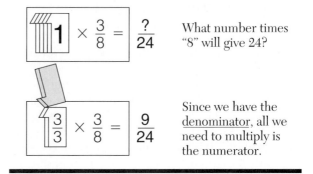

Manipulative for Independent and Small-Group Activity

Changing a fraction to a known denominator using Identity

What number times "8" will give 24?

Since we have the denominator, all we need to multiply is the numerator.

FIGURE 9.19

as a part of number theory **prior** to work with fractions. This process is logical, since both concepts are used when working with fractions. Teachers must remember, however, that the topics will need to be reviewed once students start working on addition, subtraction, multiplication, and division of fractions.

Developing GCF Using an Intersection-of-Sets Approach

There are several advantages in using an intersection-of-sets approach to introduce finding the greatest common factor. The most obvious advantage is that finding **all** the factors of a number is one way of practicing division skills, reviewing the basic division facts, and applying divisibility rules. Perhaps a more important advantage is that the term itself—"greatest common factor"—is easily explained. When students find the factors of two sets and then find the numbers that appear in both sets, they recognize that they have found a set of "common factors." When pupils identify the "largest" or "greatest" number, they understand that it is the **greatest** of the set of **common factors**.

As with earlier exercises when pupils worked with factors (see Chapter 7), a GCF introductory activity associates factors with the multiplication equation. For example, an exploratory activity may have pupils find all of the whole number factors that could be used in the sentence "$a \times b = 12$." After placing all of the factors of 12 (written on index cards) along the chalk tray, pupils would find all of the factors for "$a \times b = 18$." Once the two sets of factors were displayed, students would be directed to see if any of the factors of one set also could be found in the other set. Those "pairs of factors" (1, 2, 3, 6) would be placed into a new set which would be called a "set of COMMON factors." To find the greatest common factor the pupils would be directed to find the number that represented the largest or greatest number (6). (See Figure 9.20.)

Teachers may wish to use the intersection-of-sets approach as an exploration to find the greatest common factor for three or four numbers. While such an activity is an interesting enrichment exploration, the application of such a skill is limited, and so as a general rule, students only find the GCF of two numbers using this method. Finding GCF using prime factors is of value when working with larger numbers and may be used as enrichment in many classrooms. (The prime factor approach for identifying the greatest common factor—and simplifying a fraction—is developed in Section 9.13 of this chapter.)

Finding LCM Using Intersection of Sets of Multiples

If students learn to find greatest common factor using an intersection-of-sets approach, then they generally find work with **least common multiples (LCM)** very similar. To find the least common multiple, students identify the set of multiples for each number and then find those numbers that appear in all sets. From this set of COMMON multiples,

students select the smallest (mathematically, this is called the "least") number in this set.

There are a few considerations, when working with multiples, that differ from working with GCFs. While the set of whole number factors for a number is limited (a finite set), the set of multiples for a number continue forever (an infinite set). There are multiples of five in the hundreds (235), thousands (8,480), millions (3,032,325), and on without end. Therefore, when instructing students to write out the set of multiples for a number such as five, the teacher must restrict the number by giving an upper limit—such as "all the multiples of five through 70 (or through 100)." A second consideration that must be taken into account is the problem that occurs because the number zero is a multiple of every number ($N \times 0 = 0$, so 0 is a multiple of N). If we are going to look for the smallest or **least** of the common multiples, zero will ALWAYS be the smallest. Therefore, when defining least common multiple, the teacher will restrict the numbers to "all multiples larger than zero" or "only counting number multiples (which excludes zero)."

There is another practical matter that the teacher must consider: Many students have not completely mastered ALL of the multiplication facts. When a pupil is asked to find the multiples of six less than 100, he/she must recall not only the basic facts through 10×6, but also be able to determine that the next multiples AFTER 60 would be 66, 72, 78, 84, 90, and 96. Many youngsters find that their inability to recall combinations severely impedes progress in finding common multiples.

It is possible to develop the **concept** of finding the least common multiple even though a student is handicapped by limited recall of the basic multiplication combinations. Figure 9.21 shows how a teacher might provide strips of multiples so a pupil would not be required to recall those facts. Such strips might be reproduced on heavy paper for the student to cut apart, or the student may copy the multiples onto craft sticks for a more durable manipulative device. To find the LEAST common multiple of two numbers, such as six and eight, the pupil would select the strips for six and eight. Then the strips would be placed side by side and moved until the first common multiple is matched. This would then be the least common multiple.

It is important for the teacher to emphasize that the **set of common multiples** is infinite and that the least common multiple is just the first or smallest of the set. When finding the set of common multiples for six and eight (as in Figure 9.21), the student will see that 24 is the first multiple, but 48

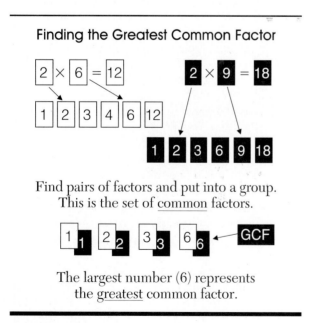

Finding the Greatest Common Factor

2 × 6 = 12   2 × 9 = 18

1 2 3 4 6 12

1 2 3 6 9 18

Find pairs of factors and put into a group.
This is the set of common factors.

1 2 3 6 ← GCF

The largest number (6) represents
the greatest common factor.

FIGURE 9.20

Independent Learning Activity

Using Intersection of Sets to Find the Least Common Multiple

Use the multiple strips to find the Least Common Denominator for pairs of multiples at this station. Select 10 pairs of sticks. Write them on your paper and then find the LCM for each pair.

Multiple strips for 6 and 8

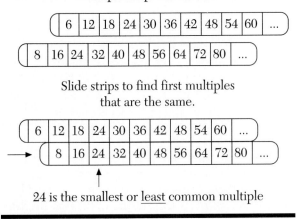

Slide strips to find first multiples that are the same.

24 is the smallest or least common multiple

FIGURE 9.21

is also found in both sets. The teacher may have students name two or three more multiples in the set so they realize that 24 is not the only common multiple. For instance, the set of common multiples for six and eight would include 24, 48, 72, 96, 120, etc. Students will **apply** this knowledge when they begin working with the addition and subtraction of fractions with unlike denominators (such as $\frac{1}{6}$ + $\frac{1}{8}$). While the **best** choice as a denominator would be the least common multiple for six and eight (24), other multiples—48, 72, 96, 120, etc.—could be used.

In common practice, once students understand the concept of finding common multiples, they no longer will be constructing the sets of both numbers. Pupils may take a shortcut, using the multiples of the greater number, comparing each multiple, to see if it is found in the other set. For instance, to find the least common multiple of nine and 12, the pupil would first determine if 12 was a multiple of nine. The pupil would then try 2×12 (or 24) to see if it were a multiple of nine and then 3×12 (or 36). When the student reaches the first multiple of the greater number which is also a multiple of the second set, the LCM has been found. (Finding the least common multiple by using prime factors is developed in Section 9.13 of this chapter.)

Simplifying Fractions

Students first learn to simplify fractions by using manipulative materials. As they gain more experience they find fractions can be simplified mathematically. Some textbooks call this simplifying process reducing fractions. However, since the word "reducing" suggests the number is getting smaller, contemporary texts avoid using the term. To determine if a fraction is in its simplest form (reduced) the numerator and denominator must be **relatively prime** (they have **only** the number one as a common factor).

Students will first simplify fractions by relating them to the process used when naming a fraction in higher terms. To change a fraction to higher terms pupils multiplied by the number one (identity). When the fraction has already been "changed to higher terms," pupils find a simpler or lower term by identifying the name for one that may have been used to get the higher terms and taking those factors out of the name. In the fraction $\frac{4}{6}$, pupils recognize that 2×2 is a name for "4" and that 2×3 is a name for "6." Since 2 is the common factor, it could be used as a name for one $(\frac{2}{2})$, leaving $1 \times \frac{2}{3}$ or $\frac{2}{3}$. As pupils learn to write fractions in lower terms they find that the simplest name is found when they use the GCF as a name for identity (Figure 9.22).

The process used to find the GCF is first introduced using intersection of sets of factors. When first exploring GCF, naming **both** sets of factors was important so the student would understand the process. When students start using GCF to simplify

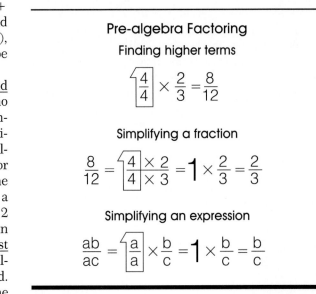

Pre-algebra Factoring

Finding higher terms

$$\frac{4}{4} \times \frac{2}{3} = \frac{8}{12}$$

Simplifying a fraction

$$\frac{8}{12} = \frac{4 \times 2}{4 \times 3} = 1 \times \frac{2}{3} = \frac{2}{3}$$

Simplifying an expression

$$\frac{ab}{ac} = \frac{a}{a} \times \frac{b}{c} = 1 \times \frac{b}{c} = \frac{b}{c}$$

FIGURE 9.22

fractions, a shortcut is introduced. Pupils learn that it is unnecessary to write out both sets if one wants to find the <u>greatest</u> common factor. Starting with <u>the largest factor of the numerator</u>, students **compare** each factor to see if it is <u>**also**</u> a factor of the denominator. The pupils work back through the factors of the numerator—the first factor found in this manner is the GCF. (See Figure 9.23.)

To make the process of simplifying fractions even <u>more efficient</u> the teacher must help students see that the renaming process (identifying the common factor, expressing each number as a factor expression, replacing the name for one (using the GCF) with one and then simplifying the fraction) can be accomplished by using the INVERSE OPERATION FOR MULTIPLICATION—division. Since renaming each part of the fraction requires finding the GCF and then the other <u>missing factor</u>, the teacher can relate this to the division operation. (See Figure 9.24.) To shorten the process, the student will divide the numerator and the denominator by the identity (renamed using the GCF). If the pupil reaches the factor 1, then the fraction is already expressed in its simplest term.

9.7 TEACHING ADDITION AND SUBTRACTION OF FRACTIONS WITH LIKE DENOMINATORS

Addition and subtraction of fractional numbers is generally introduced using fractions with **like denominators**. Although many teachers prefer to introduce addition of fractions a few days before introducing subtraction, it is possible to explore **both** operations concurrently since students are already familiar with addition and subtraction of whole numbers. In Figure 9.25 the fractions $\frac{1}{5}$ and $\frac{2}{5}$ both have the same denominators. Students relate this kind of problem to that of putting together one penny and two pennies (or one pint and two pints).

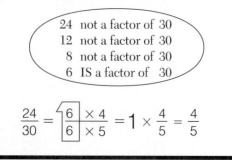

FIGURE 9.23

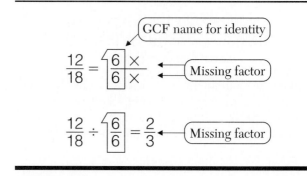

FIGURE 9.24

The use of models to demonstrate the problem not only helps students learn how to add fractions, but also reinforces the concept that addition is associated with <u>joining</u> things. Both region models and fractional number lines may be used in these early activities.

When illustrating addition using fractional parts of a region as a model, it is a good practice to place the "base units" under the fractional parts. These base units serve to remind the pupil that the fraction—such as $\frac{2}{5}$—is only <u>part</u> of a region. For example, Figure 9.25 illustrates $\frac{1}{5} + \frac{2}{5}$ using two base units to hold the fractional parts. Notice that $\frac{2}{5}$ is put together with the one-fifth just as two would be put together with one to illustrate $1 + 2$. Activities like this help pupils recognize that the numerators are "how many pieces we have" and that they should be added together. The denominators tell the <u>size</u> of the pieces, just as we might say "one

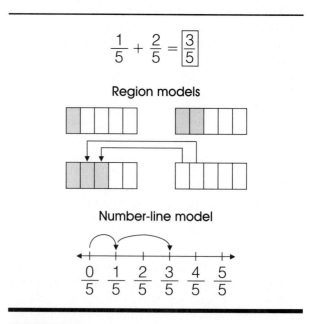

FIGURE 9.25

red thing plus two red things gives us three red things.''

The models used for subtraction of fractional numbers are similar to those used in addition of fractional numbers. When working with fractions, the teacher may find that ''take-away'' subtraction is easier for pupils to recognize. However, it is important that the other meanings related to subtraction (comparing, adding-on, and subset) are also developed. Figure 9.26 shows how these models are used.

The number line is particularly helpful when demonstrating subtraction of fractional numbers. In the subtraction problem $\frac{5}{4} - \frac{3}{4}$, the teacher may choose to illustrate the problem as ''take-away'' by

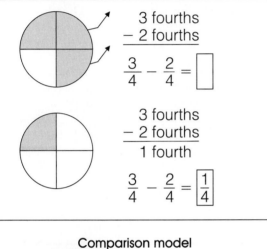

$$\begin{array}{c} 3 \text{ fourths} \\ -\ 2 \text{ fourths} \end{array}$$

$$\frac{3}{4} - \frac{2}{4} = \boxed{}$$

$$\begin{array}{c} 3 \text{ fourths} \\ -\ 2 \text{ fourths} \\ \hline 1 \text{ fourth} \end{array}$$

$$\frac{3}{4} - \frac{2}{4} = \boxed{\frac{1}{4}}$$

Comparison model

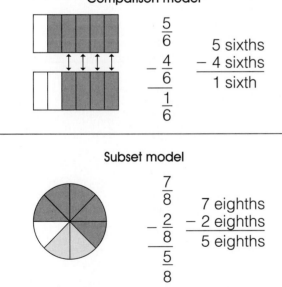

$$\begin{array}{r} \frac{5}{6} \\ -\ \frac{4}{6} \\ \hline \frac{1}{6} \end{array} \quad \begin{array}{c} 5 \text{ sixths} \\ -\ 4 \text{ sixths} \\ \hline 1 \text{ sixth} \end{array}$$

Subset model

$$\begin{array}{r} \frac{7}{8} \\ -\ \frac{2}{8} \\ \hline \frac{5}{8} \end{array} \quad \begin{array}{c} 7 \text{ eighths} \\ -\ 2 \text{ eighths} \\ \hline 5 \text{ eighths} \end{array}$$

7/8 of graph is colored. Two colors are used— red and green. If 2/8 is red, then what part of the graph is green?

FIGURE 9.26

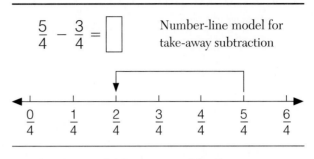

$$\frac{5}{4} - \frac{3}{4} = \boxed{} \qquad \begin{array}{c} \text{Number-line model for} \\ \text{take-away subtraction} \end{array}$$

Number-line model for missing addend.

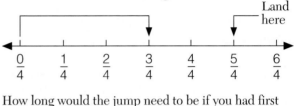

How long would the jump need to be if you had first jumped to 3/4 and now want to get to 5/4?

$$\frac{3}{4} + \boxed{} = \frac{5}{4}$$

FIGURE 9.27

starting at $\frac{5}{4}$ and ''jumping back'' $\frac{3}{4}$ (three steps of $\frac{1}{4}$). It also would be possible for the teacher to use the same number line to find how much more must be added to $\frac{3}{4}$ to reach $\frac{5}{4}$ by using the missing addend model (Figure 9.27).

Working with the Addition and Subtraction Algorithm

Shortly after students learn to add and subtract numbers written as proper fractions, those operations are reexplored using mixed numerals. While it is possible to use the number-line model with larger numbers, actions with region models are more closely parallel to the algorithm (see Figure 9.28). When illustrating adding mixed numerals, the teacher should **first** put the fractions together showing the corresponding step on the algorithm. Then students should add the whole numbers and record the sum.

Addition and Subtraction of Fractions with Like Terms (Regrouping)

Just as models help children understand regrouping in whole number operations, models provide students with a visual reference when working with mixed numerals. To build understanding, students begin working with a developmental algorithm. Since fractional number operations are not used as

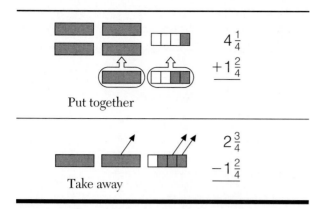

$4\frac{1}{4}$
$+1\frac{2}{4}$

Put together

$2\frac{3}{4}$
$-1\frac{2}{4}$

Take away

FIGURE 9.28

frequently as whole number operations, many students never feel the need to progress to a more efficient algorithm.

When adding fractions—or mixed numerals—regrouping generally is performed **after** the initial sum is found. That is to say, all addition will be completed and **then** the regrouping will take place—rather than regrouping within the algorithm. Figure 9.29 illustrates the development of the addition algorithm with regrouping after the adding is completed. This process is eventually shortened so that the student goes directly from three and five-fourths to four and one-fourth. (More able students <u>may</u> simplify the process and regroup within the <u>algorithm</u> as they become more proficient with the operation.)

Similarly, Figure 9.30 shows subtraction algorithm with regrouping. Unlike addition, the regrouping in subtraction must occur **before** the subtraction can take place. Therefore, the developmental algorithm **renames** the mixed numeral, writing an <u>improper fraction</u> to show the regrouping. In developing the algorithm the teacher will carefully <u>rewrite the renamed numeral rather than crossing through the figures</u>. This process helps pupils recognize that the whole number is being regrouped for fractional parts—not TEN (as in whole number operations). Again, the more able students <u>may</u> find shortcuts after understanding is developed—but it is a better practice to discourage any shortcuts until **after** subtraction of mixed numerals with <u>unlike</u> denominators is introduced.

9.8 ADDITION AND SUBTRACTION OF FRACTIONS WITH UNLIKE TERMS

When students encounter fractions with <u>unlike</u> denominators they must employ additional skills that

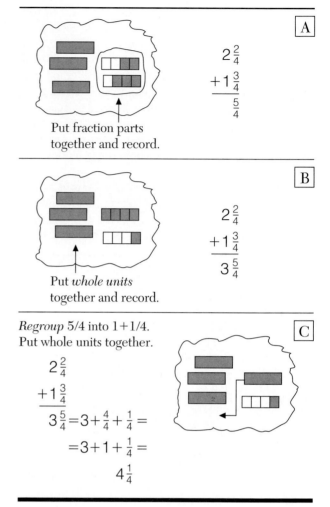

A

$2\frac{2}{4}$
$+1\frac{3}{4}$
$\overline{\frac{5}{4}}$

Put fraction parts together and record.

B

$2\frac{2}{4}$
$+1\frac{3}{4}$
$\overline{3\frac{5}{4}}$

Put *whole units* together and record.

C

Regroup 5/4 into 1+1/4. Put whole units together.

$2\frac{2}{4}$
$+1\frac{3}{4}$
$\overline{3\frac{5}{4}}=3+\frac{4}{4}+\frac{1}{4}=$
$=3+1+\frac{1}{4}=$
$4\frac{1}{4}$

FIGURE 9.29

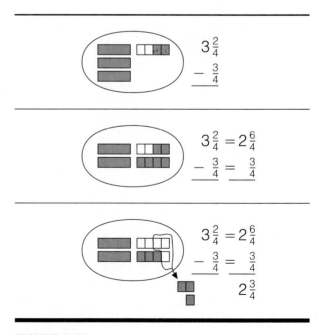

$3\frac{2}{4}$
$-\frac{3}{4}$

$3\frac{2}{4}=2\frac{6}{4}$
$-\frac{3}{4}=\frac{3}{4}$

$3\frac{2}{4}=2\frac{6}{4}$
$-\frac{3}{4}=\frac{3}{4}$
$\overline{2\frac{3}{4}}$

FIGURE 9.30

were not required when fractions with the same denominators were used. These first experiences require the student to return to manipulative materials to understand WHY it is appropriate to change to like denominators. These early activities, since they utilize manipulative materials, do not require the pupil to be proficient in finding common denominators, though the skill would make the exploration less time-consuming.

When possible, a teacher should endeavor to introduce skills in problem situations. In the lesson fragment that follows the teacher has chosen to develop the skill of adding fractions with unlike denominators without using a specific problem. Children have used their **fraction kits** to explore addition with like denominators and so the lesson is really an extension of a skill that pupils recognize and apply.

Teacher-Guided Interactive Learning Activity

LESSON FRAGMENT

M: Addition of fractions with unlike denominators

A: Fourth-grade class

T: Analysis

H: Addition of fractions with like denominators (equivalent fractions are helpful but not required)

CONCEPT DEVELOPED USING FRACTION NUMBER KITS

Teacher: Today we are going to learn to add fractions with unlike denominators. (THE TEACHER WRITES ON THE BOARD $\frac{1}{3} + \frac{1}{2}$.) Let's show these fractions with our fraction kits. (STUDENTS SHOW $\frac{1}{3}$ AND $\frac{1}{2}$—EACH ON A BACKGROUND UNIT.) In our kits, the $\frac{1}{2}$ is represented with a red region and our thirds are made of orange paper. To add, we want to put parts together. What do you THINK we will get if we put the two regions together? Gayla?

Gayla: Well, I can see that it will be <u>less than one</u>, because we have our fractional pieces. But I could have reasoned that—because $\frac{1}{3}$ is less than $\frac{1}{2}$ and it would take two halves to make a whole unit. So the answer MUST be less than one.

Teacher: Thank you for giving a reason for your estimate, Gayla. Well, looking at your kit, what do you have?

Gayla: When I put my fractions together I get two pieces.

Teacher: Good, Gayla. But what are you going to call

those two pieces. Do you have two halves?

Gayla: No—I have one red and one orange—so I can't call the sum two halves and I can't call it two-thirds. I don't know what to call the sum.

Teacher: When we added fractions **before**, the fractions were always the same denominators—they were the same color. Now we have fractions with <u>unlike</u> denominators. It would be easy to add the fractions if they had the <u>same</u> denominators. Does anyone have a suggestion how we could get the same denominators?

Tamara: We could take $\frac{1}{2}$ and add it to $\frac{1}{2}$.

Teacher: But Tamara, our problem was $\frac{1}{2} + \frac{1}{3}$. Is $\frac{1}{2}$ the same size as $\frac{1}{3}$?

Tamara: No. Maybe we could trade our $\frac{1}{2}$ in for thirds.

Teacher: Class, let's see if we can do that. Can we get an equal trade?

Bobby: No, $\frac{1}{2}$ is greater than $\frac{1}{3}$ and not big enough for $\frac{2}{3}$. Maybe we could trade for fourths. Yes, we can trade $\frac{1}{2}$ for $\frac{2}{4}$, but they still won't have the same denominators.

Rachel: We could trade $\frac{1}{2}$ for sixths and we can trade $\frac{1}{3}$ for sixths. Then they will have the same denominator. See, I have all blue fractional pieces.

Teacher: Good idea, Rachel. Let's all use our fraction kits and make that change. I will record what we have done on the chalkboard. (THE TEACHER RECORDS ON THE CHALKBOARD. SEE FIGURE 9.31.) We traded in $\frac{1}{2}$ for $\frac{3}{6}$ and $\frac{1}{3}$ for $\frac{2}{6}$. We can put these sixths together. How many sixths do we get? Gayla?

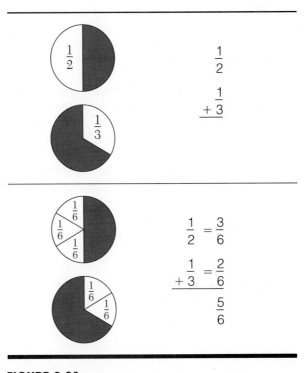

FIGURE 9.31

Gayla: I have five of the sixths.

Teacher: Good, I will record it on our algorithm. We can add the numerators two and three, getting five, and the denominator is sixths so our answer is $\frac{5}{6}$. Now we have a way of working with fractions that have <u>unlike</u> denominators. We can change them into like fractions by finding the equivalent fraction for each of the addends. Then the problem is just like the ones we have been working in the past.

Teacher: (THE TEACHER AND CLASS WORK TWO OR THREE MORE PROBLEMS TOGETHER.) Now that we have an idea how to use our fraction kits to help us, and we have a way of recording what we are doing, I am going to have you work in your groups with your kits. I would like half of the group to use the kits to work the problems I have written on the board. The rest of the group will be your "recorders"—writing down, in algorithm form, exactly what you do with your kits. After you have done a few of the problems, trade jobs so all will have a chance to use the kits.

In the lesson above, the use of fraction kits made it possible for students to find a sum even though they were not skillful in finding equivalent fractions. Before pupils can <u>efficiently</u> add or subtract unlike fractions, they <u>must</u> be able to find common denominators and equivalent fractions. It is beneficial for a teacher to review least common multiples before beginning extensive work with unlike denominators.

Subtraction of mixed numerals with unlike denominators again requires pupils to find common denominators. While <u>any</u> common denominator can be used when working with unlike fractions, using the <u>least common denominator</u> will reduce the number of sums and differences that require simplifying. (If the LCD is NOT used, the sum or difference will <u>never</u> be in its simplest terms.) Subtracting fractions is generally more difficult than adding fractions, since regrouping may be needed in order to complete the algorithm. When a subtraction problem contains mixed numerals with unlike denominators and **also** requires regrouping, the student has many more opportunities to make errors. <u>This makes these problems the most difficult type of subtraction problem that the intermediate student encounters.</u>

Let us examine a fragment of a subtraction lesson that involves several steps in finding the difference. (While the lesson uses a subtraction example, the skill of finding the least common denominator is identical for both addition and subtraction.)

Teacher-Guided Interactive Learning Activity

LESSON FRAGMENT

M: Subtraction of fractions requiring the finding of least common denominators

A: Fifth-grade

T: Analysis

H: Addition and subtraction of unlike fractions (without regrouping)

PROBLEM-SOLVING SITUATION:

THE CLASS HAS BEEN WORKING ON A PLAY AND NOW IS GETTING READY TO PREPARE SOME OF THE COSTUMES. THE TEACHER RECOGNIZES THAT THIS WOULD BE AN OPPORTUNITY TO PRESENT A MEANINGFUL PROBLEM TO INTRODUCE REGROUPING IN SUBTRACTION.

Teacher: We bought $3\frac{1}{4}$ yards of ribbon for the two costumes for our play. Dixie will need $1\frac{2}{3}$ yards to go around her skirt. How much will we have left for our other costume? How could we find out, Dixie?

Dixie: We could cut the $1\frac{2}{3}$ yards off and measure the amount left.

Teacher: True, but the ribbon isn't here right now.

Dixie: We could subtract $1\frac{2}{3}$ from $3\frac{1}{4}$ and that would give us the amount left.

Teacher: I'll write that on the board as a subtraction problem and we will work the problem together. BEFORE we work our problem—let's see if we can get a reasonable estimate. I see that several have their hands up—remember to tell me WHY you believe your guess is a good guess.

Dixie: It will be a <u>little more than</u> 1 and $\frac{1}{4}$, because 1 and $\frac{2}{3}$ is close to two. If we took two away from $3\frac{1}{4}$ there would be $1\frac{1}{4}$ left, so this must be a little more.

Teacher: Very good analysis, Dixie. I'll write that estimate here on the board. Now, if we want to subtract $\frac{2}{3}$ from $\frac{1}{4}$ what can we do, Quinn? (FIGURE 9.32A.)

Quinn: When we worked with adding fractions we found a common denominator. We can change fourths to eighths, but we can't change thirds to eighths. So we'll have to try something else. We can change fourths to twelfths and we can also change thirds to twelfths—**so** I guess twelfths would be the best denominator.

Teacher: All right. What <u>name for one</u> could we use to change the $\frac{2}{3}$? Jackie?

Jackie: Well, $4 \times 3 = 12$ so I suppose we could use $\frac{4}{4}$. If we multiply the denominator by four we will

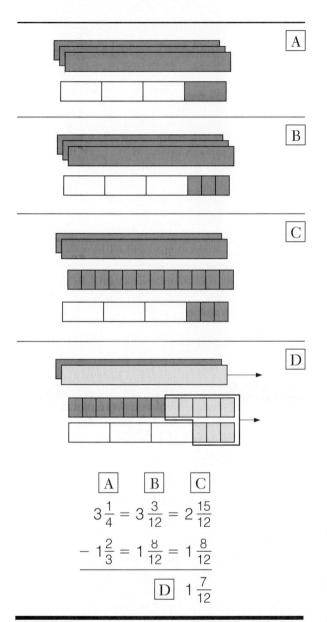

FIGURE 9.32

A B C

$$3\frac{1}{4} = 3\frac{3}{12} = 2\frac{15}{12}$$

$$-1\frac{2}{3} = 1\frac{8}{12} = 1\frac{8}{12}$$

D $1\frac{7}{12}$

get 4×3, or 12. When we multiply the numerator by four we will get 4×2, or 8. So we can change $\frac{2}{3}$ into $\frac{8}{12}$. (SEE FIGURE 9.32B.)

Teacher: I'm going to record that in the algorithm. We changed the number $1\frac{2}{3}$ to 1 and $\frac{8}{12}$. Now we can change the fraction $\frac{1}{4}$ to twelfths. If we name the number one as $\frac{3}{3}$ we can multiply the denominator by three to get 3×4, or 12. Then we will multiply the numerator—3×1—to give us three. Thus we changed the mixed number $3\frac{1}{4}$ to 3 and $\frac{3}{12}$.

Teacher: Let's work the fraction part first. If we want to take $\frac{8}{12}$ from $\frac{3}{12}$ do we have enough twelfths? James?

James: No. Teacher, it looks like we need to trade one of the three whole units in for twelfths.

Teacher: How many twelfths will you get for one whole unit? Crystal?

Crystal: One whole unit is the same as 12 twelfths.

Teacher: Good. Now if we put those 12 twelfths with the three twelfths we already had, we would get $\frac{15}{12}$. Let me record what we did. We traded one of the three—leaving two whole units. (THE TEACHER WRITES "= 2.") Now we can write the regrouped fraction—$\frac{15}{12}$. I'm going to copy the one and $\frac{8}{12}$ over to <u>remind us</u> that is the amount we need. Can we subtract the fractions now? Connie? (SEE FIGURE 9.32C.)

Connie: Yes, we'll take $\frac{8}{12}$ from $\frac{15}{12}$ and have $\frac{7}{12}$ left. Then we can take the one whole unit from the two whole units, leaving one. So our answer is $1\frac{7}{12}$. (THE TEACHER COMPLETES THE ALGORITHM ON THE CHALKBOARD.) (SEE FIGURE 9.32D.) That's really close to Dixie's guess—so our answer is reasonable.

Teacher: Let's work in our groups to practice this subtraction with our kits. Remember, when we work in our groups, our goal is to help EVERYONE on our team become proficient in subtracting. Each group use your kits to work the problems on the chalkboard and when I come around to your group I'll call upon <u>one</u> of your team to explain the process for me.

Exploring Properties and Patterns in Addition and Subtraction of Fractional Numbers

Soon after the student learns to add fractional numbers, opportunities should be provided for exploring properties and patterns associated with addition of fractional numbers. Through activities with manipulative materials and with the addition algorithm itself, students will discover that the commutative and associative properties hold for fractional numbers. They also find that the identity property of addition of fractional numbers uses a zero name. Paired problems similar to the exercises illustrated in Figure 9.33 may be used to <u>explore</u> the commutative and associative properties within the set of fractional numbers.

Children also should be guided to see that the commutative and associative properties do not hold for subtraction. Having pupils test to see if patterns such as $N - N$ and $N - 0$ hold for fractional numbers also provides an interesting exploration.

There are calculators that handle fractional operations (Texas Instruments' "Explorer," for instance). While these calculators are not expensive

Exploring Patterns

Changing the order of the addends will not affect the sum!

$$\frac{3}{7} + \frac{6}{7} = \frac{6}{7} + \frac{3}{7} = \boxed{}$$

Changing the grouping (associative law) can make a problem much easier to work!

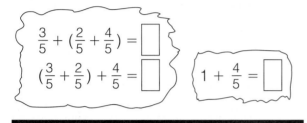

$$1 + \frac{4}{5} = \boxed{}$$

FIGURE 9.33

(about \$25), most pupils do not have access to such machines. The teacher may wish to borrow a calculator with this function so pupils can easily explore properties (commutative and associative) with larger fractions.

9.9 TEACHING MULTIPLICATION OF FRACTIONAL NUMBERS

Pupils have explored some aspects concerning multiplication of fractional numbers before the topic is formally introduced. When equivalent fractions were found using models, students developed a foundation for understanding the multiplicative identity. When pupils add two fractions with the same name ($\frac{2}{3} + \frac{2}{3}$) they build a readiness for $2 \times \frac{2}{3}$.

Typically, multiplication of fractional numbers is first explored using a whole number multiplier and a fractional number multiplicand, since the new skill can be easily associated with previously learned skills.

Illustrating a Whole Number Times a Fractional Number

When first exploring multiplication of fractional numbers by a whole number, pupils should use manipulative models. Region models may be used to show that $3 \times \frac{2}{5}$ means three <u>sets</u> the size of $\frac{2}{5}$ or three <u>jumps</u> the size of $\frac{2}{5}$ when using the number

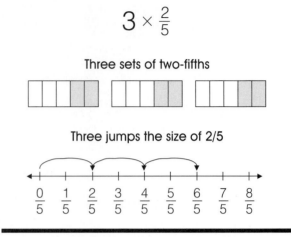

$$3 \times \frac{2}{5}$$

Three sets of two-fifths

Three jumps the size of 2/5

FIGURE 9.34

line. If the denominator is named by a written word (two-<u>fifths</u>), the teacher can show the relationship of fractional numbers to whole number multiplication. Notice how the whole number concept of three equal-sized sets is used to develop three times two-fifths in Figure 9.34.

Illustrating a Fraction Times a Whole Number

Multiplying a whole number by a fraction ($\frac{2}{3} \times 6$) often is introduced by using the commutative property of multiplication. Students reason that $6 \times \frac{2}{3}$ is $\frac{12}{3}$, or 4—so $\frac{2}{3} \times 6$ is four. However, <u>illustrating</u> multiplication this way is a little more difficult. If $6 \times \frac{2}{3}$ is interpreted as six sets of $\frac{2}{3}$, then $\frac{2}{3} \times 6$ would be $\frac{2}{3}$ <u>of a set the size of six</u>. When illustrating $6 \times \frac{2}{3}$ on the number line it is easy to show six jumps of $\frac{2}{3}$. However, $\frac{2}{3} \times 6$ would mean $\frac{2}{3}$ of a jump the size of six or that a jump the size of six would be divided into three parts and two of those parts kept. This would mean that the student would really need to know that the answer to $\frac{2}{3} \times 6$ was 4 <u>before</u> drawing the illustration! For this reason, the number line is not usually chosen as a model when illustrating a fraction times a whole number. (See Figure 9.35.)

Sets of objects (paper, pencils, etc.) can be used to illustrate a problem such as $\frac{3}{4} \times 9$ in such a manner that meaning <u>can</u> be established. Selecting four students to represent four groups, a pupil may distribute nine strips of paper (as if they were cookies) so that each person gets the same amount. After eight of the strips are gone, the last strip will be cut into equal-sized pieces so each person will get an "equal share." Once all of the strips are distributed, the teacher can point out that <u>each person</u>

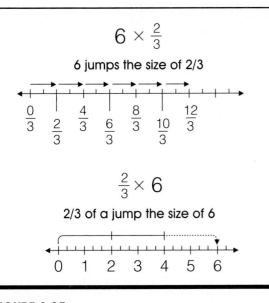

$$6 \times \frac{2}{3}$$

6 jumps the size of 2/3

$$\frac{2}{3} \times 6$$

2/3 of a jump the size of 6

FIGURE 9.35

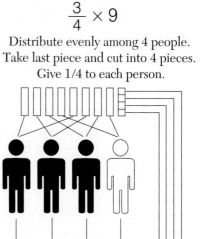

$$\frac{3}{4} \times 9$$

Distribute evenly among 4 people.
Take last piece and cut into 4 pieces.
Give 1/4 to each person.

Each person will get 2 1/4 pieces.
So 3/4 of the people will get
2 1/4 + 2 1/4 + 2 1/4 or 6 3/4.

FIGURE 9.36

has $\frac{1}{4}$ of the strips—or that each person has $2\frac{1}{4}$ strips of paper. To illustrate $\frac{3}{4}$ of 9, <u>three</u> of the students would combine their strips to end with $6\frac{3}{4}$. This process illustrates two aspects of the multiplication with fractional numbers—first, equal-sized groups are found (divide by the denominator). Then three of the equal-sized groups are put together. The teacher may need to remind pupils that multiplication is the <u>putting together of equal-sized groups</u> so they recognize that multiplication really does take place. (See Figure 9.36.)

To illustrate that $9 \times \frac{3}{4}$ and $\frac{3}{4} \times 9$ BOTH have the same product, the teacher may direct half of the class to use the unit regions of their fraction kits to model $\frac{3}{4}$ of a set of nine ($\frac{3}{4} \times 9$), while the rest of the class uses fraction kits to model nine sets of $\frac{3}{4}$ ($9 \times \frac{3}{4}$). Comparison of products—as illustrated by the fraction-kit pieces—will help pupils recognize that either order will end with the same number.

Using Array Models to Illustrate Multiplication of Fractional Numbers

While problems such as $3 \times \frac{2}{5}$ can easily pictured as three sets of two-fifths and $\frac{2}{5} \times 10$ can be seen as $\frac{2}{5}$ of a set of ten, visualizing $\frac{2}{3} \times \frac{2}{5}$ can be confusing for pupils. <u>The computational aspect of multiplying fractions is much easier than that of addition or subtraction. However, building an understanding of why one multiplies the denominators (when in addition they are not added) is much more difficult. It is possible to illustrate a</u> fraction times a fraction using the equivalent-sets

model, but students find it easier to understand the development when problems are illustrated using the array model. The array model has the added advantage of helping students see **why** each part of the algorithm is performed.

Before illustrating a fraction multiplied by a fraction, the teacher may wish to review the use of the array with whole numbers. An array model for N × M had N rows with M objects in each row. To change the manner used to illustrate the array may create confusion for some pupils, so when illustrating $\frac{2}{3} \times \frac{2}{5}$ the teacher should consistently picture the sentence showing that the first factor <u>still</u> indicates the rows and the second factor shows the columns. Teachers may develop the array by showing a unit region first divided into fifths (vertically). After identifying two of the fifths, the teacher would draw lines to divide the region into thirds (horizontally). (See Figure 9.37.) Once the "dimensions" of the array (two-thirds × two-fifths) are drawn, the region may be shaded so pupils can see what part of the whole region is named. Each of the rectangular regions created by the crossing of thirds and fifths are the same size, so the teacher may identify each part of the array as "$\frac{1}{15}$." The teacher will then point to the shaded part of the region—which represents $\frac{2}{3}$ of $\frac{2}{5}$—and count the number of the fifteenths. Since there are four of the shaded regions, the size of the array would be $\frac{4}{15}$. Some teachers develop the array for $\frac{2}{3} \times \frac{2}{5}$ by <u>coloring</u> $\frac{2}{5}$ (two of the

| Using an array to show 2/3 × 2/5 | Using colors to find 2/3 of 2/5 |

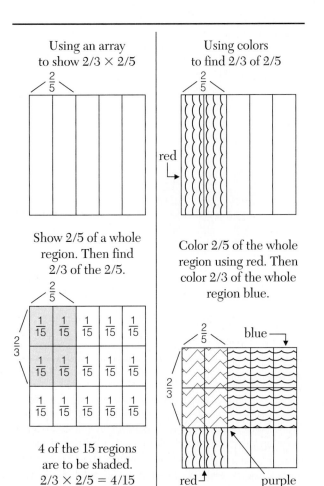

Show 2/5 of a whole region. Then find 2/3 of the 2/5.

4 of the 15 regions are to be shaded.
2/3 × 2/5 = 4/15

Color 2/5 of the whole region using red. Then color 2/3 of the whole region blue.

FIGURE 9.37

vertical regions) with one color—perhaps <u>red.</u> They then color $\frac{2}{3}$ (two of the horizontal regions) with a second color—<u>blue.</u> When pupils look at $\frac{2}{3} \times \frac{2}{5}$, it will be the part of the array that is <u>purple</u>!

Once students learn to create an array, the teacher can use the model to develop "rules" for finding the product. Using the example above, the teacher would point to the whole region and note how many equal-sized regions are illustrated. The **size** of each region is found by the 3 × 5 array (three rows of five)—which is the same as the denominators. Students thereby recognize that multiplying the denominators will give the size (denominator) of the regions. When the teacher points to the shaded part of the region, pupils may describe that section as two rows of two—or a 2 × 2 array. From this development, the pupils find that multiplying the numerators will give the number of shaded parts. A "discovered rule" might be stated as "To find the size (denominator) you multiply the denominators; to find how many (numerator) you have, you will multiply the numerators."

Multiplying Numbers Named as Mixed Numerals

Multiplication of numbers stated as mixed numerals seldom occurs in real-life situations. If such multiplication is required, individuals generally change the fraction to decimals and use the calculator to find the product. When small mixed numerals are encountered it usually is easier to restate the mixed numerals as improper fractions and work the problem the customary way. There is value, however, in exploring an algorithm that does not require changing the fractional name. When the vertical mixed numeral algorithm is developed <u>using a drawing</u> to help find each of the partial products, pupils reexamine the use of the distributive property of multiplication over addition. For pupils who have not recognized the value of this property in the set of whole numbers, this provides another opportunity to strengthen their appreciation of this important property. The renaming and distributing used in the figure for mixed numerals is almost identical to that used in whole numbers and that which will be used in decimals and algebraic formulas such as $(a + b)^2 = a^2 + 2ab + b^2$.

To develop the algorithm, a "blank array" (an array without individual items displayed) is drawn

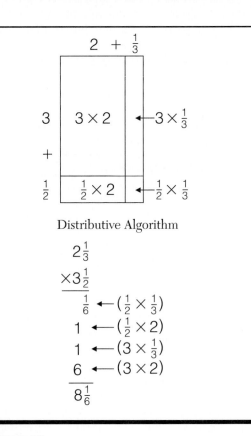

Distributive Algorithm

$$2\frac{1}{3}$$
$$\times 3\frac{1}{2}$$
$$\frac{1}{6} \leftarrow \left(\frac{1}{2} \times \frac{1}{3}\right)$$
$$1 \leftarrow \left(\frac{1}{2} \times 2\right)$$
$$1 \leftarrow \left(3 \times \frac{1}{3}\right)$$
$$6 \leftarrow (3 \times 2)$$
$$\overline{8\frac{1}{6}}$$

FIGURE 9.38

to show the two factors. In Figure 9.38 the problem $3\frac{1}{2} \times 2\frac{1}{3}$ is illustrated. The first factor $(3\frac{1}{2})$ is associated with the rows and renamed as "$3 + \frac{1}{2}$." The number of columns is indicated with "$2 + \frac{1}{3}$." By pointing to the four cells identified in the blank array, the teacher directs attention to the fact that the algorithm must contain a product for each cell—$\frac{1}{2} \times \frac{1}{3}$; $\frac{1}{2} \times 2$; $3 \times \frac{1}{3}$; and 3×2. To find the product, all of the parts must be put together (added).

Teaching Properties and Patterns of Multiplication

Just as pupils explore properties when working with addition and subtraction of fractions, they need to verify that certain properties are still applicable when multiplying fractional numbers. Examination of the commutative, associative, and distributive properties with fractional numbers need not be extensive. However, insights gained by these early explorations provide a strong foundation for algebraic proofs. Figure 9.39 illustrates fragments of exercises that have been structured to promote such explorations.

The identity property for multiplication is used so extensively to generate equivalent fractions that its mention will seem almost anticlimactic to the students. Though identity was developed via models prior to multiplication of fractional numbers, it may be reexplored once the algorithm has been developed.

Another exploration that helps pupils appreciate

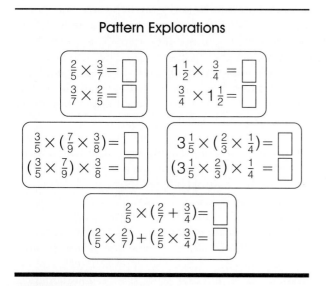

$$\frac{8}{15} \times \frac{5}{6} = \frac{8 \times 5}{15 \times 6} = \frac{5 \times 8}{15 \times 6} =$$

$$\frac{\boxed{5} \times \boxed{2} \times 4}{3 \times \boxed{5} \times \boxed{2} \times 3} = \frac{4}{3 \times 3} = \frac{4}{9}$$

$$\overset{4}{\cancel{8}} \times \overset{1}{\cancel{5}} = \frac{4}{9}$$
$$\underset{3}{\cancel{15}} \times \underset{3}{\cancel{6}}$$

FIGURE 9.40

the properties of multiplication is an investigation of "cancellation." Cancellation is used to simplify the multiplication by factoring out names for one (identity) before multiplying—thereby making the numbers used smaller and easier to compute. For example, $\frac{8}{15} \times \frac{5}{6}$ can be simplified by finding names for one. Figure 9.40 shows how eight can be renamed as 2×4 and six renamed as 2×3 so that $\frac{2}{2}$ (a name for one) can be "cancelled out." Cancellation usually is examined near the end of a study of fractional number multiplication.

Introducing the Reciprocal as Readiness for Division

The reciprocal property of fractional numbers, $(a/b \times b/a) = 1$, is a property that students did not encounter when they worked with whole numbers. The reciprocal (multiplicative inverse) is a property that has many applications in mathematics. For example, when studying division of fractional numbers the reciprocal may be used in the explanation of why one "inverts the divisor and multiplies" to find the quotient of two fractional numbers. The concept of reciprocal may be introduced by exploring a set of exercises in the form of $a/b \times b/a = \triangle$. Pupils soon recognize a pattern and discover that the answer is <u>always</u> one. The teacher may then change the expression to $? \times a/b = 1$. To complete the number sentence "$? \times \frac{5}{6} = 1$," the pupils asks, "What number can we use to multiply $\frac{5}{6}$ by in order to get a product of one?" Reflecting upon their experience with $a/b \times b/a = 1$, students recognize that the denominator and the numerator will change places in the fraction needed. After pupils recognize the pattern, the teacher may wish to provide a name—reciprocal—for this property.

Pattern Explorations

$$\frac{2}{5} \times \frac{3}{7} = \square$$
$$\frac{3}{7} \times \frac{2}{5} = \square$$

$$1\frac{1}{2} \times \frac{3}{4} = \square$$
$$\frac{3}{4} \times 1\frac{1}{2} = \square$$

$$\frac{3}{5} \times (\frac{7}{9} \times \frac{3}{8}) = \square$$
$$(\frac{3}{5} \times \frac{7}{9}) \times \frac{3}{8} = \square$$

$$3\frac{1}{5} \times (\frac{2}{3} \times \frac{1}{4}) = \square$$
$$(3\frac{1}{5} \times \frac{2}{3}) \times \frac{1}{4} = \square$$

$$\frac{2}{5} \times (\frac{2}{7} + \frac{3}{4}) = \square$$
$$(\frac{2}{5} \times \frac{2}{7}) + (\frac{2}{5} \times \frac{3}{4}) = \square$$

FIGURE 9.39

9.10 TEACHING DIVISION OF FRACTIONAL NUMBERS

Division of fractional numbers is one of the more difficult concepts to teach and it is generally the last fractional number operation taught in the intermediate grades. Since division of fractions is seldom used in everyday life, students have little opportunity to practice this skill. Of course, the division of fractional numbers algorithm is used in more advanced mathematics, so introducing this skill lays a foundation for later use. It is important that the teacher develop an understanding of why the algorithm works.

The computational complexities required to divide fractions are far fewer than those of dividing 2- and 3-digit divisors in the standard algorithm. In fact, once students learn the "shortcut" of multiplying by the reciprocal of the divisor, computational errors seldom occur. In the past some teachers actually introduced division of fractions by simply stating the rule and allowing students to practice. When students learn to divide in such a manner, they can easily find a quotient. However, the pupil has not learned much about mathematics—other than memorizing a rule. Therefore, teachers should avoid such an approach, emphasizing instead the mathematical principles employed and building estimation skills.

Division of fractional numbers may be introduced using the measurement concept. While such an approach does not lead to the standard algorithm, it does show concretely why the quotient is a reasonable number. Such an understanding is es-

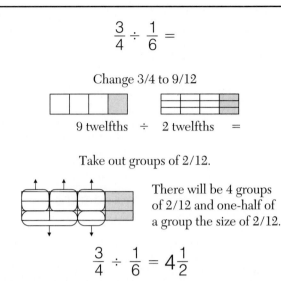

FIGURE 9.42

sential when encouraging students to estimate before working the problem. Later, when the standard algorithm is introduced, students will see that the shortcut is a faster way of calculating a quotient. Figure 9.41 illustrates how division of fractional numbers may be introduced using a measurement approach. Since both the divisor and the dividend are changed to a common denominator before dividing, this technique is often called the "common denominator approach."

The common denominator approach is frequently introduced with whole number dividends, but occasionally the teacher may need to verify that a quotient is reasonable when using fractions. Figure 9.42 shows how the problem $\frac{3}{4} \div \frac{1}{6}$ would be changed to twelfths and groups the size of $\frac{2}{12}$ measured out. Such a demonstration is helpful when students cannot understand why the answer $(4\frac{1}{2})$ is greater than the dividend $(\frac{3}{4})$. (The measurement approach is also very effective in helping students realize why a/b ÷ a/b = 1. For example, in the problem $\frac{2}{3} \div \frac{2}{3}$ the teacher could ask, "How many sets of $\frac{2}{3}$ can you get from $\frac{2}{3}$?")

To develop meaning for the standard procedure for finding a quotient, a different algorithm may be employed. Students are directed to write a problem such as "$\frac{5}{8} \div \frac{2}{7}$" as a complex fraction. The complex fraction approach has the advantage of moving the student to the standard algorithm through the use of mathematical properties. Such a technique is excellent for those students who can follow an analytical approach. Since the approach requires the student to be familiar with several mathematical properties, it is wise for the teacher to review those

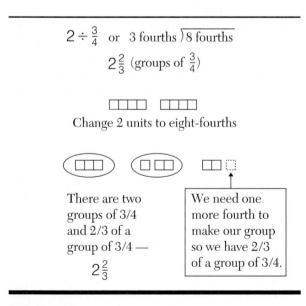

FIGURE 9.41

skills prior to introducing the algorithm.

For students to understand the complex fraction approach they must recognize that:

1. a fraction is implied division (in order to write $\frac{5}{8} \div \frac{2}{7}$ as a complex fraction)
2. multiplying by the reciprocal will give the product "one"
3. multiplying by the identity will not change a number (fraction)
4. the number one (identity) can have different names
5. a fraction can be used as a numerator and a denominator
6. any fraction with a denominator of one can be rewritten as the fraction $(\frac{2}{3})/1 = \frac{2}{3}$.

Once the student exhibits these understandings, then the steps within the complex fraction approach are easily followed.

In the problem $\frac{5}{8} \div \frac{2}{7}$ the teacher first writes the division problem into a complex fraction (see Figure 9.43). The lesson fragment below illustrates how a teacher might develop the algorithm.

Teacher-Guided Interactive Learning Activity

LESSON FRAGMENT

M: Rule for dividing fractional numbers: Multiply the dividend by the reciprocal of the divisor

A: Group of sixth-grade children

T: Guided questions leading to reasons for a rule

H: Multiplication of fractions, division by 1, $a/b \div a/b = 1$, the compensation property for division of fractional numbers, and the reciprocal property

PROMOTING DISCOVERY WITH CAREFULLY CRAFTED QUESTIONS

Teacher: I have written the problem $\frac{5}{8} \div \frac{2}{7}$ on the chalkboard. Who has an estimate of the quotient—Greg?

Greg: Since $\frac{2}{7}$ is less than $\frac{5}{8}$ we can get at least 1. If the problem were $\frac{6}{7} \div \frac{2}{7}$ we could get 3 pieces the size of $\frac{2}{7}$. Since $\frac{5}{8}$ is less than $\frac{6}{7}$, I THINK the answer will be more than two but less than three.

Teacher: Very good, Greg—I'll write that on the board. Thank you for explaining your process so we could see how you estimated. I am going to rewrite

Complex Fraction

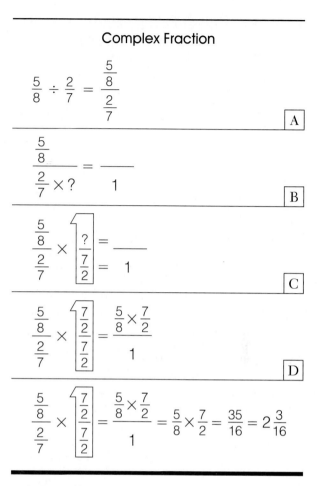

FIGURE 9.43

our problem into a COMPLEX FRACTION and we will calculate an answer. We can write our problem in this form because we know that fractions are a way of writing division. (Figure 9.43A.) Now we can see that $\frac{5}{8}$ over $\frac{2}{7}$ is not a name that we readily recognize like $\frac{2}{3}$ or $\frac{3}{4}$. IF we had $\frac{5}{8}$ over one then we could say that the fraction was a name for $\frac{5}{8}$, but $\frac{5}{8}$ is not over one. How can we change the denominator so that it will equal one? (THE TEACHER WRITES "=" AND THEN A "1" IN THE DENOMINATOR OF A NEW FRACTION. SEE FIGURE 9.43B.) Darlyne?

Darlyne: It sort of looks like the problems we did earlier this week. We had some that said $\frac{2}{7} \times ? = 1$ and we used the reciprocal to give us the product of one. So I think we should try $\frac{7}{2}$.

Teacher: Good, Darlyne. But won't we change a fraction if we multiply the denominator by $\frac{7}{2}$? (SEE FIGURE 9.43C.)

Darlyne: It won't change the fraction if we make $\frac{7}{2}$ as part of a name for one. We can write $\frac{7}{2}$ over $\frac{7}{2}$ because that is a name for one.

Teacher: All right, let's try it. I'll write that name for one in my fraction. That will give us a "1" in the denominator and a $\frac{5}{8} \times \frac{7}{2}$ in the numerator. (SEE FIGURE 9.43D.)

Teacher: Now we have $\frac{5}{8} \times \frac{7}{2}$ over one and we know that we rewrite that as simply $\frac{5}{8} \times \frac{7}{2}$ because any number over one is the number itself. Is that right, Carl?

Carl: Yes—and now we can multiply $\frac{5}{8} \times \frac{7}{2}$ to get $\frac{35}{16}$. We can simplify $\frac{35}{16}$ into the mixed numeral $2\frac{3}{16}$. That is more than two and less than three, as Greg said.

Teacher: Excellent, Carl! (THE TEACHER WOULD CONTINUE THE LESSON, TRYING A FEW MORE EXAMPLES BEFORE ENCOURAGING STUDENTS TO PRACTICE THE SKILL— EITHER INDIVIDUALLY OR AS PART OF A CO-OPERATIVE LEARNING GROUP. LATER IN THE LESSON—PERHAPS THE NEXT DAY— THE TEACHER MAY WISH TO SUMMARIZE IN ORDER TO SHORTEN THE PROCESS.)

Teacher: We have been doing a lot of writing to find a quotient. Let's see if we can find a way to shorten the process. Let's use the problem "$\frac{7}{8} \div \frac{5}{6}$." First let's estimate to get some idea what the quotient might be. Will the quotient be more than one or less than one? Carl?

Carl: Since $\frac{5}{8}$ is smaller than $\frac{7}{8}$ we'll be able to get a little more than one piece the size of $\frac{5}{6}$.

Teacher: Good—now can anyone suggest a way of speeding up the computation? Darlyne?

Darlyne: I don't bother to do all that work with the denominator anymore, teacher. It's going to change into a one anyhow. I just multiply the divisor by the reciprocal.

Teacher: Let me see if I can work the problem that way. What will we do first, Darlyne?

Darlyne: First you look at the second number (divisor). You find its reciprocal. Then you multiply the first number (dividend) by that reciprocal and you'll get the quotient! (SEE FIGURE 9.44.)

Once students learn to divide with fractional numbers, the teacher may find it helpful to explore some of the properties that are applicable to fractions. Dividing a fraction by one, as used in the lesson fragment above, can be reasoned by most

students. For those who have difficulty, the teacher may wish to apply the partition concept to the problem. For example, if two-thirds of a set were to be placed into one set, what would be placed in that one set? Using $\frac{2}{3}$ of a sheet of paper, students find that $\frac{2}{3}$ will be in the set. For pupils who are more analytical the generalization of $a/b \div 1 = a/b$ can be developed with similar questions. The measurement approach can be used to help pupils see that $a/b \div c/d = (a/b \times r/s) \div (c/d \times r/s)$. In other words, the compensation property for division of whole numbers <u>also</u> applies when dividing fractional numbers.

Using Calculators to Teach Fractional Number Concepts

Although there are calculators that compute using a fractional form, most inexpensive calculators will not display numbers in a fractional numeral form. Therefore, the use of the device to help students understand fractions is somewhat limited until the pupil has been introduced to the decimal form of fractional numbers (decimal fractions and the division meaning of the fraction). Before the development of decimals, many of the activities relating to fractions involve the intermediate steps that reflect whole number operations. For example, the calculator is a good device to verify the prime factorization of a denominator or to test the divisibility of both the numerator and denominator in the process of simplifying (reducing) fractions. Once decimal equivalents for fractions have been introduced, then the calculator can be used to work fractional number problems. Since these applications require an understanding of decimals, they will be developed in Chapter 10.

9.11 COMPUTERS

It is possible to write programs that generate fractional number exercises for the student and verify that the answers are correct. It is also possible to write programs that identify the type of error that a pupil is making and provide remedial instruction specific to that type of error. However, most teachers find that the commercial software available is efficient and therefore it is unnecessary to personally write instructional programs that are capable of teaching the various conceptual nuances inherent in teaching fractional numbers. (See the listing at end of this chapter.)

The computer, however, is an excellent tool that

Darlyne's Rule

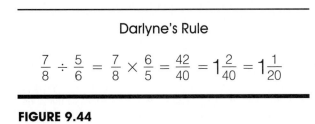

$$\frac{7}{8} \div \frac{5}{6} = \frac{7}{8} \times \frac{6}{5} = \frac{42}{40} = 1\frac{2}{40} = 1\frac{1}{20}$$

FIGURE 9.44

1. Bring program to the screen.
2. Select "none" as background for the pattern.
3. Select rectangle pattern using arrow and create a small rectangle on screen. 
4. Select lasso with the arrow and draw a ring around the rectangle so it can be copied.
5. Select the COPY command with the arrow — and the rectangle will be copied.
6. Select the paste command and a rectangle will be pasted on the screen. Move the rectangle (by using the arrow) and place it beside the first rectangle. 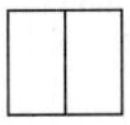
7. Repeat process until the desired number of parts have been constructed. (If you want to show fifths, then select 5 rectangular regions). 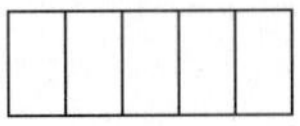
8. Select a pattern for shading the appropriate number of regions — to show 2/5 shade 2 regions. Select the paint bucket and the pattern can be "poured" into two of the regions.

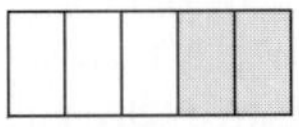

FIGURE 9.45

can be used by a teacher to design manipulative materials for teaching fractional number concepts. There are many "paint" and "draw" programs that permit even the teacher with a limited computer background to quickly generate fractional number models for use in the classroom: The MacDraw™, MacPaint™, and SuperPaint™ are three graphic programs that can be used with the Macintosh™ line of computers to create fractional materials for use in the classroom. Figure 9.45 describes how rectangular fractional regions can be quickly constructed using the SuperPaint™ computer program.

9.12 EVALUATION AND INTERVENTION

Due to the complex nature of the numbers and operations involving fractions, the misunderstandings and the types of errors children make are quite varied. Evaluation of student skill in fractional number situations requires a variety of evaluative methods ranging from observations to individual pupil interviews. While there are some similarities in the nature of the models the child will use in constructing problem-solving strategies, the attributes of the models that are unique to common

fractions, percent, and ratio will have to be evaluated in the context of fractional number problem-solving activities. For example, while the student may associate the idea of putting sets together and finding the number of the resulting set with addition, situations involving different fractional parts, such as halves and thirds, adds elements that are quite distinct from the problem-solving skills related to addition of whole numbers.

Identification of the reason a particular error is occurring may require the teacher to listen to a student talk through the problem as it is worked (oral interview). This method of isolating errors is especially useful when the pupil is making several types of errors. As with all oral interviews, the teacher must refrain from "correcting" the student during the interview, so the pupil will feel free to describe the process. Remediation of the error should take place later—after the teacher has had time to collect any materials needed.

Fractional number errors generally fall into three categories: (a) errors related to whole number concepts, (b) errors related to fractional number concepts, and (c) errors related to operations on fractional numbers. Each error requires its own remedial approach. For example, a commonly occurring mistake in operations using fractional numbers (addition, subtraction, multiplication, and division) is the failure of the student to simplify (reduce) a fraction. To overcome this error, the teacher would have the pupil reestablish the skill of simplifying fractions, working with GCF and manipulatives if necessary. Once the skill is reestablished, the pupil works multistep exercises that include as one step the act of simplifying the fractions.

If a student makes errors relating to whole number concepts, such as factorization, least common multiples, multiplication, addition, subtraction, etc., then the teacher must redevelop these concepts with the pupil. For example, if a pupil records the product $\frac{24}{49}$ for the problem $\frac{3}{7} \times \frac{6}{7}$, then it would appear that the student understands the operation and the algorithm, but is having difficulty with the basic multiplication combination 3×6. In this case, mastering the basic fact 3×6 not only will help the student obtain the correct problem when multiplying fractions containing these facts, but also will help overcome errors occurring in division of fractions, whole number multiplication and division, and changing fractional names.

Many errors result from a student's poor conceptual foundation of fractional numbers. For example, addition or subtraction of numerators and denominators ($\frac{1}{3} + \frac{1}{3} = \frac{2}{6}$), indiscriminately using one of the unlike denominators in the sum or difference ($\frac{2}{7} + \frac{3}{8} = \frac{5}{8}$), and adding the numerator to the whole number in mixed numeral addition ($2\frac{2}{3} + 1\frac{2}{3} = \frac{7}{3}$) are kinds of errors that will require the teacher to go back to the basic meanings of fractional numbers with children.

Failure to understand the operational process or reason behind the process can result in errors such as inverting <u>both</u> the dividend and divisor in division ($\frac{2}{3} \div \frac{3}{4} = \frac{3}{2} \times \frac{4}{3}$); converting both denominators to least common denominators when multiplying ($\frac{2}{3} \times \frac{1}{2} = \frac{4}{6} \times \frac{3}{6} = \frac{12}{6}$); and failure to regroup properly in addition and subtraction of fractional number exercises ($3\frac{2}{3} = 2\frac{12}{3}$).

9.13 MEETING SPECIAL NEEDS

From scale drawings in art to classroom cooking projects, the teacher has a wide variety of activities that lend themselves to extending fractional number concepts for both the student who has a strong conceptual foundation and the gifted student. For example, let's assume that the class wants to print a newspaper. As part of the project children have submitted their designs for logos for the paper. The winning logo is $2\frac{1}{4}$ inches by $1\frac{1}{4}$ inches. The teacher may request that the design be redone at a scale equal to three-fourths of the original size. The problem of reducing the design is proposed to the class. If a class plans to make cookies to take to a nursing home during the holiday season they will need to change the amounts for each ingredient in the recipe when more than one batch is needed. When planning to take a field trip to a nearby state park students may find the mileage on the map is based on a ratio of one inch to five miles. These activities give the pupils an opportunity to extend their skills with multiplication of fractional numbers.

Finding numbers represented by sums and differences of fractions from sequences of fractions also makes an interesting small-group learning activity. The teacher might pick a number and ask the children if they can find some combination of adding and subtracting fractions from the set $\{\frac{1}{2}, \frac{2}{3}, \frac{3}{4}, \frac{4}{5}, \frac{5}{6},$ etc.$\}$ that would equal this number, not using the same fraction more than one time. [For example, if the teacher specified the number one, $1 = \frac{11}{12} + (\frac{5}{6} - \frac{3}{4})$].

Magic squares with fractional numbers make interesting individual learning activities that use addition of fractional numbers. For example, a student may be asked if he can place the fractions $\frac{1}{9}, \frac{2}{9}, \frac{1}{3}, \frac{4}{9}, \frac{5}{9}, \frac{2}{3}, \frac{7}{9}, \frac{8}{9},$ and $\frac{3}{3}$ into a 9-by-9 array so that

the sum of any horizontal row, vertical row, or diagonal equals the sum of any other row, column, or diagonal.

Using Prime Factors to Find GCF and LCM

For most commonly used fractions, the GCF of the numerator and denominator is easily found by testing the factors of the numerator against the factors of the denominator. Students can gain a better understanding of the use of identity and simplificaton of fractions by working with larger numbers. When larger numbers are used, the intersection-of-sets approach—even in its modified form—is not efficient. If given $\frac{144}{360}$, a student would need to find the GCF of 72 to express the simplest or lowest terms. Such a process not only is frustrating for many students, but also requires the student to use multiplication facts that are not normally memorized.

More advanced students can learn to use a prime factor approach when finding the greatest common factor (GCF). When students express both the numerator (144) and the denominator (360) as PRIME FACTOR EXPRESSIONS, they will see several "names for one" within the fraction. When the teacher uses "factor cards" for each expression, students may suggest moving factors around so that names for one are more easily recognized (see Figure 9.46). Exchanging each "name for one" with the whole number "one" leaves the expression $1 \times 1 \times 1 \times 1 \times 1 \times \frac{2}{5}$, or $\frac{2}{5}$. While a few

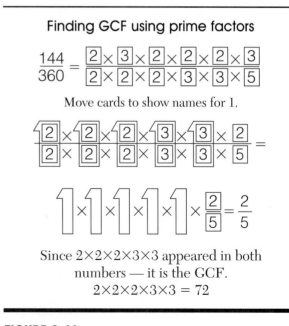

Finding GCF using prime factors

$$\frac{144}{360} = \frac{\boxed{2} \times \boxed{3} \times \boxed{2} \times \boxed{2} \times \boxed{2} \times \boxed{3}}{\boxed{2} \times \boxed{2} \times \boxed{2} \times \boxed{3} \times \boxed{3} \times \boxed{5}}$$

Move cards to show names for 1.

$$\frac{\boxed{2} \times \boxed{2} \times \boxed{2} \times \boxed{3} \times \boxed{3} \times \boxed{2}}{\boxed{2} \times \boxed{2} \times \boxed{2} \times \boxed{3} \times \boxed{3} \times \boxed{5}} =$$

$$1 \times 1 \times 1 \times 1 \times 1 \times \frac{\boxed{2}}{\boxed{5}} = \frac{2}{5}$$

Since $2 \times 2 \times 2 \times 3 \times 3$ appeared in both numbers — it is the GCF.
$2 \times 2 \times 2 \times 3 \times 3 = 72$

FIGURE 9.46

students can see that the "names for one" (2 × 2 × 2 × 3 × 3) really is 72, or the GCF, most students will need teacher guidance to see this relationship. The relationship may be easier for some to see if simple fractions are chosen. For example, if $\frac{8}{12}$ is selected, students quickly recognize that "4" is the GCF when primes are used to rename $\frac{8}{12}$ = (2 × 2) × 2/(2 × 2) × 3 = $\frac{4}{4}$ × $\frac{2}{3}$ = 1 × $\frac{2}{3}$ = $\frac{2}{3}$.

Renaming the numerator and denominators as prime expressions—as in the example above—is not commonly used when reducing fractions. However, the process of using primes when simplifying a fraction—rather than the GCF—can make a complex problem much simpler. When calculators, such as the Texas Instruments Explore™, simplify fractions, they do not use GCF—they factor out primes until the simplest expression is found. Trying to determine how such a calculator "simplifies" fractions is an interesting exploration for some pupils and leads them to recognize the value of using prime expressions. The problem illustrated in Figure 9.47 illustrates simplifying a fraction with primes. Care must be used with this technique because even after taking several steps to simplify the fraction, some students will state that they used TEN as the GCF (2 + 2 + 3 + 3). They do not recognize that the actual GCF was **2 × 2 × 3 × 3**, or 36.

A similar "prime factor approach" can be used to find the least common multiple (LCM). In fact, using prime factors is perhaps the most efficient technique when finding the least common multiple for three or more numbers. If the LCM of the numbers 42, 60, and 99 were desired, simply multiplying the numbers together would give a common multiple of 249,480—but this is not the LCM. Finding the least common multiple by the intersection of sets of multiples would be a frustrating task. Even with a calculator, recording and comparing multiples of 42, 60, and 99 would be very time-consuming until the intersection of 13,860 is reached. However, by using the prime factor expressions for each number, the construction of an LCM is a relatively simple task.

To help students understand the process, the teacher may use index cards, which will allow the prime factors to be moved around in an expression. Each number (42, 60, and 99) could be written on index cards using different colored cards. Once the expressions are displayed, students then may construct a common multiple by combining the factor expressions. The teacher will need to stress that any unnecessary prime factor cards should be eliminated in order to make the number the LEAST common multiple. For example, starting with the prime expression for 60—3 × 2 × 2 × 5—a student would move any prime cards that can be matched with 60 to a position behind the first card. (See Figure 9.48.)

Finding LCM using Prime Factors

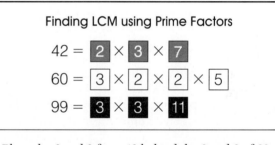

Place the 2 and 3 from 42 <u>behind</u> the 3 and 2 of 60. Move the 7 as a new factor.

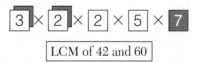

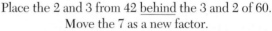
LCM of 42 and 60

Place the "3" of 99 <u>behind</u> the other 3s. (They are different colors). Move the second "3" down into the line as a factor. (You can have <u>no more than one card of each color in a stack</u>.) Move the "11" to the end of the line as another factor.

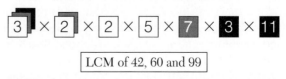

LCM of 42, 60 and 99

FIGURE 9.48

Dividing by prime number expressions for identity

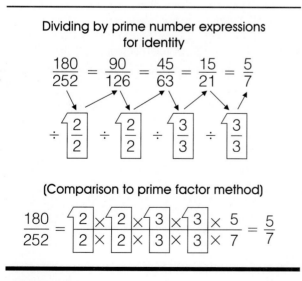

$$\frac{180}{252} = \frac{90}{126} = \frac{45}{63} = \frac{15}{21} = \frac{5}{7}$$

$$\div \frac{2}{2} \quad \div \frac{2}{2} \quad \div \frac{3}{3} \quad \div \frac{3}{3}$$

(Comparison to prime factor method)

$$\frac{180}{252} = \frac{2 \times 2 \times 3 \times 3 \times 5}{2 \times 2 \times 3 \times 3 \times 7} = \frac{5}{7}$$

FIGURE 9.47

Using $3 \times 2 \times 7$—the expression for 42—the student would move a "3" behind the three of $3 \times 2 \times 2 \times 5$ and the "2" behind one of the twos in $3 \times 2 \times 2 \times 5$. Since the "7" is left over, it would be moved to the expression to make the common multiple of 42 and $60 = 3 \times 2 \times 2 \times 5 \times 7$. Now, all that is left is to move the factor cards for 99, following the same rules. Since $99 = 3 \times 3 \times 11$, ONE of the threes could be moved behind the other color index cards for "3." That would leave a "3" and an "11" to be moved into the expression, making $3 \times 2 \times 2 \times 5 \times 7 \times 3 \times 11$, or 13,860.

Providing for the Learning-Disabled Student

Fractional numbers are among the most complex concepts taught at the intermediate level, particularly for the learning-disabled student. Therefore, the teacher may find it necessary to modify the curriculum for such a pupil. The very complexities that make fractional number concepts difficult for a learning-disabled child offer many opportunities to challenge a gifted child by slightly extending the concepts taught in the regular curriculum.

It is important to give the learning-disabled child as sound a foundation as possible in the many meanings of fractional numbers: parts of a whole, parts of a set, ratios, rate pairs, percents, and the fraction as indicated division. While equivalent decimal fractions and the use of a calculator can be used to restructure the curriculum for some learning-disabled children, functional problem-solving literacy requires the child to understand the nature of the fractional number. Functional literacy is developed by extensive use of hands-on activities with models. It may be desirable to permit learning-disabled children to develop model strategies as a way of bypassing their learning deficits before developing ways to augment learning capacities through the use of technological devices (calculators). For example, Figure 9.49 and 9.50 illustrate some rate-pair charts that have been constructed for learning-disabled children to use in problem-solving situations.

Providing for the Gifted Student

The teacher will not have to look very far afield to find fractional-number activities that will challenge the gifted child. Activities previously described that allow students to simplify fractions and to find least common denominators using prime numbers are excellent for the gifted pupil. While the average pupil might use primes for fractions such as $\frac{48}{60}$, gifted students want to simplify fractions such as

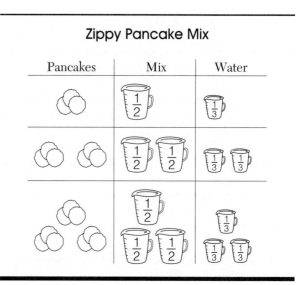

FIGURE 9.49

$\frac{324}{418}$ and find the sum for $\frac{7}{18} + \frac{5}{21} + \frac{7}{15}$. Cancellation, as a way of simplifying multiplication, is readily embraced by the talented.

Increasing or decreasing the size of a drawing by multiplying each dimension by a fraction (or mixed numeral) combines both mathematical, measuring, and art skills. A design—with dimensions indicating fractional parts of an inch—is displayed. The class is challenged to draw the same design, but to make it $\frac{3}{4}$ the size of the original. In early activities of this nature, the teacher may allow students to place their drawings on top of the reduced master drawn by the teacher to see if the two correspond. In later activities, the students would compare to see if two <u>similar</u> figures have been constructed. The activity (see Figure 9.51) of reducing a design—or increasing its size—can be used by the teacher with the whole class, but the talented student will want to make many different sizes—or will want to create a new design. Such work makes an interesting bulletin board display encouraging a pupil to "make a drawing $2\frac{2}{3}$ times the size of the

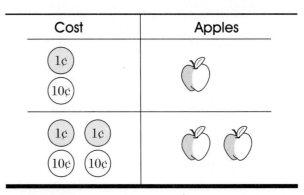

FIGURE 9.50

original'' because that picture is "missing" from the display.

Gifted students enjoy exploring the use of fractions in historical number systems. The ancient Egyptian numeration system—since it used a numerator of one for all fractions (except $\frac{2}{3}$) presents a challenging situation. Recognizing that the Egyptians showed $\frac{3}{4}$ as $\frac{1}{2} + \frac{1}{4}$ and $\frac{3}{8}$ as $\frac{1}{4} + \frac{1}{8}$, students may be challenged to find a way to depict the fractions $\frac{7}{8}$ and $\frac{13}{16}$.

Operations involving fractional numbers in other bases present interesting challenges for the gifted child. For example, having a child explore the advantages of adding and subtracting fractions expressed in base twelve ($\frac{9}{10}_{\text{twelve}} + \frac{9}{10}_{\text{twelve}} = 1\frac{6}{10}_{\text{twelve}}$) presents an interesting and challenging activity. Problems commonly found at the post-intermediate level provide interesting challenges, for instance:

> Julia can cut the lawn in $\frac{1}{2}$ an hour. Her brother can cut the lawn in $\frac{1}{3}$ of an hour. If they cut the lawn together, how long will it take them to cut the lawn?

Two cups of water are added to three gallons of lemonade. After half the lemonade is drunk, two quarts of lemonade and one-third of a cup of sugar are added to the remaining lemonade. What is the ratio of sugar to lemonade that is now in the lemonade? (This type of problem makes an excellent program for the computer, when the process is repeated N times.)

Beth has an agreement with her parents. At the end of each year they will add to her savings account an amount equal to one-fifth of the amount in it. Before the parents make their determination they wait until the bank has added its yearly interest to the account. Each year the account earns one twentieth of the amount that is in the account after the parents made the contribution for the previous year. For example, if there is 100 dollars in the account on December 31, 1988, including interest, then the parents would deposit 20 dollars to the account and the account would earn interest equaling one-twentieth of this amount during the year. If Beth started with 1,000 dollars, how much would she have at the end of five years after her parents made their annual contribution?

9.14 SUMMARY

The development of fractional number concepts at the primary level emphasizes hands-on explorations. These explorations involve parts-of-a-whole and parts-of-a-set models for fractional numbers. Children also use models to learn the nature of fractional numbers, comparing fractional numbers, and the concept of equivalent fractions.

At the intermediate level, concepts relating to parts-of-a-whole and parts-of-a-set are maintained and extended to include mixed numerals. Intermediate-level students learn that fractions are also used to indicate division and to express ratios, rate pairs, and percents. Comparison and equivalence concepts are extended with students learning mathematical techniques for generating equivalent fractions. Students learn to use GCF to simplify (reduce) fractions and the LCM to find lowest common denominators.

Students at the intermediate level become skillful in adding, subtracting, multiplying, and dividing fractional numbers. Though the application of fractions in everyday situations has diminished as the metric system incorporates into everyone's daily life, students still find a need to use fractions and fractional operations in problem-solving situations.

Copy this design — but make it only 1/2 the size!

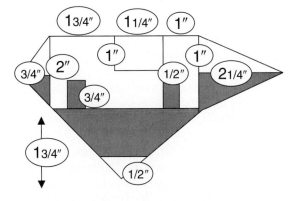

Check your design by placing it on top of the drawing taped to the window.

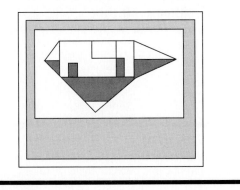

FIGURE 9.51

EXERCISES

1. Illustrate the following using drawings appropriate for primary pupils:
   a. $\frac{1}{2}$, $\frac{1}{3}$, and $\frac{1}{4}$ (using circular regions)
   b. $\frac{1}{2}$, $\frac{1}{3}$, and $\frac{1}{4}$ (using triangular regions)
   c. $\frac{1}{2}$, $\frac{1}{3}$, and $\frac{1}{4}$ (using a number-line model)
   d. equivalent fractions ($\frac{8}{12} = \frac{2}{3}$, using a set model)

2. Use a manipulative material to illustrate the fraction $\frac{1}{4}$ as
   a. implied division
   b. ratio

3. Show how to use cross-multiplication to determine which fraction—$\frac{13}{16}$ or $\frac{7}{9}$—is greater.

4. Construct a "fractional renamer" to find five equivalent fractions for $\frac{5}{8}$.

5. Find the greatest common factor for the numbers 48 and 72 using
   a. the intersection-of-sets approach
   b. the prime factor approach.

6. Find the least common multiple for the numbers 18 and 24 using
   a. the intersection-of-sets approach
   b. the prime factor approach

7. When possible, new skills should be introduced in a meaningful situation. Suggest a classroom situation which could be used to introduce
   a. addition of two fractions with like denominators (Example: $\frac{5}{8} + \frac{7}{8}$)
   b. subtraction of two mixed numbers with unlike denominators and regrouping (Example: $4\frac{1}{3} - 2\frac{3}{4}$)
   c. multiplication of a whole number times a fraction (Example: $4 \times \frac{2}{3}$)
   d. multiplication of a fraction times a whole number (Example: $\frac{3}{4} \times 9$)
   e. multiplication of a fraction times a fraction (Example: $\frac{3}{4} \times \frac{7}{8}$)
   f. division of a mixed number by a fraction (Example: $3\frac{2}{3} \div \frac{3}{4}$)
   g. division of a fraction by a whole number (Example: $\frac{3}{4} \div 6$)

8. Show how a teacher might use manipulative materials and/or drawings to illustrate each of the items listed in question 7.

9. Examine the errors made in the computational exercises below. Determine the probable cause of the error and suggest an instructional procedure which might be used to help the student.
   Myrtle: $\frac{2}{3} + \frac{5}{8} = \frac{7}{11}$ Roberto: $\frac{3}{4} \div \frac{2}{3} = \frac{8}{9}$

10. Several pupils in your class have used a distributive algorithm to find the product of $6\frac{1}{2} \times 4\frac{1}{3}$ (they did not change to improper fractions). Their answer—$24\frac{1}{6}$—is incorrect, but they cannot understand why. Use a drawing to show the pupils why their product is incorrect.

11. Select a currently published elementary school mathematics series. Look through the books to determine the grade level in which
    a. fractions are first illustrated as a part of a set
    b. fractions are shown as a ratio
    c. fractions are explored as implied division
    d. addition of common fractions is introduced
    e. greatest common factor and least common multiple are introduced
    f. subtraction of mixed numbers with regrouping is introduced
    g. multiplication of common fractions (fraction times a fraction) is explored
    h. multiplication of mixed numbers is introduced
    i. division of fractions is developed

12. Look through a current mathematics textbook for the fifth or sixth grade. Locate story problems which involve fractions and decide how each should be illustrated using concrete materials.

13. Choose one of the articles in the References section. After reading the article, write down three ideas which might be shared with a fellow teacher.

RELEVANT COMPUTER SOFTWARE

Benton Arithmetic: Fractions. 1986. IBM PC/PCjr & Apple II family. Quality Educational Designs, P.O. Box 12486, Portland, Or. 97212.

Conquering Fractions. 1988. Apple II family. MECC,

3490 Lexington Avenue North, St. Paul, Minn. 55126.

Fraction Concepts, Inc. 1987. Apple II family. MECC, 3490 Lexington Avenue North, St. Paul, Minn. 55126.

REFERENCES

Bezuk, N. S. "Fractions in the Early Childhood Mathematics Curriculum." *Arithmetic Teacher* 35 (February 1988): 56–60.

Bitter, G. G.; M. M. Hatfield; and N. T. Edwards. "Rational Numbers—Common Fractions." Chapter 10 in *Mathematics Methods for the Middle School*. Boston: Allyn and Bacon, 1989.

Curcio, F. R.; F. Sicklick; and S. B. Turkel. "Divide and Conquer: Unit Strips to the Rescue." *Arithmetic Teacher* 35 (December 1987): 6–12.

Jensen, R. J. "Common Multiples: Activities on and off the Computer." *Arithmetic Teacher* 35 (December 1987): 35–37.

——. "Ratios." *Arithmetic Teacher* 35 (April 1988): 60–61.

Levin, J. A. "Estimation Techniques for Arithmetic: Everyday Math and Mathematics Instruction." *Educational Studies in Mathematics* 12 (1981): 421–434.

Rees, J. M. "Two-Sided Pies: Help for Improper Fractions and Mixed Numbers." *Arithmetic Teacher* 35 (December 1987): 28–32.

Woodcock, G. E. "Estimating Fractions: A Picture is Worth a Thousand Words." In *Estimation and Mental Computation: NCTM Yearbook. 1986*. Reston, Va.: National Council of Teachers of Mathematics, 1986. Pp. 112–115.

CHAPTER 10

TEACHING DECIMAL FRACTIONS, RATIO, AND PERCENT

INTRODUCTION

If one were to look at the curriculum described in textbooks 20 years ago, a formal study of decimal fractions would not appear until the intermediate grades. Today the widespread use of calculators and computers by primary-level pupils has moved the formal study of decimal notation into the primary grades.

Since children in the primary grades have limited experience with fractions and place value, teachers must rely heavily upon the use of base ten models to help children recognize that the places to the right of the decimal are an extension of place value. Manipulative materials will also be used to relate pupils' growing understanding of common fractions to decimal fractions.

Decimals are employed when writing money amounts and pupils have a natural interest in learning about money, but using money as the sole model for decimals gives children a very narrow perspective of decimal notation. More generalized models must be used to broaden the pupils' perspective.

This chapter will show how to extend children's knowledge of place value to digits to the right of the decimal point. Operations with decimal fractions may be related to the equivalent operations with common fractions, thus linking any concepts previously learned with the study of decimal fractions.

Techniques for teaching percent were examined in Chapter 9. This chapter will extend and complete the discussion of teaching percent in the elementary school. Until students have attained some mastery of decimal fractions the development of percent is restricted to concepts developed from a common fraction perspective (primarily as a ratio of parts per hundred). While some fractions are easily converted to equivalent fractions with denominators of hundredths, many situations will require the full power of decimal fractions to fully exploit the use of percent notation.

10.1 DEVELOPING READINESS FOR DECIMAL FRACTIONS IN THE KINDERGARTEN AND PRIMARY LEVELS

Decimal notation for hundedths, using money notation, has long been a part of primary programs, but a hands-on development of tenths and hundredths independent of money notation represents a comparatively recent change in the curriculum. The greater use of the metric system in the primary grades is one reason for earlier examination of decimal fractions. As children measure with decimeters and centimeters, a need for understanding the relationship of those units to the meter grows. When working with money, children recognize that it takes 100 pennies to make one dollar, but seldom note that a penney is $\frac{1}{100}$ and a dime is $\frac{1}{10}$ of a dollar. The growing acceptance of calculators and computers into the curriculum is another factor that encourages early examination of decimals. Even first-grade pupils recognize that calculators display "a dot and digits to its right." Curiosity will motivate many to seek out explanations of this phenomenon.

When tenths and hundredths are introduced at the primary level, hands-on-explorations with models will be used. Formal development of operations (addition, subtraction, etc.) using decimal fraction notation is usually not explored until the intermediate grades.

The following illustrates a typical sequence for developing decimal and percent concepts:

Kindergarten through Second Grade

Examine decimal usage
- Tenths (as related to a dime)
- Hundredths (as related to money and centimeters)
- Calculator usage of decimals

Third Grade

Maintain and extend previously learned concepts
Recognize role of the decimal point
Construct models for tenths and hundredths

10.2 EXPLORING THE MEANING OF DECIMAL FRACTIONS

Once an understanding of place value (ones, tens, hundreds) is established, pupils can explore decimal fraction notation involving tenths and hundredths.

The lesson fragment below uses metric measurement to introduce the concept of tenths written as a decimal fraction.

Teacher-Guided Interactive Learning Activity

LESSON FRAGMENT

M: Tenths as a decimal fraction

A: Third-grade class

T: Models, involvement

H: Place value and common fraction for tenths

PROBLEM-SOLVING SITUATION:
LAST WEEK THE CLASS MEASURED WITH THE METER STICK AND FOUND THAT ONE OF THEIR TABLES WAS 120 CENTIMETERS LONG. THE TEACHER HAS ARRANGED THIS LESSON TO USE METRIC MEASUREMENT TO INTRODUCE RECORDING TENTHS IN DECIMAL NOTATION.

Teacher: We measured the table last week and found it to be 120 centimeters long. We also said that we COULD call the length one meter and 20 centimeters—if we wished. Today we are going to explore another way of reporting the length. Jose, I would like you to use this new meter stick to measure the length of the table again. (JOSE TAKES THE METER STICK—MARKED IN DECIMETERS—AND REMEASURES THE TABLE.) How long is the table, Jose?

Jose: It is one meter long and then two centimeters more.

Teacher: Are those centimeters, Jose?

Jose: Oh, no! They are too big for centimeters. Besides—it takes 100 centimeters to make a meter and there are only ten of these things in a meter.

Teacher: If it takes ten parts to make a WHOLE UNIT, what would we call one part, Rachel?

Rachel: We could call it a tenth. On the meter stick it would be a tenth of a meter.

Teacher: Very good! We could report the length of the table to be one and two-tenths meters. I'll write that on the board—using a fraction to show the two-tenths. (TEACHER WRITES $1\frac{2}{10}$ METERS ON THE CHALKBOARD.) I have adding-machine tape strips for each group and I would like everyone to copy this tenth ruler so we can measure things to the nearest tenth of a meter. (SEE FIGURE 10.1A.)

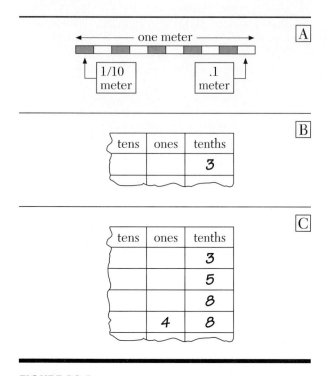

FIGURE 10.1

(EACH COOPERATIVE LEARNING GROUP TAKES OUT METER STICKS MARKED IN TENTHS. THEY ARE DIRECTED TO FIND THE HEIGHT AND LENGTH OF VARIOUS ITEMS—LESS THAN A METER IN LENGTH.)

Teacher: I see that each of your groups has recorded several measurements in tenths—writing the lengths as fractions. Today we are going to learn to write tenths in a <u>new way</u>. Look at the chart at the bottom of the sheet I handed your group. Notice the place-value chart has a new word to the right of the ones called <u>tenths</u>. Write a 3 in the tenths box to show that the length of our sheet of paper was three-tenths meters. (SEE FIGURE 10.1B.) Now let's look at some other measures—Bill's group found that the aquarium is about $\frac{5}{10}$ of a meter long. Record that on your chart. Link's group found that it was $\frac{8}{10}$ of a meter from Link's nose to his outstretched thumb, so let's record that on our chart, too. Gretchen's group measured the cabinet beneath the windows. How long is it, Gretchen?

Gretchen: We measured four and eight-tenth meters long.

Teacher: All right, let's record that amount on a new line. (SEE FIGURE 10.1C.) I am going to take the 4 and 8 out of the chart and write them on the chalkboard. Since we do not have our chart to show that the "8" means tenths we may easily mistake

it for eight ones. To remind us that the "4" is the ones, I am going to place a little man holding a sign to indicate which numeral is the ones. (SEE FIGURE 10.2A.) See how he is pointing to the ones. When we know which position is the ones, we also know that the tens are to the left and the tenths are to the right. We can read this numeral as "4 and eight-tenths." Let's all of us read this numeral together.

Class: Four and eight-tenths.

THE TEACHER DEVELOPS SEVERAL MORE EXAMPLES. THEN SHE EXPLAINS THAT HAVING TO DRAW A "LITTLE MAN" EVERY TIME YOU WANTED TO SHOW THE TENTHS WOULD BE VERY TIME-CONSUMING, SO INSTEAD WE USE A POINT THAT IS CALLED THE **DECIMAL POINT**. <u>THE JOB OF THIS DECIMAL POINT IS TO **LOCATE WHERE THE ONES COLUMN IS.**</u> (SEE FIGURE 10.2B.)

Teacher: Now that we know how to record numbers using a decimal point, let's use that skill with our calculators. Take out your calculator. (PUPILS GET CALCULATORS FROM THEIR DESKS.) Here are five single sheets of paper and one with only three-tenths colored. Press the "5" key on your calculator to show that we have five whole units. To separate our ones from our tens we will want to use a DECIMAL POINT. Find that key and enter the point and then we can enter the three to show tenths. Does your display agree with the numeral that I am writing on the chalkboard? (THE TEACHER WRITES "5.3" ON THE CHALKBOARD.)

Teacher: Go back to your **small groups**. You will find a set of materials and directions for organizing your group's activity.

Calculator Usage

When working with hundredths, money is often used as a model. Children learn to write three pennies as 3¢ <u>and</u> as $.03. While the money model is

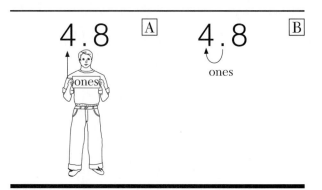

FIGURE 10.2

a convenient model for developing <u>hundredths</u>, it is important to also represent hundredths as parts of a whole in a way that <u>ten hundredths can be related to one tenth</u>. When pupils use calculators there will be frequent situations where .10 is displayed as .1. When adding 3.05 and 2.05 <u>on the calculator</u>, the **display** will show 5.1—not 5.10. This can be a source of confusion if the model is not used to show that 10 of the .01 can be written as .10 or .1.

Ten-by-ten squares of graph paper can be easily cut out to make the hundredths. If these square regions are copied onto one side of a sheet of paper, when the squares are cut out the other side will be blank and can be used to represent whole units. These same square units may be cut into tenths— showing .1 on one side and ten of the .01 on the back. (See Figure 10.3.)

10.3 TEACHING DECIMAL FRACTION CONCEPTS AT THE INTERMEDIATE LEVEL

Many students develop an interest in decimal fractions through explorations with the calculator. When the calculator divides, it does not display remainders—it shows decimal fractions. To be able to interpret and round these numbers pupils must be familiar with this form of recording numbers. Operations using common fractions are most frequently calculated on widely available calculators ONLY after changing the common fractions to decimal fraction notation.

At the intermediate level, pupil proficiency in the use of decimal fractions is extended to include decimal fraction names for common fractions (terminating and nonterminating decimals) and operations using these decimal fractions. By the time students complete the elementary school program they will have mastered most of the basic concepts of decimal fractions.

The following represents a typical sequence for teaching decimal and advanced percent concepts at the intermediate level. (See Chapter 9 for the development of introductory percent concepts.)

Grade 4

Maintain previously learned concepts
Explore thousandths
Add and subtract decimal fractions
Estimate sums and differences
Examine decimal concepts related to use of calculators

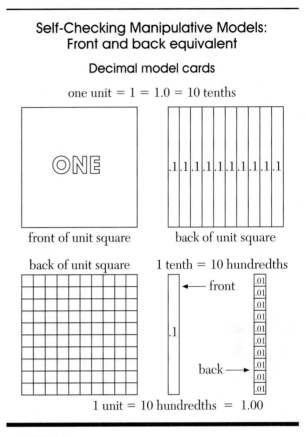

Self-Checking Manipulative Models: Front and back equivalent

Decimal model cards

one unit = 1 = 1.0 = 10 tenths

front of unit square   back of unit square

back of unit square   1 tenth = 10 hundredths

1 unit = 10 hundredths = 1.00

FIGURE 10.3

Solve problems requiring addition and subtraction of decimals

Grade 5

Maintain previously learned concepts
Estimate products
Extend ratio concepts
Multiply decimal fractions
Extend percent concepts
Extend concepts related to calculator usage
Solve problems using decimals and percent

Grade 6

Maintain previously learned concepts
Divide decimal fractions
Estimate quotients
Change percents to fractions/decimals and fractions/decimals to percent
Examine percent as a ratio
Explore terminating, repeating and nonterminating decimals
Extend decimal concepts related to calculator usage
Apply decimal and percent to problem situations

Grades 7 and 8

Express rational and irrational numbers using decimal notation
Approximate square roots using calculators
Find percent/rate/base
Use decimal fractions and percent as related to consumer mathematics

10.4 MAINTENANCE AND EXTENSION OF THE MEANING OF DECIMAL FRACTIONS

It is the intermediate teacher's responsibility to extend the pupil's understanding of decimal notation. In examining decimals students will reexplore many concepts that were first developed with common fractions. For example, students will learn to compare and find equivalent names for decimal fractions in a way similar to that used for comparing common fractions. In addition, pupils must learn to make the **connections** between the sets of common fractions and decimal fractions.

Developing Number Sense with Decimals

When first working with decimal fractions pupils will experience difficulty deciding which of two decimal expressions names the larger number. When comparing .13 to .2, students tend to focus upon the size of the numeral and not the positional value of the digits. Since .13 has two digits and .2 has one digit, the pupil believes .13 <u>must</u> represent the greater amount. It is important that the teacher structure hands-on explorations using decimal fraction models so pupils can develop the appropriate thinking strategy.

Let's examine a fragment of a lesson structured to help students develop a "sense" of the relative size of two decimal fractions.

Teacher-Guided Interactive Learning Activity

LESSON FRAGMENT

M: Comparison of decimal fractions

A: Fourth grade

T: Models

H: Concept of tenths and hundredths expressed as decimal fractions

Teacher: I have written two decimal fractions on the chalkboard—.2 and .13. Which numeral names the largest number? Darcy?

Darcy: Thirteen-hundredths.

Teacher: How did you arrive at that answer?

Darcy: Thirteen is bigger than two.

Teacher: Let's see if we can use a model to <u>verify</u> what you said. Everyone take out your 100 grids that we use to illustrate hundredths. Let's shade 13 of the hundredths to illustrate .13. Darcy, you can place your illustration in the chalk tray. Now take one of your unit regions that is marked into tenths. Shade two of the tenths. Barbara, bring your model and place it in the chalk tray next to Darcy's. Now, do our models show that 13 hundredths is larger than two tenths, Darcy?

Darcy: No, it looks like the two-tenths is larger. (SEE FIGURE 10.4A.)

Teacher: Barbara, you have your hand up—do you have an observation?

Barbara: I knew that two-tenths was larger.

Teacher: How did you know, Barbara?

Barbara: Well, my mother told me I could just put a zero after a decimal number and then I could compare them. So I put a zero after the two and I saw that it was 20. I knew 20 was larger than 13.

Teacher: Does that always work, Barbara?

Barbara: No, you can't put a zero after a whole number because it moves it over into the tens. But that doesn't happen when you work with the decimals.

Teacher: All right, let's test Barbara's procedure using our models. Take out your tenth strips and let's show two-tenths. We would write that as

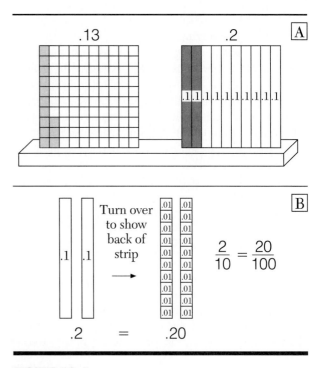

FIGURE 10.4

"point two." Now how can we rename this into hundredths?

Darcy: Look, teacher—if you turn the strips over <u>this</u> way you can trade each tenth in for 10 hundredths. That makes 20 hundredths—just as Barbara said. (SEE FIGURE 10.4B.)

Teacher: Very good! Let's try seven-tenths. Will it be renamed 70 hundredths?

Bill: It's easy—you just trade each tenth in for ten hundredths and you'll get 70 hundredths. When you write it you just put a zero behind the seven and you have 70.

Teacher: Do .7 and .70 name the same amount? Bill?

Bill: Yes.

Teacher: How did your trade show that?

Bill: We traded seven tenths for 70 hundredths.

Teacher: I have written a few numbers on your practice sheets. Each group should use its materials to model each amount. For each pair of numbers, draw a ring around the greater number.

Equivalent names for decimal fractions are developed as children learn to compare fractions. For example, in the previous lesson fragment the student learned that .2 and .20 name the same decimal fraction. The concept of equivalent names is also developed through <u>trading tasks</u> similar to the trading activities that are used with whole numbers. For example, ten hundredths (.10) can be traded for one tenth (.1), and ten tenths (1.0) can be traded for one unit (1). Trading activities become important foundations for adding and subtracting decimal fractions—especially when regrouping is required.

When students understand the nature of tenths and hundredths, extension of this skill to thousandths, ten-thousandths, and so on, is simply using previously learned skills with the new decimal names. While some pupils may need models to make this transition, most students can bypass models by using their understanding of the place-value system.

Small-Group Learning Activity

Small groups of students may explore the relationship between tenths and hundredths as they compete in decimal spinner games. Figure 10.5 illustrates how a spinner can be constructed for a game activity that requires players to trade hundredths for tenths and tenths for units. After flipping the pointer, a player collects decimal models to illustrate the amount indicated on the spinner. Each time the player spins, models will be added to his/her collection. When a student collects ten or more tenths, the player must trade ten of the tenths for

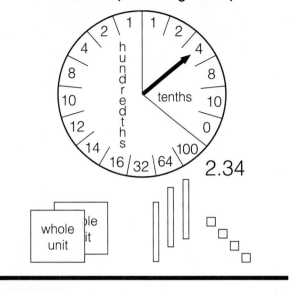

Small-Group Learning Activity

FIGURE 10.5

one whole unit. Anytime a player accumulates ten or more hundredths a trade must be made for one tenth. In the event a student spins "100 hundredths," a trade may be made for one whole unit. After each spin and trade the player must record the amount as a numeral. The first student to record <u>any</u> numeral with three consecutive digits (1.23; 2.34; 3.45; etc.) is the winner.

Reading and Writing Decimal Fractions

Pupils will need help learning to read decimal fractions. A numeral written as 0.52 may have "5" in the tenths place and "2" in the hundredths position, but is **read** as "fifty-two hundredths." When reading digits <u>to the right of the decimal point</u>, students consider the entire numeral and say the "whole number name" for the digits—THEN look at the <u>position</u> of the last digit and name its value. For example, in 0.3845 the pupil would read the digits as "three thousand, eight hundred, forty-five" and <u>then</u> say the name of the position in which the "5" is found—"ten-thousandths."

When reading whole numbers and decimal amounts—as in 26.086—a pupil should read the whole number ("twenty-six") and then the separating point, saying "**and**." Once the decimal point is named, the pupil reads the decimal amount "eighty-six" and the position name, "thousandths." Teachers should recognize that students may have acquired poor habits in earlier grade levels. The reading of the amount "123" often is orally given as "one hundred **and** twenty-three." Such a practice causes difficulty when reading an amount such as 100.023. When the amount "one hundred and twenty-three thousandths" is read many pupils will write .123 instead of the proper numeral. To avoid confusion, some individuals <u>choose</u> to read an amount as "one hundred **point** twenty-three thousandths" or "one hundred **point** zero two three."

Small-Group Learning Activity

Students quickly recognize the importance of properly reading decimal amounts if given lists of figures to be "dictated" to a group using calculators. A teacher can assemble "teams" to compete in a gamelike activity. Each member of the team is given a list of numerals to be communicated to the rest of the group. For each correct numeral displayed on the team's calculators, the team gets a point. Each team member is given an opportunity to read the list of numerals and to check to see how many recorded it properly. (The teacher may wish to set restrictions such as "only read the amount once," "do not use the word—point," etc.) The game can be made more meaningful if each list of numbers is to be added on the calculators and only correct sums receive a point. Pupils soon recognize how important it is to listen carefully, record properly, and to **communicate** efficiently.

When developing places to the right of the dec-

imal point, the teacher may find it useful to display a decimal value chart so pupils may see the relationship between the positions to the right and to the left of the decimal point. As developed in the primary lessons, students should see the role of the decimal point as a "locater." <u>The decimal point locates where the units position is.</u> The <u>tens</u> position is found by moving one position to the <u>left</u> of the ones—and the <u>ten**ths**</u> are found by moving one position to the <u>right</u> of the ones. In a similar manner, the teacher may help pupils see that two places to the <u>left</u> of the units position would be <u>hundreds</u> and two places to the <u>right</u> of the units is the <u>hundredths</u>. With encouragement, pupils see that the pattern is the same for all positions. (See Figure 10.6.)

When pupils explored whole numbers in earlier grade levels, they learned different ways of expressing an amount—in expanded notation, with exponents, as fractions, etc. At the intermediate level, students extend these skills to include expressing decimals with various notations. Some of the notations for 26.843 that are commonly examined are illustrated in Figure 10.7.

When naming decimal amounts in expanded notation using exponents, pupils benefit greatly by again examining the relationship illustrated in Figure 10.6. A pattern is easily recognized in the chart—as one moves to the left (from the units) the powers go up by a positive one; while moving to the right the powers behave in a similar manner, but the powers are negative numbers. In classrooms that introduce writing amounts in expanded

Decimal Position Relationship Chart

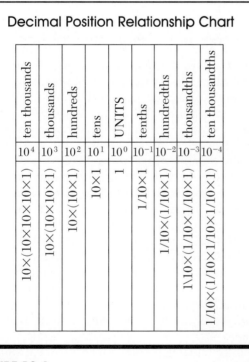

ten thousands	thousands	hundreds	tens	UNITS	tenths	hundredths	thousandths	ten thousandths
10^4	10^3	10^2	10^1	10^0	10^{-1}	10^{-2}	10^{-3}	10^{-4}
$10\times(10\times10\times10\times1)$	$10\times(10\times10\times1)$	$10\times(10\times1)$	10×1	1	$1/10\times1$	$1/10\times(1/10\times1)$	$1\backslash10\times(1/10\times1/10\times1)$	$1/10\times(1/10\times1/10\times1/10\times1)$

FIGURE 10.6

Rewriting a decimal fraction in expanded notation

$$\boxed{26.843}$$

Using Words:

2 tens + 6 ones + 8 tenths + 4 hundredths + 3 thousandths

Using Numerals:

20 + 6 + .8 + .04 + .003

Using Fractions:

20 + 6 + 8/10 + 4/100 + 3/1000

Using Exponents:

$$(20\times10^1) + (6\times10^0) + (8\times10^{-1}) + (4\times10^{-2}) + (3\times10^{-3})$$

FIGURE 10.7

notation with exponents, some pupils question the need for negative exponents. A mathematical explanation of why any number raised to the zero power is the number 1 and the treatment of negative exponents usually are delayed until pupils have had many experiences with exponents. However, pupils can recognize that "0" and the negative exponents are appropriate as they examine the **pattern** of each position to the left being one less than the right adjacent position.

Individual Learning Activities

A teacher can use a learning station to extend individual skills. Material at a station might consist of one set of cards illustrating models of decimal fractions and another set of cards on which decimal fractions are written. Such materials would allow the teacher to vary the activity by using different directions, such as:

1. Match each numeral card with its model.
2. Separate the numerals cards (or model cards) into piles representing tenths, hundredths, and thousandths.
3. Place the cards (numeral or model) into a sequence from least amount to greatest amount. (Letters may be written on the backs of the numeral cards so that a correct sequence of the numerals can be turned over to spell out a message.) (See Figure 10.8.)

Individual research questions may be assigned that require a pupil to find applications of decimals in his/her environment. For example, "Bring in a list of the many different ways you see decimals being used in your home," or "How many ways can you find decimals being used with respect to an automobile?", or "How many ways can you find decimals being used with respect to sports?" Individual pupils may be asked to bring in examples of decimals found in magazines and newspapers to contribute to a bulletin board depicting the ways decimals are used in the media.

10.5 TEACHING THE MEANINGS OF ADDITION AND SUBTRACTION OF DECIMAL FRACTIONS

Most students have no difficulty applying the whole number addition and subtraction skills to these same operations using decimal fractions. Pupils already recognize that addends can be placed into an algorithm so that the units are lined up in the ones

Independent Learning Activities

Arrange numeral cards in order — least to greatest. Turn cards over for secret message.

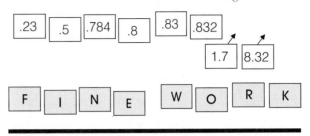

FIGURE 10.8

column, the tens in another, etc. When working with decimal fractions pupils must apply this understanding to the positions to the right of the decimal point (tenths, hundredths, etc.). When adding columns of whole numbers, students encountered "ragged" lefthand columns. For example, when adding 4,322 + 27 + 327, only in the ones and tens columns do the numerals have the same number of digits. When pupils work with decimal fractions they will find that righthand columns can also be "ragged," as in 4.17 + 23.9 + 4.017.

Developing the Meaning of Addition in a Problem-Solving Context (With and Without Regrouping)

It is the teacher's responsibility to help students recognize how properties and skills of whole numbers may be extended to numbers written as decimal fractions. As pupils reexplore these operations the teacher has another opportunity to strengthen students' background in place value. Activities should be planned that use models to help students both to transfer the skills learned when using the addition and subtraction algorithms with whole numbers and to build skill in reading and writing decimal fractions. Figure 10.9 illustrates how 2.17 + 1.36 might be set up with a model to represent the various fractional parts. Using the small square regions, pupils would trade in ten of the 13 hundredths for one strip representing the tenths. The teacher might also move the addends to show that while the order of addends may change, the sum will still remain the same (commutative property).

Once pupils learn to associate numerals with their models and learn to construct models to fit a given numeral, they will be ready to deal with the operation at a more abstract level. Some students

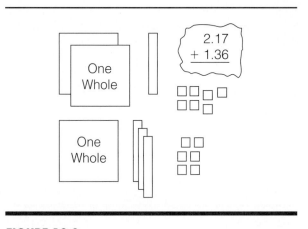

FIGURE 10.9

can readily recognize addition when performed with manipulative materials, but cannot associate the actions with the algorithm. In the activity that follows, the pupils are learning how to take a problem such as 2.38 + 18.4 + 7 + .95 and line up units, tenths, and hundredths into columns. Note that the teacher emphasizes the importance of adding like values rather than telling pupils to "line up the decimal points."

To prepare for this activity, the teacher has assembled teams of five pupils. Each team member has reached into the teacher's "grab bag" and pulled out a decimal picture card.

TEAM COMPETITIONS

Teacher: Each of you have a picture card illustrating some amount. I have also given your team several numeral "grid slips" on which you are to write your amount. However, before we write the numeral I am going to give you SPECIAL instructions for this activity. (THE TEACHER SHOWS THE CHART ILLUSTRATED IN FIGURE 10.10.) You can see that you will need to use your crayons to write the numeral because the digit for the tenths is going to be colored red—the digit for hundredths will be blue—the decimal will be black—the units will be yellow and so on. Billy, do you have a question?

Billy: The grid slips have a lot of spaces. What should we do with the extra spaces?

Teacher: A good question, Billy. We are going to write our digits—one to a space. When you are finished, you should cut off the unfilled grids. Now look at your model card and write your numeral. When you finish, give your card and numeral to another member of your team to make sure you have written it correctly. If you need another grid slip, ask your team leader.

Teacher: (AFTER ALL TEAMS FINISH THE TASK

THE TEACHER HAS EACH TEAM CAPTAIN COLLECT THE GRID SLIPS.) We are now ready to get a score to see how the teams compare. The team captain should shuffle the slips and then give each member a slip—it does not matter whether you have your own slip or not. We are going to combine the amounts. What operation will we use, Ezra?

Ezra: If we want a total, we'll add.

Teacher: Good! If we are going to add, we will need to put all of the units together, and all of the tenths together—won't we?

Ezra: We can just line up the colors, teacher. All the tenths are red and the hundredths are blue. We can add the blue column and the red column and all of the columns.

Teacher: Very perceptive, Ezra. All right, teams—find your totals and send your leader to write it on the chalkboard.

To make the game more "competitive," the teacher could have teams replace the model cards in the grab bag and try again. The score of four "heats" (games) could be used for team standings. As a follow-up activity, the teacher may have each team paste their numeral strips onto a sheet of paper (in a column format) along with their model cards and display the work on the bulletin board.

After an activity such as the one described in the team competition, the teacher would explore how pupils might line up their columns when color coding <u>was not used</u>. In the previous activity the decimal point was colored black, so students quickly pointed out that lining up the black dots would be a way of getting the columns in order. The teacher should use this pupil-suggested "rule"

Independent Learning Activity

Write numerals for model cards.
Use crayons to write digits and use this color code!

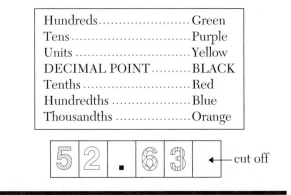

Hundreds	Green
Tens	Purple
Units	Yellow
DECIMAL POINT	BLACK
Tenths	Red
Hundredths	Blue
Thousandths	Orange

 ← cut off

FIGURE 10.10

as an opportunity to reinforce the role of the decimal point—"it points to where the ones are located and if we line up the ones, then everything else falls into place." Whenever possible in later lessons, the teacher should again question why lining up the decimal point makes the addition easier (it puts like values into a column).

Problem Solving in a Small-Group Activity

Small-group activities can be as simple as teaming children to review the meaning of addition of decimals by having one student explain the process to another student. A more complex activity would group several students into a team to investigate a problem that will require the use of addition of decimals. A challenging team activity can be constructed by using an adding-machine tape. Fifteen to 20 numbers (with differing numbers of digits to the right of the decimal) can be entered and shown on an adding-machine tape. On machines with a "floating decimal point" the "columns" do not line up so the activity becomes more challenging. The teacher will print out the tape and then cut the strip into several segments. The segments will be distributed to teams. They will cooperatively find the total of the original tape by finding the totals of each segment and then combining the subtotals. Even when pupils use handheld calculators the activity can be challenging—for entry errors do occur and team totals often do not correspond with the grand total (which the teacher removed from the tape).

Individual Learning Activities

Procedures, such as the ones listed above in the team competition, and small-group activities, can be modified into individual learning activities. A learning station might include:

1. Student chooses any five decimal model cards; uses color-coding to write numerals; and finds the sum.
2. Student takes four separate segments of adding-machine tape and finds the total of each segment. Then the segment totals are added to find the grand total.
3. Student works a problem similar to the problem in "b" but the total is given and ONE of the addends is missing from one of the segments. The student is to find the missing addend.
4. Student finds the perimeter of polygons whose sides have decimal measures. (Note: Since all measures will have the same de-

gree of precision—tenths, hundredths, thousandths—students will not build skill working with "ragged' decimals.)

Individual research projects are also valuable for individual study. A pupil might be encouraged to find out when scientists use decimal fractions. A student might be directed to cut out segments from the newspaper where decimals are used. Some student could be encouraged to construct problems using numbers found in the newspaper segment.

Developing the Meaning of Subtraction

Subtraction of decimal fractions is often taught concurrently with addition. Since pupils already know how to subtract whole numbers with three and four digits, applications to decimal fractions are easily acquired.

When exploring subtraction, manipulative models are used more to reinforce decimal concepts than to develop the subtraction algorithm. Since the "take-away" subtraction model easily illustrates the algorithm, modeling activity begins with only the minuend modeled. For example, in $5.41 - 1.32$ only the "5.41" is modeled with the manipulative materials.

Base ten blocks are often used when exploring decimals. The large block (1,000) is selected to illustrate a <u>whole unit</u>; the flats (100) are used to illustrated tenths (since it takes ten to make a large cube); a rod is used to show a hundredth; and the small single blocks show thousandths (since it takes 1000 small blocks to make one large block). In classrooms where base ten blocks are not available, teachers use flat models (sheets of paper and strips), place-value charts, or a 20-bead computing abacus to model the subtraction algorithm. Figure 10.11 illustrates a flat model set up for $5.41 - 1.32$. The teacher should emphasize the trading in of one tenth for ten hundredths when using manipulative materials. The use of materials in this case not only helps pupils visualize the decimal fractions but will also strengthen pupil understanding of regrouping.

While the algorithm for subtraction of whole numbers and decimal fractions is almost identical, students do experience difficulty when they encounter a situation where there are more digits in the subtrahend than in the minuend—for example $5.1 - 3.417$. When the pupil writes the problem into the algorithm format, there will be no digits above the one and the seven of the subtrahend! Some pupils recognize that they had similar problems when they subtracted common fractions, when there were unlike denominators. In this problem the 5.1 is written in tenths and the 3.417 is

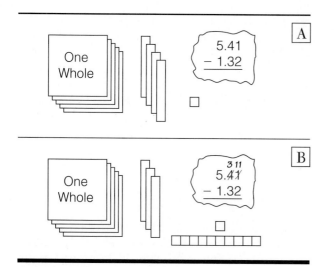

FIGURE 10.11

written in thousandths. If thousandths were chosen as the common denominator, then 5.1 would become 5.100 (since $\frac{1}{10} = \frac{100}{1000}$). It is important for pupils to explore this kind of problem—using a fraction algorithm or using concrete models so they will understand how "affixing" zeros behind the "1" of 5.1 does not change the value of the number.

In the lesson fragment that follows the teacher is using a 20-bead computing abacus to help pupils learn how to subtract a decimal fraction from a whole number.

Teacher-Guided Interactive Learning Activity

CONCEPT INTRODUCED FROM PROBLEM-SOLVING SITUATION

LESSON FRAGMENT

M: Subtracting a decimal fraction from a whole number. Affixing zeros to find a common denominator.

A: Fifth-grade class

T: Models

H: Addition of decimals with regrouping

PROBLEM-SOLVING SITUATION:

LAST WEEK, AS A PART OF A JOB AWARENESS PROGRAM, A PARENT VISITED THE CLASSROOM AND DESCRIBED SOME ASPECTS OF HER JOB. SHE LEFT WITH THE CLASS SOME METAL PIECES OF STEEL THAT HER MILLING MACHINE PRODUCES.

Teacher: You remember that Kim's mother operates a computerized milling machine that cuts off pieces of metal from bars of steel. We all examined the metal bars her machine can produce. How narrow would one of her metal bars become if Kim's mother places a steel cube, five inches on a side, in the milling machine and programs the machine to take 1.29 inches from one size?

Maya: If she milled $1\frac{1}{2}$ inches she would have $3\frac{1}{2}$ inches left. 1.29 is less than $1\frac{1}{2}$ inches—but it's close. So I would estimate that the bar would be ABOUT 3 and $\frac{3}{4}$ inches.

Teacher: I'll write that down to check the reasonableness of our answer later, Maya. To help us work through this problem, I am going to use the abacus. Let's write the problem on the board. We want to subtract 1.29 from 5. Since we are going to need tenths and hundredths, I will put five beads on this third wire and place the decimal point to identify which column is the ones. Since we do not have any beads on the tenths wire, we can record a **zero** in the tenths column. And since we do not have any beads on the hundredths wire we can record a **zero** in the hundredths place. (SEE FIGURE 10.12A.)

Teacher: We want to remove nine hundredths, but we do not have any hundredths. We will need to **regroup** from the tenths. Since we don't have any beads in the tenths to regroup to hundredths, what can we do to get some tenths? Jules?

Jules: When we used the abacus for whole numbers we just traded in one hundred for ten tens, so I guess we can trade in one of the units for ten of the tenths.

Teacher: That's a good observation, Jules—it is much like whole number subtraction and regrouping. I can trade one unit for ten tenths. (TEACHER SLIDES ONE BEAD FROM THE UNITS ON THE FRONT OF THE ABACUS AND BRINGS TEN BEADS FROM THE BACK OF THE ABACUS TO THE FRONT OF THE TENTHS WIRE.) Let's record what we did. We do not have five units anymore. How many do we have, Maya?

Maya: Four ones.

Teacher: I'm going to record that on the algorithm by crossing out the "5" and writing a "4" to show that we **now** have four ones. I traded the unit for ten tenths. What can I record now, Nell?

Nell: You can mark through the zero and record that there are ten tenths.

Teacher: (TEACHER RECORDS AS DIRECTED. SEE FIGURE 10.12B.) Now I still need to get hundredths, but I have some tenths now. We can trade one of the tenths for how many hundredths, Wilhelm?

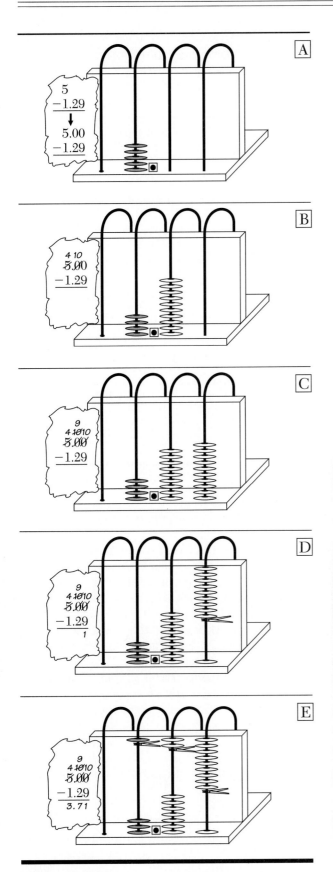

FIGURE 10.12

Wilhelm: You can get ten hundredths and you only have nine tenths left so you ought to record that.

Teacher: Excellent, Wilhelm. We do not want to forget that we traded in one of the tenths, so I will mark out the "10" and write a "9" in the tenths column. I should also show that I now have ten hundredths, so I'll mark out the "0" and record a "10" in the hundredths column. (SEE FIGURE 10.12C.)

Teacher: Now we have enough hundredths that we can take nine away. Merta, how many hundredths will we have left if we subtract nine hundredths?

Merta: One hundredth.

Teacher: (TEACHER PUSHES UP NINE HUN-DREDTHS AND HOLDS THEM IN PLACE WITH A PIN. THESE ARE LEFT ON THE **FRONT** OF THE ABACUS SO THE PUPILS CAN SEE THE AMOUNT TAKEN AWAY AND THE AMOUNT REMAINING.) We'll record the one hundredth on our algorithm. Now, Charlene, how many tenths will be left if we subtract two-tenths from nine-tenths?

Calculators allow students to explore mathematical relationships.

Charlene: Seven-tenths.

Teacher: (PUSHES UP TWO-TENTHS AND PLACES A CLIP TO HOLD THEM.) I'll record that we have seven-tenths left. (SEE FIGURE 10.12D.) And now, Cindy, how many units will be left if we subtract one unit from four units?

Cindy: There will be three left.

Teacher: (PUSHES UP ONE UNIT AND PLACES A CLIP TO HOLD IT.) Now let's record what happened. First we will want to place a decimal point to show that we are now working with the ONES. When we took one unit from four units we had three units left, so we can record a "3." (SEE FIGURE 10.12E.) How narrow will the metal bar be after the computerized milling machine takes off a piece 1.29 inches wide? Nat?

Nat: Three and seventy-one hundredths inches will be left, which is close to Maya's estimate.

Teacher: Very good, Nat. Now, to help us learn to subtract with decimals, I have problems which would require Kim's mother to use different sizes of metal. Each group should appoint someone to be the "materials verifier," working the problem using the abacus, decimal blocks, or place-value chart. You will also need a "calculator verifier" to check your work with a calculator. The rest of the group will be the "recorders"—writing out the problems and recording the work. After one or two problems, you might wish to trade jobs so everyone has a chance to use the materials and the calculator.

10.6 TEACHING MULTIPLICATION OF DECIMAL FRACTIONS

Since intermediate-level students are already familiar with the algorithm used for multiplying whole numbers and common fractions, the development of skill in multiplying decimal fractions is directed toward extending these skills and deepening the meanings associated with decimals. In life encounters, individuals **generally use calculators** when multiplying decimal fractions so skill development should be directed toward **understanding the operation** and **estimating products**. Rules such as "count the number of places to the right of the decimal in the problem and put that many places to the right of the decimal in the product" seem to have little application when working with a machine that will "round" excessive digits and not display unnecessary zeros. For instance .25 × .48 may be .1200 when calculated using paper and pencil, but it will appear as .12 on a calculator display. Pupils who count four places to the right of the decimal point in the factors will not see

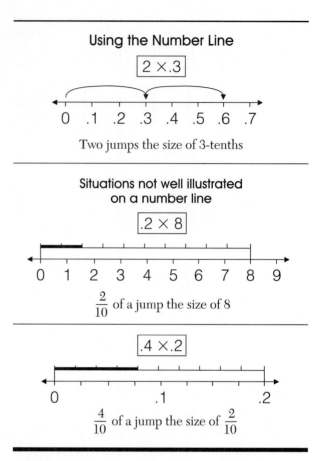

Using the Number Line

$2 \times .3$

Two jumps the size of 3-tenths

Situations not well illustrated on a number line

$.2 \times 8$

$\frac{2}{10}$ of a jump the size of 8

$.4 \times .2$

$\frac{4}{10}$ of a jump the size of $\frac{2}{10}$

FIGURE 10.13

four places when the calculator computes the product.

Students should first explore multiplication as applied to decimal fractions by using manipulative materials. While a number line can be used to illustrate problems that have a whole number multiplier (2 × .3), it is not very effective when showing decimal fraction multipliers (.2 × 8) or problems in which both factors are decimal fractions (.4 × .2). (See Figure 10.13.)

The array (or area) model, first used when multiplication of whole numbers were introduced, is a valuable tool for illustrating problems in which both factors are tenths. The drawing allows pupils to see why the product is hundredths. The algorithm also helps the pupils to see why it is possible to "ignore" the decimals until the final product is determined. Looking at the diagram (Figure 10.14) the student will recognize that ".2 × .4" produces a shaded section that is a 2-by-4 array and that the size of the square regions is found by multiplying tenths times tenths.

While it is possible to draw diagrams that would illustrate tenths times hundredths (thousandths) or hundredths times hundredths (ten thousandths),

Multiplying Decimal Fractions

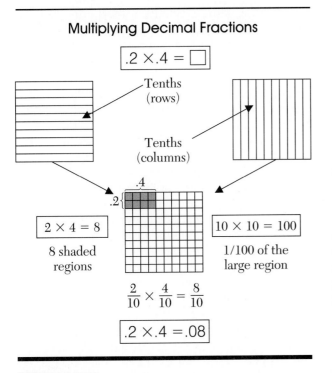

FIGURE 10.14

the number of small regions to be drawn makes the illustrations a little cumbersome. Therefore teachers generally use tenths times tenths to help pupils recognize that the drawings for decimal fractions are really just a special case of common fractions (denominators are multiples of ten). Once this relationship is established, teachers use the common fraction algorithm to help pupils find the proper placement of the decimal in the product. Figure 10.15 illustrates a typical fragment of a practice exercise that may be used at a learning station, as a

Small-Group Learning Activity

Find the missing denominators and use this information to place the decimals in the product.

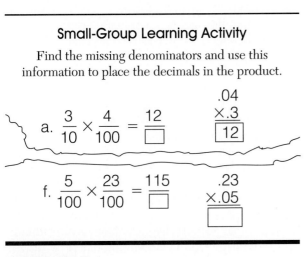

FIGURE 10.15

Exploring Patterns

$$1 \times \frac{1}{10} = \frac{1}{10} \qquad\qquad 1 \times .1 = .1$$

$$\frac{1}{10} \times \frac{1}{10} = \frac{1}{100} \qquad\qquad .1 \times .1 = .01$$

$$\frac{1}{10} \times \frac{1}{100} = \frac{1}{1000} \qquad\qquad .1 \times .01 = .001$$

$$\frac{1}{100} \times \frac{1}{100} = \frac{1}{10,000} \qquad .01 \times .01 = .0001$$

FIGURE 10.16

cooperative group activity, or as a part of a teacher-directed lesson. The exercises are designed to promote discovery of a pattern and build a readiness for developing a "rule" for multiplying decimal fractions.

Once pupils can associate a decimal fraction multiplication problem with an illustration and with the common fraction algorithm, attention should be directed to the patterns found multiplying decimal fractions. Figure 10.16 illustrates the way a teacher might arrange examples to help pupils formulate a "rule" that could be used without changing the number to a common fraction. Teachers should have students **formulate** a rule since such a procedure builds mathematical thinking skills. While student-discovered rules may not be as precise as those found in textbooks ("The number of decimal places in the product will correspond to the sum of the decimal places in the factors"), they are more meaningful and will be more useful to the student.

Small-Group Calculator Activities

Small groups are often employed to develop problem-solving skills, but many teachers do not recognize that small groups also can be utilized when exploring mathematical patterns. Since calculators will quickly give a product—and place the decimal point properly—they may be useful in examining patterns for the placement of the point in products. Calculators can mislead pupils in the formulation of procedures, but a teacher can overcome some of these obstacles by carefully choosing the numbers which will be used. For initial explorations with calculators, it is wise to avoid multiplying factors which end in five since the product of a multiple of five and any even digit will result in zero (which calculators often do not display).

The following illustrates one way a small group of students might discover a rule for placing the decimal in the product. The group is given the directions:

Each person in your group should—

1. Pick a whole number from the list and multiply it by one-tenth. Write down your answer and share your answer with the other members of your group. Did you discover anything in common with all the answers?

2. Pick a whole number from the list and multiply it by one-hundredth. Write down your answer and share your answer with other members of your group. Did you discover anything in common with all the answers?

3. Pick two decimals, either both tenths, both hundredths, or one tenth and one hundredth. Multiply your two decimal fractions. Write down an equation that describes what you did and the result you got. Share your equation with the members of your group. Discuss the location of the decimal in your products. Try to make up a rule that will help you determine where the decimal will appear in your answer. Test your rule with other examples.

4. Pick two numbers that involve either tenths, hundredths, or thousandths. Ask another member of the group to **estimate** where the decimal will occur in the product. Test the estimate by using your calculator.

5. Make up a number that ends in five. Try out your rule. Does this product fit your rule? Try several numbers that end in five. Do they always fit your rule? Can you give a reason why they may not fit the rule?

Individual Learning Activities Using Calculators

Estimation is an essential skill when calculators are used to find products (and quotients). Failure to record a decimal may result in an incorrect product. Estimation helps establish **the reasonableness of a product.**

Learning stations lend themselves to developing the pupil's decimal number sense. A station may display a list of problems. When the student visits the station he/she is directed to estimate the product of each problem. A suggestion may be given that each number (such as 6.73 and 8.54) be rounded to the nearest whole number and the product be used as an estimate. After all estimates are written on the sheet, the pupil is directed to compute the product using the calculator. Each estimate would then be checked to see if it falls within an "acceptable" range.

Learning-station activities may also be constructed that require the pupil to identify which products from a list of completed problems seem reasonable and not reasonable. After recording their **guesses**, pupils may use the calculator to see if they were "close." The teacher may wish to create a gamelike environment by awarding "points" for the estimate falling within a certain range.

Common fractions also may be used when estimating products. For example, in .25 × 16.4 the child may remember that .25 is equivalent to $\frac{1}{4}$. Since one-fourth of 16 is four, a good estimate of the product would be four. Pupils should also recognize that a fraction that is close—but not equivalent—may be helpful when estimating. When estimating the product for .37 × 90, it might make the "guessing" easier to think $\frac{1}{3}$ of 90 is 30.

Pupils can also learn to estimate products based on the leftmost nonzero digit of each factor. The product estimate is based on these two 1-digit factors. Once the estimate is made, the pupil would find the product using a calculator to check the appropriateness of her estimate. For example, in the problem .0378 × .0422 the child would estimate the product using three-hundredths times four-hundredths (12-ten-thousandths) and then find the product using the calculator (.001596).

10.7 DEVELOPING AN UNDERSTANDING OF DIVISION OF DECIMALS

Division with decimal fractions provides the teacher with another opportunity to strengthen pupil understanding of the division operation and its relationship to multiplication. Explorations on the number line can be used to illustrate the measurement concept of division, while base ten blocks and the 20-bead abacus can illustrate the partition concept and develop the division algorithm (using a whole number divisor). (See Figure 10.17.)

Whole number operations serve as a foundation for developing skills with decimal fractions. Before pupils encounter the division operation with decimal fractions they should already be reasonably proficient in dividing whole numbers with 2- and 3-digit divisors. Problems requiring money quotients have established a readiness for decimal fraction division, so learning to divide decimal fractions with a whole number divisor seldom gives difficulty to the student who is already proficient with division of whole numbers.

Measurement Division Illustration

How many jumps the size of .3
can you take from 1.2?

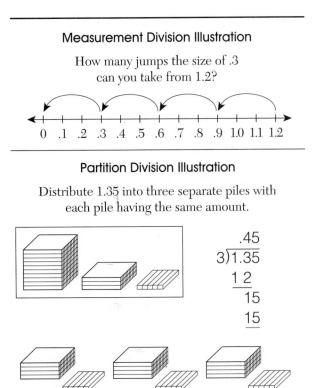

Partition Division Illustration

Distribute 1.35 into three separate piles with
each pile having the same amount.

$$
\begin{array}{r}
.45 \\
3\overline{)1.35} \\
1\ 2 \\
\hline
15 \\
15 \\
\hline
\end{array}
$$

FIGURE 10.17

Precalculator Concept Development

Problems with a decimal fraction divisor are generally not introduced until pupils can perform division involving a decimal fraction dividend and a whole number divisor (for example, 4.86 ÷ 2). In problem-solving situations, a **calculator will usually be employed to work more complex division problems,** but pupils still need to be reasonably proficient with decimal fraction division when calculators are not available.

When a teacher introduces problems such as .24 ÷ .3, **estimation** will be the first strategy employed. Using the measurement model for division, the pupils should recognize that .24 is **less** than .3 so the quotient must be less than one. Some students may see that 24 ÷ 3 will be 8 and then reason that it cannot be eight whole units, so it must be $\frac{8}{10}$. It is important that division be developed from an **estimation perspective** in order to strengthen the **estimation skills** that will be vital when using calculators. Once an estimate is made, development of a procedure for calculating quotients may be more thoroughly explored.

The most commonly used procedure for calculating quotients when the divisor is a decimal fraction is to restructure the problem so that the divisor

becomes a whole number. Since pupils are proficient using whole number divisors, the calculation is simply an application of previously learned skills. To help the student visualize how the problem is restructured, a process similar to that used when teaching division of fractions (the complex fraction approach) is used. In Figure 10.18 the teacher first rewrites the division algorithm into a complex fraction form. Using identity, a name for "1" is chosen that will rename the denominator (divisor) into a whole number. Once a fractional name for one is chosen, the numerator (dividend) and the denominator (divisor) are multiplied—changing the position of the decimal point. The divisor and dividend are then moved back into the algorithm and divided as with whole number divisors.

Before formally beginning work with decimal fraction divisors, it will be helpful to have pupils review multiplying decimal fractions by tens, hundreds, thousands, etc. For example, students can complete exercises such as 10 × .45, 100 × .45, 10 × 6.4, 1000 × .003, etc. Concurrent with these exercises teachers may wish to ask questions such as, "What would you multiply 3.046 by to get

Converting a Decimal Fraction Divisor to a Whole Number Divisor

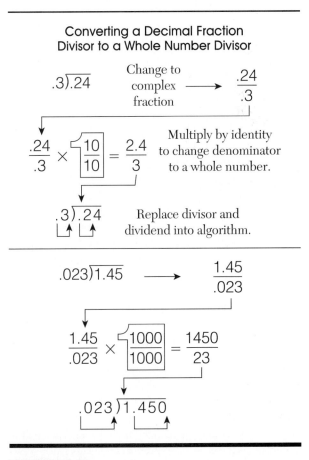

FIGURE 10.18

3046? What number times .14 will give you 14?,'' etc. After such a review, students are ready to apply this skill to the process of changing decimal fraction divisors into whole numbers.

Developing the Meaning of Division in a Problem-Solving Context

Let's examine a fragment of a lesson that introduces the child to the meaning associated with the standard division algorithm using decimals.

Teacher-Guided Interactive Learning Activity

LESSON FRAGMENT

M: Decimal division algorithm, estimation

A: Sixth-grade class

T: Models

H: Estimating quotients using leading digits, division of decimals related to division of fractions, converting a decimal divisor to a whole number divisor

PROBLEM-SOLVING SITUATION:

AN ELECTRICIAN FOUND THAT A BOX FOR A SWITCH WAS RECESSED IN THE WALL ONE-QUARTER OF AN INCH. HE HAD TO USE SOME WASHERS THAT WERE .042 OF AN INCH THICK TO SHIM THE SWITCH, SO THE SWITCH WOULD BE FLUSH WITH THE WALL WHEN IT AND THE WASHERS WERE SCREWED INTO THE BOX. HOW MANY WASHERS WILL THE ELECTRICIAN HAVE TO USE?

Teacher: Let's begin by converting our common fraction to a decimal. Questa, what is a decimal name for one-fourth?

Questa: Point, two, five.

Teacher: Good. We are trying to find out how many forty-two thousandths there are in twenty-five hundredths. Can anyone guess how the electrician might be able to **estimate** the number of washers he would need? Nick?

Nick: He could think how many four-hundredths are in two-tenths, or four-tenths in two, or fours in 20. He would **estimate** five.

Teacher: That was very creative. I could see how you were moving the decimal point over one place at a time until you got two numbers you could use. Very good.

Teacher: Before we work it with paper and pencil let's use our calculators and see how good Nick was at estimating the answer. Vera, what did you get?

Vera: I got 5.95. It's going to take six washers.

Teacher: Why do you say that?

Vera: Because the electrician is only working with whole washers and he would be off by almost a whole washer if he used five.

Teacher: That's true—but Nick's estimate was still very close, wasn't it! Remember—estimating gives you an idea of whether an answer is reasonable. It is not an exact answer. Let's see if we could work out our answer without a calculator—because sometimes even electricians leave their calculators in the truck. I'll write our problem on the board in an algorithm form. Our basic problem is 25-hundredths divided by 42-thousandths. Now if this had been simply a problem of 42 divided into 25, we could have worked through the problem just like the ones we did last week. However, this problem has a decimal fraction divisor. Is there a way of changing a decimal fraction into a whole number so that we could work this more easily? Beth?

Beth: You could multiply it by 1000—but wouldn't that throw the rest of the problem off?

Teacher: Good point! Let's rewrite our division problem into a fraction form. (THE TEACHER WRITES A FRACTION WITH A NUMERATOR OF .25 AND A DENOMINATOR OF .042.) What happens to the fraction if we multiply the denominator by 1000? (THE TEACHER WRITES "× 1000" BESIDE THE DENOMINATOR.) Beth?

Beth: We get 42, but that changes the fraction. You would **also** need to multiply the numerator by 1000.

Teacher: Can you explain why, Beth?

Beth: Well, 1000 over 1000 is a name for one and that will not really change the number—but if you multiply ONLY the denominator you would be multiplying by $\frac{1}{1000}$ and that really would change the number.

Teacher: Excellent explanation, Beth. We can multiply a number by one and the product will not change. So let's us rewrite our fraction. Our numerator is now 250 and our denominator is 42. We can record that change in our division algorithm by using this little "carat" to show how we moved the decimal when we multiplied both the divisor and the dividend by 1000. Since we have a whole number divisor we can now work the algorithm as we did last week. Just in case someone asked how we did these problems, let's work through each step together. (NOTICE THAT THE TEACHER HAS GONE TO A PARTITIVE EXPLANATION CONSISTENT WITH THE DEVELOPMENT OF THE STANDARD DIVISION ALGORITHM, EVEN

THOUGH THE BASIC NATURE OF THE ORIGI-NAL PROBLEM WAS A MEASUREMENT PROB-LEM. THE TEACHER WILL NEED TO RETURN TO THE MEASUREMENT NATURE OF THE PROBLEM AFTER DEVELOPING THE ALGO-RITHM CONCEPT.) Can we distribute two of the hundreds so that each of 42 groups will each have at least one hundred? (NO!) Can we distribute 25 tens to the 42 groups so that each has at least one ten? (NO!) Can we divide 250 ones into 42 groups so that each will have at least one? (YES) How many will each get? (5) (TEACHER RECORDS IN THE ALGORITHM AS IT PROGRESSES.) That will use up 210 and we will have 40 left. We can trade in the 40 ones for 400 tenths. Can we divide 400 tenths into 42 groups? (YES) What is the largest number of tenths that can be placed in each group? (9) That will take 378 of the tenths, leaving 22. If we wished, we could trade in the 22 tenths for 220 hundredths and continue, but we don't need to go any farther because we can see that it will take 5.9 and a little. We only have whole washers—so we can take the nearest whole number and get six washers.

When developing the algorithm, teachers should devote time to teaching pupils **how to estimate** the quotient. In 1.45 ÷ .023 the pupil might initially learn to use the **leading digit approach,** before proceeding to learn a rounding approach. In this instance, the pupil may look at the "1" of the dividend and the "2" in the hundredths place of the divisor and think, "There are 50 of the $\frac{2}{100}$s in one unit. Since I have a little more than one unit, the quotient will be a little more than 50, but less than 100." By further reasoning the pupil could see that if the lead digit were two then he would have 100 two-hundredths in two. Thus the child could decide if an answer obtained on the calculator (64.0435) seemed reasonable.

Some pupils use money as a referent when estimating quotients. They reason (in the problem above) that .023 is close to .02 or two cents. Looking at 1.45 as $1.45 students sense that there would be *about* 70 sets of two cents in $1.40, so the answer (64.0435) would be a <u>reasonable</u> quotient. In the problem 3.741 ÷ .87 the pupil might reason, ".87 is close to nine dimes and 3.741 is nearly 37 dimes, so how many sets of nine dimes can I get out of 37 dimes—four? I can get about four sets."

When developing the division algorithm, teachers should look for opportunities to deepen the pupils' understanding of both the division operation and its relationship to multiplication. Examining the relationship between the quotient and the div-

Small-Group Learning Activity

Where would the decimal point be placed in each of the problems below?

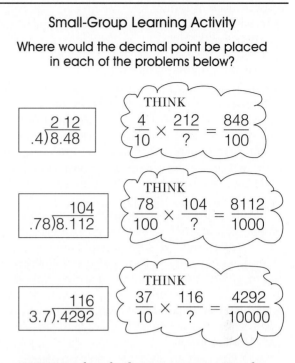

HINT: Look at the fraction sentence. Decide what denominator would replace the "?".

FIGURE 10.19

isor not only emphasizes the inverse or undoing relationship of multiplication and division, it also helps pupils develop a **"checking" technique** for the proper placement of the decimal point in the division algorithm. The development illustrated in Figure 10.19 could be used in a small group, a learning station, or a teacher-guided interactive learning activity.

Calculator Usage

Most applications requiring division of decimals (especially when the divisor has two or three digits) will be computed using a calculator. Therefore it only will be necessary for students to develop "reasonable" proficiency with paper-and-pencil calculations. Increased calculator usage for division makes it crucial that students know when to divide, when the quotient obtained is reasonable, and how and when to round decimal fractions.

Calculator Explorations with Repeating Decimals

Most calculators are limited by the number of spaces that can be displayed on the screen. Many quotients obtained when using calculators give the

appearance of terminating, as in $1 \div 3$. A calculator with only an eight-digit display will print this quotient as "0.3333333," leading pupils to believe that the decimal numeral ends after seven places or that the quotient ends in the ten-millionth position. Most calculators display a figure **rounded** to the last displayed position. For example, $2 \div 3$ will register as 0.6666667 on a calculator with an eight-digit display. Students can verify that the number is rounded when they multiply the quotient by the divisor ("undo the division"). Pupils find that instead of getting "2," they get a number greater than 2—(2.000001).

While calculators are useful in exploring terminating, repeating, and nonterminating decimals, pupils may need work with manipulative materials to understand **why** such quotients will keep repeating. Figure 10.20 shows a learning-station activity for discovering the repeating decimal for one-third. This activity may be explored by either a small group of children working cooperatively or by each student individually. At the station, pupils are given a large square of paper and instructed to divide the paper into tenths. They then distribute the tenths into three stacks, finding that each stack has three tenths and there is one tenth left over. This single tenth is traded in for hundredths and they distribute these hundredths into the three stacks.

Learning Station

Change 1/3 into a decimal.
Can you find a pattern?

Remember: 1/3 also means — 1 divided by 3
Use sheet marked in hundredths.

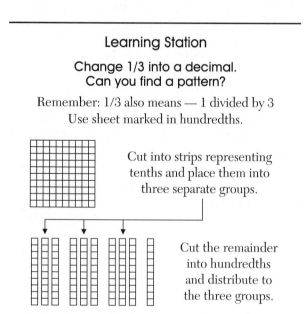

Cut into strips representing tenths and place them into three separate groups.

Cut the remainder into hundredths and distribute to the three groups.

Continue this process until you either get a remainder of zero or see a pattern.

FIGURE 10.20

1st step	$1 \div 3 = .3 + .1 \div 3$
2nd step	$1 \div 3 = .33 + .01 \div 3$
3rd step	$1 \div 3 = .333 + .001 \div 3$

Continue in a like manner!

FIGURE 10.21

Pupils continue the process until they either get a remainder of zero or see a pattern developing. (Figure 10.21 shows the mathematical model for this activity.)

Exploring Square Roots with a Calculator

Many calculators have a square root key ($\sqrt{\ }$). Pupils can easily find the square root of any number simply by pressing a key on the calculator. However, to use the square root key efficiently the pupil must understand the **concept** of the square root. First activities should require the pupil to find a number to make an open sentence true (for example, $\Delta \times \Delta = 4$). When other square numbers (9, 16, 25, 36, 49, 64, etc.) are used, the student simply recalls the multiplication facts. These early activities help establish a meaning for square root and reinforce the relationship between multiplication and division.

The teacher may need to use leading questions to get children to see that a square root might be found by "undoing multiplication." Since the number (for example, 289) is the product of a number times itself, the square root might be found by **estimating.** An **upper/lower boundary estimate** would show that the number must be between 10 and 20 because $10 \times 10 = 100$ and $20 \times 20 = 400$. After estimating the upper and lower boundaries the pupil would try out "guesses" using a calculator. When a product is found ($15 \times 15 = 225$), it is compared to the original number (289) to see if it is "too small," "too large," or "just right." Since 15×15 was too small, a greater number would be tried the next time—$17 \times 17 = 289$.

After finding square roots of square numbers, calculators can be used to extend understanding to finding square roots for numbers that are not square numbers. Since these numbers are not squares, students soon realize that no whole number can be found that will be a square root of the number. However, they will find whole numbers useful in making their first estimate. For example, to find the square root of 20, the pupil may think,

"4 × 4 = 16 and 5 × 5 = 25—so the square root of 20 will be somewhere between 4 and 5. Since 20 is nearly halfway between 16 and 25, I will try 4.5." When 4.5 is squared on the calculator, the product is 20.25, so the "guess" was just ".25 too much." The pupil continues to take successive estimates, testing each estimate by finding the product. If such an activity were performed as a paper-and-pencil activity it would be burdensome, but a calculator makes it interesting and challenging. From a teaching aspect, such an activity also provides a meaningful situation for pupils to develop estimating skills using decimals while developing an appreciation of the calculator's square root key. Figure 10.22 illustrates a learning-station activity designed to teach a child to approximate a square root.

Frequency Versus Length of String

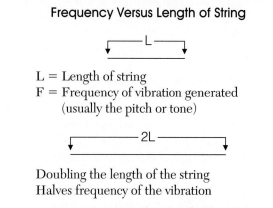

L = Length of string
F = Frequency of vibration generated
(usually the pitch or tone)

Doubling the length of the string
Halves frequency of the vibration

Frequency is <u>inversely</u> related to length — the longer the string, the lower the frequency of vibration.

FIGURE 10.23

10.8 EXTENDING RATIO CONCEPTS

Ratios have fascinated man for thousands of years. Almost everywhere man looked he could find ratios at work. Early makers of stringed musical instruments found that the frequency of the tone doubled as the length of a string was halved (see Figure 10.23). The early Greek mathematicians found countless interesting ratios that existed among geometric figures—for instance, the ratio of the circumference of a circle to its diameter (π). Early scientists found that as they discovered things about their world, the discovery could often be expressed in terms of ratios. For example, scientists expressed the electrical amperage flowing through a wire as a ratio of the voltage to the resistance, and they expressed velocity in terms of the ratio of distance traveled to the time needed to travel the distance, etc.

Ratios are also found in the student's world. For example, every time a student rides a ten-speed bicycle, makes a purchase at a store, discusses baseball batting averages, receives a test score (expressed as a percent), or converts from one unit of linear measure to another he is encountering ratios.

A bulletin board is an interesting way to build students' awareness of the applications of ratios in everyday situations. Pupils can search newspapers and magazines to find situations in which ratio is used. The teacher may divide the bulletin board into sections with labels such as "Sports," "Home," "Workplace," "Recreation," "Science,"

Learning Station

Approximating Square Roots

Select one of the following numbers:

2, 3, 5, 7, 8, 10, 11, 13, 14, 35, 99

Use the calculator to approximate the square root of a number above.

Try to estimate a number that will make the following equation true.

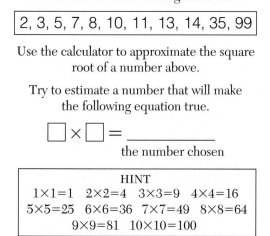

□ × □ = _____
the number chosen

HINT
1×1=1   2×2=4   3×3=9   4×4=16
5×5=25   6×6=36   7×7=49   8×8=64
9×9=81   10×10=100

1. Guess (estimate) what number goes in the box. (The "Hint" may help you make your first guess).

2. Test your guess with the calculator. Make a new guess and try to get a closer approximation.

3. Keep repeating this process until you have approximated an answer to the nearest thousandths. Check your approximation with the answer written on the answer key at this station.

FIGURE 10.22

etc. Teams may "compete" to fill their sections first. (See Figure 10.24.)

Developing Number Sense with Ratios

Ratio is first introduced as common fractions are being developed. The meaning of ratio is seen as a relationship of subsets to the set. For example, in a handful of eight jelly beans, three of the candies are red. Students learn to express this relationship as "three out of eight are red" or the ratio of red to the set is three to eight. (See Section 9.6.)

Early experiences with ratio tend to be **reflective**—reporting what is observed in an illustration. In the example above pupils would record the ratio of red beans as $\frac{3}{8}$ or 3:8. As students mature, they will apply their understanding of ratio to **predictive situations.** For instance, in the previous example there were three red jelly beans in every set of eight—then one might **_predict_** that IF the same ratio held there would be six red beans in 16, nine in 24, 12 in 32, etc.

One way of exploring this concept consists of providing pairs of students with sets of construction paper square-inch regions. Each pupil would be instructed to choose a number (between one and ten) and take that many regions (of a single color) every time his/her partner took a turn taking their "favorite number." Students are instructed to "predict" how many regions each would have after five selections, after seven, etc. The teacher may wish

to have a pair of students share its results with the class after several selections—but NOT reveal their "secret numbers" (ratio). The class then tries to determine what the simplest expression of the ratio would be. For example, if a team reported a ratio of 48 red to 84 green, the class may surmise that the original ratio was 4:7 and that the pair took 12 turns to get to that point. (A teacher might "suggest" that the class try to decide how many greens would be needed if 32 reds were chosen. Such a situation provides application of a fraction skill—cross-products—$\frac{4}{7} = \frac{32}{n}$).

Small-Group Experiment

Materials: Ten-speed bicycle

Step 1. Estimate how far the wheel will travel through one turn of the pedals. Do this for each of five gears.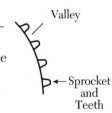

Step 2. Place a chalk mark at some point on the tire and measure distance traveled through one turn of the pedals. How close was your estimate to the actual distance traveled?

Chalk mark

Step 3. Now measure and record the diameter of each gear. Measure from the valley of the sprockets— through the center to the valley of the sprockets on the opposite side. Record the number of teeth on each of the gears used.

Valley

←Sprocket and Teeth

Step 4. Make a chart to show the data you have collected. Make a column for each of the following:
  a. distance wheel traveled
  b. diameter of front gear
  c. diameter of rear gear
  d. sprockets on front gear
  e. sprockets on rear gear

Step 5. See if you can use the chart you made to make better estimates for the remaining 5 gears. Test your new estimates by repeating steps 1 through 4 for the last five gears.

Bulletin Board
Small-Group Project

Each group is responsible for providing examples of the application of ratios for its assigned area. Groups can use clippings from newspapers and magazines—as well as illustrations and models.

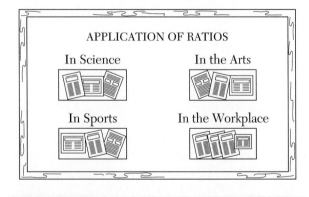

FIGURE 10.24

FIGURE 10.25

It is important that a student appreciate the "effects" caused when one aspect of a ratio changes. For example, in Figure 10.23, increasing the length of a string decreases the frequency of the vibration (sound)—an <u>inverse</u> ratio. Increasing the ratio of the two gears will increase the distance a bicycle wheel will travel when the larger-sized gear is turned once—a <u>direct</u> ratio.

There are many **experiments** that can be used in **cooperative learning groups** for the purpose of discovering ratios. Figure 10.25 illustrates an activity that studies the ratios associated with a ten-speed bicycle.

Extending the Concept of Percent

Though students explore some percent concepts when they study common fractions (see Chapter 9), percent concepts will be developed in greater depth once pupils understand decimal fractions. When first introduced to a percent, pupils learned to associate the "%" symbol with a fraction (or ratio) in which the denominator is 100. For example, they learned that five per hundred is expressed as $\frac{5}{100}$ or 5%. During the initial explorations of percent pupils may have <u>also</u> learned the word comes from the Latin "*per centum*" which means "per one hundred," and have drawn a parallel with words having the same root—a penny is called a "cent" and $\frac{1}{100}$ of a meter is called a <u>centimeter</u>.

Throughout school students repeatedly are exposed to data using percents. For example, a grade may be reported as 90% when a student gets nine out of ten problems correct on a social studies test. Students see ads in newspapers advertising "25% off." Through such exposure, pupils will enter the intermediate grades being able to recognize many percent equivalents to common fractions; for example, $\frac{1}{3}$ is $33\frac{1}{3}$%, $\frac{1}{4}$ is 25%, and $\frac{1}{2}$ is 50%. Such background knowledge, while useful, must not mislead the teacher into believing that the pupils understand the many percent concepts or know how to convert common fractions to percents.

Teachers should employ **manipulative models** to extend students' conceptual understandings of percents. While such a procedure is especially necessary for those pupils with weak conceptual backgrounds, this approach also will deepen the level of understanding of pupils with stronger backgrounds.

A "hundred region" is an excellent model for percent. Material used to introduce decimal fractions (tenths and hundredths) may easily be employed when illustrating percent. Since pupils already associate this material with decimals, the

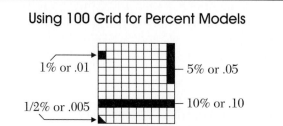

Using 100 Grid for Percent Models

FIGURE 10.26

relationship between percent and decimal fractions is readily recognized by most students. When using the hundred grid, the teacher should have pupils color regions to illustrate percents such as 1%, 5%, 10%, 25%, etc. Once simple percents are related to decimal representations, teachers may include drawings of 100%, 150%, and even 300%. Percents that are less than 1% are a little more difficult for pupils to understand. Illustrating $\frac{1}{2}$% by coloring $\frac{1}{2}$ of a square region helps pupils recognize that $\frac{1}{2}$% is *not* 50%! (See Figure 10.26.)

Models should be used to illustrate percents of amounts greater (or less) than 100 as a foundation for later computational activities. Pupils may illustrate 6% of a 100 grid by coloring six regions. Using TWO of these regions the teacher can show 6% of 200; THREE of the regions will illustrate 6% of 300, etc. Pupils CAN recognize that 6% of 50 would be a 100 grid cut into two equally-shaded parts with three colored grids in each 50. (See Figure 10.27.)

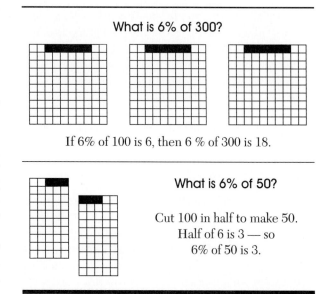

What is 6% of 300?

If 6% of 100 is 6, then 6 % of 300 is 18.

What is 6% of 50?

Cut 100 in half to make 50.
Half of 6 is 3 — so
6% of 50 is 3.

FIGURE 10.27

For amounts less than 100, however, it is more effective to have pupils <u>estimate</u> and then use a grid cut into 100 separated regions to verify their estimate. The lesson fragment below illustrates this method:

Teacher-Guided Interactive Learning Activity

LESSON FRAGMENT

M: Percent of amounts less than 100

A: Sixth grade

T: Modeling, involvement

H: Percent of 100, use of models to illustrate percent

DEVELOPING ESTIMATION SKILLS

Teacher: What might we do if we wanted to find a percent of a number less than 100%? Suppose we wanted 12% of 50. Who has a guess at what it might be? Bertha?

Bertha: I think it would be more than five, because 10% of 100 is ten and that would give us five per 50.

Teacher: Good, Bertha! That's good reasoning. Anyone else have a guess?

Teddy: I think it's six.

Teacher: Can you tell us why you think that's a better guess, Teddy?

Teddy: Well, 12% of 100 is 12. Fifty is half of 100 so 12% of 50 must be half of 12 or six.

Teacher: That's good reasoning, too! Let's see if we can verify that response with our cut out grids. Let's try Teddy's estimate. Everyone take 50 grids and turn six of them over to show the red backing. Now we will have six per 50. Put another group just like it to see if there will be 12 reds in the 100.

Teddy: That's so easy we don't need to get 100, teacher. There are going to be 12 reds.

Teacher: All right, let's try a slightly harder problem. Can we estimate and then verify our guess for 8% of 40? I'm going to warn you—it MIGHT not come out even!

Percent Expressions

When pupils first work with percent they write a numeral for the model illustrated. As pupils recognize the relationship between decimal fractions and percent, they can convert from a decimal fraction (written as a hundredth) to a percent. To strengthen this understanding a teacher may wish to have pupils first convert a decimal fraction into a common fraction and then into a percent (.17 = $\frac{17}{100}$ = 17%). Such an activity prepares students for renaming fractions to percent, for they see that it is necessary to rename the common fraction into an equivalent fraction with a denominator of 100.

An alternate approach might be to rename the % sign as meaning "times one-hundredth" ($\times$ .01). In a number such as 17% the pupil would think "17 $\times$ .01 = .17." With this approach the pupil can recognize how a calculator may be used when working with percents. A percent may be entered as a whole number and renamed to a decimal expression keying "$\times$" and ".01." Initial explorations using the calculator will lead many pupils to discover that percents can be renamed to decimal fractions "by shifting the decimal point two places to the left." To convert a decimal to a percent, pupils find that multiplying by 100 gives the percent—or "moves the decimal place two places to the right."

Solving Problems with Percent

Historically, percentage was taught as three situations—"rate," "base," and "percentage." In the example "7% of 300 = 21," a "rate" problem would have the percent (%) missing; a "base" problem would have the 300 missing; and a "percentage" problem would ask how many regions would be shaded. To learn these three "cases" pupils *memorized rules* and applied these rules when the situation warranted. Today, "cases" are seldom mentioned. Pupils learn a basic relationship for percent and then apply an understanding of this relationship to identify missing information. In pupils' texts, one of two approaches is generally emphasized—the number sentence approach <u>or</u> the ratio proportion approach.

When using the **number sentence approach,** the teacher applies the pupil's understanding of the multiplication sentence—"factor $\times$ factor = product." The percentage relationship is stated in a mathematical sentence (see Figure 10.28) and the percent is then converted to a decimal fraction. If the "product" is missing, the two factors are multiplied. If the product is given and a factor is missing, then the multiplication must be "undone" using the inverse operation, division.

When the percent relationship is expressed as a **ratio proportion** the student expresses the percent as a common fraction with a denominator of 100. In the example given in Figure 10.28, the "base" is expressed as the denominator since the proportion is perceived as "23 is to 100 as what number is to 17." Using cross-products, the pupil finds that "100 $\times$ n = 23 $\times$ 17," then "100n = 391" or "n = $\frac{391}{100}$ = 3.91."

What is 23% of 17?

Number Sentence Approach

Change percent into decimal fraction and then express relationship in multiplication sentence.

$$.23 \times 17 = \boxed{}$$
$$\text{factor} \quad \text{factor} \quad \text{product}$$
$$\text{(missing)}$$

$$.23 \times \boxed{} = 3.91$$
$$\text{factor} \quad \text{factor} \quad \text{product}$$
$$\qquad \text{(missing)}$$

$$\boxed{} \times 17 = 3.91$$
$$\text{factor} \quad \text{factor} \quad \text{product}$$
$$\text{(missing)}$$

If a product is missing, multiply — if a factor is missing, divide the product by the factor.

Ratio Proportion Approach

Express as a proportion. Use cross-products to solve for missing number.

$$\frac{.23}{100} = \frac{P}{17}$$

$$100 \times P = 23 \times 17$$
$$100\,P = 391$$
$$P = 391 \div 100$$
$$P = 3.91$$

$$\frac{23}{100} = \frac{3.91}{B} \quad \textbf{OR} \quad \frac{R}{100} = \frac{3.91}{17}$$

FIGURE 10.28

Throughout the development of percent problems the teacher should emphasize **estimation**. Some guidance might be necessary to help pupils develop effective estimation procedures. For example, suppose it is known that 40% of some number is 1600. This means that 10 percent of that number is 400, so 100% of that number would be 4000. Thus 1600 is 40% of 4000. If one tries to find 35% of 60, a student <u>could</u> think "10% of sixty is six and I need three-and-one-half sixes, or 21." Encouraging students to develop **estimation strategies** and share their "thought processes" with others in cooperative learning groups not only develops **number sense skills,** but also helps pupils recognize that many ratio problems can be solved without the aid of calculators or paper and pencil.

10.9 COMPUTERS

Computers can be used to teach students decimal concepts. While a teacher could construct a program in BASIC language to help students learn to use percent, interest, decimals, etc., many readily available software programs already exist that utilize sophisticated graphics to explore introductory decimal, percent, and ratio concepts as well as more advanced decimal, ratio, and percent concepts (see references at the end of this chapter). If a classroom computer has sufficient memory capability, students can organize and manipulate decimal, percent, and ratio data using one of the commercially available **spreadsheet** programs. (See Chapter 5.)

Once students begin a study of decimals (ratios and percents), they should explore (through field trips or guest speakers) how computers are used by business and industry to perform routine computations involving decimals (ratios and percents). For example, before the advent of computers, store clerks hand-marked the selling price on items. Many work hours were devoted to this task. Now a manager can program a computer to mark up merchandise by a percentage of the cost of the item and the computer will price the items as they are obtained from wholesalers. This information is then stored in the computer together with the items' inventory numbers. When a customer brings an item to the checkout counter, the inventory number of each item purchased is keyed into the computer through the cash register terminal. The computer then "looks up" the price and displays it on the cash register screen. Each item being purchased is processed in a similar fashion. When the clerk concludes the transaction, the computer is told to calculate the sum of the costs of the purchases. It assigns the appropriate amount of sales tax, computes the total bill, and then shows the amount on the cash register screen. When the customer hands the clerk an amount of money, the clerk enters this amount into the computer/register and it displays the amount of change the individual is to receive. On some registers, the computer will also count out the change (not bills) to be returned to the customer. Concurrent with this process the computer keeps track of the items still in the inventory and when the items fall below a certain number the computer will automatically make up an order to get new items. (See Figure 10.29.)

Using Spreadsheet Sort Functions

Most spreadsheet programs can sort a list of numbers in order from largest to smallest (or vice versa).

Teaching Students Computer Applications

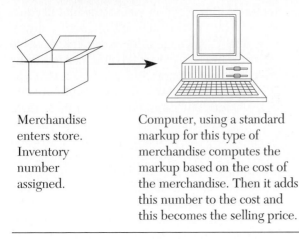

| Merchandise enters store. Inventory number assigned. | Computer, using a standard markup for this type of merchandise computes the markup based on the cost of the merchandise. Then it adds this number to the cost and this becomes the selling price. |

Example: Item cost the business $3.72. Normal markup is 30%.

The computer calculates the markup as $1.12 to the nearest cent.

The computer adds the markup to the cost to obtain a selling price of $4.84.

FIGURE 10.29

When decimal fractions are entered into such a program, the generated list can be used to help students understand decimal place-value notation, equivalent names for decimal fractions, and relative size of decimal fractions. Figure 10.30 illustrates a spreadsheet exercise designed to help a student learn concepts relating to the relative size of decimals (ordering) and equivalent names. The activity described assumes a student has learned how to input a series of numbers into a spreadsheet column and how to instruct the computer to list the numbers from smallest to largest. (See Chapter 5.)

10.10 EVALUATION AND INTERVENTION

Evaluation of pupils, instruction, and the curriculum with respect to decimals, percent, and ratio has always been a complex task. Part of this complexity is due to the many mathematical skills and concepts that must be satisfactorily demonstrated before a student can be deemed to have mastery of decimals, percents, and ratios. For example, to solve a problem involving multiplication of decimal fractions, the pupil will need to apply the skills used in multiplying whole numbers plus an understanding of decimals plus understandings associated with multiplying common fractions (tenths times tenths equal hundredths, etc.).

While the student may be required to demonstrate computational proficiency in using decimal fractions in paper-and-pencil tasks, most future requirements for calculation will be performed using calculators. Assessment of computational and problem-solving skills involving decimals, percents, and ratios should therefore involve both paper-and-pencil assessments and calculator usage assessments. Paper-and-pencil assessments, interviews, and observation of the child at work will provide the teacher with a means to identify the types of conceptual misunderstandings that cause a student to fail to meet a learning objective. For example, when paper-and-pencil computational exercises are employed as an assessment device, teachers should carefully analyze any errors that occur. Suppose a pupil fails to "line up the decimal points" in an addition exercise. Did this error occur because the pupil does not understand the positional value of the numeral? Such a weakness may also be present in adding common fractions, adding measurements, etc. A follow-up interview may be necessary to determine the basis of the conceptual misunderstanding.

Exploring the Relative Size of Decimals and Equivalent Names Using a Spreadsheet Program

TASK:

1. Write out—in a column—the following decimals —listing them from smallest to largest.

>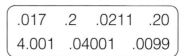
> .017   .2   .0211   .20
> 4.001   .04001   .0099

> Hint: If you find two equivalent names—list them in either order.

2. Now input the list into your spreadsheet program in the first column.

3. Tell the computer to sort your list from smallest to largest. Did the order of your list change? (If the order changed, see if you can tell why it changed.)

4. Where in your list did you find .2 and .20 listed? Why?

FIGURE 10.30

Sometimes when items are missed on a carefully prepared evaluative instrument that is designed to measure understanding, follow-up diagnostic procedures may be required. While an incorrect response may give a direction, the teacher will still need to interview a student to clarify a response. For example, consider the item in Figure 10.31, designed to determine if a student understands that "the product of two decimals, both of which have values between one and zero, will be equal to a number that is <u>less</u> than either decimal."

If a student chose "b" ("a" is the correct response), a teacher would still need to know <u>how</u> the student arrived at that solution before determining an appropriate strategy for remediation. Perhaps the student misread the problem and answered the question as if it were related to addition instead of multiplication; of course, the pupil <u>may</u> have read the question correctly but did not understand the relationship between a product and two factors less than one. At this point the teacher must interview the student to determine which intervention strategy is appropriate.

As with all computational errors, it is possible to classify errors into many different "kinds" or "cases." The chart (Figure 10.32) looks at some types of errors that are significant, since each type of error shows a lack of conceptual <u>understanding</u>.

Significant paper-and-pencil calculation errors are those which relate to a student's understanding of the decimal system. Since addition and subtraction problems can be "ragged" (not line up) on both the left- <u>and</u> righthand sides of the algorithm, the teacher can anticipate that pupils with weak understandings of positional value will incorrectly calculate these problems. Typically, pupils do not recognize that .2 and .20 name the same number—therefore they misplace the column or they fail to regroup. When a pupil calculates the product of .23 and .044 properly but fails to place the decimal properly, the teacher will need to test the pupil's understanding of hundredths times thousandths (multiplying the denominators in common fractions).

Errors that occur when using a calculator generally fall into two categories. Most commonly an error is made when the pupil improperly inputs the data and the pupil's estimation skills are not sufficiently developed to enable him/her to recognize the unreasonableness of the answer. A second major error occurs when a pupil chooses an inappropriate operation or keys the operation incorrectly into the machine (for example, pressing ".35," then "÷," then ".42," for the problem .42 ÷ .35).

Assume you are multiplying two decimals represented by points A and B on the number line. Would the product be found:

    a. To the left of both A and B.
    b. To the right of both A and B.
    c. Between A and B.
    d. It can't be determined.

FIGURE 10.31

Paper and Pencil Activities

Errors that have as their basis conceptual misunderstandings that pre-date the teaching of decimals.

Example	Type of error may indicate that the student
$\begin{array}{r} 3.9 \\ +\ 4.6 \\ \hline 7.15 \end{array}$	does not understand the regrouping process.
$\begin{array}{r} .18 \\ \times\ .6 \\ \hline .112 \end{array}$	has not mastered the basic facts.
$\begin{array}{r} .22 \\ 13\overline{).2626} \\ \underline{26} \\ 26 \\ \underline{26} \\ 0 \end{array}$	did not or cannot estimate quotients.
In May Athens had 9.72 inches of rain. This was 3.46 inches more than the average rainfall for May. How much is the average rainfall? Student's answer: 13.18 inches.	has not mastered strategies for selecting appropriate operations in problem solving.

FIGURE 10.32

10.11 MEETING SPECIAL NEEDS

The special needs of learning-disabled students are quite different from those of gifted students when the development of decimal, percent, and ratio concepts and their application in problem-solving activities are concerned. The learning-disabled student may need more **extensive hand-on manipulations** of concrete materials to reduce the level of abstraction and will need more concentrated work applying the decimal skills that are required to make the pupil a functionally literate problem solver. Additionally, some learning-disabled children may profit by skipping the writing steps and going directly to calculator usage in working with decimals.

Most learning-disabled pupils will use calculators to compute with decimal fractions, percents, and ratios. Therefore, the teacher will need to assist the students in making the appropriate associations between manipulative model activities and calculator activities. Special attention should be devoted to the manner in which a calculator drops unnecessary zeros in numbers. For instance, when adding $4.25 and $3.75 the screen will display the sum as 8, not 8.00. Therefore the teacher will need to use manipulative models to ensure an understanding that numbers such as 8 and 8.00 or .4 and .40 are really the same number. A model, such as the 100 grid, can be used to show that coloring four-tenths is the same as coloring 40 hundredths. Money (dimes and pennies) can also be used.

Since estimation skills may be beyond the capacities of some learning-disabled children, the teacher may wish to have these children check the reasonableness of an answer by working it twice. This technique will only provide for checking inputting errors, not conceptual types of errors. Development of specific calculator routines may be desirable for some learning-disabled children to make them functionally literate. For example, establishing a set procedure for keeping track of the total cost of their purchases as they select items for purchase in a store, in order to ensure that they do not get to the checkout counter with insufficient funds for their purchases.

Since most calculators record amounts as decimal fractions rather than common fractions, hand-held calculators are valuable tools when working with the high-ability pupil. Computational exercises are performed so easily using calculators that more advanced pupils abandon the written form as soon as they recognize how to modify standard algorithms. **Estimation** as a means of verifying the calculation becomes a major skill for these students. Upper and lower boundary checks (mental operation) can set limits for many problems, but multiplication and division skills may require additional practice before students become proficient.

"Chase Me" is an interesting two-player game that can be used to build both multiplication or division estimation skills for the high-ability student. To work on multiplication skills, each student secretly enters a 3-digit number into his calculator. The object of the game is to guess a factor which, when combined with your displayed number, will give you your opponent's number. Once the number is entered, the player who chooses to go first looks at the opponent's "display" and tries to convert his number to the other player's number by inputting the factor he thinks will convert his number to his opponent's number. (The product is ROUNDED to the nearest whole number.) If he is able to match his opponent's number the game is over. If not, the opponent gets to repeat the process trying to obtain the new product. For instance, suppose you are trying to get to 127, starting with 786 displayed on your calculator. If you chose to multiply by .15 (because $\frac{1}{10}$ of 786 would be about 80), then the product would be 118 (rounded from 117.9). Since you did not get the opponent's number, your opponent tries to make his 127 into the 118 by multiplying by his estimate of the factor. The student must first recognize that 127 is more than 118 so the multiplier would need to be greater than one. Since .1 × 118 would be about 12, 1.1 would be about 130, so the pupil might choose a slightly smaller number: 1.05, giving 124 (rounded from 123.9). This gives the first player a NEW "secret number" to chase. The first player to "catch" his opponent wins. (The game may be changed to work on division estimation skills by requiring the "chase" to be accomplished by DIVIDING the secret number.)

10.12 SUMMARY

In the primary grades children explore hundredths not only as they relate to money and metric measurement concepts, but they also engage in hands-on manipulations with models depicting both tenths and hundredths.

By the time students complete the intermediate grades they have been introduced to all the major aspects of decimal fractions, including operations and a wide variety of problem-solving activities. In addition the concepts of ratios, proportions, and percents have been extended to include decimal fraction applications.

Because students will do many of their problem-solving activities that involve decimals, ratios, percents, and proportion using calculators, a large amount of time is devoted in the intermediate grades to developing calculator skills.

EXERCISES

1. How might a teacher use manipulative materials to help a pupil recognize that .3 is greater than .24?
2. Describe how a teacher would emphasize "adding like values" rather than telling pupils to "line up the decimal points" when adding the numbers 2.3 + .984 + .53.
3. When pupils are familiar with the whole number subtraction algorithm, the problem 8.2 − 2.873 should not cause difficulty. However, many pupils compute and find the difference to be "5.473."
   a. Analyze the error—telling how you "suspect" pupils get this difference.
   b. Describe how manipulative materials may be used to overcome this difficulty.
4. In the problem 7.5 × 8.24 the product should have three places to the right of the decimal.
   a. What problem can the teacher anticipate when pupils "verify" their product with a calculator?
   b. What prerequisite skills are needed before a pupil can understand this seeming discrepancy between the "rule" and the calculator product?
5. Show how a teacher can help a pupil recognize that .3 × .4 = .12 using
   a. manipulative materials (or drawings)
   b. multiplication of fractions.
6. Describe the development of a procedure for "moving the decimal point" in the problem .91 ÷ .3.
   a. Describe a problem situation that might be used to introduce this skill.
   b. Suggest how pupils might use estimation to "verify" the quotient. (How might the pupil "justify" the estimating process?)
   c. Describe how a teacher might structure the lesson to develop the "rule" for moving the point.
7. Describe how a calculator might be used to help pupils understand "square root."

RELEVANT COMPUTER SOFTWARE

Conquering Decimals. 1988. Apple II family. MECC, 3490 Lexington Avenue North, St. Paul, Minn. 55126.

Expanding Your Math Skills, Level 2. 1986. Apple II family. Random House School Division, 201 E. 50th Street, New York, N.Y. 10022.

REFERENCES

Allinger, G. D. and J. N. Payne. "Estimation and Mental Arithmetic with Percent." In *Estimation and Mental Computation: NCTM Yearbook. 1986.* Reston, Va.: National Council of Teachers of Mathematics, 1986. Pp. 141–155.

Behr, M. J., and T. R. Post. "Teaching Rational Number and Decimal Concepts." Edited by T. R. Post. Chapter 7 in *Teaching Mathematics in Grades K-8: Research Based Methods.* Boston: Allyn and Bacon, 1988.

Hannick, F. T. "Using the Memory Functions on Hand-held Calculators." *Arithmetic Teacher* 33 (November 1985): 48–49.

Rolenc, E. J., Jr. "The Computer and Approximate Numbers." In *Estimation and Mental Computation: NCTM Yearbook. 1986.* Reston, Va.: National Council of Teachers of Mathematics, 1986. Pp. 186–189.

Vance, J. H. "Estimating Decimal Products: An Instructional Sequence." In *Estimation and Mental Computation: NCTM Yearbook. 1986.* Reston, Va.: National Council of Teachers of Mathematics, 1986. Pp. 127–134.

CHAPTER 11

TEACHING GEOMETRY

INTRODUCTION

Geometry is all around us. It is found in the design of our buildings, the examination of nature, the appreciation of artistic endeavors, and the function of most mechanical devices. Pupils are immersed in geometric applications from infancy. Awareness of geometric concepts, however, will require children to examine their environment and seek out similarities, differences, consistencies, etc. This "awareness" is an important foundation for a more mature examination and development of formal proofs.

Prior to the 1950s, elementary school instruction was primarily concerned with "arithmetic" (the study of numbers) and geometry was seldom explored. During the 1960s, the "modern mathematics" movement brought much more geometry into the curriculum. Such a change allowed children many more opportunities to explore geometric topics as they progressed through the elementary curriculum.

Today, instruction in geometry is being guided by the ***van Heile model of geometric thought.*** This model, proposed by two Dutch educators—Dina van Heile-Geldof and her husband, Pierre Marie van Heile—suggests that individuals go through five levels of understanding as they study geometric topics: visualization, analysis, informal deduction, formal deduction, and rigor. Perhaps the most significant element of the model is that progress through the levels is dependent more upon the instruction the pupil receives than the pupil's age. The van Heiles noted that no method of instruction allows a pupil to skip over a level of understanding (though some instruction may help pupils move more rapidly through the levels). (Crowley, 1987)

First Level: (*Visualization*) Children recognize a geometric shape by its overall appearance. They can identify a shape and even reproduce it. They know a shape is a square because "it looks like a square—like the floor tiles."

Second Level: (*Analysis*) Pupils begin to look at specific characteristics of a figure. They recognize that certain characteristics set a shape apart from other shapes. They know that a figure is a triangle because "it is a closed figure and it is made with three line segments."

Third Level: (*Informal Deduction*) Pupils look at properties within figures and recognize the value of a definition. Subsets within categories are identified. Students find that "an equilateral triangle is isosceles because an isosceles triangle has two congruent sides—and an equilateral triangle has three sides that are congruent—so it must have at least two sides congruent."

Fourth Level: (_Deduction_) The pupil can construct proofs—not just recall those illustrated. This is the level that is used most often in high-school geometry courses (although some students are not yet at this level).

Fifth Level: (_Rigor_) Geometry is perceived as an abstract system of logic. Pupils explore and construct axiomatic systems—and compare different geometries. (This level is most often found at the college instructional level.)

Most instruction in the primary program occurs at the first level—"visualization." However, before pupils leave the elementary program, many will have progressed through the second and third levels—"Analysis" and "Informal Deduction." Teachers must recognize that there will be pupils in the upper grades who are still at the "visualization" level. Indeed, some instructional programs never take students beyond this level. Since pupils generally cannot move from one level to a more advanced level without carefully planned instruction, teachers must assess the level of a group and/or individual prior to introducing a new geometric topic.

In planning an instructional lesson (or series of lessons) the van Heile model would suggest that five "phases" be included when organizing instruction.

INQUIRY: Students and teachers should use objects in activities and observations should be made. Teachers should encourage conversation, leading pupils to examine how things are alike—and how they are different.

DIRECTED ORIENTATION: In this phase, the teacher should carefully sequence instruction to direct pupils to examine specific characteristics of the object under study.

EXPLICATION: In this part of the lesson, the teacher encourages pupils to share their perceptions of structures developing their language skills. The teacher's role is to help pupils use accurate and appropriate language.

FREE ORIENTATION: Activities that can be completed in many different ways will follow teacher explication. While the pupil may be directed to use a material to complete a task, each pupil works with the materials in his/her own way.

INTEGRATION: This phase of instruction is designed for review and summary. It does not explore any new ideas, but rather tries to "integrate" what has been explored and discussed.

Most teachers utilize an instructional plan that incorporates the essentials of the van Heile model. They propose a new exploration and provide some time for early discussion. Teachers then guide part of the instruction to prepare for independent or group activity. In small groups or as a total class, children share what they find from their explorations, and finally the teacher guides pupils to organize these findings into a logical structure.

11.1 TEACHING GEOMETRY IN THE KINDERGARTEN AND PRIMARY GRADES

Geometry at the kindergarten level is exploratory in nature. Children examine the shapes around them—things that roll, things that are flat, things that are hollow, things drawn on a sheet of paper, etc. They also develop a vocabulary that can be used to describe things in their environment—inside, outside, above, under, straight, curved, etc. These concepts serve as a foundation for later explorations.

Geometric topics are introduced in a more systematic manner in the primary grades. While shape identification (circle, square, rectangle, and triangle) is a part of most kindergarten programs, children in the first grade refine that skill to include rudimentary definitions of those shapes. They learn that the shapes are **closed** figures. They recognize that triangles are made up of three line segments.

Most geometric concepts taught in the primary level have a direct application to other areas in the elementary curriculum. Plane figures and terms associated with them have many applications, including an extensive use when the concepts of fractional numbers are developed. Many of the terms (edge, side, diagonal, etc.) are used when giving directions in subjects such as art or physical education. Concepts related to positive coordinates have immediate and direct applications in reading maps during social studies and graphing data. Activities with space figures serve as readiness for geometric concepts to be developed in the intermediate grades.

Not every school program initiates all of these geometric concepts in the primary grades. Careful examination of each school's scope and sequence will identify which of these concepts is developed at each grade level. A typical scope/sequence is illustrated below.

Kindergarten

Informally explore geometric shapes
Develop vocabulary and concepts related to spatial location
  • below, above, between, on, under, etc.
Identify geometric shapes: square, rectangle, circle, and triangle

Grade 1

Identify open and closed figures
Two-dimensional shapes
  • identify characteristics of shapes
      circle, rectangle, square, triangle
  • locate interior (inside) and exterior (outside)
Three-dimensional shapes
  • sort using similar attributes (curved surfaces, flat surfaces, etc.)
  • identify shapes
      sphere (ball), cone, cylinder (can), pyramid, prism (box)
  • locate interior (inside) and exterior (outside)

Grade 2

Name points on coordinate graph
Identify right corners
Two-dimensional shapes

  • identify and name squares, rectangles, circles, triangles
  • identify congruent figures using slides, rotations, or flips
Three-dimensional shapes
  • identify and name cone, sphere, cylinder, pyramid, prism, cube

Grade 3

Identify line segments, rays, angles, right angles
Identify lines of symmetry
Use tracings to show congruency
Two-dimensional shapes
  • identify and name squares, rectangles, circles, triangles
  • compare shapes made with line segments (polygons)
  • identify right corners in polygon
Three-dimensional shapes
  • identify and name cone, sphere, cylinder, pyramid, prism, cube
  • identify faces, edges, vertices (corners)

11.2 INFORMAL EXPLORATIONS IN THE KINDERGARTEN

Children enter kindergarten with some knowledge of pregeometry terms. Of course, this background may need to be extended to incorporate new meanings. A child may play inside or go outside to play. When playing "Go In and Out the Window," the child will learn that he/she can be inside or outside the ring of children. When doing an art project, many children wish to color inside the lines. (After geometric shapes have been introduced, the vocabulary associated with pregeometry can be incorporated into activities such as the "Jack Be Quick" game.)

The concepts of curved and straight are used during art activities. Most marks a child makes on paper will be curved. The teacher may draw attention to this fact with comments such as, "You drew some nice curved figures." To help the child draw straight segments the teacher may hold a straight-edge while the child traces along its edge to make a straight mark. The teacher may emphasize "straightness" by saying, "That is straight, isn't it?" Some art projects may be drawings with straight lines only. Through contrast, the child learns to distinguish between the concept of straight and curved.

Developing Spatial Concepts with Game Activities

One activity that might be used to develop spatial words is the "Place It" game. In this game the teacher lays out several toys on the floor. Children are called upon to "put the ball on the top shelf." Other directions are given, such as "Put the doll to the right of the ball" and "Put the bird between the ball and the doll." After all of the toys are placed, the teacher can reinforce some of the words by involving the class in an "I Am Thinking of a Toy" activity where a pupil encourages other children to guess the toy they are thinking about by using statements such as "I am thinking of a toy on the top (bottom, middle, etc.) shelf."

Developing Names of Geometric Shapes

In kindergarten, instruction related to geometric concepts is generally limited to naming common shapes and identifying objects that have these shapes. This doesn't mean the teacher is prohibited from pointing out or naming line segments, angles, etc. These terms, if used with real objects, provide a strong foundation for later experiences. Kindergarten programs usually build a child's ability to recognize and identify shapes such as squares, rectangles, triangles, and circles. A child may recognize that a stop sign has a different shape (octagon), but would not be expected to recall its name. At the kindergarten level the less precise term "shape" is used because the model being used by the teacher is composed of the figure and its interior. In geometry, a polygon made of three line segments is a triangle while the inside of the triangle is its interior (interiors of polygons are not part of the polygon). The triangle and its interior forms a triangular shape (mathematically called a triangular region). In most instances the teacher will be using cut-out pieces of paper or pieces of flannel to represent the shapes. Children should also see these shapes illustrated as "frames" so they are ready for a more precise definition.

Many geometric concepts are developed by using "examples and counterexamples." The child learns that some "curved things" are called circles—but not all things that have curves are circles. As children develop a vocabulary for these concepts, they find many opportunities to use those words throughout the day. A tricycle has wheels that are circles and floor tiles are square shapes. Teachers in kindergarten look for examples in everyday objects and activities to maintain the child's understanding and vocabulary.

Art projects offer kindergarten teachers many opportunities to integrate the study of geometric shapes with creative experiences. For example, when pupils study triangular shapes they can use cut-out triangular shapes to paste a picture using only triangle shapes. After several shapes have been introduced, the children can construct pictures showing where they live, someplace they have visited, etc.

Some kindergarten children are ready to extend their understanding of geometric shapes to include those figures which are **closed** and those which are **open.** Children first may relate those terms to an "open door" or a "closed jar." This understanding may be extended to include the concept of open and closed curves.

In the child's world, not all geometric shapes are flat. Some of those shapes are really space figures like the cone, cylinder, sphere, prism, and pyramid. While these words generally are not formally introduced in a kindergarten program, children do like to explore some of the properties of these figures. When a set of play blocks includes cylinders, cones, cubes, and prisms, children discover many of the relationships without teacher direction. A teacher may deepen a child's awareness by posing questions during play with the blocks. Questions can include, "Can you find other things that roll?", "What do you have at home that is that shape?", "Does the cone roll the same way?", "That block doesn't roll at all, does it?"

Children are not expected to remember the geometric names for the space figures. However, there is no real reason to avoid the specific geometric name for a given shape. Hearing the geometric term may develop a child's listening vocabulary and builds a readiness for later exploration with the shapes. If the teacher uses specific geometric terms, it is helpful to "link" the geometric vocabulary with a common word. "That round block is a sphere. It's like a playground ball, isn't it?", "That box is a cube.", "That pointed block with the flat sides is called a pyramid. You may have seen pictures of pyramids in books."

11.3 TEACHING GEOMETRIC FIGURES AND THEIR ASSOCIATED TERMS

From the first time a child picks up a crayon or pencil and makes marks on paper, he/she is making **models** of geometric figures. At first these marks are only curved segments, but at some point the child learns to close the curves and add some line segments for arms and legs. Soon the child uses other marks for facial features and draws his/her first picture of a person.

The primary teacher must take the child's perceptions and conceptions of geometric figures and refine them. During this process the child will develop the technical vocabulary (terms associated with the figures), which will facilitate further study of geometry.

While the following development is organized around a sequence, starting with simple figures with few attributes and proceeding to figures with many attributes, organization should be dictated by a child's need to be familiar with particular concepts. For example, it may be necessary for a teacher to explain the concept of symmetry early in the first grade when an art project that requires an understanding of symmetry is introduced. A teacher may need to review geometric shapes prior to the study of fractional numbers.

Point, Curve, and Simple Curve

Even as toddlers, with crayons in hand, children begin making representations of points, curves, and simple curves. This is not to say they know they are creating geometric figures; on the contrary, they are having fun. Making marks seems to satisfy some innate need in children.

Points are the building blocks upon which many geometric concepts are built. Therefore, it is essential to minimize the distortion of the attribute when illustrating the term. One critical attribute of a point is that it has no dimension or "width." Children learn that a "point" is a location, but in order to talk about the location, a teacher must draw a dot to represent the point. Children must recognize that the point takes up no space at all. (**The smaller the dot the better the representation of the point.**)

Since a point is defined as a location, it really does not exist except in one's mind. This concept is difficult for young children to comprehend. It is generally sufficient to establish the fact that a "point" is smaller than the dot and that we can "draw a picture" of a point by using a dot. As pupils mature they will see that this "location" has no dimension at all.

Another geometric concept developed early in the child's formal study of geometry is that of a **curve.** A curve is pictured as a path of points (locations) that may have no starting point and no ending point (goes on forever). Of course, most curves drawn by children have a starting point and an ending point. The term "curve" includes straight paths (such as line segments and lines). Since "straight" and "curve" seem to be opposites, some teachers prefer to use the word "path" instead of curve. By using a wide variety of models of paths children will see that some paths "wander all over the place," some "cross over" themselves, and some are "straight" (lines and line segments).

The **closed curve** is one special curve explored by children early in the primary level. A closed curve is a path that "starts and ends" at the same point. As children explore constructing different closed curves, they find that some cross themselves and some do not. When a closed curve does not cross itself, it is called a **simple closed curve.** One activity that promotes this concept is to have children build "fences" with string or sticks and place a toy animal inside their structure. When the animal is inside a simple closed curve, it cannot get out (without jumping the fence). If the fence "crosses itself," the animal cannot get to the other part of the field. (After children are able to identify simple closed curves, they recognize that the figures identified in kindergarten as squares, circles, rectangles, and triangles are really special kinds of simple closed curves.)

Two attributes that play important roles in sorting or classifying geometric figures are the properties of **straightness** and the **number of endpoints.** Some paths have no ending point—they go on forever in both directions while others begin at a point and go on forever in a single direction. Still other paths have both a starting and ending point.

If a path (curve) is straight but has only one endpoint it is called a **ray.** Rays start at a point and "go on forever." A flashlight beam is a useful illustration for a "ray." When the flashlight is held on the chalkboard children can trace the beam and see that the ray would continue on and on. To illustrate a ray with a drawing, a point is identified to show where it starts. An arrow point is drawn at the other end to show that the ray keeps right on going. (Example, ⟶)

Straight curves with no endpoints are called **lines.** (A line is straight and goes on forever in BOTH directions.) To indicate that a line goes on forever, an arrow point is drawn at each end of a drawing. (Example, ⟵⟶) Examples of lines are difficult to find in the child's environment. Commonly used textbook examples include "a straight highway," "the horizon," and "a railroad track." Some children have difficulty with these examples because they recognize that all roads **must** turn eventually and that the horizon is really curved since the earth is not flat.

Curves (paths) that are <u>straight</u> and have <u>two</u> <u>endpoints</u> are called **line segments.** Pupils see examples of line segments everywhere—the edge of their desks, straight marks on their paper, the edge of a book. Two balls of string stretched tightly between two students can be used to represent a line segment. (Some pupils imagine the string unwinding in a straight line and never ending as a model for a line.)

Some primary programs teach children how to use symbols when identifying geometric terms since it limits the number of written words that must be "read" by youngsters. To name a line segment, a pupil writes the letters of the two <u>endpoints</u> and draws a "miniature" line segment <u>above</u> the letters. (Example, $\overline{KT}$) In naming a line segment it is not important which letter is written first—line segment KT and line segment TK are two names for the same thing. To name a <u>ray</u>, the letter of the endpoint is written first and then any other point on the ray is identified. A "mini<u>ature</u>" ray is drawn above the two letters. (Example, $\overrightarrow{RS}$) (The ray symbol **always** faces right, regardless of the direction of the ray.) To name a line, **any** two points on the line can be used. The symbol for a line is a "miniature line," drawn above the two identifying le<u>tters</u> to indicate that the figure is a line. (Example, $\overleftrightarrow{JM}$)

When developing these models it is important for the teacher to use representative models that convey the desired attributes. Figure 11.1 illustrates a possible set of models from the child's world that conveys one aspect of the attributes of these three figures.

Closed Figures—Circle, Square, Rectangle, Triangle

Children may enter first grade with misunderstandings about circles, rectangles, squares, and triangles. For example, some children identify *any* round shape as a circle. If a square is tipped up on one corner, pupils do not identify it as being a square. Children first recognize that circles, triangles, squares, and rectangles are simple closed curves—that "animals that are inside the fence cannot get out." They find that SOME of the simple closed curves are made entirely of line segments. Children must learn how to identify the features that <u>distinguish one shape from another</u>.

Circles are first explored as a special kind of closed curve that does not use any line segment. As pupils examine the shape more carefully, many will see that every spot on the border of the circle is the same distance away from the center of the

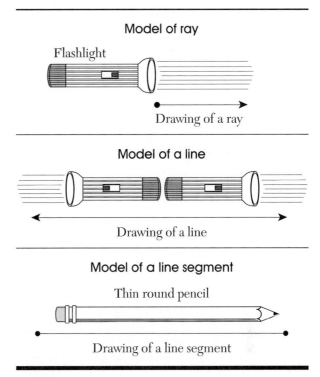

FIGURE 11.1

circle. Teachers sometimes help pupils see this by having a child hold on to a length of rope that is tied to a pole and walk all the way around the circle—just as a minute hand would sweep around the clock.

There are several important features to explore when primary children examine a **rectangle.** Pupils should recognize that the shape is a "closed path" made out of "four line segments." They should also recognize that the line segments opposite each other stay the same distance apart (<u>parallel</u> line segments). With primary children, the <u>meaning</u> of parallel is emphasized but generally the word "parallel" is not used. Children should also recognize that rectangles have a "special corner" that may be identified as a "right corner." As children explore rectangles some may recognize that a square has ALL of the features of a rectangle—so it would be a "special kind of rectangle." (A square is a rectangle made of four congruent line segments.)

First activities with **squares** and rectangles should allow children to construct squares using strips of paper (toothpicks, drinking straws, etc.) and a model of a right corner (see Figure 11.2) to ensure the corners of the squares determine right angles. Some of the distinguishing features that are first identified by primary children through these manipulative activities include:

Right-corner model.

FIGURE 11.2

- "Squares are closed figures."
- "They are made with four sticks." (Four line segments)
- "They have special corners called 'right corners.'"
- "All the fences used in a square are the same length."
- "A square is really just the border."
- "There is an inside and an outside of each figure."

When exploring **triangles** children discover that they are closed figures made with three "fences" (line segments). When pupils first construct triangles with straws they tend to make equilateral triangles. However, as the teacher emphasizes that a triangle is made of three line segments, pupils will try fences that are not the same length and see that they too are triangles.

A primary program may teach children to identify and write the names of these figures using symbols instead of written words (for example, the symbol for "triangle" is Δ). Polygons may be named by writing the symbol (or word) in front of the letters of the corners (vertices). The points representing the corners are commonly listed in a clockwise (or counterclockwise) order, beginning with any letter. (See Figure 11.3.)

Angles and Right Angles

In the latter part of the primary level, children learn about **angles.** Most children have heard and used the word "angle" on occasions, but many times in an improper context. They have learned that there are "angles" that allow people to get around rules. They may know there are "angle irons" that support shelves in their basement. They have gone fishing and "angled" with a fisherman. They watch their mother try to get the right "angle" when she rolls her ball down the bowling alley. And they have heard that there are three "angles" in a triangle.

However, none of these uses of the word helps the child recognize the geometric meaning of the word.

Most texts define an angle as **two rays that have a common endpoint** (vertex). To build this idea, a teacher may use two flashlight beams directed out from a single point. By tracing the path of the beams, children can see the ray will go through many points, but it never really ends. (Note that it takes rays—not line segments—to create an angle. Line segments can determine an angle if we think of the line segments being extended to form a ray, but they do not make an angle.)

Angles are named by identifying a point on each of the rays and writing the name of the vertex (the beginning point of the two rays) **between** the two letters. When teaching children to write the name of an angle, a teacher will find it helpful to first write the letter of the **vertex** to show the starting point for each ray. Then a point on one of the rays should be identified and that letter written in front of the vertex letter. After one ray is named, the teacher may then identify a point on the second ray and write that letter after the vertex letter. The following lesson fragment describes one way a teacher might develop the naming of an angle.

Teacher-Guided Interactive Learning Activity

LESSON FRAGMENT

M: Naming an angle

A: Third-grade class

T: Modeling, definition

H: Pupils recognize rays

Teacher: On the chalkboard I traced the rays of the flashlight to indicate the rays which have a common endpoint. We have several points indicated on each ray. We see one ray that starts at A and goes **through** B, C, and D. We have a second ray that starts at A. What points does it go through, Georgia?

Georgia: It starts at A and goes through E, F, and G.

Teacher: Good. We could call that ray AE, or ray AF, or ray AG (FIGURE 11.4A.). If we wanted to talk about **both rays** we would call that an **angle.** An angle is two rays with a common endpoint. We call that endpoint the **vertex** of the angle. Note that the angle is only the rays, not the interior or the exterior.

Teacher: How could we write the name for this angle, Turk?

Turk: We could just write "angle A."

Teacher: That's a good idea. With the drawing on the

Naming Polygons

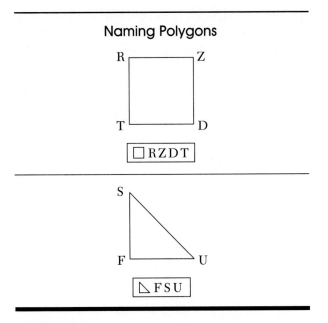

FIGURE 11.3

board, there would be no confusion about which one we meant. But suppose we had another ray—AH. Then we might have some difficulty distinguishing between the different rays. (FIGURE 11.4B.)

Turk: We could write a "1" and a "2" inside the angles and talk about them that way.

Teacher: Excellent, Turk! Sometimes we do just that. But today I'm going to show you another method that we can use to make it clear exactly which angle we want to talk about. First we will draw a "miniature" picture of an angle so we will not need to write the word "angle." This symbol is used just like the plus and minus signs are used so we don't have to write the words. (THE TEACHER WRITES THE SYMBOL FOR ANGLE ON THE CHALKBOARD.)

Teacher: Now we will use some of the letters to name the angle. I'm going to name the vertex of the angle. What letter indicates the vertex of the angles, Vicki?

Vicki: The letter A.

Teacher: So I'll write the letter "A" to show the vertex. Now we need to show that one ray goes through B, C, and D. I can choose any of those letters since it is the same ray. Which one would you name, Will?

Will: Let's use C.

Teacher: Okay, Will, we'll write "C" **before** the vertex letter to show that one ray goes through C. Now we need a letter to indicate the second ray. Bea, would you care to name a point?

Bea: Let's use G.

Teacher: Good, Bea. We could have used E, F, or G, but Bea chose to use G. We'll write the letter G on the other side of the vertex letter. So now we have

the angle that has a ray that starts at A and goes through C (TEACHER POINTS TO THE RAY) and a ray that starts at A and goes through G (TEACHER POINTS TO THE RAY). We read the angle's name from left to right as "angle CAG." (FIGURE 11.4C.)

Pupils do not generally measure angles until they reach the intermediate level. Then the terms "acute" and "obtuse" will be introduced. One special angle, the **right angle,** is introduced in the latter part of the primary level. Children first encounter the concept of a "special corner" in first grade as they explore squares and rectangles. When angles are explored, model "right corners" are used to name the special angle that fits this model. (Since children have not learned to measure angles, pointing out that the angle has "90 degrees" has little meaning to them.)

Teaching Congruency

In order to classify the polygons and to work with fractional parts, children must recognize when two

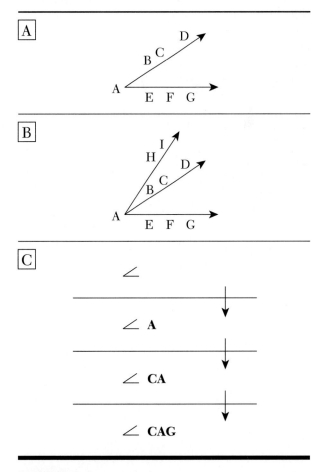

FIGURE 11.4

figures are congruent. To be **congruent** means the figures must be the same shape and size. Congruency is taught at the primary level by having children place one figure on top of a second figure to see if they fit exactly. (At the intermediate level, pupils will explore the motions needed—slide, flip, and rotate—to determine congruency.)

Care must be exercised when working with congruency to prevent the undermining of another geometric concept. The first-grade teacher carefully establishes the concept of interior, exterior, and square (by standing inside the circle and on the circle). If a teacher then cuts out a square shape to place on a second "square," some children revert to thinking of the square as the border **and** its interior. It is better for the teacher to place one sheet of paper on top of a second sheet and hold them both up to the light to see if they fit, or trace one square and place the tracing on top of the second square. (See Figure 11.5.)

When children work with fractions they will cut sheets of paper into congruent regions to show that a half is one part of a sheet cut into two equal-sized pieces. Teachers again must be careful in the use of geometric shapes when illustrating fractional parts. Since a square is simply the OUTLINE—not the interior—dividing of a square into fourths will result in **four line segments.** When illustrating fractional parts of geometric shapes, most teachers are really using "circular regions," or "square regions." The term "region" is developed at the intermediate level to denote the figure (border) **and its**

interior. Since primary children do not know this term—and since they are just beginning to understand that a square or circle does not include the interior of the figure—it is probably **best** to refer to circular shapes as "cookies" or "cakes." If it is necessary to use geometric terms the teacher should make sure that children realize they are working with the figure **and** its interior.

Lines of Symmetry

An interesting attribute of some geometric figures that has an artistic as well as a mathematical application is that of a curve (path) having lines of symmetry. Children see symmetrical objects all around them in their everyday world. As they learn their "letters" they discover many (especially capitals) are symmetrical. The hearts they cut out for Valentine's Day are symmetrical.

Figures can have **line symmetry** or they may have "point" symmetry. Lines of symmetry can be compared to fold lines or the place on a figure where a mirror could be placed to duplicate the image of the figure. The letter "A" has line symmetry since it can be folded down the middle into duplicate parts of the letter. The letter "S" has point symmetry. It is possible to find a point that would divide the letter into two similar parts, but the letter cannot be folded to fit one part on top of the other.

Primary children explore figures that have line symmetry. A figure may have several lines of symmetry. (A circular region has an infinite number of lines of symmetry!) Teachers often use art projects that help children appreciate the beauty of symmetrical designs. Figure 11.6 illustrates the lines of symmetry for several figures.

11.4 TEACHING SPACE FIGURES AND RELATED TERMINOLOGY

Space figures surround the preschool child. Toddlers play with balls (spheres), cans (cylinders), and blocks (prisms). Children eat ice cream from a cone, and see a pyramid roof on their church steeple. They come to first grade with a wealth of experience with space figures, but they have not learned the vocabulary that is used to describe these objects. The introduction of space figures generally focuses upon learning the names for the figures, comparing the different space shapes (those that roll, etc.), associating the geometric figures with real-world models, and learning the vocabulary associated with the figures (such as face, base, edge, vertex).

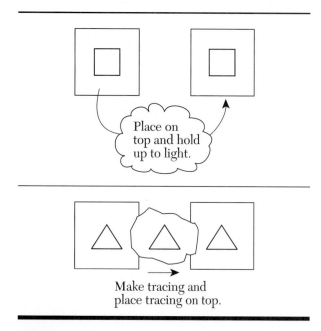

Place on top and hold up to light.

Make tracing and place tracing on top.

FIGURE 11.5

Exploring Lines of Symmetry

FIGURE 11.6

Comparing the Shapes

Even in kindergarten, children are making discoveries with space figures. Cans and balls roll, but blocks don't. This kind of exploration is used in a more formal way at the primary level. Classifying activities help children see ways that shapes are both alike and different. Teachers may place a wide variety of space figures on a table (or in a play area) and ask children to put all of the things that roll in one box. Questions may be asked, such as "Can you find something that can roll in any direction?" (sphere) or "Can you find an object that will roll itself back to the place you pushed it from?" (cone)

If children are told to "put the blocks that are alike" into boxes, the cone and pyramid may be found in the same box. Children realize that both figures have "points." (This observation will prove valuable when children are required to find the volume of those shapes.) Early work with space figures should lead children to compare and contrast shapes. "How are these two shapes alike?" and "How are these things different?" are questions that the teacher can use to focus on this aspect.

Children also explore shapes that have flat sides. Youngsters are already familiar with building blocks. Of course, they call them blocks, not cubes. When developing an understanding of a cube, teachers are not introducing a new shape; they are simply giving a familiar shape a more technical name—"cube." The cube is examined in comparison with other shapes. Children find that, unlike the cylinder, cone, or sphere, a cube does not roll. They look at the flat sides (faces) and find that they all are congruent. When sorting blocks, children generally place the cubes with the rest of the "flat blocks" (prisms).

Children readily recognize some objects that fit into the "box" category. Most boxes are rectangular (or square) prisms. A prism has two bases (bottom and top) that are congruent. Some prisms do not look like boxes. When those bases are rectangular, the prism is called a "rectangular prism." If the bases are triangular, the shape is a "triangular prism." When children reach the intermediate level, they will explore prisms that have hexagonal regions as bases (hexagonal prisms) and octagonal regions as bases (octagonal prisms).

Pyramids have flat sides (faces), but they only have one base. The most commonly recognized pyramid is a square pyramid—it has a square region as a base. Children have seen pictures of the Egyptian pyramids (square pyramids). When they use their building blocks, a pyramid is used as a roof. Primary-grade children generally explore only pyramids with square (or rectangular) bases, but when they reach the intermediate level, they will discover triangular, hexagonal, and octagonal pyramids. (See Figure 11.7.)

Children can learn geometry in non-mathematical settings.

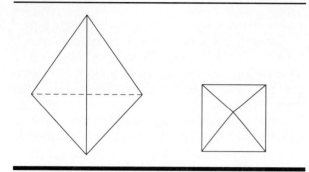

FIGURE 11.7

Associating Space Figures with the Environment

As children learn the names and shapes of space figures, they become aware that there are many examples of these geometric objects in their everyday world. The teacher must direct the attention of the class to shapes in the room or on the playground and note how they are similar to the geometric space figures that have been explored. As children become more familiar with the shapes, there are many more opportunities to use the vocabulary to describe everyday shapes. If children describe an object, the teacher should encourage the use of geometric terms. If a child shows his "round" pencil, the teacher might ask the class what geometric shape is represented by the pencil. When studying the Plains Indians the teacher might point out that an Indian teepee—which looks like a cone—is really closer to a pyramid shape (with an octagon base).

When children make an observation about an object in the room, there may be a need for "qualifying" in order to make it a good model. For instance, a baseball may be spherical in shape, but

the teacher will want to point out that spheres are hollow, while a baseball is not. (Space figures have a surface and an interior—everything outside is called the exterior.) If a child suggests an ice cream cone, the teacher should accept it as a "cone-shaped" thing, but should point out that the geometric figure called a cone is closed. The hole in the top of an ice cream cone is needed, since the ice cream must fit somewhere, but a geometric cone would have a lid on it. (See Figure 11.8.)

A teacher must become familiar with the shapes in the neighborhood so attention can be directed to these figures. Children may bring in items that are not commonly recognized models. For example, the milk cartons often found in lunchrooms are like pentagonal prisms; the "base" (not the bottom) is the five-sided end of the carton. (See Figure 11.8.)

Each classroom and individual building will of-

sphere
playground ball; classroom globe, some bubbles and balloons

cylinder
empty pop can; round pencil (hollow); hockey puck (hollow)

cone
ice cream cone (with lid); front of a rocket; cheerleader's megaphone (is not pointed)

cube
hollow dice; child's plastic block; Rubik's cube

rectangular prism
shoe box; cereal carton; textbook (hollow); hollow door

triangular prism
pup tent; roof of a house (with floor); wedge (hollow)

hexagonal prism
hollow yellow pencil; a 6 sided gazebo

octagonal prism
thick stop sign (hollow); terrarium (8 sides, covered)

square or rectangular pyramid
Egyptian pyramid (hollow); center pole tent; roof of church steeple (with floor)

hexagonal pyramid
Indian tepee with 6 poles and a floor; roof of 6-sided gazebo

octagonal pyramid
Indian tepee with 8 poles and floor; perhaps the base of a gemstone (8 sides)

Lid

FIGURE 11.8

FIGURE 11.9

fer different examples. A bus shelter may have a "pyramid" roof. A swing set may be shaped like a triangular prism. Some examples that might be considered are listed in Figure 11.9.

Building a Technical Vocabulary

As pupils become familiar with space figures, the need for a more technical vocabulary grows. Children become frustrated when describing the features of a figure because their terms are not specific. In describing an Aztec pyramid, a child may say, "I saw a pyramid where the top part was gone. I mean that part where all those slanted parts come together. You know, the opposite part from the base, if you come right up straight." At this time it might be appropriate for the teacher to provide the more technical term "apex" to the child's vocabulary.

Since the need for a more technical vocabulary occurs as children talk about space figures, teachers must structure the classroom environment so students feel that need. By asking questions that require more specific terms, teachers help children learn new words. When a child describes one of the "corners" on a prism, a teacher may point to an edge, and then a vertex, to ask which one is being described. Once the child identifies the corner (pointed part), the teacher may give the term "vertex" to clarify the name.

By the end of the third grade, most children know that the flat parts on prisms and pyramids are called **"faces."** They recognize that when two faces come together, it is similar to the edge of a knife and is called an **"edge."** Where three or more faces come together the "pointed part" is called a **vertex** (the plural form is vertices). The bottom of a figure is generally called the base, and that point where all surfaces from the base come together (on a cone and pyramid) is called an **apex.** (See Figure 11.10.)

11.5 TEACHING GEOMETRY AT THE INTERMEDIATE LEVEL

Explorations of geometry that began in the primary grades continue at the intermediate level, but at a more formal stage. Here students will look at the specific characteristics of a shape (van Heile second level), explore subsets of triangles and quadrilaterals, and examine specific properties of figures (van Heile third level).

Intermediate-level students are introduced to construction of simple geometric figures using

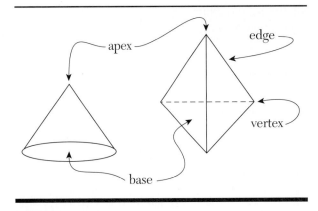

FIGURE 11.10

compass and straightedge. Students learn to bisect angles, inscribe and circumscribe figures, erect perpendiculars, and copy angles and line segments. Transformations of geometric figures are introduced and students explore the effect of using "slides, flips, and turns" upon a figure.

The following illustrates a typical scope and sequence of geometry topics taught at the intermediate level.

Grade 4

Maintain and extend concepts introduced in primary grades
Explore planar figures and their attributes
  • angles (right, acute, obtuse)
  • circles (diameter, radius, center)
  • lines (parallel, intersecting)
  • line segments
  • polygons (vertex, side, diagonal, perimeter) classification by sides (quadrilaterals, pentagons, etc.)
  • similar and congruent figures
  • line symmetry
Explore space figures
  • identify shapes (cylinder, cone, sphere, pyramid, rectangular solid)
  • apply terms (face, edge, vertex)
Maintain skill in coordinate graphing

Grade 5

Maintain and extend planar figure concepts
  • lines (extended to include perpendicular)
  • triangles classified by angles (right, obtuse, acute)
  • quadrilaterals classified (square, rectangle, parallelogram, rhombus, trapezoid)
  • circle (extended to include arc, circumference)

Maintain and extend space figure concepts
Examine geometric constructions
- copy line segment, circle
- bisect line segment, angle

Explore transformations (slides, flips, and turns)

Grades 6, 7 and 8

Maintain and extend planar figure concepts
- triangle (relationship of hypotenuse explored)
- polygons (classified and compared)
- circle (circumference and pi explored)

Maintain and extend space figure concepts
- prism family (triangular prisms, rectangular prisms, etc.)
- pyramid family (triangular pyramid, square or rectangle pyramid, etc.)
- polyhedrons explored (tetrahedron, pentahedron, octahedron, etc.)
   regular and nonregular figures
   truncated figures, right and oblique figures

Use geometric constructions
- copying angles
- erecting perpendiculars
- inscribing and circumscribing figures

11.6 COMPARING AND CONTRASTING GEOMETRIC FIGURES

Students entering the intermediate level are familiar with many of the attributes of geometric figures. For example, most can discern straight paths from nonstraight paths, paths that do or do not cross, paths with endpoints, and simple closed figures. Teachers <u>may</u> need to associate pupil awareness of "same shape and same size" with the mathematical term "congruent."

Teaching Similarity

Students at the intermediate level explore the concept of **similar figures**. (<u>Similar</u> means the figures have the same shape, but not necessarily the same size.) Congruency of figures can be verified simply by placing a figure (or its tracing) upon a second figure, but the verification of similar figures is more complicated. Early explorations with similar figures are designed to develop an <u>intuitive</u> understanding and do not emphasize geometric proofs. Therefore, initial activities lead students to recognize that when two figures look "alike," one may be "larger than the other." Most students will focus their at-

tention primarily upon the "appearance" of the figures: "Do they look alike?" In these first experiences, the teacher can accept this kind of observation, but may want to point to features that are the same and those that are different in the figures. Leading questions such as—"Are the corners the same in each of the figures? Are the sides the same? Are ALL corresponding line segments in the second figure <u>twice as long</u> as the first figure?"—lay the foundation for more formal geometric proof of similar figures.

An interesting technique for generating figures of the same shape (similar) is to project a figure onto the chalkboard with an overhead projector. Figure 11.11 illustrates a child replicating a similar figure from an image of a figure drawn on a transparency.

Grids of various sizes can be used to generate similar figures. Figure 11.12 illustrates the transferring of similar designs from one grid size to another. Students enjoy "enlarging" or "reducing" figures, especially when the original figure appears to be an "artistic drawing" of an automobile or rocket, etc.

Independent Learning Activity

Making similar figures.

FIGURE 11.11

Small-Group Learning Activity

FIGURE 11.12

Teaching the Concept of Parallel and Intersecting Lines and Planes

While primary-level children may have difficulty envisioning lines as "unending," the more mature intermediate-level pupil readily accepts the fact that lines can go on forever, reaching far out into space. The concept that parallel lines are two lines (in the same plane) that will NEVER cross is easily accepted by these students. Parallel line segments also are recognized as being the "same distance apart" since they are a part of parallel lines. However, students sometimes have difficulty accepting that lines that coincide with the parallel line segments also must be parallel. Teachers may need to reinforce pupil understanding of the relationship of lines and line segments, demonstrating that the lines that extend from the line segments must be STRAIGHT (they can't start curving), and therefore will never come any closer together!

When first working with parallel line segments, students may choose to use congruency to verify that two line segments are parallel. Tracing points at one end of the parallel line segments, they slide the "copy" to the other end of the segments to see that the segments "stay the same distance apart." Teachers may need to point out that the pencil "tracing" may be in error since lines have no thickness. Therefore, "measuring" to see if two line segments are parallel may not always identify line segments that are not parallel, especially if the lines (of which the segments are just a subset) intersect "way out in space."

Teachers can demonstrate that two sides of a polygon are not "parallel" by extending the line segments to the point that they intersect. Figure 11.13 offers one way of illustrating the concept of parallel and nonparallel line segments.

Parallel planes are planes in space that do not intersect. Sometimes a teacher will refer to faces of a space figure as being parallel. This is analogous to referring to line segments as being parallel. What is really meant is that the faces are part of planes that are parallel.

However, once students recognize faces for polyhedrons as parts of planes, it is possible to refer to the faces being parallel. Students will discover that some faces on space figures are not parallel (as in a pyramid). When planes intersect, that intersection forms a line. When segments of planes (plane regions, faces, etc.) intersect, they form a line segment. On space figures, intersecting faces form an edge, which is a line segment.

11.7 USING SLIDES, FLIPS, AND TURNS TO EXPLORE GEOMETRIC TRANSFORMATIONS

Geometric transformations have a wide variety of applications. One of the most interesting is the way anthropologists classify designs used in various cultures. Artifacts are often sorted by the way their designs were generated in terms of transpositions (slides), inversions (flips), and rotations (turns). Figure 11.14 illustrates designs found on three sets of pottery. Some designs may involve multiple combinations of slides, flips, and turns.

Transformations are used in art, engineering, and computer graphics, as well as mathematics. Explorations at the elementary school level are generally limited to helping children interpret visual transformations using the simple classifications of "slides," "flips," and "turns." Such explorations create an awareness of this aspect of geometry and encourage pupils to see its application in the world around them.

Instruction in transformations involves manipulations and design activities that incorporate slides, flips, and turns. An overhead projector is a

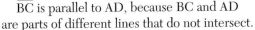
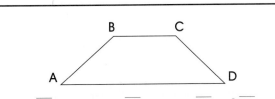

$\overline{BC}$ is parallel to $\overline{AD}$, because $\overline{BC}$ and $\overline{AD}$ are parts of different lines that do not intersect.

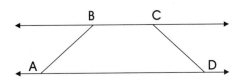

$\overline{AB}$ is not parallel to $\overline{CD}$, because $\overline{AB}$ and $\overline{CD}$ are parts of different lines that intersect.

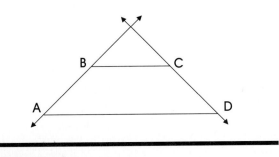

FIGURE 11.13

Design using slides.

Design using turns.

Design using flips.

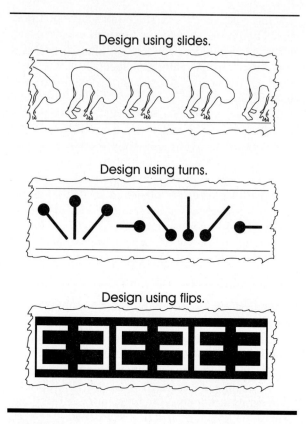

FIGURE 11.14

good device for introducing this idea. As the teacher describes the activity (a slide, a flip, or a turn) children watch the transformation on the screen. Follow-up projects might involve designs pasted onto a sheet of construction paper using some specific child-created rule to form a design pattern. Transformations can be found in the art of M. C. Escher (1898–1972) whose tessellations are fascinating to students. (Tessellations are developed more fully in the enrichment section of this chapter.)

11.8 MAINTENANCE AND EXTENSION OF CONCEPTS RELATED TO FIGURES IN A PLANE

Students leave the primary grades with limited mastery of geometric concepts and vocabulary. Therefore, the intermediate-level teacher must review those skills before new concepts can be introduced. To maintain interest in such a review, the teacher can present the material in a different manner, combining two or three terms in a single illustration. Though children explored points, planes, lines, line segments, rays, and angles during the

first three grade levels, they usually used simple drawings to build single concepts.

Extending Understanding of Geometric Terms

At the intermediate level, more complex drawings are used. For example, in a drawing such as that found in Figure 11.15A, students recognize the importance of a notational system to identify parts of the drawing. If the teacher asks a pupil to point to **the** line in the illustration, the student has difficulty identifying WHICH of the four lines the teacher means. More information is needed. Iden-

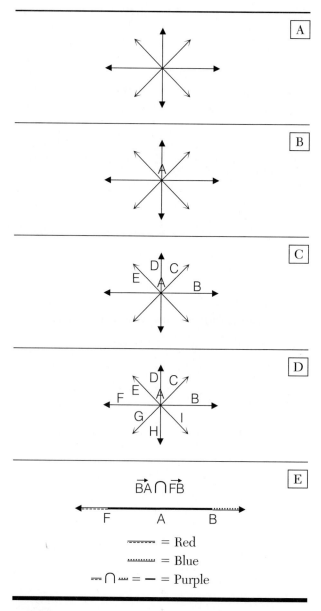

FIGURE 11.15

tifying the point of intersection as "A" will give some information (Figure 11.15B). The teacher can then say that the **line** passes through point A. But, since all four lines pass through A, another point needs to be identified. By asking different students to identify points on the lines with letters as labels (Figure 11.15C), the teacher emphasizes the value of using symbols to identify lines. The line that passes through A <u>and</u> B would be called "line AB" while the line that passes through A <u>and</u> C would be designated "line AC." The symbol for the line (as illustrated in Figure 11.15C) gives the student a simple way of writing identifying information. The teacher can also identify **rays** with the same drawing. Using one of the rays that originates at "A,"the teacher can help pupils recognize the importance of labeling <u>other</u> points in order to identify WHICH ray, starting at A, is being described (Figure 11.15D). Once other points have been identified on the drawing, pupils can quickly find the ray that starts at A and passes through point G (ray AG).

In numeration, children first learned to identify an amount, such as five. Then pupils learned that 3 + 2 was also another way of looking at five—or <u>another name</u> for five. This same concept is explored when examining geometric figures. In Figure 11.15D the teacher directs students to "find another name" for the union of ray AB and ray BF (line AB). Pupils also may identify the intersection of ray BA and ray FA as line segment FB. When using activities of this nature, students generally are directed to "trace" ray BA with a <u>red</u> crayon and ray FA with a <u>blue</u> crayon. The resulting "purple" part is identified as the intersection and recognized as a line segment since it has a "beginning <u>and</u> ending point" (Figure 11.15E).

Children explored angles in the primary grades, and right corners (right angles) were used when describing squares and rectangles. In the intermediate grades, students learn to identify angles that are "smaller" than right angles (acute) and angles that are "larger" than right angles (obtuse). Since students have worked with "right corners" in the primary grades, the use of such a model for comparison purposes is effective when determining whether an angle is right, acute, or obtuse. Angles that "fit the model right corner" are classified as "right angles"; those that are "wider" are classified as **obtuse**; and those that are narrower (or hidden by the model) are **acute** (Figure 11.16). Since pupils have not yet learned to <u>measure</u> angles with a protractor, the teacher should not define acute as "less than 90 degrees" and obtuse as "greater than 90 degrees." Such a definition is an outgrowth of

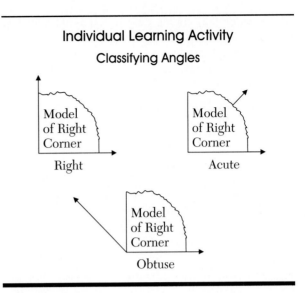

Individual Learning Activity

Classifying Angles

Right

Acute

Obtuse

FIGURE 11.16

measuring angles and will <u>extend</u> the pupil's understanding of acute and obtuse.

Recognizing Special Polygons

In the primary grades children classified shapes based on attributes such as the number of sides (triangles, quadrilaterals, pentagons), special characteristics (quadrilaterals with right corners—rectangles), and combinations of features (quadrilaterals with square corners <u>and</u> congruent sides). At the intermediate level students refine their classification skills using more specific characteristics— parallel line segments and/or angular measure determined by using a protractor. Pupils also learn to recognize how these geometrical concepts apply in their everyday environment and how they are applied in problem-solving situations.

Exploring the Triangle Family

When children first examined triangles, they recognized them as a particular shape. Their attention was later directed to the fact that triangles are <u>closed figures</u> that are made of three line segments and that these shapes were "separated" (classified) from the shapes that used four, five, six, and more line segments. At the intermediate level, students learn that triangles may be further classified by their corners (right, obtuse, or acute) or by their sides (equilateral, isosceles, or scalene).

At the primary level students were satisfied simply to classify all three-sided things as triangles. Intermediate-level students are more mature and explore the relationship of angles and triangles.

They recognize that angles are defined as "the union of two rays with a common endpoint (vertex)." Since triangles are the union of three <u>line segments</u>—<u>not rays</u>, some pupils cannot understand how the triangle can have <u>any</u> angles. Such observations provide an opportunity for the teacher to clarify how corners of polygons are "determiners of angles." Teachers develop this concept by drawing a picture of an angle on the chalkboard. Since the rays of the angle go on forever and the picture of the angle stops at the edge of the chalkboard, students recognize that the drawing is just a PART of the angle. By using a large sheet of paper to conceal the rays so that they appear to be "shorter," the teacher can show pupils that the rays are really DETERMINED by the first part of the ray (the line segment) that is left exposed on the board. As the paper is moved closer and closer to the vertex, students recognize that the angle is not getting smaller; they just cannot see as much of the rays. (Figure 11.17.)

To help students learn to classify triangles by their sides, the teacher may distribute strips of paper or sticks and have students construct different triangles by pasting them together. As various triangles are collected, the teacher may direct the class to "sort" triangles into "like" groups, describing WHY each went into a selected pile. One of the first groups usually identified is that set of triangles made by using strips that were <u>congruent</u>. Students then find that there are triangles that have <u>NO congruent sides</u>. This leaves a set that has two congruent sides. Once classified, the teacher may introduce the mathematical terms for (a) all congruent sides—**equilateral triangles**; (b) two congruent sides—**isosceles triangles**; and (c) no congruent sides—**scalene triangles**. Since equilateral triangles have <u>at least</u> two sides which are congruent, they **also** are isosceles. The teacher should direct students' attention to the fact that equilateral triangles are a subset of the set of isosceles triangles.

Students may sort triangles by their corners (angles). They easily sort triangles into two groups,

those that have right corners and those that <u>do not</u> have right corners. A further sorting of the "non-right corner" triangles reveals triangles with a "fat" corner (obtuse angle) and those without a "fat" corner (acute). Students who have explored right, acute, and obtuse angles will recognize that corners are "determiners" or "starting sides" for these angles. Once students can sort triangles on the basis of corners (angles), then the names for those categories—**right triangles, acute triangles,** and **obtuse triangles**—may be introduced. When sorting by angles teachers should help pupils recognize that ALL triangles will have AT LEAST two corners that are acute; only in the acute triangle are ALL corners acute.

Sorting activities can be used to develop an excellent bulletin board display. Students are encouraged to search newspapers and magazines for pictures to add to the bulletin board. Pupil understanding is deepened when they must decide whether a picture showing the end of an A-frame house should be displayed as an isosceles triangle

---

Small-Group Learning Activity
Triangles

Take the cards given to your group.

A. Sort the cards into three piles on the basis of their sides. Label your groups.

SORT BY SIDES

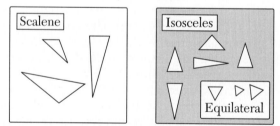

B. Sort the cards into three piles on the basis of their corners. Label your groups.

SORT BY CORNERS

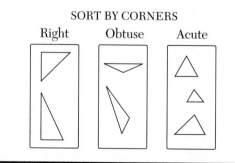

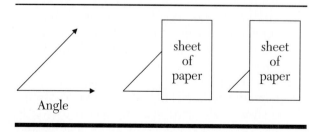

Angle

FIGURE 11.17

FIGURE 11.18

Independent Learning Activity

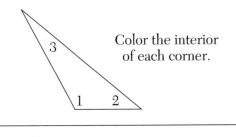

Color the interior
of each corner.

Tear off the corners and match their
edges. Find the sum of the measures
of the corners. (180 degrees)

FIGURE 11.19

or as an acute triangle (see Figure 11.18).

Once pupils have learned to classify triangles, the teacher may explore other relationships within triangles. Examining the angles of an isosceles triangle allows students to discover that isosceles triangles have two <u>congruent</u> angles as well as two congruent sides. Students may use tracing paper to replicate the sides or corners when checking for congruency. Once students learn to measure angles, a protractor may be used to verify that a triangle is right, acute, or obtuse.

Another interesting exploration for intermediate-level pupils is the examination of the sum of the measures of the interior angles of polygons. Using protractors, students can measure various triangles and discover that the sum of the interior angles of a triangle equals 180 degrees. Another way to explore this relationship of a triangle to its interior angles is illustrated in Figure 11.19. In this activity students color the corners (interior) of a triangle. These colored corners are then cut off and pasted together to demonstrate how they will form a line segment (determine a straight angle).

Late in the intermediate level, students reexamine right triangles to discover new relationships. The special relationship between the side opposite the right corner and the sides that form the determiners of the right angle is a valuable study. The side opposite the right corner is called the <u>hypotenuse</u>. By comparing the hypotenuse to the other two sides pupils can discover an interest-

ing relationship—the Pythagorean Theorem (Figure 11.20).

Exploring the Quadrilateral Family

In the primary grades children used congruency and right corners to classify squares and rectangles. In the intermediate grades, students examine new relationships, properties, and attributes when clas-

Independent Learning Activity

Pythagorean Theorem

Look at the drawing. Side A has a square tile pattern. How many tiles will it take to tile in the pattern for side A? How many tiles will it take to tile in side B?

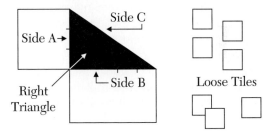

Now use the tiles from sides A and B. How many of the tiles will it take to make a square pattern for side C?

Try your pattern on right triangles
— with sides of 6, 8, and 10
— with sides of 9, 12, and 15

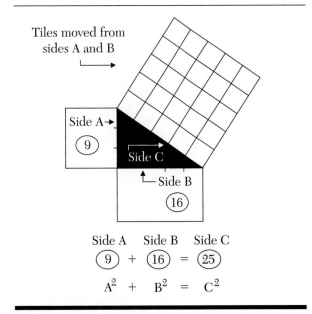

Side A   Side B   Side C
  9 + 16 = 25
  A^2 + B^2 = C^2

FIGURE 11.20

sifying quadrilaterals (quadri means four; lateral means sides).

Once pupils understand parallel, the quadrilaterals can be classified in terms of the opposite sides being parallel line segments. If a quadrilateral is made with two pairs of parallel line segments it is a member of the **parallelogram** family. When one and only one pair of parallel line segments is used, the quadrilateral is a **trapezoid**. Figure 11.21 illustrates some members of the parallelogram and trapezoid families.

Although children are familiar with rectangles, they generally do not identify rectangles as a subset of the parallelogram family. Protractors may be used when exploring members of the parallelogram family. Parallelograms whose angles measure 90 degrees are also called **rectangles**. Students also learn that the same family can be described in different ways; for example, "rectangles have congruent opposite sides and right corners"; "rectangles have opposite sides that are parallel and have four right corners"; or "rectangles are quadrilaterals with two congruent diagonals." In describing rectangles, students find that some "descriptors" are not precise enough to eliminate other figures. For instance, the isosceles trapezoid (bottom right-hand shape in Figure 11.21) has diagonals that are congruent, yet it is not a rectangle. The teacher might accept from a pupil the definition "the opposite sides are parallel and the figures have four right angles."

Intermediate-level students learn that **squares** are members of several families. Since squares have "opposite sides parallel and have four right corners, they must be rectangles (and parallelograms). Since many pupils incorrectly perceive that rectangles have a "pair of long sides and a pair of short sides," they find it difficult to accept squares (which have all sides the same) as part of the rectangle family. Once they reconcile the fact that squares are "special" rectangles, they can more easily accept that a square also can be a **rhombus**, since the rhombus family consists of those parallelograms which have four congruent sides.

As students classify various figures, they often question the importance of having different categories. Suggesting that a student "describe a square to someone over the phone" may help pupils recognize the value of a more precise vocabulary. Since the person on the other end of the phone can only "see" a square through the oral description, one must be very careful in the choice of words. Descriptions can get quite lengthy and can easily be misinterpreted. If a pupil only says, "A square is made with four congruent line segments," then

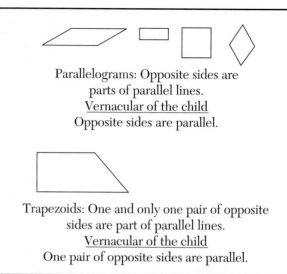

Parallelograms: Opposite sides are parts of parallel lines.
Vernacular of the child
Opposite sides are parallel.

Trapezoids: One and only one pair of opposite sides are part of parallel lines.
Vernacular of the child
One pair of opposite sides are parallel.

FIGURE 11.21

four "sticks" that are unattached would fulfill the description (see Figure 11.22).

Exploring Other Polygons

While intermediate-level explorations deal mainly with polygons within the triangle and quadrilateral families, some time is devoted to examining the general classification of polygons that have more

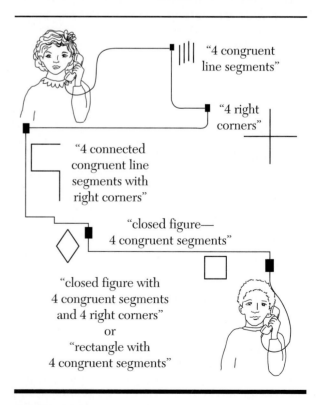

"4 congruent line segments"

"4 right corners"

"4 connected congruent line segments with right corners"

"closed figure— 4 congruent segments"

"closed figure with 4 congruent segments and 4 right corners"
or
"rectangle with 4 congruent segments"

FIGURE 11.22

than four sides. Pupils learn that polygons with more than four sides are named by the number of sides in the figure. For example, five-sided polygons are called <u>pentagons</u>, six-sided polygons are <u>hexa</u>gons, eight-sided polygons are <u>octagons</u>, ten-sided polygons are called <u>decagons</u>, etc.

Two explorations are frequently conducted when studying polygons. One activity studies the pattern associated with the <u>diagonals</u> (a line segment joining two nonadjacent <u>vertices</u>) of polygons. For example, a triangle has no diagonals, while a quadrilateral has two diagonals. When the diagonals are shown on a pentagon (connecting the vertices of the figure) the student will discover there are five diagonals (2 + 2 + 1); a hexagon has nine diagonals (3 + 3 + 2 + 1); and other polygons show similar patterns. By exploring the <u>patterns</u>, the pupil may be able to determine a "rule" for <u>predicting</u> the number of diagonals for ANY polygon (Euler's formula).

A second exploration, finding the sum of the interior angles of a polygon, provides a much more challenging activity. Once students recognize that the interior of the polygon may be broken into a series of triangles, many can reason through the remaining steps to find the number of degrees for the entire figure. Pupils need to be reminded that the sum of the interior angles of a triangle is 180 degrees. Others may need to recognize that the sum of all the angles around the center of the shape will be 360 degrees. Figure 11.23 shows a learning-station activity that explores the relationship between the sum of the interior angles of a polygon and its number of sides.

While concave figures are not a <u>major</u> focus of the intermediate program, students do explore the relationship of **convex** and **concave** figures. A <u>geoboard</u> is an excellent device for investigating these <u>figures</u>. Geoboards are available commercially, but inexpensive models can be constructed with nails and a board. Figure 11.24 illustrates a geoboard using rubber bands to exhibit a quadrilateral that has the property of concaveness, and another quadrilateral that has the property of convexness. Using rubber bands, pupils find that some figures have diagonals that <u>stay within the figure</u>. These figures are called convex. When ANY diagonal <u>crosses outside the figure</u>, the figure is called concave.

Exploring Circles and their Properties

Some of the earliest human artifacts indicate an awareness of the circle. From the circular arrangement of the stones at Stonehenge to the circular petroglyphs left behind on the rocks by prehistoric

---

Independent Learning Activity

What is the sum of the angles of a square?

Hint: four triangles.
The sum of the interior angles
of a triangle equals 180 degrees.

What is the sum of angles A,B,C,D?
How can this help you find the sum of
the interior angles of a square?

---

5 triangles

Can you find the sum of the
interior angles of a pentagon?

The sum of the five angles in the
center will still be 360 degrees!

---

6 triangles

Can you find the sum of the
interior angles of a hexagon?

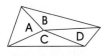

Can you find the sum
of the interior angles
of this figure?

Independent Learning Activity

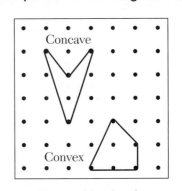

Using rubber bands:
Make a convex quadrilateral
that encloses only 1 nail.

Make a concave quadrilateral
that encloses only 1 nail.

FIGURE 11.23   **FIGURE 11.24**

American Indians, humans have demonstrated an awareness of this geometric figure. The utilitarian nature of the circle can still be seen today in the most primitive of cultures. Many tribes make a circle on the ground as the first step in erecting a shelter. Sitting in a circle to share folk tales and make council is almost a universal tradition among primitive cultures.

The circular shape occurs often in nature, from the circular patterns on certain flowers to the ripples that are made when a rock hits calm water. Many teachers introduce the study of circles by having students find places where they encounter the circle in their environment.

When developing meaning for a circle at this more mature level, the definition should also be developed. The teacher may call upon different pupils to find locations that are all the same distance from a point on the chalkboard. After several locations have been identified, the teacher should ask students to find ALL points that are the same distance from the identified point. As more and more points are found, the pupils see that the shape which emerges is that of a **circle**. To identify ALL points on a plane which are equidistant from a given point (center), a circle must be drawn. The distance from the center to the edge of the circle is given the name **radius**. While working with the diagram, pupils also see that a line segment drawn from one side of the circle, through the center, and touching the other side of the circle would be two times the length of the radius. The teacher may identify this line segment as the **diameter**. Any line segment that <u>starts on</u> the circle and <u>ends on</u> the circle is called a **chord**. Since the diameter starts and ends on the circle—it is a chord. Students should explore to find that <u>the diameter is the longest chord of the circle</u>. The circumference is the distance around the circle, or for some students, it is the "length" of the path that makes up the circle. Figure 11.25 illustrates the technical vocabulary that is used with children in the intermediate grades.

An exploration of the relationship between the circle's diameter and circumference is an interesting activity for most intermediate-level students. A learning station that presents many different circular objects provides a good environment for discovering **pi**. Students can select four or five round objects and measure the distance around (circumference) by rolling each object. Pupils then measure the distance across (diameter). Using a calculator, pupils may divide the circumference by the diameter and find that the same ratio—about $3\frac{1}{7}$—exists whether the object is a penny or a bicycle

wheel! Because of measurement inaccuracies, pupils generally will only get "near" 3.14. As more measurements are made, the numbers may be AVERAGED to come closer to pi.

Applications of Geometric Shapes

The polygons and circles studied in school are found in a wide variety of applications. Students may look around the classroom and find rectangular chalkboards and sheets of paper, circular clocks, triangular supports for shelves, and many other shapes. Discussion can lead to speculation on why the shapes are found so often in our world.

Quadrilaterals—rectangles in particular—are an integral part of a wide number of everyday objects. Many can be seen easily—the frame of the door or window—while some are not immediately recognizable. For example, when walls in a house are constructed, carpenters use wood frames in a series of rectangles. When lumber is put into the frame, the carpenter can <u>predict</u> where to place his nails

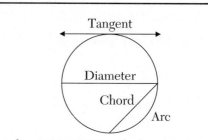

The DIAMETER is the longest chord
and goes through the center of the circle.

The RADIUS is a line segment from the
center of the circle to the "edge" of the circle.

The CIRCUMFERENCE is the distance
around the circle.

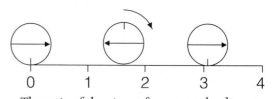

The ratio of the circumference to the diameter
has a special name called pi (π).

The circumference is approximately 3 and 1/7
times the length of the diameter.

In decimal form—pi is <u>about</u> 3.14

FIGURE 11.25

even when the boards are covered by sheets of ply-wood due to the parallel nature of the sides of the rectangles.

While the parallel nature of the sides of a rectangle have great advantages in building, they lack the rigidity of form of the triangle family. To investigate this property of shapes, students can put strips of posterboard together with paper fasteners to see how "strong" they are. When a quadrilateral is used the shape "collapses" or "tilts over," but triangles are always very rigid. Pupils discover that if they place a diagonal on a rectangle, they have formed two triangles and that will make the rectangle much stronger.

Because of the triangle's structural rigidity, it is often used in the construction of bridges, towers, and highrise buildings. The teacher may wish to have a bulletin board display of student-furnished pictures that highlight triangles in use in everyday situations. Construction projects with toothpicks and glue also offer an opportunity for the child to discover the structural advantage of using triangular shapes.

Polygons are found in art, architecture, engineering, and the sciences. Graphic artists make extensive use of polygons to create interesting designs. Architects utilize a variety of polygons to provide efficient traffic flow within a building, and chemists use polygons to create models for the study of crystalline structures and chemicals.

Circles play an integral part in the study of longitude and latitude in social studies. In addition, navigational routes taken by explorers are often plotted on the basis of **great circle** routes (the shortest distance between two points on a globe). **Arcs** of circles are used to study pendulums in science, while both circles and arcs are used to form intricate designs in art. Circular shapes are an integral part of many machines and tools of everyday life from wheels and gears to the sockets for electric lights.

11.9 TEACHING GEOMETRIC CONSTRUCTIONS

Intermediate-grade students enjoy creating simple constructions with a straightedge and compass. Pupils are taught to draw arcs and circles, copy angles, erect perpendiculars, construct lines parallel to other lines, and bisect angles and line segments. These skills are used to construct congruent and similar triangles and quadrilaterals. (This section presents only a few of the more common constructions.)

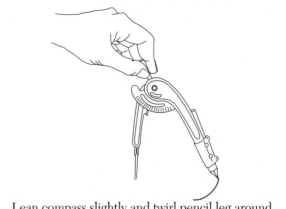

Lean compass slightly and twirl pencil leg around, making arc or circle.

FIGURE 11.26

Drawing an Arc and a Circle from a Fixed Point

To draw an arc with a compass, the needle end of one of the legs is placed on a point and an arc (or circle) is drawn by the pencil leg (Figure 11.26). Pupils should be taught to "twirl" the knob to make a smooth circular path.

Copying an Angle

Being able to copy an angle is a skill fundamental to reproducing similar and congruent polygons. Figure 11.27 illustrates a step-by-step procedure for using a straightedge and compass to copy an angle.

Bisecting an Angle

A common construction taught at the intermediate level is that of bisecting an angle. Figure 11.28 illustrates the following four steps in bisecting an angle:

1. Place the needle leg of the compass on the vertex of the angle and swing the pencil in an arc that crosses both rays.
2. Move the needle leg to the point where the arc crosses a ray. Swing the pencil to form a new arc on the interior of the angle. (The compass may need to be spread further for this step.)
3. Move the needle leg to the intersection of the first arc and the second ray. Swing a new pencil arc—crossing the arc drawn in step 2.
4. To bisect the angle, draw a ray starting at the vertex of the original angle, which passes through the intersection of the arcs drawn in steps 2 and 3.

Constructing Congruent Angles

1. Place needle leg of the compass on the vertex and swing an arc through each ray of the angle.

2. Draw a ray where you wish to construct the new congruent angle. **A**

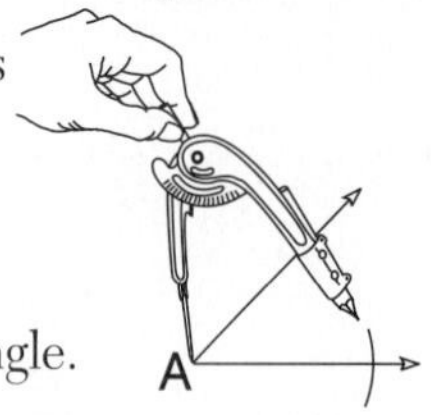

3. Keep the spread of compass legs the same as in step 1. **B**

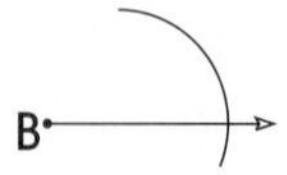

4. Place needle end of compass on the endpoint of ray and swing an arc.

5. Return to the original angle and adjust the spread of the compass legs so that the needle leg pivots on the intersection of one ray **A** and the pencil leg crosses the intersection of the arc and the other ray of the original angle. (Swing an arc to make certain the measure is accurate.)

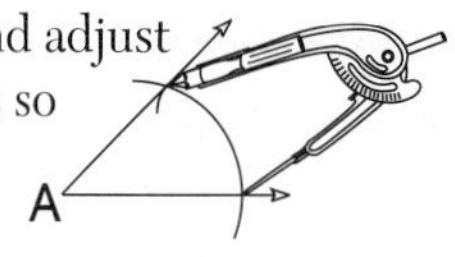

6. Keep the same compass setting as in 5 and move compass to new ray. **B**

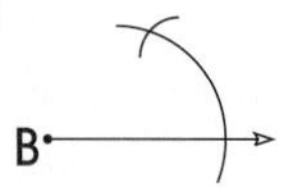

7. Set needle leg on intersection of arc and ray. Swing new arc with pencil so it intersects with first arc. **B**

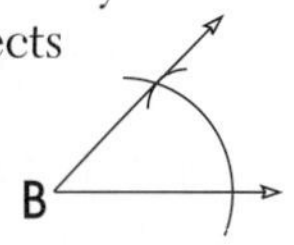

8. Use straight edge to construct a ray from the vertex (B) through this intersection of arcs.

FIGURE 11.27

Constructing Perpendicular Bisectors, Perpendiculars at a Point, and Perpendiculars from a Point to a Line

Being able to construct perpendiculars plays an important part in constructing right triangles and members of the rectangle family. Figure 11.29 illustrates how these basic constructions are made. (The steps of making arcs and line segments are indicated by number.)

11.10 EXTENDING UNDERSTANDING OF SPACE FIGURES

The intermediate-grade student will learn more precise ways of classifying space figures (van Heile's second level of understanding). While the

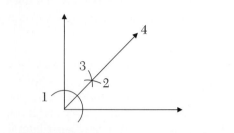

FIGURE 11.28

primary child was satisfied to label a wide variety of figures as "boxes" or "prisms," the intermediate pupil classifies prisms by their bases—triangular, rectangular, pentagonal, hexagonal, octagonal, etc. Pyramids are now classified as triangular pyramids, rectangular pyramids, square pyramids, hexagonal pyramids, etc.

The terms "edge" and "face" were introduced at the primary level. Students now will recognize that a face is a "plane region" (a shape with its interior). The edge will be described as the intersection of two faces that results in a line segment. Students also learn to use the name "vertex" (plural, vertices) for the "pointed corners" of the space figure. More specifically, the **vertex** will be identified as the intersection of three or more faces. The result of this intersection is a point. Pupils learn to identify the apex and base of a space figure. For most pupils, the **apex** is that point on the figure where all line segments drawn from the boundary of the base meet. Cones and pyramids will be examined and found to have only one **base** (a surface that is perpendicular to the altitude of the space figure), while prisms and cylinders have two bases. Spheres—since they have only curved surfaces—have no bases at all!

As students look around the environment they observe that some objects look similar to the space models, but parts are "missing." They will learn that such figures can be described as **truncated**. Truncated figures are used in the study of new geometric plane figures, such as the ellipse or parabola family of curves, which are generated by certain truncations caused by planes passing through cones. (See Figure 11.30.)

Pupils are introduced to a new way of classifying a space figure that has only faces (no curved surfaces)—**a polyhedron**. Sorting polyhedra (plural) is a way of classifying figures based on the number of faces. For example, a four-faced space figure is called a **tetrahedron**, a five-faced shape is a **pentahedron**, a six-faced figure is a **hexahedron**, an eight-faced figure is an **octahedron**, a twelve-faced figure is a **dodecahedron**, and a 20-faced figure is called an **icosahedron**. (While figures with seven and nine faces also have names, they are seldom used.) Polyhedra that have all faces congruent and the same number of faces that meet at each vertex are called **regular** polyhedra or **Platonic solids**. (Space figures are hollow. They have an exterior, an interior, and the surface itself. When someone wishes to include the interior and surface, then the figures are called **solids**.)

Pupils can learn much about space figures by constructing the various models. Patterns—provided by the teacher—can be cut out, folded into a space model, and taped together. Using these models, identifying the vertices, faces, and edges becomes much more understandable. Students sometimes play a guessing game with a set of space models. A pupil chooses a polyhedron and hides it from view. The figure is then described in terms of

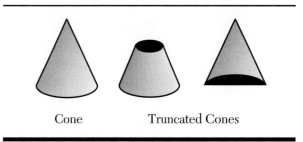

Cone   Truncated Cones

FIGURE 11.30

edges, faces, and vertices. The opponent takes the given data and gives the precise shape name. For instance, if a pupil said, "I have a figure with twelve vertices, eight faces, and 18 edges," the opponent must identify the shape as a "hexagonal prism" (not an octahedron). Figure 11.31 illustrates a few common patterns for making space figures.

Many pupils encounter difficulty with drawings used to "represent" space figures in textbooks. To show that the space figure is "three-dimensional" the pictures may show a perspective drawing in which the pupil sees "through" the figure. In such drawings, the faces, edges, or vertices are commonly "miscounted." Instructional time must be devoted to associating this kind of perspective drawing to the actual space models.

11.11 COMPUTERS

While there are a number of computer programs that teach aspects of geometry to children, the most widely used of these programs at the elementary level is the LOGO program. LOGO is a computer language that was developed by Seymour Papert, a professor at the Massachusetts Institute of Technology (M.I.T.), and his fellow workers. Not only does LOGO provide many interesting avenues for explorations with geometric concepts, but it also introduces the pupil to computer programming.

Once the LOGO program has been loaded in the computer (the first programming step in using LOGO), the pupil tells the computer to "show the turtle." (Type SHOWTURTLE and press key marked enter or return.) Now the student can program the "turtle" (a small triangular figure on the screen) to move a certain number of spaces and specify direction of movement. If no direction is specified the turtle will move forward in the direction it is pointing. For example, FORWARD 25 (enter), RIGHT 90 (enter), FORWARD 25 (enter), RIGHT 90 (enter), FORWARD 25 (enter), RIGHT 90 (enter), FORWARD 25 (enter) will generate a square.

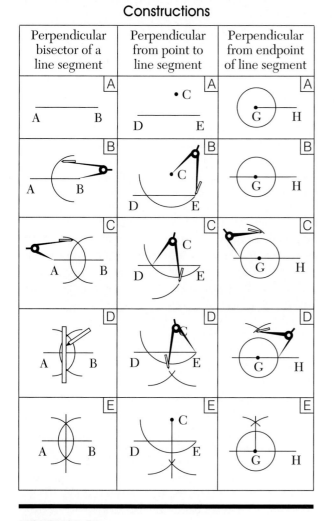

Constructions

Perpendicular bisector of a line segment	Perpendicular from point to line segment	Perpendicular from endpoint of line segment

FIGURE 11.29

Patterns for Space Figures

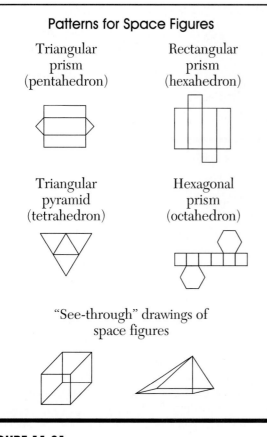

Triangular
prism
(pentahedron)

Rectangular
prism
(hexahedron)

Triangular
pyramid
(tetrahedron)

Hexagonal
prism
(octahedron)

"See-through" drawings of
space figures

FIGURE 11.31

It would be very cumbersome to program each individual movement of the "turtle" by writing a direction for each movement and each change in direction. Fortunately LOGO allows one to give the computer directions to replicate a step. For example, the previous example can be shortened to RE-PEAT 4 (FORWARD 25, RIGHT 90).

LOGO makes it possible for the teacher to design problems that will lead to interesting student discoveries. For example, what would be the directions you give in LOGO to generate six-sided (nine-sided, ten-sided, 12-sided, 18-sided) regular polygons? (Hint: How do the exterior angles relate to the "turtle" turning, and how does the number of sides of the regular polygon relate to 360 degrees?) Explorations with triangles and angles also lead to some interesting discoveries. For example, if the pupil programs "FORWARD 20 (enter), RIGHT 60 (enter), FORWARD 10 (enter)" and then looks at the screen, what angle might the pupil speculate would take him/her back to the beginning? If this process were repeated with other movements, always taking a 60-degree turn and always moving half the number of spaces on the first movement, what generalization might the pupil discover about triangles formed by 30-, 60-, and 90-degree angles?

LOGO lets the pupil explore the nature of programming a computer in a relaxed atmosphere while experiencing many of the attributes of other computer programs to be learned later. Students will learn how to set up a program, set up subprocedures, use terms such as print, load, count, and, or, if, not, save, end, copy, and random—which are terms and procedures common to many computer programs.

Of course, commercial software is available to explore various geometric figures and their properties. These programs are useful when teaching students to classify figures and to help them learn the terminology associated with these figures.

11.12 EVALUATION AND INTERVENTION

Because the nature of the geometry is different than that of number and number operations, the assessment and diagnoses of conceptual understandings of geometric concepts are also different. In assessing the pupil's understanding of geometric concepts, the student's developmental level must be considered. The average child enters the primary grades knowing the names of some shapes (circular, square, triangular), some properties (straight and curved), and some vocabulary related to spatial location (top, bottom, under, over, and between). Assessment at this level involves determining if the child can identify shapes, properties, and spatial locations.

At the intermediate level pupils will analyze spatial figures using more specific properties (congruence, endpoints, closed). For example, the students learn to classify figures based on simple analysis, such as "a quadrilateral is a <u>closed</u> figure formed by four line segments." Assessment at this level may require the pupil to test a figure to see if certain properties hold. For instance a student would check a rectangle to see if the corners are square. The assessment procedure may require sorting or drawing objects having a specific property or characteristic.

At the intermediate level the pupil studies the planar figures and learns multiple names for two- and three-dimensional objects. For example, students may classify a space figure as either a triangular pyramid based on its base, faces, and apex, or as a tetrahedron based on its number of faces. Assessment should include construction tasks, identification tasks, sorting tasks, and identification of specific parts, elements, or properties of the figure.

In a sense, remediating incomplete mastery of geometric concepts is easier than remediating concepts relating to numeration or number operations. Frequently, the pupil's weakness is the result of not having been exposed to the concepts being assessed. In these instances, the teacher will plan an instructional program that provides the student with an opportunity to learn these concepts. In other instances, pupils will not master geometric concepts because they have deficits that relate to learning spatial information. (This type of remediation will be addressed in the section on teaching exceptional children.)

11.13 SPECIAL NEEDS

The area of geometry is rich in meaningful explorations for the gifted and more able student. In school systems where the emphasis is on vertical enrichment the teacher can plan explorations of relationships that will be examined more formally in plane geometry courses—for example, "which components of angles and sides determine unique triangles?" The teacher may choose designs and patterns such as tessellations (mosaic patterns) as explorations or assign independent research studies that investigate how engineers, architects, or artists use the planar or space figures that have been studied.

Horizontal enrichment through activities with tessellations can be approached either from a mathematical perspective, art perspective, or social studies perspective (for example, how the Moors of North Africa used tessellations to decorate their buildings). An interesting way to explore tessellations is to start with a simple tessellation and have the child modify it to develop a new tessellation. For example, notice in Figure 11.32 how a square-shaped figure has been modified to generate a new tessellation. Teachers can choose a wide variety of tessellation building blocks to help children explore tessellations. Triangles, parallelograms, rectangles, and other regular patterns that can be used as "unit" figures provide good exploration materials for modifying into new tessellations.

Providing for the Gifted Student

Geometry has many topics that present challenges to the gifted student. The teacher can choose topics about the early mathematicians who developed geometry, such as Euclid; or study contemporary topics, such as the application of geodesic domes in construction; or accelerate the pupil's study by picking more advanced topics.

In the following lesson fragment a group of gifted children discover the sets of conditions that are necessary and sufficient to construct a unique triangle.

Teacher-Guided Interactive Learning Activity

LESSON FRAGMENT

M: Necessary and sufficient conditions for construction of unique triangles

A: Gifted sixth-graders

T: Discovery, construction of models

H: Geometric constructions using a straightedge and compass

Constructing a Tessellation Using Square Regions

Start with a square region and draw a design. Move "cut off" parts from one square to an adjacent square region.

Cut this part and move.

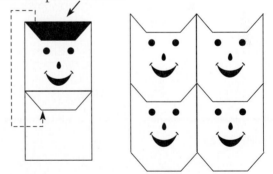

By cutting and moving from one square region to another many interesting designs may be created.

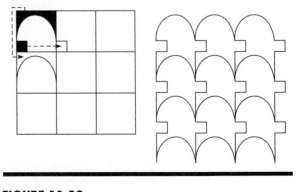

FIGURE 11.32

Small-Group Learning Activity

Copy the line segment and
angles illustrated.

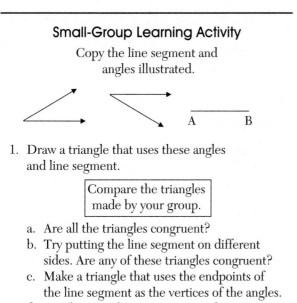

1. Draw a triangle that uses these angles
   and line segment.

   > Compare the triangles
   > made by your group.

   a. Are all the triangles congruent?
   b. Try putting the line segment on different
      sides. Are any of these triangles congruent?
   c. Make a triangle that uses the endpoints of
      the line segment as the vertices of the angles.
   d. Are the triangles now congruent?

2. Copy the line segments below. Construct a
   triangle using the line segments. Compare
   the triangles made in your group.

   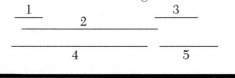

   a. Are all triangles congruent?
   b. Can you make a triangle with these segments
      that is not congruent?

3. Copy the line segments below. Use any three to
   make a triangle. Are there any combinations
   that will not make a triangle?

   $$\underline{\hspace{1.5cm}}^{1} \qquad \underline{\hspace{2cm}}^{3}$$
   $$\underline{\hspace{3cm}}_{2}$$
   $$\underline{\hspace{3cm}}_{4} \qquad \underline{\hspace{1cm}}_{5}$$

FIGURE 11.33

Teacher: Each of you were given a series of exercises
in which various conditions relating to angles and
sides have been specified. You were also given angles and line segments for each exercise. (FIGURE
11.33 ILLUSTRATES SOME OF THE EXERCISES
PRESENTED BY THE TEACHER.) When you finished, you were directed to compare your work with
others in your group to see if you could discover
which conditions are necessary and sufficient to determine a triangle.

Teacher: In exercises 1 and 2 did anyone discover
which of these conditions resulted in a series of
congruent triangles? Yes, David?

David: When the two angles were started at each end
of the line segment.

Teacher: Good. So we have found one condition that
will always give us congruent triangles, or—an
angle-side-angle determines a triangle. Are there
any other conditions that will determine a triangle?
(THIS TYPE OF INQUIRY IS DEVELOPED WITH
THE OTHER PAIRS OF EXERCISES. WHAT
WOULD THE STUDENTS DISCOVER WORK-
ING EXERCISES 3 AND 4?)

Providing for the Learning-Disabled Student

Geometry may be difficult for learning-disabled
children—especially when their deficit areas are related to spatial orientation and memory. In some
cases, making the learning tasks multisensory may
improve the child's ability to learn the geometry
concepts being presented. In fact, many of the
same kinds of activities recommended when learning to configure numerals may be used to teach
geometric concepts. For example, walking through
large geometric figures taped to the floor or feeling
sandpaper outlines of the figures will assist certain

Individual Learning Activity
Geometric Sorting Tasks

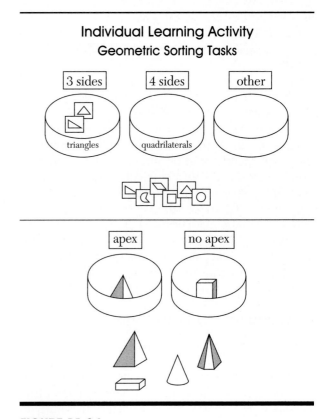

FIGURE 11.34

children with spatial memory deficits to get a feel for the geometric shapes. Other pupils benefit from "limited" sorting tasks. In such activities the pupil is given picture cards of geometric figures and asked to sort the objects into sets by a specified characteristic. A student might be asked to sort the cards by the "number of sides" in one activity. On another occasion, a pupil may be given ONLY quadrilaterals and asked to group those which have "four right corners." Figure 11.34 illustrates sorting tasks based on the specific criteria being remediated.

11.14 SUMMARY

Geometry begins with the study of shapes in the kindergarten. In the primary grades the child has many hands-on explorations with some of the more common figures in a plane and is introduced to some elementary properties of figures (congruency, figures with square corners). Children also learn some basic vocabulary associated with these figures. In addition to planar figures the child learns to identify and name the more common space figures (cone, pyramid, sphere, and cube).

At the intermediate level pupils use a more analytical approach to classifying plane and space figures. Students learn to form groups and subgroups of figures based on specific sets of properties. New properties are introduced and incorporated into the classification systems being developed.

At both primary and intermediate levels the pupil learns to recognize geometric figures in his/her environment and appreciate the role played by these figures in everyday life. The explorations that take place at the elementary school level serve also as readiness for the more formal study of geometry at the postelementary school level.

EXERCISES

1. The van Heile model of geometric thought presents five levels. Name the levels and give an example of a pupil behavior at each level.
2. Describe how a teacher might help pupils recognize the difference between a "dot" and the definition of a "point."
3. For each geometric term below, suggest an object from the child's environment which might be used as a physical "model." If an object does not "exactly" fit the definition of the term, give the modification that would be necessary. (For example: an ice cream cone is "nearly" like a geometric cone, but it would need a lid to cover the opening since space figures are closed.)

   a. ray
   b. line
   c. angle
   d. rectangle
   e. square
   f. triangle
   g. circle
   h. sphere
   i. cone
   j. cylinder
   k. simple closed curve
   l. rectangular prism
   m. square pyramid
   n. hexagonal prism
   o. octagonal pyramid

4. Describe an activity that might be used by a teacher to introduce each of the following concepts:

   a. congruency
   b. similar figures
   c. parallel lines

5. Describe a beginning activity in which a teacher introduces classification of angles (right, obtuse, and acute).
6. Describe the characteristics of each of the following figures:

   a. the triangle family (classified by sides and classified by corners)
   b. the quadrilateral family (parallelogram, rectangle, square, rhombus, trapezoid)
   c. concave and convex plane figures
   d. truncated space figures
   e. polyhedra (tetrahedron, pentahedron, hexahedron, etc.)

7. When possible, new skills should be introduced in a meaningful situation. Suggest a classroom situation which could be used to introduce

   a. geometric constructions (perpendicular, bisecting angles, etc.)
   b. transformations (flips, slides, and turns)
   c. tessellations

8. If available, explore the use of a LOGO program for exploring geometric relationships. What strengths and/or weaknesses could you recognize from your use of the program?
9. Select a currently published elementary school mathematics series. Examine the geometry topics presented in the first, third, fifth, and eighth grades. Try to determine

which of the van Heile levels of geometric thought are being developed with those exercises.

10. Often geometric topics are explored simply as textbook exercises. Suggest several ways that a teacher could help pupils recognize

the importance of geometry in activities outside of school.

11. Choose one of the articles in the References section. After reading the article, write down three ideas that might be shared with a fellow teacher.

RELEVANT COMPUTER SOFTWARE

Inside Outside Shapes. 1986. Apple II family. Random House School Division, 201 E. 50th Street, New York, N.Y. 10022.

REFERENCES

Bright, G. W. "Logo and Geometry." *Arithmetic Teacher* 36 (January 1989): 32–34.

Bright, G. W., and J. G. Harvey. "Learning and Fun with Geometry Games." *Arithmetic Teacher* 35 (April 1988): 22–26.

Burger, W. F. "Geometry." *Arithmetic Teacher* 32 (February 1985): 52–55.

Campbell, P. F. "Microcomputers in the Primary Classroom." *Arithmetic Teacher* 35 (February 1988): 22–29.

Crowley, M. L. "The van Heile Model of the Development of Geometric Thought." In *Learning and Teaching Geometry, K-12: NCTM Yearbook. 1987.* Reston, Va.: National Council of Teachers of Mathematics, 1987. Pp. 1–16.

Heukerott, P. B. "Origami: Paper Folding—the Algorithmic Way." *Arithmetic Teacher* 35 (January 1988): 4–8.

Jensen, R. J. "Concept Formation in Geometry: A Computer-aided, Student-centered Activity." *Arithmetic Teacher* 35 (March 1988): 34–36.

Jensen, R., and D. C. Spector. "Geometry Links the Two Spheres." *Arithmetic Teacher* 33 (April 1986): 13–16.

Kaiser, B. "Explorations with Tessellating Polygons." *Arithmetic Teacher* 36 (December 1988): 19–24.

Larke, P. J. "Geometric Extravaganza: Spicing Up Geometry." *Arithmetic Teacher* 36 (September 1988): 12–16.

Pappas, C. C., and S. Bush. "Facilitating Understandings of Geometry." *Arithmetic Teacher* 36 (April 1989): 17–20.

Smith, R. F. "Coordinate Geometry for Third Graders." *Arithmetic Teacher* 33 (April 1986): 6–11.

Terc, M. "Coordinate Geometry: Art and Mathematics." *Arithmetic Teacher* 33 (October 1985): 22–24.

CHAPTER 12

TEACHING MEASUREMENT

INTRODUCTION

An understanding of measurement is essential to function in a modern society. People structure their day around time schedules; make purchases with money; and select items by length, area, or volume. We dress according to the predicted temperature for the day; celebrate holidays according to a calendar; and go on diets to reduce weight.

The seven basic types of measure commonly examined in the elementary school program include time, weight (or mass), money, length (including perimeter), area, volume (both liquid and dry), and temperature. Both the English (customary) and metric measurement systems usually are taught in elementary programs because the child will encounter each system in everyday activities. (Soda pop **may** be purchased in pint or quart bottles, or may be found in 1-, 2-, and 3-liter containers.)

The fact that the United States uses two measurement systems (English and metric) means children must become "bilingual" in measurement. Children should not be taught to convert from one system to the other, but they do need to compare English and metric units (a liter is a "little more" than a quart; a meter is a "little longer" than a yard). As pupils learn the metric units, they will find that some fields, such as science, medicine, photography, and international track events, use only metric measures. When purchasing foods, packages show both the English measurements and the metric units.

12.1 TEACHING MEASUREMENT IN THE KINDERGARTEN AND PRIMARY GRADES

Kindergarten children explore measurement concepts as circumstances present themselves in the routine of daily activities. When children enter the primary level explorations with measurement concepts become more systematic. The nature of measuring is explored using nonstandard units **before** standard English and metric units are studied.

Children are taught to recognize the names of standard units and the relative size of these units in terms of items in their environment. Pupils should know that a yard is "about" the distance from an adult's nose to the tip of his/her outstretched hand. As children become more familiar with the relative size of measures they will begin estimating measures.

While learning different measuring units children recognize why different-sized units (inch, yard, mile, etc.) are needed. Being able to *select* the appropriate unit when measuring is a skill with many applications. Children will also need to change from one unit to another (one foot equals 12 inches, etc.).

The primary-level child must recognize and be able to use a variety of instruments for measurement. For example, a tape measure and a ruler may be used when making linear measurements. When finding weight, a scale (balance scale or spring scale) is used. A measuring cup helps us determine liquid measure, and a thermometer is used to check temperature.

The order in which measurement skills are introduced may vary from school system to school system. The outline below gives one of many possible sequences for developing measurement skills in the kindergarten and primary grades.

Kindergarten

Identify items that are equal and not equal in measure
Recognize measurement instruments and their use

Grade 1

Money
- identify penny, nickel, dime, and quarter
- count collections of coins (pennies, nickels, dimes—no more than one quarter)

Time
- tell time to the hour and half hour
- write o'clock and half past
- recognize days of the week on a calendar

Length
- measure with inch or centimeter ruler

Liquid Measure
- identify cup, pint, quart
- compare measures by pouring liquids

Angles
- identify figures with right corners

Weight Measure
- use balance scale
- read weight scale

Temperature
- associate warmth and coldness with seasons

Solve measurement problems

Grade 2

Money
- identify coins through half dollar
- count coins through 99¢
- write money with cents and dollar sign
- choose amount from collection of coins

Time
- tell time to the nearest five minutes
- write time to nearest five minutes

Length
- measure and record to nearest inch and centimeter

Liquid Measure
- identify cup, pint, quart, liter
- compare cups to pints; pints to quarts
- recognize equivalent measures

Angles
- draw right corners using model

Weight
- identify and compare pound and kilogram

Temperature
- read a temperature scale (thermometer)

Solve measurement problems

Grade 3

Money
- identify coins and bills
- count money through $5
- write money through $5 with dollar sign
- select most appropriate coins for purchase

Time
- tell time to the nearest minute
- write time to nearest minute
- identify minutes before and minutes after
- identify A.M. and P.M.
- identify months of year

Length
- measure to the nearest inch, foot, yard
- measure to nearest centimeter and meter

Liquid Measure
- identify cup, pint, quart, gallon
- identify liter measures
- compare measures (within system)
- compare cups to pints; pints to quarts; quarts to gallons

Perimeter/Area/Volume
- count units of length around a figure
- count tiles needed to cover region
- count blocks needed to fill a box

Angles
- identify and draw right corners with model

Weight
- measure to nearest pound or ounce
- measure to nearest kilogram

Temperature
- read a thermometer to nearest degree
- recognize typical temperature readings

Solve measurement problems

12.2 TEACHING MEASUREMENT CONCEPTS IN THE KINDERGARTEN

Children enter kindergarten with many misconceptions regarding measurement. Some misconceptions are developmental—for example, many children will not be able to conserve measure (length, area, volume). Children have great difficulty in perceiving equality of measure under transformation. For example, many children believe that when a liquid in a short, fat container is poured into a tall container there is more liquid in the taller container. A child may believe that when one of two matched cookies is broken and spread out, the broken cookie represents more cookie than the whole cookie. (See Figure 12.1.) Of course, some misconceptions stem from misinterpreting vocabulary they hear being used by others. For example, parents frequently use measurement terms idiomatically and not mathematically. For example, "I'll be there in a second" is an idiomatic expression for "I'll be there in a little while" and adults don't mean one second in the measurement sense.

Building Premeasurement Skills

Part of the kindergarten teacher's responsibility is to provide pupils with experiences that help them develop a conceptual understanding of measurement. The teacher must enlarge and refine the general measurement vocabulary, since it also serves as a vehicle for communicating other mathematical concepts. Premeasurement vocabulary (smaller-larger, shorter-longer-taller, big-little, heavier-lighter, faster-slower, and more-value and less-value) are developed as part of structured kindergarten lessons, games, playground, and free-time activities.

In early school experiences, children will explore the concept of equal (and not equal) in measure and recognize instruments used to make these determinations. Although children enter school with some awareness of both of these aspects of measurement, the teacher must identify and correct misconceptions about measurement. When children leave the kindergarten they should recognize things that are equal (and not equal) in measure. They also will know that a ruler is used to measure length, a clock and a calendar are used to keep track of time, and a scale (generally a balance scale) is used to measure weight. Since children will use money in their everyday lives, they also must learn to recognize coins (by their names) and know that a quarter is worth more than a dime, a dime is worth more than a nickel, and a nickel has more value than a penny.

When developing equal (and not equal) concepts the teacher will utilize examples where children see the attribute in "action." For example, two children balancing on a teeter-totter, two objects that take up the same amount of space in glasses of water, or two objects that just match when laid end to end. Figure 12.2 illustrates an activity in which equality of <u>time</u> can be examined in terms of a playground activity.

One of the child's first experiences with length occurs when the child's height is measured. Teachers use this opportunity to construct height strips and make rudimentary graphs of each child's height by taping these strips to a wall. (Some teachers trace around children on large sheets of paper. These are saved so children can see how much they grew during the year.) Hands and feet can be traced and a ruler used to find out about how many inches across a hand is, or a foot is. It should be noted that the objective of such lessons is primarily to make the child aware of the instrument used to measure length—the ruler.

Learning to read a clock is not a skill usually developed in the kindergarten program although some children learn to identify particular hand settings. When kindergarten activities begin at a <u>particular</u> time each day, these fixed time activities sensitize the child to the purpose of a clock. Teachers may display paper clock faces to show how the hands will look when various activities are supposed to begin during the day. (See Figure 12.3.)

The calendar is used to note the date, the day of the week, when someone is having a birthday, and to study how many more days until a given

Cookies

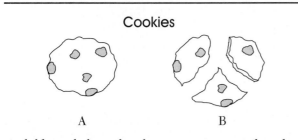

A B

A child may believe that there is more to eat when the cookie is broken into parts (B) than when it is one single piece (A).

FIGURE 12.1

Time

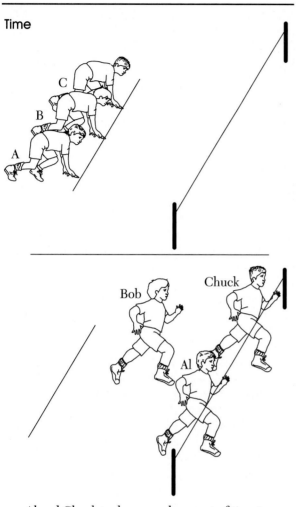

Al and Chuck took an equal amount of time to run the race.

FIGURE 12.2

event. Many teachers use the calendar each day—counting the days of the month that have already passed as a rational counting experience. Some teachers have children record the weather by placing a cloud for a rainy day, a sun for a sunny day, a snowflake for a snowy day, etc. This provides many different rational counting opportunities as the month ends. More formal instruction on the number of days per week and months per year is delayed until later in the primary grades (although some kindergarten programs teach children the names of the days of the week).

Money value is only taught superficially at the kindergarten level. In addition to developing the concept that when two people are willing to trade objects then equal value is established, children are taught to recognize coins. One of the first money

activities is simply sorting coins into pennies, nickels, dimes, and quarters. Figure 12.4 illustrates a sorting task where each sorting cup has one of the coins taped to the cup to serve as a guide for sorting. Notice that the sorting cups also have the word name taped to the cup. Kindergarten programs usually do not stress the exchange of two nickels for one dime, etc.

As a part of the health program in a school, children generally are weighed several times throughout the year. Such an activity will help pupils see how scales are used to measure weight. In the classroom, balances and spring scales will be used to compare various common objects. It is probably <u>best</u> to restrict the weight of the objects to the numbers being developed in the kindergarten (0–10). The balance scale—since it dramatically illustrates that two objects are not equal—is probably more useful than spring scales. When using a balance, children can "measure" the weight of various toys by finding how many "blocks" or "washers" it takes to make the balance even. Children should recognize that BOTH instruments are used to measure weight.

A good kindergarten program should include activities that encourage pupils to pour things (water, sand, etc.) from one container to another. If the pupil does not recognize that the amount of liquid does not change the teacher may need to suggest that the liquid might be poured back into the original container to verify this fact. These "pouring" activities in kindergarten are important foundations for pupils who later will learn that a pint is

FIGURE 12.3

Individual Learning Activity

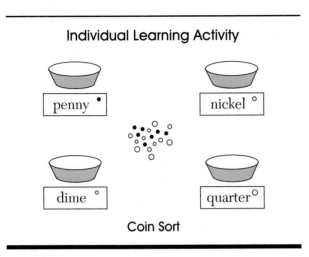

Coin Sort

FIGURE 12.4

the <u>same</u> as two cups and that two cups measure the same amount as one pint.

12.3 TEACHING MONEY

While a child's first contact with measurement occurs when being weighed shortly after birth, his/her first conscious recognition of measurement generally is of a parent purchasing some item for him/her with <u>money</u>. Some preschool children use an "allowance" to buy candy or gum at a grocery store. Through these experiences the child comes to recognize that money has <u>value</u> and it can be <u>traded</u> for other items he or she wants. To strengthen a child's understanding that <u>value</u> is associated with the willingness of two individuals to trade items, teachers may begin the study of money by encouraging children to trade pencils, toys, or other items (provided by the teacher). Such "trades" permit children to recognize that the equality of value is established by the two individuals doing the trade, <u>not by what others may think about the trade.</u>

By the time many children enter the first grade they have had many experiences with coins and often with paper money, but children differ greatly in their experiences. Some children have things bought **for** them—they never really handle the money. Others have been "shopping" with their own money for two or three years. Therefore, a first-grade classroom may have some children who can name <u>all</u> the coins through a half-dollar, while other children only recognize a penny. Even when children have the ability to name the coins, they often

do not recognize the *relative value* of the coins. For example, many children believe a nickel is worth more than a dime because it is "bigger."

One of the first skills taught by the primary teacher is **coin recognition**. Classifying activities (sorting) may be used to develop recognition skills. Given a set of coins that includes <u>only</u> pennies, nickels, and dimes, the child sorts them into boxes—pennies in one box, nickels in a second box, and dimes in a third box. Since classifying is relatively simple for children, the task may be combined with a counting activity. Once the coins are sorted, the child is directed to count the number of pennies or is asked, "How many pennies do you have?"

While there is merit in using **actual coins**, teachers must recognize that some children cannot resist the temptation of pocketing the money for their own use. To remove this temptation, teachers may substitute **play money** when working with coins. Textbooks used in primary classrooms usually provide a set of "punch out" play coins for <u>each</u> child. Since these photographically reproduced coins are quite realistic, they may be used very effectively in both directed lessons and in free-play situations.

Although first-graders may recognize the coins—**penny** and **nickel**—many have not learned their relative values. Early lessons with coins may work concurrently on these two skills; for example, two children may be paired, with one child given a set of pennies and the other child a set of nickels. The children are directed to "trade" their coins following the teacher's directions. Every time one child counts out five pennies the other person must <u>trade</u> them a nickel. The appropriate dialogue when trading is, "Here are your <u>five pennies</u>," while the other child says (as he tra<u>des</u> a nickel for the five pennies), "Here is your <u>nickel</u>." After all the pennies have been traded for nickels the process is reversed, and the child who was trading a nickel for five pennies exchanges his pennies back for nickels.

Trading activities are usually followed with "toy store" activities in which a penny will purchase **one** item and a nickel will give the child **five** of those items. As children become more proficient with the values of the penny and nickel, the teacher can use the toy store to develop money names and use these names to label items to be purchased. In this development, the **cents sign** is used, but not the decimal notation for money. (See Figure 12.5.)

When a teacher chooses to use a counting strategy to develop the relative value of a penny, nickel, dime, and quarter, then the <u>initial compar-</u>

Small-Group Learning Activity

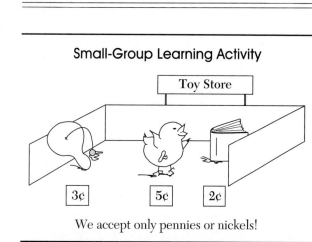

We accept only pennies or nickels!

FIGURE 12.5

isons will be done counting by ones. For example, ten pennies will be traded for one dime; 25 pennies get traded for a quarter. (After the child learns to count by fives the relationship of two nickels to a dime and five nickels to a quarter can be used when trading coins.)

Once children recognize the coins and their relative values they develop strategies for **counting collections of coins**. Several prerequisite skills must be developed before a child can effectively determine the value of a collection of pennies, nickels, and dimes. Of course, children first must recognize the coins and their relative values. Beyond this, children must also be able to count-on. For example, if given a nickel and three pennies, the child should first point to the nickel and say, "Five." Then the child will touch each penny, counting-on after the five, saying, "Six, seven, eight." If a set of coins has several nickels, the child must also be able to count by fives. If the set contains dimes, then counting by tens will be required. When a set of coins contains pennies, nickels, and dimes, children must be able to count by tens, then count-on by fives, and then count-on by ones.

The most effective strategy for counting a set of coins begins the counting process with the coins that have the highest value. For example, when counting dimes, nickels, and pennies the child should **first** count the value of the dimes, **then** count-on using the value of the nickels, and **finally** the pennies. The coins employed for initial instruction in counting two types of coins will be determined by the counting skills possessed by the child. For example, if children have been counting by tens and ones for place-value development (but have not yet learned to count by fives), then the teacher may begin by counting sets that contain only dimes and pennies. However, if children know

how to count by fives, the teacher may introduce counting money with nickels and dimes. In any case the child must be able to count by both fives and tens before introducing counting activities involving nickels and dimes.

Traditionally, first-grade instruction in counting coin sets restricted the collection to dimes, nickels, and pennies. More recently, programs have included **one** quarter in the collection. Since children normally do not learn to count by 25s until third or fourth grade, the inclusion of several quarters is deferred until after children have learned this skill.

There are a variety of counting skills that can be developed once children recognize the coins and their values. For example, given a handful of coins a child should be able to select and count out a specific amount. When making a purchase, sometimes one does not have the exact coins needed. In this case, the child must find an amount that is greater than the purchase amount (but not too large). This skill is much more difficult than finding the exact amount among a set of coins.

Teaching a child to count out either a specific amount from a set or—when the exact amount cannot be found within a set of coins—an amount just larger than the specified amount is developed using the same strategy. Let us examine a fragment of a lesson that develops this skill:

Teacher-Guided Interactive Learning Activity

LESSON FRAGMENT

M: Selecting the proper coins from a set of coins to make a purchase

A: A group of third-graders

T: Involvement, analogy, rules, problem solving

H: Counting a fixed amount of money involving pennies, nickels, dimes, and a quarter

PROBLEM-SOLVING SITUATION:
THE CLASS HAS BEEN USING A "PLAY STORE" IN WHICH THE PRICES WERE MULTIPLES OF TEN OR FIVE. AS THE NEW WEEK BEGINS, THE TEACHER HAS "CHANGED THE PRICES" SO NEW AMOUNTS ARE REQUIRED.

Teacher: Take out your play coins and put four dimes and three nickels on your desk. We are going to the store to buy some items. We want to give the clerk the exact amount of coins to make the purchase. If we do not have the exact amount, we will want to give the clerk an amount so we get the fewest number of coins back. Today I am going to let you use any coins you want to use, providing they are either the exact amount or just over what you need. Before we start let's plot our strategy. If something costs five cents, show me the coin you would give the clerk. (EACH CHILD HOLDS UP A NICKEL.) If something costs ten cents, what coin would you give the clerk? (EACH CHILD HOLDS UP A DIME.) If something costs 15 cents, which coins would you give the clerk? (THE TEACHER FOLLOWS THIS PROCEDURE UP THROUGH 35 CENTS, ALLOWING A VARIETY OF COMBINATIONS TO BE ACCEPTABLE, PROVIDING THEY ARE EXACTLY EQUAL TO THE AMOUNT SPECIFIED.)

Teacher: Here is one of the new prices at our store. (TEACHER HOLDS UP A PRICE CARD SHOWING 11¢.) How could we buy this item, Buddy?

Buddy: We can use a dime and then put a penny with it.

Teacher: Good idea, Buddy. That is a lot better than eleven pennies, isn't it? But look at the coins you have on your desk. We do not have any pennies. What could we use to pay for our purchase? Who has a suggestion?

Marion: You could give the clerk a quarter, but we don't have a quarter.

Mitch: You could give the clerk two dimes.

Teacher: Mitch, that is a good solution if all you have are dimes. Can someone find another solution? Melony?

Melony: We could use a dime and a nickel—then we would get only four pennies back.

Teacher: Those were all good responses. (NOTE THE PROBLEM-SOLVING NATURE OF THE ACTIVITY OFFERING DIFFERENT PATHS TO THE SOLUTION.) Would Melony's or Mitch's solution result in the fewest number of coins being returned in change? Jeff?

Jeff: Melony's choice results in the fewest number of coins being returned in change.

Teacher: Now I am going to play the part of the clerk. I'll show you a picture of the item we want to purchase, along with its new price. Count out the coins you would need to buy this item, then place them in your "show-me card holder." (THE TEACHER DISPLAYS A CARD WITH A PICTURE OF AN ITEM COSTING 17 CENTS, AND THE CHILDREN COUNT OUT THE AMOUNT NEEDED AND DISPLAY THEIR ANSWERS.) (SEE FIGURE 12.6.) (LATER—DURING FREE PLAY—THE

Evaluation

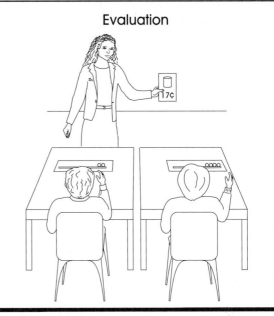

FIGURE 12.6

STORE WILL OPEN WITH ITS NEW PRICES FOR CHILDREN TO PLAY THE SHOPPING GAME.)

When children are able to determine at least one set of coins (from among a set that offers many possible correct choices), then the teacher may have children examine the choices to determine if some are more appropriate than others. For example, if a person feels he/she is carrying around too many coins, then the best choice for 17¢ might be four nickels rather than two dimes. On the other hand, if time is of the essence, then two dimes would be the best choice since the individual will be handling the fewest number of coins.

Writing Money Amounts

The dollar sign and dollar amounts also are introduced in primary grades and their development closely parallels the development of place value. Once the child has learned to compute and has developed some skills with the concepts associated with money, these skills are applied in problem situations involving adding, subtracting, and multiplying amounts of money. Models for this activity are the same models that have been developed for whole number operations, except that the sets involve money. For example, putting together a set of three cents with a set of four cents suggests addition, just as it would if one were talking about the objects being blocks. Likewise, money can be taken away or compared, or one can be talking about a set and a subset of money or—in the case of a multiplication model—equal sets of money. Teachers should include problems involving all types of money situations.

12.4 TEACHING TIME

Time is an integral part of school life. Children go to school in the fall, winter, and spring, and take a vacation in the summer. They attend school Monday through Friday and get Saturday and Sunday off. Their activities—from the time they awaken, through the school day, and when they go to sleep at night—are organized around scheduled time. While the importance of understanding time is recognized by children, mastery of these concepts will, to a great extent, depend upon (1) the child's maturity, (2) the child's mastery of the prerequisite concepts, (3) the opportunity to practice these skills, and (4) the skill with which the teacher presents these concepts.

Time is an abstract concept involving the simultaneous comparison of two events taking place. For example, the child was born at some point in the earth's orbit around the sun. When the earth returns to the same spot, we say that the child is now one year old. In other words, when we state a person's age we are really comparing that person's existence with the number of trips (years) the earth has taken around the sun. In a similar manner, if something—say a flower—exists for a day, we mean that it has lived through one rotation of the earth on its axis. Since we cannot even sense the motion of the earth on its axis, let alone its travel around the sun, this abstract idea is somewhat difficult for a child to comprehend. (While time—as a concept—is abstract, the teacher needs to find ways to at least give the child some understanding of the concept. One way of making children aware of equal and unequal time was suggested in the premeasurement discussion in Section 12.2.)

Teaching Months, Days of the Week, and other Calendar Concepts

For children in kindergarten and even first grade, the calendar is an important measuring device. Indeed, the calendar generally becomes a central focus for the morning exercises. Each month teachers prepare colorful bulletin board displays on which children will record the weather (sunny, rainy, etc.) by pinning on cut-out pictures. Pupils count in unison (rational counting) as the teacher touches each block on the calendar identifying "today's date." Special days (Halloween, Billy's birthday, etc.) are noted and children count the number of days until those important events. These daily experiences help children associate the calendar with a way of keeping track of days.

Pupils may also learn the days of the week by using a calendar. To identify "Friday" the teacher will point to the labels—Monday, Tuesday, Wednesday, Thursday, Friday—while having the class say the days of the week in unison. Teachers also use the names of the days of the week in nursery rhyme songs that emphasize the days of the week. By the time the teacher is ready to teach children the names for the days of the week many children will already be able to:

1. recite the words in order,
2. identify the written words, and
3. recognize that there are seven days in one week.

Children know the names of some months of the year before entering the first grade, but they generally do not recognize the order of the months or the number of days in each. First-grade children generally know the name of the present month, since they hear it at home. They also can recall the name of the previous month. However, after several months have passed, they cannot remember which month came before or after a given month. Learning the order of the months and the number of days in each is not a formal part of the first-grade mathematics program, but children will work on this skill sometime during the second and third years.

When the child is ready to associate the number of days with each month, mnemonic devices are effective. Rhymes such as "Thirty days hath September, April, June and November. All the rest hath thirty-one, except February, it has twenty-eight," are fun to learn as well as useful in remembering days and months. A teacher might want to use a model to assist in this memorization process. Figure 12.7 illustrates how "knuckles and notches" may be employed as a model. (February must still be taught as an exception, even when this device is employed.)

Teaching a Child to Read a Clockface

Some children learn to tell time very easily while others experience great difficulty. There are several reasons why telling time using a clock may be difficult.

Start on left—touch a knuckle and say "January." Continue across the valleys and knuckles saying the months in order. (There will be no valley where the two hands touch—July and August.)

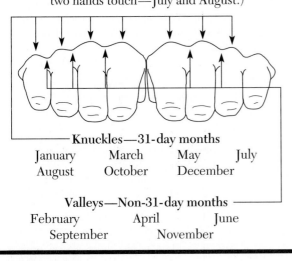

Knuckles—31-day months

| January | March | May | July |
| August | October | December | |

Valleys—Non-31-day months

| February | April | June |
| September | November | |

FIGURE 12.7

1. There are a variety of ways to <u>read</u> the same visual image on a clockface. For example, 5:15 on a clockface can be read, "quarter past five," "fifteen minutes past five," or "five fifteen."
2. Clocks have many different shapes and configurations. Faces may be round, square, oval, diamond, or many other shapes. Some clocks have second hands, while others do not. Clockfaces may be written in Roman numerals or Arabic numerals. Some clocks have numerals identifying only 3, 6, 9, and 12 and others have no numerals at all.
3. Some clocks (digital) do not have hands; numerals are given to indicate the time (e.g., 3:30). While children can "read" the times from this kind of clockface easily, they may have difficulty associating those times with hour-and-minute-hand models and time phrases such as "half past three."
4. After the half hour, the hour hand is closer to the next hour. When the time is really 5:55, the hour hand points almost directly toward the "6," causing many children to read the time as "6:55."

Most children learn to identify some times before formal instruction. They know that their favorite TV program comes on at four o'clock, so they have learned to watch for that time on the clock. Formal instruction in telling time usually begins in first grade when children learn to tell time to the

hour and half hour. Teachers use model clockfaces to illustrate how the clock hands move. When using a clockface model it is <u>best</u> to use one where the movement of the minute and hour hands are coordinated. These models are geared so that a teacher can move the minute hand all the way around the clock and the hour hand will slowly move between two numerals. The teacher should focus pupil attention on the movement of the hands while moving the minute hand, noting the <u>direction</u> the hands are moving (preparing children for the concept of <u>clockwise direction</u>) and the fact that the hour hand is constantly moving, yet ever so slowly. As the minute hand gets closer to the 12, the teacher should point out that the hour hand is getting closer to the next numeral, but has not reached that numeral yet. Only when the minute hand reaches the 12 will the hour hand complete its journey from one numeral to the next.

In teaching children to tell time to the hour, a teacher should emphasize that the minute hand must go all the way around the clockface (emphasizing a clockwise direction) to show one hour. A time is read as "o'clock" (a contraction which means "of the clock") when the minute hand reaches the point indicated by the 12. The "little" hand points to the hour. A child should be directed to look at the hour hand and read the numeral and, when the minute hand reaches the 12, to say "o'clock." Practice should be given on times when the minute hand does not touch the 12 to show that the time cannot be read "o'clock." For instance, after showing three o'clock, the teacher could move the minute hand to show one minute past three and ask the class if it is still "three o'clock." As the teacher points out times past three, he/she may wish to indicate that it is "one minute past three" or "five minutes past three" in preparation for later development of reading time to the nearest minute.

While an understanding of the fraction "half" is helpful when teaching children to read times such as "half past three," many children learn to read this time before they encounter fractions. Since the fractional numeral is not used in writing time amounts, children are not handicapped by their limited background in fractional number concepts. Teachers can illustrate "half past" by showing a cut-out circular clockface. By folding the paper cutout so that the crease lines up on the 12 and 6, a child can see that the region has been "folded in <u>half</u>." Children often associate this with getting a "half of a cookie." They must then associate the lining up of the minute hand at the "crease" with being "half past" the hour. When working with the geared clockface, a teacher should point out that the hour hand moved halfway between the two numerals (at half past three the <u>hour</u> hand will be <u>halfway</u> between the three and the four. The teacher also may want to show that the minute hand has raced "halfway around the clock."

Children learn to write time using either words or numerals. When the clockface shows ten o'clock, children should be able to write "ten o'clock" and "10:00." Since the hour hand points to the hour and the minute hand says "o'clock" when it reaches the 12, children do not experience difficulty recognizing the written word for time. When learning the numeral form for time, many children simply learn that "10:00" is another way of writing "ten o'clock" and that "10:30" is another way of writing "half past ten." They generally do not associate the ":00" and ":30" with the number of minutes past the hour. Teachers can build this understanding by setting the geared clockface at the hour (for example, ten o'clock) and moving the minute hand to show one minute at a time. Children are encouraged to count <u>in unison</u> as the minute hand touches each minute. When the hand reaches the "6," children will have counted to 30 and the teacher will write the hour, colon, and then the "30." Pointing out that this means "thirty minutes <u>past</u> the hour," the teacher then has the class read the time as "ten-thirty." While the activity is designed to help children learn to write "half past ten" as 10:30, some children also learn to read times to the nearest minute from these experiences.

Telling time in terms of "quarter past" or "quarter to" is not taught until the child has worked with the fractional concept of fourths. Since fractional concepts are not explored until the end of the first grade, teaching "quarter past" and "quarter to" is normally deferred until second grade. Again, teachers find that a folded "clockface" is effective when illustrating fourths since similar "pie pieces" were used to introduce fractions. Children have little difficulty learning "quarter <u>past</u>," since they have already learned "half <u>past</u>." Learning "quarter <u>to</u>" does create difficulty since it really involves counting backwards. The time "quarter <u>to</u> five" is written as 4:45. Some teachers have children count by fives backward— counterclockwise—from the "next" hour to show that "quarter to five" is also "fifteen minutes until five o'clock." (Some children may get confused by the term "quarter." In <u>money</u> a quarter means 25 cents, while in <u>time</u> a quarter means 15 minutes.)

Most children count by fives before they leave the first grade. The skill is used as a "timing de-

vice" in games such as "hide-and-seek." Children use counting by fives in counting collections of coins and telling time. While children usually learn to tell time to the nearest five minutes in the second grade, some children do not yet efficiently count by fives. When planning introductory lessons to teach telling time to the nearest five minutes, it is a wise practice to first review counting by fives. A review may become a part of the telling-time lesson, but counting by fives is an essential prerequisite skill. Let's look at a fragment of a lesson where a teacher introduces telling time by five-minute intervals.

Teacher-Guided Interactive Learning Activity

LESSON FRAGMENT

M: Five-minute intervals on a clockface

A: Second-grade learning team

T: Choral counting, physical involvement

H: Prerequisite skills of being able to count by fives, being able to identify the minute hand and hour hand, being able to tell time by hour and half-hour. (After a review of "counting-by-fives" using just the minute hand, the teacher places the hour hand back on the clock.)

Teacher: Watch the hour hand as I move the minute hand slowly around the clock. (THE TEACHER STARTS THE MINUTE HAND AT 12 AND MOVES THE HAND SLOWLY AROUND THE CLOCK UNTIL THE HAND RETURNS TO THE 12.) What happened to the hour hand, Ezra?

Ezra: It moved <u>very slowly</u> from the 4 to the 5.

Teacher: Very good observation, Ezra. The hour hand is slowly <u>moving</u> while the minute hand is moving. Now, let's watch as I move the minute hand. We'll start at five o'clock. When the minute hand reaches the 1, it shows five minutes past 5. When the minute hand touches the 2 it will be ten minutes past 5. As I touch each numeral I am going to stop and <u>you can tell me the time.</u> (THE TEACHER MOVES THE HAND SLOWLY AROUND THE CLOCK— STOPPING AT THE 1, 2, 3, 4, 5, AND 6 WHILE THE PUPILS ORALLY RESPOND.)

Teacher: Let's see how we can record this time on the chalkboard. First I will write the "5" to show the hour. Then I will PUT a colon—two dots like this—to separate the hour from the minutes. Now I must write the minutes past 5—"30." We can read this as "five-thirty."

Teacher: Let's continue to move our minute hand. Count-on with me by fives from the 30 as I move the minute hand. We were at 30, so now it is 35, 40, 45, 50. (THE TEACHER MOVES THE HAND TO THE 7, 8, 9, 10, AND STOPS.) Now it is 50 minutes past five. Note that the hour hand has not reached the 6 yet! We would write the time as five (AS THE TEACHER SAYS "FIVE" SHE WRITES THE NUMERAL "5") fifty (AS THE TEACHER SAYS "FIFTY" SHE WRITES ":" AND "50.").

Telling time to the nearest minute is a skill children should master before they leave the third grade. To be proficient the child must be able to:

1. Recognize that the hour hand moves slowly between the numerals, but is read as the last hour passed. (For instance, when the time is 5:50 the hour hand is really closer to the 6, but the time is read as 50 minutes past five.)
2. Count by fives to 60.
3. Count-on (by ones) from any multiple of five less than 60. (For example, when the time is 5:18 the child counts by fives to 15 and then counts on to 18 by ones.)

Children learn to read and record time to the nearest minute in a manner similar to learning to tell time to the five minutes. They first count by fives around the clock until reaching the numeral at or just before the minute hand. If the minute hand points to some location between two numerals, children will stop counting by fives and count-on by ones until they reach that point. For example, if the clock shows 4:37, the child will count, "5, 10, 15, 20, 25, 30, 35" and then count-on by ones, "36, 37." Having this information, the child then looks at the hour hand and observes that it has not yet reached the 5, so the time is read as "37 minutes past four." To write the time, the child indicates the hour before the colon ("4:") and the minutes after the hour immediately to the right of the colon (":37") making the time 4:37.

12.5 TEACHING LINEAR MEASURE (LENGTH)

Though many linear measurement skills are needed as children get older, there are few out-of-school activities to reinforce the skills which are taught in the classroom. However, the spiral nature of the school mathematics curriculum (topics are repeated, with each new visit promoting a higher and broader development than before) frequently introduces a skill before the child needs to apply these concepts in out-of-school problem-solving situations. Because of this, it is important that the teacher involve students in classroom activities that utilize these skills (constructing bulletin boards, measuring paths for various types of playground games, constructing items for various projects, etc.).

Using Nonstandard Units

Since the child's background is so limited in linear measure, a teacher will begin instruction by exploring the nature of linear measure. Here a distinction must be made between two different kinds of measurement. Sometimes, when a person measures length, that person is the only person using the data. If a ruler is not available, the individual can measure with "homemade" or nonstandard units. For example, if Susie wants to cut a board to fit a hole in the floor she could employ a ruler displaying inches or centimeters, but she just as easily could use a straw or a narrow strip of paper as a measuring instrument. She might find how many "straws" long the hole is and then use the straw to transfer this measurement to a board. However, if Susie wanted to buy a window shade to fit her window she would need to communicate that length to another individual—a clerk at the store. It would be possible to take the straw and show it to the clerk, but it would be much more convenient to use a measuring unit (inch or centimeter) with which the clerk was familiar.

Nonstandard units help children explore the nature of measuring without the distracting element of learning standard measurement names (inch, foot, yard, centimeter, etc.). Giving children brief explorations with nonstandard units promotes understanding of linear measurement and helps children recognize the value of standard units.

Early explorations using manipulative materials will use terms such as "about," "between," "almost," and "a little more than." For example, in measuring the width of a book with paper clips, the child may find that his/her book is between seven and eight paper clips wide, or perhaps a little more than seven paper clips wide, or almost seven paper clips wide. This type of observation helps children see the need for smaller units. Using larger nonstandard units can show how the measuring task is simplified with a concurrent loss of precision. Using different nonstandard units will help children to see the difficulty when communicating measurement information to each other.

Teaching Measurement with Standard Units of Measure

The English unit—the inch—is the first standard unit normally developed in the primary grades. The inch, which originally was the width of a man's thumb, is used when introducing standard units since it is small enough to measure many items and yet large enough so children can handle separate units easily.

Inch units, if illustrated with narrow strips of cardboard one inch in length, are quite effective when helping children understand measurement to the nearest unit. Separate models can be used to measure the length of various items. For example, if a child is measuring the top of a book with cardboard pieces (inches) and he/she puts the last piece down, it may or may not end right at the edge of the book. If the child can place the last unit <u>and it stays on</u> (although it may stick out over the edge), the child counts the units and gives that as its length. On the other hand, <u>if the last unit falls off</u>, <u>only the units that stay on the book can be counted</u>. Figure 12.8 illustrates this activity and the resulting measurement. (Notice how this activity gives the child a hands-on experience in choosing which measurement is "closer." The activity also strengthens the child's understanding that in reporting measures you are always "off a little," but the measurement is <u>within a half of the unit used in measuring</u>.)

One advantage of using individual units is that they can be pasted on a longer strip of cardboard so children can see how a scale is developed. Pupils quickly discover that a scale (ruler) increases the efficiency of the task of taking a measurement. Figure 12.9 shows a child using a "homemade" scale to measure length. If a teacher has used the analogy of the units "falling off," then children learn

---

Individual Learning Activity

Pupil constructed ruler using strips of paper as units.

FIGURE 12.9

how to measure to the <u>nearest</u> inch.

Most children are familiar with a ruler as a commonly used instrument for measuring length, but they generally do not recognize its relationship to the units measured. The lesson fragment below uses a nonstandard unit—a child's hand—to help children learn about a ruler.

Teacher-Guided Interactive Learning Activity

LESSON FRAGMENT

M: Measuring with nonstandard units and constructing a ruler

A: First-grade class

T: Involvement

H: Rational counting to 10; conservation of length

Teacher: Yesterday, Jason told us that his grandmother called from Hawaii and said that she was coming to visit next month. She asked Jason how much he had grown. What did you do, Jason?

Jason: I showed her, but she couldn't see me because she was on the telephone.

Teacher: How do you suppose you can let your grandmother know how tall you are before she visits?

Jason: I could make a tracing of me lying down, like we did at the beginning of this year.

Teacher: Very good, Jason. But if we talked to grandmother on the phone, she would not be able to see our drawing, would she? How else might we tell her how we've grown?

Lance: We could measure Jason and tell her how tall he is.

Teacher: Good idea! Let's try some measuring here in class, so we can measure accurately. Suppose we use our hands and measure the tops of our desks. (CHILDREN MOVE THEIR HANDS ACROSS THEIR DESKS.) How many hands wide is your desk, Jamie? (SEE FIGURE 12.10.)

Jamie: I measured nine hands.

Billy: My desk is only seven hands, teacher.

Individual Learning Activity

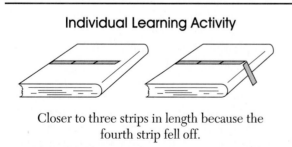

Closer to three strips in length because the fourth strip fell off.

FIGURE 12.8

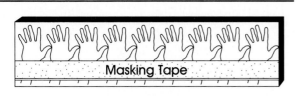

Desktop being measured with a "Billy hand ruler."

FIGURE 12.10

Teacher: Your desks <u>look</u> the same length, don't they? Why do you think you have different amounts, Billy?

Billy: She has little hands!

Teacher: Good observation, Billy. Your hands are not the same size as Jamie's hands. How else could we check the desks, Billy?

Billy: Let me use my hands; then they'll be the same. (THE TEACHER LETS BILLY MEASURE THE DESK AND FINDS THEM TO BE THE SAME. THE TEACHER THEN TAKES "BILLY'S HAND" AROUND THE ROOM TO MEASURE DIFFERENT OBJECTS. AS BILLY TIRES, THE TEACHER SUGGESTS THAT THEY MAKE A COPY OF HIS HAND. BILLY'S HAND IS TRACED AND SEVERAL COPIES ARE MADE.)

Teacher: Instead of having loose copies of Billy's hand, let's tape them together so then it will be easier to use. (TEN TO 12 COPIES OF BILLY'S HAND ARE PLACED ON MASKING TAPE AND MADE INTO A RULER.) Now let's measure how tall Jason is. (THE "HAND RULER" IS USED TO FIND JASON'S HEIGHT.) Look everyone, Jason is ten "Billy hands" tall. Now he can call his grandmother and tell her how tall he is.

Christy: But, teacher, Jason's grandmother doesn't know Billy so she won't know how big his hand is!

Teacher: Good point, Christy. We need something that she does know. When people want to measure things, they don't usually use "Billy hands"—they use inches. (THE TEACHER HOLDS UP A MODEL OF AN INCH FOR ALL TO SEE.) Just as we put Billy's hands together so they were easier to use, inches are put together and numbered so the inch is easier to use. (TEACHER HOLDS UP A RULER.) We call this measuring instrument a <u>ruler</u>. <u>This</u> ruler is marked in inches. I'm going to pass out some rulers that have inches marked on them and we will practice measuring with inches.

When first measuring length the teacher should distribute rulers that <u>only</u> show the unit of measure. For instance, when learning to measure length

to the nearest inch, the ruler should NOT show $\frac{1}{2}$ or $\frac{1}{4}$ inches. When measuring with centimeters, the ruler should not be marked with millimeters. When objects do not line up "exactly" on a mark, then the pupil is <u>forced</u> to decide which mark is closest. (Before measuring to the nearest half-inch or quarter-inch, the child must be fluent in the use of fractional numbers. Therefore, measurement with these more precise units usually is not developed at the primary level. The concept being developed for measuring to the nearest half-inch, however, is exactly the same as measurement to the nearest inch; only the unit—half-inch—is different.)

Children must be taught how to use the ruler properly. A ruler commonly does not show zero; the end of the ruler is assumed to be the starting point. Pupils must be taught to line the end of the ruler up with one end of the object being measured. They then look for the nearest unit to determine the length. On rulers that show intermediate marks ($\frac{1}{2}$ inch, $\frac{1}{4}$ inch, mm, etc.) students must learn to ignore all marks except the unit indicators.

Measuring lengths that are longer than the ruler is especially difficult for children. By observing some children measure, a teacher can readily understand how they get confused. When measuring a line segment a child will place the ruler next to the segment and mark the end of the ruler (12 inches). Then the child moves the ruler and finds that the line segment then ends at the "4," so a length of <u>four inches</u> is reported.

To help a child learn how to measure longer segments teachers may wish to begin measuring longer segments with a ruler that has only <u>ten inches</u> (rather than a foot). Counting the number of rulers (tens) and the part that is "left over" not only helps a child recognize that previous "ruler lengths" must be considered in the total length, but also reinforces the child's skill in place value. Once the student recognizes the importance of counting the "ruler lengths," a teacher can use different rulers (six-inch and 12-inch rulers) to show how "counting on from the last amount" is needed to determine the total length.

Using Reference Units to Estimate Lengths

As children work with new measuring units they need to be able to approximate the size of those units. Teachers usually point out a <u>reference unit</u> that can be used to help children develop a feel for the unit's relative size. For example, a teacher might show the child that the width of one's thumb is "close to" an inch; the thickness of a little finger is "just about" a centimeter; the distance from the school to the local grocery is a mile, etc. Children should be encouraged to find their own reference units to use for inch, centimeter, foot, yard, etc.

Using reference units, children will be able to estimate the length of various objects. To build estimating skills children should first use their reference units to measure an object and then check by using a ruler with the standard unit. Later, children should be advised to look at the object and imagine how many of their reference units can be used in the measuring.

Comparing Units of Measure

As a child's understanding of units of measure (inch, foot, centimeter, etc.) grows, attention is focused upon the comparison of length units. If an object is two inches long, it is not the same length as an object that is two feet long. Inches are smaller units of measure. Children also must recognize that the length of an object does not change when the object is measured with two different units. A piece of construction paper that is two feet long does not change size when measured with inches, even though its measure is 24 inches.

Comparison of units of measure is developed at two skill levels. Not only must the child recognize that a foot is longer than an inch, but he/she also must know the proportional amount longer one unit is than another unit (for example, one foot is 12 times longer than an inch). Initially, a teacher develops this concept by placing one unit upon another unit. To compare inches to feet, children place model inches atop a model foot to cover the measure. The inches are then counted and children discover that 12 inches measure the same as one foot. The teacher may find it easier to show the proportions of these measurements by using two rulers—one marked in inches and the other a foot ruler (without any indication of the inches).

The foundations for equivalent measure occur in the primary grades with extensive hands-on activities. Children learn that 12 inches are the same as one foot and that three feet are the same as one yard by comparing the units. Many pupils will remember these numbers, but development of equivalent units involving purely abstract conversions is generally deferred until the intermediate grades. There the child is expected to recall measures such as:

12 inches	is equal in measure to	1 foot
3 feet	is equal in measure to	1 yard
36 inches	is equal in measure to	1 yard

Small-Group Learning Activity

FIGURE 12.11

Figure 12.11 illustrates an activity using both a yardstick with foot units and a yardstick without units marked. The children record measurements made with the foot ruler in threes—which will be added later.

In addition to learning to measure with various units, children learn to read and write the names of the units and their abbreviations in both their singular and plural forms. During early explorations a teacher introduces the names and displays them in association with measurements taken by the students. When George's group finds the length of the room to be about 28 feet, the teacher records "28 feet" on the chalkboard. When teaching abbreviations the teacher will point out that the abbreviation for singular and plural is the same and that a period completes the abbreviation.

Teaching Metric Lengths

The activities used to develop a child's understanding of the metric system closely parallel the activities used when developing the English system. Indeed, the inch and centimeter are often introduced in the same lesson as two different units used in measuring. Since children are learning a ten system in numeration, the metric system makes much more sense to them than the English system. Unfortunately, children will not see metric measures used as often as the English measures. Therefore, most of the child's experience with metric lengths must occur in classroom situations.

The most commonly used metric lengths are the millimeter, centimeter, meter, and kilometer. Only the centimeter and meter are formally developed at the primary level. The millimeter, which is about $\frac{1}{25}$ of an inch, is much too precise for most measurements used by young children. The kilometer (which is a little more than six-tenths of a mile) is difficult for children to visualize. While the meter is the basic unit in the metric system, it is too large for children's beginning measurements. Therefore, children begin metric length using the centimeter—$\frac{1}{100}$ of a meter.

The metric system is a measurement system based upon ten. The prefixes that are used for length also are used for all measures within the system (capacity, mass, etc.). Children informally learn some of the commonly used prefixes while working at the primary level and will systematically explore the organization of the system at the intermediate level.

kilo	thousand	**milli**	$\frac{1}{1000}$
hecto	hundred	**centi**	$\frac{1}{100}$
deka	ten	**deci**	$\frac{1}{10}$

One unit—the decimeter—is a valuable reference unit. For many measurements, the centimeter (little finger) is too small and the meter (height of a door handle) too large. Children need some measure that is between these two units. The decimeter—which is equivalent to ten centimeters—is a handy unit. Most children use the width of a hand as a model of a decimeter. They approximate the width of a sheet of paper by using "two hands and two little fingers." Recognizing that a decimeter is ten centimeters, a child would convert this approximation to 22 centimeters.

The metric system also differs from the English system in the way measurements are written. In the metric system symbols rather than abbreviations are used to represent the measurement word. The symbol for millimeter is "mm," for centimeter it is "cm," and for meter it is "m." The symbols are not followed by a period. In the English system three miles is abbreviated "3 mi." while in the metric system three kilometers is written as "3 km" (without an ending period).

Making Comparisons between Systems

Comparisons between units at the elementary school level are limited to developing a general feel for ideas such as "a centimeter is less than an inch," and "a meter is slightly longer than a yard," etc. Part of this awareness may come from the reference unit used by the teacher. For example, the teacher may choose to use the tip of her nose to the end of an outstretched hand as a rough approximation of a yard. A meter might then be illustrated by changing the yard reference, turning her head away from the outstretched hand, and showing that the meter is "a little longer than a yard."

Pupils are not taught to convert from inches to centimeters or yards to meters. The two systems are taught as separate measuring units. Just as children learn that ten is written as "10" in our conventional system and as "X" with Roman numerals, they learn that their ruler is 12 inches—it is one foot—and it is close to 30 centimeters. Children learn that a meter is "a little longer" than a yard—not that it is 39.37 inches.

12.6 TEACHING LIQUID CAPACITY

From a very early age, children have used some units of measure including the cup, pint, quart, liter, and gallon in play situations. These containers are found in most homes. Children watch their parents using measuring spoons and measuring cups in the kitchen, buying gallons of gas for their car, and taking home quarts or liters of soda pop. The words for these units are familiar to children in first and second grade, but they generally cannot associate the name of the unit with the model.

Children who enter the primary grades have limited experience pouring liquids (or sand) from one container to another. Some will believe the quantity of "juice" changes if it is poured from a tall, narrow glass to a short, fat glass. They do not yet understand "conservation of volume." These children need many "pouring" experiences before they are confident the amount does not change. Rather than individually test each child to ascertain whether he/she can conserve volume, a teacher may provide pouring activities for all when teaching liquid capacity. For those who have not yet learned to conserve, such experiences provide a valuable foundation and for those children who can conserve, the activities reinforce and strengthen their knowledge.

Most kindergarten programs try to provide opportunities for children to experiment with variously shaped containers. In the first grade a more formal study of capacity of units is undertaken. First-graders still need hands-on activities as they learn about the cup, pint, and quart. Common containers may be used to associate the child's home experiences with the formal study of units. Measuring cups and $\frac{1}{2}$-pint milk containers are used to show the unit "cup." Children see a "pint" bottle of pop, milk, or even salad dressing. Quart canning jars and "large" bottles of soda pop are also used.

Children need to pour from one container to another to see that a unit quantity will stay constant even though the containers differ in shape. A pint bottle of cola and a pint jar of mayonnaise look different, but they contain the same amount of liquid (or sand). Since commercial containers often allow for expansion of the product, the teacher will want to prepare the containers by pouring from one to another and showing—with a marker—where the top of the liquid should end.

Equivalence of units (2 cups = 1 pint) is initially developed from pouring activities in which the child "discovers" that two cups are the same as one pint. Likewise, the number of pints in a quart and quarts in a gallon are first explored by filling containers. (See Figure 12.12.) When working with these hands-on activities the teacher will first require the child to **estimate** the number of quart containers it will take to fill a gallon. The child then checks the estimate by pouring quarts of liquid into a gallon container.

Once a child explores and finds equivalent measures, practice activities will be necessary so the child will recall that information. Practice sheets that illustrate those equivalences are used to remind the child of the measures explored. Often a lengthy period passes before the children encounter those liquid measures after the first experience with equivalence. Teachers may find it necessary to demonstrate the equivalence again for those who have forgotten. Such activities are helpful not only for those who are forgetful, but also for those were not ready for the first measuring activities.

12.7 READINESS ACTIVITIES FOR PERIMETER, AREA, AND VOLUME

Primary teachers build a foundation for finding perimeter, area, and volume. While children will play with blocks and tiles in kindergarten or first grade, they will use these materials more formally in the second and third grades. Pupils will use "tiles" of construction paper to "cover up" things as a preparatory activity for area. They "stack blocks" into brick shapes or flat roof buildings as a readiness for volume.

Perimeter is a measure of the distance around a figure. Primary teachers construct activities which require children to "walk about the outside" or "put string around the edge" of the figure. Written exercises with perimeter are largely confined to working with objects in which the distance around each object is a whole number of units. Frequently children use guide marks to facilitate a counting of the number of units around the unit. (See Figure 12.13.) In the illustrated activity, the child simply counts the number of units around the figure. Some children will recognize that the process of

FIGURE 12.12

counting could be speeded up by determining how far the ant would go to get halfway around, and then doubling that amount. Children at this level are not yet expected to develop the formula for finding the perimeter of a rectangle, $P = 2(L + W)$.

Most children at the primary level do not recognize that the area can stay the same even though the appearance of the shape changes. Many believe that a long narrow cake offers more to eat than a cake cut and placed into a "fatter" shape. (See Figure 12.14.) Those children will need many experiences with regions before they recognize that the areas are the same. Working with **tangrams** may help some children see that the same region can be arranged many different ways, but most second- and third-graders work more effectively with square-shaped regions. Children are given "tiles"

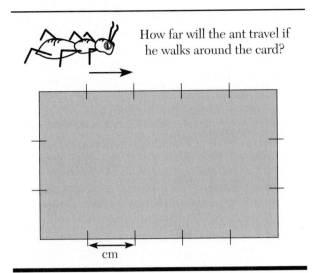

How far will the ant travel if he walks around the card?

cm

FIGURE 12.13

Individual Learning Activity

Do the shapes below cover the same space as the white tiles? Do they have the same number of tiles?

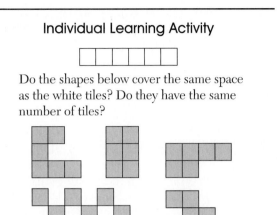

FIGURE 12.15

to arrange into many different shapes, and then return to the original shape. (Figure 12.15.) Follow-up paper-and-pencil activities simply have children count the number of "tiles" illustrated.

Though children work with volume when learning units of liquid capacity, formal instruction in finding the volume is limited to the construction of solids where the number of blocks in each layer can be counted. The finding of volume (by formula) requires multiplication skills that usually are not well developed before children leave third grade. In addition, children will need many experiences with capacity measures before they are able to conserve volume.

Several construction activities designed for the second and third grades build a strong foundation for later experiences with volume. Children may be directed to put blocks into different configurations. They may make "bricks," using smaller blocks (1-inch cubes). Bricks are made with two or three layers and children must tell how many blocks were used in making the bricks. Children also make block "towns" with "flat-topped" buildings. When finished, the group must decide how many cubes were used to make each building. (See Figure 12.16.)

Follow-up activities that use drawings of "bricks" or "buildings" can cause pupils difficulty.

Which cake is larger?

FIGURE 12.14

Group Learning Activity

Building Block Village

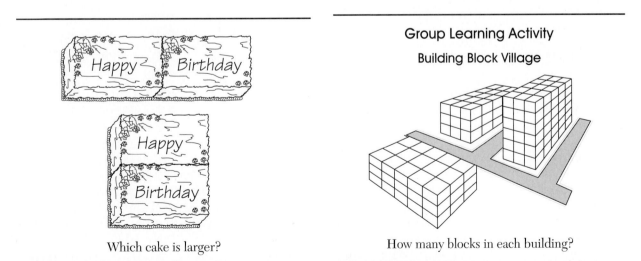

How many blocks in each building?

FIGURE 12.16

Since children cannot see <u>all</u> of the bricks in a drawing, there is a tendency to count the faces of the cubes. Some children may see that a textbook drawing is a "picture" of their bricks, but others will need to use the cubes to construct the pictured prism to verify their response.

12.8 TEACHING ABOUT ANGLES

Most children do not learn to measure angles until they reach the intermediate level. However, the geometric figures—square, rectangle, triangle, and circle—are identified in kindergarten and more precise descriptions are used as early as first grade. Squares and rectangles differ from other quadrilaterals in that they have four "right angles," so the idea of right angles is explored when first-graders describe these two figures. Since the geometric concept of angles is not usually developed in the first grade, teachers use the term "right corner" to describe the special corners of rectangles and squares.

To build the concept of "right corner" the teacher may choose a model right corner—a corner of a book, corner of a sheet of paper, etc. Once the corner is displayed, children are asked to find shapes in the room that have this special kind of corner. As children identify various objects, the model corner is placed on the object to verify that the two are congruent. When children identify squares and rectangles they will use the model right corner to verify that the figures have the correct corners. Other shapes—triangles and parallelograms—also may be used to show that some corners are "bigger" than a right corner and some are "smaller," but the terms "obtuse" and "acute" generally are not introduced at this time.

12.9 TEACHING TEMPERATURE

The concept of temperature is developed both in mathematics and science programs in elementary school. First-grade children observe that when the weather gets warmer, the temperature goes up. When the weather gets colder, the thermometer reading (temperature) goes down. Children learn that people wear different clothing when it is cold than when it is warm.

By the end of the primary grades children can read a thermometer and record temperatures. They also learn the freezing and boiling points of water, and develop a relative knowledge of common temperatures. Most weather reports now give the temperatures in <u>both</u> Fahrenheit and Celsius, so children recognize there are two different ways of reporting the temperature. This dual reporting also helps the child associate the two scales. Children who hear that it is 32 degrees Fahrenheit or 0 degrees Celsius begin to recognize the freezing temperatures of each scale.

The thermometer scale is similar to a number line, but there is a significant difference for children. A number line usually shows a mark for every number. <u>Thermometers</u> are marked in increments of two, five, or ten, so reading temperatures requires new skills. When reading a thermometer a child will find the temperature often falls <u>between</u> two marks on the scale. On a thermometer marked in two-unit increments, the child may see that the mercury is halfway between 74 and 76 degrees Fahrenheit. To read the thermometer a child must recognize that the number halfway between 74 and 76 is 75, so the temperature would be 75 degrees. On a thermometer that shows increments of five, there are four locations to be identified with the numbers between 70 and 75.

Because of the nature of the temperature scale, children are not expected to be proficient in reading the thermometer until they leave the primary grades. Let's examine a fragment of a lesson that involves learning to read the thermometer scale.

Teacher-Guided Interactive Learning Activity

LESSON FRAGMENT

M: Reading the thermometer scale

A: Group of third-graders

T: Demonstration, involvement, model

H: Counting by twos; other scales; knowledge that a thermometer is used to determine temperature; understanding of fractional parts on a linear scale

Teacher: Here we have a large model of a thermometer. Notice there are only four marks between each tens mark. (SEE FIGURE 12.17A.) Listen as I count these marks. I will start at 70. Seventy, 72, 74, 76, 78, 80. You will notice that I was not counting by ones. What number did I use, Jan?

Jan: The twos.

Teacher: Correct. Our thermometer is marked to show **twos**. While there are marks for every two,

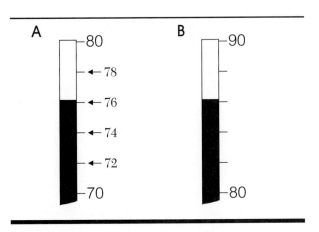

FIGURE 12.17

only the tens are identified. Let's see if we can read the temperature as I move the marker. (THE TEACHER SLIDES THE 'MERCURY' TO INDICATE 86 DEGREES—SEE FIGURE 12.17B.) Who can read the temperature for us? Bernie?

Bernie: It is 86 degrees.

Teacher: Can you explain how you found that temperature?

Bernie: (BERNIE COMES TO THE THERMOMETER AND POINTS TO THE SCALE.) Well, it is between the 80 and the 90, so I'm going to start at the 80 and count by twos. It is 80, 82, 84, 86.

Teacher: Excellent explanation, Bernie. You can sit down and let us try a different temperature. This time I am going to show the "mercury" between two marks. We are going to have to estimate where our one-degree marks might be when we read the thermometer. Let me place several examples on the board and see if we can estimate whether we should read the temperature as an even degree or an odd degree. (SEE FIGURE 12.18.) In model A the mer-

cury is almost on the marks that indicate an even temperature, so we would read this as 76 degrees. The temperature indicated on thermometer B would be 72 degrees. On C the "mercury" is between the marks. Since the mark is <u>nearly halfway</u> <u>between</u> 74 and 76 we would read the temperature as 75 degrees. (THE TEACHER WOULD THEN USE THE LARGE THERMOMETER TO HAVE CHILDREN MOVE THE INDICATOR TO **SHOW** DIFFERENT TEMPERATURES.)

A wide variety of science activities supplement the study of temperature in the primary grades. Children have weather study projects where the recording and graphing of temperatures is a routine activity. Experiments involving high and low temperatures frequently are also included in the primary curriculum (freezing, boiling, temperatures needed for germination of seeds, etc.).

12.10 TEACHING WEIGHT (MASS)

Children encounter many units of weight before they enter kindergarten. They know they weigh more now than when they were a baby. They have eaten a burger that was a "quarter-pounder" and they helped put away the five-pound bag of sugar. The weights have little meaning for them, however. They are unable to estimate the approximate weight of objects and cannot pick out an object which weighs approximately one pound. They can tell when one object is "a lot" heavier than another, however.

First activities with weight concepts begin in kindergarten when children sit on the teeter-totter and find that they can't seesaw with a person who is much heavier. Weight is explored more formally in the first grade when children use balance scales to compare two objects. Children should first **estimate** which object is heavier by "hefting" (putting objects in opposite hands to see which feels heavier), but when comparing two objects that weigh nearly the same a balance scale is more efficient.

Children initially explore measuring weight measurement using nonstandard units. A marble weighs less than an apple, so children find how many marbles it will take to balance an apple, a ball, a book, etc. Such activities help children discover the principles of measuring weight before the standard units are introduced. (See Figure 12.19.)

The standard units of ounce, pound, and kilogram are used in everyday activities long before the units are formally introduced in the curriculum. Children may know how much they weigh in

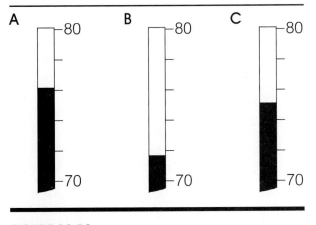

FIGURE 12.18

Nonstandard Units

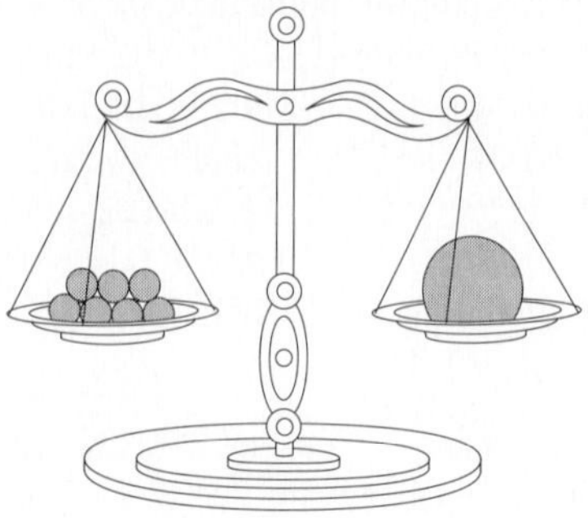

The ball is equal in weight to seven marbles
because the scale is evenly balanced.

FIGURE 12.19

pounds and kilograms because they were weighed
by the school nurse. Children should recognize that
their weight does not change simply because it was
reported in kilograms or pounds. To build an understanding of standard units, activities similar to
those for standard units of length would be used.

It is difficult for a child to develop reference
units for an ounce, pound, or kilogram. Perception
of weight is influenced by the density of the object
to be weighed. A lead weight for a pound seems to
be heavier than a pound bag of potato chips. Older
children may develop some reference units for
weight.

12.11 TEACHING MEASUREMENT IN THE INTERMEDIATE GRADES

Measurement is an integral part of most applications of mathematics at the intermediate level.
Problem solving using operations invariably contains some aspect of measurement. Even problem
solving using geometry frequently involves angular
measurements. At the intermediate level, science
and social studies activities frequently have measurement components.

Most measurement concepts that one needs to
function efficiently are developed at the intermediate level. Skills relating to money, time, and
length and perimeter, area, volume, weight, temperature, and angular measurement are for the
most part completed at the intermediate level.
Because of the large number of concepts to be
taught, measurement becomes a major part of the
intermediate-level mathematics curriculum.

Since the measurement skills developed at this
level are so important, intermediate teachers must
make a concerted effort to ensure that each child
has mastered all of the measurement concepts developed at this level. The following is a typical scope
and sequence of measurement concepts developed
at the intermediate level:

Grade 4

Money
- maintain previously taught money concepts
- make change
- add, subtract, and multiply money measurement

Time
- maintain previously taught time concepts
- tell time to and past the hour
- determine elapsed time (hours only)

Length (Standard and Metric Systems)
- measure to nearest quarter-inch
- develop reference measures for mile and
  kilometer
- maintain linear and perimeter measurement
  skills
- explore perimeter of polygons using sum of
  sides concept

Capacity, weight, and temperature (Standard and
  Metric Systems)

Weight
- maintain weight measuring skills and explore ounces as units

Liquid
- maintain capacity measuring skills and
  explore the unit—ounce
- convert measures within system (ounces to
  cups, etc.)

Temperature
- measure temperature with Fahrenheit and
  Celsius scales

Area (Standard and Metric Systems)
- explore area of triangle, rectangle, square,
  and parallelogram

Volume (Standard and Metric Systems)
- measure volume of rectangular prisms using
  blocks

Angle measurement
- maintain previously taught angular measurement skills (right angle)

Solve measurement problems

Grade 5

Money

- maintain previously taught money concepts
- divide using money amounts

Time
- maintain previously taught time concepts
- explore calendar concepts including—century, decade, score
- examine time zones
- find equivalent time measures (hours/days; minutes/hours)

Length
- maintain linear and perimeter measurement skills (Standard and Metric Systems)
- measure to nearest eighth-inch
- convert length within system (inches/feet; feet/yards)
- find perimeter for rectangles and squares using formulas

Capacity, weight, and temperature (Standard and Metric Systems)
- maintain previously developed skills
- examine measuring units (ton and metric ton)
- convert equivalent measures within the system
- examine capacity unit—milliliter—and determine equivalents (1000 mL = 1 L)
- recognize common temperatures in both Fahrenheit and Celsius
- perform operations involving capacity, weight, and temperature

Area (Standard and Metric Systems)
- explore surface area of space figures
- determine area triangles, rectangles, and squares using formulas

Volume (Standard and Metric Systems)
- find volume of rectangular prisms using blocks
- find volume of rectangular prisms using formula

Angle measurement
- maintain previously taught skills related to angular measurement
- use a protractor to measure angles

Solve measurement problems

Grade 6

Money
- maintain previously taught money concepts

Time
- maintain previously taught time concepts
- add and subtract time
- read time schedules
- use 24-hour clock

Length

- maintain linear and perimeter measurement skills (Standard and Metric Systems)
- find greatest possible error
- measure to nearest sixteenth-inch and millimeter
- change to smaller and larger metric units
- use operations involving linear measurements
- find perimeter of regular polygons using formulas
- find perimeter of concave figures
- find circumference of a circle

Capacity, weight, and temperature (Standard and Metric Systems)
- maintain previously developed concepts
- read Fahrenheit and Celsius scales and recognize common temperatures
- use operations involving capacity, weight, and temperature
- convert metric units using division

Area (Standard and Metric Systems)
- find area of triangles, rectangles, squares, and parallelograms using formulas
- find surface area of rectangular prisms, cubes, and pyramids

Volume (Standard and Metric Systems)
- find volume of rectangular prisms by counting units
- find volume of rectangular prisms and cylinders using formula
- convert to metric units using division/multiplication of decimals

Angle measurement
- maintain previously taught concepts related to angular measurement
- use a protractor to measure and draw angles

Solve measurement problems

Grades 7 and 8

Money
- examine comparative pricing
- explore checking accounts
- determine the costs of installment buying

Area
- find area of trapezoids and concave figures
- find surface area of prisms, cylinders, spheres, cones, and regular space figures

Volume
- find volume of prism, pyramid, cone, sphere

General measurement concepts
- determine greatest possible error
- explore concepts of precision, range of error, and relative error

Solve measurement problems

12.12 TEACHING GENERAL MEASUREMENT CONCEPTS

Pupils must be able to select the best unit of measurement to be used when measuring a particular item. This is really a problem-solving skill since there are many paths to a solution and the best path depends on the situation. When great **precision** is needed, very small units should be employed because they result in smaller measurement errors. For example, a machinist making a gear for a car may need measurements to the nearest millimeter or the nearest hundredth or thousandths of an inch in order for the part to function properly. However, when the lengths being measured are large, such precision may be unnecessary. When a homeowner wants to order a fence, measurements to the nearest millimeter or nearest hundredth of an inch would be inappropriate.

Before children are able to select the best unit for a particular task they must recognize that measurements are not exact, no matter how small the measurement unit, and that the **range of error** will depend on the unit being used. Figure 12.20 illustrates the range of error that might occur for an object that measures one and one-half inches to the nearest half inch. Notice that the **greatest possible error** is always one half of the unit being used; in this case, one-half of one-half inch, which equals one-fourth inch. The true measurement <u>can</u>

be anywhere in the range of plus or minus one-fourth inch from the stated measurement of one and one-half inches.

When examining the nature of measure students are introduced to the concept of **relative error**. For example, the greatest possible error after measuring the distance of 82,000 inches is still $+/- \frac{1}{2}$ inch, but this error is a relatively small error when compared to the 82,000 inches measured. However, an error of $+/- \frac{1}{2}$ inch when measuring an object six inches across is a relatively large error. How tolerant one can be with the relative size of the error will depend upon how the measurement data is to be applied. Mathematically, relative error (R.E.) is found by dividing the greatest possible error (G.P.E.) by the number of units used in the measurement (R.E. = G.P.E./Measure).

Let's look at a lesson where some of these general concepts are informally integrated. Students will determine which units are selected in terms of **precision** and **relative error**.

Small-Group Learning Activities

LESSON FRAGMENT

M: Selecting appropriate measurement units for a task

A: Teams of sixth-graders

T: Involvement, problem solving

H: Skills measuring with inches and feet and yards, the concepts of precision, and the greatest possible error for a unit being used

PROBLEM-SOLVING SITUATION:
PUPILS HAVE BEEN EXPLORING LINEAR MEASURE, BUT CANNOT SEE THE NECESSITY OF THE MANY DIFFERENT SIZE UNITS—INCHES, FEET, YARDS, ETC. THE TEACHER HAS DESIGNED AN OUTDOOR ACTIVITY TO HELP PUPILS RECOGNIZE THE NECESSITY OF MATCHING A MEASURING UNIT WITH THE PURPOSE OF MEASURING.

Teacher: I have divided you into three teams. We have some bushes along the wall outside our classroom. Let's pretend we are going into the business of selling plants and we are going to base our price on the height of these bushes. I have given each group a different unit of measure, and all three teams should select a different bush. One group will measure a bush to the nearest inch, another group should measure their bush to the nearest foot, and the last group will measure a bush to the nearest

A measurement which is reported as <u>one and one-half inches</u> may fall anywhere between these two marks on the ruler.

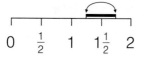

$$0 \qquad \frac{1}{2} \qquad 1 \qquad 1\frac{1}{2} \qquad 2$$

Range of Error

<u>No smaller than</u> 1 and 1/4 inches
and
<u>No larger than</u> 1 and 3/4 inches.

Greatest Possible Error

GPE is <u>1/2 of the unit being used.</u>
The unit on the ruler is 1/2 inch. So
$1/2 \times 1/2 = 1/4$
The greatest possible error
is plus or minus 1/4 inch.

FIGURE 12.20

yard. As soon as each group finishes I want them to return because time will play a role in our decision-making process. (THE FIRST GROUP TO RETURN IS THE TEAM THAT MEASURED TO THE NEAREST YARD, THE SECOND GROUP BACK TO THE CLASSROOM USED A FOOT UNIT, AND THE LAST GROUP TO RETURN MEASURED THEIR BUSH TO THE NEAREST INCH.)

Teacher: The group measuring to the nearest yard was the fastest. Why might this be important if you were running a business, Phyllis?

Phyllis: Because the owner would have to pay somebody to do the measurements and the shorter the time it took the less money it would cost her.

Teacher: Good: Can anyone think of a problem that might develop with customers if you were pricing your items by the nearest yard, Kenneth?

Kenneth: If the bush were just over one-half a yard tall it would be rounded to a yard. The person buying it might object to having to pay for a bush one yard tall when it was a lot shorter.

Teacher: That sounds reasonable. This problem probably wouldn't occur for which unit of measurement and why, Hasti?

Hasti: The inch measure because a person wouldn't be able to tell whether it was just under or just over an inch by looking at it.

Teacher: Good. What would be the disadvantage of using inches? Anyone?

George: It takes too long and the movement of the plant makes it very hard to measure to the nearest inch.

Teacher: Good. Would it make any difference if we were selling very short bushes instead of very tall ones? Anyone?

Kenneth: You would want to use smaller units with the small bushes because customers wouldn't want to pay by the foot if the bush was only seven or eight inches tall.

Teacher: That's a very good point, Kenneth. The smaller the object being measured, the smaller the units we are going to use. That's a good general rule, but we are still going to have to decide the best unit for our task.

Kenneth: Last year we bought an eight-foot tree for the holidays. I told my dad that it was not quite eight feet, because it didn't hit our ceiling—but it was close.

How precise one wants to make a measurement is related to the concept that measurement is imprecise and the degree of imprecision is tied inexplicably to the size of the unit being used. Pupils should recognize that units of measure that are dis-

crete—like dozen and gross—are counted and may be measured "exactly." However, _most_ measuring is not of discrete items and therefore imprecision is inherent in the process. Pupils should be directed to measure <u>accurately</u>—but still measure to the "nearest" chosen unit.

12.13 TEACHING MONEY CONCEPTS

Concepts about money are among the most important measurements a child will learn. Lack of basic money skills will make an individual functionally illiterate in a society that uses money in almost every aspect of daily living (work, recreation, and securing basic human needs).

Some tasks requiring money skills are now done by computers and automated cash registers. For example, determining how much change an individual gets when the shopper hands a clerk a cash payment is almost universally handled in department stores and franchised food establishments by automated cash registers. However, the student will need money skills in situations where automated devices are not available and to verify the correct amount of change. With the advent of the electronic era, many new instruments, such as credit cards, cash cards, and automated teller cards, became viable for widespread use. These credit instruments require schools to teach new skills to students.

By the time students enter the intermediate level, they recognize the names and values associated with coins, can find the value associated with a collection of coins, and can select from a set of coins the amount required to make a purchase (either the exact amount or an amount just sufficient to make the purchase). The pupil will also recognize and use either the cent sign or decimal notation to denote amounts.

The intermediate-level student must learn to make change and to compute with money notation. In addition to becoming skillful in consumer mathematics skills such as comparative shopping and price discounts, the postelementary student will learn how to balance a checkbook, make installment purchases, look for investment values, etc.

Learning How to Make Change

Efficient procedures for making change are learned in much the same way as grammar rules. Students already have a sense of how to make change, just as they have developed a feel for language by hearing it spoken correctly. In teaching students to make change, the teacher will use change-making activities to systematize and extend those skills. Formal instruction will reveal any inefficient strategies.

Making change requires counting-on from the amount of purchase to reach the given amount. Before pupils can become successful making change they must be able to count by fives, tens, and twenty-fives AND be able to count-on by ones, fives, or tens. These counting skills are usually developed in primary programs, so making change is an application of these counting skills. However, before initiating an instructional lesson in making change, the teacher should review these skills to make certain the group is ready.

The most efficient strategy for making change is one that reaches multiples of twenty-five, ten, or five and then counting-on using these denominations. For example, if a purchase price was seven cents and the amount given was 25 cents—the student would <u>first</u> try to reach ten by sliding a penny at a time to count-on "eight, nine, ten." Upon reaching ten, the pupil can count by tens—sliding a dime across the desk—saying "twenty." Since tens would be <u>now</u> too much, the fives will be used—sliding a nickel across the desk and saying "twenty-five." Figure 12.21 illustrates one possible teaching sequence that involves using a "rule" for pennies and lets the pupil discover the rest of the process using hands-on explorations. The teacher <u>may</u> wish to point out that a store clerk would use the pennies, nickels, and dimes to make change; whereas a person making change on a paper route or at a garage sale may not have some coins and would be required to substitute other combinations. Students should recognize that some employers may prescribe specific ways of making change, so it is possible to anticipate how many coins will be needed during any given workday. Teachers may permit a wide latitude of approaches in the initial hands-on explorations. As students become more skillful, they should be led to use the fewest possible coins when making change.

After students learn to make change (when amounts are less than $1.00), the teacher will extend those skills to include situations where the person making the purchase has handed the clerk an unusual amount (so as to limit the coins they receive in change). For example, a customer hands the clerk a five-dollar bill and a quarter when purchasing an item for $4.24. This will minimize the amount of change received. Under these circumstances pupils are taught to view the change mak-

---

Cost of item: 7¢
Amount paid: 25¢

Rule: Use pennies to get to a multiple of five. Then see what coins you will need to get 25¢.

Alice's solution: 3 pennies, 1 nickel and 1 dime.

$\left(1¢\right)\left(1¢\right)\left(1¢\right)\left(5¢\right)\left(10¢\right)$

Betty's solution: 3 pennies and 3 nickels.

$\left(1¢\right)\left(1¢\right)\left(1¢\right)\left(5¢\right)\left(5¢\right)\left(5¢\right)$

Teacher: Both are correct solutions! Who used the fewest coins? When would three nickels and three pennies be the best solution?

FIGURE 12.21

---

ing process as a two-step process. The coins and paper currency become separate change-making processes. Change is made with the coins first, returning a penny to make $4.25 and then the paper currency to change the four dollars to five dollars, saying "$5.25."

Teaching Operations with Money Notation

The development of operations (addition/subtraction/multiplication/division) involving money closely parallels the development of the operations in general. For example, soon after children learn to add numbers and to use the cent notation (¢) for recording money, they are taught to perform addition using the cent sign to denote money values. When writing "money," the decimal is introduced as a "separating point." After multiplying and dividing whole numbers, money values requiring these operations are introduced. Since students have not yet worked with multiplication and division of decimals, they have not learned procedures for placement of the decimals. Since money values are written with a "point" to separate the dollars and cents, students are directed to place the point in the final answer to indicate which part of the answer indicates dollars and which indicates cents. In early work with multiplication of money, the teacher may indicate where the "separating point" will be written as the problem is developed. In Figure 12.22 the teacher has reached the step in the algorithm when the separating point should be indicated.

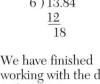

We have finished working with the cents and now we are ready to work with the dollars, so we will place a dot to separate the dollars and the cents in the answer.

We have finished working with the dollars and now we are ready to work with the cents, so we will place a dot to separate the dollars and cents.

FIGURE 12.22

12.14 TEACHING TIME CONCEPTS

Children entering the intermediate level are able to "read" the time on a clock, can name the days of the week and months of the year, and possess a few other general concepts related to time. The intermediate-level student is taught some of the more subtle but nonetheless important concepts related to time—such as telling time "until the hour"; identifying A.M. and P.M.; computing elapsed time; reading time schedules and 24-hour clocks; and recognizing the time periods of decade and century. Some students already have learned many of these concepts prior to classroom instruction. For example, if pupils use a VCR at home they may learn to read a 24-hour clock when they program the machine to record programs.

Teaching Until and Past the Hour

Students should to be able to tell time in a variety of ways. For example, the pupil will recognize that when the minute hand is on the three and the hour hand is just past the four, time can be reported as "quarter past four," "four-fifteen," or "forty-five minutes until five." There are a number of reasons why different ways of reporting time will be important to the pupil. Knowing different ways of viewing time will help pupils when they determine elapsed time. In addition, these skills are used in both everyday communications and planning for daily events. For example, "I will meet you at 20 to four," "It is now four-fifteen," and "I have to be home by five, so I have forty-five more minutes before I have to be home."

Telling time after the hour is a natural extension of the way the child has been taught to tell

time. The minute hand points to the minutes AFTER the hour. Reading minutes BEFORE the hour requires the pupil to count-on from where the hand indicates—ignoring the minutes generally associated with that position on the clock. First activities should encourage the pupils to place their fingers on the minute hand and count by fives, until they reach the 12. To avoid problems in initial instruction, teachers should position the minute hand <u>on a numeral</u> so the pupils will be saying a multiple of five each time they touch a numeral. Students find times such as five or ten minutes to the hour much easier to determine than those that are more than 30 minutes from the hour. When the minute hand does not point to a numeral, students may be more successful counting counterclockwise—counting by five to the last numeral before the minute hand, then counting-on to the minute hand using ones. For example, when using the counterclockwise method for 1:47 the child will count the interval between 12 and 11 saying "five," then that between 11 and 10, saying "ten." From this point on the pupils will count by ones to the 47 saying, "eleven, twelve, thirteen." Students eventually become so skillful using this method that they "sight read" the time—recognizing the amount except for the odd minutes, then mentally adding this amount to get the total minutes until the hour.

Telling time until the hour using a digital clock requires a different skill, since students cannot touch the numerals as they count around the clockface. To successfully determine time until the hour using a digital clock, the student must mentally subtract the displayed time from the hour. For younger students, this is difficult because it involves the more difficult subtraction problems—those that involve double zeros.

Teaching Elapsed Time

The skills pupils develop when learning to read time until the hour are used in teaching elapsed time. In a sense, minutes until an hour is a special case of how many minutes must elapse before the minute hand arrives at the twelve.

Teachers begin the study of elapsed time by reviewing telling time until the hour. Questions are used to focus pupils' attention upon the number of minutes that must elapse before the minute hand reaches the twelve. Teachers then have pupils find the time that will elapse between a set time and five or ten minutes BEFORE the hour. For example, Bill began his music lesson at 3:10 and finished at 3:50. How long did Bill practice? (In other words, how much time had elapsed from the time Bill started his lesson until he had finished?) Students start by touching the minute hand (which points toward the "2") and count-on repeating the multiples of five as they touch each numeral on the way to the "10"—five, ten, fifteen, twenty, twenty-five, thirty, thirty-five, forty." Determining elapsed time beyond the hour is a simple extension of the previous skill. When counting elapsed time that includes hours—for example, three hours and 15 minutes—pupils should count the hours first and then the minutes.

Computing elapsed time when a clockface is not used (as with digital clocks) is much more difficult for pupils. Such cases require the pupil to use computation with denominate numbers (see Section 12.20—Working with Denominate Numbers). These denominate number operations ask the student to regroup one hour for 60 minutes. Students confuse this regrouping process with the regrouping process in the decimal system in which one hundred is regrouped for ten tens.

Teaching Terms Associated with a Calendar

Terms associated with the calendar are taught by reviewing the definition of the term. For example, a child is taught that a century is one hundred years, a decade is ten years, and a leap year has 366 days, with the extra day being added to the days in the month of February.

Working in cooperative-learning groups allows children to reflect and clarify their thinking on measurement concepts.

Some calendar concepts, particularly those associated with decade and century, are first encountered in social studies rather than mathematics. When developing the terms in mathematics lessons, the teacher will wish to associate these words with the prefixes from the metric system. The word "century" can be matched with "centi"—as used in centimeter—to remind pupils that it takes one hundred units to make a single unit. Students may also recognize that the word "cents" also is related to century in that it takes 100 cents to make a dollar and 100 years to make a century. The word "decade" is from the same root word as deka in dekameter—and means ten in both cases. In the metric system a dekameter is ten meters while in a time system a decade means ten years. (Some students may confuse deka with deci since they sound and look much the same. "Deka" comes from the Greek word *deka* while "deci" is from the Latin *deci*, but both words mean ten.)

Application of Time Concepts (Reading Schedules)

Students apply time skills whenever they read time schedules. There are many schedules that are meaningful to pupils—school schedules; schedules in the TV program guide; and bus, train, and airline schedules. Since pupils already are very familiar with school and TV schedules, many teachers prefer to develop the skill of reading time schedules in a new situation by using schedules obtained from airline, bus, and train companies. Travel schedules offer the opportunity to study aspects such as lay-over times, connecting times, departing times, arrival times, time from one scheduled stop to another; connecting times between different carriers, times (days) service is offered, check-in times, total travel time, and other considerations that relate to travel (meals, type of equipment, etc.). Planning trips using schedules and other travel information permits the class to explore related travel considerations such as discounted fares when tickets are purchased a given number of days in advance, or when travel is restricted to certain days, or a trip limited to a specified number of days.

One way of teaching students to read schedules is to use a "guided look" method. After a general discussion in which students identify the kinds of information found in the rows and columns, the teacher may direct pupils to find some specific information that the teacher has identified on the schedule. The following illustrate some questions that guide pupils to look for specific information:

If you wanted to go to Syracuse, New York, but couldn't leave until two o'clock, when would be the next bus you could get?

Would it make any difference in how you would plan your departure time if you were taking the bus to Syracuse on a holiday?

If you left on the 8:30 evening flight to Charlotte, on what kind of plane would you be flying?

Should you eat a snack before you take Flight 301 to Tallahassee?

Teaching the Conversion of Units of Time

While a variety of approaches may be used when converting from one time unit to another, all offer a teacher the opportunity to build readiness for a ratio approach that is used extensively at the post-elementary school level, not only in mathematics but in the sciences. When using a ratio approach students learn basic ratios and then chain these relationships together to arrive at the desired conversion. For example, assume the student knows the following conversion units:

$$60 \text{ seconds} = 1 \text{ minute}$$
$$60 \text{ minutes} = 1 \text{ hour}$$
$$24 \text{ hours} = 1 \text{ day}$$

When the number of seconds in seven days is required, the student first finds the ratio of seconds to one day using a chain of ratios:

$$\frac{60 \text{ seconds}}{1 \text{ minute}} \times \frac{60 \text{ minutes}}{1 \text{ hour}} \times \frac{24 \text{ hours}}{1 \text{ day}}$$
$$= \text{seconds in 1 day}$$

To find seven days, the student multiplies by seven.

$$7 \times \frac{60 \text{ seconds}}{1 \text{ minute}} \times \frac{60 \text{ minutes}}{1 \text{ hour}} \times \frac{24 \text{ hours}}{1 \text{ day}}$$
$$= \frac{604,800}{\text{seconds in 7 days}}$$

12.15 EXTENDING CONCEPTS RELATED TO LINEAR MEASURE, PERIMETER, AND CIRCUMFERENCE

In the primary grades the child measured objects to the nearest inch and centimeter. In making these measurements, the pupil learned that objects often do not end at the exact mark on the ruler and that a measure is reported to the <u>nearest</u> unit. When the student enters the intermediate level he/she recognizes the need for more precise measurements, so smaller units are introduced. Intermediate-level pupils learn to measure to the nearest quarter-inch, eighth-inch, and sixteenth-inch in the conventional (standard English) system and to the millimeter in the metric system. As each smaller unit is introduced, students recognize that measurements only can be made to the nearest mark on the ruler so the resulting measurement still may be plus or minus a half of the unit being used. (This would mean that a line segment that measured $5\frac{7}{16}$ inches long might be as short as $5\frac{13}{32}$ inches or as long as $5\frac{15}{32}$ inches, since $\frac{1}{2}$ of the unit $\frac{1}{16}$th inch is $\frac{1}{32}$nd of an inch.)

At the intermediate level a greater emphasis is placed on developing an understanding of the greatest possible error of the measurement and its importance when performing operations with denominate numbers. For example, a class wants to hang Valentine decorations from a string in the hall. One student reports the distance from the water fountain to the door as nine yards and a second student finds that it is 14 feet from the door to the end of the hall. Since the measurement using yards can be $1\frac{1}{2}$ feet shorter than nine yards (plus or minus $\frac{1}{2}$ yard to the nearest yard), adding the measures could result in a string that would not reach!

Not only do students learn to use smaller units at the intermediate level, but they also explore larger units such as the mile and kilometer. Using a trundle wheel, teachers may measure a mile and a kilometer to a location near the school so pupils will have a visual referent to use when studying these measures. A referent along a path to school will give students a constant reminder of the length of these two units.

Extending Perimeter Concepts

Primary-grade children found "perimeter" by counting marks along the edge of various polygons. Such activities generally were more effective for practice in counting than in developing the concept of perimeter, but they do provide a readiness for later exploration. Intermediate-level pupils develop both an understanding of the concept and a familiarity with formulas commonly used when working with perimeter.

Students seldom have difficulty finding perimeter with formulas, but they often confuse perim-

Individual Learning Activity
Finding Perimeter

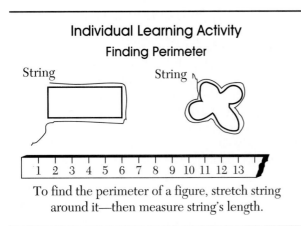

To find the perimeter of a figure, stretch string
around it—then measure string's length.

Perimeter of a Square

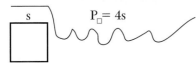

All sides congruent in square, so measure
one side and then get four times this length.

Perimeter of a Rectangle

L + W is halfway around, so get two
times the length of the string.

$$P_{\square} = 2(L + W)$$

FIGURE 12.23

eter and area by choosing the wrong formula.
Therefore, it is important for the teacher to focus
on the underlined concept of perimeter and not on formulas.
Activities should emphasize that perimeter is a
length. Pupils develop a basic strategy by "putting
a string around the shape." Such a strategy is helpful even when the perimeter of an irregular shape
is found (see Figure 12.23).

Once pupils understand that perimeter is finding the distance AROUND a figure, instruction
may be directed toward "shortcuts" in the measuring process. When measurements for the sides of
a figure are already known, it is unnecessary to use
string. Simply adding the lengths together will give
the same measure. String again may be helpful for
the purpose of deriving a formula when students
explore the perimeter of squares, rectangles, and
regular polygons. Pupils can see that only one

measure is needed in regular polygons, since ALL
sides are congruent. Using a number sentence to
record this information helps pupils see a formula
as a way of recording the relationships discovered
in finding perimeter of figures such as squares, rectangles, and other polygons. (See Figure 12.23.)

After students learn to find the perimeter of various convex polygons, they should explore perimeters for concave polygons. Determining the distance around such shapes when ALL dimensions
are listed is an easy task for most pupils. However,
when one or more of the lengths of a concave polygon are missing, students frequently record incorrect perimeters. Pupils tend to ignore a side when
a dimension is missing. To help students find the
area of concave figures, teachers must again emphasize the concept of perimeter. Since perimeter
of a polygon is the measure of the line segments
which make up the polygon, the length of EVERY
line segment must be found. This may require the
use of deductive reasoning to determine some of
the unlisted lengths. In Figure 12.24, a bug crawling around the figure has reached one of the "unknown" distances. In such an example, students
could be asked to help the bug find how far he will
crawl by using some information about the length
of segments he has already traveled.

Finding the Circumference of a Circle

Most programs teach the circumference of a circle
as a part of an exploration of geometry. Pupils learn
that the "distance" from the center of a circle to its
edge is called the radius, the distance from one side
of the circle through its center to the other side is
called the diameter, and that the distance around
the circle is called the circumference. When students find the circumference they really are finding
the "perimeter of the circle" or the distance around
the circle.

To find the circumference as a length, a student
first needs to have explored the relationship between the circumference and the diameter—pi (π).
Once these relationships have been established
($C \div D = \pi$) then the circumference can be found
by examining the mathematical sentence. Pupil attention is directed to the sentence "$C \div D = \pi$."
The circumference (C) is the product of $D \times \pi$.
(Students learned the relationship of multiplication
and division in the third grade when division was
introduced—but the intermediate-level teacher
may need to review the idea.) To find the circumference (C) of a circle, the student would multiply
the diameter (D) times pi (π).

Perimeter of Concave Polygons

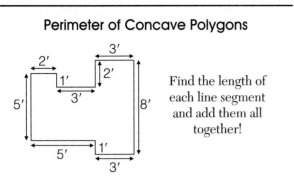

Find the length of each line segment and add them all together!

How far will Blackie Bug travel around the outside of the room?

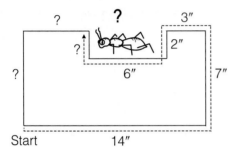

Start   14″

— If Blackie crawled DOWN 2″, will he now need to crawl UP the same amount?
— If Blackie crawled 14″ to the right when he started, will he need to crawl 14″ back?

FIGURE 12.24

Teaching Conversions of Length

As pupils progress through the intermediate level they will learn to convert within the standard (or metric) system from one unit of length to another. Primary-level children learned to change units by adding or multiplying units. For example, to convert from two yards to feet, they recall that one yard is equal (in measure) to three feet—so 3 feet + 3 feet = 6 feet. To change four yards to inches, they multiply 4 × 36 inches to get 144 inches.

Intermediate-level students use ratio to generate the appropriate units in the new scale. For example, to convert feet to inches, they might use the known ratio of inches to feet ($\frac{1}{12}$) to change 84 inches to feet.

$$\frac{1}{12} = \frac{n}{84}$$

(1 foot is to 12 inches as n feet are to 84 inches)

$$12 \times n = 1 \times 84 \quad \text{or}$$
$$n = 84 \div 12 = 7$$

Students appreciate the nature of the metric system after they have studied conversion in the standard system. Converting in the metric system is simply a matter of multiplying by the proper power of ten. For example, changing 44 centimeters to millimeters is simply a matter of multiplying the 44 centimeters by 10 (or 10^1) to get 440 millimeters. To convert 440 millimeters to centimeters one would multiply by .1 (or 10^{-1}). To change from meters to millimeters (which is three places to the right) the pupil simply multiplies by 1000 (or 10^3), and to change millimeters to meters, the pupil would multiply by 1/1000 (or 10^{-3}). Because the metric system is a base ten system, students quickly find that conversion is simply a matter of shifting the decimal point; the direction and number places depend upon the relationship of the new unit to the old unit.

12.16 TEACHING MEASUREMENT OF CAPACITY, WEIGHT, AND TEMPERATURE

While skills in using money, time, and length are generally well developed before the intermediate level, skills in measuring capacity, weight, and temperature are minimal. Measures of capacity, weight, and temperature are an integral part of experiment-oriented science programs and students find many applications of these skills at that time. Units on weather, growth, simple machines, physical laws, etc., use one or more of these skills.

Because the metric system is so widely used in science, metric conversions of weight and capacity are used often in school settings. However, students encounter ounces, pounds, quarts, and gallons in their shopping/home environment, so instruction in these measures still is a part of many elementary mathematics programs.

Weight (Mass)

Pupils extend their knowledge of scales for weight by learning larger units (metric ton and standard ton) and smaller units (gram, milligram, and ounce). When first working with the smaller units, students will use these units to measure items on the balance and spring scales. Ounces and grams can easily be investigated using balance scales. However, since the milligram is only $\frac{1}{1000}$ of a gram, it is very difficult to measure with the instruments available to students in elementary school. Pupils sometimes associate the weight with that of a grain of salt, but it is sufficient at this level to recognize that the unit is VERY small.

Teachers generally are unable to find a good reference measure for a ton and a metric ton. Most students will recognize that the units would be VERY heavy. Some teachers compare student weights to a ton, showing that it would take an entire classroom of about 30 pupils (67 lbs. each) sitting on one end of the seesaw to balance a ton weight on the other end. A metric ton can then be envisioned as equivalent to having about 33 pupils on the seesaw.

The teacher should help students recognize where various units are used. For example, coal is purchased by tons and metric tons, medicines are frequently prescribed in milligrams, while candy bars are generally measured in grams or ounces. Students take great delight in searching for the appearance of the terms on products and in news articles.

Capacity

Capacity measures (liter, milliliter, and fluid ounce) are units that are explored at the intermediate level. Many pupils do not develop the ability to conserve volume until they are well into the intermediate grades; therefore earlier instruction in cups, pints, quarts, and gallons must be reinforced. Students do not need to participate in as many "pouring" activities since they are more mature, but will need to recognize why labels indicating capacity are helpful when containers differ in size. The liter—which is just slightly larger than the quart—is the most commonly used metric measure for capacity. Many companies are now producing containers that measure a liter rather than a quart, but the process of changing over to the metric system within the United States is a slow one. The 2-liter bottle is commonly available and some bottlers even distribute a 3-liter bottle! Anything less than a liter is measured in milliliters—a very small measure that is comparable to the capacity of the white Cuisenaire™ rod. Pupils who have used the cooking measure $\frac{1}{4}$ teaspoon recognize that the milliliter is even smaller $\frac{1}{5}$ teaspoon)! The standard measure—a fluid ounce—is nearly 30 milliliters so it is much larger. Pupils learn that it takes eight ounces to make one cup and 16 ounces to make a pint. As students look around their homes and the store they find many items measured in ounces and milliliters that they can share with the class.

Changing from one unit of liquid measure to another unit is fairly simple in the metric system. Once students learn to change from millimeters to meters, they see that changing from milliliters to

liters or milligrams to grams is accomplished in a similar fashion. Learning to change from one conventional (English) unit of weight (pounds/ounces) or liquid capacity (fluid ounces/pints) requires a great deal more effort. Development of conversion skills parallels the way the skills are developed for changing from one length unit to another. The pupil must first learn the different ratios between the units and then chain these ratios. For example, the tables of measure in Figure 12.25 show some of the basic comparisons that students may be required to KNOW in order to function in the everyday world.

When converting in the conventional (English) system, the student is taught to chain needed ratios. For example, to convert three pints to ounces the student would construct the following chain to determine how many ounces are in three pints: 16 ounces = 1 pint, so 3 pints would be 3×16 ounces or 48 ounces.

Temperature

Children learned to read thermometers to determine the temperature in the primary grades. Many temperature concepts have been mastered through the use of temperature terms in the child's everyday life. Before pupils leave the intermediate

Capacity

English

1 cup	= 8 ounces
1 pint	= 2 cups
1 quart	= 2 pints
1 half-gallon	= 2 quarts
1 gallon	= 2 half-gallons

Metric

1 liter	= 1000 milliliters

Weight

English

1 pound	= 16 ounces
1 ton	= 2000 pounds

Metric

1 gram	= 1000 milligrams
1 kilogram	= 1000 grams
1 metric ton	= 1000 kilograms
1 megaton	= 1000 metric tons

FIGURE 12.25

level, they will recognize the freezing point of water (32 degrees Fahrenheit or 0 degrees Celsius) and the boiling point of water (212 degrees Fahrenheit or 100 degrees Celsius). Students may also explore how these temperatures were used to establish the scales and to standardize the units for each scale.

12.17 EXTENDING CONCEPTS RELATED TO MEASUREMENT OF AREA

Before entering the intermediate level, students could find the area of rectangular regions by counting superimposed square regions. Once in the intermediate grades, student understanding of area is extended to include formulas for determining area and the use of these formulas to determine the surface area of certain space figures.

Teaching Formulas for Determining the Area of Squares and Rectangles

To prevent any confusion between area and perimeter, instruction in finding area begins with activities that emphasize COVERING UP a region. Some teachers use different shaped "tiles" (circle, triangle, rectangle, etc.) to show the covering-up process. Later, pupils recognize that square regions generally are used as a standard unit to determine area.

First explorations into area usually require the student to "tile" a figure with square regions, and then count to determine the number of regions used. Teachers direct attention to the fact that each row has the same number of tiles. Students soon discover that it is possible to determine the number of tiles needed to cover a region without placing all of the tiles. Since each row contains the same number of tiles, one only needs to find out the number of rows. Students who have used arrays as a model for multiplication recognize that area can be found by multiplying the number of tiles in a row by the number of rows. Figure 12.26 illustrates how the formulas are developed for rectangular regions.

Teaching the Formula for Finding the Area of a Parallelogram

When pupils understand the concept of "tiling" to find the area of a rectangular region, this can serve as the foundation for finding the area of other polygons. One of the first shapes encountered after rectangles is that of the parallelogram. When students

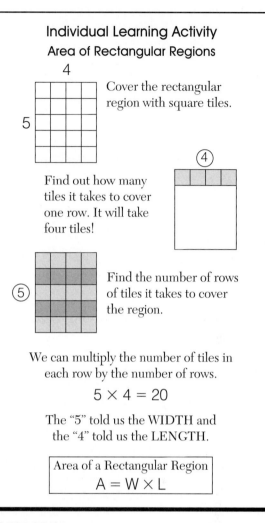

Individual Learning Activity
Area of Rectangular Regions

Cover the rectangular region with square tiles.

Find out how many tiles it takes to cover one row. It will take four tiles!

Find the number of rows of tiles it takes to cover the region.

We can multiply the number of tiles in each row by the number of rows.

$$5 \times 4 = 20$$

The "5" told us the WIDTH and the "4" told us the LENGTH.

Area of a Rectangular Region
$A = W \times L$

FIGURE 12.26

try to cover the parallelogram with tiles they find that some of the tiles "hang over." Using a paper cutout of a parallelogram (and its interior) a teacher can help pupils change the parallelogram into a rectangle by cutting a triangular corner from one end of the polygon and moving it to the other end. This process is illustrated in Figure 12.27. Students now can cover the rectangular region and find the area. The teacher should point out that the length and the width (altitude) of the parallelogram did not change when the end was moved. So the area of the parallelogram can be found by multiplying the length times the altitude, just as with rectangles.

It should be noted that while it really makes no difference which end of the parallelogram is moved, students seem to have less difficulty with the end that does not affect the "bottom" length. Teachers also may want to emphasize the difference between the altitude (width) of the parallelogram and the slant height (which is used when finding the perimeter).

Area of a Parallelogram

When tiles are placed on the parallelogram, they "hang over."

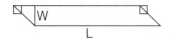

So one end is cut off and moved to the other end—turning it into a rectangle. The length does not change and the width does not change!

Thus the area of the parallelogram is equal to length times width.

A = LW

FIGURE 12.27

Teaching Formulas for Finding the Area of Triangles

Once students learn to turn a parallelogram into a rectangular region, they can use a similar strategy to find the area of a triangle. When the triangle is a right triangle, students can easily construct a rectangle by making another congruent triangle and placing it next to the original. The area of the new rectangle is found by multiplying the height (altitude) times the base. Since the rectangle is made of two congruent triangles, one of the triangles must be $\frac{1}{2}$ of the rectangle—or $\frac{1}{2}$ ab.

When the triangle is either isosceles or scalene, students have a little more difficulty visualizing how the shapes can be turned into rectangles. The most successful strategy is to make a copy of the original triangular region (a congruent triangular region). The students can then cut the congruent triangle along the altitude and use those two parts to change the original triangle into a rectangle. Figure 12.28 illustrates how students manipulate each of the three types of triangles to form a rectangle whose area is twice that of the original triangle. Notice that the student now can take any triangle and make a rectangle and regardless of what shape the triangle is, it will always be $\frac{1}{2}$ of the rectangle or $\frac{1}{2}$ ab.

Some teachers prefer to develop the area of triangles by comparing the triangular region to the parallelogram (see Figure 12.28). When using this

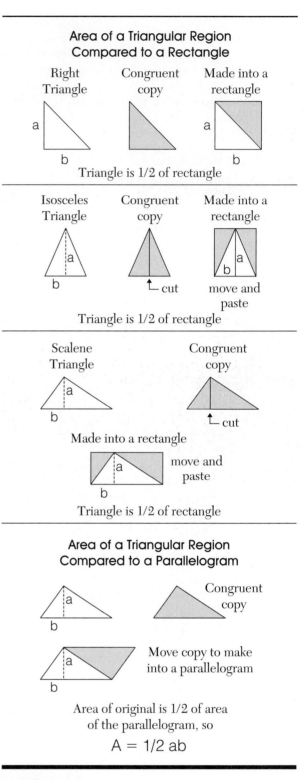

Area of a Triangular Region Compared to a Rectangle

Right Triangle | Congruent copy | Made into a rectangle

Triangle is 1/2 of rectangle

Isosceles Triangle | Congruent copy | Made into a rectangle

cut — move and paste

Triangle is 1/2 of rectangle

Scalene Triangle | Congruent copy

Made into a rectangle

cut — move and paste

Triangle is 1/2 of rectangle

Area of a Triangular Region Compared to a Parallelogram

Congruent copy

Move copy to make into a parallelogram

Area of original is 1/2 of area of the parallelogram, so

A = 1/2 ab

FIGURE 12.28

approach, a congruent triangle region is constructed and placed along one side of the original triangle, making a parallelogram. Since the triangle is $\frac{1}{2}$ of the parallelogram, the formula for the triangle will be $\frac{1}{2}$ ab.

Finding the Area of a Trapezoid

Make a congruent copy
of the trapezoid

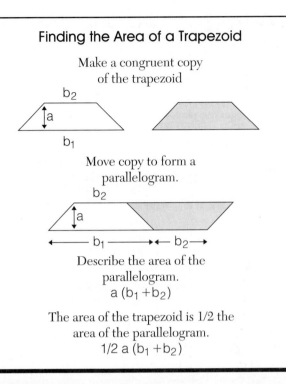

Move copy to form a
parallelogram.

Describe the area of the
parallelogram.
$$a (b_1 + b_2)$$

The area of the trapezoid is 1/2 the
area of the parallelogram.
$$1/2\, a\, (b_1 + b_2)$$

FIGURE 12.29

Finding the Area of a Trapezoid

Students find the area of a trapezoid using a strategy similar to that employed with the triangle. Pupils trace around the trapezoid to make a congruent trapezoid. This second trapezoid is cut out and moved to make a parallelogram. Pupils then discover that the area of the trapezoid (and its interior) is one half that of the parallelogram. Students may be guided to see that the parallelogram formed from the two congruent trapezoids has a base that is made by adding the bottom (b_1) and top (b_2) of the trapezoid. To find the area of the parallelogram, the pupil would write "$a\,(b_1 + b_2)$," so the area of the trapezoid becomes $\frac{1}{2}$ of that or $\frac{1}{2}$ $a\,(b_1 + b_2)$. Figure 12.29 illustrates the use of a congruent trapezoid to generate the parallelogram.

Teaching the Formula for the Area of the Circle

The strategy used to develop the formulas for finding the area of triangles and trapezoids was that of turning the shape into a rectangle or parallelogram. Therefore, it seems only natural to apply this same strategy to determine the area of a circular region. (While there are other techniques for developing the formula, the use of the parallelogram is one of the more common techniques and one that is easily understood by pupils. An enrichment activity might be used to explore the area of circles with one of the other techniques.) To turn a circular region into a parallelogram, the circle is first cut along the diameter and the halves are placed side by side. Pupils readily see that this does NOT make a parallelogram. But when each half is cut again, students see a very roughly defined parallelogram. As students cut the circular region into smaller and smaller pieces, they find that the very "thin" pieces can be put together to closely approximate the shape of a parallelogram with a base equal to one-half the circumference and a height equal to the radius of the circle. Most students recognize that if they keep cutting the "pie-shaped" sections into very thin sections, eventually a straight line would be formed. Once the area of the parallelogram is defined, students write the formula as "Area = $\frac{1}{2}$ Cr," which would give the area of a circle. However, the circumference of a circle often is not given and pupils must work with ONLY the radius given, so the formula is simplified (see Figure 12.30), ending with the standard formula.

Finding the Area of Regular Polygons

Some programs do not include the finding of area for regular polygons as a part of the regular curriculum (the topic is included as an enrichment activity). It would be a rare occasion when an individual would need to <u>recall</u> the formula for a regular hexagon or octagon.

Finding the area of a regular polygon will allow pupils to use their mastery of the area formula for triangles to find other areas. Cutting a polygon into triangular regions and finding the area of <u>each</u> triangle is an interesting problem-solving strategy. Such a strategy is useful with a large number of polygons even when the shape is not regular.

To find the area of a regular hexagon, students find the center and construct triangles that have <u>congruent</u> bases. (See Figure 12.31.) Since there are six congruent triangular regions in a regular hexagonal region, the "formula" is $6 \times \frac{1}{2}$ ab or 3ab. (A regular octagon can be divided into eight congruent triangles, so the formula would be $8 \times \frac{1}{2}$ ab or 4ab.)

Finding the Surface Area of Space Figures

Exploration of surface area for common space figures is normally a part of the seventh and eighth grade curriculum, although some programs look at

Finding the Area of a Circle

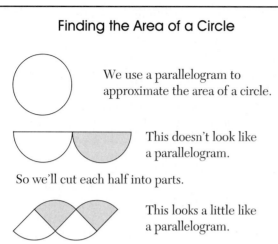

We use a parallelogram to approximate the area of a circle.

This doesn't look like a parallelogram.

So we'll cut each half into parts.

This looks a little like a parallelogram.

Cut it into even smaller parts.

radius

←— 1/2 circumference —→

Now describe the parallelogram. The length is 1/2 the circumference and the width is the radius.

$$A = 1/2C \times r$$

Since $C = 2\pi r$, we can copy that to replace C, giving us

$$A = 1/2 \times (2 \times \pi \times r) \times r$$

which we can simplify to

$$\boxed{A = \pi r^2}$$

FIGURE 12.30

the concept as early as fifth grade. Students who associate perimeter with "putting string around it" and area with "tiling it," generally think of surface area as "covering it with wallpaper." To determine the amount of paper needed to "cover" the surface of a space figure, pupils are encouraged to make a pattern by tracing around the faces of the space figure. Figure 12.32 illustrates patterns for a triangular prism, rectangular prism, square pyramid, and cylinder.

Students first find surface area by determining the area of each part of the pattern and then adding the areas together. They are encouraged to simplify the process by looking for congruent regions. For example, the combined area of the four congruent triangles in a regular tetrahedron can be expressed as $4 \times \frac{1}{2}$ ab, which can be simplified as "$2a \times b$." (It would take two or three more lines to make this

statement correct.) Exploring how the surface area of a cube can be simplified to six times the square of a side and the surface area of a square pyramid can be simplified to b × (b + 2a) make interesting enrichment activities and serve as good readiness activities for later algebraic factoring at the post-elementary level.

Teaching Conversion of Units of Area Measure

Although most pupils at the intermediate level can use a ratio approach—similar to that used in linear measurement—some will need to use a model to verify the conversion. When using model verification, the student constructs a square-foot unit and then superimposes upon it a square-inch grid, verifying that there are 144 square inches. When this approach is used, the student will see that a 12-by-12 grid is used for each square foot, so there will be 144 square inches per square foot.

Another way of teaching students to convert from one unit of measure to another is to teach conversion within the context of the formulas for area. For example, in developing a conversion ratio for converting square yards to square feet, the teacher would have the students rethink the area of a square yard. Knowing that one yard is equal in measure to three feet, the pupil would think, "The length of the square yard is three feet and the width

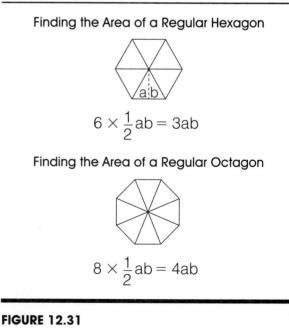

Finding the Area of a Regular Hexagon

$$6 \times \frac{1}{2} ab = 3ab$$

Finding the Area of a Regular Octagon

$$8 \times \frac{1}{2} ab = 4ab$$

FIGURE 12.31

Surface Area

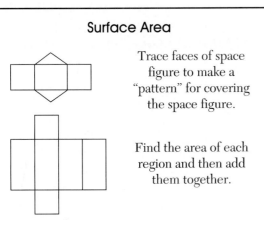

Trace faces of space figure to make a "pattern" for covering the space figure.

Find the area of each region and then add them together.

Look for congruent faces.

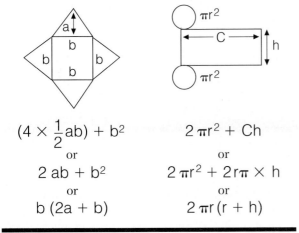

$$(4 \times \frac{1}{2}ab) + b^2$$
or
$$2\,ab + b^2$$
or
$$b\,(2a + b)$$

$$2\,\pi r^2 + Ch$$
or
$$2\,\pi r^2 + 2r\pi \times h$$
or
$$2\,\pi r\,(r + h)$$

FIGURE 12.32

is three feet, so 3×3 would be nine square feet." By a similar rethinking process one could establish that 1 cm^2 is equal in measure to $10\text{ mm} \times 10\text{ mm}$, so it would take 100 mm^2 to cover 1 cm^2.

12.18 EXTENDING CONCEPTS RELATED TO MEASUREMENT OF VOLUME

In the primary grades children counted the number of blocks it takes to fill a rectangular prism. Usually when pictured material is used, the interior regions have been marked off into cubes for the child to count. In some instances, primary-grade teachers have children fill boxes with rectangular cubes to determine the volume. At the intermediate level the concepts of volume measure are extended to include the formula for finding the volume of rectangular prisms. By the time the student leaves the eighth grade, the formulas for the volume of prisms, pyramids, cylinders, and cones will have been introduced.

Since finding volumes of any space figure (other than rectangular prisms) is seldom required in everyday life, teachers should emphasize a technique for finding volume rather than memorizing formulas. Rectangular prisms are used to establish the concept of volume. In finding volume, pupils associate volume with a process of "filling it up." Initial activities may have students fill a prism (or pyramid, cone, sphere) with beans, books, etc. As pupils work with rectangular prisms, they find that cubes fill the interior very efficiently, leaving no "empty space" around the blocks. They soon recognize that the amount that can be contained by two different boxes can be compared by filling each box with cubes and then counting the cubes.

To develop a more systematic way (a formula) of determining the number of cubes the teacher will have students describe the filling process. Pupils are directed to first "cover the bottom" with a layer of cubes. Attention is then directed to the height by asking if the next layer would have the same number of blocks. In a right prism each layer will contain the same number of blocks, so students can find the number of layers and multiply. For example, the teacher may start with a layer that appears as a 4-by-5 array of cubes. (See Figure 12.33.)

Individual Learning Activity
Volume of Rectangular Prism

Find the number of cubes it takes to cover the bottom layer.

20 blocks in the first layer.

Each layer has the same number of blocks. Count the layers. There are six layers of blocks (height).

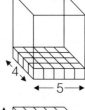

Volume = blocks to cover the base times the number of layers.

$$V = B \times H \quad \text{or} \quad V = (L \times W) \times H$$

FIGURE 12.33

The number of cubes in a box that would hold six layers of 4-by-5 arrays of blocks could be written as 6 × (4 × 5). After several rectangular prisms have been explored, the teacher may note that in finding the number of blocks in the first layer the students were "covering the base" in a manner similar to "tiling" (area). Students should—by examination—see that the volume of the prism can be found by determining the <u>area of the base</u> (L × W) and then multiplying by the number of layers (H), or V = LWH.

Once students explore the process for finding the volume of a rectangular prism, they can find the volume of any right prism in a similar manner. Of course, the pupils find that cubes do not fit well in triangular, trapezoidal, hexagonal, or octagonal prisms. However, the process of covering the base with cubes is related to finding the area of the base. Since each layer will have the same number of blocks needed to cover the base, the pupil will then count the layers (height) and multiply the area of the base. The basic formula for finding the volume of all right prisms (and the cylinder) is "area of the base" (B) times the height (h), or V = Bh. (See Figure 12.34.)

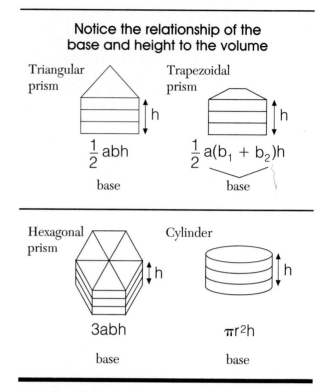

Notice the relationship of the base and height to the volume

FIGURE 12.34

Exploring Volumes of Pyramids, Cones, and Spheres

Finding the volume of space figures that do not have the same number of blocks in each layer (pyramids, cones, and spheres) calls for a new strategy. To help students understand the relationship of these space figures to those of right prisms and cylinders, teachers may employ volume models that have the same bases and heights. To discover the volume formula for a square-based pyramid, a teacher would find a square prism that has the same base and height. Once the congruence of the bases and the equal height of the two figures is established, the teacher will direct pupils to fill the pyramid with water, sand, or rice to determine how many pyramids it will take to fill the prism. Students usually estimate it will take two pyramids to fill the prism. They are surprised when actual pouring reveals that it takes THREE pyramids to fill one prism. Using this information, a "formula" may be written as V (square pyramid) = $\frac{1}{3}$ the volume of square prism. Since the volume of the square prism is L × W × H, the square pyramid would be $\frac{1}{3}$ LWH. (See Figure 12.35.)

Exploration of other pyramids is done in a similar fashion. Students find a prism with the same base and height as the pyramid. They pour the con-

tents of the pyramid into the prism and discover it takes THREE pyramids, so the volume of the pyramid (triangular, rectangular, hexagonal, etc.) will be $\frac{1}{3}$ the volume of the right prism with the same base and height.

Once students explore the volume relationship of pyramids and prisms, they can quickly devise a strategy for determining the volume of a cone. Since a cone has a circular base, it is compared to a cylinder with the same base and height. Although a few students will speculate that cones will be different than pyramids, most are not surprised when they find that it takes THREE cones to fill a cylinder. The volume of a cone is $\frac{1}{3}$ the volume of a cylinder with the same base and height; the formula $V = \frac{1}{3}\pi r^2 h$ is a recording of this relationship.

Finding the volume of a sphere presents a new situation for students. However, since the cone was compared to the cylinder, many students will suggest that spheres also should be compared to the volume of a cylinder. When the liquid in a sphere is compared to the volume of a cylinder with the same diameter and height, students discover the sphere will fill the cylinder $\frac{2}{3}$ full. Students then find that the volume of a sphere can be found by finding $\frac{2}{3}\pi r^2 h$. While this is not the standard formula, this "descriptive" formula can be used to find the volume of a sphere. Teachers may suggest substitut-

Individual Learning Activity

Pupils can pour from one container to a container with a congruent base and height to discover the formulas for cones, pyramids and spheres.

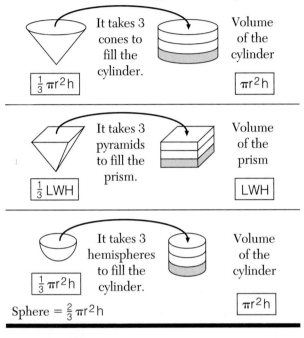

It takes 3 cones to fill the cylinder.

$\frac{1}{3}\pi r^2 h$

Volume of the cylinder

$\pi r^2 h$

It takes 3 pyramids to fill the prism.

$\frac{1}{3}LWH$

Volume of the prism

LWH

It takes 3 hemispheres to fill the cylinder.

$\frac{1}{3}\pi r^2 h$

Volume of the cylinder

$\pi r^2 h$

Sphere $= \frac{2}{3}\pi r^2 h$

FIGURE 12.35

ing "2r" for "h" (since the height of a sphere is its diameter) and then simplify the formula ($V = \frac{2}{3} \times \pi r^2 \times 2 \times r$), arriving at the standard $V = \frac{4}{3}\pi r^3$. (Some teachers prefer to compare a hemisphere when finding the volume of a sphere. It takes three hemispheres to fill a cylinder—like a cone—so a hemisphere is $\frac{1}{3}$ of a cylinder. Since a sphere would be TWO of the hemispheres, students reason that a sphere would be $\frac{2}{3}$ of a cylinder.)

Teaching Units of Volume

Intermediate-level children know there are some commonly used units for measuring volume—cubic inches (cu. in.), cubic feet (cu. ft.), cubic yards (cu. yd.), cubic centimeters (cm^3), and cubic meters (m^3). As students use the cubic units to find the volume of space figures, they should be alerted to the application of these units in industry and business. For example, cubic feet, cubic yards, and cubic meters are used in construction, cubic centimeters in the automotive industry, and cubic meters in international shipping. Pupils can be encouraged to look for examples of other applications in magazines and newspapers. A bulletin-board dis-

play will give students a place to display their discoveries, so others will benefit from what they have found.

Teaching Conversion of Units of Volume

Conversion from one metric unit of volume to another involves skill with both powers of ten and the metric scale. Metric volume conversion does not occur frequently in daily life experiences; it is usually limited to scientific and technical applications. Most metric measurements of volume are set in a specifically selected unit and this unit is not generally converted to another unit on that scale. For example, if the volume of dirt to be excavated from a construction site is calculated in cubic meters (m^3), there rarely would be a need to use cubic centimeters (cm^3). Of course, one liter (a cubic decimeter) often is compared to 1000 ml, but students generally do not associate these measures with cubic measurement.

A common way to teach conversions in both the metric and standard systems is to use a method similar to that used with square measure conversions. For example, to change from a cubic foot to cubic inches, the dimensions of a cubic foot are converted to inches ($12 \times 12 \times 12$) or 1728 cubic inches. Metrically, to convert from a cubic centimeter to cubic millimeter, one would replace each dimension of a centimeter with 10 mm and multiply ($10 \times 10 \times 10$), so a $cm^3 = 1000 mm^3$. (In some programs students master for recall some of the more common conversions such as: 1 cubic foot = 1278 cubic inches; 1 cubic yard = 27 cubic feet; and 1 $cm^3 = 1000 mm^3$.)

12.19 TEACHING THE MEASUREMENT OF ANGLES

Students first learned to classify angles as acute, right, and obtuse by comparing them to right corners (right angles). After pupils become proficient with this simple comparison, angular measurement (using a protractor) is introduced. Since students are familiar with right corners, the measurement of right angles is one of the first measurements undertaken and pupils learn that right angles measure 90 degrees. Since acute angles are "smaller" than right angles, acute angles measure less than 90 degrees while obtuse angles must measure more than 90 degrees.

Though a standard unit—the degree—will be used whenever pupils measure angles, they first should recognize that any size angle COULD have been chosen for measurement. Taking a model right corner and folding it in half will show pupils how a model of a smaller angle could be constructed. Continued folding will show students that smaller units could be used in measuring the size of angles. Using a smaller unit they find that a right corner measures four of the smaller units. Once students recognize that any sized unit may be constructed, they can be shown the "standard" unit of a degree. Further study of the unit may lead pupils to discover WHY the degree was chosen and why we use 360 degrees as a complete trip around a circle.

When using the protractor, students must be taught several skills in order to measure angles accurately. Some of these skills include being able to:

1. Align the center point of the protractor with the vertex of the angle being measured.
2. Align one of the rays (or line segments) along one of the radii represented on the base of the protractor.
3. Extend an angle's rays (or line segments) so it will extend up through the scale of the protractor if the ray does not reach the edge of the scale.

Figure 12.36 illustrates these steps.

Protractors come in a variety of designs but most have two scales that permit the reading of an angle in either a clockwise or counterclockwise direction. The pupil must be aware of <u>which</u> scale is being read. Some protractors (as illustrated in Figure 12.36) require the child to interpret when the measure of the angle is greater than a right angle. Some instruction will be required for reading the particular scale being used by the students.

All students should learn to estimate the size of an angle by comparing that angle to a right angle (90 degrees). When a measurement is taken, the pupil should check to see if the numbers are reasonable. If the angle is an acute angle—a measure of 120 degrees is <u>unreasonable</u> since acute angles are smaller than right angles. This estimating process will help pupils decide on the proper protractor scale to use with a given angle.

As with other measures, students should be made aware of the many places angle measure is required in our society. For example, students should recognize that machinists, sailors, draftsmen, surveyors, architects, artists, contractors, astronomers, and mechanics all use angle measurement in their professions.

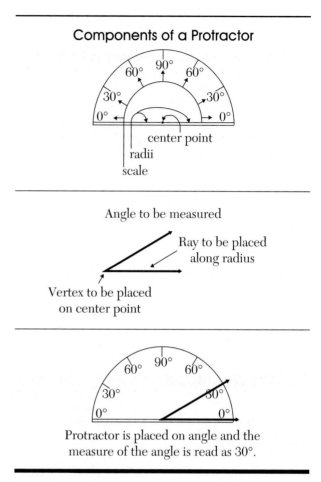

Components of a Protractor

center point

radii

scale

Angle to be measured

Ray to be placed
along radius

Vertex to be placed
on center point

Protractor is placed on angle and the
measure of the angle is read as 30°.

FIGURE 12.36

12.20 WORKING WITH DENOMINATE NUMBERS

As the metric system becomes a part of our everyday lives, the need for learning special algorithms for working with denominate numbers becomes less significant. Some occupations require more skill with measurement computation than others. For instance, a carpenter, electrician, or plumber may need to add three feet seven inches to a measure of two feet eight inches, but much of their proficiency to do this task comes from on-the-job training and not from what they learned in school. Since the need for denominate number skills is diminishing, some school programs have dropped this skill from their curriculum. When computational skill must be taught, the teacher should teach <u>general strategies</u> rather than drilling for mastery.

Several concepts can be stressed when teaching students to compute with denominate numbers.

One area for exploration is to study the effect on precision when one adds, subtracts, multiplies, or divides with measurements. Operations using measures that do not have the same degree of precision produce misleading information. For instance, adding three yards to two yards three inches would appear to produce five yards two inches. This measure reports a precision to the nearest inch—which should fall between five yards $2\frac{1}{2}$ inches and five yards $1\frac{1}{2}$ inches. However, the three yards could have an error of 18 inches ($\frac{1}{2}$ yard)! To reduce the error of measurement, the teacher should have pupils work only with measures that have the same precision. (An interesting exploration for talented pupils would be to determine the range in which the measure would be found when working with measures of different precision.)

Another aspect which might be explored by the teacher is the effect of converting from one unit to another. For instance, while six feet is equal in measure to two yards, measurements to the nearest foot do not have the same degree of precision as measurements to the nearest yard. The measure of two yards COULD be off by as much as $1\frac{1}{2}$ feet! It probably would be better to report that six feet was equal to two yards and 0 feet in order to maintain the precision of the original measurement. Similar concerns exist for work within the metric system. While 100 centimeters and one meter are equivalent measures, they do not reflect the same degree of precision.

When performing operations within the metric system, the algorithms for working with whole numbers and decimals are used. Regrouping within the metric system, since it too is based on a ten system, is handled just as in the standard algorithms. Since these operations may be performed easily on the calculator, computation within this system should concentrate upon the degree of precision that is appropriate.

Computation in the conventional (English) measurement system, since it is not based on ten, requires students to learn a new algorithm. Computing with denominate numbers is similar to working with common fractions. The denominator of a fraction "names" the size of the fractional part just as pint, inch, and foot "name" the size of the unit. Pupils who have learned to regroup when adding and subtracting fractions readily see the necessity of trading for units other than ten. When subtracting two feet nine inches from four feet three inches the students must trade one foot for 12 inches. When the 12 inches are added to the three inches, the student must record 15 inches, not 13 as when working in base ten.

Before students can become proficient working with denominate numbers they must be able to convert from one unit to another (1 yard = 3 feet; 1 gallon = 4 quarts). Once students have learned to convert within a system, then the pattern similar to that employed in teaching operations with other numbers can be employed.

Teaching Addition and Subtraction Involving Denominate Numbers

Students will encounter fewer problems if they first explore addition and subtraction of denominate numbers in situations where conversion is not required. Such problems are easy to construct in textbooks, but those that grow from the student's everyday work with measurement seldom follow such a pattern. Therefore, the teacher may need to help students learn both a format (algorithm) and a regrouping process simultaneously. Figure 12.37 illustrates some examples of the type of initial exercises that introduce the student to the denominate number algorithm.

Addition and subtraction algorithms for denominate numbers can use the expanded notation form similar to the expanded notation developmental algorithms used in the primary grades. When adding, conversions take place after the addition is completed (no internal regrouping). In subtraction, changing from one unit to another must take place when it is needed in an algorithm. Figure 12.38 il-

$$\begin{array}{lll} 3 \text{ lb.} & 2 \text{ oz.} \\ +2 \text{ lb.} & 5 \text{ oz.} \end{array} \qquad \begin{array}{lll} 3 \text{ hr.} & 17 \text{ min.} \\ +4 \text{ hr.} & 6 \text{ min.} \end{array}$$

$$\begin{array}{lll} 2 \text{ gal.} & 1 \text{ qt.} \\ +5 \text{ gal.} & 2 \text{ qt.} \end{array} \qquad \begin{array}{lll} 7 \text{ ft.} & 5 \text{ in.} \\ +6 \text{ ft.} & 4 \text{ in.} \end{array}$$

$$\begin{array}{lll} 5 \text{ sq. ft.} & 23 \text{ sq. in.} \\ +8 \text{ sq. ft.} & 55 \text{ sq. in.} \end{array}$$

$$\begin{array}{lll} 13 \text{ cu. yd.} & 15 \text{ cu. ft.} \\ -\ 7 \text{ cu. yd.} & 8 \text{ cu. ft.} \end{array}$$

$$\begin{array}{lll} 45 \text{ min.} & 16 \text{ sec.} \\ -32 \text{ min.} & 14 \text{ sec.} \end{array}$$

FIGURE 12.37

$$
\begin{array}{ll}
3 \text{ yards} \quad 2 \text{ feet} & \\
+4 \text{ yards} \quad 2 \text{ feet} & \\
\hline
7 \text{ yards} \quad 4 \text{ feet} = 8 \text{ yards} \quad 1 \text{ foot}
\end{array}
$$

> Child converts 3 feet to 1 yard.

> Child converts 1 cubic yard to 27 cubic feet.

$$
\begin{array}{llll}
8 \text{ cu. yds.} & 4 \text{ cu. ft.} & = & 7 \text{ cu. yds.} \quad 31 \text{ cu. ft.} \\
-2 \text{ cu. yds.} & 9 \text{ cu. ft.} & = & -2 \text{ cu. yds.} \quad 9 \text{ cu. ft.} \\
\hline
& & & 5 \text{ cu. yds.} \quad 22 \text{ cu. ft.}
\end{array}
$$

FIGURE 12.38

lustrates these differences between the way the algorithms are developed for addition and subtraction.

Teaching Multiplication Involving Denominate Numbers and Whole Numbers

Students can either be taught to use the distributive property with the whole number and denominate numbers or to convert the denominate numbers to the smallest unit represented, multiplying, and then converting the product back into the larger units. For example, if you wished to compute 3×4 hours 32 minutes you could use the distributive property—multiplying the minutes and then the hours. The resulting 12 hours 96 minutes can be changed to 13 hours 36 minutes. Using a second technique, the pupil would convert the 4 hours 32 minutes to 272 minutes and then multipy by 3 to obtain 816 minutes. Then the pupil would convert the 816 minutes to 13 hours and 36 minutes by dividing by 60 minutes. While this second method may seem more cumbersome, much of the computation can be handled by a calculator. (Using a calculator to convert minutes to hours will require the pupil to be able to find a REMAINDER using the machine.)

Teaching Division Involving Denominate Numbers and Whole Numbers

The right distributive property of division is used to divide denominate numbers by whole numbers (partition division) and requires the pupil to regroup within the algorithm. (See Figure 12.39.) Another common approach, especially when dividing

$$
\begin{array}{ll}
4 \text{ hr.} \quad 32 \text{ min.} & 4 \text{ hr. } 32 \text{ min.} = 272 \text{ min.} \\
\times 3 & 3 \times 272 = 816 \\
\hline
12 \text{ hr.} \quad 96 \text{ min.} = & 816 \div 60 = 13.6 \\
13 \text{ hr.} \quad 36 \text{ min.} & (13.6 - 13) \times 60 = 36 \\
& 13 \text{ hr. } 36 \text{ min.}
\end{array}
$$

$$
\begin{array}{l}
23 \text{ ft.} \quad 11 \text{ in.} \\
4\,\overline{)\,95 \text{ ft.} \quad\; 8 \text{ in.}} \\
\;\;\;\underline{8} \qquad +36 \\
\;\;\;15 \qquad\; 44 \\
\;\;\;\underline{12} \qquad -4 \\
\;\;\;\; 3 \qquad\;\; 4 \\
\qquad\qquad -4 \\
\;36 \text{ in.}
\end{array}
$$

How many 4 lb. 6 oz. packages can I get from 26 lb. 4 oz.?

4 lb. 6 oz. = 70 oz.

26 lb. 4 oz. = 420 oz.

$420 \div 70 = 6$ packages

FIGURE 12.39

a denominate number by another denominate number, is that of changing the denominate numbers to the smallest unit, dividing, and then changing the answer back into larger units, if possible. For example if a merchant wanted to make up packages weighing four pounds six ounces from a bag that weighed 26 pounds four ounces, how many packages could he get? To solve the problem, the pupil could use the calculator to change both weights to ounces and then divide.

12.21 COMPUTERS

Computer programs are available that can actually teach many of the measurement concepts, such as finding formulas for various polygonal regions. Some software programs simulate real-world situations. A simulation may take a student through an activity of running a lemonade stand, including the simulation of business conditions that can result in failure or success of the operation. (Pupils choose the amount to charge, the quantity to make each day, and determine the cost. Then they are given the conditions and the amount they sell from the simulated program.)

Commercial software programs are also available that provide materials allowing students to create graphics for linear, area, and volume problems. When the dimensions in the program are changed, new data is generated. These programs promote the student's ability to estimate and develop an intuitive feel for the effect on area (volume) when a dimension is altered.

At its simplest level, the computer may be used to classify coins, convert from one unit to another, and give abbreviations for measures in the standard system and symbols for measures in the metric system. At a more complex level, students can be given design problems related to measurement applications.

12.22 EVALUATION AND INTERVENTION

Diagnosis and remediation in the area of measurement generally falls into the following categories: (1) misconceptions related to the nature of the measurement; (2) inability to use measurement instruments properly; (3) inability to choose appropriate units and/or convert from one unit to another; or (4) inappropriate actions with operations on denominate numbers.

Methods for identifying errors in the area of measurement are similar to those techniques suggested in previous chapters. In many instances, however, measurement skills are demonstrated through physical activities. Therefore, observation is used to identify errors being made by students. For example, when measuring with a ruler, the starting point (zero) often is not the end of the ruler. A teacher must observe a pupil as the measurement is being made to detect that the student is not starting his/her measurement at the correct place. When a student reads a thermometer a teacher can, by observation, detect that a child is interpreting the marks as increments of one degree rather than two degrees only as the pupil touches and counts the marks. To detect errors in counting money, the teacher may request the child to count aloud to determine if an error is a counting-on weakness, a coin identification error, or the lack of skill in counting multiples.

Errors related to factual concepts (12 inches = one foot; the abbreviation for quart; the symbol for centimeter, etc.) can be detected by analyzing seatwork or quizzes. Errors related to operations with denominate numbers also can be identified through paper-and-pencil activities. However, the true nature of denominate number errors may require an interview with the student.

Remedial strategies are determined by the type of error a student makes and how the error originated. For example, conceptual errors are remediated by employing concrete manipulative materials. Skill errors, on the other hand, may often be corrected by relating them to previously learned (or similar) skills. Errors that represent a lack of knowledge are overcome by activities that build on that knowledge, which may require a return to manipulative models.

Before errors related to operations with denominate numbers can be corrected, a careful analysis must be made. If the error is a conceptual misunderstanding related to operations in general, then the remedial focus is on the operational concepts and skills. For instance, the student fails to regroup when subtracting a larger digit from a smaller digit. Frequently the error is in converting from one unit to another during the operation process. In such instances the remedial focus should be on reteaching conversion skills.

12.23 MEETING SPECIAL NEEDS

Measurement presents many opportunities for the teacher to provide a wide variety of activities for children with special needs. This section will only sample a few of these possibilities.

Extending Money Concepts for the More Able Student

Every day, students hear terms that can be explored to deepen their understanding of money values. As students encounter terms such as "inflation, gold standard, trade deficit, revenue, net income, value of stocks, balance of payments, barter system, time value of money, economy, etc." the teacher may suggest activities or research assignments to relate these terms to the students' world.

Monetary value is often discussed in social studies. When studying early American history or the American Indians, the barter system may be examined and even acted out in the classroom. When students examine how the United States sells and buys products from other nations; inflation, balance of payments, trade deficit, and many other terms related to the monetary system are discussed. Currency exchange rates (which often change daily) can be explored by having the class plan an imaginary trip to Europe. Allowing a more talented student to be the "head teller" at the classroom exchange center will allow pupils to use their calculators to help determine the currency (U.S. dollars to francs) to be taken on the trip.

Consumer mathematics topics offer many opportunities for enriching a program. For example, using a catalog to make out a birthday wish order—complete with tax and shipping costs—is interesting and challenging. Some students enjoy examining the price of a new automobile—comparing the cost if bought on an installment basis to the cost if cash is paid. Using calculators to determine the total cost, students apply many of the skills previously taught in the classroom. To help pupils understand profit and loss, classrooms may form corporations in which the class buys stock to fund a project. The class purchases (or constructs) items to be sold in the school and keeps a record of expenses and profit. When the company starts making a profit, "dividends" are determined and "stockholders" share in the company's success.

Extending the More Able Student's Concept of Time

If time is explored from a historical perspective, many activities can be developed. Although we use clocks and calendars today, pupils find it interesting to find out how people kept track of time in the past. Such research leads students to design their own timekeeping devices (water clocks, candles, shadow clocks).

Non-clock timing devices are another concept that students enjoy. Streetlights automatically turn on and off with regulators that sense daylight and darkness. There are devices that monitor the wash cycle in a washing machine, open or lock safes, regulate the traffic signals, and turn the lights off a short time after the garage door has been opened or closed. Students may wish to make lists of the many different places where timing devices are used.

If encyclopedias are examined, students can find that there are ultra-accurate clocks that use the vibration of atoms to measure time very precisely. They may find that scientists now can measure time to the nearest nanosecond. As pupils explore timekeeping around the world, they recognize the value of time zones, Greenwich time, and daylight saving time.

Enriching the More Able Student's Understanding of Linear Measure

While students normally learn to measure units to the nearest $\frac{1}{16}$ inch and millimeter, exploring measures that are more precise is a rewarding enrichment experience. Determining an appropriate unit for measuring the thickness of human hair makes pupils aware of the necessity of smaller units. Industry commonly uses small units such as microns in measuring the thickness of wire.

Measures for great distances are commonly discussed in science. When one wishes to determine the distance to the nearest star, kilometers or miles are inappropriate. Length may be related to the distance light travels in one year. Some pupils will find it interesting to calculate the number of miles away a star is when it is reported that it is 1000 light years away.

Concurrent with studies of linear measure, students may examine the kinds of instruments that would be used to measure small or large distances. Students may explore as out of class assignments questions such as

- "How does an auto mechanic measure spark-plug gaps to the nearest $\frac{1}{1000}$ inch?"
- "What kind of instrument would be used to measure the distance to the moon?"
- "How is ocean depth measured?"
- "How can radar (or sonar) be used to measure distance (or speed)?"

Many explorations in measurement involve other skills (ratio, proportion, similarity, congruent angles, etc.). For example, to find the height of the school flagpole (without climbing it), students may measure the shadow and use ratio concepts. Students often encounter linear measurement in problem-solving situations. When they wish to determine the height of a building, they may measure a single brick and mortar and then determine the number of layers in a wall. While the focus of such an activity is problem solving, pupils must apply their measurement skills to solve the problem.

Enriching the More Able Student's Understanding of Capacity, Weight, and Temperature

Social studies units again present an opportunity to examine how early cultures measured capacity and weight. Many students are challenged by asking questions such as "Why is a gallon measured in quarts and not fifths?", "Who made the decision and why was it made?", "How did ancient traders weigh objects?" Researching how the weight of very large objects is determined is an area ripe for exploration. For example, how do scientists estimate the weight of the moon? Or, how does a geologist estimate the number of tons of coal under the ground before a shaft is dug to mine the coal? In addition to encyclopedic sources, students may enjoy reading the story of weights and measures written by Jeanne Bendick entitled *How Much and How Many*.

Capacity and temperature offer similar possibilities for examining unusual methods of measuring.

For example, how does a geologist estimate the barrels of oil to be found underground in a given area, or how many gallons of water are trapped as ice in the arctic regions? Enrichment activities with temperature can range from research about the "Greenhouse Effect" to examining exotic ways that temperature is taken when measuring the temperature of molten steel in a blast furnace or of a rocket's exhaust.

Extending the More Able Student's Ability to Use the Calculator in Measurement-Related Activities

Students will need a strong foundation in measurement concepts before they can fully utilize calculators for measurement activities. For example, putting data into a calculator without understanding precision, greatest possible error, significant digits, and accuracy can produce a nonsensical display. For example, a bar is 32 centimeters (to the nearest centimeter) and a pupil wants to find the length of 50 bars. Keying in 50×32 will give a mathematical answer of 1600, but each measure may be "off" $+/- \frac{1}{2}$ centimeter. Therefore the actual range of 50 bars would be $+/- (50 \times \frac{1}{2}$ centimeter)—or between 1575 cm and 1625 cm.

Calculators open a whole area of scientific measurement applications to the elementary school student. While most applications of linear, area, and volume measurement are static in nature (no variations are taken into account) most applications by engineers and scientists take into account the effect of temperature on measurement. For example, "How does an engineer provide for the expansion of metals in his plans?" An interesting small-group learning project would be to measure a local bridge span on a cold day and a hot day using a temperature-neutral device and note the differences in lengths. Students would need to refer to tables of expansion coefficients for data on expansions of metals. This type of project can provide a wide range of research questions for the students to investigate using calculators and tables.

Measuring the amount of water wasted by a dripping faucet in the classroom is a project that not only utilizes measurement, but also helps students see the importance of such skills in the everyday world. If students find that a dripping faucet accumulates 43 fluid ounces of water each day—they can use their calculators to find how much water would be wasted in a week, month, and year. Calculators can also be used to convert the ounces to gallons and then find how much the water company would charge for the wasted water. Even

homeowners are amazed by how costly a constantly running commode can be in terms of a monthly water bill. Students may use volume skills to find how much money it would cost to fill their swimming pool!

Providing for the Learning-Disabled Student

All students need a thorough foundation in measurement skills. Without measurement skills an individual is functionally illiterate in our technological society. Measurement skills are especially important to the learning disabled, because these skills enable them to live independently in our society. While all children should develop an understanding of measurement concepts through hands-on explorations, the learning-disabled pupil may need a much longer period of hands-on manipulations. Applications of measurement skills should occur in situations that simulate the real world as closely as possible. For example, when learning money concepts, real money and real-life money applications should be used. While "play store" activities are useful in developing beginning skills, pupils should have many opportunities to use money at the school store, the lunchroom, and other places in their environment. Supervised out-of-school excursions to use money should also be a part of every learning-disabled child's program.

Measuring instruments for the learning disabled should be kept as close as possible to the actual devices individuals will have to master to become functionally literate in society. For example, parking meters, tape measures, kitchen timers, and devices on ovens and microwave ovens should all be a part of the learning-disabled students' curriculum.

Providing for the Gifted Child

Measurement skills are important to gifted students, because many technical and professional careers they might choose for their life work (art, science, engineering, medicine, business, etc.) utilize measurement skills and concepts extensively.

The gifted child can explore measurement problems faced by scientists and engineers who are constantly faced with the problem of measuring very small and enormously large things. To give the gifted child a flavor of this type of problem-solving activity a teacher may wish to have children create methods of measuring extremely small objects. For example, a very small object of known width can be used to measure the width of other small objects,

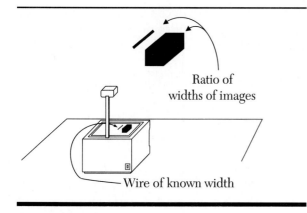

Ratio of
widths of images

Wire of known width

FIGURE 12.40

by using the magnified image of this object and the reference object of known width. In Figure 12.40 a student is using the projected image of the objects on the wall and the concept of ratios to determine the approximate width of the second object using the known width of a fine copper wire (purchased at an electrical supply store). For example, the width of the fine copper wire is .023 inches. Since the width of a thin piece of metal (image A) is four times larger than the image of the copper wire, the thickness of the metal must be about .092 inches. Students might also explore how microbiologists place grids of known widths under a microscope to estimate the width of a cell they are viewing on the grid.

An interesting exploration for the gifted student is the finding of surface area of a cone or sphere. Most students learn to find surface area of simple polyhedrons. The usual strategy for finding surface area—open the model and lay it flat—can be used to find the surface area of a cone. Once the curved portion of the cone is flattened, the student can cut the region into "pie-shaped pieces" and rearrange the pieces to form a parallelogram (Figure 12.41). The base of the parallelogram is $\frac{1}{2}$ of the circumference of the circular base and the width is the slant height of the cone. The area of the parallelogram ($s\pi r$) is added to the area of the base (πr^2) to find the surface area of the cone or $s\pi r + \pi r^2$. The standard formula SA cone $= \pi r (s + r)$ is a simplification of this description by factoring out πr.

Finding the surface area of a sphere is much more challenging than finding that of the cone. Spheres do not "flatten out" easily. Therefore the strategy of opening up the model cannot be easily adapted. A new strategy—"cover it up" with string—can be used in early explorations. An or-

ange can serve as a good model. Students may take heavy cord and find how much string it will take to cover the orange (Figure 12.42). One of the first things they discover is that they only need to cover half of the orange (a hemisphere) since they can then double the amount. Since the cord sometimes "slips" students may dampen it with water or a sticky substance. Once the cord entirely covers the hemisphere, the student can unwrap the cord and use the string to cover the area of the "center slice" of the orange (the great circle). Students find that they can cover BOTH center slices, so the surface area of the hemisphere is $2\pi r^2$. Since a sphere is TWO hemispheres the surface area of the sphere would be $4\pi r^2$.

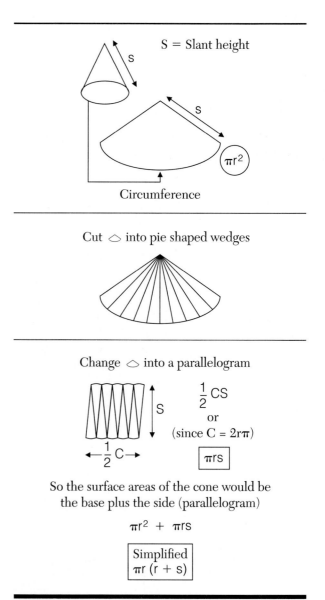

$S = $ Slant height

Circumference

Cut △ into pie shaped wedges

Change △ into a parallelogram

$\frac{1}{2}$ CS

or

(since C = 2rπ)

πrs

So the surface areas of the cone would be the base plus the side (parallelogram)

$\pi r^2 + \pi rs$

Simplified
$\pi r (r + s)$

FIGURE 12.41

Individual Learning Activity

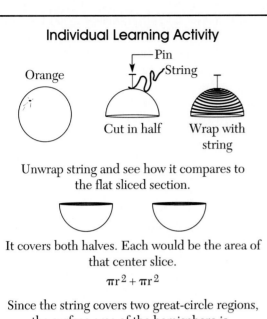

Unwrap string and see how it compares to the flat sliced section.

It covers both halves. Each would be the area of that center slice.

$$\pi r^2 + \pi r^2$$

Since the string covers two great-circle regions, the surface area of the hemisphere is

$$2\pi r^2$$

The surface area of the sphere would be 2 hemispheres

$$4\pi r^2$$

FIGURE 12.42

Finding the volume of irregular containers is an interesting problem-solving activity for the talented pupil. When given a drinking glass that is cone-shaped, but truncated so it will not tip over, the student finds he/she has no formula to derive the volume. Questions such as "Can you estimate a mark that will show when the container is half-full?" can lead to many interesting explorations. Students should be given a container and allowed

Individual Learning Activities

Can you find the halfway point on this glass?

One pupil's solution—

I filled the glass with beans. Then I counted the beans. I put half of the beans back in the glass and made a mark.

FIGURE 12.43

to experiment and then share the way they found the half-full mark with the class. Pupils take interesting approaches—some of which may be

- Fill it with beans. Empty it and count the beans. Take half of the beans and put them back into the container. Draw a mark to show where $\frac{1}{2}$ of the beans ends. (See Figure 12.43.)
- Fill it with water. Find the number of milliliters. Divide that by two. Measure out that much water and pour it back into the container. Draw a mark.
- Weigh the container. Fill the container with water and weigh it. Find the difference. Divide the difference by two and add to the weight of the container. Fill container until you reach that weight. Draw a mark.
- Pour it full of water. Get a second container of the same size. Pour the water back and forth between the two containers until they both have the same amount. When the water level in both containers lines up—place a mark.

(Students might be challenged to determine if their method would work if one wished to fill the container $\frac{3}{4}$ full.)

Measurement projects make interesting science fair projects for gifted students. The teacher may wish to expand the gifted student's conceptual understanding of measurement by exploring other kinds of measurement concepts (viscosity, surface tension, voltage, and resistance). Some interesting research projects for the gifted can be stimulated by asking questions such as "How do scientists estimate the weight of an atom; the length of a radio wave of a particular frequency; the temperature of the surface of the sun? How do scientists determine a scale for hardness, and smoothness?"

12.24 SUMMARY

In the primary grades the child learns that units of measure are manmade and are used to communicate measurement information from one individual to another. Through hands-on explorations children develop a "feel" for various units of measurement. Concurrent with their learning to read and write names for units, children learn to write abbreviations and symbols for these names. Both the metric and standard units are introduced to children at the primary level. Children learn to use a wide variety of measurement instruments. They begin developing and using scales for various types of measures. In the primary grades children estimate by developing their own "reference units" and round measurements to the nearest specified unit.

At the intermediate level students are immersed in problem-solving applications using measurement concepts. By the end of the intermediate grades the average student can convert from one unit to another in both the metric and standard measurement system. Personal reference units are developed and estimation and rounding skills applied to measuring situations. The student is formally introduced to the concept of greatest possible error, precision, and accuracy. The student progresses from hands-on explorations with measurement devices to the more abstract technique of using formulas for finding a variety of measures.

EXERCISES

1. Some "premeasurement" skills are taught in kindergarten. Identify several of these skills.
2. When counting a collection of coins to determine the monetary value of the set, what are four prerequisite skills that should be evaluated by the teacher?
3. When telling time to the nearest minute, pupils often find those times past the half hour more difficult than those before the half hour. Why?
4. What are some areas which a teacher might anticipate as difficult for pupils when learning to measure to the nearest inch or centimeter?
5. Describe the kind of activity a teacher would plan when first exploring
   a. liquid capacity
   b. weight
   c. perimeter
   d. area
   e. volume
   f. angle measurement
6. Learning to read a thermometer requires pupils to learn to read scales. What differences in a thermometer scale might give pupils difficulty?
7. When introducing new skills in measuring, teachers begin by using "nonstandard units." What nonstandard unit might be chosen for measuring:
   a. the length of the classroom
   b. the width of a desk
   c. the amount of water in a drinking glass
   d. the weight of an apple
8. For each of the measurements below identify the range of measurement error and greatest possible error.
   a. 48 inches   b. $7\frac{1}{4}$ pounds
   c. 82.5 millimeters   d. 3 quarts
9. Describe a procedure that would be appropriate when teaching pupils
   a. to make change
   b. to determine elapsed time
   c. to discover the perimeter formula (regular figures, rectangle)
   d. to determine an area formula (rectangle, triangle, parallelogram, trapezoid)
   e. to find the volume (prisms, cylinders, pyramids, cones, spheres)
10. When working with a circle, how would a teacher develop
    a. the relationship of the circumference to the diameter
    b. the area
11. Select a specific grade-level text from a currently published elementary school mathematics series. Look through the book to determine which measurement concepts are presented at that grade level. What prerequisite skills would these concepts require?
12. Look through a current mathematics textbook for fifth or sixth grade. Locate story problems that involve measurement and decide how each should be illustrated using concrete materials.
13. Choose an article in the References section. After reading the article, suggest how the ideas presented might be useful to a classroom teacher.

RELEVANT COMPUTER SOFTWARE

The Calendar. 1986. Apple family. Gamco Industries, Box 310P5, Big Spring, Tex. 79721.

Math Shop. Cary Hammer. 1986. Apple II family. Scholastic Software, 730 Broadway, New York, N.Y. 10003.

Clock Works. Susan Gabrys, Scott Jensen, Carolyn Kapplinger, and Craig Solomonson. 1986. Apple II family. MECC, 3490 Lexington Avenue, St. Paul, Minn. 55126.

REFERENCES

Baroody, A. J. "A Cognitive Approach to Writing Instruction for Children Classified as Mentally Handicapped." *Arithmetic Teacher* 36 (October 1988): 7–11.

Binswanger, R. "Discovering Perimeter and Area with Logo." *Arithmetic Teacher* 36 (September 1988): 18–25.

Brickman, M. "Food for Math." *Arithmetic Teacher* 34 (September 1986): 48–49.

Bright, G. W. "Simulations of Operating a Store." *Arithmetic Teacher* 36 (March 1989): 52–53.

Burkett, L., and E. L. Whitfield. "Store-bought Mathematics." *Arithmetic Teacher* 33 (December 1985): 36–37.

Butzow, J. W. "Y Is for Yacht Race: A Game of Angles." *Arithmetic Teacher* 33 (January 1986): 44–48.

Clason, R. G. "How Our Decimal Money Began." *Arithmetic Teacher* 33 (January 1986): 30–33.

Mason, M. "Checking Speedometer Accuracy." *Arith-metic Teacher* 33 (January 1986): 52–54.

Neufeld, K. A. "Body Measurement." *Arithmetic Teacher* 36 (May 1989): 12–15.

Reys, R. E. "Testing Mental-Computation Skills." *Arithmetic Teacher* 33 (November 1985): 14–16.

Routledge, J. "What's Cooking." *Arithmetic Teacher* 33 (October 1985): 14–15.

Souza, R. "Golfing with a Protractor." *Arithmetic Teacher* 35 (April 1988): 52–56.

Thompson, C. S., and J. Van de Walle. "Learning about Rulers and Measuring." *Arithmetic Teacher* 32 (April 1985): 8–12.

Zanelotti, G. "Estimation." *Arithmetic Teacher* 36 (January 1989): 34.

Zweng, M. J. "Introducing Angle Measure through Estimation." In *Estimation and Mental Computation: NCTM Yearbook. 1986.* Reston, Va.: National Council of Teachers of Mathematics, 1986. Pp. 212–219.

CHAPTER 13

EXTENDING NUMBER AND NUMERATION SKILLS

INTRODUCTION

Most of a student's number experiences—both in school and out of school—will use the decimal numeration system. On occasions, Roman numerals may be encountered, but there will be few occasions for a student to need any other kinds of numerals. If one perceives of the mathematics curriculum simply as providing skills that are immediately applicable to the pupil's everyday life or future vocational choices, then explorations into historical numeration systems, figurate numbers, or other number bases may not seem important. However, if the curriculum is viewed as building a way of thinking and exploring our world, then explorations into interesting "side trips" are essential.

Of course, a case may be made for many of the topics included in this chapter. Roman numerals are a part of our world and occur on clocks, in outlining, as chapter headings, on public buildings, and as copyright dates on movies. Integers are used when reporting winter temperatures and as debits in accounting. Base two is used as a machine language for computers, and figurate numbers (square, triangular, etc.) appear in science and nature.

Besides the actual application of some of these topics, exploration into systems and numbers other than those based upon ten are interesting and challenging activities for students. Being able to discover a new pattern or a way of recording numbers helps pupils build problem-solving and prealgebra skills and makes them aware of the nature of mathematical thought. Exploring historical number systems builds student appreciation of number and how numbers have allowed mankind to think with symbols.

13.1 EXTENDING NUMBER AND NUMERATION CONCEPTS IN THE KINDERGARTEN AND PRIMARY GRADES

Since children are so deeply involved in learning about the base ten system of notation, the explo-

ration of historical and nondecimal numeration systems is generally delayed until the intermediate grade levels. Children do encounter Roman numerals and integers out of school and therefore a few readiness activities and discussions may occur even in kindergarten. Systematic development of these topics, however, rarely occurs in primary programs.

Kindergarten/Grade 1

Pattern recognition
Odd and even numbers
Skip counting by twos and fives
Integers associated with walk-on number line

Grade 2

Roman numerals associated with the clock

Grade 3

Roman numerals through XXXIX
Integers associated with temperature

Exploring Odd and Even Numbers

Children <u>do</u> explore some number sequences and number patterns in the primary. Developing pattern recognition skills is an important activity in the kindergarten program. These skills are extended as pupils work with **odd** and **even numbers** in first and second grade. By placing "tiles" into rectangular patterns of two, children quickly discover that some numbers are "nice and smooth" while others have a "rough end" because one tile "hangs over." Once identified as odd and even numbers, children quickly progress to counting by evens or odds using "skip counting." These patterns are easily discovered when seen on a chart (Figure 13.1).

Children learn to count by odd and even numbers early in the primary grades. One method of teaching this skill is to have the student "silently count" every other number as they count by ones. For example, in counting by odd numbers the students would say one (loud), two (silently to themselves), three (loud), four (silently to themselves), etc. After they had heard the odd numbers several times and picked up the pattern, the silent counting of the even numbers would be dropped, leaving the odd numbers. The even numbers may be taught in a like manner.

Visual patterns may be explored through bead stringing activities, linear flat arrangements, Unifix™ Blocks, and patterns within grids. For example, attributes of objects such as big and small, geometric shapes, and a fixed number of objects followed by a fixed number of different objects may occur in different patterns or the same pattern. Patterns that develop in a line seem to be easier for children than those that develop in a curve (such as a loop of beads), so teachers generally begin with linear patterns. Blocks, mosaic-art projects, and stickers are linear-pattern materials. Figure 13.2 il-

Independent Learning Activities

Sort the tile patterns into like groups. Find a numeral card for each pattern.

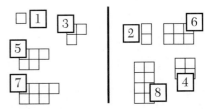

Take all of the numeral cards that are left over and decide into which group each would be placed. Can you build a tile pattern to verify your answer?

19 9 16
46 10

□ □ □ □
□ □ □

Extra Tiles

Take a Hundred Chart and color all of the "smooth" numbers found on the chart (even numbers). Would those that remain make a "ragged" tile pattern (odd numbers)? Use tiles to verify one or two of the numbers.

1		3		5		7		9	
11		13		15		17		19	
21		23		25		27		29	
31		33		35		37		39	
41		43		45		47		49	
51		53		55		57		59	
61		63		65		67		69	
71		73		75		77		79	
81		83		85		87		89	
91		93		95		97		99	

FIGURE 13.1

lustrates two types of patterns developed by a teacher at the kindergarten level.

Work with patterns is not restricted to visual patterns in the kindergarten. Auditory patterns created by clapping are also used. In these activities the teacher will clap a pattern (for example, clap, clap, pause, clap, pause, clap, clap, pause, clap, etc.) and the children will repeat the pattern. Physical movement patterns also are fun for children. Walking six steps and then touching the floor develops physical coordination, pattern recognition, and rational counting skills.

Key question: What's next?

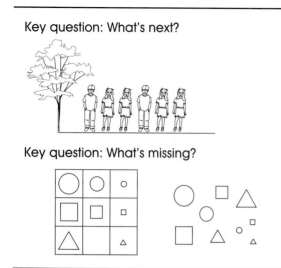

Key question: What's missing?

FIGURE 13.2

Learning to Read Roman Numerals

Since young children encounter Roman numerals on clock faces and chapter headings, small numbers written in that numeration system are examined. In the Roman system, numbers through 39 use only the symbols X, V, and I. Numbers larger than 39 require new symbols. Therefore, primary programs typically restrict instruction in Roman numerals to numbers less than 40.

Exploring Roman numerals brings children into contact with a way of writing number names that is different from those commonly used. Through this experience many begin to appreciate the merits of a place-value system of numeration. Pupils also gain a new understanding of the role played by numerals as they name the number "eight" using "five and three ones, or VIII." When writing nine, they recognize it can be viewed as "one less than ten, or IX."

Building a Readiness for Integers

Children hear "negative numbers" when they listen to television weather reports and find that the temperature in one section of the country dropped to "17 degrees below zero." Indeed, many may live in an area where such winter temperatures are common. Developmental activities in the primary, however, generally include experiences only with the positive integers.

The teacher does play an important role in preparing pupils for later explorations with integers. When children use a "walk-on number line" they start at zero and take steps to the right developing the positive integers. Such a line **should** be prepared in such a manner that pupils recognize that the line goes in <u>both</u> directions. The teacher may point out that the pupils will only be working with the "positive number" side of the number line—leaving the children with the understanding that there are numbers in the other direction. Similarly, when showing the temperature on a thermometer, the teacher may show that the numbers go in <u>both</u> directions from zero. Children should recognize that when the weather is colder than 0 degrees, a "minus" or "negative number" is used to indicate these numbers.

13.2 EXPLORING NUMBER SYSTEMS AND PATTERNS AT THE INTERMEDIATE LEVEL

By the time pupils reach the intermediate grade levels, they have had many experiences with the decimal numeration system (through 10,000) and have learned to write fractions. They are quite capable of looking at other ways of organizing numbers. Pupils in these grade levels are developing an interest in historical cultures, and investigations into historical numeration systems are explored. Since Roman numerals have out-of-school applications, most mathematics programs include this topic. Other historical systems (Egyptian, Mayan, Greek, etc.) are interesting enrichment investigations for more mature pupils.

Pupils also develop an interest in grouping by numbers other than ten. While they appreciate the fact that humans have ten fingers and therefore a base of ten is a logical grouping, they also enjoy speculating how a numeration system might have developed if only one hand had been used (base five) or if an alien race only had three fingers. Such explorations deepen pupils' understanding of the characteristics of a numeration system and <u>may</u> help some pupils gain new insight into the base ten system.

Integers are generally explored in all intermediate-level mathematics programs. The maturity of the pupil makes the development of a system of positives and negatives a rich area to build deductive thinking and reflect upon concepts used within the set of whole numbers. The development of "rules" for handling the operations in this "new" number system helps pupils form analytical procedures that are essential to mathematical thinking.

Explorations into **figurate numbers** (triangular, square, rectangular, pentagonal, etc.) have both practical applications and recreational uses. Square numbers and Fibonacci numbers are used throughout mathematics and science. Triangular, pentagonal, and other figurate numbers provide explorations rich in opportunities to build problem-solving skills.

There is a much wider range of placement of the topics in this section. Some programs make some of the skills listed below "enrichment" rather than a part of the basic program. Therefore, great discretion must be used when examining the "typical" scope and sequence that follows.

Grade 4

Roman numerals through 399
Prime numbers and Sieve of Eratosthenes

Grade 5

Roman numerals through 3999
Prime numbers and composites
Square numbers
Identification of positive and negative integers

Grade 6

Triangular numbers
Addition and subtraction of integers

Grades 7 and 8

Multiplication and division of integers
Perfect numbers
Irrational numbers

13.3 EXPLORING HISTORICAL NUMBER SYSTEMS

Most students have encountered Roman numerals on clocks and chapter headings in books. In the latter case, the numbers rarely exceeded 30. However, as the pupils' world expands they will encounter larger numbers written as Roman numerals on buildings and as film copyright dates. Teachers extend pupil skill with Roman numerals in the fourth grade and by the time students leave the intermediate level they will be able to read and write amounts as large as 3999 using Roman numerals. Some pupils may wish to write larger amounts using Roman numerals since they have been working with ten thousands, hundred thousands, and millions. These amounts <u>can</u> be writ-

Learning is a cooperative venture.

ten, but pupils will rarely encounter Roman numerals used for amounts greater than two or three thousand.

When teaching how to <u>write</u> Roman numerals from 1 to 1,000 it is important that students recognize that the <u>pattern</u> established in writing amounts from one <u>through</u> ten is the same pattern for the tens and hundreds, except different symbols are represented in the pattern.

Like our conventional numeration system, the Roman system is based upon ten. The Romans used symbols to represent 1, 10, 100, and 1000 and for points <u>halfway</u> between the powers of ten—5, 50, and 500. Unlike our conventional numeration system, the Roman numerals are not a positional system. A symbol for ten (X) always means ten—regardless of its position in the numeral. The numerals are <u>generally</u> written with the symbols for the largest amounts coming first—in a manner very similar to expanded notation. To write 2,312 one might show the thousand first, then the hundreds, the tens, and finally the ones (2000 + 300 + 10 + 2 = MMCCCXII).

In the **early** Roman system a symbol <u>could</u> appear as many as four consecutive times. That is, the number four was written as "IIII" and 40 was written as "XXXX." The Roman system was later revised to allow a symbol representing a smaller amount to be placed directly to the left of a symbol, thereby <u>subtracting</u> its value from the symbol on the right. Instead of showing 90 as LXXXX, the **revised** system would show XC. The revised Roman system did <u>not</u> allow <u>two</u> of the smaller value symbols to precede a larger valued symbol (IIV ≠ 3). It also placed another restriction on the sub-

Roman Numerals

$$
\begin{array}{ll}
\text{I} & = & 1 \\
\text{X} & = & 10 \\
\text{C} & = & 100 \\
\text{M} & = & 1000 \\
\end{array}
\qquad
\begin{array}{l}
\text{``Half-steps''} \\
\text{V} = 5 \\
\text{L} = 50 \\
\text{D} = 500 \\
\end{array}
$$

Rules

- Symbol cannot be repeated four consecutive times (i.e., XXXX).
- Smaller value to right—add.
- Smaller value to left—subtract.
- Smaller value can only precede next larger step (or half-step).

Patterns

Ones	Tens	Hundreds
I	X	C
II	XX	CC
III	XXX	CCC
IV	XL	CD
V	L	D
VI	LX	DC
VII	LXX	DCC
VIII	LXXX	DCCC
IX	XC	CM

A bar over a numeral multiplies the value of the symbol by 1,000.

$$\overline{\text{V}} = 5,000 \qquad \overline{\text{XXI}}\text{CDXV} = 21,415$$

FIGURE 13.3

Roman Numeral Cards

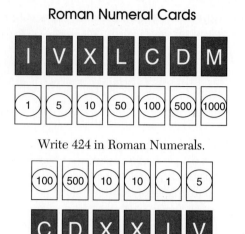

Write 424 in Roman Numerals.

Assemble 424 in conventional system —then turn the cards over.

FIGURE 13.4

---

tractive symbols. A smaller power (never a half-step) could be subtracted ONLY from its next higher power or half-step. In practice this means that an "I" can only be placed to the left of an "X" or "V"; an "X" to the left of "C" or "L"; and "C" to the left of "M" or "D." This restriction causes pupils difficulty since they often wish to incorrectly write "IC" for 99 and "IM" for 999.

Figure 13.3 illustrates the basic set of numerals for the Roman system showing the pattern for the ones, tens, and hundreds. The numerals from one through 999 are formed by selecting the appropriate symbols from the hundreds, then the tens, and then the ones. (By placing a **bar** over a numeral the value is multiplied by one thousand.)

When teaching pupils how to read and write Roman numerals, the **meaning** of the symbols; the **patterns** that exist between the ones, tens, and hundreds; and the **rules** for writing these symbols should all be incorporated into the lesson. Symbol

cards with Roman letters on the front and equivalent conventional numerals on the back are effective instructional materials (see Figure 13.4). Students assemble an amount using powers of ten (1, 10, 100, and 1000) and "half-steps" (5, 50, and 500) with conventional numerals. They then turn the cards over to see which letters would be used to write the Roman numeral.

When exploring other numeration systems, the teacher must help the students make the connection between the decimal system and other systems that are explored. Comparing and contrasting the attributes of other systems is one way in which pupils deepen their understanding of numeration.

Two historical systems frequently examined are the Egyptian and Mayan numeration systems. Each system provides contrasting attributes that help students appreciate and understand our own system. Most pupils find the Egyptian system very interesting—especially if they have been studying other cultures in social studies. The Egyptian system is perhaps the easiest historical system for pupils to explore. Figure 13.5 illustrates one of three systems used by ancient Egyptians. It used ten as a base and is additive, like our system, but did not use place value or have a symbol for zero. Symbols could be used in any order and often numerals were used in an artistic manner.

Egyptian numerals can be used to promote a better understanding and appreciation of our place-value system. A teacher might require pupils to "draw" various amounts and then suggest limita-

Egyptian Numeration

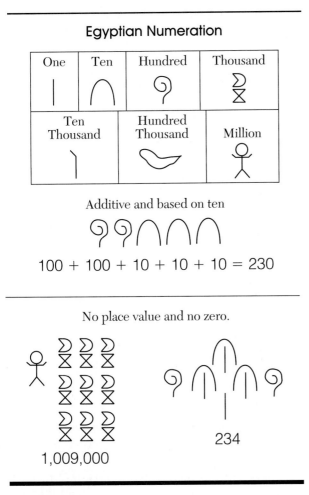

One	Ten	Hundred	Thousand

Ten Thousand	Hundred Thousand	Million

Additive and based on ten

$$100 + 100 + 10 + 10 + 10 = 230$$

No place value and no zero.

1,009,000   234

FIGURE 13.5

Mayan Numeration System

One	Five	Zero
•	—	⊕

5 + 1 = 6

twenties
units

20 + 5 = 25

20 + 20 + 0   = 40

20 + 5 + 5 + 5 + 1   = 37

Name three of the system's attributes.

FIGURE 13.6

tions or advantages of the system. Questions such as:—"If you were cutting the numeral 999 into a stone for a pyramid wall, which would be faster, the Egyptian symbols or the conventional symbols?", "Why didn't the Egyptians need a symbol for zero?", "Suppose you had to add (or subtract) using Egyptian symbols, how would you do it?"—provide the basis for lively group discussions.

The Mayan system, since it was a positional system based on twenty, is an interesting system to explore. The Mayan system only used three symbols—a dot, a dash, and a symbol for zero. The fact that it is based on twenty (at least at the beginning of the system) raises many questions such as, "What might account for a culture in a warm tropical climate adopting a system based on twenty?" Like the conventional system, it is an additive system and has place value—though the place value is "vertical" rather than horizontal. Notice in Figure 13.6 that the groupings are from top to bottom, rather than left to right.

13.4 EXPLORING NONDECIMAL NUMBER SYSTEMS

Nondecimal based systems became a part of the elementary school mathematics curriculum in the 1960s. Initially, one reason for the inclusion of this topic was the feeling by some that a knowledge of nondecimal bases would be needed to become functionally literate with computers. This justification quickly vanished as computer technology took quantum leaps forward to "user friendly" programs. A second often-cited justification was that a study of other bases would increase pupil understanding of the base ten system. While research tended to support the fact that students understood systems of numeration better after studying other number bases, it did not find that those students understood the decimal numeration system any better than those who had spent an equal amount of time studying base ten. Therefore, most mathematics programs eliminated the study of other bases from the core curriculum. A study of other number bases, however, may be appropriate for those children whose understanding of base ten has already been well-established. Exploring other systems does serve as an excellent enrichment activity.

Studying nondecimal based number systems should place emphasis upon the <u>manner</u> in which the grouping system develops. In the decimal system 10 ones are grouped to form 1 ten, and 10 tens to form 1 hundred, etc. If a number other than ten were chosen, say four, then 4 ones would be grouped to form 1 <u>four</u>, and 4 <u>fours</u> would be grouped to form 1 <u>sixteen</u>, and 4 <u>sixteens</u> would be grouped to form 1 <u>sixty-four</u>, etc.

One way of introducing other number bases is to pose a "what if" question. "What if man only had eight (six, four, etc.) fingers instead of ten? How might man have developed a number system?" To explore the implications of this question the teacher may set up a "grouping" activity or a "chip trading" task activity. In **"Chip Trading"** the rules are set so that no individual can keep a group of eight objects (or whatever base is chosen). As soon as a pupil gets "8" of something it must be traded in for "1" of the next kind of object and passed on. In Figure 13.7 Abe will pass his circular chips to Bob—one at a time. When Bob gets eight <u>circular</u> chips, he will put them in his bag, take a <u>square</u>-shaped chip from the cup, and pass it to Chuck. When Chuck gets eight <u>square</u>-shaped chips, he puts these in his bag, takes a <u>triangular</u>-shaped chip out, and passes it on to <u>Dave</u>. This process will continue until Abe passes all of his chips. Then the number of each kind of chip is recorded in a chart similar to the one indicated in Figure 13.8. (To see how many objects this base eight numeral records, Bob's bag of chips could be emptied and counted.)

To help students remember to use <u>only</u> those

Small-Group Learning Activity

Sixty-fours	Eights	Ones
2	3	1

231 eight ← Required information when you are not grouping by tens.

Question: If B dumped his bag, how many circular shapes would you find?

FIGURE 13.8

symbols that are appropriate to a given base, teachers may use special "recording sheets" on which numerals are constructed by gluing on symbols. For example, when working in base five, pupils are furnished strips of numerals containing only the digits 0, 1, 2, 3, and 4. (See Figure 13.9.) When the base of the system is greater than ten the teacher can provide additional "made-up" symbols or let the children create their own symbols. For example, in base twelve two additional symbols (T and E, for example) will need to be created.

Some lessons in other bases are designed to <u>expand</u> student understanding of an algorithm. By exploring addition in a different base system, the

Small-Group Learning Activity

Eight of these ● are traded for one of these ■

Eight of these ■ are traded for one of these ▲

Eight of these ▲ are traded for one of these ⬬

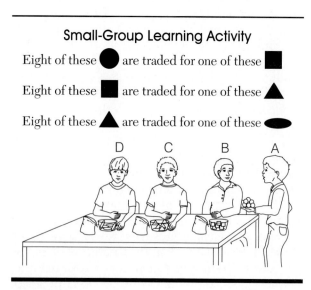

FIGURE 13.7

Paste the digits furnished to name the number in base five.

1. 37ten = [1][2][2] five

2. 79ten = _____ five

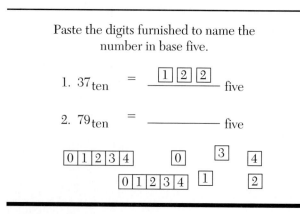

FIGURE 13.9

student recognizes the similarity of the regrouping process operation in the base ten addition algorithm. In the lesson fragment that follows, students explore the addition algorithm in base four.

Small-Group Learning Activity:

LESSON FRAGMENT

M: Base four addition algorithm

A: Gifted group of fourth-graders

T: Models, rules

H: Students have mastered base four notation and place value in base four

Teacher: (STUDENTS WILL HAVE A SET OF BASE FOUR MODELS.) Each team has been given base four blocks. Use your blocks to show the addends. Once you have set up the problem—put the blocks together to find the sum. Remember—whenever you get four of something, trade for one of the next highest group. You can trade four blocks for one rod; four rods for one flat, four flats for one cube. Have

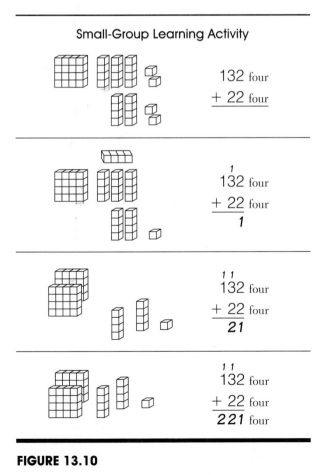

Small-Group Learning Activity

$$132 \text{ four}$$
$$+ 22 \text{ four}$$

$$\overset{1}{132} \text{ four}$$
$$+ 22 \text{ four}$$
$$\overline{1}$$

$$\overset{1\,1}{132} \text{ four}$$
$$+ 22 \text{ four}$$
$$\overline{21}$$

$$\overset{1\,1}{132} \text{ four}$$
$$+ 22 \text{ four}$$
$$\overline{221} \text{ four}$$

FIGURE 13.10

one team member record each step of what you do onto the algorithm. Work as a team. If you need help, raise your hand and I will come to your group. (FIGURE 13.10 ILLUSTRATES THE STEPS THE STUDENTS WENT THROUGH IN THE EXERCISE.)

In addition to studying numeration and operations in different number bases, some pupils—especially more talented students—find a study of **modulo arithmetic** challenging because it deals with a <u>finite</u> number system (fixed quantity of numbers) rather than an infinite system with which pupils are familiar. One might explore a modulo system because of its similarity to the 12-hour clock commonly used in everyday life. Students are often confused when adding time on a clock because adding five hours to 9 o'clock does not end up at 14 o'clock—it becomes two o'clock!

Exploring modulo systems is better justified as an exploration into mathematical thinking. Modulo systems are not familiar to students—they must adjust their thinking patterns to **reason outcomes.** They must **postulate** and then **verify** their speculations. In the process, they may also develop some deeper insights into operations and properties within the set of whole numbers. For example, suppose the only numbers you have are zero, one, two, and three—what happens when you add two of the numbers? Can you create a set of addition facts? Would this number system have an identity property, a commutative property, and an associative property? Figure 13.11 illustrates one way a student constructed a set of facts that would follow the rules and obey the properties. Can you find another way? Can you discover how the student's understanding of the difference between a number concept and its name plays a role in creating this system? (Hint: Ignore the names given the number ideas and think of what number idea is being represented by trips from zero in a clockwise direction.)

13.5 EXPLORING THE SYSTEM OF INTEGERS

Students entering the intermediate level recognize that there are positive and negative numbers, but they have not really explored these amounts as a related system of numbers. They know that $-7°$ is a lot colder than $+7°$ and that a score of -7 is less than zero. When pupils reach the intermediate grades they begin exploring positive and negative

Independent Learning Activity

A child made this "creative clock."

She worked out the "basic facts" using her clock and they were very consistent with her clock. Can you see how she got her answers using the clock?

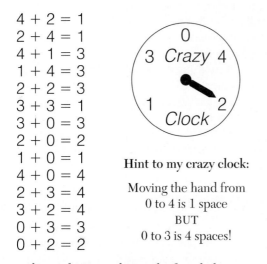

$4 + 2 = 1$
$2 + 4 = 1$
$4 + 1 = 3$
$1 + 4 = 3$
$2 + 2 = 3$
$3 + 3 = 1$
$3 + 0 = 3$
$2 + 0 = 2$
$1 + 0 = 1$
$4 + 0 = 4$
$2 + 3 = 4$
$3 + 2 = 4$
$0 + 3 = 3$
$0 + 2 = 2$

Hint to my crazy clock:

Moving the hand from
0 to 4 is 1 space
BUT
0 to 3 is 4 spaces!

She made 2 mistakes in the facts below.
Can you find them?

$0 + 1 = 1$ $2 + 1 = 0$ $0 + 0 = 0$
$0 + 4 = 1$ $1 + 2 = 0$ $1 + 3 = 2$
$4 + 4 = 1$ $4 + 3 = 0$ $3 + 1 = 4$

Is Crazy Clock commutative?

Would the associative property work
with Crazy Clock?

FIGURE 13.11

numbers as a part of a number system and they learn how to add, subtract, multiply, and divide using these integers.

Establishing a Model for Integers

The most commonly used model for illustrating integers is the number line. This model is used in kindergarten and all through the primary grades when illustrating whole numbers. When first using a walk-on number line pupils recognized that there were numbers to the <u>left</u> of zero—but that they would use only the righthand portion of the line. Later, when fractions were introduced, the number line model was again used to illustrate the relationship between the whole numbers and rational numbers. Therefore, this model is readily accepted by pupils when exploring the set of integers.

While pupils in the primary grade levels enjoyed performing before the entire class and would quickly volunteer to take "trips" on the walk-on number line, pupils in the intermediate grades are more self-conscious. Therefore, the walk-on number line, which is an excellent tool to develop negative numbers as those in the "opposite direction" from the positive numbers, may not be as effective as an instructional tool. Of course, when a teacher works with a SMALL group some pupils will act out operations and find both positive and negative integers on the walk-on number line, whereas they would not think of participating in such a "juvenile" activity when used as a class activity.

The teacher must be sensitive to student perceptions and choose an instructional model that effectively demonstrates the concept and also meets the student at his/her maturity level. There are many models that may be used to illustrate positive and negative integers. A teacher-illustrated number line may incorporate many of the strengths of the walk-on number line and yet not be perceived by pupils as being childish. Since pupils explore electricity in the intermediate level, picturing the integers as positive and negative "electrical charges" may kindle student interest when a number line is not effective (Figure 13.12). A teacher may find many other models or examples that bring meaning

Models for Exploring Integers

Primary Number Line

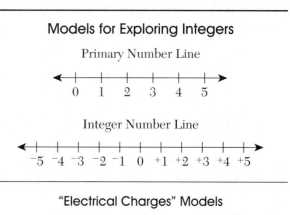

Integer Number Line

"Electrical Charges" Models

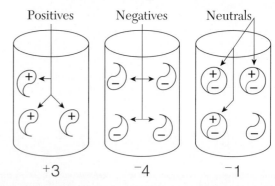

FIGURE 13.12

to positive and negative numbers (paychecks are "positive" amounts while "bills" that must be paid are "negative" amounts, etc.).

Throughout the development of integers, especially when using the number line model, the teacher will establish that for each positive number ($+3$ for example) there is a corresponding negative number (-3) that is the SAME DISTANCE from zero, but in the opposite direction. When illustrating $+5$ on the walk-on number line, the teacher would have the pupil face the "positive direction" (to the right on most number lines) and walk five steps. To illustrate -5 the pupil would face the OPPOSITE direction (to the left on most number lines) and walk five steps.

Using the Number Line to Develop Integer Operations

Operations with integers do not differ greatly from those with whole numbers. However, teachers should take care in developing an understanding of each operation and how it behaves. Rules for adding, subtracting, multiplying, and dividing integers are easily "memorized," but understanding takes careful development. When exploring operations with integers, the teacher should **always** explore and develop understanding, **before** attempting to develop rules. In this manner, pupils may rediscover a rule, should there ever be any misunderstanding in its use.

Pupils who have used the number line with whole numbers find very little difference when working with integers. When acting out operations on the walk-on number line, pupils would illustrate addition as "walking forward." Since subtraction is the inverse operation, to subtract one "walks backward." (To compensate for pupils who may dislike "acting out" actions on the number line, the teacher may wish to illustrate the actions by using a "walking man" on a magnetic chalkboard.)

To illustrate $-2 + -3$, the teacher may place the walking man facing the negative direction and then move the figure two spaces to the left. After stopping at -2, teacher would show the walking man still facing the negative direction and continuing forward for three more steps to land at -5. To illustrate $-1 + {}^+4$, the teacher would illustrate with the man facing the negative direction and walking one step (ending on -1). Then the walking man would turn to face the positive direction (to illustrate $+4$) and walk forward four steps. (See Figure 13.13.)

Subtracting on the walk-on number line is illustrated in a similar fashion (See Figure 13.14). To illustrate $-1 - -3 = N$, the teacher would show

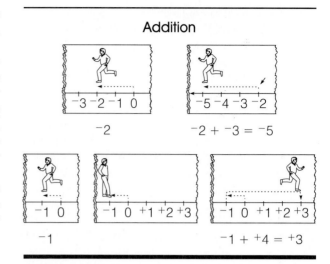

Addition

-2

$-2 + {}^-3 = {}^-5$

-1

$-1 + {}^+4 = {}^+3$

FIGURE 13.13

the walking man facing the negative direction and walking one step to reach -1. Since -3 will be subtracted, the walking man will continue to face the negative direction (to illustrate -3) but walk backward ending at $+2$ to illustrate subtraction. In $-2 - {}^+4 = N$, the walking man would face the

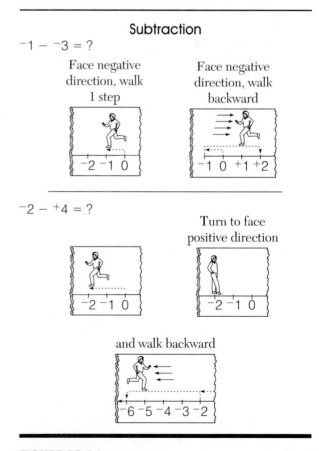

Subtraction

$-1 - {}^-3 = ?$

Face negative direction, walk 1 step

Face negative direction, walk backward

$-2 - {}^+4 = ?$

Turn to face positive direction

and walk backward

FIGURE 13.14

negative direction and walk two steps ending on ⁻2. Since the number to be subtracted is a positive number, the walking man is turned to face the positive direction. However, the <u>operation</u> is subtraction, so the man will <u>walk backward</u>.

Multiplication of integers may also be illustrated on the number line. To illustrate ⁺3 × ⁻2, the walking man is shown facing the negative direction to take "jumps" the size of ⁻2. The ⁺3 indicates how many <u>forward</u> jumps the man will take. After taking three jumps the size of ⁻2, the man would land on ⁻6. When the multiplier is a negative number (as in ⁻3 × ⁻2) the walking man would face the negative direction (because the size of the jumps are to be ⁻2), but would jump three jumps in the <u>backward direction</u>! (See Figure 13.15.)

Division is probably best illustrated as the inverse of multiplication. To reestablish this relationship, the teacher would illustrate the ⁺6 in the sentence "⁺6 ÷ ⁺2 = N" as the destination the walking man wants to reach (the product). The

man will be taking jumps the size of two and facing the positive direction (since the divisor is ⁺2). Students recognize that it will take three jumps—<u>forward</u>—to get to ⁺6. To illustrate ⁻6 ÷ ⁻2 = N, the man would face the negative direction (since the divisor is ⁻2) and wish to get to ⁻6. To get to ⁻6, the man will jump <u>forward</u> (positive) and it will take three jumps so the quotient will be ⁺3. If the division sentence were ⁺6 ÷ ⁻2 = N then the man would face the negative direction to show the "⁻" part of the "⁻2" and then find that he would need to <u>jump backward</u> for three jumps or a quotient of ⁻3 (for jumping backward) (for the number of jumps). (See Figure 13.16.)

Using "Electrical Charges" to Develop Integer Operations

More mature students seem to grasp more meaning from an "Electrical Charges" model than a number-line model. Indeed, the model will help many recognize "why" subtracting a negative is the same as adding a positive as found in "rules" for subtracting integers. Pupils are first taught to visualize a "jar" filled with charges—some positive and some negative. Each negative will balance out a positive—creating a "neutral" charge.

To illustrate addition, charges are placed into the jar. If the number sentence ⁺2 + ⁻5 = N were to be illustrated, the pupil would place two positive charges and five negative charges into the jar. Since there are both positive and negative charges in the jar, the two positives will link up with two of the negatives to make two neutrals (zeros). This makes the jar a negative three since there are three negative charges that are unmatched. (See Figure 13.17A.)

To illustrate subtraction, the pupils place the minuend "charges" into the jar and then remove (take-away) to show subtraction. Sentences such as ⁻5 − ⁻2 = N (see Figure 13.17B) or ⁺4 − ⁺1 = N are easily illustrated by removing the amount of the subtrahend from the jar. In the sentence ⁺2 − ⁻4 = N the student cannot take out four negatives because there are <u>only</u> positives in the jar. Such a situation may temporarily be frustrating until the pupil recognizes that "neutrals" (which have both a positive and a negative) may be added to the jar without changing the number. Therefore, if four "neutrals" are added, the jar remains a "⁺2 jar." Now it is possible to remove four negatives—leaving four of the positives unmatched. The jar now has six positives. (See Figure 13.17C.) Pupils soon recognize that it would be unnecessary to add the neutrals and then take back the negatives—they just add the opposite (the positive).

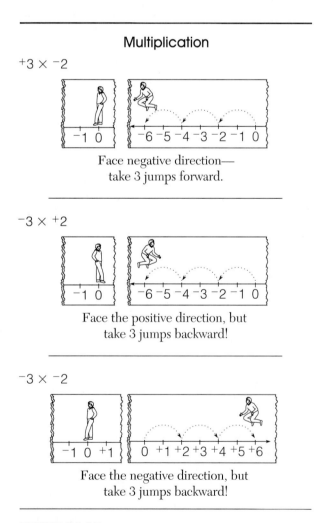

Multiplication

⁺3 × ⁻2

Face negative direction—
take 3 jumps forward.

⁻3 × ⁺2

Face the positive direction, but
take 3 jumps backward!

⁻3 × ⁻2

Face the negative direction, but
take 3 jumps backward!

FIGURE 13.15

Division

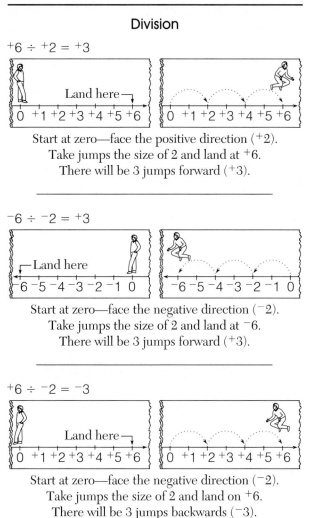

$^+6 \div ^+2 = ^+3$

Start at zero—face the positive direction ($^+2$).
Take jumps the size of 2 and land at $^+6$.
There will be 3 jumps forward ($^+3$).

$^-6 \div ^-2 = ^+3$

Start at zero—face the negative direction ($^-2$).
Take jumps the size of 2 and land at $^-6$.
There will be 3 jumps forward ($^+3$).

$^+6 \div ^-2 = ^-3$

Start at zero—face the negative direction ($^-2$).
Take jumps the size of 2 and land on $^+6$.
There will be 3 jumps backwards ($^-3$).

FIGURE 13.16

When using an electrical charges model, a multiplication sentence such as $^+4 \times ^-2 = N$ is interpreted as putting four groups of two negatives into the jar (Figure 13.18A). Therefore, $^-4 \times ^-2 = N$ would be taking out 4 groups of $^-2$. Since the jar starts empty, this would mean that four groups of two neutrals would be placed into the jar. It is then possible to take out four groups of $^-2$, leaving the jar with $^+8$. (See Figure 13.18B.)

Division with the charges model would be illustrated as related to multiplication. In this case, we know how many we want to have in the jar and we know the size of the groups we want to use—but we do not know how many to use. This is a little more difficult to visualize and the use of manipulative materials is necessary for many students. To illustrate $^-6 \div ^-3 = N$, the pupils would take an empty jar (it may have several "neutrals" in the jar and it would still be considered "empty") and try

to put enough groups of three negatives to make the jar become $^-6$. This is done by gathering up two groups of three negatives and putting them into the jar. (See Figure 13.19A.) To illustrate $^-6 \div ^+2 = N$, the student will take an "empty" jar (this time the jar will need several "neutrals"). The pupil is asked to determine how many groups of two positives would it take to make the jar a negative six. Pupils should recognize that adding positives to the jar will not make the jar a negative. The only way to make the jar a negative six is to remove six positives from the neutrals. Removing from the jar is associated with negative numbers, so it would be possible to remove three groups of two positives or $^-6 \div ^+2 = ^-3$. (See Figure 13.19B.)

13.6 EXPLORING FIGURATE NUMBERS AND NUMBER PATTERNS

Early explorations with figurate numbers are generally restricted to those numbers that can be put

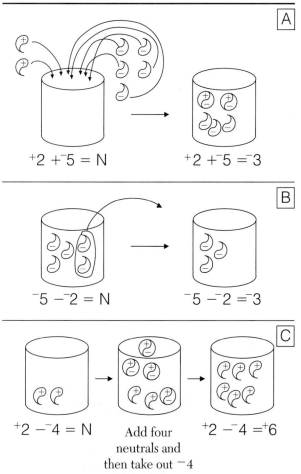

$^+2 + ^-5 = N$ $^+2 + ^-5 = ^-3$

$^-5 - ^-2 = N$ $^-5 - ^-2 = ^-3$

$^+2 - ^-4 = N$ Add four neutrals and then take out $^-4$ $^+2 - ^-4 = ^+6$

FIGURE 13.17

Using Positive and Negative Charges to Illustrate Multiplication of Integers

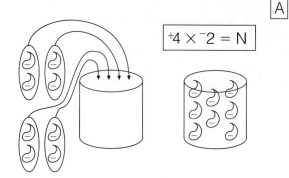

$$^+4 \times ^-2 = N$$ [A]

Put in four sets of $^-2$. This will make $^-8$.

$$^-4 \times ^-2 = N$$ [B]

A negative four is the opposite of a positive four, so $^-4 \times ^-2$ means take out 4 sets of $^-2$.

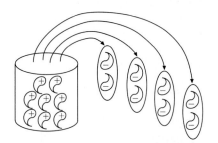

There is nothing in the jar, so neutrals will be placed into the jar.

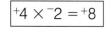

Now four sets of $^-2$ can be taken out of the jar. The jar will now contain eight positives.

$$^+4 \times ^-2 = ^+8$$

FIGURE 13.18

into $2 \times n$ rectangular arrays—even numbers. While pupils should explore even numbers as related to a figure, many pupils only recognize the numbers as those that end in 0, 2, 4, 6, and 8. Having only worked with the decimal numeration system, they do not generally recognize that an even number is not defined by the ending digits.

In the Roman numeral, 16 (XVI) does not end in 0, 2, 4, 6, or 8—it ends in "I." In base five, the even number sixteen might be written as 31_{five}, which ends in a 1!

As pupils become more mature, they enjoy examining numbers that develop from different patterns or figures. The most familiar set of numbers explored are those that might be placed into square patterns (**square numbers**). Pupils discover these numbers when they find the products of 1×1, 2×2, 3×3, 4×4, etc. While a mathematical meaning for square numbers can be developed without using a square pattern, the arranging of tiles into square patterns is a much more meaningful activity and one that provides many opportunities to look for patterns.

The square is not the only figure that produces a set of interesting numbers. Number tiles (or counters) can be placed in triangular figures (triangular numbers), rectangular figures (rectangular numbers), pentagonal figures (pentagonal num-

$$^-6 \div ^-3 = N$$ [A]

$^-6$ describes the charges needed in the jar. If we have sets of $^-3$, we will need to put in two sets (+2) to make $^-6$.

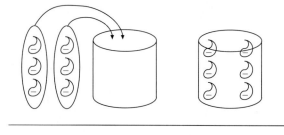

$$^-6 \div ^+2 = N$$ [B]

$^-6$ describes the charges needed in the jar. If we have sets of $^+2$, putting sets into the jar will not make $^-6$, so we will take out three sets ($^-3$) from the neutrals that are in the jar.

FIGURE 13.19

Independent Learning Activity
Exploring Number Patterns

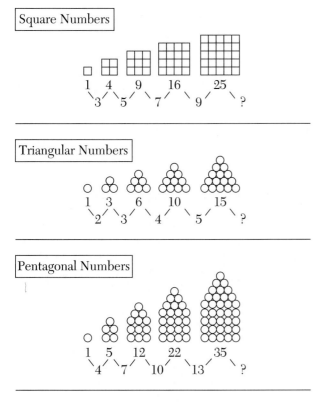

What numbers less than 50 can be placed
into rectangular patterns?

FIGURE 13.20

bers), etc. Each figure produces an interesting pattern and pupils are challenged to find larger and larger numbers in the set (see Figure 13.20). With more mature pupils, determining a pattern which could be used to predict the 15th or 100th triangular number builds more sophisticated mathematical thinking skills. Indeed, a talented pupil may become interested in developing a <u>formula</u> that could be used by a computer to find 1000 triangular (rectangular, pentagonal, etc.) numbers!

There are number patterns that are unrelated to figures. A pattern may follow an arbitrary "rule" proposed by a student (double the number and add three; add two and multiply by three, etc.) or may be related to the previously reported numbers—"take the last two numbers and add them together" as in 1, 1, 2, 3, 5, 8, 13, 21, etc. (Many students see this pattern first when they examine the Fibonacci numbers. See Section 13.7.) The exploration of number patterns will provide many opportunities

for pupils to **speculate, postulate,** and **check out hypotheses.**

Pattern identification, which begins with bead stringing and other pattern-recognition activities in kindergarten, often becomes a favorite activity of pupils in the intermediate grade levels. Pupils can examine simple patterns found in the multiplication tables (multiples of fives end in zero and five) and can extend that activity to locate "hidden patterns" that exist for the nines (add the digits of the product and the sum will always be nine), the threes (sum of the digits will always add to three, six, or nine), the sixes (even multiples of three), eleven, etc.

Pupils also may generate their own patterns by employing a rule such as "2a + 3." Such an activity can be presented in a gamelike atmosphere with a "panel of experts" taking numbers from the class and presenting the result of applying their rule. The class can then try to determine the rule from the pattern that is recorded on the chalkboard. (See Figure 13.21.)

Individuals also enjoy developing their own "secret rule" for generating patterns. When the sequence of numbers that is generated from the pupil's rule is recorded onto a two- to three-foot strip of adding-machine tape, the sequence may be placed in a "Number Pattern Machine" and revealed one number at a time for classmates to analyze. When the tapes are to be used on other occasions, pupils are instructed to write their names and their rule at the end of the tape. Many students who participate in this and similar sequence identification activities seek out ways of entering their rules into computers so that new number se-

Group Learning Activity

Give us 2 numbers—
We'll use our rule and
give you the result.

What's My Rule ?		
In		Out
a	b	
7	4	18
9	6	24
8	5	21
2	13	17
	6	6
		?

Panel of Experts

FIGURE 13.21

quences may be generated. The pupil quickly learns that mathematical sentences—formulas—may be used as a means of giving directions to computers. (See Figure 13.22.)

Developing Prealgebra Concepts from Patterns

Foundations for algebra are developed throughout the elementary school. When open sentences are used in the first grade, children are developing a readiness for the formal study of algebra.

Patterns offer an opportunity to further students' prealgebra skills. Patterns develop a need to efficiently communicate the nature of the pattern to others. (To **generalize** the nature of the pattern into an **equation**.) Once the pattern is communicated to others there will be a need to see if the communication has been accurate. (A need to **regenerate** the pattern using the equation. In algebraic terms the student will be finding solutions to the equation.)

Let's examine a pattern exploration activity that develops children's ability to communicate pattern information in an abbreviated format (equation).

Teacher-Guided Interactive Learning Activity

LESSON FRAGMENT

M: Constructing and solving equations from number patterns

A: Sixth grade

T: Models, discovery

H: Open sentences, variables, functions, patterns

Teacher: I have placed two EMPTY boxes in the left pan of our scale and adjusted the balance so the two pans are even. (SEE FIGURE 13.23A.) Now I am going to hide some washers in the boxes—but I will put the same amount in each box. Then to make it more difficult—I am going to place three more washers out where everyone can see them. Larry, can you come up and put enough washers in the other pan so they will balance? (LARRY PLACES 13 WASHERS ON THE RIGHTHAND PAN TO MAKE THE PANS EVEN.)

Teacher: I am going to write down what we have in an equation form. We have two boxes with the same amount in each box—which I am going to call "2B." We also have added three loose washers. That amount equals the 13 washers that Larry put in the righthand pan. (SEE FIGURE 13.23B.) Without

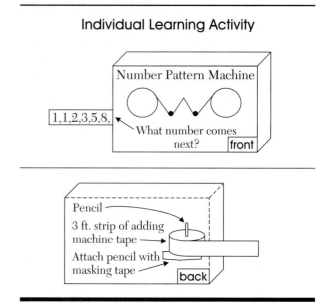

Individual Learning Activity

Number Pattern Machine

1,1,2,3,5,8,   What number comes next?   front

Pencil
3 ft. strip of adding machine tape
Attach pencil with masking tape
back

FIGURE 13.22

opening the boxes, how can we tell how many washers are in each one?

Jan: We could start by taking off the three loose washers.

Teacher: Won't that make the pans uneven?

Jan: Oh yes—we will need to take three from the righthand pan, too.

Teacher: All right, Larry—take three from each side and I'll write that we subtracted the same amount—three—from each side of the equation. (SEE FIGURE 13.23C.) Now what can we do?

John: We have ten in the righthand pan. Since ONE box is $\frac{1}{2}$ of the number of boxes in the left pan, we could get $\frac{1}{2}$ of ten, which is five, and we would have the amount in each box. (SEE FIGURE 13.23D.)

Teacher: Very good. I'm going to let each group work with the balance scales we have and try to act out the equations written on the board. When you get ready to work a problem, send a representative to see me and I'll tell that person how many to "hide" in the boxes to set up your equation.

"Box" problems can be used by students to generate exercises where other children transcribe communications into equations and then solve them. For example: Write the equation for the following and then solve it:

I have a mystery number of marbles in a box. I take half of them and throw them away. I put three marbles out where you can see them. It takes eight marbles to balance this. How many marbles did I start with in the box?

While most prealgebra activities at the elementary level grow out of hands-on explorations with models, similar to the "box" problem, more able students may be able to progress to creating and

Developing a Foundation for Algebra

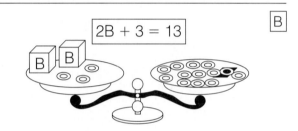

A

Empty boxes placed on scale and scale adjusted.

$$2B + 3 = 13$$

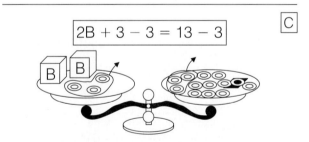

B

Same number of washers placed in each box. Three extra washers. Put enough on right to balance.

$$2B + 3 - 3 = 13 - 3$$

C

Take three washers from each side and it will still balance—so two boxes will equal 10 washers.

$$2B = 10$$
$$1/2 \text{ of } 2B = 1/2 \text{ of } 10$$
$$B = 5$$

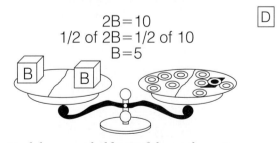

D

Each box must hold 1/2 of the washers. One half of 10 washers is five washers.

FIGURE 13.23

Original Price	Sale Price
$ 1.00	$ .75
2.00	1.50
10.00	7.50
35.00	
47.00	
51.00	

What was the original price of the merchandise if the sale price is $15.00?

FIGURE 13.24

solving problems involving both number patterns and equations in the absence of concrete models. For example, once students have mastered the concept of percent, then equations and patterns involving discount can be explored. Problems such as: A store has advertised that it is having a sale in which all items are discounted 25%. Complete the following table (see Figure 13.24) to indicate how each item would be priced for the sale.

13.7 COMPUTERS

Many software programs practice and explore number, numeration concepts, integers, and nondecimal bases. The computer is also an ideal device for generating a wide variety of patterns. Probably the most efficient method of generating patterns is to use spreadsheet programs which replicate formulas, sequences, series, etc.

We will use as an example a sequence of numbers known as the Fibonacci numbers. This sequence of numbers is derived by starting with two ones which are added together to get a third number (2). The second number (1) and the third number (2) are added together to get the fourth number (3). Continuing in this manner will produce the sequence 1, 1, 2, 3, 5, 8, 13, etc. Scientists have discovered many places in nature in which this sequence of numbers applies. Leaves on certain plants grow in this sequence; a pine cone can be related to this sequence as well as the shells of some mollusks. While this sequence is being chosen because of its interesting applications, any patterned sequence could just as easily be used with students. For example, 1, 3, 4, 7, 11, 18, etc., or 1, 3, 5, 7, 9, etc.

The spreadsheet programs previously mentioned can all be used to generate a sequence of numbers in a column. Of course, each commercial program has its own method of setting up the data. The following example was generated using a spreadsheet program from Microsoft Works™.

The procedure for generating Fibonacci numbers in a spreadsheet is:

1. Record a "**1**" in cell A1 and a "**1**" in cell A2.
2. Record "**= A1 + A2**" in cell A3.
3. **COPY** cell A3.
4. Use cursor to select cells A3 through A14. (Any number of cells can be used.)
5. "**FILL DOWN**" command. (The Fibonacci numbers will be generated through cell A14. See Figure 13.25.)

One of the more interesting explorations students conduct using the ratios of Fibonacci numbers follows. The procedure for setting up the

spreadsheet to calculate the ratios of adjacent pairs of Fibonacci numbers is as follows:

1. Set up a column of Fibonacci numbers using the procedure above.
2. In cell B2 record "= A1/A2."
3. **COPY** cell B2.
4. Drag down cell B3 to B14.
5. "**FILL DOWN**" command. (The computer will generate approximations of the Golden Ratio in the column. See Figure 13.26.)

Adjacent pairs of ratios may be examined. Students are quick to notice that the sequence of ratios alternate: first bigger than the next number, then smaller. Each adjacent pair of ratios turns out to be located on either side of a number called the Golden Ratio. The farther down the sequence of ratios one

---

Individual Learning Activity
Computer Spreadsheet

In cells A1 and A2 enter the number "one." In cell A3 enter the command "=A1+A2" instructing the program to add adjacent cells.

1	← Cell A1
1	← Cell A2
=A1+A2	← Cell A3

Copy

Use cursor to select Cell A3 and copy the command.

1	Select Cell A3
1	to A14 by dragging
=A1+A2	cursor down.

1	Key the fill down
1	command and the
2	computer will
3	generate the
5	Fibonacci number
8	series.
13	
21	
34	

FIGURE 13.25

Individual Learning Activity
Computer Spreadsheet

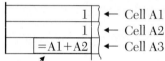

1	
1	=A1/A2
2	
3	
5	

Generate the Fibonacci series in the first column—(see Figure 13.25). In Cell B2 record the command "=A1/A2"

Copy the command in cell B2. Then use cursor to select (by dragging down) cells B3 through B14.

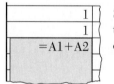

1	
1	=A1/A2
2	
3	
5	

1		Enter the fill down
1	1	command and the
2	0.5	computer will generate
3	0.6666666666	approximations of the
5	0.6	Golden Ratio.
8	0.625	
13	0.6153846153	
21	0.6190476190	
34	0.6176470588	
55	0.6181818181	
89	0.6169775280	
144	0.6180555555	
233	0.6180257510	
377	0.6180371352	

FIGURE 13.26

goes the better the approximation of the Golden Ratio. The 0.6180 is a good approximation of the Golden Ratio. The Golden Ratio has been widely used in architecture and other areas. An interesting research project for individual students is to have them find applications of the Golden Ratio as well as the Fibonacci numbers.

Once students have been taught how to generate a basic sequence of numbers using a spreadsheet, many sequences can be explored. For example, the figurate numbers generated from models can be generated in spreadsheet columns. This type of activity will help develop the student's "feel" for numbers (number sense). For example, record a "1" in cell A1. Enter "= A1 + 1" in cell A2. Copy A2. Drag across A2 to some cell down the column. Give the FILL DOWN command. This will generate a series of counting numbers starting with one. By using this base set the square numbers can be generated in the next column, by recording in cell B2, "= A1*A1. Then B2 is copied—the column is dragged and filled down, thus generating a sequence of the square numbers. In the next column a sequence of the differences of the square numbers can be generated by simply repeating the process beginning in cell C3 with the recording of "B2 − B1," copying, dragging, and filling down.

More able students can explore the concept of limit. Pupils may examine—at an intuitive level—the sequences of decimal fractions associated with sequences such as $\frac{1}{2}, \frac{2}{3}, \frac{3}{4}$, etc., as they are generated in decimal form on the spreadsheets.

13.8 EVALUATION AND INTERVENTION

Observations of students actively engaged in explorations with number and numeration and patterns can help the teacher identify students with special talents and aptitudes in the area of mathematical reasoning. The teacher should encourage such students to engage in further explorations after they have identified the basic nature of a pattern. Carefully phrased questions can guide students into extending their discoveries when a teacher observes them gaining insight into a process: For example, "What do you suppose would happen if you doubled each number in the sequence?" or "What do you suppose would happen if you started with 1 and 3, instead of 1 and 1?" or "What do you suppose would happen if you used multiplication instead of addition?"

Observations of some students may indicate

that they have reached an impasse in their search for a pattern, and that no productive learning is taking place. In these instances, the teacher may need to provide clues that will reignite the learning process. For example, if the student does not see a pattern associated with the ratios of Fibonacci numbers, then the teacher might further the learning process by asking the student if he or she notices anything interesting about the size of the different ratios.

Evaluation of students' understanding of the advanced number and numeration concepts may reveal that the students have conceptual misunderstandings about number and numeration systems. For example, work with addition in nondecimal bases may show that the child does not really understand the regrouping process for addition. In such cases the teacher should remediate the student's misunderstandings by redeveloping the conceptual understandings of the less advanced concepts.

13.9 MEETING SPECIAL NEEDS

Many of the topics discussed up to this point in this chapter were at one time considered topics for the more advanced student. To some extent, topics such as nondecimal bases and ancient numeration systems are still viewed as topics only for the more advanced student or to be used in enrichment situations. However, due to their everyday applications, topics such as integers and Roman numerals must be included in the curriculum even for learning-disabled students.

Providing for Gifted Students and Students with Strong Mathematical Foundations

Each topic covered in this chapter could be expanded to provide valuable experiences for gifted students and students with strong mathematical foundations. For example, the more able student could explore operations other than addition in nondecimal bases. Figure 13.27 illustrates such an exploration in subtraction in base five.

Not only can students with a strong background explore ancient numeration systems (Roman, Egyptian, and Mayan) but they can also create their own numeration system. To do this they would have to decide on the attributes they wanted their numeration system to have. (What base? Will it be additive, subtractive, multiplicative? Will it be a

Independent Learning Exploration
Subtraction in Base Five

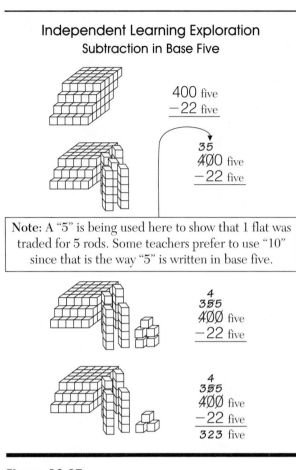

$\begin{array}{r} 400 \text{ five} \\ -22 \text{ five} \\ \hline \end{array}$

$\begin{array}{r} \overset{35}{4\cancel{0}0} \text{ five} \\ -22 \text{ five} \\ \hline \end{array}$

Note: A "5" is being used here to show that 1 flat was traded for 5 rods. Some teachers prefer to use "10" since that is the way "5" is written in base five.

$\begin{array}{r} \overset{4}{3}\overset{35}{\cancel{5}}5 \\ 4\cancel{0}0 \text{ five} \\ -22 \text{ five} \\ \hline \end{array}$

$\begin{array}{r} \overset{4}{3}\overset{35}{\cancel{5}}5 \\ 4\cancel{0}0 \text{ five} \\ -22 \text{ five} \\ \hline 323 \text{ five} \end{array}$

Figure 13.27

place-value system? What symbols will be needed?) This activity lends itself to small-group learning activities in which the group is trying to create a new model culture.

Once students understand the integer system, they have enough background with the concept of variable and calculator usage that they can be asked to explore questions such as:

- Can you find four integers that satisfy the following equation?
$$A^B \times C^D = ABCD$$
- Using any combination of the negative integers ($^-1$, $^-2$, $^-3$, $^-4$) and any operations, can you find names for the positive integers from one through ten? (You are not allowed to use any integer more than once in any one name.)
- Can you find four integers that give the same result when added together as when multiplied together?
$$A + B + C + D = A \times B \times C \times D$$

Irrational numbers (decimal expressions that cannot be represented as the quotient of two inte-

gers, for example π) offer another avenue for exploration. For example, after studying repeating decimals, a student may be asked to find the quotient of two numbers that will generate a decimal expression with the following pattern, "abaabaaabaaaab . . . ," where the pattern continues with one more digit, represented by "a" each time the pattern repeats. When the pupil thinks a pair of numbers has been found, she would be asked to perform the long division using a paper-and-pencil method (beyond the number of digits that can be represented on the calculator) to verify the finding. Activities of this form lead pupils to recognize the existence of irrational numbers and where they might be found on the number line.

Providing for the Learning-Disabled Student

The learning-disabled student needs some proficiency with both Roman numerals and integers to function in today's society. Roman numerals are necessary because they are widely employed as chapter headings, used when outlining, and appear on clock faces in public buildings. Integers are important because they are used when the temperature drops below zero, when reporting debt, and when describing a checking account that has been overdrawn.

Activities for the learning-disabled should emphasize hands-on explorations with manipulative materials that relate the activities directly to applications that will make the student functionally literate. To work with integers pupils should read thermometers when the temperature is below zero (thermometers can be used in the school's freezer when the temperature outside is not conducive to this activity). When working with Roman numerals pupils should look at the chapters in a book—relating the symbols to chapters 1, 2, 3, etc. Often children can use the table of contents to see the order of the numerals.

While activities for the handicapped focus upon those skills that students need to be functionally literate, it is still important to develop basic understanding of the concepts. The walk-on number line is equally useful with learning-disabled students. When working with a thermometer pupils can "act it out" by letting their fingers do the walking along the scale.

The concept of owing someone money may be acted out with individuals playing the role of the debtor and creditor. Discussions of the effects of overdrafts on a checking account and similar problems can be explored through similar activities.

13.10 SUMMARY

Many of the topics developed in this chapter are included in an elementary school mathematics curriculum as enrichment activities for the purpose of building ways of thinking about mathematics and exploring our world. However, Roman numerals and integer concepts have direct applications and are usually included as a regular part of elementary school programs.

While a study of historical and nondecimal numeration systems is studied at the intermediate level, the kindergarten and primary grades develop some "readiness" activities with Roman numerals and integers. In addition, the study of patterns and prealgebra concepts based on these patterns starts in kindergarten and continues throughout the student's study of mathematics.

At the intermediate level students continue study of Roman numerals in more depth. They learn to add, subtract, multiply, and divide integers using hands-on-explorations. The inclusion in the curriculum of topics related to nondecimal bases and ancient numeration systems may differ among school systems. In some systems these topics are included as enrichment topics, only at the teacher's discretion. Even when these topics are included in the curriculum their placement varies.

EXERCISES

1. Recognizing patterns is a skill developed as early as kindergarten that continues throughout the primary and intermediate grade levels. Describe an activity that might be appropriate for developing pattern recognition skills
   a. at the preschool or kindergarten level
   b. at the primary level
   c. at the intermediate level
2. Children often do not recognize the value of exploring historical number systems.
   a. Name four "out of school" situations in which a pupil might encounter a need to read Roman numerals.
   b. Suggest a classroom situation that might be used by a teacher to introduce the skill of writing Roman numerals.
3. How would the following amounts be written using Roman numerals?
   a. 49   b. 999   c. 1492   d. 1992
   e. 12,245   f. 1 million
4. In modern Roman numerals a symbol is never repeated four times consecutively—however, there are amounts which may have four Ms, four Cs, or four Xs in the numeral. Show a properly written Roman numeral that would have four repetitions of a single symbol.
5. A parent has asked you—as a teacher—to explain why his/her daughter needs to study number systems that are not commonly used, such as the Egyptian, Mayan, or other number base systems. What are some educational reasons for exploring these systems?

6. Integers are informally introduced in the primary grades, but operations with integers are developed at the intermediate level. Describe how a teacher would use concrete materials to develop addition and subtraction of integers
   a. using a walk-on number-line approach
   b. using an "electrical charges" approach.
   c. Suggest a classroom situation that might be used to introduce addition (or subtraction) of integers.
7. Describe how a teacher might use figurate numbers to extend pupil skill in recognizing number patterns. Make sure to describe the use of manipulative materials in developing this skill.
8. The text describes the use of a spreadsheet program (Microsoft Works™) to explore patterns. Some classrooms do not have access to a Macintosh computer. Explore other spreadsheet programs (Appleworks™ for the Apple IIc™) to see how patterns may be explored using that software.
9. Describe how a teacher might assess a pupil's UNDERSTANDING of the mathematical concepts in
   a. writing and reading Roman numerals
   b. adding and/or subtracting integers
   c. pattern recognition
10. Choose an article (in References) that appears in *Arithmetic Teacher*. Identify two major ideas or suggestions given by the author. Try to convince a fellow classmate of the value of those suggestions.

RELEVANT COMPUTER SOFTWARE

Freddy's Puzzling Adventures. 1984. Apple II family. Developmental Learning Materials, One DLM Park, Allen, Tex. 75002.

REFERENCES

Arcavi, A. "Using Historical Materials in the Mathematics Classroom." *Arithmetic Teacher* 35 (December 1987): 13–16.

Balka, D. S. "Digit Delight: Problem-solving Activities Using 0 through 9." *Arithmetic Teacher* 36 (November 1988): 42–45.

Blattner, J. "Microcomputer Arithmetic." In *Computers in Mathematics: NCTM Yearbook. 1984.* Reston, Va.: National Council of Teachers of Mathematics, 1984. Pp. 202–204.

Ronau, R. N. "Number Sense." *Mathematics Teacher* 81 (September 1988): 437–440.

Vacc, N. N. "Individualizing Mathematics Drill and Practice: Variations on a Computer Program." *Arithmetic Teacher* 34 (March 1987): 43–47.

CHAPTER 14

TEACHING GRAPHING, PROBABILITY, AND STATISTICS

INTRODUCTION

The age of information and technology requires that individuals be able to process and translate information into formats useful to the individual and also that the individual be able to communicate this information efficiently to others. For example, the weatherman must take very complex data and translate it into graphs and charts that the layman can understand. The geologist must be able to organize data from seismic readings into graphs that corporate officers can understand and act upon when deciding to drill for oil. The nurse must collect data on patients that can be interpreted by doctors when managing postoperative patients and the business manager must be able to organize information about her business and competitors' businesses so she can decide when to expand. The homeowner must collect and organize data to determine the most efficient way to manage home energy usage. Individuals who are overweight collect and organize data on caloric intake to better manage their diets.

In an age of technology almost all vocations require individuals to have <u>some</u> information processing and translation skills. However, the need to interpret information goes beyond a vocational need. All types of media communicate information in formats that permit efficient transmission of summarized data (graphs, charts, etc.). An informed citizen must be skillful in interpreting data in these abbreviated formats.

Sometimes the information being communicated is derived from statistical samples taken from a large population. For example, "1100 persons were surveyed and 52 percent said they will vote for Sue Smith, while 48 percent said they will vote for Joe Brown." If there is a 3 percent error range, the percentage of people favoring Sue Smith is somewhere between 49 percent and 55 percent, whereas those favoring Joe Brown is somewhere between 45 percent and 51 percent. The media reports data in the form of probabilities. For example, "There is a 40 percent chance of rain tomorrow." Informed citizens will need a wide variety of skills and understandings with graphs, probability, and statistics.

At the elementary school level these understandings and concepts should develop from the student being **actively involved** in—

Helping establish a reason for collecting information (data). (What is the question we want to answer? What is the problem we are trying to solve?)

Setting up the procedure for gathering information (data). (How do we sample and gather data from the whole population?)

Gathering the data. (How are observation, questionnaires, and experiments used to gather data?)

Organizing data for communication. (In what form—charts, graphs, ranges, averages, means, mode—should the data be presented?)

Interpreting data. (What are the implications of the data? What conclusions can be drawn from the data?)

Applying the data in problem-solving activities. (We found that 60% of the students surveyed preferred chocolate chip cookies, 25% liked oatmeal cookies, and 15% liked frosted cookies. How should we use this data in preparing for our booth in the school festival?)

14.1 TEACHING GRAPHING, PROBABILITY, AND STATISTICS CONCEPTS AT THE PRIMARY LEVEL

At the primary level children learn to collect, organize, interpret, analyze, and describe data arising out of a need to communicate, to understand, or to apply data in problem-solving situations. Teachers must initiate classroom activities that create these needs, allowing pupils to use these skills in real-world situations. Activities should involve:

Collection of data—which may range from counting events or members of a set to collecting information about an aspect of that set (such as the weight of each object).

Organization of data—which may be simply displaying objects or constructing charts or graphs.

Interpretation and analysis of data—which range from identifying some characteristic (least/most or largest/smallest) to specific numerical aspects (months that have the fewest days of rain) and include interpretations that help pupils make appropriate decisions in light of the data obtained. Interpretations may also lead to predictions based on data obtained.

A general overview of the graphing, probability, and statistics skills introduced at the primary level is listed below:

Grade 1

Informal explorations with coordinates
Collection of data
  • using tallies
  • using blocks
Graphing with real objects and pictures
  • bar graphs
  • pictographs
Problem solving with graphs

Grade 2

Locating coordinates
Collection of data
  • construction of charts and tables
Graphing with pictures and symbols
  • pictographs using 2s, 5s, or 10s
  • reading line graphs
Problem solving with coordinates and graphs

Grade 3

Plotting coordinates
Collection of data
  • surveying and sampling
  • analyzing data
  • making predictions
Graphing
  • bar graphs
  • pictographs
  • constructing line graphs
  • construct individual progress charts
Examine statistical terms in daily activities
Problem solving with coordinates and graphs

Children enter school with a very limited background in graphing. This means the teacher must look for meaningful situations where graphing is appropriate in order to develop the foundation for later statistical work. Pupils will use real objects in beginning graphing activities. In kindergarten a teacher may have pupils group themselves accord- ing to the color of their shirts, hair, or shoes. When pupils line up—each standing in one floor tile— they construct a "living" bar graph. Teachers may then have each pupil take off ONE shoe and place it on a tile to find which kind of shoe—cloth, leather, etc.—was worn most often that day. (Figure 14.1.)

Calendars are also used as a source of data. Pupils are encouraged to keep track of sunny days, cloudy days, rainy days, and snowy days by record- ing the weather in "picture" form. Data produced by this daily activity is an excellent source for graphing. If the teacher makes each symbol (sun, cloud, rain, etc.) approximately the same size, the symbols themselves may be removed from the cal- endar and used to make a pictograph. (Figure 14.2.)

There are many events that may be used to de- velop a bar graph—even as early as kindergarten. The teacher may find out "our favorite color" by placing square regions cut out of the various colors and asking the children to come and take a "tile" of their favorite color. Each child would then come to the bulletin board and paste the color in a line with others. Children observe the resulting "color trains" and determine which color was chosen by most pupils, by the fewest pupils, etc. (Figure 14.2). Pupil-height strips (adding-machine tape copies of pupil heights) may also be used in a graphing activity.

14.2 INITIATING CONCEPT DEVELOPMENT FROM PROBLEM-SOLVING ACTIVITIES

As children become more mature, the teacher will be able to use more **small-group learning activi- ties** when developing graphing skills. Working in small groups, pupils develop an ability to commu- nicate information involving data—a major goal of mathematics education. Let us examine a typical class project that could be utilized to develop many skills in collecting, organizing, interpreting, and communicating data or information.

Small-group Learning Activities

PROBLEM-SOLVING SITUATION

THE CLASS DECIDED TO COLLECT ALUMINUM CANS, WHICH CAN BE SOLD AT THE RECY- CLING CENTER TO HELP RAISE MONEY FOR A CLASS PROJECT. A STUDENT HAS ASKED HOW TO KEEP TRACK OF THE NUMBER OF CANS

FIGURE 14.1

EACH PERSON COLLECTS AS A WAY OF RECOG- NIZING THE EFFORT OF EACH PERSON.

Group discussion (TRIGGERED BY TEACHER QUESTIONS): "Let's keep track of the number of cans each person collects as a way of recognizing the effort of each person. How can we keep track each day of the number of cans collected?"

The following idea is agreed to by the group: Name tags in front of each person's stack. (SEE FIGURE 14.3.)

Problem: Stacks get so high they keep falling over.

Teacher's suggestion: Let's use a box in which to

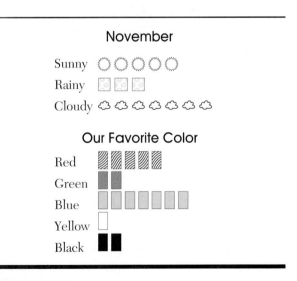

FIGURE 14.2

keep the cans, but we will give each person a pic-ture for each can they bring in and then they can paste it beside their name on a chart.

Problem: Sue brings in so many cans that her pictures will not fit on the chart. The class offers some suggestions—(SEE FIGURE 14.4.)

• Start a second row for a person when the row gets used up.

• One picture could represent two cans.

Discussion: A student raises a question related to using one picture to represent two cans. "How could we represent one can if a picture represents two cans?" A pupil suggests using only half a can. Two cans represented by each picture is adopted with a picture of half a can being used to represent one can.

Project Conclusion: At the end of the project the teacher suggests using strips of paper to record the number of cans collected in all by each person. Pupils choose a "one-inch length" to represent each can when a strip of paper is used to represent the number of cans collected. The strip for Sue is too long for the piece of poster board and someone suggests that one inch can represent <u>two</u> cans, just as we let one picture of a can represent two cans collected. The teacher suggests that we include a scale beside the strips to remind everyone how many cans are represented by the strips. A bar graph is constructed. (SEE FIGURE 14.5.)

The project described illustrates <u>one way</u> a teacher may initiate a study of graphs. Of course, children need to see a variety of ways that data are collected and learn how to apply that data in

decision-making processes and problem-solving activities.

Let us examine a second activity that provides students with a different insight into data collection techniques and the application of data in the decision-making process.

PROBLEM-SOLVING SITUATION
THE CLASS VOTED TO USE THE SALE OF ICE CREAM AT THE SCHOOL FAIR AS A CLASS PROJECT. THE TEACHER HAS IN-

Pictograph
Using pictures to represent the objects

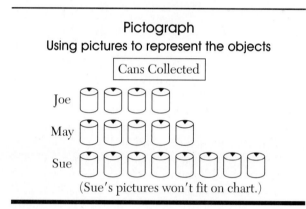

(Sue's pictures won't fit on chart.)

FIGURE 14.4

Initial Activity
Using a collection of real objects to create a visual image that permits rapid communication of data.

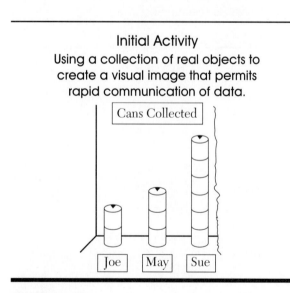

FIGURE 14.3

Bar Graph
A bar graph used at the end of project

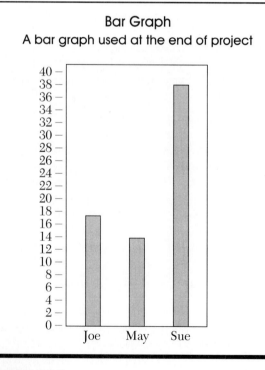

FIGURE 14.5

DICATED THAT THERE WILL BE ROOM IN THE BOOTH TO SERVE THREE KINDS OF ICE CREAM AND THE CLASS HAS INDICATED THAT THEY WOULD LIKE TO STOCK VANILLA, CHOCOLATE, AND STRAWBERRY. NOW THE PROBLEM BECOMES HOW MUCH OF EACH FLAVOR TO ORDER.

Class suggestions are as follows:

- Use the preferences of the class as an indication of what flavors the buyers are going to want.
- Survey all the children who will be coming to the fair to find out each person's favorite flavor.

The class decides to **survey** all the children coming to the fair, because a survey will also tell people that ice cream will be available at the fair.

Committee is assigned to construct a survey instrument: The committee decides that they should interview each person to see if he or she will be coming to the fair, since it is only these people they really want to survey further. A student suggests that they need to determine whether a person will be buying ice cream, since they really don't care what flavor a person likes if they aren't going to buy any.

Everyone agrees that when a person indicates he or she will be coming to the fair they might decide to buy ice cream. Then they should be asked which of the three flavors they prefer. A pupil suggests that a child might not like <u>any</u> of the three flavors and suggests that this information should also be noted on the survey.

Committee is assigned to plan how the survey will be administered. It decides to survey students as they are entering the school in the morning.

Survey taken and recorded. Students are assigned in teams to collect information at each of the school entrances.

Group discusses the results of the survey. Were some people, who will be buying ice cream, not covered by the survey? What about parents and preschool children coming to the fair? A suggestion was made to expand the survey to include a telephone follow-up to parents. Group decides to go with the data they have. Twice as many children have indicated they will buy chocolate as have indicated they will buy either vanilla or strawberry, so the class decides to buy twice as much chocolate as vanilla or strawberry. Someone suggests that some people will want two scoops. They decide to buy enough to sell everyone one and one-half scoops. If they see they are not going to have enough to get through the day they can make the scoops of ice cream smaller. If they find they bought too much they can make the scoops larger.

At the end of the fair day they find that they had some chocolate left over and the vanilla ran out in the early afternoon.

Actual results compared to predictions. The next day the group discusses why their **predictions**—based on their survey—did not match the actual **results.** They discuss how they can use this experience to help them improve their data-collection procedure. The teacher leads the group to discuss how well the sample matched the **population** (the group that would be eating the ice cream).

Using Data to Make Predictions

Sometimes data is collected for the purpose of making predictions. Explorations with chance are kept simple and intuitive at the primary level. Two initial concepts developed at this level relate to being able to answer questions such as "Which event has the greater chance of happening?" and "What do you predict will be the composition of the population based on recorded events?" While these questions look at probability from two different viewpoints, children can build a strong foundation for later mathematical explorations in probability and statistics by exploring these ideas.

The following **small-group learning activity** addresses the first question—"Which has a greater chance of happening?" While it is perhaps more meaningful for children if such explorations grow out of a classroom situation, there are occasions when teachers must construct an event where meaning can be developed.

Small-group learning activity

PROBLEM-SOLVING SITUATION
CHILDREN ARE GIVEN A PAPER BAG AND

TOLD IT CONTAINS 25 YELLOW AND 5 RED M & M'S™. THEY ARE ASKED TO GUESS WHAT COLOR THEY WOULD GET IF THEY DREW ONE CANDY FROM THE BAG WITHOUT LOOKING. THEY ARE TO RECORD THEIR GUESSES.

Activity: Each group of pupils makes selections and records their results. Children repeat this selection several times, always placing the candy back in the bag and shaking the bag before repeating the process. When they have reached one hundred selections they total the number of times they drew out a red and the number of times they drew out a yellow. What did they observe? Did they tend to predict yellow would be selected more than red? (THE DATA ACCUMULATED BY SEVERAL SMALL GROUPS MAY BE COMBINED TO GET EVEN LARGER SAMPLINGS. THE TEACHER MAY WISH TO EXTEND THE ACTIVITY OVER TWO OR THREE DAYS TO SEE IF THE RESULTS DIFFER.) The activity may be repeated with an equivalent amount of each color and pupils then must reexamine their predictions.

Spinner cards as illustrated in Figure 14.6 can be used for similar activities. A question such as "Which is greater, the chance that the spinner will fall in the black area or the white area?" may be followed by having the children record the results of repeated spins of the pointer. Such an activity provides an opportunity for children to gain an intuitive feel for the concept of chance.

The earlier activity with candy leads children to see results of generating a series of events, when one **event** is more likely to happen than another event. It is also important for children to participate in explorations where they don't start out knowing information about the **population**. In other words, they have to make predictions about attributes of a whole population based on data obtained from a sequence of observations of individual members of the population.

The **small-group learning activity** that follows has children predict the attributes of a **population** (in this case, the number of pieces of popcorn kernels that have been lightly spray-painted black in a paper bag containing twenty pieces of unpopped popcorn) based on a sequence of observations of individual members of the population.

Small-group learning activity

Materials: Several paper bags, each containing twenty pieces of unpopped popcorn, with a different number of the pieces in each bag spray-painted black.

Two teams: Each team designates a person to keep track of the results of each withdrawal from the paper bag.

Game rules: Each group is told that 20 pieces of popcorn have been placed in the bag. Children then try to **predict,** within one piece of popcorn, the number of pieces in a paper bag that have secretly been spray-painted black by the teacher. Each team shakes the bag and

Small-Group Learning Activity

Is there a greater chance of the pointer falling on a white space or a black space?

FIGURE 14.6

Children systematically organize and describe using tables, charts, and graphs.

then withdraws a piece of popcorn and records if it is white or black. Then the popcorn is placed back in the bag and shaken and the other team withdraws a piece of popcorn and records the color, before replacing the popcorn. This process is repeated until a team, upon getting its turn, says it is ready to guess the number of pieces of black-painted popcorn. If the team guesses within one piece they win a point. If not, the other team gets a point. The game is repeated with other distributions of black-painted popcorn.

14.3 TEACHING GRAPHING, STATISTICS, AND PROBABILITY CONCEPTS AT THE INTERMEDIATE LEVEL

Pupils at the intermediate level encounter statistical concepts outside of school. They play board games with spinners and dice. They listen to predictions on radio and television. From these experiences they recognize the importance of exploring statistical concepts and probability. A teacher can heighten this interest by posing questions such as "How do networks determine which programs we will see on television? How do manufacturers determine which products we will get to choose from at a grocery store? How can weather forecasters predict there will be a 40% chance of rain tomorrow? How do traffic control engineers decide how long to leave traffic signals in the "go" and "stop" positions? How do baseball managers decide which pinch hitter to send to the plate? How can newscasters predict who will win an election even before all the ballots are counted?"

In the intermediate grades students solve problems using the tools of graphing, probability, and statistics. After identifying a problem, pupils collect, organize, and describe data in order to make inferences. Sometimes statistical explorations occur when designing and executing projects for a school—a science fair, contest, or social studies project. On other occasions, the problem-solving projects stem from an interest of a group or individual within the class, such as sports, cooking, or elections.

Graphing concepts and skills that were developed at the primary level, such as the construction of pictographs and bar graphs, are extended at the intermediate level to include line and circle graphs.

Measures of central tendency are examined (mean and median). Other descriptors of data (mode, range, and standard deviation) may also be explored at this time.

Skills and understandings related to probability are developed at this level. The student will move from the concept of events being "more likely" and "less likely" into trying to predict the nature of populations from samples. Students will also learn to make predictions based on theoretical or experimental probabilities.

A general overview of the graphing, probability, and statistics skills introduced at the intermediate level is listed below:

Grade 4

Plotting coordinates
Extend bar and pictographing skills
Construction of line graphs
  • examining trends
  • determining scale
Analyze circle graphs
Probability
  • independent events
Finding mean (average) using calculator
Problem-solving with graphs

Grade 5

Locating coordinates
Collection of data
  • construction of charts and tables
Graphing with pictures and symbols
  • pictographs using 2s, 5s, or 10s
  • reading line graphs
Examining mean, median, and range
  • using redistribution
  • using calculator
Probability
  • independent events
  • tree diagrams and tables
  • described as fractions
Problem solving with graphing and probability

Grade 6

Plotting positive and negative coordinates
Collection of data
  • surveying and sampling
  • analyzing data
  • making predictions
  • analysis of data bias

Construction of graphs
- double bar graphs
- multiline graphs
- percentage and/or circle graphs

Finding mean, median, mode, and range
- using redistribution
- using calculator

Probability
- two or more independent events
- described as percentages

Problem solving with graphing, probability, and statistics

Grades 7 and 8

Extending graphing, probability, and statistical skills
- sample space
- bias and unbiased sampling

Explore graphing on computers

14.4 EXTENDING GRAPHING CONCEPTS AND SKILLS

Students at this level become very interested in displaying data in a graphic form. The teacher must recognize that the construction of graphs is not an end in itself. While students may learn from constructing graphs, they must <u>also</u> learn to use graphs to resolve problems, answer questions, and communicate data efficiently.

Developing Line-Graph Concepts

Prior to the development of line graphs the child will have been introduced to the concept of coordinates. In many programs children will have encountered the basic concept of finding points in a plane through the problem-solving activity of finding locations on a map in their social studies activities. However, a slightly more formal approach is presented as part of the elementary mathematics curriculum, because graphing of data is commonly found in both scientific and business presentations. Figure 14.7 illustrates coordinate plotting concepts developed through an independent learning activity.

When constructing graphs at the primary level children dealt with discrete sets, things that could be counted. At the intermediate level, students

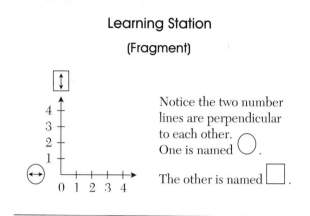

Learning Station

(Fragment)

Notice the two number lines are perpendicular to each other. One is named ◯.

The other is named ▢.

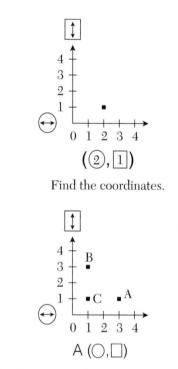

(②, ①)

Find the coordinates.

A (◯, ▢)

FIGURE 14.7

learn to represent <u>continuous</u> data using **line graphs.** For example, if the temperature of the air is measured now at 78 degrees and three hours later at 81 degrees, during those three hours the temperature went *through* every number *between* 78 and 81 degrees. <u>When data are continuous in nature, line graphs are a better choice in presenting this information.</u> A wide variety of measures studied at the intermediate level are continuous in nature. For example, the weight and height of individuals from birth, the air temperature from one point in time to another, time, and speed are all continuous in nature and are best represented by line graphs. The science fair project illustrated in Figure 14.8 uses a line graph as a tool for displaying the results of the study.

When developing line graphs the teacher will wish to:

1. Discuss that line graphs are used when data is either continuous, or reported in very small increments (such as the average sales price of a stock traded on the New York Stock Exchange).
2. Develop the concept of an axis (including how decisions are made about which axis to use for a particular variable).
3. Discuss how decisions are made concerning the scales that will be used on each axis.
4. Examine how line graphs show <u>trends</u> and give students opportunities to analyze trends from line graphs.

Developing Circle-Graph Concepts

A circle graph is generally used when one is trying to report fractional parts of the whole unit (usually when those fractional parts have been expressed as a percent). For example, when a city wishes to report the various percentages of expenditure of its budget, then a circle graph provides a visual means for transmitting this information. (See Figure 14.9.) Circle graphs are excellent devices for developing students' analytical skills. Questions such as "Did the city spend more for safety than they did for human services?" and "What area of the city budget received the least amount of city resources?" require the student to analyze the graph and the relationship of each part to the whole.

In developing circle graphs the teacher will wish to:

1. Teach children how to partition a circle into the appropriate fractional parts using a protractor. For example, in order to make a "pie" shape representing 10% of the circular shape, the degrees in the arc to be used would be determined by first finding 10% of 360 degrees. Using a protractor, the student would mark off the 36 degrees of arc on the circle. Then line segments would be drawn that connect the center with the ends of the arc.
2. Assist students in learning to analyze the implications associated with various aspects of circle graphs.

Science Fair Project

Student Identification Number: 79
Science Fair Site: Corning, Ohio

Hypothesis:
There will be no significant difference between the growth of bean plants subjected to acid rain and those not subjected to acid rain.

Procedure:
Sample "A" subjected to watering with mine runoff every third day.

Sample "B" subjected to watering with distilled water every third day.

Sample "B": _____ Sample "A": ....

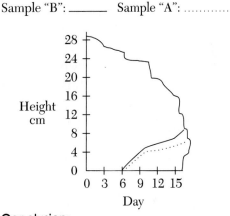

Conclusion:
Hypothesis rejected. Acid rain stunts bean plant growth.

FIGURE 14.8

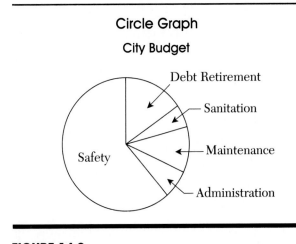

FIGURE 14.9

14.5 EXPLORING STATISTICAL CONCEPTS (MEAN, MEDIAN, MODE, RANGE)

Unfortunately, many students know <u>how</u> to find the **arithmetic mean** (average) before they really understand the concept. As early as the third and fourth grades pupils are "adding their scores and dividing by the number of tests" to determine their "grade." Most can readily apply a procedure, but cannot estimate an average when given three numbers such as 82, 86, and 84. Since students will encounter the statistical concepts of mean, median, and mode many times throughout their lives, it is essential that a firm foundation be established early in their school program.

When exploring the concept of **mean**, pupils should first be involved in activities that require them to "even up" groups by moving objects from one pile to another. Only after pupils thoroughly understand this model for "average" should they put together groups (add) and then redistribute (divide) them. When working with the **median**, pupils should line up groups from smallest to largest and then count in from <u>both</u> ends to reach the middle (median). Using the same ordering activity, pupils can see the **range** as being the breadth of distribution (smallest to largest) and the **mode** as the amount that appears most often in groups.

The lesson below shows one way of using manipulative materials to explore statistical concepts.

Teacher-Guided Interactive Learning Activity

LESSON FRAGMENT

M: Mean and median

A: Fifth-grade class

T: Experiment/modeling

H: Column addition, division

PROBLEM-SOLVING SITUATION

LAST MONTH PUPILS TRACED AROUND THEIR HANDS AND USED GRID PAPER TO APPROXIMATE THE AREA OF THEIR PALMS. TODAY THE TEACHER HAS SUGGESTED ANOTHER EXPERIMENT—DETERMINING HOW MUCH EACH PUPIL'S HAND CAN HOLD.

Teacher: I have a box of Unifix™ blocks. Before I give instructions, I want the groups to assemble around their work tables. (PUPILS GATHER AROUND WORK TABLES.)

Theodore: Teacher, should we have the blocks in rods or loose?

Teacher: Let's keep the blocks loose, because we will want to find out how many we can grip in our hands. Now I would like each person in the group to take a handful of blocks. <u>Once you get a handful</u>, put those blocks into a ROD and place the ROD on your worktable. I will come around and see how you are doing. (TEACHER MOVES FROM GROUP TO GROUP AND HELPS PUPILS ASSEMBLE RODS.)

Lucy: Teacher, we put our rods in order and mine is the longest.

Theodore: If I had another grab at the blocks, I could get a whole lot more!

Teacher: Theodore has a good suggestion, class. Sometimes we seem to grab more than other times. To be fair, let's grab five different handfuls. Then we'll put each handful into a rod and line the rods up from the smallest to the largest—as Lucy suggested. Do that for ONE member of your team and then we'll talk about what happened. (TEACHER WALKS AROUND AS PUPILS SELECT ONE MEMBER AND LET THAT INDIVIDUAL GRAB BLOCKS.)

Gregory: I didn't get the same number of blocks each time, teacher! Look at the rods. A couple of times I only got four and then one time I had eight!

Teacher: All right, class. What could we do in this case?

Lucy: Why don't we try to even up the piles by taking some from the eight and putting it with the four. That will give us <u>about</u> what he would get each time.

Teacher: Very good idea, Lucy! Everyone in your group—try to even out the rods.

Gregory: I had rods of four, four, seven, seven, and eight. I took two from the eight and put them with the four to make six. Then I took one from each of the sevens and put them with the other four, making all sixes.

Clifford: Teacher—I can't make all the rods the same length because I had a five, six, six, six, and eight. When I take one from the eight and put it with the five—I have four of them the same length—but that last rod is seven. (SEE FIGURE 14.10.)

Gabby: Just call it six, Clifford! We really ought to cut the block and distribute it between the five rods so we would have $6\frac{1}{5}$. But we can't cut the block so we will have to round to the nearest number.

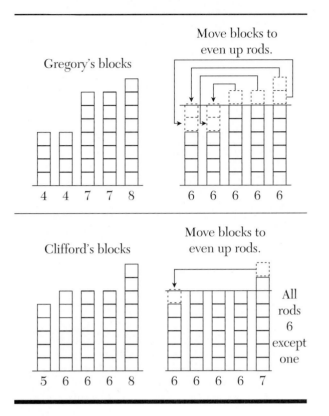

FIGURE 14.10

Teacher: O.K.—let's use Gabby's suggestion—let's redistribute and round to the nearest block. Now I want each group to find the number of blocks for <u>each</u> member of the team. (THE TEACHER CIRCULATES AROUND THE ROOM AS PUPILS FIND THE "GRIP AMOUNT" FOR EACH TEAM MEMBER.)

Lucy: Teacher, we found a shortcut. We don't bother to put the blocks into a rod. We just put all of the rods together. Then we sort them into piles for the five tries. Then we put them into rods.

Teacher: Good idea—let's all try that.

Gabby: This is sort of like finding average—isn't it, teacher?

Teacher: Good observation, Gabby. It <u>is</u> finding ***average***. When we want to find average, we want to "even up the rods" by taking from the longest and putting it with the shortest until they are all the same length. Lucy's group found a <u>shortcut</u> by adding all the amounts and then dividing by the number of trials. Now let's see if we can find the AVERAGE size of the team. Each team member take one grab and then find the average grab for the team. Instead of putting the blocks into rods and redistributing, I'm going to let you use your calculators

to *compute* the average. (THE TEACHER THEN HAS EACH TEAM CONTINUE THE ACTIVITY SEVERAL TIMES TO FIND THE "GREATEST GRAB," THE "LEAST GRAB," ETC.)

While the activity above was used to develop only the concept of arithmetic mean (average), it could have been extended to develop median, mode, and range. In developing the concept of median, pupils arrange the blocks from the shortest stack to the tallest stack (Figure 14.11). Then students move from both ends until they reach the middle. This middle stack would represent the **median.** (Such an activity prepares pupils for the eventuality of dealing with even numbers of stacks—where the median would fall <u>between</u> two numbers.) Looking at the entire set of blocks—from the shortest stack to the tallest stack—pupils can determine the **range.** If the teacher wishes to point out the **mode,** pupils only need to find the stack size that <u>appears most often</u>—in the illustration it would be <u>12</u>.

Extending Statistical Skills

At the intermediate level, students explore the concepts of samples, sample space, biased and unbiased sampling, as well as determining the probability of events. In these activities hands-on explorations are used to give students an intuitive

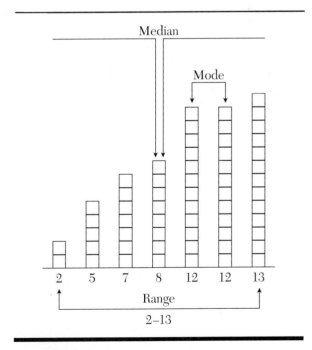

FIGURE 14.11

feel for the concepts that will be developed later in the curriculum.

Let us examine a small-group learning experience that explores some of the concepts related to sampling.

Small-group learning activity

PROBLEM SITUATION
  THE CLASS PLANS TO STRING POP-
  CORN TO DECORATE THE ROOM. THE
  TEACHER POSES THE QUESTION, "HOW
  MANY PIECES OF POPCORN WILL WE
  NEED TO MAKE STRINGS FOR THE
  HALL?"

  Materials: A large pail of popped popcorn and a large sheet of cardboard folded into a "V" shape, marked off in inches, with one end taped across. (SEE FIGURE 14.12.)

  Procedure: Teams will construct samples from the pail of popcorn. Each sample will make a ten-inch row of popcorn (the last piece of popcorn must be touching the ten-inch mark.) Then the number of pieces will be tabulated. After each sample measurement is recorded the popcorn will be replaced in the pail and the popcorn mixed. Eleven samples will be taken by each group.

  Requirements: List the sample counts from the smallest to the largest.

  • Which number occurred most often? (This number is called the **mode.**)
  • What is the middle number in your sequence of numbers? (This number is the **median.**)
  • Use your calculator to find the average of the 11 numbers. (This number is the **mean.**)
  • List the smallest and largest of the numbers in your list. (This is the **range** of the data.)
  • How might stirring the popcorn, after you took each sample, bias your later samples? (Hint: What might happen to pieces of popcorn as they are stirred?)
  • Do any of the sample sizes provide you with a clue for predicting the size of the next sample that would make ten inches? Does the mode help you? In what way? Does the mean help you? In what way?
  • Take 11 more samples. Find the mean of the 11 samples. How does this mean compare with the mean of the first samples? Is it close to the other mean? Far away?
  • Similar types of activities can be used to help

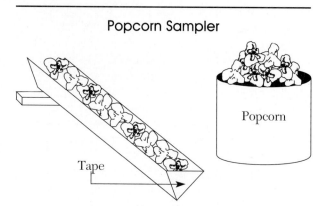

Popcorn Sampler

Dip into can with sampler. Count the number of pieces in the ten-inch row. Return the pieces after each sampling. Take eleven dips.

FIGURE 14.12

students formulate an intuitive feel for statistic and probability concepts.
  • Similar activities may be constructed using unpopped kernels and finding out:
    • Which MICROWAVE brand will pop the greatest quantity?
    • Which leaves the fewest unpopped kernels? (Must start with the same number of kernels)
    • Which has more kernels per tablespoon (before popping)?

14.6 EXPLORING PROBABILITY CONCEPTS

By the time pupils reach the intermediate grade level they have played games in which "chance" was a factor. Many board games use spinners or dice to determine the number of spaces a player may move. Students, however, generally believe that everything is based upon "luck"—and have learned little about mathematical probabilities. Students also hear items reported in terms of probabilities—"70% chance of rain" and "the odds of winning are 1 chance in 1,890,000." Election results may be "predicted" on the basis of statistical samplings.

When exploring the fundamental concepts of probability pupils should use many manipulative materials, including spinners, bags of colored blocks, coins, and dice. A teacher may encourage students to speculate what color block would be more likely to be randomly selected from a bag containing three red blocks and one white block in a bag. Teams may experiment and record their find-ings—selecting a block, recording its color, and re-turning it to the bag each time. The findings may then be compared to their speculations.

As pupils try to predict outcomes they become more interested in discovering ways to make those predictions more reliable. In a bag containing one white and three red blocks pupils generally decide that there are better chances of getting a red block—since there are more reds. Since there are four blocks, the **probability** of drawing a red block would be three out of four, or $\frac{3}{4}$. The probability of drawing a white block from the bag would be one out of four, or $\frac{1}{4}$. Since there are no green blocks in the bag, the probability of drawing out a green would be zero out of four, or $\frac{0}{4}$.

By placing more blocks into the bag, pupils will see that the distribution may change. Placing one more white would mean that there would be five blocks in all, and the probability of drawing a white would be $\frac{2}{5}$. If still another white block were placed into the bag there would be three white and three red, so there would be three chances out of six ($\frac{3}{6}$) of getting a white. Pupils recognize a similarity to fractions and find that $\frac{3}{6}$ could be simplified to $\frac{1}{2}$. To verify this with the blocks, the teacher may wish to arrange the set so pupils can see that both sets are equivalent (Figure 14.13).

To describe event probabilities the ratio of a sub-set to the total set is reported. When working with two independent events, the pupil must develop a much more systematic way of recording the possi-ble outcomes. While it would be possible to list every possible outcome, students seldom are sys-tematic in such an approach and often omit one or

two possibilities. The teacher may teach students to use a tree diagram or a table as an organizational aid. Such devices not only make the recording more systematic, they provide a background for deter-mining probability by the means of a mathematical formula.

Using a Tree Diagram to Find Probabilities

Figure 14.14 illustrates two spinners. To determine the probability of the two spinners resulting in a sum of four, the pupil may construct a **tree dia-gram**. To guide the construction, the teacher may suggest that the student show all possibilities by writing down the possibilities of the first spinner (one and two). Then the pupil would match each possible outcomes with the possible outcomes of the second spinner (one, two, and three). On spin-ner A, "1" would be matched with one, two, and three and then "2" would be matched with one, two, and three—making six possible outcomes. Two of those six outcomes would give a sum of four, so the probability of getting a sum of four would be $\frac{2}{6}$, or $\frac{1}{3}$.

Students may recognize that an event on Spin-ner A had a probability of $\frac{1}{2}$ and an event on Spinner B had a probability of $\frac{1}{3}$. The probability of two events can be seen as one out of six, or $\frac{1}{6}$. From this students may speculate that the probability of the two events could be found by multiplying the two

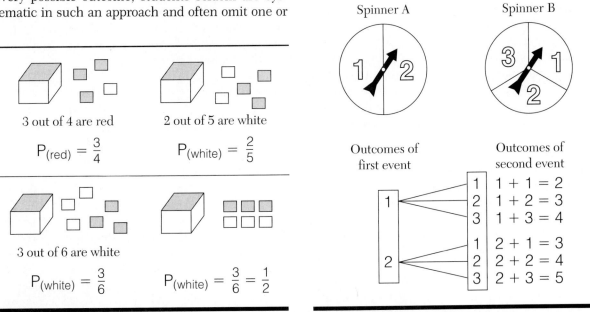

FIGURE 14.13

FIGURE 14.13

FIGURE 14.14

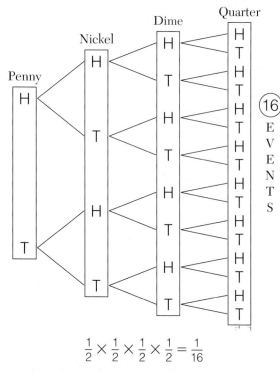

$$\frac{1}{2} \times \frac{1}{2} \times \frac{1}{2} \times \frac{1}{2} = \frac{1}{16}$$

FIGURE 14.15

fractions together. Before reaching a mathematical procedure, pupils should try different combinations of events answering questions such as "What would happen if we used three spinners?" Figure 14.15 illustrates a tree diagram for four coins—each with an independent probability of a head or a tail appearing when dropped onto a table ($\frac{1}{2}$). The figure shows the possible outcomes if four coins are used. As pupils construct the tree diagram, they find that two coins will give four outcomes; three coins will give eight outcomes; and all four coins will give 16 outcomes. Some pupils prefer to construct a tree just for heads and then double the result since there will be both heads and tails. Others will predict that multiplying the probabilities of each event ($\frac{1}{2} \times \frac{1}{2} \times \frac{1}{2} \times \frac{1}{2} = \frac{1}{16}$) will give the probability of a single outcome of the multiple event.

Constructing a Table to Show Outcomes

When the outcomes of two events are to be examined, pupils may choose to construct a table rather than a tree diagram. In Figure 14.16, a chart has been constructed to find the most likely sum of a pair of number cubes. After constructing a chart as a class activity, small groups may test the mathematical probabilities using the cubes. As each

What sum is most likely when rolling two number cubes?

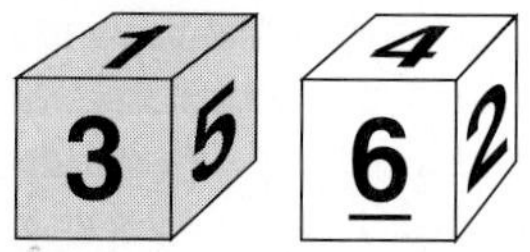

	Red Die					
	1	2	3	4	5	6
1	2	3	4	5	6	7
2	3	4	5	6	7	8
3	4	5	6	7	8	9
4	5	6	7	8	9	10
5	6	7	8	9	10	11
6	7	8	9	10	11	12

(White Die — left column labels 1–6)

A group rolls the two number cubes 36 times—making a tally for each sum. The table below shows the result of the 36 sums.

Sample

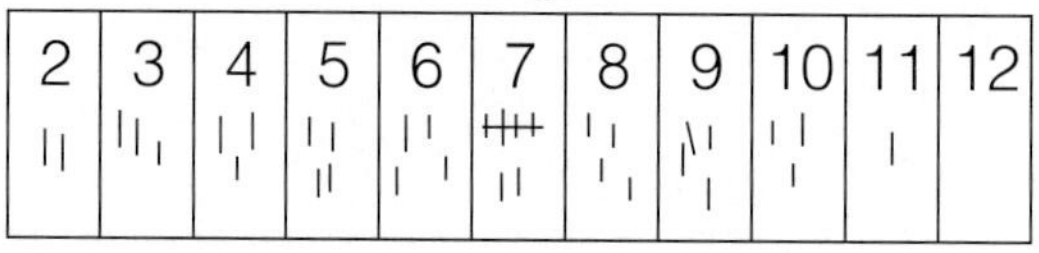

2	3	4	5	6	7	8	9	10	11	12
II	III	III	III	III	HHH	II	IIII	II	I	

FIGURE 14.16

group records its 36 trials they may post those on a bulletin board chart to show how the groups differed. Pupils may wish to use calculators to find the total number of trials and compare the class findings with the predicted probabilities.

14.7 COMPUTERS

Programs ranging from LOGO to some of the more sophisticated spreadsheet programs can sort the data, find various attributes of central tendency such as mean and median, and generate a wide variety of graphs from data. However, the student should have a strong understanding of how various graphs are generated before automating the process by using computer programs. Similarly, a pupil should have a good understanding of how measures of central tendency and other statistical terms are generated with physical models before letting the computer generate this information as a routine part of a statistical program.

Once the basics of graphing are mastered, then the computer may be used as a **tool** for providing students with a wide variety of graphs for analysis. For example, the computer can quickly generate line graphs to analyze trends that are developing over time, or compare two sets of line graphs that may have been generated from class experiments. (See Figure 14.17.) Some computer programs, (Cricket Graph™) for example, will permit students to display the same data on various graphs, thereby allowing pupils to compare graphing forms to determine which more effectively conveys the data.

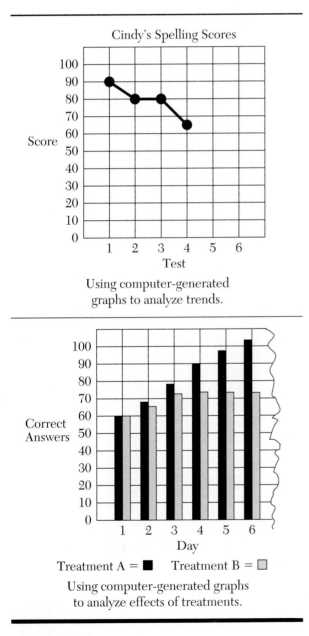

Cindy's Spelling Scores

Using computer-generated
graphs to analyze trends.

Using computer-generated graphs
to analyze effects of treatments.

FIGURE 14.17

14.8 EVALUATION AND INTERVENTION

When students are involved in activities involving graphing, statistics, and probability the teacher will have an excellent opportunity to evaluate their ability to think logically, interpret data, and communicate information to others. Observation will be the primary method of gathering information on the extent to which children are able to communicate mathematical information to others. Interviews and test instruments provide valuable assessment data on students' ability to construct and interpret graphs.

Explorations with probability concepts at the elementary level are primarily designed for building a student's foundation for a more formal study at the postelementary level; therefore evaluation of a student's understanding of probability concepts is informal in nature. When students express ideas that represent probability misconceptions, remediation will consist of setting up experiments to test the student's assertions. For example, a child may think that because an event has happened several times in a row (for instance, the first three times a coin is flipped a head comes up), that a different outcome will be more likely on the next trial. An experiment should be constructed to record the next event whenever a certain event has happened N times. (For example, recording the next event every time three heads in a row occur.)

Evaluation of statistical concepts taught at the elementary school level examines a student's understanding of meaning of statistical terms (median, mean, range, mode, sample) and how these terms are derived and applied. Remediation with respect to the meanings associated with the terms may require constructing models to illustrate the terms.

As a student explores statistical concepts and probability, there are occasions where basic computational skills are required. Since such explorations are applications of computational skills, calculators are generally used. Such situations allow the teacher to evaluate a pupil's understanding of the operation (rather than the algorithm). Even with a calculator, errors occur when entering data, choosing an operation, verifying through estimation, and applying the results. When calculators are NOT used, a teacher may analyze the computational errors to determine if they occurred due to poorly understood concepts or because errors were made in the algorithm.

14.9 MEETING SPECIAL NEEDS

The areas of graphing, statistics, and probability present many concepts that can be explored with the more able student. For example, examining the subtleties of sample bias, the concept of trends, color gradients used in graphing (used in projecting temperatures, location of minerals, etc.), and transmission and reconstruction of digitized satellite data are just a few of the many productive avenues available for individual and small-group learning activities for the more able student.

Let's examine an activity that explores the concept of sample bias.

Small-Group Learning Activity

Procedure: A small group of students are given a series of cards depicting surveys being taken. They are asked to identify how each survey is being biased. A sample card is pictured in Figure 14.18.

Providing for Gifted Students

Individual research projects are an effective means to provide for the needs of gifted students. A study of data collection and transmission via satellite is an excellent project. Investigations can identify how satellites gather and transmit data about the

FIGURE 14.18

Earth's natural resources or they may speculate on how satellites record the temperature of far-distant planets.

Talented students also examine how graphs are produced and used in different professions. The electrocardiograph is one example of electronically collected data that is displayed in a graphic form. Students may also examine how video screens help a doctor during heart surgery; how a business tracks its sales; how agriculturists determine the yield of a new hybrid corn; how a farmer keeps track of the nutrients being taken in by cattle; how an athlete uses charts and graphs to track his/her performance; or how a naturalist monitors the activity of a polar bear.

Providing for Learning-Disabled Students

Learning-disabled students need to develop an understanding of basic concepts of graphing, statistics, and probability since much of the data necessary to be functionally literate in a technological society is transmitted in these forms.

Graphing activities for learning-disabled students should concentrate on those skills which prepare students to function as consumers and citizens. Adults must read and interpret graphs that they encounter in everyday activities. Seldom will a learning-disabled student be required to construct a graph, but making graphs (with teacher guidance) may help the student interpret data that is presented in this form. Hands-on activities, such as plotting an individual skill progress chart; graphing weight and height over the school year; and reading graphs in social studies and science are frequently used to help students gain graphing skills. Learning-disabled pupils readily participate in the construction of bulletin boards that display graphs found in newspapers and magazines. Indeed, learning-disabled students often find far more examples than their classmates.

14.10 SUMMARY

At the primary level children learn a variety of ways to collect and organize data into charts and graphs. They learn to construct bar graphs and pictographs. Once the data is organized children interpret and analyze the data, making decisions based on their analysis of the data.

Intermediate-level students identify and solve problems using the tools of graphing, statistics, and probability. To solve problems, they collect, organize, and describe data in order to make inferences. Construction of line and circle graphs are mastered at this level. Intermediate-level students also learn the meaning and application of the statistical terms (mean, median, mode, and range) and explore the basic concepts of probability and sampling.

EXERCISES

1. Which kinds of graphs are commonly developed
   a. at the primary level?
   b. at the intermediate level?
2. Which kind of graph is most appropriate when plotting data
   a. that are continuous?
   b. that compares one item to another?
   c. that compares parts to the whole?
3. What is the major focus of the activity used to develop the statistical concept of
   a. mean?
   b. median?
   c. range?
   d. mode?
4. In a bag there are 15 blue jelly beans and five red jelly beans. What is the probability of drawing out a blue jelly bean? A red jelly bean?
5. There are two tetrahedron "dice" (four sides). On their faces are the numerals 1, 2, 3, and 4.
   a. Draw a tree diagram to show the probability of rolling a sum of eight.
   b. Construct a table to determine the most likely sum (when rolling both dice) and give the probability.
6. Raisins are sold in one-ounce packages as a snack food. Since the product is sold by weight (rather than amount), the boxes differ in the number of raisins contained. Describe an activity in which a teacher might distribute a package to each pupil and then use these packages in small (cooperative) groups to explore statistical concepts.
7. A group of students have become interested in toy cars. Each is convinced his/her car is the "best." How could a teacher use this interest to devise a lesson in which statistical concepts are developed?
8. On a written test, Tommy was able to "compute" the mean. How might a teacher test to determine whether Tommy understood the concept of mean?
9. Examine current listings of computer programs. What commercial software is available that would be appropriate for elementary school pupils? Which do you like best? Why?
10. Examine the readings found in References. Choose an article (or selection) and summarize the major points in the article.
11. Material is constantly being written about teaching statistics and probability in the elementary schools. Examine the Education Index and choose a recently published article (not listed in the References below). Find and read your chosen article. Share with your colleagues ways in which the article can contribute to their growth as professionals.

RELEVANT COMPUTER SOFTWARE

What's the Chance? 1987. Apple II family. Educational Materials and Equipment Company, Old Mill Plain Road, P.O. Box 2805, Danbury, Ct. 06813.

Cricket Graph. Jim Rafferty and Rich Norling. 1986. MacIntosh family. Cricket Software, 3508 Market Street, Suite 206, Philadelphia, Pa. 19104.

REFERENCES

Anno, M., and M. Tuyosi. *Socrates and the Three Little Pigs*. New York: Philomel Books, 1986.

Bright, G. W. "Probability Simulations." *Arithmetic Teacher* 36 (May 1989): 16–18.

Dickinson, J. C. "Gather, Organize, Display: Mathematics for the Information Society." *Arithmetic Teacher* 34 (December 1986): 12–15.

Freeman, M. *Creative Graphing*. New Rochelle, N.Y.: Cuisenaire Company of America, 1986.

Liao, T. T., and E. J. Piel. "The Yellow-Light Problem: Computer-Based Applied Mathematics." Chap. 13 in *Computers in Mathematics: NCTM Yearbook. 1984*. Reston, Va.: National Council of Teachers of Mathematics, 1984.

Vissa, J. M. "Probability and Combinations for Third Graders." *Arithmetic Teacher* 36 (December 1988): 33–37.

Whitin, D. J. "More Patterns with Square Numbers." *Arithmetic Teacher* 33 (January 1986): 40–42.

INDEX

Guide for using index: Vocabulary associated with each of the following categories is indexed under that category.

Games and activities
Graphing
Manipulative devices
Measurement topics by type of measurement
Number systems
Operations by type of operation
Probability
Problem solving
Statistics

All other vocabulary is indexed separately.